WORLD RELIGIONS TODAY

WORLD RELIGIONS TODAY

Sixth Edition

JOHN L. ESPOSITO
Georgetown University

DARRELL J. FASCHING
University of South Florida

TODD T. LEWIS
College of the Holy Cross

New York   Oxford
OXFORD UNIVERSITY PRESS

Oxford University Press is a department of the University of Oxford. It furthers the University's objective of excellence in research, scholarship, and education by publishing worldwide. Oxford is a registered trademark of Oxford University Press in the UK and certain other countries.

Published in the United States of America by Oxford University Press
198 Madison Avenue, New York, NY 10016, United States of America.

Library of Congress Cataloging-in-Publication Data

Names: Esposito, John L., author. | Fasching, Darrell J., 1944– author. |
  Lewis, Todd, 1952– author.
Title: World religions today / John L. Esposito, Georgetown University,
  Darrell J. Fasching, University of South Florida, Todd T. Lewis, College
  of the Holy Cross.
Description: Sixth Edition. | New York: Oxford University Press, 2017.
Identifiers: LCCN 2016051083 | ISBN 9780190644192 (student edition)
Subjects: LCSH: Religions—Textbooks.
Classification: LCC BL80.3 .E88 2017 | DDC 200—dc23 LC record available at
https://lccn.loc.gov/2016051083

9 8 7 6 5 4 3
Printed by Webcom, Canada

This edition is dedicated to the memory of our colleague and co-author Darrell Fasching, a masterful teacher and scholar

BRIEF CONTENTS

CONTENTS

Chapter 4   CHRISTIAN DIVERSITY AND THE ROAD TO MODERNITY   125

OVERVIEW   125

Chapter 5 ISLAM: THE MANY FACES OF THE MUSLIM EXPERIENCE **183**

OVERVIEW **183**

Chapter 6   HINDUISM, JAINISM, AND SIKHISM: SOUTH ASIAN RELIGIONS

Chapter 8   EAST ASIAN RELIGIONS: CONFUCIANISM, DAOISM, SHINTO, BUDDHISM   413

PREFACE

Religion is unquestionably a dynamic spiritual and political force in the world today. Around the globe religious experiences and beliefs profoundly change individual lives even as they influence politics and play a powerful role in international affairs. This sixth edition of *World Religions Today* addresses this reality with an introductory volume for college and university students.

Although this is a multiauthored text, with each author taking primary responsibility for different chapters (John Esposito: Islam; Darrell Fasching: Judaism, Christianity, and New Age Religions and Globalization; and Todd Lewis: Hinduism, Buddhism, East Asian Religions, and Indigenous Religions), it has truly been a collaborative project from start to finish. Throughout the entire process we shared and commented on each other's material.

World Religions Today grew out of our several decades of experience in teaching world religions. It is a product of our conviction that, for our students to understand the daily news accounts of religions in our global situation, they need more than just the ancient foundations of the world's religions. Textbooks on world religions have too often tended to emphasize historical origins and doctrinal developments, focusing on the past and giving short shrift to the "modern" world. Many stressed a textual, theological/philosophical, or legal approach, one that gave insufficient attention to the modern alterations of these traditions. Most gave little attention to their social institutions or their connections to political power. As a result, students came away with a maximum appreciation for the origins and development of the classical traditions but a minimum awareness of the continued dynamism and relevance of religious traditions today. So, despite the growing visibility and impact of a global religious resurgence and of the unprecedented globalization of all world religions, most textbooks have not quite caught up. *World Religions Today* began with our commitment to address this situation.

World Religions Today, Sixth Edition, continues our hallmark approach of using historical coverage of religious traditions as a framework to help students understand how faiths have evolved to the present day. Indeed, we open most chapters with an "Encounter with Modernity." These encounters illustrate the tension between the premodern religious views and the modern/postmodern world. Each chapter then returns to the origins of the tradition to trace the path that led to this confrontation with "modernity." We attempt to show not only how each tradition has been changed by its encounter with modernity but also how each religion in turn has influenced the contemporary world.

NEW TO THE SIXTH EDITION

The book's major theme and chapter structure have been retained from the earlier editions, though they have been updated and revised. We have also updated chapter content to reflect recent events at the time of writing. In response to reviewer suggestions, we have:

- reduced, by approximately 20 percent, the complexity of detail that often overwhelmed students
- expressed complex ideas as clearly and directly as possible
- updated the timelines

FEATURES

Each chapter is enriched by a wide variety of thematic and special-topic boxes that explore particular ideas or practices in some depth. It is our hope that these lively and interesting boxes are seen as an integral part of the text, allowing students to imagine how religion today is among the most colorful, lively, and striking of human endeavors.

- "Gender Focus" boxes present additional information, beyond that in the regular text, about different practices by believers of different sexes.
- "Rituals and Rites" boxes describe the ritual practices of believers, often with a focus on ways these rites have changed over time.
- "Contrasting Religious Visions" boxes compare the beliefs of two significant adherents of a faith who both see the demands of their religion calling believers in very different directions, demonstrating that, no matter what religion we are examining, that very same religious tradition can be used to promote either peacemaking or conflict.
- "Teachings of Religious Wisdom" boxes offer some of the primary texts and formal teachings of different religions.
- "Tales of Spiritual Transformation" offer descriptions of religious experiences in the believers' own words.

SUPPLEMENTARY MATERIALS

For the instructor: Supplementary materials are available on the Oxford University Press **Ancillary Resource Center (ARC),** a convenient, instructor-focused single destination for resources to accompany your text. Accessed online through individual user accounts, the ARC provides instructors with access to up-to-date ancillaries at any time while guaranteeing the security of grade-significant resources. In addition, it allows OUP to keep instructors informed when new content becomes available. Available on the ARC:

- The **Instructor's Manual**, which includes the following:
  Chapter summaries
  Chapter goals
  Lecture outlines
  Key terms with definitions
  Suggested web links and other resources
- A **Computerized Test Bank**, including 40 multiple-choice, 40 true/false, 40 fill-in-the-blank, and 12 essay/discussion questions per chapter
- **Lecture outlines** as PowerPoint-based slides

A link to the ARC is available on the **Companion Website** (www.oup.com/us/esposito).

For the student: The **Companion Website** (www.oup.com/us/esposito) includes the following student resources:

- Chapter goals
- Flashcards of key terms
- Suggested web links and other resources
- Self-quizzes, containing 20 multiple-choice, 20 true/false, 20 fill-in-the-blank, and 6 essay/discussion questions per chapter, selected from the Test Bank in the ARC

The Instructor's Manual and Computerized Test Bank, as well as the student material from the Companion Website, is also available in **Learning Management Systems Cartridges**, in a fully downloadable format for instructors using a learning management-system.

ACKNOWLEDGMENTS

This sixth edition of *World Religions Today* has been substantially revised in light of the valuable comments we continue to receive from colleagues across the country who have used it and in light of our own subsequent experiences and reflections. We offer special thanks to the following professors and to the other, anonymous, reviewers. This edition is much stronger because of their thoughtful comments:

Kenneth Bass, Central Texas College
Todd M. Brenneman, Faulkner University
Clayton Crockett, University of Central Arkansas
Dennis G. Crump, Lindsey Wilson College
Jonathan Ebel, University of Illinois–Urbana Champaign
Jim Gustafson, Florida Southwestern State College
B. N. Hebbar, George Washington University
Samuel Hopkins, Northern Arizona University
Ernest P. Janzen, University of Winnipeg
Scott Kenworthy, Miami University of Ohio
Kristin Beise Kiblinger, Winthrop University
Lee Krahenbuhl, Mercy College of Ohio
Andrew Pavelich, University of Houston–Downtown
Judith Poxon, California State University–Sacramento
Bassam Romaya, University of Massachusetts–Lowell
Patricia Walters, Rockford University
Alice L. Wood, Bethune-Cookman University

Thanks also to the reviewers of the previous editions for their lasting input on the work: Constantina Rhodes Bailly, Eckerd College; Herbert Berg, University of North Carolina–Wilmington; Sheila Briggs, University of Southern California; Robert Brown, James Madison University; Terry L. Burden, University of Louisville; Dexter E. Callender Jr., University of Miami; David Capes, Houston Baptist University; James E. Deitrick, University of Central Arkansas; Sergey Dolgopolski, University of Kansas; Joan Earley, State University of New York at Albany; James Egge, Eastern Michigan University; John Farina, George Mason University; Debora Y. Fonteneau, Savannah State University; Liora Gubkin, California State University–Bakersfield; William David Hart, University of North Carolina–Greensboro; William Hutchins, Appalachian State University; Father Brad Karelius, Saddleback Community College; Sandra T. Keating, Providence College; Mohammad Hassan Khalil, University of Illinois; David Kitts, Carson-Newman University; Louis Komjathy, University of San Diego; Peter David Lee, Columbia College—California; Ian Maclean, James Madison University; Sean McCloud, University of North Carolina at Charlotte; Tim Murphy, University of Alabama; Nancy Nahra, Champlain College; Jason Neelis, University of Florida; Patrick Nnoromele, Eastern Kentucky University; Catherine Orsborn, University of Denver; Robin L. Owens, Mount St. Mary's College; Linda Pittman, College of William and Mary; Kris Pratt, Spartanburg Methodist College; Rick Rogers, Eastern Michigan University; Barry R. Sang, Catawba College; Brooke Schedneck, Arizona State University; D. Neil Schmid, North Carolina State University; Paul Schneider, University of South Florida; Martha Ann Selby, University of Texas at

Austin; Caleb Simmons, University of Mississippi; Theresa S. Smith, Indiana University of Pennsylvania; Yushau Sodiq, Texas Christian University; Phillip Spivey, University of Central Arkansas; Bruce Sullivan, Northern Arizona University; Aaron J. Hahn Tapper, University of San Francisco; James H. Thrall, International College–University of Bridgeport; Eglute Trinkauske, Nazareth College; Peter Umoh, University of Bridgeport; Hugh B. Urban, Ohio State University; Anne Vallely, University of Ottawa; Andrew Christian Van Gorder, Baylor University; Glenn Wallis, University of Georgia; Tammie Wanta, University of North Carolina at Charlotte; Mlen-Too Wesley, Penn State University; Catherine Wessinger, Loyola University New Orleans; Mark Whitters, Eastern Michigan University; Simon A. Wood, University of Nebraska–Lincoln. John Esposito would like to acknowledge the invaluable contributions to the Islam chapter of Tasi Perkins, his research assistant.

We have been fortunate to work with an excellent, supportive, and creative team at Oxford University Press, led by Robert Miller, Executive Editor in Oxford's Higher Education Group. Senior Production Editor Barbara Mathieu, Editorial Assistant Kellylouise Delaney and Assistant Editor Alyssa Palazzo, and Senior Development Editor Meg Botteon have been extraordinarily supportive throughout the writing process. Our thanks also to Robin Tuthill, who prepared the student and instructor support materials for the first four editions of the book, and to Kate Kelley, who updated them for the fifth and sixth editions.

John L. Esposito
Darrell J. Fasching
Todd T. Lewis

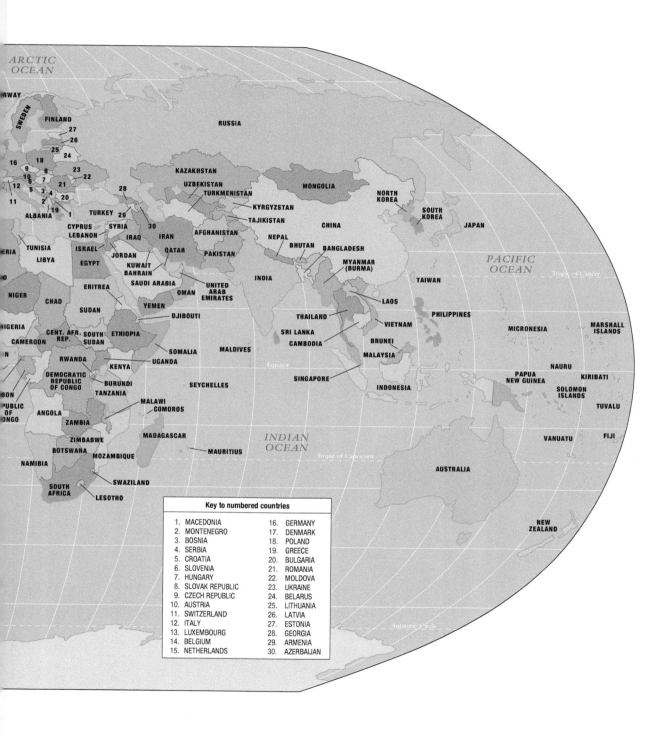

ARCTIC OCEAN

NORWAY
SWEDEN
FINLAND
27
26
25 24
16 18
9 8
10 23 22
6 7 21
12 5 3 4 20
11 2
19 1
ALBANIA
CYPRUS TURKEY 29
LEBANON SYRIA 30
ISRAEL IRAQ IRAN
JORDAN
TUNISIA QATAR
LIBYA EGYPT KUWAIT
BAHRAIN
NIGER SAUDI ARABIA
ERITREA OMAN
CHAD YEMEN
SUDAN DJIBOUTI
NIGERIA
CENT. AFR. SOUTH ETHIOPIA
CAMEROON REP. SUDAN
RWANDA SOMALIA
KENYA UGANDA
DEMOCRATIC
REPUBLIC BURUNDI
OF CONGO TANZANIA
GABON
PUBLIC MALAWI
OF ANGOLA COMOROS
CONGO ZAMBIA
ZIMBABWE MADAGASCAR
BOTSWANA
NAMIBIA MOZAMBIQUE MAURITIUS
SWAZILAND
SOUTH
AFRICA LESOTHO

RUSSIA

KAZAKHSTAN
UZBEKISTAN
TURKMENISTAN
KYRGYZSTAN
28 TAJIKISTAN
AFGHANISTAN
NEPAL
PAKISTAN BHUTAN
UNITED
ARAB INDIA
EMIRATES

MONGOLIA

CHINA

NORTH
KOREA
SOUTH
KOREA JAPAN

BANGLADESH
MYANMAR
(BURMA)
LAOS TAIWAN

THAILAND VIETNAM
SRI LANKA
CAMBODIA PHILIPPINES
MALDIVES BRUNEI
MALAYSIA
SINGAPORE
INDONESIA
SEYCHELLES

PACIFIC
OCEAN
Tropic of Cancer

MICRONESIA
MARSHALL
ISLANDS

NAURU
PAPUA KIRIBATI
NEW GUINEA
SOLOMON
ISLANDS
TUVALU

INDIAN
OCEAN
Tropic of Capricorn

VANUATU FIJI

AUSTRALIA

NEW
ZEALAND

Antarctic Circle

Equator

Key to numbered countries

1.	MACEDONIA	16.	GERMANY
2.	MONTENEGRO	17.	DENMARK
3.	BOSNIA	18.	POLAND
4.	SERBIA	19.	GREECE
5.	CROATIA	20.	BULGARIA
6.	SLOVENIA	21.	ROMANIA
7.	HUNGARY	22.	MOLDOVA
8.	SLOVAK REPUBLIC	23.	UKRAINE
9.	CZECH REPUBLIC	24.	BELARUS
10.	AUSTRIA	25.	LITHUANIA
11.	SWITZERLAND	26.	LATVIA
12.	ITALY	27.	ESTONIA
13.	LUXEMBOURG	28.	GEORGIA
14.	BELGIUM	29.	ARMENIA
15.	NETHERLANDS	30.	AZERBAIJAN

WORLD
RELIGIONS
TODAY

INTRODUCTION

Understanding World Religions in Global Perspective

1

n an age of **globalization**, human events reach through time and around the world to transform our personal, social, economic, and political lives. Until the modern period, the great world religions had largely divided the globe among them, with some modest overlap. But in our postmodern era, all the world's religions have members in every country or society. Just as Christians had migrated to every city in the world by 1850, today Hindus, Buddhists, and Muslims are now found in significant numbers in all large American and European cities and increasingly in smaller ones. Today, anyone using the Internet can observe and even participate in live webcam services in major temples, shrines, churches, mosques, and monasteries from around the world; devotees can offer prayers, order rituals, or make monetary offerings through their websites. This is globalization.

Essential to understanding globalization in the United States is the Immigration Act of 1965, signed by President Lyndon Johnson. This act abolished the immigration system set up in 1924 and modified in 1952. The earlier system heavily favored immigration from Europe and severely restricted immigration from other parts of the world, especially Asia. The 1965 legislation dramatically changed the face of America. As of 1950 in the United States, according to government figures, about 3.6 percent of immigrants were from Asia; by the year 2000, more than 30 percent were.

In the 1950s, when people thought about religious diversity, it was limited largely to Protestants, Catholics, and Jews. In the twenty-first century the situation is

globalization:
in terms of world religions, the idea that all the world's religions have members in almost every country or society; and that technology affords access to all key religious sites, practices, and teachers

---

◀ With the Space Age, awareness that all humans share life in a global village has come to the religions and cultures of the earth.

dramatically different. Almost daily the media takes note of new religious members of the community—for example, a meditation retreat at a Korean Zen center in the suburbs of Providence, Rhode Island; the opening of an Islamic mosque in St. Louis, Missouri; or the dedication of a Hindu temple in Tampa, Florida.

Figure 1.1, compiled from Pew Foundation reports, census data, and other studies, offers an approximation of the number of adherents of the various religions found in the world today, and their numbers in relation to one another. There is no reliable exact count available or even possible for many reasons: the lack of surveys utilizing the same criteria; disagreements about what is a branch of a world religion and what is a "new religion"; and the paucity of census/survey data from the world's two most populous nations, India and China. Existing surveys that summarize religious identity on a global level are extremely problematic due to these issues of definition, limited global scope, and affiliation.

Central to any survey data is the assumption that a person can be listed under one variable and be only that; but such an exclusive choice of one and only one religion does not very well capture the reality of world religions today. (For this reason, the estimated percentages assigned to each tradition in Figure 1.1 exceed 100%.) Even among those professing to be monotheists, there are now many hyphenated identities (such as Buddhist Jew, Zen Christian, or agnostic Yoga devotee). Singular identity is even more problematic for representing the religious reality for most people in Asia and the various indigenous peoples across the world, where many follow more than one tradition. Demographers too often give a false sense of certainty to the pluralistic and fluid boundaries of the world's religions today. ◯ ◉ ◯

Why Study World Religions?

In the emerging global economy, most neighborhoods, workplaces, and schools reflect this diversity as well. The beliefs and practices of world religions have become part of the mosaic of American society. It is more and more likely that our neighbors, classmates, and colleagues are ethnically, politically, and, yes, even religiously diverse—coming from many parts of the globe (see Map 1.1). Understanding diverse religions is necessary because it is now about understanding our neighbors. If we do not understand each other, our misunderstandings may well lead to prejudice, conflict, and even violence.

The academic study of religion is one of the newest disciplines in the modern university. Its beginnings go back to the emergence of the social sciences in the nineteenth century, with the appearance of such fields as anthropology, sociology, and comparative linguistics. One of the great founding fathers of this study was the Indologist Max Müller (1825–1900), who argued that "the person who knows only one religion understands none."[1] It is only by studying the diverse expressions of religion throughout history and across cultures that we come to understand its unity and diversity.

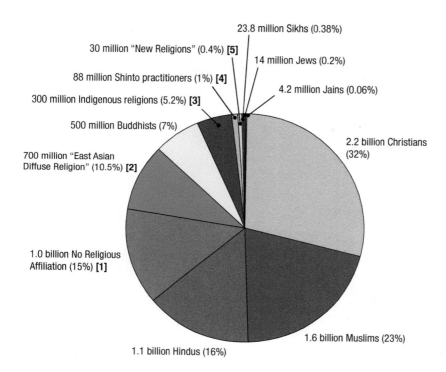

23.8 million Sikhs (0.38%)

30 million "New Religions" (0.4%) **[5]**

14 million Jews (0.2%)

88 million Shinto practitioners (1%) **[4]**

300 million Indigenous religions (5.2%) **[3]**

4.2 million Jains (0.06%)

500 million Buddhists (7%)

2.2 billion Christians (32%)

700 million "East Asian Diffuse Religion" (10.5%) **[2]**

1.0 billion No Religious Affiliation (15%) **[1]**

1.6 billion Muslims (23%)

1.1 billion Hindus (16%)

Figure 1.1 The world's major religions (percentage of global population).

Notes:

[1] Includes atheists, agnostics, and people who do not self-identify with any particular religion in surveys. Studies have also revealed that many of the "religiously unaffiliated" do have some religious beliefs. Some of the religiously unaffiliated, for example, do express belief in God or a higher power, a view shared, for example, by 7% of Chinese unaffiliated adults, 30% of French unaffiliated adults, and 68% of unaffiliated U.S. adults. Some of the unaffiliated also engage in certain kinds of religious practices. For example, 7% of unaffiliated adults in France and 27% of those in the United States say they attend religious services at least once a year.

[2] A combination of Confucian, Daoist, and local religious devotions. This figure was estimated based on a Chinese government statistic indicating that 44% of adults reported that they had worshipped at a graveside or tomb in the survey year.

[3] Practice various folk or traditional religions, including African traditional religions, Indian tribal traditions, Native American religions, and Australian aboriginal religions.

[4] This number for adherents to Shinto in Japan is based on recent surveys that have shown that 80% of Japanese register their newborn children at a Shinto shrine, and that roughly the same number visit these temples on New Year's Day and other major traditional holidays.

[5] The formation of new religions has been a key hallmark of global religious life since 1750, and it has been recorded on every continent. Some have come and gone (such as the "Shakers" in Colonial America); some have arisen but to this day command the loyalty of few; most have arisen and spread in a particular region; a few have become global in membership.

Prior to the 1960s, in the United States, one could not have studied religions comparatively in secular and state universities. Only religious colleges and universities offered courses and degrees in religion, and these were typically on the teachings of their own denominations. If other religions came up for discussion it was usually to

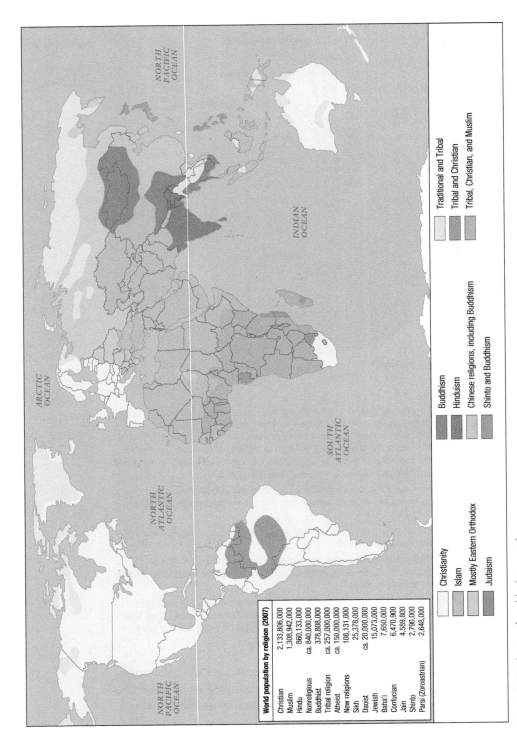

World population by religion (2007)

Christian	2,133,806,000
Muslim	1,308,942,000
Hindu	860,133,000
Nonreligious	ca. 840,000,000
Buddhist	378,808,000
Tribal religion	ca. 257,000,000
Atheist	ca. 150,000,000
New religions	108,131,000
Sikh	25,378,000
Daoist	ca. 20,000,000
Jewish	15,073,000
Baha'i	7,650,000
Confucian	6,470,900
Jain	4,589,800
Shinto	2,790,000
Parsi (Zoroastrian)	2,648,000

Christianity

Islam

Mostly Eastern Orthodox

Judaism

Buddhism

Hinduism

Chinese religions, including Buddhism

Shinto and Buddhism

Traditional and Tribal

Tribal and Christian

Tribal, Christian, and Muslim

Map 1.1 Distribution of world religions today.

point out their "errors." Then in the 1960s departments of religious studies began to appear in nonreligious colleges and secular state universities. Responding to the new diversity brought on by globalization, these departments began to offer courses on non-Western as well as comparative religions. What they attempted was completely new in history: They sought to understand and appreciate the diverse religious traditions of the world without prejudice toward any of them.

The academic study of religion requires the courage and compassion to empathetically understand the diverse worldviews of others and the willingness to learn from each. Its goal is not to show one religion is "right" and all others "wrong," but rather to show what humans have found compelling in each and how each tradition has shaped history. The task in the study of world religions today is to overcome stereotypes and glimpse the wisdom found in each of these traditions. To judge another's religion without understanding it and what it means to its members is to "prejudge" them—that is the meaning of the word *prejudice*. When encountering beliefs and practices we do not understand, it is easy to fall into the trap of ridiculing them, saying, "How can anyone possibly believe that?" Certainly each of us wants to be understood and respected, not stereotyped and dismissed. We need to extend that same courtesy to all others as well. So in the academic study of religion we agree to set aside our own beliefs and prejudices and to simply try to understand and appreciate the meaning others find in their beliefs and practices.

> In surveying world religions today, we shall not be able to cover everything that could be said about them. Our selection will be governed primarily by the following question: What do we need to know about the past to understand the role of religion in the world we live in today?

Our Task

In this book we focus on the diverse ways in which human beings have been religious in the past and are religious today. Indeed, the last decades of the twentieth century brought a global religious resurgence. This development defied earlier predictions that civilization was becoming more secular, with a worldview increasingly based on modern science. As a result, many scholars believed that religion would inevitably disappear. The ongoing clash of traditional religions with contemporary scientific and secular society is a major concern of this textbook. Awareness of this conflict is essential if we are to understand the interactions between religions and cultures in the world today. Every chapter thus begins with examples of a major controversy or significant tension each religion now faces.

We describe our present time as one in transition between "modernity" and a new "postmodern" era of globalization. To understand what is "new" about postmodernity, we first have to understand the premodern period of the different religious traditions and how the premodern worldview of each relates to and contrasts with the modern period. In particular, we will have to compare the premodern period in each tradition with the changes brought about by the "modern" era, which began with the rise of modern science after 1500 and declined after World War II. In surveying world religions today, we shall not be able to cover everything that could be said about them. Our selection will be governed primarily by the following question: What do we need to know about the past to understand the role of religion in the world we live in today? In order to understand many of the conflicts that we hear about in the news, we need to understand how religious traditions profoundly shaped the world to be the way it is today. Since religious beliefs are often at the center of the individual's identity, and because religious communities are major actors in our world today, studying world religions provides crucial insights for understanding our world. And to do that, we must begin by introducing some basic concepts.

Understanding Religious Experience and Its Formative Elements

Wherever we find religious practice, we will find certain key elements:

The Experience of Sacredness
Myth or Symbolic Story (typically embodied in sacred writing or *scripture* and expressed in a system of *beliefs*)
Ritual
Community
Morality
Religious Leaders/Experts

religion: the sense of being tied or bound by sacred obligations to powers believed to govern our destiny

Let us begin with a working definition of the term **religion**. The word *religion* has its roots in Latin, the language of the Romans. Although its exact root is uncertain, it is probably derived from the Latin *religare*, which literally means "to tie or bind" and has the connotation of "acting with care." It expresses our sense of being "tied and bound" by relations of obligation to whatever powers we believe govern our destiny—whether these powers are natural or supernatural, personal or impersonal, one or many. Because our word *religion* comes from the Roman, it will be helpful to understand their use of the word.

If you were to ask a group of Romans in the first century CE, "What religion are you?", they would not understand the question. However, if you asked instead, "Are you religious?", they would understand immediately. They might even respond: "Of course, but who isn't?"

In the first version of the question, the word *religion* is used as a noun. It suggests that *religion* is a social group to which people can belong, and that you can be a member of a specific religion only if you are not a member of another. This way of understanding religion naturally arises among monotheists, who by definition have chosen one god and excluded all others. However, the Romans did not have such an exclusive concept of religion. In rephrasing the original question as "Are you religious?" you are no longer treating *religion* as a noun, describing something you join. Instead, you are treating it as an adjective, describing a way of seeing, acting, and experiencing all things. In most times and places throughout history, people did not think of their practices as "a religion"—a separate reality they had to choose to the exclusion of all others. Today in Japan, for instance, it is possible for a person to practice Buddhism, Daoism, Confucianism, and Shintoism. This may seem odd from the monotheistic perspective of Western religions, where one can be, for instance, a Muslim or a Christian or a Jew but not two or more at the same time. And yet, paradoxically, Jews, Christians, and Muslims all claim to worship the same God.

The Sacred

Religion is about what people hold sacred, what matters more than anything else to them—namely, their destiny individually and collectively. For all human beings in all places and all times throughout history, religion has been about power and meaning in relation to human destiny. The word *religion* is derived from the Latin word *religio* that had two roots: the verb *religare*, which literally means "to tie or bind," and the adjective *religere*, meaning "careful or respectful [to the supernatural]."

Ancient peoples everywhere believed that the powers governing their destiny were the forces of nature. Why? Because nature was experienced as that awesome collection of powers that surround and, at times, overwhelm human beings. On the one hand, nature provides life and many of its necessities (food, clothing, shelter, etc.); but on the other hand, nature may turn on people, destroying them through earthquakes, storms, or floods. Therefore the forces of nature evoke in human beings the ambivalent feeling of both fascination and dread. Rudolf Otto (1869–1937), a pioneer in the comparative study of religions, argued that the presence of these two ambivalent emotions is a sure sign that one is in the presence of the sacred. A defining mark of religious experience across cultures, these emotions are stirred by the uncanny experience of being in the presence of a power (or powers) that determines not only how well one lives, but whether one lives or dies.

Religion as a form of human experience and behavior, therefore, is not just about purely "spiritual" things. Nor can the study of religion globally be defined only by gods or God. People's religiousness has proven to be as diverse as the forms of power they believe govern human destiny. These powers have ranged from gods as forces of nature to the unseen ancestral spirits or spirits associated with sacred places, to more impersonal sacred forces or energies; or even the mysterious power(s) that govern history. Hence, whatever powers we believe govern our destiny will elicit a religious response from us and inspire us to wish "to tie or bind" ourselves to these powers in relations of ritual obligation. Thus tied or bound, we will act respectfully and carefully in relation to these powers, to ensure that they will be on our side.

How do we know what our obligations to these powers are? Throughout history this knowledge has been passed down from one generation to the next through myth and ritual.

Myth, Scripture, and Beliefs

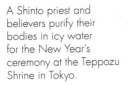

myth: symbolic story about the origins and destiny of human beings and their world

Our word **myth** comes from the Greek *mythos*, which means "story." Myth, we could say, is a symbolic story about the origins of the world and destiny of human beings. Myth "ties and binds" human beings in relations of obligation to whatever powers they believe govern their destiny and explains what these powers expect of them. Unlike the contemporary English use of *myth* to indicate an untrue story or a misunderstanding based on ignorance, every religious tradition uses myth to convey the deepest and most profound truths about life. These truths are expressed through grand stories of creation and destiny rather than in abstract theories. After the invention of writing (about 3000 BCE), these stories came to be written down, creating what we now call the "scriptures" of the various religions. Because these scriptures tell the stories about the power or powers that govern human destiny, they have been treated as sacred scriptures and passed on from one generation to the next.

For students of world religions, understanding the symbolic nature of much of religious language is a key challenge. To understand a religious story literally can often lead to misunderstanding its meaning and so make it seem false. For example,

A Shinto priest and believers purify their bodies in icy water for the New Year's ceremony at the Teppozu Shrine in Tokyo.

in Western biblical tradition, the Psalms say: "God is my shepherd," just as Buddhist scriptures refer to their founder, the Buddha, as "a bull of a man." We know such statements are not meant literally: God is not literally a shepherd, nor is the Buddha literally a bull.

Statements like these are metaphorical. They use familiar things to help explain what is less familiar—a reality that is mysterious or even beyond human language. Shepherds and bulls we can see and know something about, but God or a Buddha is more mysterious. A person who says "God is our shepherd" has expressed the thought that God is like a shepherd, in the sense that God watches over and cares for persons in the same way a shepherd tends his sheep. Similarly, "Buddha was a bull of a man" expresses the conviction that the man who achieved enlightenment was strong and powerful. These metaphors both assert that the Buddha and God are realities that can always be relied upon.

Not all religious experiences are theistic, reflecting belief in one or more gods. Theravada Buddhists in ancient India refused to use the Hindu words roughly equivalent to the English word *God* to describe their religious understanding. Instead they spoke of the emptiness and inadequacy of all spoken metaphors to explain their goal, the blissful state of *nirvana* (see Chapter 7). And yet they too used metaphors to try to help people understand what they had experienced as the "blowing out of the flame of desire," which leads to liberation from all suffering.

In fact, the word *God*, which is so central to the Abrahamic religious traditions (Judaism, Christianity, Islam), is just one of many diverse terms used in different religions and cultures across the world to designate the **ultimate reality**, that which is the highest in value and meaning for the group. This class of terms includes not only the personal God of Western theism but also the impersonal Brahman of Hinduism, the transpersonal nirvana of Buddhism, and the impersonal power of the *Dao* at work in all things that is central to Chinese religions.

To live well, have many descendants, and live a long life—these are three great treasures in Chinese culture. A Chinese woman prays for prosperity, posterity, and longevity at a Buddhist temple on the island of Lantau.

ultimate reality: that which has the highest value and meaning to a group

sympathetic imagination: empathy; necessary to understand the religious languages and messages of different times and places

via analogia: a way of explaining spiritual reality by using analogies from particular finite qualities and characteristics

via negativa: a way of explaining spiritual reality by negating all finite qualities and characteristics

transcendent: beyond all finite things

Here lies the challenge, mystery, and fascination of studying the religions of the world: Do differences in religious terminology reflect experiences of different realities? Or are they different expressions or ways of describing the same reality? Because religious metaphors come out of particular historical contexts and because they are symbolic forms of expression, to understand the religious languages and messages of different religious traditions requires that we put ourselves in the time and place of their origins. We must use our **sympathetic imagination** to understand the metaphors used. Different cultures and different generations have each contributed to the rich variety of metaphors used to illuminate the mystery and meaning of human existence.

Religious language, as symbolic language, can take one of two forms: analogy or negation. The metaphor "God is my shepherd" is an example of the way of analogy (*via analogia*). In these metaphors, we use familiar words to create an analogy that describes something less familiar. However, there is another form of religious language, the way of negation (*via negativa*). This way of speaking religiously proceeds not by asserting what God or ultimate reality is (or is like) but by saying what it is not. This approach is very typical of mystical traditions. The Muslim mystic declares that Allah is "nothing," stating that Allah (God) is beyond (i.e., transcends) or is different from anything in our material universe and experience. Allah is not this thing and not that thing. Allah is in fact no "thing" at all. Being beyond all finite things and thus **transcendent**, Allah must be said to be no-thing.

In general, Western monotheism has emphasized the way of analogy by saying that there is one God who is like humans, able to "know" and to "love," but in a superior fashion. Thus, God is described as all-knowing, all-loving, or all-powerful. By contrast, Buddhism, of all the religions, has emphasized most strongly the way of negation, insisting that what is most valuable or true cannot be either named or imaged. Yet both ways are found in all traditions. Some Jewish, Christian, and Muslim mystics have referred to God as a "Nothingness," even as some Hindus have referred to the ultimate reality as a cosmic person rather than an impersonal power. Moreover, we should note that these two ways do not really conflict, for the way of analogy itself implies the way of negation. That is, every time we say God is *like* some thing, we are at the same time saying God is not literally that thing. Every analogy implies a negation.

Our discussion of religious language should help us to appreciate just how challenging it can be to study and compare various religious traditions. Just as religious communities and religious traditions from different parts of the world use different metaphors and symbols, they also mix the way of analogy and the way of negation. Therefore, two different traditions sometimes talk about the same human experience in ways that seem to be totally contradictory. For example, it may seem that a Jewish theist and a Theravada Buddhist hold diametrically opposed religious beliefs, for Jews believe in a personal God who created the universe and Theravada Buddhists do not. Yet, when we look more closely at Jewish beliefs, we discover that Jews believe that God can be neither named nor imaged, even as Theravada Buddhists believe that ultimate truth is beyond all names and images. And yet, in both traditions, experiencing the nameless is said to make one more human or compassionate, not less.

After learning about the traditions covered in this book, you might conclude that perhaps theistic and nontheistic religious experiences are really not far apart. However, it is also possible that they might be seen as truly different. To pursue this great human question, we must begin by withholding judgment and simply try to understand how stories and rituals shape people's views, values, and behavior. Perhaps the real measure of comparison should be how people live their lives rather than the apparently diverse images and concepts they hold. If both Jews and Buddhists, for example, are led by their religious experiences and beliefs to express compassion for those who suffer or are in need, then clearly the two faiths are similar in that very important respect.

Ritual

Ritual actions, like myths, "tie and bind" the individual and the community to the sacred. Such actions often involve the symbolic reenactment of the stories that are passed on from one generation to the next. Typically myth and ritual are closely tied to the major festivals or holy days of a religious tradition and illuminate the meaning of human destiny in relation to sacred powers. By celebrating a cycle of festivals spread throughout the year, people come to dwell in the stories that tell them who they are, where they came from, and where they are going.

> **ritual:** actions that link the individual and the community to each other, through the sacred

Religious rituals recall important events in the history of each faith: the "Night Journey" of the Prophet Muhammad, the enlightenment of the Buddha, the death of Jesus Christ, the birthday of Confucius. In other rituals, the faithful offer gifts to the supernatural beings to whom they ascribe a power to profoundly affect their lives. Still other rituals require circumcision, tattoos, or burn marks to set the believers off from nonbelievers, fostering in-group solidarity. The consumption of certain foods as part of some rituals suggests that the believer can acquire the "same essence" as the **divine** through ingestion, as in the Christian communion, Hindu puja, or tribal eating of a totemic animal to affirm common identity.

> **divine:** highest spiritual reality; representative of the gods

We should not assume that rituals only communicate ideas or beliefs. Religions are not confined to doctrines regarding the sacred. Rather, they include rituals that, in their own right, tie and bind people to each other and to cosmic meaning. Being religious thus entails taking decisive action at certain times, while abstaining from activities at other times. For example, at specific times gifts may be offered to supernatural beings or pilgrimages made to sacred places. At other times, religion might require abstaining from food (fasting).

For many believers, acting in the prescribed manner, called **orthopraxy** (correct practice), is more important than **orthodoxy** (correct belief)—acceptance of the doctrines set forth in texts and formulated by scholars. Performing the five daily Muslim prayers, visiting a Buddhist or Hindu temple to offer flowers on the full moon day, cleaning a Chinese family's ancestral grave during the spring festival, or being baptized

> **orthopraxy:** practice of "right actions" as prescribed by sacred traditions
>
> **orthodoxy:** acceptance of "right beliefs" based on sacred texts as explained by religious authorities

as a Christian—all these acts are as central to "being religious," as is adopting beliefs or doctrines defined as orthodox.

The great annual festivals in the world's religions give devotees a break from the profane time of normal working life and reinforce important ties with family and fellow devotees. The need to orchestrate such crucial ritual actions leads followers to create the religious institutions that occupy central places in their societies.

Community and Morality

Myth and ritual shape unique communities to foster the way of life that emerges out of their religious experiences. Religion not only ties us to the sacred powers we believe govern our destiny; it also binds us to each other. Consequently, in most religious traditions, ritual and **morality** have been closely intertwined. "Right" is often defined by "rite"—the ritual patterns of behavior that keep life sacred. Morality is an inherent dimension of religious experience, for religion not only concerns sacred powers but also describes the way of life to be followed.

morality: right action

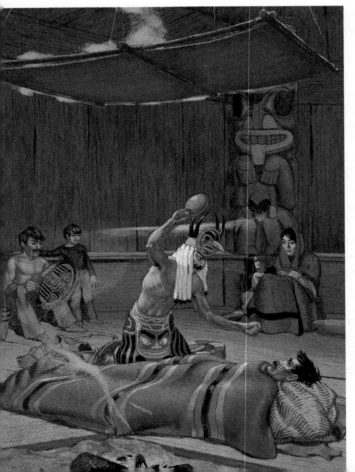

A Tlingit shaman performing a healing ceremony.

The sacred—what matters most to a given community—provides the ground for the moral experience of the virtuous life. The blueprint for what is just or moral is expressed in myth and ritual. Take, for example, the Jewish festival of Yom Kippur. This is the occasion at the beginning of a new year for each person to repent, to seek and offer forgiveness for the ways each has harmed others. Each person also resolves to live more compassionately and justly in the new year.

Once we realize that religion is about what people hold sacred and the way of life that is called for by such beliefs, then it makes sense to say that all morality has a religious dimension, because every morality is grounded in religious experience, namely in the experience of what is held sacred in a given community. In this sense even the morality of atheists or others, who may not think of themselves as religious, can be said to have a religious dimension—to the degree that certain values are held sacred. Such an observation still leaves open the philosophical question of the degree to which a tradition's sacred morality is truly ethical, for ethics is the questioning of sacred moralities, asking whether what people customarily say is good or virtuous really is good or virtuous.

Religious Leaders/Experts

In every religion we will find specialists: the shamans, priests, ministers, monks, rabbis, scholars, and teachers who mediate between the sacred power(s) and the community by explaining the myths and performing the rituals. The world's oldest religious specialist is the shaman. This man or woman goes into a trance to leave his or her body and go to the spirit realm. There, he or she communicates with sacred ancestors and supernatural beings (spirits, gods, demons, ghosts). Practitioners of this art (also called mediums or oracles) are depicted on cave walls across Eurasia from the Neolithic period 25,000 years ago. Shamans still exist in many parts of the world, not only among indigenous peoples but also within or alongside the great world religions (see Chapter 2).

Since the invention of writing in 3000 BCE, the great world religions have relied on written materials and on scholars who have learned to write and read and thereby interpret the sacred texts. These keepers of the sacred writings translate their meanings for the great majority of followers, most of whom, until the modern era, were illiterate. The Confucian masters, the Muslim ulama, and the Hindu brahmin are examples of this religious specialist. And then there are those who specialize in being spiritual teachers, such as the Hindu guru, the Jewish rabbi, or the Sufi Muslim shaykh. Although we can point to interesting comparative patterns among religious rituals and between religious teachers, it is also true to say that each tradition can and must be known by its own unique set of religious practitioners and institutions.

A two-year-old Muslim boy, living in predominantly Catholic East Timor, prays alongside his father at a mosque in Dili.

The Great Religious Stories of the World

As human beings, we are not just storytellers, we are "storydwellers." We live in our stories and make sense of the world through them. Even our understanding of what is good and evil is shaped by the kind of story we see ourselves in and the role we see ourselves playing in that story. Although religious stories need not be about gods and other spiritual beings, most of the earliest stories that have shaped human religious life have been.

There are four main types of religious stories, each of which presents a symbolic story of the origins and destiny of human beings and the challenges they face in striving to realize their sacred destiny. (Consult Figure 1.2, the "World Religions in Perspective" chart, when reading this section.) These four main types of sacred story are:

myths of nature
myths of harmony
myths of liberation
myths of history

Myths of Nature

The earliest religious stories are myths of nature. These are stories about the powers of nature that govern human destiny and portray them as either personal beings (gods, spirits, and sacred ancestors) or impersonal powers. Such religions tend to see time as cyclical, always returning to the moment just before creation. Just as winter and death are followed by spring and new life, starting the earthly cycles all over again, time is an endless loop. Myth and ritual are the means to erase the distance between "now" and the time of origins, "in the beginning," when the gods or ancestral spirits first created the world. In such stories the problem of life is time. Time inevitably brings sickness, decline, and death. The ideal in human life is to return to the newness of life at the beginning of creation, before time began.

The means for bringing about this return is the recitation of the myths and the performance of rituals reenacting creation. Hunter-gatherer stories emphasize the fertility of the earth, the relations with animals and plants, the need for the ritual renewal of life in harmony with the seasons, and the role the tribe plays in maintaining the eternal cosmic order. In many of these societies, a shaman is the spiritual leader; as will be seen in Chapter 2, the shaman's trance journeys restore harmony between the human community, spirits, and the forces of nature.

China and the Myths of Harmony

In China the great cosmic story was that of the Dao (sometimes rendered Tao). The universal Dao, which all beings share, is the source of harmony in the universe.

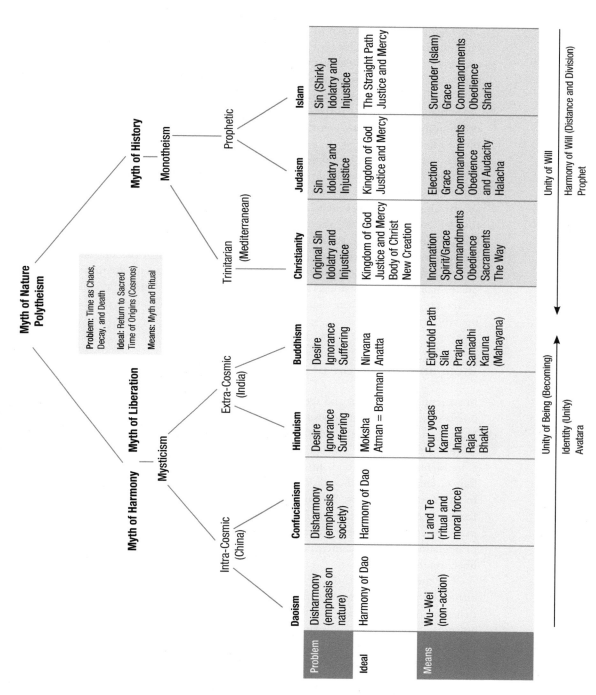

Figure 1.2 The world's religions in perspective.

17

The Dao is at work, hidden in all the forces of nature. One's true self is knowable only in relation to the Dao. All of creation works through combinations of complementary opposites of *yin* and *yang*, of dark and light, of earth and heaven, of female and male. Yin and yang are never polar opposites; rather, each flows into the other with no absolute division, the way day flows into night and night into day. The ideal for human life, then, is balance and harmony. The great problem of existence is the disharmony that occurs when the elements of self, society, and/or the universe are out of balance.

To restore balance, two different religions emerged in China: Daoism and Confucianism. Both sought to bring harmony between heaven and earth, self and society. These two traditions offered very different means to overcome the problem and realize the ideal. Daoist sages urged humans to seek harmony with the rhythms of nature through cultivating *wu-wei*, the art of "not doing," or not interfering with the natural flow of life. By contrast, the Confucian sages urged humans to establish harmony in society through the practice of *li*, the ritual observance of obligations attached to one's station in society. They taught that people can be in harmony with the rhythms of the universe only when individuals know their place in the social order, (as child, parent, citizen etc.), cultivate their character, and sacrifice their self-interest for the good of the whole society.

India and the Myths of Liberation

In ancient India, life was also seen in relation to the cycles and rhythms of nature. Its priests enacted powerful rituals to control the gods behind all cosmic activity. But in India these rhythms were ultimately to be escaped, not affirmed. Human existence is seen as unsatisfactory not because there is nothing good about life but because it is transient and always ends in old age, sickness, and death. The problem of life is human entrapment in an endless cycle of suffering and rebirth; the highest goal was to overcome these traps. The ultimate goal of all the great religions originating in India is to destroy the delusions fostered by our selfish desires, for only when these are mastered can humans be freed from the wheel of death and rebirth. In that moment of liberation or enlightenment, one will find blissful union with ultimate reality and liberation from rebirth.

For most Hindus, the true self (*atman*) is the same as the eternal Brahman in either the personal or impersonal form. Buddhism suggests that an eternal self is a delusion, for all selves are empty; one who realizes the illusion of a permanent self advances on the path to nirvana or enlightenment, and closer to liberation from rebirth.

Hinduism and Buddhism developed a variety of means, called yogas, for achieving liberation or enlightenment. These range from disciplined ritual activity and the selfless performance of one's duties, to seeking spiritual knowledge through meditation, or cultivating selfless devotion toward a particular god or goddess.

The Middle East and the Myths of History

The myths of nature, of harmony, and of liberation use the human experience of the rhythms and cycles of nature as the basis for religious metaphors and symbolic language expressed in sacred stories. In the myths of history, by contrast, it is not nature but history from which the metaphors for religious experience are primarily drawn. While all religions communicate their traditions by telling stories, only the religions of the Middle East, beginning with Judaism, make "story" itself the central metaphor of religious expression. Unlike the eternally cyclical rhythms of nature, stories have a beginning and an end. Ancient Judaism conceived of the cosmos as a great unfolding story told by a great divine storyteller (God): In the beginning God spoke, the world was created, and the story of revelation began.

Three versions of this story of revelation arose in the Middle East—first the Judaic, then the Christian, and finally the Islamic. For each of these, human beings are considered human by virtue of being children of the one God who created all things. All three traditions tell the myth of Adam and Eve as the first human beings, and venerate the patriarch Abraham, whom each considers the true model of faith and obedience to divine revelation. In all three, the problem of life is viewed as "sin"—failing to

Hindu women pay homage to the god of the sun during the Chat Puja festival on the banks of the Hooghly River in the eastern Indian city of Calcutta. Thousands of Hindu devotees reached the riverside at sunset and will spend the night praying.

All that remains of the great temple in Jerusalem, destroyed by the Romans in 70 CE, is the Western Wall. It is considered to be the holiest of sites where observant Jews come to pray.

follow God's will or laws, a combination of idolatry and human selfishness that leads to injustice. The ideal goal of life is for humans to be in harmony with the will of God, whereupon peace and justice will reign and death will be overcome.

While all three religions believe that the means for bringing about this era of peace and triumph over death are obedience to the will of God, each has its own unique complement to that obedience. In Judaism, it is study and debate over the meaning of God's Word; in Christianity, acceptance of divine aid through the incarnation of God; and in Islam, submission to the will of God. Although each of the three Abrahamic religions has its own story of the cosmos, full of many trials, triumphs, and tragedies, each tells of the human-divine story having a happy ending. In contrast to the myths of nature, harmony, and liberation, traditions founded on myths of history regard time not as the enemy but as the vehicle for encountering the ultimate reality, which is God. The goal is not to escape time by returning to the beginning through ritual, nor rising above time in mystical ecstasy, but to meet God in time and make a journey with God through time. Time for the faithful is promising, and the future is ultimately hopeful.

Religious Diversity and Historical Change: The Structure of This Book

Each of these religious traditions speaks to the problem of morality by helping the individual to get beyond the self-centeredness that came with urban individualism and to grasp the essential unity and interdependence of all human beings. And each sought to provide life with meaning by depicting individuals and communities as participating in a great cosmic story that gives drama and purpose to human life. In addition, these stories show individuals a way to overcome the finality of death.

We need to refine the picture of the world's religions we have just created. When we stand back at a great distance we can use the four types of myth or story—those of nature, harmony, liberation, and history—to classify the various religions. As we get closer, we discover that each of these stories has variations expressing internal differences in doctrine and in practice.

In the chapters to come we will examine how human beings struggle to continue the religiousness of their ancestors in a radically different, fast-changing, and globalizing world. We will see how Western civilization gave birth to modernity and, through its colonial expansion, spread its religious and cultural influence around the world, disrupting premodern religious cultures everywhere. **Colonialism** is part of the story of virtually all religions and civilizations, East and West. But after 1492, modern Western colonialism came closest to achieving global domination. Propelled by European colonialism, Christianity became the first faith to spread globally, forcing every religion to reckon with its beliefs, its practices, and its critiques of other religions.

We will also describe how colonialism, in turn, provoked postcolonial reactions that have divided those in each religious tradition into three groups:

1. *Fundamentalists*, who reject important aspects of modernity and want to go back to what they perceive as the purity of an "authentic" social/political order manifested in the sacred way of life of their ancestors.
2. *Modernists*, who seek an accommodation of their religious tradition to the insights of science and the social and political realities of modern life.
3. *Postmodernists*, who, while rejecting the dominance of science and Western modernity, seek a new situation that affirms the role of religion in public life in a way that embraces religious and cultural diversity. Postmodernists are open to change in their religious tradition in this regard.

While some fundamentalists reject everything modern, most accept modern technology while rejecting changes suggested by the sciences that would call into question the fundamentalists' religious worldview. Earlier we spoke of "orthodoxy" as "right belief," and while many fundamentalists would consider themselves orthodox, not all those who call themselves orthodox would consider themselves fundamentalists. Very often orthodox movements will interpret their scriptures allegorically or symbolically, while fundamentalists tend to interpret their scriptures literally. For instance, an orthodox Christian might interpret the seven days of creation as symbolic periods of undetermined length. A fundamentalist, however, would be inclined to say, "No, we are talking about creating the world literally in seven 24-hour periods of time, so scientific accounts of the origin and development of the universe over millennia are false."

colonialism: the political, social, cultural, and economic domination of one society by another

fundamentalist: one who rejects aspects of modernity and wants to return to the perceived foundational purity of an ancestral sacred social/political order, or way of life

Figure 1.3 Mapping the typical spectrum of believers in religious communities.

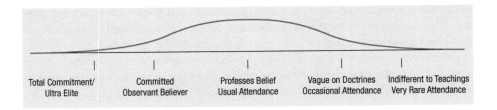

Total Commitment/ Ultra Elite	Committed Observant Believer	Professes Belief Usual Attendance	Vague on Doctrines Occasional Attendance	Indifferent to Teachings Very Rare Attendance

Among modernists and postmodernists, most argue that some parts of the religious tradition must change. What is distinctive about the modernist view is that human understanding of religious truth and practice is subject to historical change and development, a notion that fundamentalists find abhorrent, even blasphemous.

As Figure 1.3 indicates, religions should not be studied as abstract beliefs but as the beliefs and practices of real people. The range of beliefs that humans adopt in any religious tradition range from the virtuosos to the average believers and the hardly observant. The elite have a complete commitment and lifestyle to the highest religious ideals. At the other extreme are those who are indifferent to doctrine or who disbelieve. In learning about world religions, being attentive to this variance offers clues about how religion has brought out the best and worst of humanity in history.

Our treatment of the history of each tradition in each chapter will be organized as follows:

- Overview
- Encounter with Modernity
- Premodern
- Modern
- Postmodern
- Conclusion

The overview at the start of each chapter introduces the basic worldview of the religious tradition. The section that follows, "Encounter with Modernity," describes a particular moment in which premodern religious traditions clashed with the modern worldview and explains the diverse responses that emerged from that encounter. Next, each chapter will shift back to the premodern period and the origins and development of the tradition, to better explain why modernity represents a challenge to it. This period is accounted for in two phases—a formative period, which traces the origins of the traditions, and a classical period, which explains its fully developed premodern beliefs, rituals, and institutions.

The section on modernity traces the diverse fundamentalist and modernist responses that developed in each tradition as it was challenged and threatened by Western colonialism and its modern scientific/technological worldview. This is followed by a postmodern section, in which we survey the most recent reactions to the adaptations each tradition has made to the modern world. These reactions tend to be postcolonial revolutions (in most regions, after 1945) to reclaim religious and cultural identities that existed before the advent of modern Western colonialism. In this way we show why the world, with all its possibilities for coexistence and conflict, is the way it is today. The conclusion to each chapter addresses the implications of this history for the future of each tradition.

Historical Overview: From Premodern to Postmodern

The structure of this book revolves around two great transitions in human history:

Premodern to Modern
Modern to Postmodern

The first began with urbanization, and the second begins with globalization.

From about 8000 BCE the domestication of plants and animals made village life possible. Acquisition of agricultural skill then allowed the development of the first great cities, from approximately 3000 BCE, bringing about a great transformation in human experience. Urban life drew people together out of different tribal groups. In the earliest indigenous human groups, everyone lived close to the rhythms of nature, in extended families or clans that shared a common way of life and lived by the same myths and rituals. In the cities people came together from different groups, bringing with them different stories, different rituals, and different family identities.

The complexities of urban life led to the specialization of labor. Whereas in indigenous societies everyone shared in hunting and gathering or simple agriculture, in the cities society became more complex and differentiated into classes (peasants, craftsmen, noblemen, priests, etc.). In a parallel fashion, elaborate and detailed new mythologies emerged in the cities, assigning special powers and tasks to each of the many gods and spirits of the different tribes now embraced as the gods of the city.

These changes fundamentally transformed the economies and cultures of the new urban centers. In earlier indigenous groups, identity was collective because everybody shared the same stories and hunting and gathering activities. The cities, by contrast, were communities of strangers. People did not automatically share a collective sense of identity.

The loss of collective sense of identity and the emergence of large, impersonal urban city-states in Egypt, India, China, and Mesopotamia led to growing populations for whom the experience of the world was marked by suffering and cruelty. Populated by strangers and ruled by emperors, kings, or pharaohs considered divine or representatives of the gods, these new city-states eventually faced a threefold crisis.

First, indigenous tribal collective identity was experienced as eternal—the tribe never dies. However, in urban contexts, humans began to think of themselves as individuals, and death suddenly loomed as a personal problem even as life seemed more cruel and uncertain. With the greater development of individual self-awareness, death presented people with a new and unsettling problem: What happens to my (individual) "self" when I die?

Second, urban life created the new problems of law and morality. In the indigenous group the right thing to do was prescribed by ritual, and the same rites were known and respected by all. In cities, people from a variety of religious traditions lived together; yet as individuals, each looked out for his or her own good, if necessary at the expense of others. Thus in the cities law emerged to set the minimum order necessary to sustain human life. It also became necessary to develop a system of ethics to persuade people to live up to even higher ideals.

Third, life in the city-state evoked a crisis of meaning. Can life really have any meaning if it is filled with injustice and ends in a meaningless death? The first written expression of this great question appeared in the ancient Near East at the beginning of the urban period (ca. 3000–1500 BCE) and is known as the *Epic of Gilgamesh*.

The great world religions emerged in the three centers of civilization in the ancient world—China, India, and the Middle East—as their founders and prophets responded to critical questions about the meaning of life, mortality, and morality. Between 800 BCE and 600 CE all developed their classical expressions, dividing much of the world among them (see Map 1.2) in the context of the formation of great empires that united peoples of various tribes and city-states into larger political entities. These new political orders created a need for a more inclusive understanding of human identity. Sages and prophets arose who redefined the meaning of being human in terms beyond the boundaries of the tribe and the city-state, seeing a higher unity to reality beyond the many local gods and spirits. These ideas about the meaning of the divine–human relationship remain central to the world's great religions.

Today the secularizing influences of modernization and unprecedented international migration are transforming the ancient geographic division of the world's religions. Before we can move on to explore the struggle of peoples everywhere to continue the religiousness of their ancestors in today's very different world, we need to be clear about the terms **premodern**, **modern**, and **postmodern**.

In general, premodern history describes a range of cultures in which religion played the decisive role in explaining and ordering life. In premodern societies, religion provided the most certain knowledge one could have of the world, and consequently religious authority played a central role in each culture's social, political, and economic ordering of public life. In this respect, all premodern cultures have more in common with each other than with modern **secular** (i.e., nonreligious) culture.

With the advances in science made in the eighteenth century, the scientific worldview spread globally and, for many, came to replace religion as the most certain form of knowledge. The modern period is marked by a tendency for individuals to view religion as a matter of personal faith or opinion. Gradually most areas of public life

premodern: civilization in which there is no separation between a dominant religion and society

modern: civilization that separates its citizens' lives into public and private spheres, restricting religion to private life

postmodern: society typified by accepting public diversity in both religious beliefs and social practices

secular: sociologically used to mean "nonreligious"

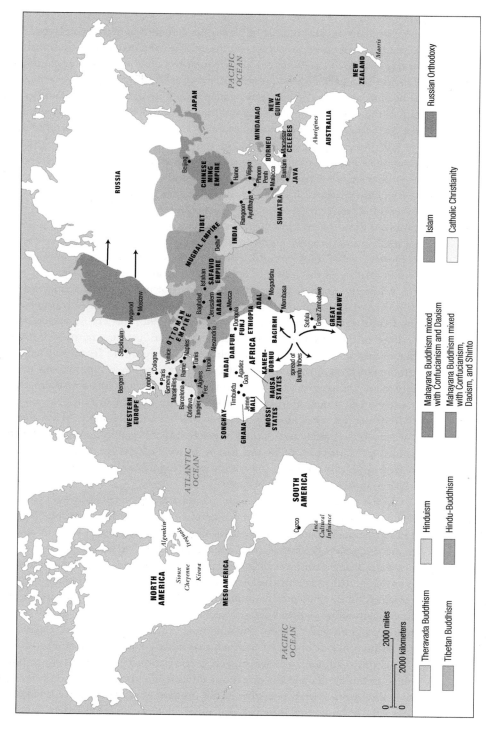

Map 1.2 Distribution of world religions circa 1500 CE.

The map legend includes:

- Theravada Buddhism
- Tibetan Buddhism
- Hinduism
- Hindu-Buddhism
- Mahayana Buddhism mixed with Confucianism and Daoism
- Mahayana Buddhism mixed with Confucianism, Daoism, and Shinto
- Islam
- Catholic Christianity
- Russian Orthodoxy

Labeled locations on the map include:

NORTH AMERICA — Algonkin, Iroquois, Sioux, Cheyenne, Kiowa, MESOAMERICA

SOUTH AMERICA — Cuzco, Inca Cultural Influence

WESTERN EUROPE — Bergen, Stockholm, Novgorod, Moscow, London, Cologne, Paris, Geneva, Venice, Rome, Naples, Barcelona, Marseilles, Córdova, Tangier, Fez, Algiers, Tunis, Tripoli

AFRICA — SONGHAY, GHANA, MALI, Timbuktu, Jenne, Agadez, MOSSI STATES, HAUSA STATES, KANEM-BORNU, WADAI, DARFUR, BAGIRMI, FUNJ, Dongola, ETHIOPIA, ADAL, Mogadishu, Mombasa, Sofala, GREAT ZIMBABWE, spread of Bantu tribes

Middle East — OTTOMAN EMPIRE, Baghdad, Jerusalem, Alexandria, Mecca, ARABIA, SAFAVID EMPIRE, Istahan

RUSSIA

India/Asia — MUGHAL EMPIRE, TIBET, Delhi, INDIA, Rangoon, Ayutthaya, Vijaya, Hanoi, Phnom Penh, CHINESE MING EMPIRE, Beijing, JAPAN

Southeast Asia/Pacific — SUMATRA, JAVA, Bantam, Malacca, BORNEO, CELEBES, Macassar, MINDANAO, NEW GUINEA, AUSTRALIA, Aborigines, NEW ZEALAND, Maoris

Oceans — PACIFIC OCEAN, ATLANTIC OCEAN

Scale: 0 – 2000 miles / 0 – 2000 kilometers

were secularized. That is, religious doctrines and officials no longer played central roles in politics, economics, or public education. The most dramatic institutional expression of this change in the West was the emergence of the separation of church and state. The secular state was the expression of "modern" reality—politics governed a society's public life, and religion was a private matter for individuals and their families. From the end of the nineteenth century up until the early 1970s, many scholars even predicted the end of religion and a coming nonreligious, or secular, stage in world history.

Every premodern society saw the universe through explicitly religious eyes and pronounced its vision of life sacred. Since all premodern societies were dominated by the influence of religious authority, they all understood their worlds through religious myths and rituals that had been passed down for many generations. Modern culture, by contrast, tends to emphasize the centrality of rational and empirical science. In addition, the modern view held that history represented inevitable progress toward an ideal future, progress that could only be accomplished through science, with its "objective view" of the world. For modernists, science and the progress of history would finally end the centuries of human bloodshed caused by religions.

While the contrast between premodern and modern is dramatic and clear, our third term in this sequence—postmodern—needs clarification. According to the postmodernist thinker Jean-François Lyotard (1924–98), this era is characterized by the collapse of the all-encompassing sacred stories or "grand narratives" through which human beings interpreted life in their respective cultures.[2] In ancient societies, these **metanarratives** (to use another of Lyotard's terms) were the religious myths of the four types we have described; the notion that they were true for all times and places went virtually unquestioned. In modern culture the primary metanarrative has been the story of history as progress driven by science and technology. However, the globalization of religious and cultural interaction that began in the twentieth century has tended to "relativize" them all—that is, to see each as a historical construction, and regard none as ultimately, universally true. Significantly, this includes the modern myth of inevitable scientific progress.

In the premodern world a single grand narrative or religious worldview was typically experienced as true and meaningful by the majority of people. It is this kind of metanarrative that has collapsed for many in our day. For Lyotard, "postmodern" is more a style of thinking than a stage of history. It invites pluralism and rejects imposing a single truth on all. In our postmodern world a new type of metanarrative is arising globally, an anti-metanarrative accepting the reality of religious and cultural pluralism. In this anti-metanarrative, no single story is all-encompassing for all people in a given culture—especially as a global culture emerges. The grand stories of the world religions have thereby become miniaturized and globalized. Everyone has his or her own stories, and acknowledges that other people live by other stories.

In this textbook, we also suggest a correlation between the postmodern challenge to modernity and the postcolonial challenge to colonialism. A postcolonial era typically begins with a rejection of the modern Western historical metanarrative of scientific-technological progress, opening the door to postmodern awareness and critiques. However, that door swings two ways: Some seek a return to premodern

metanarrative: grand cosmic and/or historical story accepted by majority of a society as expressing its beliefs about its origins, destiny, and sacred identity

fundamental notions of religious truth and practice, insisting that there is only one true religious
story and way of life; while others embrace the
postmodern situation and seek to accommodate
the reality of diversity. What these fundamentalisms and postmodern pluralisms have in common
is a rejection of the modern strategy of privatizing
religion. Both insist that religion ought to play a
role in influencing not only private but also public
life. Fundamentalists advocate accomplishing this
by returning to an absolute religious metanarrative
and work to impose a political order that should
shape public life for everyone. In contrast, postmodernists accept a plurality of narratives, recognizing the public benefits of embracing religious

An adult pilgrim is
baptized in the Jordan
River, Israel.

pluralism in an age of globalization. Today, all the world's religions are caught up in the
struggle between their premodern, modern, and possible postmodern interpretations.

Because Christianity is the dominant religion of Western civilization, the civilization that produced modernization, it went through the trauma of accommodation
to modernity first. Being the first, it had the luxury of embracing modernization in
slower stages than those religions that did not encounter modernization, until it had
attained a more developed form. Therefore Chapter 4, on Christianity, will have to
tell two stories. One is an outline of the intellectual and social history of the West
that resulted in modernization, and the other is the story of the role that Christianity
played in that history, both in promoting modernization and in resisting it.

Some have charged that modernization is a form of Western cultural and perhaps
even religious imperialism that has been forced on other cultures. However, modernization and secularization challenge all sacred traditions and identities, including
those of Western religions. As we shall see in this book, modernization did not have
an impact on all religions simultaneously, nor did all react in exactly the same way,
although there are striking similarities. Therefore, we should not expect all religions
and societies to exhibit exactly the same patterns and responses.

The Modern/Postmodern Transition: Colonialism, Socialism, and the End of Modernity

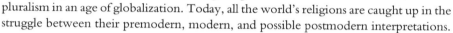

In the nineteenth century the synergy of Western science, economics (capitalism), and
technology fostered among the dominant European nations, especially England and
France, a thirst for building colonial empires. These colonial ambitions were paralleled

in the modern period by only one Asian nation—Japan. By 1914 most of the world was under the domination of Western European culture. Geographically the Russians and the British controlled about a third of the globe. In terms of population, the British Empire controlled about a fifth of the human race—nearly 400 million people—while France controlled over 50 million colonial subjects (see Map 1.3).

Colonial dominance, and often governance or rule, and paternalism (the British spoke of "the white man's burden" and the French of their "mission to civilize") were accompanied by the spread of science, technology, and capitalism, which proved traumatic to indigenous cultures and their religious traditions. The impressive achievements of Western civilization often prompted elites to initially embrace modernization and secularization. Almost inevitably, however, there was a religious and political backlash, seen in struggles for national liberation as indigenous peoples sought to reclaim their independence and autonomy and to reaffirm the value of their original ways of life. This backlash often included a resurgence of religious influence as a force in anticolonial struggles. Most independence movements readily adopted a key element of Western civilization—**nationalism**—in their attempts to resist foreign occupation and to protect their religious and cultural identities by resisting exploitation.

nationalism: Belief in the nation as a sacred entity

Many of these movements paradoxically struck an alliance with socialism, the philosophical and political movement that arose in the nineteenth century in Europe among the new urban working class as a protest against the poverty and social dislocation created by early capitalism and the Industrial Revolution. Socialism was itself a modernist movement, sustained by a vision of scientific progress, yet it also championed premodern values of community against the rampant individualism of modern capitalism. In Karl Marx's formulation of "scientific socialism," it became an international movement that had an impact on world history as profound as that of any world religion. Indeed, as religious societies around the globe revolted against European imperialism, most experimented with some form of socialism as a modern way of protesting modernity itself. The twentieth century produced examples around the world of Jewish, Christian, Islamic, Hindu, Buddhist, and neo-Confucian forms of socialism. In its secular form socialism or communism became the dominant element in Russian culture, spreading throughout Eastern Europe and across Asia like a new missionary religion, most prominently "converting" China, the largest country of Asia, by 1949.

Consistent with the myth of modernity, the German socialist Karl Marx (1818–83) saw history as progressively unfolding in three stages defined in terms of a class theory of society:

1. First, primitive communism (tribal societies), in which all were equal
2. Next, the rise of complex urban civilizations, which led to societies ruled by bureaucracies and pitted privileged classes against the masses
3. Finally, the last stage of history in which society would once more be communistic. In this last age all would once again be equal—for all complex, class-defined institutions would wither away, and people would live together in spontaneous harmony.

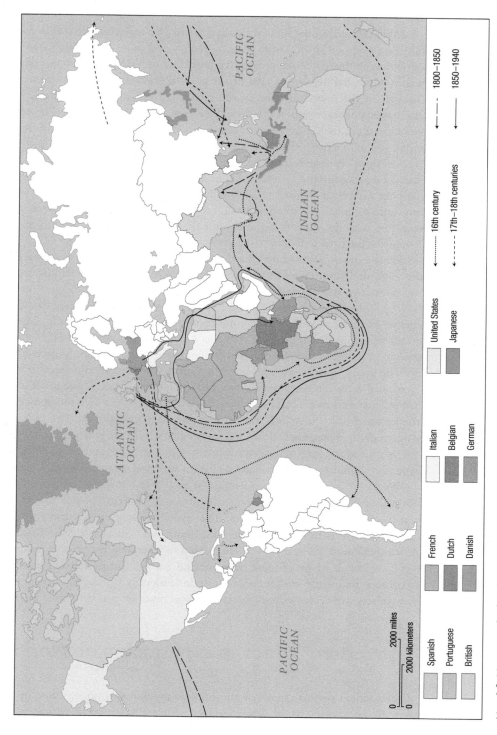

Map 1.3 Missions and colonialism.

PACIFIC OCEAN

INDIAN OCEAN

ATLANTIC OCEAN

PACIFIC OCEAN

1800–1850

1850–1940

16th century

17th–18th centuries

United States

Japanese

Italian

Belgian

German

Spanish

Portuguese

British

French

Dutch

Danish

0 2000 miles

0 2000 kilometers

29

Marx secularized the biblical myth of history by replacing the will of God as the directing force of history with what he maintained were "scientific" laws of social development that guide the progressive unfolding of history. Marx believed that capitalism depended on a large class of urban workers, who, once they were gathered together in the industrial cities of the modern world, would organize, creating an international workers union that would lead a worldwide revolution. This revolution would result in the replacement of capitalist societies, based on hereditary wealth and privileges, with a new, classless society of freedom, equality, and social justice for all.

Socialism represents an ambivalent rejection of a modern scientific world dominated by an economic system, capitalism, that seemed to make the rich richer and the poor poorer. It claimed to be "modern," "secular," and "scientific." Yet Marxism, unlike capitalism, retained much of the religious and ethical power of biblical tradition, with its emphasis on justice for the poor, the widow, the orphan, and the stranger as the final outcome of history.

While socialism challenged the impact of modernity on society, two world wars decisively undermined belief in inevitable progress toward greater scientific understanding, prosperity, and benevolent coexistence. World War I (1914–18) and World War II (1939–45) shattered this myth. Science and technology, which had been viewed as the engines of progress, were now the means of unprecedented destruction. The utopian dream of technological progress ended as a nightmare in August 1945, when newly invented atomic bombs were dropped on the Japanese cities of Hiroshima and Nagasaki.

The use of nuclear weapons brought World War II to an end, only to usher in a "cold war" between the Soviet Union and the United States. Throughout the second half of the twentieth century, an armed standoff between these two superpowers threatened a third and final world war of thermonuclear annihilation. The makers of the modern myth of progress had failed to foresee that a technology that increases efficiency can be applied not only to the improvement of public health and the production of less expensive consumer goods, but also to the invention of weapons of mass destruction.

Finally, it is important to note that World War I and especially World War II not only called into question the "scientific age of progress" but also brought an end to the modern age of empires. The twentieth century saw the withdrawal of European powers from the Middle East, South Asia, Southeast Asia, East Asia, and Africa. European colonial powers left behind independent nation-states whose rulers were unelected. Many of these new political entities had boundaries drawn by the colonizers, frequently without regard to ethnic identity or religious communities. In many places, the legacy of exploitative colonial practices was economic poverty.

Postmodern Trends in a Postcolonial World

In the modern period the social authority of religion was undermined by the new scientific rationalists, whose descriptions of reality, they believed, explained how the world "really is," in contrast to the fantasies of religions. In the postmodern world, many have argued that not only religious knowledge but also scientific knowledge is relative. That is, science too can be seen as an imaginative interpretation of the world based on faith (faith that the world can be "known") and cannot offer the final truth about reality. These arguments are similar to the disputes between premodern religious philosophers (defending religion) and the new secular scientists (challenging religion) at the beginning of the modern period. No matter who is ultimately correct, the re-emergence of such disputes suggests that the postmodern situation is one in which unquestioning faith in science, which characterized the modern era, no longer exists.

From the perspective of postmodernists, all knowledge is relative, including religious and scientific knowledge. Postmodern trends seem to promote cultural and ethical relativism. Some rejoice in this, arguing that it means the end of absolutes that have been used by some to justify violence. Still others are afraid that total relativism will lead to the end of civilization and the beginning of a new barbarism—that once we have relativized the absolute distinction between good and evil, we will plunge into an ethical void in which any atrocity can be justified.

Thus for individuals living in the postmodern period, scientific knowledge now competes on equal intellectual footing with religious knowledge. They are equally relative and equally subject to criticism by those who reject their main precepts. Therefore the position that scientific secularism is a source of public and certain knowledge, while religious knowledge is subjective, non-empirical, and private, no longer seems as valid as it once did. Consequently, the appearance of postmodern trends has been accompanied by a resurgence of religion in the public realm—a resurgence whose diverse forms are responses to both the threat and promise of postmodernity.

Conclusion: We Are All Heretics in Our Postmodern Situation

In the premodern period, most people acquired their religious identities because of where they were born. But in the postmodern world, however, most individuals are faced with what sociologist Peter Berger (b. 1929) calls "the heretical imperative."[3] *Heretic* comes from an ancient Greek word that means "to choose." In our postmodern world every religious person becomes a **heretic**, that is, one who is no longer simply born into a given religion or identity but must choose it, even if it is only to retain the identity offered by the circumstances of his or her birth.

In this world of "heretics," all the world's religions have been forced to take account of each other. Today global media allow distant viewers to experience the positives and negatives, both exemplary and scandalous actions, of individuals acting in the name of their religions. Around the world, religious adherents and skeptics encounter their own uniqueness amid the undeniable reality of the world's enduring diverse faiths.

heretic: from the ancient Greek term for "one who chooses," used to communicate the postmodern idea that everyone has no choice but to choose one's beliefs since there is no longer a single center of "taken-for-granted commonly shared truth" in society

"Modernity multiplies choices. . . . The modern individual is faced not just with the opportunity but with the necessity to make choices as to his beliefs. This fact constitutes the heretical imperative."

—Peter Berger

Before the era of postmodernism, other people's religions could be readily dismissed in a series of negative stereotypes. When people of diverse religions are neighbors, this option is both more difficult and more dangerous. To the degree that stereotyping and discrimination persist, they promote prejudice, conflict, and violence. The alternative is to develop new understandings of the relation between world religions and the societies around the world—one that tolerates all people following their chosen faith traditions, including nonbelief, yet also share their wisdom with each other in an atmosphere of mutual respect and understanding. This alternative—to appreciate what we have in common as well as to acknowledge our distinctive differences—has been explored brilliantly by two of the great religious figures of the twentieth century, Mohandas K. Gandhi and Martin Luther King Jr. Each spiritual leader "passed over" from his native religion and culture to the religious world of the other and came back enriched by that second tradition without having abandoned his own. You are invited to embark on a similar journey through the study of the world's religions today.

Discussion Questions

1. Define religion in terms of its six characteristics—sacred, myth, ritual, community, morality, and religious leaders—and explain the possible relations among them.

2. What do the authors mean when they argue that all morality is religious, even that of atheists?

3. In what way does religious language complicate the question of whether there is agreement or disagreement among religions on various issues? Describe in terms of the *via analogia* and the *via negativa*, giving examples of each.

4. Explain the four types of religious story and give a historical example of each.

5. Why did urbanization lead to the emergence of the great world religions? That is, what new urban problems did these religions address?

6. What is colonialism, and what is its significance for religions and cultures in the modern period?

7. How are the terms *premodern*, *modern*, and *postmodern* being used in this text, and how are they related to modern colonialism?

8. According to the authors, modernization privatizes religion, whereas in premodern and postmodern religious movements religion plays a public role in society but in different ways. Explain.

9. Explain Marxist socialism, and tell why it was an attractive option to religious movements protesting modernity.

10. How might you justify the statement that both postmodernist and fundamentalist religious movements are examples of Peter Berger's "heretical imperative"?

Key Terms

colonialism
divine
fundamentalist
globalization
heretic
metanarrative
modern
morality

myth
nationalism
orthodoxy
orthopraxy
postmodern
premodern
religion
ritual

secular
sympathetic
  imagination
transcendent
ultimate reality
via analogia
via negativa

Notes

1. F. Max Muller, *Lectures on the Origin and Growth of Religion as Illustrated by the Religions of India* (London: Longmans Green, 1880), p. 218.
2. Jean-François Lyotard, *The Postmodern Condition: A Report on Knowledge* (Minneapolis: University of Minnesota Press, 1984).
3. Peter Berger, *The Heretical Imperative* (New York: Doubleday, 1979), p. 60.

INDIGENOUS RELIGIONS

2

Overview

ndigenous peoples are ethnic groups whose ties to their lands go back a millennium or even longer. Found on every continent except Antarctica, some indigenous peoples have migrated to new homelands and changed their ways of life in recent centuries; others have been relocated to "reservations" within modern states; still others (in growing numbers) live in two worlds, moving between life in their modern countries and their native group.

All surviving indigenous peoples (or "first peoples") have been affected by the modern world. The cultural traditions and religious lives of all these peoples have been altered, often dramatically, by outsiders encroaching on their lands, exposing them to new diseases, and forcefully assimilating them into the majority citizenry. Around the world, hundreds of indigenous groups have succumbed or been assimilated, their religions (like their languages) lost forever.

The religious traditions discussed in this chapter are different from those of the great world religions covered elsewhere in this book. Yet these indigenous peoples and their religions remain a noteworthy part of the world's religious landscape today, despite their small populations. Although few possess scriptures or temples, these independent, ethnic, and land-bounded religions are worthy of study for three reasons. First, they help us understand the general phenomenon of humanity as a religious species. Second, the treatment of indigenous peoples by the great world religions provides insights about the latter's role in the historical expansion of early states and

◀ Wearing feathers to suggest soul flight, adorned with body paint and ornaments to array the power of his ancestral protectors, an Amazonian shaman enters a healing trance.

modern nations. Finally, we can see beliefs and practices of the world's indigenous religions being assimilated into the new religions forming across the globe today.

This chapter begins by looking back to prehistory to understand some of the common worldviews, religious roles, and ritual practices evident among early *Homo sapiens*. We then examine case studies of the world's last living hunter-gatherers and simple agriculturalists. Although it is impossible for any textbook to represent the richness and diversity of the world's surviving indigenous religions, these case studies convey an awareness of the spiritual vitality and the neglected histories of these extraordinary indigenous traditions. Understanding religions today is enriched by seeing how all humanity, even in isolated nonliterate groups, has always been "religious." ○ ● ○

Origins of *Homo religiosus*: Prehistory

Around a hundred thousand years ago, *Homo sapiens* emerged from a 4-million-year process of hominid evolution to become the animal who makes tools, controls fire, buries its dead, speaks, and thinks symbolically. Long before agriculture and urbanization, the first *Homo sapiens* lived in hunter-gatherer societies. By studying their artifacts as well as the small-scale societies that still subsist in this mode of life, we can imagine what their existence was like. We know our ancestors usually lived and ate well, and that they made efforts to communicate with the spirits of their ancestors and with animals. Most likely, they regularly sought assistance from these spirits through trance and altered states of consciousness, which may have been the origins of religion.

Although the earliest humans used language, writing had not yet been invented. Consequently, these societies had oral cultures in which everything that was known was known only because someone remembered it. And memories were made readily accessible because they were expressed in stories—stories of sacred ancestors, spirit beings, and heroes. Not recorded in written texts, these stories were kept alive in song and dance.

Moreover, time and space were not abstractions but were reckoned according to ancestral myths and sacred experiences. Religion likely began at sites where people believed the powers that govern the universe first appeared. Humans experienced such places of revelation as "centers of the world" (*axes mundi*). In the indigenous religions, most everything is spiritually alive. The trees, the mountains, the rivers, special stones, animals, and, of course, humans are said to have souls or spirits that give them life, or *animate* them. Anthropologists once used the term **animism** to describe a worldview in which a measure of conscious life is attributed to these entities.

Each of the thousands of indigenous peoples have (or had) a unique **cosmogony**, or account of the world's origins and its essential powers. Because in most cosmogonies the group telling the story was a part of the everlasting cycle of nature's rhythms, the group is assumed to be an integral part of the cosmos. Everything in premodern indigenous group life reinforced a collective sense of common identity: All shared the

animism: belief in an inner soul that gives life and identity to living things and emphasizes rituals in which humans interact with other souls

cosmogony: mythological account of the world's creation

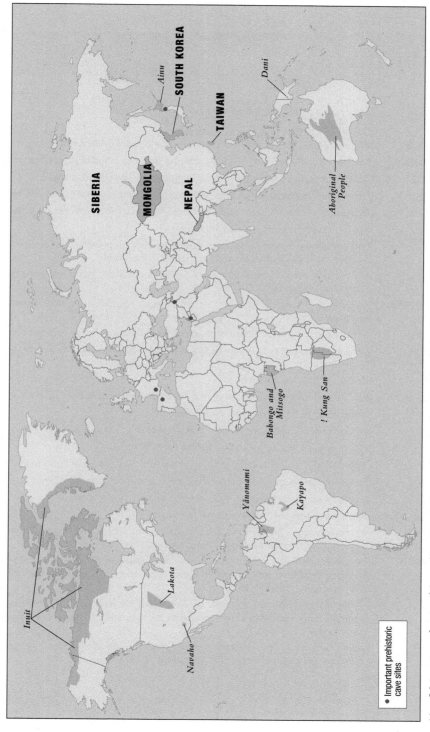

Map 2.1 Locations of some of the prehistoric and ethnographic cultural groups discussed in this book.

- Important prehistoric cave sites

SIBERIA

MONGOLIA

SOUTH KOREA

TAIWAN

NEPAL

Ainu

Dani

Aboriginal People

Babongo and Mitsogo

! Kung San

Yãnomami

Kayapo

Inuit

Lakota

Navaho

37

Timeline

2 million	Early hominids use the first stone tools
½ mill	Fire domesticated
100,000	*Homo sapiens*: Neanderthals and another line present evidence of ritual burial
40,000 BCE	Modern man biologically; hunting-gathering societies found across Africa and Eurasia
30,000	Human language and symbolic thought reach new level of advancement
20,000	Human burials across Africa and Eurasia with offerings, reflecting afterlife belief
10,000	*Homo sapiens* from Siberia disperse across North and South America via Bering Strait
7,000	Beginnings of settled agriculture, first cities
5,000	Earliest archaeological evidence of Australian aboriginal belief connected with the Rainbow Serpent, perhaps the oldest continuing belief in the world
2,000	Major states arise on the Yellow River, China; Indus River, India; Babylon on Tigris–Euphrates; Nile in Egypt
800 BCE–200 CE	Era of lasting formulations of social-spiritual teachings defining ethical modes of human existence in cities
100 BCE	States expanding into wilderness frontiers; assimilation of indigenous peoples
1400 CE	Growing populations in Americas live in hierarchically organized chiefdoms or small kingdoms
1492	Columbus reaches America
1492–1600	Europeans make first contact with native peoples of Western Hemisphere continents
	Introduction of the horse to the New World
	90 percent indigenous mortality in many settlements
	Christian missionaries fan out across the New World
1546	"New World" colonists form societies and economies dependent on slave labor
1606	Earliest recorded contact between Europeans and Australian Aborigines
1616	Smallpox epidemic decimates native tribes in New England region
1709	Slave market erected on Wall Street in New York
1716	Alamo Mission in San Antonio is authorized by the viceroy of Mexico. The mission becomes an educational center for Native Americans who converted to Christianity.
1808–1811	Tecumseh, chief of the Shawnees, organizes a defensive confederacy of Northwest frontier tribes, attempting to make the Ohio River a permanent boundary between the United States and indigenous peoples' land
1811	William Henry Harrison, governor of Ohio, leads the ferocious Battle of Tippecanoe, which destroys Tecumseh's town as well as the remnants of Tecumseh's indigenous confederacy
1830	Indian Removal Act passed; over next ten years U.S. government forcibly removes thousands of indigenous peoples west of the Mississippi

1838	"Trail of Tears": Native Americans force-marched by U.S. military to settle in Oklahoma
1850–1875	Hunting by American colonists leads to near extermination of buffalo herds, undermining Plains Indians' survival
1871	1871 Indian Appropriation Act specifies that no tribe thereafter would be recognized as an independent nation
1876	Lieutenant Colonel George Custer leads army attack on assembled native tribes; he and all 250 of his soldiers are killed. Afterward, U.S. Army orders troops "to attack and kill every male Indian over twelve years of age."
1888	The White Australia Policy articulated
1889–1890	Paiute spiritual leader has vision and spreads message of the Ghost Dance
1890	Massacre of Sioux at Wounded Knee, South Dakota
1910	Bwiti, a West Central African religion, is founded among the forest-dwelling people of Gabon and Cameroon
1918	Native American Church founded in Oklahoma
1920	Santo Daime is begun in western Brazil
1930–1989	Soviet repression of shamans in Siberia and Outer Mongolia
1950	People's Republic of China labels shamanism a "superstition" and represses spirit mediums across China
1951	Australian government formally adopts assimilation policy toward aboriginal peoples
1975	The Australian Senate acknowledges prior ownership of country by aboriginal people and seeks compensation for their dispossession. The World Council of Indigenous People is founded.
1978	Religious Freedom Act promises to "protect and preserve" for Native Americans "freedom to believe, express, and exercise" traditional religions, "including but not limited to access to sites, use and possession of sacred objects, and the freedom to worship through ceremonial and traditional rites"
1989	Kayapo people joined by international indigenous group rights advocates to protest dam project at Altamira
1992	Australian High Court rules that native title to land has not been extinguished, rejecting 200-year-old settler claims that aboriginal lands were *terra nullius*, "no one's land"
2004	National Museum of the American Indian opens in Washington, DC
2008	Australian and Canadian governments issue formal apologies to aboriginal peoples for policies detrimental to integrity of lives, including forcibly sending children to Christian boarding schools
2013	Kayapo clans oppose new Amazon basin dam project on the Xingu River that will flood tribal lands
2016	Native Americans across the United States stage massive sit-in demonstration to protest placement of oil pipeline on Standing Rock Sioux native lands

same occupations (hunting and gathering, simple agriculture), the same myths, and the same rituals; and all were integral to the group. As a result, a person's identity was embedded in the collective identity and fate of the group. The group lives on and the individual can stay connected to it, even after his or her own death.

This collective worldview is very different from the individualism and social fragmentation that is common today. In the following chapters on the world's great religions, we will show how each pushed humanity, out of the collective community mind-set and toward greater individualism. Comprehending the features of indigenous religions will make it clear how the world's religions have some of the basic features of the earliest religious traditions, yet also how they have simultaneously reinterpreted them as human existence has changed.

Human nature features qualities that underlie the most basic expressions of religion. These include a tendency for repetitive behaviors (ritual), an ability to create meaning (symbols, ritual acts), the enhancement of survival by identification with land or territory (sacred space), and a strong mother–child bond (devotion). Archaeologists have determined that about 30,000 years ago, humans with biological traits the same as our own established themselves across Eurasia. They wove cloth, used finely wrought fishhooks, constructed boats, and were experts in subsistence wherever they lived. The record of human life indicates that in every society over the last 100,000 years, the mastery of tools was accompanied by the development of language and the unmistakable presence of religion.

Homo religiosus:
religious humanity

The universality of religion in human societies even led Mircea Eliade (1907–86), a pioneering scholar of comparative religions, to call our species ***Homo religiosus***, or "religious humanity." In fact, religion has always been at the center of human culture. Thus, we can say that religion has always been an integral part of humanity's path. It supported the success of small hunter-gatherer groups, the domestication of plants and animals, and later reinforced the creation of cities, empires, and superpowers. We now turn to the very beginning of this extraordinary story.

The Limitations of the Term *Animism*

The term *animism*, though still in widespread use, is rooted in a problematic distinction in earlier scholarship. An *animist* was said to see the world as inhabited by a host of souls (*anima*) that are embodied in a variety of life-forms. By applying the term only to indigenous peoples, who usually worship a polytheistic pantheon, early scholars tried to distinguish between them and peoples adhering to the major monotheistic religions. But does belief in souls truly separate humanity's religious belief systems and its thousands of believers? All three Abrahamic faiths hold that human beings possess souls (*anima*), as do traditional Indian and Chinese religions. In that sense, most world religions are animist. Furthermore, even the monotheistic religions hold that a multitude of nonhuman "souls" inhabit the world alongside human beings: angels, ghosts, *jinn*, demons, and so on. A second limitation with the term *animism* is that it also masks the large array of very different conceptions of "soul" recorded in human religious history.

Religion's Origins Among Hunter-Gatherers

For nearly all of our species' history, humans lived as nomadic hunter-gatherers. However, our world has been so drastically transformed that few if any people anywhere on the planet still live that way.

The earliest *Homo sapiens* existed much like the people we refer to today as belonging to indigenous or simple subsistence societies. Small groups of related individuals (usually fewer than fifty) lived off the land, moving with the seasons to find wild fruits and nuts and to be close to the animals they hunted for food. Close-knit bonds within these groups were essential to everyone's survival, with individuals sharing the food and relying on each other for protection. Also typical was a division of labor, with men predominantly the hunters and women the gatherers. Compared to the permanently settled societies that began in recorded human history, most of these societies were (and are) highly egalitarian, with food and wealth shared equally.

In choosing the term *indigenous religions*, we are implying that the social and religious lives of a given people are rooted deeply in a given place. The reader should note that we are not equating modern hunter-gatherers with humans living in this mode of life 30,000 years ago or suggesting that these contemporary groups are "living fossils," since none today live isolated from the developed world and all have distinct histories. In growing numbers, indigenous peoples today are quickly learning about the legal systems of modern states and selectively adopting modern technologies in an attempt to preserve their lands, ease the burdens of subsistence, and ensure their culture's adaptation and survival.

The Kung San of southern Africa, one of the most studied, late-surviving hunter-gatherer groups, are typical. A nomadic people, the Kung utilize simple tools and build temporary houses. An intricate knowledge of their environment is expressed in a language that recognizes 500 species of plants and animals, yielding a diet that consists of 105 different foods. Mastery of an environment shared with large predators is typical of such groups. Once scholars gained firsthand knowledge of hunter-gatherers like the Kung, they began to appreciate the highly skilled nature of this mode of life, the clear rationality of the people, and the very sophisticated languages and cultures that had evolved among them. This new understanding disproved the theories of nineteenth-century social scientists, who had speculated that religion had its origins in the fear and ignorance of humans facing a threatening and incomprehensible world.

The human capacity for language and symbolic thought was almost certainly present by 100,000 BCE among the Neanderthals and those who succeeded them, the *Homo sapiens*. Around this time, humans began performing ceremonial burials, painting with carefully mined red ochre and other pigments, and carving art, keeping records on bone and stone plaques, and crafting personal adornments. They also made music with flutes and drums. It was by this time that humans acquired the capacity to think symbolically, almost certainly as a result of their development of more complex languages.

Prehistoric cave art: the first shaman. Over fifty examples of animal–human figures like this one suggest that shamanism had its origins in the prehistoric era.

As we saw in the first chapter, religion is centered on humans establishing and expressing life's ultimate truths. Scientists, therefore, have suggested that this development changed the destiny of our species: "categorizing and naming objects and sensations in the outer and inner worlds, and making associations between resulting mental symbols . . . for only once we create such symbols can we recombine them and ask such questions as 'What if . . . ?'"[1] The simultaneous emergence of modern humans and religion indicates that many "what if" questions attempted to explain the unseen powers of life, the inner world of personhood, and the mystery of death. Many artifacts of prehistoric religion have been found that reflect human engagement with each of these realms.

Fertility, Childbirth, and Survival

"Venus" figurines: prehistoric Eurasian small stone figures with exaggerated female characteristics

One striking kind of object found across Eurasia in late prehistory is what scientists have called **"Venus" figurines**, small stone sculptures of females with large breasts and hips, often with their genitalia emphasized. To understand these objects, we must enter into the reality of prehistoric human life. Small tribes were greatly concerned with ensuring the regular birth of healthy children to keep their own group numerous enough for success in subsistence, hunting, and warfare. Further, since at that time all pregnancies and all childbirths were high-risk events, it is likely that the figurines are related to concerns about birth and the survival of children in small groups. Some scholars therefore interpret the Venus figurines as icons representing a protecting, nurturing "mother goddess."

Added to this evidence of veneration of a mother goddess is another important archaeological find: After 15,000 BCE the dead were uniformly buried in mounds or graves in the fetal position, suggesting that people perceived the earth as a womb from which some sort of new birth was expected.

The makers of Venus figurines revered a special female power that lay behind the mystery of conception and birth. They focused on the miracle of females producing beings from their own bodies and celebrated the ability of women to perpetuate human life.

Religion in Prehistory: The Secret of Early Cave Rituals

In the cave paintings of Eurasia, hunted animals such as bison, bear, and deer are carefully rendered in a variety of styles. Humans are also shown, some in poses that are still puzzling, challenging us to understand who created the images and the meaning of their context.

Caves could be dangerous places, and groups of individuals taking the trouble to go several hundred yards under the earth engage in no ordinary task. Archaeologists surmise that these sites were related to the hunts undertaken by bands of able-bodied men. These men hunted to secure the meat essential for their diet, the skins for clothing, and the bones and sinew used for tools and adornment. Some painted cave scenes indicate the dangers of hunting: Wild bison, cave bears, and large cats are shown inflicting lethal injuries on humans.

Scholars believe that prehistoric hunting-group initiation ceremonies were held in underground sanctuaries decorated with carefully rendered images of animals like this early masterpiece of painting from the Chauvet cave in southern France.

The hunt required group coordination for success, since tracking, stalking, encircling, and using spears or stones to make kills at close range could not be achieved without coordinated action. A hunting expedition could fail if a single member failed. Based on similar rites among modern hunting tribes, scholars view some of the prehistoric caves as ritual theaters for initiating adolescent boys into the ranks of hunters. Through this initiation ritual, young men bonded with the other adult males with whom they would risk their lives.

Such practices in the service of human survival formed the basis of the first religions according to the definitions we discussed in Chapter 1: They helped *bind* a group critical to the society's success, and they reinforced the human need to *be careful* with regard to the unseen powers surrounding them. The second point is especially important if we assume that the elders taught that each animal, like every human being, has an inner spirit or soul, one that must be respected in death. We now turn to this topic and trace its frequent presence in a variety of modern indigenous groups.

TEACHINGS OF RELIGIOUS WISDOM: The Dreamtime

In this creative era, a host of supernatural beings from an unspecified somewhere arrived and set out to populate and transform the previously flat and featureless Australian landmass. By their activities . . . they created diverse, religiously-charged landforms, richly imprinted with meaning and replete with fauna and flora. During their wanderings and numerous adventures, they established rituals and human institutions. These set in place for all time the various groups, their languages, cultural characteristics, and bound the first humans to a kind of contract. Through obedience to the laws of Dreaming, and the proper and regular performance of rituals, living Aborigines are charged with keeping the whole cosmic system of order going. This occurs under the watchful and caring gaze of the creative beings . . . who monitor human affairs without direct interference, but stay in touch via spirit-being messengers through whom they channel new knowledge and ritual elements into human society. [Humans] remain keenly aware of the proximity and relevance of the spiritual powers to their well-being and future existence. Failure by humans to uphold the human blueprint will cause the inhabitants of the spiritual realm to cut off the flow of power into human society and bring all life to an end. . . . Each succeeding generation is charged with enormous responsibility for society's continuing reproduction.

Source: Robert Tonkinson, "The Mardu Aborigines: On the Road to Somewhere," in George Spindler and Janice E. Stockard, eds. *Globalization and Change in Fifteen Cultures* (Belmont, CA: Thomson, 2007), p. 233.

Indigenous Religious Traditions: Soul Belief and Afterlife

There are indigenous peoples today who subsist primarily as hunter-gatherers, shifting slash-and-burn agriculturalists, or settled agricultural cultivators, as well as those who have assimilated in various ways into the world's modern states and economies. The traditions of these indigenous groups relating to the sacred, though uniquely grounded in each people's separate historical existence, have been an integral part of their survival and remain an important part of the story of the world's religions today.

Studies of the myths of indigenous peoples recount what is sacred to the group: the origins of life, its relations with animals, its connections to landforms, and the origination of the norms governing the members of the group. The religious experiences cultivated among these groups also show the great extent of humanity's experimentation with altered states of consciousness and extremes of bodily endurance. The rituals performed to heal, revere, and express group solidarity reveal the ways our species has conceptualized and faced the dual mysteries of birth and death.

The presence of a human belief in some sort of afterlife emerges from the earliest archaeological records of ceremonial burials. In hundreds of excavations, burial clearly was done to preserve the body and provide it with decoration (colors, jewelry, flowers, animal skulls, or antlers), foods (meat, grain), and tools (spears, sticks). These

"The first thing when we wake up in the morning is to be thankful to the Great Spirit for the Mother Earth: how we live, what it produces, what keeps everything alive."

—Joshua Wetsit, an Assiniboine from Montana

SOURCE: The Sacred Ways of Knowledge, Sources of Life.

Awakening the Spirits: A Bullroarer

Bullroarers are powerful ritual tools that convey the bond between living and dead members of scattered aboriginal groups, from those in prehistory up to those still used among native peoples in Australia. A bullroarer is a sphere that has a hole at one end, and when the device is swung around on a string, air passes through, resulting in a booming-whirring sound. The sound waves vibrate at a frequency that evokes a strange feeling, one that conveys the presence of sacred time and space.

A bullroarer painted with a serpent motif. Swinging the roarer produces a deep, piercing sound that elicits a numinous feeling in ritual participants.

arrangements suggest that early humans felt that there was a nonmaterial component of the self, a soul or spirit that "lived on" after the physical body had died. Death seems to be likened to sleep, and the function of burial seems to be to open a gateway to an afterlife.

More recent studies of surviving indigenous religions focus less on belief in vaguely defined souls or spirits and more on the phenomenon of how indigenous peoples actually perceive relations with a range of others, human and nonhuman, through their sensory experience. For them, being religious is not about creeds or texts that need interpreting. Instead, people are engaged with the environment around them, in which certain stones, animals, trees, and the dead may "speak" to the living. Most indigenous people sustain a very close relationship with the natural world, one in which the ecosystem is sensed as alive and part of a larger, ordered cosmos.

In hunter-gatherer societies today, people still live by the rising and the setting of the sun, the phases of the moon, and the seasons of the year. Time is circular. This **circular time** follows the pattern of the celestial and natural world. Human lives, too, revolve like the seasons. In myth and ritual and in contact with their sacred centers of revelation, indigenous peoples seek equilibrium with the environment.

This relatedness with the natural world is realized through the engagement of all five senses and is guided by myth, mind, and emotions. Resident spirit beings that have souls are believed to see, hear, and even speak. Indigenous traditions vary by the ways these spirit beings speak, their personalities, and the landscapes they occupy through the seasons. The human community's attuning of its senses to these entities through ritual ensures their successful survival. Many groups believe these ties with a spirit world extend into an afterlife. Some assume that souls of the dead reincarnate

circular time: awareness, especially in hunter-gatherer societies, that time and life follow the same recurring cycle of time determined by the sun, moon, and the seasons

as humans or other life forms. Relating with spirit beings (or souls) requires ongoing connections with them. These connections are maintained by the careful practice of communal rituals.

Among most indigenous peoples today, dreams or visions support the idea that the dead can "return" in nonmaterial form. As we will see, this belief is supported by spirit mediums who serve as communicators with the dead, enabling a departed soul to speak to the living from the other side. Indigenous peoples today, like most humans before the modern era, regard dreams and visions as significant sources for understanding the ultimate meanings and purposes of life.

For indigenous societies, death is not an ultimate end. On the contrary, death is an elevation of one's status to that of sacred ancestor. Ancestors, in turn, are venerated as spirits who can help the living by guiding them in successful hunts or by invigorating wild foods and cultivated crops. At the same time, misfortune in a community may be the fault of the living, who have incited the ancestors' anger and punishment by breaking a moral law or neglecting a ritual. In such situations, harmony between the living, the dead, and all of nature needs to be restored.

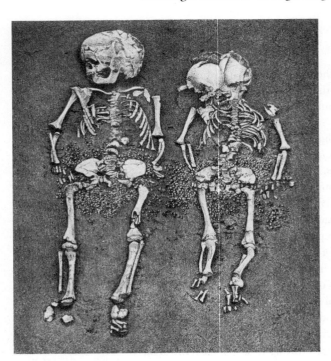

Burial of children from 20,000 BCE: With the remains are perforated shells and remnants of decorated clothing found in Grottes des Enfantes, France.

Ancestral spirits are seen as custodians of tradition. They may harm those who disregard custom and bless those who are faithful to it. Some scholars believe that later religions evolved from early animist views of the world and efforts to manage the activities of supernatural spirit-beings. Recent archaeological evidence suggests that the most elaborate burials in late prehistory were conducted to protect the living from the power of malevolent souls. Perhaps powerful ancestral spirits (both the kindly and the dangerous) became the world's first gods.

Among the Dani, a simple agricultural group in highland New Guinea, belief that the soul survives into an afterlife shapes the ways of the living. In their death rituals, the Dani try to direct the soul of a person who has just died to a distant ghost land. Yet many ghosts are thought to return to cause problems, especially if their last rites were not done properly or their death is not avenged in timely fashion. Thus Dani elders take great care when performing funerals, and they maintain small guest houses to accommodate, and pacify, the occasional ghost visitors.

Further, rival Dani villages engage continually in lethal warfare, whose main purpose is for the men to satisfy a newly departed kinsman's spirit by killing someone on the enemy's side. The Dani moral code includes the precept of "a life for a life."

Moreover, since losing a kinsman inevitably weakens the collective community and each individual's soul, avenging the loss of the deceased by killing an enemy tribesman is the only means to restore the vitality of the survivors' souls. In fact, Dani kinship and food production is organized around the central need for supplying the feasts that must be held to mark deaths and celebrate revenge killings. Appeasing ancestral ghosts is always in mind.

The Dani are representative of the many indigenous groups in which shamans are absent or marginal. Lacking a class of priests, every adult learns to perform the most common rituals. But there are in Dani society wise religious leaders who are looked to for leading major communal festivals based on their ready knowledge of the intricate rites. Dani religious leaders are thoughtful in hosting the regular visits of ancestral ghosts.

Totemism: Australian Aboriginal Religion

Anthropologists have noted that many indigenous groups use a symbol, or totem, to establish their fundamental identity, identify proper marriage partners, promote collective solidarity, and regulate relations with outsiders. A **totem** is an animal, reptile, insect, or plant that is emblematic of the community and is treated as sacred. The relationship between totems and groups reveals a special circle of kinship and a primal connection between humans and the rest of nature.

Totemism is still found among some Native Americans and is common among the various aboriginal peoples of Australia. The latter believe that their origins occurred in the **Dreamtime**, when the world as we know it was being created from a previously flat and featureless landmass by a host of spirit-beings. Their myths inform them that their clan consists of the descendants of their totemic progenitors, who created them from their own bodies and essence and established their existence as humans. Each then led them to their current home territories, creating spiritually charged landforms including rivers, mountains, and other creatures, richly imprinting them with meaning. During their wanderings, they also bound them to a contract of sorts: In return for humans obeying the laws of Dreaming and performing prescribed rituals, the spirit-beings continue to maintain connections to their living "kin," sending blessings and power. Each totemic group faces the serious task of keeping the cosmic order going through its faithfulness to established traditions and morality.

To understand this belief system, we can take an example from the latter: members of the aboriginal kangaroo clan. Its group members ritually decorate their bodies with kangaroo drawings, and before its children are considered to be adults, they must learn the distinctive dances and songs recounting the group's totemic kangaroo story. Elder men pass down these secrets to the young men through initiation. The group is also protective of its own "songlines," the myths that are sung to trace in detail the progenitor's trail of creation over the land. These oral records give the group a shared identity and territory; celebrating them faithfully enables the group to propagate and prosper.

totem: symbol taken from natural world to represent common origin and essence of a social group

Dreamtime: for Australian Aborigines, the time when the world was created, and which exists in another realm

RITUALS AND RITES: Shamans Across the World

The shaman remains the key religious specialist in many societies today. The term *shaman* comes from the Evenk, a group of hunters and reindeer herders in Siberia. The term was later adopted by early scholars for all similar practitioners. Shamans are still found among peoples on every inhabited continent and in the earliest records of our direct forebears.

Though differing in details of clothing and techniques, shamans are found across the world today: left, a Yanomami shaman in the Amazon; right, a Korean shaman in Seoul.

Elders pray to and invoke the totemic kangaroo spirit for healing and guidance. Women of the kangaroo clan who want to become pregnant visit the places where the totemic spirits reside, for they believe that conception—via spirit/soul acquisition—cannot occur without exposure to the totem's life force.

taboo: action or object that is normally forbidden

Although harming or eating a kangaroo is almost always forbidden, or **taboo**, to members of the kangaroo clan, there is a regularly performed ritual that unifies the totemic group. In addition to singing and acting out their myth of origins, all the "kangaroos" in the group, on this one annual occasion, gather to renew their primordial identity by hunting and killing a kangaroo and eating its flesh. These rites are performed to increase the totemic species and give spiritual strength to individuals in the group. Although the design of the world was fixed once and for all in the Dreamtime, it is the task of humans, through this and other totemic rites, to maintain and renew this creation.

"We are all visitors to this time, this place. We are just passing through. Our purpose here is to observe, to learn, to grow, to love . . . and then we return home."

—Aboriginal proverb

The French sociologist Émile Durkheim (1858–1917) argued that totemism points to a key feature in all religious life. It is the sacred totem (in our example, the kangaroo) that gives the group a singular focus and by extension stands for the group itself. For Durkheim, religion is about making a group's own identity, survival, and worth sacred by focusing on and identifying with a common symbol. What human groups felt as an unseen but sacred force was really, he argued, the power of group unity. This sense of unity, he argued, allows for social stability. Durkheim's influential theory is that whatever else has come to define religious beliefs across the world's human groups, religion's power to bind us together is what established it and keeps it central to human life.

Shamans: "Technicians of the Sacred"

In the event of failed hunts, debilitating illness, or other misfortunes, members of indigenous societies turn to a **spirit medium**, or **shaman**, who can intervene with the unseen powers. Many traits and skills are attributed to shamans.

The role of the shaman varies across the world: In some indigenous societies they dominate in the group's religious life; in others, the medium remains a marginal, often-distrusted figure resorted to only in dire circumstances, while chiefs, priests, or healers perform the group's ritual and healing functions. And some indigenous societies have no tradition of spirit mediums at all.

The most common shaman's role worldwide is the ability to heal (both literally and metaphorically) through **spirit flight** achieved in a trance or an altered state of consciousness. The trance state can be reached by fasting or by drumming and singing, but shamans worldwide have discovered a long list of psychotropic agents for altering consciousness to their purposes. Practices may also involve the inhaling of incense, snuffs, smoke from tobacco or other psychoactive herbs, or the ingesting of mushrooms or potent plant concoctions. The shaman's trance may be marked by bodily fever, loud breathing, protruding eyes, insensitivity to temperature or pain, convulsions, or trembling. In many

The art of contemporary Australian Aborigines depicts totemic beings and their role in creation during the "Dreamtime."

spirit medium/ shaman: person who communicates with deities and spirits through ritually induced trance

spirit flight: shaman's attempt to locate another person's soul in another realm

traditions, the shaman's soul is thought to leave the physical body, free to fly to the heavens, beneath the earth, or under the sea. On these spirit flights, shamans attempt to locate another person's lost soul, perhaps because it has wandered off in this world or passed on to the afterlife. Another common belief is that the dead person's spirit needs a shaman's assistance to reach the afterlife dwelling place of the clan's ancestors.

sorcerers: mediums who manipulate the spirit world, often for their own benefit rather than on behalf of the community

Shaman healers usually cooperate with spiritual beings and in this way are distinct from **sorcerers**, mediums who manipulate the spirit world and coerce spiritual and supernatural beings without their consent, often for the sorcerer's own benefit and against community values.

Where found, shamans are ritual specialists. Through ritual, they unite the community in the face of the chaos of disease, death, and discord. Many shamans through their spirit flights return to teach their communities, and through trance rituals they demonstrate that the daily, ordinary world is not all there is. In most indigenous societies, the living and the dead, the community and its sacred ancestors, form one great community. Binding it all together, the shaman uses his or her body as a bridge to connect these two worlds. If harmony in an indigenous group has been shattered by troubling ancestral ghosts, only the shaman, who is able to visit both worlds and communicate the needs of one to the other, can restore balance.

tutelary spirit: supernatural agent, often an ancestral spirit, who helps a shaman

Through initiation, shamans find connection with a protective spirit, or **tutelary spirit**. This is a supernatural agent, often an ancestral spirit, whose help is required to perform the difficult spirit flights, negotiate with evil spirits, compel a soul to return, or increase the shaman's healing powers. In many tribes, shamans have human helpers who watch over their unconscious bodies during trance states, for they, too, can remain stuck as spirits if their souls cannot return to their bodies.

numinous: human perception of the sacred

The shamanic world is one in which spirits coexist with humans in a layered cosmos, with humans occupying the earth between an upper and a lower world. The spirits are particularly accessible to humans around sacred physical objects or unusual places. Each culture regards these locations as being connected to the "center of the world" (*axis mundi*). Most commonly, such sites are actual or symbolic sacred mountains or sacred trees, revered as places of original revelations, intensely alive with spiritual power, or **numinous** presence. Several examples show how shamanic traditions from around the world today share common traits.

Case Studies in Indigenous Religious Practices Today

Healing Trance: Kung San Healers

The Kung San of southern Africa believe that the dead go to an afterlife, a "next world" populated by ancestors, one that is similar to this world and is linked closely to the living. Souls that miss the living return to earth as ghosts and try to sicken friends and family members in an effort to hasten their arrival in the next world. The most accomplished Kung shamans (***n/um kausi***) have the ability to enter into a trance

n/um kausi: shamans of the Kung people

during night-long dances, in which everyone joins in ceremonies of rhythmic drumming and singing around a fire. With this group support and social purpose, anthropologists suggest, the Kung shamans activate a natural force within their bodies, the *n/um*, a power that "boils" in and moves up the spine. The body shakes and sweats, and inhalations grow forced and deeper as the shaman slips into a trance state. Thus empowered, the shaman begins to touch the bodies of others to transfer the healing force of the boiling *n/um* into them. Expert healers can also identify and suck out poisons from the bodies of the sick; some may massage the patient with a mixture of the shaman's own sweat and blood. Healers who perceive the ghosts of troublesome ancestors watching the dance outside the community circle may shriek or hurl stones at deities in the shadows who are identified as causing difficulties. The most effective Kung shamans are honored, but they are otherwise typical members of the tribe; while most are men, some are women.

A Kung healing ceremony. The trancing and healing performed by Kung shamans depends on the community's participating in drumming, singing, and dancing.

The shaman's role is universally regarded as mortally dangerous. The Kung call entering trance "being half-dead" and with great care guard a shaman's physical body while the healer's soul journeys to "the other world." Like many indigenous peoples, the Kung are also careful not to startle sleeping individuals, for fear that souls wandering during sleep will not have time to return to a person who has been awakened suddenly.

Men and women who become shamans in the Kung or other cultures must train through long apprenticeships. But in most groups it is common for shamans to feel that they were chosen for the role by a tutelary spirit, often in spite of their own resistance. Novice shamans must prove their ability by surviving an initiation ordeal that may require fasting and acts of extraordinary physical endurance. Each must demonstrate the capacity for trance, the grace of a tutelary spirit, and evidence of supernormal powers. Many shamans feel that they wear out their bodies by repeatedly undergoing near-death experiences in the course of spirit flights.

Sioux Vision Quest for a Spirit Ally

The Lakota Sioux of North America believe, as do the Kung, that every human being has the potential for supernatural connection and that all should be encouraged to develop this ability. Among the Lakota, young men go to a sacred wilderness region

"You dance, dance, dance, dance. Then *n/um* lifts you up in your belly and lifts up in your back, and you start to shiver. In trance, you see everything, because you see what's troubling everybody. . . . Then *n/um* enters every part of your body, right to your feet and even your hair. . . . Then *n/um* makes your thoughts nothing in your head."

—Kinachau, a Kung San healer

SOURCE: Richard Katz, *Boiling Energy: Community Healing Among the Kalahari Kung* (Cambridge, MA: Harvard University Press, 1982).

on a vision quest in search of a personal protector spirit. After preparatory training, the apprentices fast and purify themselves in a sweat lodge. Then each one ventures out alone into the wilderness.

Those contacted by strong spirit allies in dreams and those who have vivid visions of the ancestors may go on to become shamans after further training with an elder practitioner. Apprentices learn the techniques of trance, the myths of the tribe, the location of "power places" in the landscape, and other healing arts that involve the use of medicines. Shamans are never the same after initiation; many receive a new name, a new identity, and in the myths they even obtain a new body. Shamans encounter evil spirits that must be tricked, seduced, or killed to complete the healing task. Given these arduous demands, becoming a shaman is often described as a death-and-rebirth experience.

Bear Sacrifice: A Widespread Arctic and Pacific Rim Tradition

We have noted how shamans can serve as mediums who bring the spirits down to earth for ritual negotiations. An example of this practice is the bear sacrifice, once one of the most widespread rituals in the world and common across the upper Pacific Rim and the vast circumpolar region from northern Japan to North America. As observed in modern times, shamans carefully manage the sacrificial rituals, offering gifts from humans in exchange for an animal's life. A common belief in hunter-gatherer societies is that animals are actually spirits in disguise who assume animal bodies to interact with humans. This may have been the earliest example of humanity conceptualizing divine incarnation, the embodiment in earthly form of a supernatural being.

Among the Ainu people on Hokkaido Island in northern Japan, spirits that incarnate themselves as animals are called *kamui*. They mostly dwell in an "other world" but can have contact with humans by coming to earth and assuming life in a bear's body. The Ainu conception is that humans and *kamui* are of equal status. Although the latter (when unencumbered by a body) can fly and have magical powers, only humans can give them what they really need and want: sake (a wine made from rice) and *inau*, fragrant willow sticks. In the Ainu understanding, the spirits don animal bodies to acquire their fur as "clothes" to trade, for *inau* and sake from humans. This transaction requires that they be ritually hunted and have their bodies killed to complete the exchange that benefits both parties.

The Ainu shaman performs special rituals to attract a spirit in its bear incarnation. Knowing that an exchange has been requested and consenting to it if humans have kept up their part in earlier exchanges, a bear cub leaves trail signs that allow hunters to track and capture it. Villages then raise the specially chosen animal until it becomes fully grown. Afterward, the shaman addresses the bear respectfully, makes the proper offerings, performs a ritual execution, and releases

Ainu elders celebrating a Bear Feast. Offerings of food and sake are placed before the dead bear; swords and sacred quivers hang on the altar behind the men. This photograph was taken by the anthropologist Bronislaw Pilsudski (1866–1918), who lived with an Ainu community for several years in the early twentieth century.

the *kamui* spirit to return to the other world, presumed to be happy with its gifts. The Ainu believe that if the sacred conventions of the exchange are duly observed, the *kamui* just released and other spirits will continue to assume animal form. Thus the shaman ensures that the people will have a continuous supply of meat and shelter.

Shamans Who Repair the World

A shaman's expertise can also be effective when a human group acts improperly. The practices of the Inuit (who dwell around the Arctic region) illustrate the shaman's role in repairing the world. The Inuit believe that the great goddess Takanakapsaluk, Mistress of Sea Animals, lives on the ocean floor and releases whales, seals, fish, and other marine creatures so that they may be killed for human use. But the Inuit believe that when their community performs the

"The greatest peril in life lies in the fact that human food consists entirely of souls. All these creatures that we have to kill and eat, all we have to strike down to make clothes for ourselves, have souls, souls that do not perish and which must be pacified lest they revenge themselves on us for taking away their bodies."

—Ivaluardjuk, an Inuit healer

SOURCE: *The Sacred Ways of Knowledge, Sources of Life.*

ritual improperly or someone breaks a moral taboo, the goddess's hair "becomes soiled" and she burns in anger, holding back all creatures in her domain. The Inuit shaman must then be called for a séance. To follow one account, when the shaman encounters the goddess:

> . . . the shaman finds her angry, with hair uncombed, filthy, and hanging over her eyes. The creatures of the ocean sit in a pool beside her. The shaman gently turns the goddess toward the animals and a nearby lamp, combing and washing her hair. He then asks why the animals are not coming, and she replies that they are being withheld because the people have eaten forbidden boiled meat and because the women have kept their miscarriages secret, failing to purify their homes afterward. Mollified by praises and promises to make amends, goddess Takanakapsaluk releases the animals and they are swept back into the ocean. The shaman's return is marked by a distant, then louder call of "Plu-a-he-he!" as he finally shakes in his place, gasping for breath. After a silence, he demands, "Your words must rise up," and then the audience members begin to confess their misdeeds. By the end of the séance, there is a mood of optimism.[2]

The Yanomami shamans of the Amazon rain forest also illustrate how mediums repair community life by communicating with the spirits. The village shaman (always male) locates and returns the disoriented souls of sick or dying villagers. If others have acted to weaken or steal someone's soul, it is the shaman who must identify both the misdeed and the perpetrators. To be initiated as shaman and to achieve such abilities, an individual must memorize chants, drumming, and struts to attract the support of his special ancestral spirits. The Yanomami shaman must also master the use of the hallucinogenic snuff called *ebene*, a powerful substance thought to be a spirit ally that is essential for opening the shaman's body to perceive, feel, and contact his tribe's spirit allies.

The Yanomami shaman has the power to conduct the spirits into the human world. The spirits can then be induced to enter the shaman's body and respond to questions about matters of concern, small or great. At times and without invitation, the shaman's mouth may speak the spirit's messages about group origins, life's meaning, or any hidden facts relevant to recent events.

The reliance on psychoactive substances to assist the shaman to achieve altered states of consciousness, as found among the Yanomami, is not universal. Drug-induced trances are limited mostly to groups in the Americas, where the use of the cactus peyote, the vine extract ayahuasca, and plants such as jimson and datura have long been in the shaman's medicine bag. What is universal for shamans across the world, even among shamans utilizing psychoactive drugs, is reliance on the impact of rapid rhythmic drumming, dancing, chanting, and fasting to induce trance experiences. Thus, the drum or the rattle is a universal symbol of the shaman's extraordinary religious practice.

TALES OF SPIRITUAL TRANSFORMATION: The Peyote Ceremony

Divine Communion

From that time, whenever they held peyote meetings, we all attended and . . . one time something happened to me. . . . I was sitting with bowed head, . . . we prayed, . . . then I saw Jesus standing there. . . . I will pray to him, I thought. I stood up and raised my arm. I prayed. I asked for a good life—thanking God who gave me my life. And as the drum was beating, my body shook to the beat. I was unaware of it. I was just very contented. I never knew such pleasure as this. There was a sensation of great joyousness. Now I was an angel. That is how I saw myself. Because I had wings I was supposed to fly but I could not quite get my feet off the ground. . . . I knew when I ate peyote that they were using something holy. That way is directed toward God. Nothing else on earth is holy, . . . and if someone sees something holy at a peyote meeting, that is really true. I understood that this religion is holy.

—Shirley Etsitty, Native American Church

Source: *The Sacred: Ways of Knowledge, Sources of Life* (Tsaile, AZ: Navajo Community College Press, 1996).

Indigenous Religions Today

The Cataclysms of Colonialism

A theme that runs throughout this book is the disruptions to life and religious traditions caused by modern European colonialism. For indigenous societies across the planet, this global expansion of invading outsiders and the political dominance they imposed have been disastrous. Native peoples of the New World and other remote regions were decimated by the diseases of Eurasia, to which they had no natural resistance. Often simultaneously, the disease-bearing outsiders plundered the native people's riches, utilizing horses and superior weapons technology to achieve their aims. In the early colonial era, millions of people in small-scale subsistence societies were killed or enslaved. The outsiders appropriated and transformed the native lands when natural resources were discovered there. Ways of life that had evolved over centuries were destroyed. Since religion is closely related to a community's way of life, the epidemics and genocide suffered by the world's indigenous peoples inevitably included environmental devastation in their home territories.

Representative of this pattern is the series of events in nineteenth-century North America. In 1811, Tecumseh, chief of the Shawnees, organized a defensive confederacy of Northwest frontier tribes that attempted to make the Ohio River a permanent boundary between indigenous peoples' land and the United States territory. In response, William Henry Harrison, governor of Ohio, led the U.S. army to fight the ferocious Battle of Tippecanoe, destroying Tecumseh's town and confederacy. In 1830, the Congress passed the Indian Removal Act, empowering the government to forcibly remove all indigenous peoples west of the Mississippi River.

The U.S. military force-marched all known native Americans to reservations in Oklahoma, an episode of ethnic cleansing in 1838 known as "the Trail of Tears."

Indigenous survivors of colonialism and their descendants faced stark choices. Would they risk the chaos of migration by retreating into remote lands still untouched by the colonizers? Would they acquiesce to a nineteenth-century government's program of forced resettlement on reservations? Or would the best choice be for individuals to assimilate with the dominant society and submit to the national laws and social customs of others? Whatever the choice, the solidarity and cultural integrity of most of these displaced groups worldwide has weakened over every generation. It has inevitably been the young who have seen the limits of their minority status, rejected the old dialects and religious customs, and responded to the allure of the dominant culture by embracing assimilation.

Exposure to missionary religions and their alien exponents often contributed to the downfall of the indigenous religions. Governments in the Americas and Australia forced indigenous children to attend missionary schools, where Christianity was aggressively taught and in which traditional practices were ruthlessly banned. Students who spoke their native languages were subject to punishment. Missionaries viewed shamans as obstacles to the advance of the colonizing powers, and often accused the native healers of combining evil with fakery: acting as "servants of the devil" while also being imposters or religious charlatans who exploited their own people. For the Euro-American Christian immigrants, shamanism represented the chaotic wilderness, the shaman a source of disruptive chaos that threatened the colonial order. Under these circumstances, native peoples in many cases had to hide their drums, medicines, and sacred images. They believed that the only way to preserve their culture was to take it underground.

Ghost Dance: nineteenth-century Native American religious revitalization movement led by spirit mediums

Other native peoples, however, organized in attempts to restore their place in the world and give new life to their traditions. In North America, shamans revitalized native peoples in the nineteenth century through a movement called the **Ghost Dance**. After the decimation of the buffalo by white hunters, which contributed to the destruction of the indigenous way of life on the Great Plains, several elders had the same visionary revelation: Their tutelary spirits announced a way to restore the lost world by bringing back the ancestors and causing the whites to disappear. Native American religious leaders then preached that this could be accomplished if all the people performed a new dance ritual as prescribed by the spirits. Soon this Ghost Dance was practiced with fervor across the Great Plains by those whose kin had died, with the dancers falling unconscious in hopes of experiencing reunion with their deceased relatives. One leader in this movement had this vision of the Ghost Dance recorded:

All Indians must dance, everywhere, and keep on dancing. Pretty soon in the next spring, the Great Spirit come. . . . The game be thick everywhere. All dead Indians come back and live again. . . . White can't hurt Indian then. Then big flood come like water and all white people die, get drowned. After that, water go away and then nobody but Indians everywhere and game animals of all kinds thick.[3]

The pain of engagement with outsiders is unmistakable in the Ghost Dance movement, which sought to bind a vision of ecological renewal with the restoration of traditional religious consciousness. In 1890 the U.S. Cavalry was ordered to end this nationwide movement by massacring the men, women, and children gathered for a Ghost Dance at Wounded Knee, South Dakota.

By the twenty-first century, no indigenous societies remain that have not been exposed to the world of outsiders. Some have even been the targets of genocidal persecution. Most of the Kung people have been relocated onto reservations, forced to give up hunting, and directed to adopt agriculture or simple craft production. The Ainu of northern Japan have suffered land seizures and discrimination and are so stigmatized today that few are willing to profess knowledge of the old traditions and shamanic practices. Native peoples of the Amazon rain forest have been displaced by land-clearing settlers and threatened by multinational mining and oil drilling projects. The history of Native Americans since 1500 is a story of genocide and land taking, made worse by legal discrimination by the United States government against Native American religious practices. In the twenty-first century, hundreds of indigenous languages and religious traditions will likewise decline in use and disappear forever.

Some indigenous groups that have survived with their cultures most intact are those living far from resources the modernizing world has sought, although even these most remote places and peoples are increasingly threatened by climate change. Others have found successful means of assimilating, with members gaining education and employment outside the group and integrating modern economic life with indigenous tradition. Those groups that have retained autonomy, resisted assimilation, and worked to revitalize their identity show both the adaptability of human culture and the resilience of the human spirit. An example of this indigenous vitality is in groups like the Kayapo in Brazil, who now use the Internet to share their anti-expropriation strategies and principles of cultural revitalization with other groups across the globe. Their experience emphasizes the role of the young as bicultural actors who negotiate with the world outside the indigenous group.

Shamans in some indigenous groups were pivotal figures who led their people in facing the crises of modernity. Because traditionally they were entrusted with mediating between spirits and humans, shamans have been the natural choices to act on behalf of the group when the outside world intruded. In the face of repression, many shamans saw confrontation as the only hope for their group, led rebellions, and died in vain defense. Siberian and Mongolian shamans under Soviet rule from 1939 to 1980, for example, retreated to the deep wilderness and continued to practice there.

Religious leaders found other creative responses. Some advocated **syncretism**, in which indigenous religious beliefs and practices were woven together with those of outsiders. In present-day Mexico, for example, shamans have integrated Catholic saints and sacramental theology into healing rites that utilize peyote. Another example of combining elements from different traditions to create a new religion is **Bwiti**, a West Central African religion. Organized in the early twentieth century

> "The Catholic church is a beautiful theory for Sunday, the iboga on the contrary is the practice of everyday living. In church, they speak of God; with iboga, you live God."
>
> —Nengue Me Ndjoung Isidore, Bwiti religious leader in Africa
>
> SOURCE: S. Swiderski, *La religion Bouiti*, vol. 1 (1990–91).

syncretism: combination of elements from different belief systems

Bwiti: West Central African syncretic religion

The Native American Church

In the United States today, over 550 Indian nations are recognized by the U.S. federal government, each with its own history and tribal land and each practicing its own distinct traditional religion. In the last century, there have been successful efforts to draw scattered Native Americans into new religious groups in what scholars have identified as

the "pan-Americanization" of indigenous peoples. The Native American Church is a major example of this phenomenon, one that has had one faction drawn into the orbit of Christianity and another that remains independent. But the two are united in their ceremonial use of the cactus peyote as a communal sacrament. This "melting pot" movement remains controversial among some Native Americans, who criticize how the Native American Church draws tribal members away from their own group's traditions. An additional problem this group encounters is the drug enforcement laws of the U.S. government. Similar indigenous peoples' new religions have started in South America. Two examples are Santo Daime and União do Vegetal; both are syncretistic, influenced by Christian morality and folk religion, and centered on a traditional psychotropic herb, in this case, ayahuasca. Both also have now spread across the globe, attracting nonindigenous devotees from Japan to Europe.

Source: https://nativeamericanchurches.org/

Native American Church: modern religious group uniting native peoples of North America

Religious leaders in the Bwiti movement creatively combine regional and Christian traditions.

among the forest-dwelling Babongo and Mitsogo people of Gabon and the Fang people of Gabon and Cameroon, Bwiti incorporates animism, ancestor worship, and Christianity into its belief system. As with the **Native American Church**, a mild hallucinogen plays a role, in this case the root bark of the iboga plant, which is now specially cultivated for its religious purpose. Individuals joining the Bwiti community are taught that iboga induces a rich spiritual experience, one that allows the disciple to be healed and solve problems.

In a world in which the ancestral spirits clearly failed to protect the group or safeguard its territory, radical change was inevitable. Over generations, many shamanic traditions themselves have been diminished or reformulated to match the new life circumstances. Under colonial conditions and until today, cultures that were thriving only a few centuries ago exist only in dimming memory. What has proven the most enduring of these indigenous traditions, even in regions that came to be dominated by one or more world religions, is shamanism.

Kayapo chiefs act as religious and political leaders, trying to retain control of the land that is essential to the continuation of tradition.

The Kayapo of Brazil: Selective Modernity and the Survival of Tradition

The Kayapo until recent decades killed all intruders on their lands, whether lumberjacks, gold miners, or rubber-tree tappers, and were regarded as the most dangerous natives of the Amazon rain forest. Outsiders made every effort to exterminate the Kayapo, going so far as to fly over them to drop blankets infected with smallpox onto their villages. But in the middle of the twentieth century, Kayapo chiefs changed their relationship with outsiders, and in 1982 they regained ownership and control of most of their indigenous lands, the largest tract held by native peoples in South America. On a limited scale, their leaders have sold rights to cut timber and to allow outsiders to mine for gold, using the substantial rents and taxes collected to sustain and protect their culture.

The Kayapo consider themselves an integral part of the universe, bound to the cycles of the natural year and nature's ongoing rebirth. Returning from their hunts, men sing to the spirits of the game they killed in order for the animal or reptile spirits to remain in the forest. Each species is connected to a distinctive song that begins with the cry of the dead animal. A "center of the world" is located in each village's central plaza, where rituals and public life take place. To go back to the time of mythical origins and stimulate the energy required for life's prosperity and continuance, the Kayapo dance the myths recounting their origins and subsequent incidents, recalling their past to reaffirm their identity and innate vitality.

Now that some of their young men have gained an education and attracted the support of international organizations upholding the rights of native peoples, the Kayapo have secured a firm legal existence in modern Brazil. Their chiefs have acted decisively and creatively to selectively modernize yet preserve their religious traditions. From their taxes on tenant miners, they brought the group into the national cash economy, even going so far as buying airplanes and hiring Brazilian pilots to police their territory. They invested in radios and video equipment for recording group rituals and communicating with other Kayapo across their large territory, all to cultivate their common identity, ritual celebrations, and cultural survival. Traditional lip plugs and body painting remain common in village life, and group hunts keep male and female jungle survival skills honed; yet these have been integrated alongside the adoption of Western medicine, canned foods, and business connections in the global economy (such as supplying Brazilian nut oil to the corporation The Body Shoppe). As material wealth has increased, Kayapo chiefs, by adapting to the possibilities of modern life, have been outspoken in having their group maintain their jungle traditions; like many surviving indigenous peoples, they have realized that preserving the ecological vitality of their lands is essential to guarding their sociocultural integrity.

Shamanism in Modern Asia: Division of Labor Within the World Religions

Shamanism continues to be an integral part of the pluralistic religious cultures of Asia. In most settlements across the region, there is a shaman who can enter into the trance state, if called on to heal or to solve practical problems. Such shamanic practice today

Protest against modern states is a regular fact of life among indigenous peoples in the world today. Struggles to retain control of the land, secure their legal rights, and ensure the education of the young are central to the survival of indigenous religious traditions today. Here, Australian Aborigines demonstrate in Sydney for the restoration of lands annexed from them by the national government.

"Look around. . . . So much of nature has been ruined. Spirits of trees and rocks are displaced and haunt humans because they have nowhere else to go. No wonder the country is a mess."

—Kim Myung, a Korean shaman

SOURCE: *New York Times*, July 7, 2007.

has been harmonized with the doctrines of the dominant religions and is tolerated by the Hindu, Buddhist, or Islamic religious establishments that are also by now deeply rooted in these areas.

This pattern of coexistence also includes East Asia, where shamans augment popular Confucian beliefs and ancestral rituals, a tradition of pluralistic accommodation there going back to the beginnings of recorded history (see Chapter 8). Given the widespread belief across East Asia in deities inhabiting this earth and in the soul's afterlife destiny, it is not surprising that East Asians still recognize the utility of spirit mediums who attempt to communicate with the dead. In addition, the shamanic skill of divination provides answers to such problems as where grandmother's soul might be residing, whether the ghost of a dead child is causing family troubles, or what might be done to gain the favor of a god who could help end a drought. Unhappy spirits are also thought to cause distress to the living, so here, too, shamans have had an important role in healing the sick.

Typically, a client approaches a spirit medium today because of the suspicion that an illness is due to ghost possession. The medium goes into trance in the sick one's presence and speaks or acts after having made contact with one or more spirits. The medium's communications are usually interpreted by an assistant, who acts as the intermediary for the family and community members present. For example, contemporary mediums in Taiwan, called *dangki*, become possessed and rapidly write divinely inspired characters in red ink on yellow papers. Sometimes these writings become amulets for their patients; alternatively, they may be burned, whereupon their ashes are mixed with water that is then drunk as medicine. The role of these spirit mediums has, if anything, *increased* with the modernization and rising prosperity of Taiwan. The same phenomenon has been reported in modern Korea as well.

Global Neo-Shamanism: Expropriation by "White Shamans"

Traditional shamanistic practices now appeal to those in the dominant societies who want to explore the mysteries of life outside the practices and normative worldviews of the major world religions. With their esoteric qualities, shamanic practices are seen by some in the West as "uncontaminated," the last remaining spiritual frontier on earth. Now growing numbers of people from urban civilizations seek out shamanic experience as the representative of nearly lost worlds, hoping to recover something of value. Thousands of Euro-Americans each year sign up for tours to Siberia, the Amazon, or the Himalayas to observe and even be initiated by local shamans. A number of Westerners (hence "**white shamans**") have created global organizations propagating a purported "universal" shamanic tradition, charging high fees for tours, courses, initiations, and healing services, pledging to use some of the proceeds to assist local shamans.

white shamans: Westerners who claim to be practitioners in a "universal" shamanic tradition

In indigenous societies, the shaman has a social rather than a personal reason for entering into trance and contacting the spirits, with a primary concern for the community and its well-being. This is an orientation that contrasts sharply with that of the neo-shamans, whose primary interest is in personal development and a self-healing disconnected from any wider community.

Some native peoples regard this development as an attempt by the conquerors to take the last of their possessions, their culture. Well aware of how much their peoples have lost and ever zealous to guard their traditional secrets, many shamans both distrust the outsiders and doubt their sincerity. Responding to these postmodern possibilities, the indigenous shaman is again mediating between worlds in creative ways.

GENDER FOCUS: Women Healers and Shamans Today

In most hunter-gatherer societies, both women and men worked as healers. As indigenous societies became more complex and settled, and adopted forms of pastoralism and simple agriculture, women were subject to greater restrictions, but in some societies they still serve as healers and noted spirit mediums. In most urban communities of China and Japan, shamans are typically regarded as marginal figures of low status, but in South Korea their practices are uniquely honored and sought by people of all faiths. Korean shamans called *mudang* tend to be predominantly women, drawn into the role from one of two backgrounds: troubling personal experiences that led them to initiation; or inheritance of the role through kinship lines. An estimated 100,000 Korean shamans practice their healing arts today. Their séances, called *kut*, are usually held to contact a deity to request economic blessings, healing, restoration of good marital relations, or help in becoming pregnant. The *mudang* enters a trance and then begins to speak with voices attributed to deities. Typically the first statements are complaints of deficiencies in the offerings laid out or about impurity, which Korean supernaturals particularly dislike. When sponsors apologize and promise to do better next time, the divinities usually entertain the sponsor's request(s). A second type of ritual has the most proficient *mudangs* go to the next world with the soul of someone who has recently died or to check the status of a newly departed soul.

Assimilating indigenous animistic and shamanistic traditions into urban-based civilizations goes back to the very beginnings of recorded human history, as we saw in Chapter 1. We will see in subsequent chapters how world religions from antiquity onward performed a central role in absorbing tribal peoples into states by "converting them" away from their indigenous religions. It will also be seen in the final chapter that the "civil religions" of modern nations focused on legitimating the often violent work of assimilating indigenous peoples. Recently, some modern governments have issued formal apologies to indigenous peoples for their treatment of them and their ancestors: in 2008, for example, the Australian and Canadian governments issued formal apologies to aboriginal peoples for policies "detrimental to integrity of lives, including forcibly sending children to Christian boarding schools."

In the next chapters, we can find repeatedly the imprint of indigenous religions, especially soul belief and trance. Soul beliefs remain nearly universal in the great religions, with East Asia's widespread ancestor veneration an important example of archaic practices that remain compelling. Death rites continue to be powerful expressions of religious tradition, and states of altered consciousness are still central to spiritual growth. The metaphor of human life existing on a plane between heaven above and a netherworld below is found in all major world religions. Finally, sacred places that are believed to be at the center of the world (the *axis mundi*) in the early indigenous traditions continue to be revered in the great world religions. As for the connection with shamans, when examining the lives of the founders of the world religions, prophets as well as sages, we can notice the performance of miracles such as healing the sick and ascending to the heavens on magical flights, in both cases demonstrating the mastery of what began as the chief shamanic arts.

In the last chapter of this book, we will trace further this now-global arc of interaction between indigenous religions, their leaders, shamanism, and "white shamans." We will also see how the shamanic experience of trance, communication with other worlds, and spirit flight have again found their way into the syncretistic practices of many of the "new religions" that have arisen across the world.

Conclusion

For at least the last 30,000 years, humans have evolved primarily through their cultures. Art, religious practices, and complex symbols were all present among modern *Homo sapiens* from the beginning. And all three emerged simultaneously. What should we understand from this circumstance? Religion is an essential element in the evolution of our species. It has helped humanity bond more tightly, face the unknown, hunt more effectively, and reconcile with death. Cultural historians see all these factors as having helped human groups maximize the quality of their diet, which in turn enabled them to better organize, understand, and adapt to their environment as well as to each other. With more free time, there were greater possibilities for individuals to specialize, experiment, and so introduce cultural innovations.

Evidence of religion in prehistory reflects the major concerns of our species as hunter-gatherers. Fertility was important for group survival, the need to hunt for prey was a constant and central fact, and there was ongoing concern to maintain group and gender boundaries. Indigenous religions among hunter-gatherers and early settled cultivators clearly aided group survival.

To the extent a group adopted religious beliefs and practices, that group obtained advantages compared to other groups. As a force binding communities, as a means of being careful about the unseen, and as a decisive factor in helping human groups adapt to their environment, the world's indigenous religions point out the central issues we face in understanding the continuing and universal role of religion in later human life.

Finally, we can also discern the emergence of the first religious specialist, the shaman, who cultivates the universal human capacity for entering altered states of consciousness. Both serving and leading the people, the shaman has given peoples confidence and direction in dealing with the world's unseen forces. Shamanism is still widespread in the world today. Even where one or more of the great world religions has been adopted by a population, shamanic traditions continue to find patrons. In some cases, shamans express concepts associated with one of the now-dominant world religions (e.g., the soul, hell, the force of karma). In other instances, a shamanic cosmos exists side by side with that of a world religion. Today, shamanism is practiced "underground" if there is reason to fear persecution. In most places, however, it is integrated with the dominant world religions.

Discussion Questions

1. What are the problems in knowing and understanding the religions that existed before the development of written language?

2. How might the history of religions be written by a member of an indigenous people?

3. In many hunter-gatherer groups, the people often refer to themselves as "the true people." How might sudden awareness of the existence of other people in itself undermine the cosmos posited in such indigenous religious traditions?

4. Do you think it is valid to generalize from modern hunter-gatherers back into the past to reconstruct the origins of religion? Why or why not?

5. How might a modern shaman explain the endurance of her tradition and the attraction of shamanic practices by those living in modern industrial societies?

6. Some scholars have noted that the practices of modern sports fans in the West often resemble the totemic practices of indigenous peoples. Describe these commonalities in the case of your college or for a professional team such as the Chicago Bears. How do mascots and symbolic practices function to achieve group unity and individual identity?

7. Scholars who have studied tribal peoples now counsel sympathetically imagining indigenous religions as "lived through the body" and involving the entire spectrum of human perception. Explain why this approach has value, given the practices of Kung shamanism.

8. The scholar of comparative religions Joseph Campbell once suggested that the dominant world religions all differed from the indigenous religions by their requiring followers to distance themselves from the powerful personal religious experiences that were routine in many indigenous societies. While you are invited to test this assertion in the following chapters, can you see any problems with traditions that invite everyone to have regular immersions into the sacred as described in this chapter?

9. In 1985, the anthropologist Michael Harner founded the nonprofit Foundation for Shamanic Studies, which seeks to foster "greater respect for the knowledge of indigenous peoples and ultimately help to preserve and dignify this wisdom for future generations." What questions would you have for this organization, given that they also offer workshops to train Western peoples in shamanic practices?

Key Terms

animism	*n/um kausi*	syncretism
Bwiti	Native American	taboo
circular time	Church	totem
cosmogony	numinous	tutelary spirit
Dreamtime	sorcerers	"Venus" figurines
Ghost Dance	spirit flight	"white shamans"
Homo religiosus	spirit medium/shaman	

Suggested Readings

Beck, Peggy, Anna Lee Walters, and Nia Francisco. *The Sacred: Ways of Knowledge, Sources of Life* (Tsaile, AZ: Navajo Community College Press, 1996).

Buyandelger, Manduha, *Tragic Spirits: Shamanism, Memory, and Gender in Contemporary Mongolia.* (Chicago: University of Chicago Press, 2013).

Gardner, Robert. *Gardens of War: Life and Death in the New Guinea Stone Age* (New York: Random House, 1969).

Grim, John. *The Shaman: Patterns of Religious Healing Among the Ojibway Indians* (Norman: University of Oklahoma Press, 1983).

———. *Indigenous Traditions and Ecology: The Interbeing of Cosmology and Community* (Cambridge, MA: Center for the Study of World Religions, 2001).

Harris, Marvin. *Our Kind* (New York: Harper & Row, 1989).

Hayden, Brian. *Shamans, Sorcerers and Saints: A Prehistory of Religion* (Washington, DC: Smithsonian Institution Press, 2004).

Katz, Richard. *Boiling Energy: Community Healing Among the Kalahari Kung* (Cambridge, MA: Harvard University Press, 1982).

Kendall, Laurel. *The Life and Times of a Korean Shaman* (Honolulu: University of Hawaii Press, 1988).

———. *Shamans, Housewives, and Other Restless Spirits* (Honolulu: University of Hawaii Press, 1988).

Lame Deer, and R. Erdoes. *Lame Deer: Seeker of Visions* (New York: Simon & Schuster, 1972).

Lawson, E. Thomas. *Religions of Africa: Traditions in Transformation* (San Francisco: Harper & Row, 1984).

Olupona, Jacob K. *Beyond Primitivism: Indigenous Religious Traditions and Modernity* (New York: Routledge, 2003).

———. *African Religions: A Very Short Introduction* (New York: Oxford University Press, 2014).

Pfeiffer, J. E. *The Creative Explosion* (New York: Harper & Row, 1982).

Ritchie, Mark. *Spirit of the Rainforest: A Yanomamo Shaman's Story* (New York: Island Lake Press, 1996).

Spindler, George, and Stockard, Janice E., eds. *Globalization and Change in Fifteen Cultures* (Belmont, CA: Thomson, 2007).

Sullivan, Lawrence A., ed. *Native Religions and Cultures of North America: Anthropology of the Sacred* (New York: Continuum, 2003).

Taylor, Timothy. *The Buried Soul: How Humans Invented Death* (Boston: Beacon, 2002).

Vitebsky, Piers. *The Shaman* (New York: Macmillan, 1995).

Notes

1. Ian Tattersall, "Once We Were Not Alone," *Scientific American*, January 2000, p. 62.
2. Summarized from Piers Vitebsky, *The Shaman* (New York: Macmillan, 1995), p. 125.
3. Quoted in Sherman Alexie, *The Lone Ranger and Tonto Fistfight in Heaven* (New York: Atlantic Monthly Press, 1993), p. 104.

Additional Resources

Aboriginal Culture (http://www.aboriginalculture.com.au/index.shtml). A detailed site that contains information about traditional Australian Aboriginal Cultures, including material culture, social organization, art, and Aboriginal religion.

Foundation for Shamanic Studies (http://www.shamanism.org/). Website by the nonprofit organization dedicated to preserving shamanic cultures and spreading their beliefs and practices across the world.

Native Languages of the Americas (http://www.native-languages.org/religion.htm). A website written by Native American scholars and practitioners, with links to other sites on a variety of themes in religion and spiritual culture.

Survival International (http://www.survivalinternational.org/). Web site documenting and advocating for indigenous peoples globally.

Virtual Religion Index: American Studies (http://virtualreligion.net/vri/america.html). A rich and exhaustive listing of Web resources on every aspect of Native American religious traditions.

THE MANY STORIES OF JUDAISM

3

Sacred and Secular

Overview

Jews, like all other religious people, are divided on whether diversity is a good thing or a problem. In fact, that issue is a constant theme throughout this book. To appreciate diversity in Judaism, we can start by painting a clearer picture: In a neighborhood in Jerusalem, on a Friday evening as dusk approaches, ultra-Orthodox Jewish men, dressed in black suits and hats, close off their streets and neighborhoods to traffic in strict observance of the rules of the Sabbath as a holy day. The majority of Jerusalem's inhabitants are secular Israelis in modern Western dress who do not consider themselves to be religious Jews. They see themselves as only ethnically Jewish and choose to ignore the Sabbath and most other religious rules. Meanwhile, in a New York City neighborhood, a male rabbi leads the traditional worship at an Orthodox **synagogue**, a role not permitted to women among the Orthodox. Nevertheless, three blocks away a woman rabbi leads her more liberal, Reform congregation in a Friday night prayer service. There is, indeed, great diversity in Judaism today. And while, since the Holocaust, the majority of Jews worldwide reside either in **Israel** or in the United States, one can still find communities of Jews throughout Europe and scattered throughout the Middle East, Africa, Latin America, and Asia, including India and China.

synagogue: community centered on prayer and study of Torah; the building in which the community meets for these activities

Israel: Jews as a religious people; also the land and state of Israel, depending on the context

◀ Hasidic Rabbi carrying the scrolls of the Torah.

67

Rabbinic: Judaism
of the postbiblical
premodern period

Behind this modern diversity and the conflicting understandings of how to live a Jewish life that they express lies premodern **Rabbinic** Judaism, which provided the model for Jewish life from about the sixth century CE until the emergence of modern forms of Judaism in the nineteenth century. Indeed, ultra-Orthodox Jews see themselves as preserving premodern Judaism against the onslaught of modern Jewish diversity. Judaism is the smallest of the great world religions; its 14 million adherents comprise 0.2 percent of the world's population. Yet Jews have had, and continue to have, a major impact on history. Over the millennia, Judaism has been many things to many people in different times and places. Moreover, as we have said, some people today who consider themselves to be Jewish do not identify themselves as religious. Yet secular or ethnic ways of being Jewish, as we shall see, have had profound effects on the Jewish religion and vice versa. Therefore, they must be included in our survey to help us understand the religion of Judaism. We will find great diversity among the Jewish people, but we shall also discover a common thread. That is the task of this chapter.

Judaism Timeline

2000 BCE	The approximate time for the events attributed to Abraham
1280	The time of the events attributed to Moses—Exodus and the Covenant
1240	Conquest of land of Canaan under Joshua
1004–965	King David
721	Fall of northern kingdom of Israel to Assyrians
586	Fall of southern kingdom of Judah to Babylonians
538	Return from Exile
198–167	Maccabean revolt against enforced Hellenization
63	Beginning of rule by Rome
ca. 30 CE	Hillel and Shammai—first of the Tannaim
70	Destruction of the second temple
73	Fall of Zealot fortress at Masada
90	Emergence of the Academy at Yavneh
90–200	Formation of the Mishnah
200–500	Formation of the Gemara
1070	Founding of Talmudic academy by Rashi in Troyes, France
1095	First Crusade; beginnings of pogroms—mass slaughter of Europe's Jews
1306	Jews expelled from France; beginning of pattern repeated throughout Europe
1700–1760	Hasidic leader Israel ben Eliezer, the Ba'al Shem Tov
1729–1786	Moses Mendelssohn, leading figure in Jewish *Haskalah* (Enlightenment) movement/Reform Judaism

Jews believe that the highest reality is the God of creation and history, who revealed himself at Mount Sinai, and they believe that to act in harmony with the will of this God is the highest goal of life. Indeed, the monotheism of both Christianity and Islam is rooted in this most ancient of the three traditions. Christianity and Islam also follow Judaism in seeing the gravest problem in human life as sin—the failure to live in harmony with the will of a God who demands justice and compassion. The ideal of life is living in harmony with the will of God. Sin disrupts that life-giving harmony. In Judaism, one overcomes the problem and realizes the ideal by means of the study and practice of God's teachings or revelation: **Talmud** Torah.

Talmud: the oral Torah and its written commentaries

In Judaism, each and every human being is free to choose good or evil because each person stands before God in the same relationship that Adam and Eve did. The idea that the sin of the first two human beings, Adam and Eve, was inherited by all descendants, the Christian concept of original sin, does not exist in Judaism (nor in Islam). In creating the people Israel, God gave them a gift to tip the balance between

1808–1888	Samson Raphael Hirsch, leading figure in emergence of Orthodox Judaism
1860–1904	Theodor Herzl, founder of modern Zionism
1917	Balfour Declaration—proposal for Jewish homeland in Palestine endorsed by British government
1933–1945	Rise and fall of Nazi Party; the Holocaust, 6 million Jews murdered
1939–1945	World War II
May 14, 1948	Birth of state of Israel
May 11, 1949	Israel admitted to United Nations
1967	Six-Day War, followed by emergence of Judaism of Holocaust and Redemption
1973	Yom Kippur War, followed by growth of ultra-Orthodox movements
1979	Camp David peace treaty between Egypt and Israel
1980s	*Intifada*: Palestinian uprising and escalation of conflict between Palestinians and Israelis
1993	Oslo Accord, developing increased autonomy for Palestinians and the framework for negotiating peace with Israel, followed by continued violence on the part of radicals on both sides who view compromise as betrayal; also, continued tension between secular Israeli Jews and ultra-Orthodox haredim and between Israeli haredim and Conservative and Reform Jews of the Diaspora
1995	Oslo II agreement establishing an independent Palestinian Authority
2002	Israeli construction of a wall of separation between Israel and the territories of the Palestinian Authority; conflict between Israelis and Palestinians continues in the following years
2012	U.N. General Assembly upgrades Palestine to non-member observer-state status

dual Torah: the scriptures of Rabbinic Judaism, composed of the written Torah (Tanak) and the written formulation of the oral Torah (Talmud)

covenant: agreement between God and Israel promising God's protection in exchange for Israel's obedience to God's commandments

halakhah: religious commandments or laws of Talmudic Judaism; God's 613 commandments

mitzvot: God's commandments requiring deeds of loving kindness

good and evil in favor of good. This was the **dual Torah**, the sacred oral and written teachings concerning God's revelation to his people. In giving Israel the Torah, God established a **covenant** (i.e., a binding agreement) with Israel, making them a holy people and reminding them: "I will be your God and you shall be my people, I will guide and protect you and you will obey my commandments." According to the story of Torah, God set before Israel the choice between life and death and made it possible for the people to choose life. This could be accomplished by following the 613 commandments that are God's law and called *halakhah*, which means "to walk in the way of God." These commandments can all be reduced to two: loving God above all and one's neighbor with the same compassion you expect for yourself. These commandments require deeds of loving kindness, or *mitzvot*, by which the people embody in their lives the justice and mercy of God as a model for all the world.

It would be misleading, however, to think that this summary sketch of the religious worldview of Judaism would be agreed to by all Jews. In the remainder of this chapter we shall try to understand both the unity and the diversity of Judaism as a religious tradition and the profound impact of the emergence of modernity on its development. We begin by discussing the twentieth-century encounter of Judaism with modernity that gave rise to ultra-Orthodoxy. We then go back to the historical beginnings of Judaism and trace its history, to understand the sources of the diverse threads of contemporary Judaism and the ongoing struggle to define its future. Because our goal is to understand Judaism's encounter with modernity, we shall focus primarily on those aspects that reveal the diversity of Judaism today and show how that diversity developed. ○ ● ○

The interior of the Touro Synagogue in Newport, Rhode Island, the oldest synagogue in the United States, consecrated in 1763.

Encounter with Modernity: Modern Judaisms and the Challenge of Ultra-Orthodoxy

Premodern Rabbinic Judaism was a world unto itself. It embraced every aspect of life and offered safe haven from the non-Jewish world that largely rejected it while greatly restricting the role of Jews in the larger society. The modern world, by contrast, seems to offer Jews a new option—the possibility of sharing in its citizenship. Thus all modern forms of Judaism draw a line between the secular (i.e., nonreligious) and the religious and allow Jews to participate in both worlds.

Ultra-Orthodox Jews (the **haredim**) seek to recapture, as far as possible, the way of premodern Jews. And they hope to see the day (at least in Israel) when all modern forms of Judaism will disappear and their own communities will be the model for the whole of society. The goal of "deprivatizing" Judaism, so that its religious vision can shape all of public life, sets ultra-Orthodox Judaism apart from other modern forms of Judaism. At the same time, ultra-Orthodoxy rejects pluralism, a key characteristic of "postmodernity." They rebel against modern religious pluralism. For the ultra-Orthodox there cannot be many ways to keep the covenant—only one way. And that one way is all-encompassing. It does not permit a Jew to parcel out his or her life into separate secular and religious portions. Nor does it permit men and women to redefine their gender roles in new and "liberating" ways. Such redefinitions, they argue, will inevitably lead to moral chaos and the collapse of the family. Although only a minority of the world's Jewish population have opted for ultra-Orthodoxy, this way of being Jewish offers a challenge to Jews the world over to examine the implications of their modern spiritual and political beliefs: Can one be both modern and Jewish without sacrificing the essence of one's religious identity?

Haredim: the communal name for the ultra-Orthodox coming from eastern Europe

The Conflict over Public Life: Religion and Politics in the State of Israel

The conflict created by ultra-Orthodoxy is most obvious in the state of Israel, where public life was shaped initially by secular Jews with a nonreligious socialist-Zionist worldview. **Zionism** is a nineteenth-century Jewish secular political movement that promoted giving Jews their own national homeland. However, especially since the mid-1970s, the ultra-Orthodox minority, approximately 24 percent of the Israeli population, have formed increasingly influential religious parties that seek to undo this secularity and place the public order under the rule of *halakhah*, the religious commandments or laws of premodern Talmudic Judaism.

Zionism: nineteenth-century Jewish secular political movement that promoted giving Jews their own national homeland

Although a minority with considerable diversity and disagreement among themselves, the ultra-Orthodox share in the desire to make the public life of the secular state of Israel more religiously observant. They insist, for example, that all businesses be closed on the Sabbath, and they succeeded in having the Israeli legislature, the Knesset, pass a law requiring that all marriages be performed by Orthodox rabbis. In the eyes of the ultra-Orthodox, their secular, Reform, and Conservative brethren are not really Jews, and Orthodox Jews are not orthodox enough. All non-ultra-Orthodox Jews are urged to repent and return (*teshuvah*) to the true Judaism. Consequently, both Orthodox and ultra-Orthodox Jews have campaigned to amend an Israeli law enacted in 1950, two years after Israel achieved statehood. The act, called "the law of return," assures all post-Holocaust Jews that Israel is their homeland and grants automatic Israeli citizenship to all Jews, born of a Jewish mother, who apply. Orthodox and ultra-Orthodox partisans have repeatedly tried to have the law modified to prevent anyone who has not undergone an Orthodox conversion from being accepted for citizenship.

Despite the minority status of ultra-Orthodox Jews in Israel (and despite the anti-Zionist stance of most of them), the various political parties that represent them have managed to play a significant role in Israeli public life, because typically neither of the major secular parties—Labor and Likud—is able to secure enough votes to form a majority government without entering into a coalition with at least some of the religious parties. This state of affairs has given such religious parties bargaining power disproportionate to their numbers.

Ultra-Orthodoxy as a Form of Fundamentalism

The rise of ultra-Orthodoxy in Judaism is part of a larger religious resurgence that has been going on in all religions and cultures around the globe since the mid-1970s. The late 1960s and early 1970s were a time of radical cultural disruption in Western urban secular societies—a time when the youth of the Western world, the children of those who experienced World War II, were rejecting what they described as the emptiness of modern secular culture. In their rejection, large numbers turned to various Eastern and Western religious movements as a way of recovering a sense of meaning and purpose in life. Indeed, the less modern and secular the movement, the more attractive it appeared.

One form that this religious resurgence took was distinctively fundamentalist. What all religious fundamentalist movements have in common is a desire to return to the foundations of belief and action that existed in their respective traditions prior to the coming of modernity. These movements see in contemporary culture, where many view all truth and all values as relative, the decadence of the modern period. So they think that this is a period in which most human beings have lost their way and have ended up in a world without standards and norms.

The total immersion in a deliberately premodern way of life represents to the ultra-Orthodox a definitive break with what it views as the decadence of Western civilization. And while the completeness of their immersion experience emulates that of the premodern tradition of Rabbinic Judaism, its self-consciousness does not. These "new" Jews have chosen to engage in an experiment, and in this sense their religion, too, belongs to the range of forms of Judaism of the modern/postmodern period. They, like all other religious persons of the modern era, have no choice but to choose. Their choice is between withdrawal from and involvement with the modern world, either back to what they somewhat romantically view as the "one way" of premodern Judaism or forward into pluralism. To understand the implications of this choice, we must return to the beginnings of premodern Judaism in the biblical period and work our way forward.

Premodern Judaism: The Formative Era (2000 BCE–500 CE)

The Biblical Roots of Judaism

Judaism, along with Christianity and Islam, is shaped by the myth (i.e., symbolic story) of history, a concept we learned in Chapter 1. Indeed, the myth of history begins with Judaism. Judaism finds its roots in the story of the God who made promises to Abraham and his descendants that were fulfilled centuries later. This happened when the God of Abraham sent Moses to deliver his people from slavery in Egypt and lead them into the "land of promise"—the land of Canaan. From these beginnings the story blossomed into the full myth of history, which tells of the God who acts in time (i.e., in history) and leads his people on a journey through time toward a day of final resurrection in which all injustice, suffering, and death will be overcome.

While all religious traditions pass on their vision of reality through stories, story plays a unique role in Jewish religion. (In this chapter, depending on context, *Israel* refers either to the country or to "the people Israel"—to the biblical people of the Mosaic covenant from which Judaism developed.)

Indeed, for Judaism God is the divine storyteller, and the unfolding of creation in history is God's story. In the beginning God said, "Let there be light," and the story began. And the unfolding story will continue to play out in history until God brings it—after many trials and tribulations—to a happy conclusion at the end of time, when the dead are raised to enjoy a new heaven and a new earth.

The Story Begins: One God Above All Others

The religiousness of ancient Israel that gave birth to Judaism developed against the background and influences of two great ancient polytheistic civilizations: Egyptian and Babylonian. Indeed, the names of the two greatest figures of the Torah, "Abraham" and "Moses," are, respectively, Babylonian and Egyptian names. And the biblical stories of both reflect this. Abraham is said to have migrated from Ur in Babylonia down into the land of Canaan, while Moses is born in Egypt, where the descendants of Abraham had migrated, seeking refuge from famine in their own land.

The great sociologist Max Weber (and many scholars since) argued that the beginning of the secularization of Western society began with the ancient Israelite religion

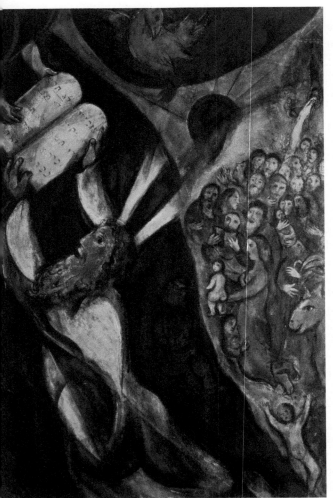

In this 1953 painting, *Moses Receiving the Tablets of the Law,* the Russian painter Marc Chagall portrays Moses receiving the Ten Commandments at Sinai. Jews trace the beginnings of Judaism to the covenant made between God and Israel at Sinai.

that gave birth to Judaism. Although influenced by the religions of the Egyptians and Babylonians, ancient Israelite religion was strikingly different. For the Egyptians and the Babylonians, the world was the sacred embodiment of the gods (i.e., the waters, the land, the sun, etc., were all gods); then biblical religion came along and by the time of the Prophets had declared there is but one God and he is not the world but creator of the world. Therefore the world is secular, and God alone is holy—although the world can be sanctified, or made holy, by serving this God.

The story of the past, as it was imagined by the people Israel, proceeds from the creation of the first man and woman, Adam and Eve, to the near annihilation of humanity, as related in the story of Noah and the flood. Then came the division of humans into many language groups at the tower of Babel, God's call to Abraham to be a father of many nations, and God's promise to give the land of Canaan to the descendants of Abraham (Genesis 15). The story moves on to the migration of the family of Abraham's great-grandson Joseph into Egypt at a time of famine. It relates how the tribes of Israel, Abraham's descendants, became enslaved in Egypt and how God sent Moses to deliver them from slavery.

In the story of the Exodus, God assists Moses by sending down ten plagues on the Egyptians and then parting the waters of the Red Sea to enable the Israelites to escape to the land God gives them, in keeping with a promise made to Abraham (Genesis 15:18–21). According to this story, on the way to this land of promise God brought the people to Mount Sinai, gave the Torah to Moses, and formed a covenant with the people. As the book of Exodus (19:3–6) describes it:

Moses went up to God, and the Lord called to him from the mountain [Mount Sinai], saying, "Thus shall you say to the house of Jacob, and tell the people of Israel; You have seen what I did to the Egyptians, and how I carried you on eagles' wings, and brought you to myself. Now therefore, if you will obey my voice indeed, and keep my covenant, then you shall be my own treasure among all peoples; for all the earth is mine; And you shall be to me a kingdom of priests, and a holy nation. These are the words which you shall speak to the people of Israel."

This description of the delivery of the covenant at Mount Sinai is a climactic moment in a powerful and dramatic story about a journey that created a holy people—the people Israel. In fact, the Hebrew word for holy (*qadosh*) suggests that to be holy is to be "set apart." So Israel was chosen out of all the nations and set apart to be God's people as an example, or light, for other nations.

The story goes on to tell how the tribes of Israel wandered in the desert for forty years, entering the land of promise under the leadership of Joshua only after the death of Moses (see Map 3.1). For the next 200 years they lived on the land as a loose confederation under military leaders called *judges*. However, as threats of conquest from their neighbors became more frequent, many among the tribes began to demand a king like other nations, with a standing army to protect Israel. Some, however, argued that there could be only one king over Israel—the God of Abraham, Isaac,

> "I am the Lord your God who brought you out of the land of Egypt, out of the house of slavery: You shall have no other gods before me."
>
> —NRSV, Exodus 20:2–3

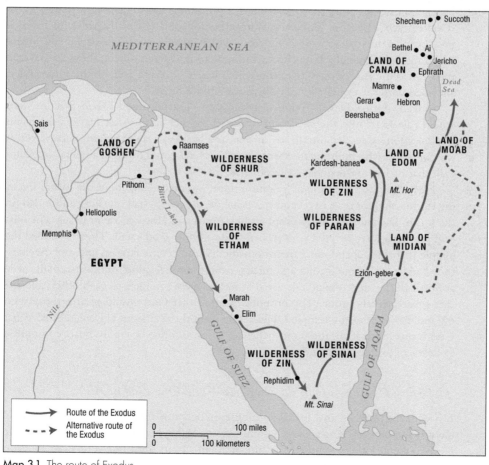

Map 3.1 The route of Exodus.

and Jacob. According to the story, God agreed to allow the people to have a king. And so Saul, chosen by God, was anointed with oil by a prophet, as a sign that the first king over Israel had been selected by God, not the people. Indeed, the concept of messiah (*mashiah*) has its beginnings here, for *messiah* means "anointed one," and it was understood that the one so anointed had been chosen to rule over the kingdom of God, the kingdom of Israel (1 Samuel 9:11–11:15).

Saul, however, proved to be a weak king. It was David, the second king over Israel, who established Israel as a nation. Under David and later his son Solomon, Israel claimed, for a brief time, to be the greatest nation in the Middle East. Stories were told of David's rise to power—how even as a young boy he had saved the tribes by slaying the Philistine giant, Goliath. When Saul died in battle against the Philistines, David was proclaimed by the people and anointed as their king. Later, the northern tribes, called Israel, visited David and asked him to be their king, too. Soon he would consolidate the monarchy, becoming known as the king of all Israel and Judah.

David used his army to capture Jebus, a Canaanite city, renaming it Jerusalem, or "God's peace." Because Jerusalem had not belonged to any of the tribes of Israel, it gave David a neutral vantage point from which to rule over both Israel and Judah. David made his capital a holy city by bringing to it a sacred object, the gold-covered chest called the Ark of the Covenant, which was believed to contain the stone tablets inscribed with the commandments given at Mount Sinai.

Indeed, during David's reign it is said that God promised David that his heirs would rule Israel into the far distant future (2 Samuel 7:16). After David's death, his son Solomon succeeded him to the throne, and Israel was at the height of its power. It was Solomon who built the first **temple** so that God could dwell in a splendor greater than that of any of the gods of the other nations.

However, after the time of Solomon there was quarreling about the succession to the throne, and for over two centuries Israel (in the north) had one king and Judah (in the south) had another. Soon prophets like Amos and Hosea arose in Israel. The biblical prophets were revered persons believed to know God's will. They reminded the people that since abandoning their nomadic life to become farmers and city dwellers, they had been drifting further and further from the tribal values of the covenant made at Sinai. In the cities the people acted as if they were strangers to each other, and the rich mistreated the poor. The prophets warned that God would punish those who offered sacrifices in the temple while acting unjustly as citizens and neighbors. What God wants most of all, the pious believed, is the sacrifice of a pure heart committed to deeds of justice and compassion.

The Story Continues with the Prophets—The One God of All

It is with the prophets that Jewish monotheism becomes fully formed, for in the tribal days of the time of Moses, Israel's commitment had been *henotheistic*—that is, to one God above all others. Thus the commandment "I am the Lord your God . . . you shall have no others beside me" did not mean that there were no other gods, only that

temple: the place in Jerusalem where the people Israel worshipped

Promise to David: "Your house and your kingdom shall be made sure forever before me; your throne shall be established forever."

—NRSV, 2 Samuel 7:16

Israel was forbidden to follow them. God was their tribal God. But after Israel was established as a great nation in the time of David, the prophets forced Israel to see that Israel's God was the only God of all the nations. Moreover, he would use the other nations, if necessary, to punish Israel for any failure to keep the covenant.

Out of the prophetic experience came the pure and simple creed of Judaism, the **Shema**: "Hear O Israel, the Lord our God, the Lord is one" (Deuteronomy 6:4). This confession is completed by reminding the people to love this God with all their heart, soul, and strength; to pray the *Shema* on arising and retiring; and to bind its words on their hands, foreheads, and doorposts to ensure that the awareness of the one true God might permeate their every thought and action.

Shema: in Judaism, the essential confession of monotheistic faith

The prophets warned the people that if they strayed from the covenant, the God of Israel would punish them. And that is exactly how the misfortunes of Israel and Judah came to be interpreted. For in 721 BCE the Assyrians conquered the kingdom of Israel and carried its inhabitants off into slavery. In 621 Judah's king, Josiah, is said to have discovered in the temple what he believed to be the long-lost book of the law (the biblical book of Deuteronomy). These writings echoed the teachings of the prophets about the need to practice justice to please God. On this basis Josiah initiated a reform that included a renewal of the covenant and designated the temple in Jerusalem as the only proper site for sacrifices. However, according to the biblical story, the reforms were not observed conscientiously, and God again allowed the people to be punished. In 586 the Babylonians conquered the Assyrians and their territories, destroyed the temple Solomon had built, and carried off the inhabitants of the southern kingdom of Judah into exile and slavery.

Thus says the Lord to his anointed (messiah), to Cyrus, . . . "For the sake of my servant Jacob, and Israel my chosen, I call you by your name, I surname you, though you do not know me."
—NRSV, Isaiah 45:1 & 4

As the time of the Babylonian exile approached, another generation of prophets arose—Jeremiah, Ezekiel, and Isaiah—spanning the time of exile and eventual return. These prophets asserted that God was indeed punishing Israel for its failure to keep the covenant, but they added that the punishment would be temporary (to teach them a lesson). As it happened, the Persians soon conquered the Babylonians, and after only fifty years, in 538, the Israelites were permitted to return to the land. This turn of events was due to the benevolent policy of the Persian king, Cyrus. That a pagan king should so favor the Israelites was seen as miraculous, and Cyrus was declared a messiah, that is, one anointed by God to carry out God's will to return his people to their land (Isaiah 45:1–13). Cyrus himself, of course, was not aware of this role attributed to him in the destiny of Israel. Thus we see that even in the biblical period, Judaism was capable of finding religious significance in secular political events.

The Story Becomes One of Exile and Return

The first wave of exiles returned to the land (520–515 BCE), but it was not until Ezra, a priest, and Nehemiah, a gifted layman, led a second wave of exiles (458 BCE) in a return to the land of Israel that a clear pattern for a postexilic Judaism emerged. These leaders demanded that the people repent: They had married citizens of other nations and sacrificed to other gods, and now they must rededicate themselves to the covenant and re-purify themselves as a holy people by separating themselves from their neighbors. It is with this priestly reform that Judaism adopted the experience of exile and return, in which they saw the liberation from slavery in Babylon as a repeat of the liberation from slavery in Egypt. So exile and return became the normative pattern through which to interpret all past and future Jewish experiences. Whenever Jews felt persecuted and exiled they would hope for the day of return—"Next year in Jerusalem" became their cry. In this sense, the experience of exile and return gave birth to Judaism.

In the fourth century BCE, Alexander the Great conquered the ancient world, and after his death in 323 his empire was divided among his generals. The Seleucid generals (198–167) began a policy of enforced Hellenization, requiring all their conquered peoples to adopt Greek customs and beliefs, including veneration of many gods. The Jews, who refused to abandon their worship of the one God of Abraham, Isaac, and Jacob, were severely persecuted for their noncompliance. Thus in the middle of the second century, Judas Maccabaeus and his brothers led a revolt against the cruel Seleucid ruler Antiochus Epiphanes IV. This effort, the Maccabean revolt, was successful in bringing about a status of semi-independence, which lasted into the first century CE. However, in a bid to resist new efforts at control by the Seleucids, the Jews in 63 BCE invited in the Romans to protect them. After the Exile, the temple was rebuilt on a modest scale and then later, between 20 BCE and 60 CE under the domination of Rome, the second temple was rebuilt on a grander scale. It is from the time of Alexander through the time of the Roman Empire that the religion of ancient Israel splintered and developed into a variety of religious movements, each claiming they represented the true practice of faith.

A model of the city of Jerusalem centered around the temple as it might have looked in 50 BCE.

The Historical Roots of Diversity

By the first century CE, the most important of these new movements were the Sadducees, the Pharisees, the Hellenists, the Samaritans, the Zealots, the Essenes, and the Nazarenes—all of which were engaged in ongoing debate. Today we would be tempted to say the debate was about the right way to be Jewish, but the idea of Judaism as a religion did not yet exist. Rather, the partisans of the first century saw the debate as about an attempt to define how one must live to be the "true Israel," or the true people of God. To understand this debate it is important to remember that at the beginning of the first century there was no official Bible and no set of practices and commitments accepted as normative by all Jews (see Timeline on pp. 68–69). It was only at the end of the first century that the **Tanak**, or the Bible of Judaism as we have it today, came into existence, along with Rabbinic Judaism as the normative pattern of Judaism for the next 1,800 years.

Now, let's consider each of these movements in a little more detail. The *Sadducees* came from the wealthy upper class, were associated with the temple tradition that was exclusive to Jerusalem, and saw their task as keeping peace with Rome. They accepted only the five books of Moses as sacred scripture and insisted on literal adherence to the written Torah.

The *Pharisees* were teachers associated with the synagogues (houses of study and prayer) found in every city and village; they accepted not only the five books of Moses but also the historical and wisdom writings and those of the prophets. Both the Jewish Bible (Tanak) and the Christian Old Testament are largely derived from the Pharisees' selection of scriptural materials. The Pharisees taught that God revealed himself in the written Torah and through oral traditions that accompanied the giving of the Torah to Moses. Moreover, they insisted that the written word could not be properly interpreted without the oral traditions. In these teachings the Pharisees offered a precursor to the later Rabbinic doctrine of God's revelation through the dual Torah, the oral and the written. Politically, the Pharisees were neither cozy with the Romans nor openly hostile to them.

Jews who were dispersed in the Roman Empire (i.e., outside the protectorate of Palestine) were known as the Jews of the **Diaspora**. The leaders of their synagogues were Hellenistic Jews who used a Greek translation of scriptures that closely corresponded to the Hebrew scriptures of the Pharisees, with some important exceptions. The *Hellenists* were the great missionaries of Judaism, who used Greek philosophy to explain the meaning of the biblical stories. They were anxious to promote Judaism as a religion that had a place for **gentiles**, and they adapted Judaism to Greek customs whenever feasible. They successfully encouraged large numbers of gentiles to come and worship the one true God of Israel.

Finally, there were sectarian movements like the *Zealots*, the *Samaritans*, the *Essenes*, and the *Nazarenes* (the followers of Jesus of Nazareth). Some, like the Zealots and Essenes, were openly hostile to the gentile world, whereas the Nazarenes, like the Hellenists, were very positive toward gentiles and sought their conversion. Adherents of these movements tended to be apocalyptic, believing that God would bring the world to an end soon and so would send a messiah to judge all human beings and reward the faithful. In the first century there was no single clear definition of *messiah*. A wide variety of speculations emerged, and each sectarian group had its own ideas. Most were expecting a spiritual leader, but some, primarily the Zealots, looked for a military leader able to overthrow the Romans, whose rule in Palestine had become oppressive.

What was typical of these sectarian movements was a strong distrust of the Sadducees, who were viewed as having sold out to the Romans. The Zealots, the most hostile of all, had nothing but contempt for the Sadducees and chose to oppose them

Tanak: the written Torah, or Hebrew Bible

Diaspora: the dispersion of a religious people outside their geographic homeland

gentile: anyone not Jewish

directly. If the Sadducees urged, "Don't rock the boat," the Zealots were committed to rocking the boat as often as possible. To this end, they staged random guerrilla attacks against the Roman legions. In the second century a Zealot, Simon bar Kokhba, claimed the title of messiah and was executed by the Romans.

Finally, at least some of the sectarian groups practiced baptismal rites, that is, ritual immersion and purification. Ritual immersion was already a requirement for any gentile convert to Judaism (along with **circumcision** for males). From the first century on, however, some groups insisted that not only gentile converts were to be immersed and purified, but also Jews, if they had strayed from the true path as understood by the particular sectarian movement.

circumcision: the cutting of the foreskin as a sign of the covenant of Abraham

Exodus and Exile: Story, History, and Modernity

The difference between premodern and modern is the difference between sacred story (scripture) and secular story (history). Fundamentalists fear the incursion of time and history into their sacred story, whereas modernists welcome it. The biblical writings as we have them are organized to tell a story of God's saving journey with his people. It is, as we have noted, the story of the God who acts in time and leads his people through time toward a final fulfillment. This is a grand story that answers questions of origin and destiny for the Jews as a religious people: Where do we come from? Where are we going? When modern historians read this story, they ask different questions. Primarily they want to know if things really happened as described in the sacred texts. They try to find out by comparing the stories with what else is known about the past through ancient writings, through literary analysis of stylistic changes in the writings, and through archaeological evidence.

When historians began to read the biblical stories critically, they believed they could identify different layers of historical development in the scriptural writings. It is on this basis that they identified four major layers of historical materials: J and E (Jahwist and Elohist, from two different Hebrew names for God), from the period of the monarchy of David and Solomon (ca. 1000 BCE); D (Deuteronomic, ca. 621 BCE), associated with the prophetically rooted reforms of King Josiah; and P (Priestly, ca. 458 BCE), associated with the priestly reforms of Ezra and his administrative successor, Nehemiah. Today biblical scholars do not think that the historical materials can be sorted out quite that neatly, but the recognition of historical layers remains essential to the historical study of biblical writings.

The earliest stories (J and E) seem to have been written down in the courts of David and Solomon to tell the story of how God chose Israel, from humble beginnings, to become a great kingdom. Bringing together diverse ancient tribal narratives, the royal storytellers constructed a larger and more complex story that begins with the creation of the world and ends with the kingdom of Israel under David and Solomon as the greatest nation of the ancient Middle East. It is an unambiguous story of promise and fulfillment. However, the story had to be revised in light of the Babylonian exile.

The Priestly revision describes Israel as a people shaped by seemingly broken promises that are unexpectedly renewed, leading to new hope and new life—a story of exile and return.

If the Exodus was the founding event of the story of Judaism, the Exile was its formative event. As the distinguished scholar of Judaism, Jacob Neusner, has noted, it was the great crisis of exile and the astonishment of return that set the mythic pattern of Judaic thought and experience ever since.[1] The exile and return provided a story pattern through which all past and future events, whether of triumph or of tragedy, could be meaningfully integrated into Jewish identity. "Exile and return" shaped the imagination of all future generations. Therefore, the fall of the second temple at the hands of the Romans in 70 CE was a trauma and a deep blow to those who wholeheartedly believed the story of the God who leads his people through time, but the crisis was not without precedent or without meaning. Although the disasters that befell the first and second temples were two of the most traumatic events in the long history of Judaism, neither destroyed the faith of Jews. On the contrary, in each case Jews came to the conclusion that the loss of the temple was not a sign of God's abandonment but a prophetic call to the people Israel to be more fully observant of the covenant. Thus today Jews willingly recall these two disastrous events on the holy day of **Tisha B'Av**, for remembering brings about not despair and hopelessness but repentance and renewal.

> **Tisha B'Av:** day of mourning to commemorate tragedies affecting the people Israel

From Torah to Talmud

The Pharisaic Roots of Rabbinic Judaism

To follow the emergence of Rabbinic, or Talmudic, Judaism, we need to resume our discussion of the various Jewish sects and movements that existed in the first century. Such diversity was brought to an end by the destruction of the temple in 70 CE. Of the movements that had been vying to provide a model for religious life, only a few survived, and of these it was the Pharisees who provided new leadership. There were at least three reasons for this.

First, the political neutrality of the Pharisees in the period before the fall of the temple made them appealing to the Romans. Unlike the Zealots, the Pharisees seemed benign in their views of the Roman Empire. So the Roman authorities gave them permission to establish an academy at Yavneh on the coast of present-day Israel. There they began the task of reconstructing Judaism for a new period of exile apart from the land and the temple. Second, the Pharisees were already the leaders of the synagogue tradition and the teachers (rabbis) of the oral tradition. And finally, the oral tradition the Pharisees had espoused gave them the flexibility to interpret the requirements of Jewish life in changing circumstances. Thus when the temple priesthood disappeared, no new institutions needed to be invented. The Pharisees became the natural leaders by default everywhere in ancient Palestine.

The task of the new leadership was to transpose the priestly model focused on the temple in Jerusalem into a new key—one that would allow the people Israel, like their ancestors in Babylon, to survive as Jews apart from the land and the temple. The solution the Pharisees arrived at was a model in which the people Israel (not just the temple) were holy, and every male head of a Jewish household was in fact a priest, even as the table in every Jewish house was an altar. In this new model, the center of Jewish life shifted from written Torah to the oral tradition, from priest to rabbi, from temple to synagogue, and also from temple altar to family table.

The Pharisees transferred the priestly rituals from the temple cult to a system of ethics. The prophets had issued sweeping demands, in the name of God, for justice and mercy. The Pharisees took these demands and made them the content for the priestly rituals of holiness, working out their application in all the details of everyday life according to the best insights of the oral tradition. Between the second and fifth centuries, Rabbinic Judaism, or the Judaism of the dual Torah, emerged as the insights of the oral tradition were written down and incorporated into what became known as the Talmud. And it was this Talmudic tradition that shaped Jewish life from the sixth century until the advent of Jewish modernizing movements in the nineteenth century.

The heart of the teachings of the Pharisees was that God was a loving personal father who chose Israel and entered into the covenant with them. This is the covenant revealed in the oral and written Torah, which teaches that each and every individual who keeps this covenant can live in hope of resurrection from the dead. Although the Pharisees are depicted as legalists in some of the Christian scriptures, historians have shown quite the contrary: that the Pharisees actually taught that the sacrifices that God wants are deeds of loving kindness rooted in a pure heart, not merely external observance of divine laws.

The Pharisees asked Jews to love God above all and their neighbor as themselves. They insisted that what is hateful to oneself must not be done to one's neighbor. They insisted that humans do not live by bread alone, and therefore one should trust in God rather than worry about tomorrow. They insisted that those who would seek the will of God would find it and that those who humbled themselves would be exalted. All these teachings were adopted by Christianity as well, as we shall see in Chapter 4.

The Rabbis and the Formation of the Talmud

Hillel and Shammai were the two leading rabbis, or teachers of oral tradition, in the first century of the common era (CE). Their influence led to the development of two major schools: the house of Hillel (*Bet Hillel*) and the house of Shammai (*Bet Shammai*). The disputes between Hillel and Shammai, and their schools, eventually became the foundation of the Talmud and set the tone of disputation and dialog that is characteristic of Talmudic Judaism. Both Hillel and Shammai sought to apply the oral Torah tradition to the details of everyday life. It was the students of Hillel who were the primary shapers of the **Mishnah**—the writings that form the core of the Talmud.

It was the disciples of Hillel and Shammai and their descendants who led the Jews into the Talmudic era. A disciple of Hillel, Johanan ben Zakkai, started the academy at Yavneh on the coast of Israel. There, the first task was to settle one of the key arguments

"If water, which is soft, could hollow out the hard stone, the words of the Torah, which are hard, will certainly make an impression on my soft heart."
—Rabbi Akiva

"Do not unto your neighbor what you would not have him do unto you. This is the whole of the Jewish law. All else are but commentaries."
—Rabbi Hillel

Mishnah: the writings that form the core of the Talmud

The Talmud records the ongoing discussion of Torah by the great rabbinic minds across the ages and is meant to be studied and debated in a communal setting.

that had been going on at the beginning of the century—namely, which writings of the tradition to regard as holy and, therefore, as revelations from God. The argument, of course, was settled by default. Since the Pharisees survived to establish Rabbinic Judaism, it was the writings they revered that were selected to comprise the canon, the official set of scriptures. In addition to the five books called the Pentateuch (Genesis, Exodus, Leviticus, Numbers, Deuteronomy), the Pharisees included the books of the prophets (e.g., Jeremiah and Ezekiel, Amos and Hosea, etc.), some historical writings (e.g., First and Second Kings), and also the writings of the wisdom literature (e.g., Proverbs, Ecclesiastes, Job). Thus it was the academy at Yavneh that settled on the books that make up the Bible of Judaism, known as the *Tanak*—an acronym standing for

- Torah (teachings),
- Neviim (prophets), and
- Ketuvim (writings).

In Western culture it has often been thought that to compare the teachings of Judaism and Christianity, all one need do is compare the Tanak, or Hebrew Bible (which Christians call the Old Testament), with the New Testament. Such a view, however, is totally misleading. The Talmud and the New Testament are like two different sets of glasses for reading the Hebrew Bible. Through the Talmud glasses, certain passages seem very clear and easy to read, while other parts are fuzzy and unreadable. And with New Testament glasses, the fuzzy passages become clear, and vice versa. Both Jews and Christians read the Hebrew Bible through the eyes of a further revelation (Talmud and New Testament) that tells them how to read the Hebrew scriptures, including what is valid and what can be dismissed. Thus Jews and Christians who seem to be reading an important body of holy writings in common might just as well be reading two different books—which, in a sense, they are. Consequently, to understand Judaism one must understand the Talmud and the central role it plays in Judaism.

The Talmud and the Torah

Tannaim: the generation of sages who created the Mishnah

With the Jewish people's sacred teachings committed to writing in the written Torah, or Tanak, the **Tannaim** ("those who study") began the paradoxical process of writing down the vast and diffuse teachings of the oral tradition and transforming this material into the oral Torah. The process occurred in two phases.

First, the Tannaim, led by Hillel and Shammai, organized the wisdom of the Jewish oral tradition in the *Mishnah*, which codifies the wisdom of the oral Torah. The Mishnah was intended to show Jews how they could sanctify life (i.e., make it holy) despite their loss of the temple and absence from the land of Israel. In the second phase of Talmudic formation, the successors to the Tannaim, the *Amoraim* ("those who interpret"), set about developing a commentary on the Mishnah that would link the oral to the written Torah. The result of their work was called the **Gemara**, and these combined writings form the Talmud (meaning "learning" or "study" as related to Torah).

Gemara: commentary on the Mishnah, and part of the Talmud

Even though the Talmud (Mishnah and Gemara) is said to have been completed by the sixth century, there is a sense in which the Talmud is never complete. The tradition of Talmudic commentary, which continues from generation to generation, is integral to Judaism, leaving the Talmudic traditions, as an expression of oral Torah, open to continuous development.

Producing the Talmud by writing down the oral Torah surely seems like a self-contradictory task. And yet the genius of the Talmud is in preserving the oral character of the material in written form. To appreciate the uniqueness of the Talmud one really has to look at it and see how its pages are constructed. A typical page is made up of diverse and distinct parts, coexisting on the same piece of paper. These parts express the voices of the rabbis throughout the ages, and teachings about the same subject are juxtaposed on the same page. The Talmud is an ongoing dialog among Jews not only of the same time period but from age to age. At the core of a page you may find statement (A) from the Mishnah of the second century outlining the opposing points of view of Hillel and Shammai on a question of appropriate behavior. Above this text, on the same page, might be a section of the Gemara (B) from a period 200 or 300 years later, relating the Mishnah to relevant passages from the Tanak and to the diverse opinions of the Amoraim and of the Tannaim. Typically, as well, there will be a section (C) devoted to the commentary of the greatest of the Rabbinic Talmudic scholars, Rashi. In yet another section (D) will be the commentaries of the students of Rashi from a collection known as the *Tosafot*. Each of these expresses views on the meaning of the passages of the Mishnah in light of the comments of the others and in light of additional commentaries and writings that supplement the tradition. The sections on a given page of the Talmud might span a thousand years or more.

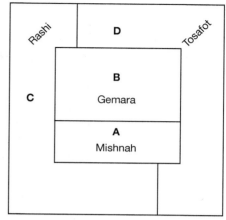

A page of the Talmud.

Although Talmudic decisions are made to guide the life of the Jewish community, it would be a mistake to think that the whole point of Talmud study is to reach a conclusion. For Talmudic study is a form of religious ritual whose purpose is nothing less than to bring the student of Torah to experience God through the thrust and parry of argument about the one thing that matters most in life—God's word. That is why it is not unheard of for a debating partner to help an opponent who is stumped for a response by suggesting a line of argument that might be able to refute the point the stronger partner has just made. In this way the Talmud sanctifies doubt and questioning as a medium of religious experience that brings one in touch with God. God is in the questions even more than in the answers. For this reason too, then, the Talmud is never finished as long as there is one more Jew ready to join the debate. It is a tradition of commentary upon commentary that guarantees that the Talmud is always both ancient and ever fresh and new. The Talmud is always about how one is to make the new day holy.

This understanding of Talmudic debate echoes the Torah story that explains how Israel got its name: According to Genesis (32:23–32), one night Jacob wrestled with a stranger who refused to tell his own name but, rather, blessed Jacob and gave him a new name, Israel, meaning "one who has wrestled with God and men and prevailed." As the sun rose, Jacob limped away, convinced that he had "seen God face to face."

So the Torah teaches Israel that the way of Torah is a wrestling with the God who cannot be named (or, for that matter, imaged), and that the one who wrestles with God (and God's Torah) and with other humans (about the meaning of Torah) can prevail. Indeed, to wrestle with the Torah is to see God face to face, to be transformed and given a new name: "Israel," which means "wrestler with God." Hence in Rabbinic Judaism there is no higher calling than to wrestle with God and others over the meaning of God's Torah. This activity is one that includes rather than excludes those who disagree. According to Talmudic tradition, when the rabbis disagree on the observance of *halakhah*, the majority opinion is to prevail for the good of order. Yet it is understood that those in the minority are not necessarily wrong. The Torah is large enough to embrace everyone.

Indeed, the story of the covenant at Sinai, through which God chose Israel, suggests just such a give-and-take relationship. According to the story, the covenant established that day was a *mutual* agreement between two parties, much like a marriage contract that is both a legal arrangement and an expression of mutual love and care. In this covenant the people promise to obey the commandments of God and walk in the

A page of the Torah in Hebrew, illustrating the use of a pointer called a *yad* (the Hebrew word for "hand") to follow the text.

"The world is suspended in space and has nothing to rest on except the breath of Torah study from the mouths of students—just as a man may keep something up in the air by the blowing of his breath."

—Talmud

kosher: what is suitable or fit, particularly in reference to Jewish dietary laws

way of the Torah, which gives life. And God promises to guide and protect them on their journey through time. Throughout this journey, God and Israel have wrestled with each other—at one moment God is reminding Israel that by their sins the people have strayed from their promise to obey the commandments, and at another moment Israel is reminding God that he appears to have strayed from his promises to guide and protect. Within the bounds of the covenant, each party can be held accountable by the other. It is this covenant that makes Israel *Israel*—wrestler with God. For the rabbis, the identity of the Jews lay not in their national or ethnic history, although within the myth or symbolic story of Torah they surely embraced that history. Nor is the people's Jewishness a function of their being, by choice, members of a religion called *Judaism*; in fact, there is no word for *Judaism* in biblical Hebrew!

Instead, the rabbis reminded the people how God had brought them to himself on eagles' wings, to be a holy people (Exodus 19:3–6), set apart to be a witness to the holiness of life. In this "setting apart" lies the ultimate meaning of the rules for **kosher** dining that forbid Jews to eat pork, to mix meat and milk, and so on. Even what one eats and the way one eats should remind the world that life is not meant to be profane and meaningless. Rather, a holy life, one that is set apart, is not one's own but belongs to God. Indeed, every act of one's life should be a witness to the One who alone is truly holy and in turn sanctifies all creation.

Torah, in the Talmudic tradition, is a multidimensional word. In its narrowest sense, Torah refers to the Pentateuch, the first five books of the Bible. In a broader sense it refers to the entire Bible, or Tanak. Broader still is its meaning as the dual Torah—that is, Torah plus Talmud. And ultimately Torah is the source and pattern for all creation, for, according to the Talmud, when God created heaven and earth he did it by consulting the Torah, which was already with God in the beginning. Hence the Torah provided the pattern for the right order of the universe, a pattern revealed in the *halakhah*, given through oral and written Torah. It was this understanding of the dual Torah (Torah plus Talmud) that shaped classical Judaism.

Premodern Judaism: The Classical Era (500 CE–1729 CE)

The Premodern Rabbinic World: God, Torah, and Israel

If human beings are not only storytellers but also storydwellers, then the Torah story of the rabbis was a magnificent dwelling indeed. If religion (*religio*) is about being "tied and bound" into the cosmic drama of life by one's story symbolically told (myth) and enacted (ritual), then Torah was, and is, just such a story. The Torah story of the rabbis created the cosmic vision of classical Judaism. It is a story that embraces not only every minute, hour, and day of Rabbinic Jewish life, providing a template to make it holy, but also the whole of time, from the creation of the world to its ultimate messianic redemption.

In the premodern world, the right to live within this story accompanied being born of a Jewish mother (and also those who were converts). While women thus determined Jewish identity, the primary guardians of Rabbinic religious life were men. Males alone had to be confirmed in their religious status through two key rituals: circumcision shortly after birth, and **bar mitzvah**, a ceremony in which they demonstrated their knowledge of the faith as they entered adulthood at age thirteen.

The Jews of the Rabbinic age of classical Judaism ate, drank, and slept Torah. The men began the day by dressing in garments with fringes (*tzitzit*) to remind them of the commandments of the covenant (Numbers 15:37–40). Before morning prayer, they wrapped the words of Torah (Deuteronomy 6:4–9) on their arms and foreheads, encased in small leather boxes known as *tefillin*, or phylacteries. Indeed, every act of the day would be couched in prayer. And every Sabbath (the seventh day of the week), all work ceased and eternity pervaded all things as the people both recalled the beginning of creation and contemplated its fulfillment to come in the messianic era at the end of time. No matter what suffering history brought to Israel, on the Sabbath an eternal people dwelled with their eternal God, savoring a foretaste of that messianic day for which all creation was made—when God will be all in all.

The meaning of the Sabbath unfolded in the portion of Torah assigned for every week of the year, organized around a great cycle of festivals from Rosh Hashanah and Yom Kippur to Purim and Hannukah (see box on festivals).

Talmudic Judaism replaced political Zionism with an apolitical spiritual Zionism. The rabbis argued that Israel had been seduced by the Zealots into trying to force the

bar mitzvah: rite of passage for Jewish boys to become full members of the religion of Judaism; the **bat mitzvah** is a parallel rite for girls

Observant Jews, like this young man putting on *tefillin*, declare God's oneness by binding the Torah scrolls to their bodies before daily prayer.

RITUALS AND RITES: Rituals of the Life Cycle

Rituals marking the important transitions in the life of the individual can be found in all religious traditions. In Judaism these are the *Bris* or *Brit milah*, the bar and bat mitzvah, and the rituals for marriage, and death.

Bris or Brit Milah

In accordance with the teachings of the Torah (Genesis 17:10–14), every male child must be circumcised when he is eight days old, as a sign of the covenant between God and his people. This ceremony is known as the *Bris* or *Brit milah* (derived from the Hebrew for "covenant" and for "circumcision"). During this ritual the child is named and the foreskin of his penis is cut off as an external sign of the covenant. This ritual ties and binds every male child's life to the eternal covenant between God and his people, renewing that covenant with each generation, child by child.

Bar and Bat Mitzvah

When a boy reaches the age of adulthood, thirteen, he is eligible to become a bar mitzvah (son of the commandments, or covenant); to this end, he is expected to demonstrate the ability to carry out his responsibilities in maintaining the religious life of the community. After intense training by his rabbi in the study of Hebrew and of Torah and Talmud, the young man is called forth at a synagogue service to read from the Torah. He may also be asked to comment on the meaning of the passages. Once he has completed this ceremony he is considered to be an adult, qualified to form part of the *minyan* (ten adult males) required for any Jewish worship service. With the appearance of the Conservative and Reform Jewish communities the ritual has been extended to include young women as well. For them the ritual is called the bat mitzvah (daughter of the commandments, or covenant).

Marriage

A Jewish wedding takes place under a *huppah*, a sort of grand prayer shawl stretched over four poles that can be said to symbolize the heavens and God's creation, even as the bride and groom stand in the place of Adam and Eve, the first man and woman created by God. In the marriage ceremony, prayers and blessings sanctify the union of a man and a woman by binding them to each other and to the story of Israel's relation to God, from creation through exiles and tribulations to joyous redemption in the new Zion. It is customary, at the end of the ceremony, for the groom to step on and break a glass, symbolizing the fall of the second temple. Great festivity and celebration follow.

Death

Jewish death rites are very simple. A person facing death is encouraged to say a prayer of confession, asking for forgiveness of sins and healing if possible. The prayer continues by asking that the person's death, if it is to come now, serve as atonement for all his or her sins. The prayer ends with requests ("Grant me a share in the world to come" and "Protect my beloved family") and commits the person's soul into the hands of God. Burial takes place on the day of death or the day after, without embalming. The immediate family of mourners remains at home for seven days and will continue to recite memorial prayers (kaddish) for eleven months and thereafter on the anniversary of the death.

coming of the messianic era by their own political activity. The truth is, the rabbis argued, that only God can initiate the messianic era, and God will bring the age of exile to an end and restore to Israel the land of promise only when all Israel is fully observant of *halakhah*. This view prevailed throughout the Middle Ages and was not seriously challenged until the coming of modern secular Zionism in the nineteenth and twentieth centuries.

The Medieval Journey of Judaism

With the Talmudic way of life described in "The Premodern Rabbinic World," Jews made their way through the Middle Ages. Medieval Judaism reveals the precarious situation of the Jews in a world dominated by the new religion of Christianity. With the emergence of the Holy Roman Empire in 800 CE, at first Jews were more or less tolerated. By the late Middle Ages, however, this toleration gave way to persecution, except in Spain. There, for a brief period in the twelfth and thirteenth centuries CE known as the "Golden Age," Jews were welcome and Judaism flourished.

Discrimination Against Jews in the Early Middle Ages

Dwelling in the great cosmic story of Torah, the people Israel survived their journey through the medieval world of persecutions and expulsions. Their unity was then splintered by the Jewish Enlightenment in the nineteenth century and nearly shattered by the Holocaust in the twentieth century. That journey is a tale of tragic precedents for the Holocaust; and yet it is also a story of amazing spiritual endurance and creativity

RITUALS AND RITES

Major Festivals: The Days of Awe and Passover

The story of Torah stretched out over the lives of Jews from the beginning of the day until the end of the day, from the beginning of the year until the end of the year, from the beginning of their lives until the end of their lives, and from the beginning of time until the end of time. In the Torah story, God and Israel dwelled—sometimes in harmony and sometimes wrestling with each other—but always within a drama that gave life meaning in spite of the brutal incursions of the profane world that surrounded and rejected the Jews.

Rosh Hashanah and Yom Kippur

The new year begins for Jews with the Rosh Hashanah synagogue service, during which the story of creation is retold and people are reminded that God is deciding who will and who will not be written in the book of life for another year, even as he will decide the fate of nations and of the whole world. So the new year raises questions of life and death and calls for self-examination. The process ends ten days later, on Yom Kippur, a day of total fasting and repentance. When Yom Kippur ends at sunset and the fast is broken, penitents consider themselves to be both cleansed and prepared to face the new year.

Passover

Passover, or *Pesach*, recalls God's deliverance of the tribes of Israel from slavery in Egypt (Exodus 1–15). Passover is celebrated in the home, usually with the extended family and friends. The Passover *aggadah* is an order of service that retells the story of the liberation from Egypt with extensive commentary from the sages of the Talmud. The male head of the household presides at this retelling, which is done around the dining table, but members of the family are invited to participate, individually and collectively, in the recitation. Prominence is given to the youngest child, who must ask four key questions, the first of which is: "Why is this night different from all other nights?" In this way the story is passed on from generation to generation. As the story is retold, certain symbolic foods are eaten to remind everyone of the events that led and still lead to liberation from slavery for every Jew.

This festival is also called the feast of unleavened bread (*matzah*), for the story indicated that only bread without yeast was used at the time of the original event, since the tribes left in a hurry and did not have time to make leavened bread.

that enriched and expanded the house of Torah in which Israel dwelled—especially through the contributions of Kabbalistic mysticism and Hasidic piety.

The situation of the Jews deteriorated with the decline of the Roman Empire and the rise of Christianity. While Jews in Palestine, the land of Israel, were under the colonial rule of the Romans in the first four centuries, they enjoyed a unique protected status as a legal religion, despite their refusal to worship the gods of the official state cult. However, when the emperors and the empire became Christian in 380, the colonial domination of the Jews became more severe, and Jews eventually lost most of the legal protection they had enjoyed under the Romans. That domination did not really end until the establishment of the state of Israel in the twentieth century. The view that Christians had superseded or replaced the Jews as God's "chosen people" led to what in later centuries would be called "the Jewish problem"—namely, the continuing existence of Jews. Jews came to be seen as an "obstinate" and "stiff-necked"

To prepare for Passover all leavened bread must be removed from the premises and all utensils cleaned. After various symbolic foods are consumed during the telling of the story of the Exodus, a full family meal of celebration is eaten. During the Passover meal it is said that ordinary time is suspended and every Jew becomes part of the liberating event and so can say, "This day I too have been liberated from slavery."

Minor Festivals

In addition to the major festivals, a variety of other festivals are celebrated through the year, including the following.

Sukkot and Simchat Torah
Five days after Yom Kippur, the Festival of Booths is celebrated. Temporary dwellings (a wooden frame covered with branches) are constructed outdoors where Jews will eat their meals and may even sleep. The dwellings are to remind Jews of their journey through the wilderness to the land of promise, during which they had no permanent shelter. Sukkot is followed by Simchat Torah or the festival of "Rejoicing in the Torah." The last words of Torah (the end of the Book of Deuteronomy) are read, followed by the reading of the opening words of the first book of Torah, Genesis. This is a festival of joyous celebration that includes a ritual "dancing with the Torah."

Purim
Jewish history is filled with many incidents of persecution. This joyous festival commemorates an occasion in Jewish history where an attempted Persian persecution is thwarted. The festival celebrates the tale of the book of Esther, who saves her community from a Persian pogrom.

Hanukkah
This is an eight-day festival of light, celebrated in the dead of winter and symbolizing the light of hope. It commemorates the reopening of the temple in Jerusalem reclaimed from the Syrian persecutors in a Jewish revolt led by the Maccabean brothers. The temple was cleansed, and the temple menorah or candle stand needed to be relighted. However, there was only enough olive oil to burn for one day. Miraculously, the oil lasted eight days, until further oil could be supplied, keeping the fire and hope in God's love and protection alive.

people who refused to acknowledge the truth of Christianity and convert (or, in later modern secular culture, refused to give up their Jewishness and assimilate).

The Carolingian Era of Tolerance

For a while in Europe, under the Frankish Carolingian kings, who founded the Holy Roman Empire (800 CE), the life of Jews improved. Jews enjoyed high positions in the courts and in the professions and experienced new opportunities for wealth. And while Jews were not considered full citizens, they prospered under so-called diplomas of protection from the king's court. They became "the king's Jews." This practice was a benefit as long as Jews were favored by the king. However, in later periods the arrangement resulted in sudden reversals of fortune whenever a king (or Holy Roman Emperor) found it convenient to rescind his protection.

Centuries of Persecution and Pogrom

In the late Middle Ages, Jewish life became truly precarious in Europe. The tide turned against Jews with the launching of the First Crusade by Pope Urban II in 1095. The announced reason for the Crusades was to free Jerusalem and all of the Holy Land from the Muslims, who had taken Jerusalem in 638. In Islam as in Christianity and Judaism, Jerusalem is a holy city.

A plenary indulgence, or guarantee of forgiveness of sins and entry into heaven, was promised by the Pope to anyone who participated in the Crusades. However, as the armies raised for this purpose passed through the cities and towns of Europe on their way to rid the Holy Land of infidels (i.e., the Muslims), they decided to use the opportunity to purge the Christian world of its other "enemy" as well.

The Christian armies passing through the Rhine Valley offered Jews the choice of conversion or death. Many responded by committing suicide; many others were massacred. Few converted. The pattern of persecution and violence against Jews continued in the centuries that followed. In 1251 the Fourth Lateran Council of the Catholic Church adopted a practice first used by Muslims in eleventh-century Egypt, that of forcing Jews to wear distinctive dress. Also at this time, the Jews were forced to live in segregated quarters called *ghettos*. To the pattern of discrimination and violence was added the periodic practice of expulsion. In 1306, in a single day, all the Jews of France were arrested and ordered to be out of the country within a month. Other countries followed suit, driving the majority of Europe's Jews into eastern Europe. In 1348, as the Black Death swept across the Continent, Jews were blamed and made the scapegoats, and the Jews of many communities were executed. In Strasbourg, in the year 1349, for instance, 200 Jews were burned alive in a cemetery on the Sabbath.

The Protestant Reformation, initiated in 1517, seemed to be characterized by a more positive attitude toward Judaism. At first, Martin Luther wrote favorably of the Jews. But toward the end of his life, the founder of the Reformation realized that Jews were no more receptive to his interpretation of the Gospel than to the Catholic interpretation. Thereafter, Luther turned viciously anti-Judaic, advocating the abuse of Jews and the burning of synagogues. Nevertheless, the aftermath of the Reformation in the sixteenth and seventeenth centuries left Christians too busy fighting each other to make the Jews a central concern. This distraction, as well as a modification of ghettos that put Jews under lock and key at night, served to reduce the violence Jews experienced at the hands of Christians.

However, at the same time, as the Jewish population of eastern Europe grew by leaps and bounds as a consequence of the expulsions from western Europe, new waves of violence broke out against Jews in eastern Europe. Between 1648 and 1658, in organized massacres called *pogroms*, over 700 Jewish communities were destroyed. Jewish deaths numbered in the hundreds of thousands. Fueling this violence in Europe was an ethos of Jew hatred that expressed itself in the rationalization that "the Jews are our misfortune" and helped prepare the way for Hitler and the Holocaust.

The Jews of Italy offer a striking exception to this history of persecution: On the whole, they fared much better than the rest of European Jewry. Rome is the only major city of Europe from which Jews were never expelled. And unlike those in the rest of Europe, the Jews of Rome experienced no punitive taxes, were free to select their occupations, and were not forbidden by law to marry Christians. Nor were Jews persecuted in Italy during the Crusades and the years of the Black Death.

There were a number of reasons for this paradoxical thread in the religious history of Europe. For example, since usury was an allowable occupation for Christian financiers in Italy, Jews were not singled out for resentment as "money lenders." But perhaps the most influential factor was the relation between the popes and the Jews.

It was widely believed by medieval Christians that the gentile followers of Jesus had replaced the Jews as God's chosen people. To explain away "the Jewish problem"—why God nevertheless permitted Jews to continue to exist—the popes, from the sixth century on, turned to a theory developed by influential Christian theologian St. Augustine of Hippo, the so-called negative witness theory. According to this theory, it was God's will for Jews to wander the earth without a home, their unhappy existence functioning as a "negative witness" that proved the superiority and truth of Christianity. Consequently, the popes preached that God had rejected the Jews while, paradoxically, acting as the legal protectors and guardians of the original chosen people, insisting that they not be physically harmed.

Although the negative witness theory shaped papal strategy for dealing with "the Jewish problem" in medieval Christendom, during the Renaissance some popes took a less biased view. Pope Sixtus IV (1471–84), for example, commissioned a Latin translation of the Kabbalah. Later Pope Clement VII sought to develop a common translation of the Old Testament by Jewish and Christian scholars, and he suspended the persecution by the Spanish Inquisition of Jews who had been forcibly baptized in Spain.

From the Golden Age in Spain to the Spanish Inquisition

In the midst of this violent history stands the Golden Age of Spain as an extraordinary interlude, when Jews were welcomed as allies against the Muslims in the portions of Spain that had been reconquered by Christians. For a time in the twelfth and early thirteenth centuries, Jews were encouraged to settle in the reconquered territories and were given unusual freedom both socially and politically, achieving important roles in the royal court and in the professions. It was a period of unprecedented intellectual exchange between the great scholars of Judaism, Islam, and Christianity.

The period came to an end in the mid-thirteenth century as a Christian backlash developed. Christians suddenly became alarmed at the growing number of Jews in high places. This fear of a "Jewish takeover" led to a new period of persecution, violence, and forced conversions, culminating in the Spanish Inquisition. Between 1480 and 1492 some 13,000 Jews, most of whom had been forcibly baptized as Christians, were condemned as **Marranos**—Jews masquerading as Christians while practicing their Judaism in secret. Many were tortured and burned at the stake. The Jews were expelled from Spain in 1492 (see Map 3.2).

Marranos: Jews of Spain who, although forced by the Inquisition to convert to Christianity, continued to practice Judaism in secret

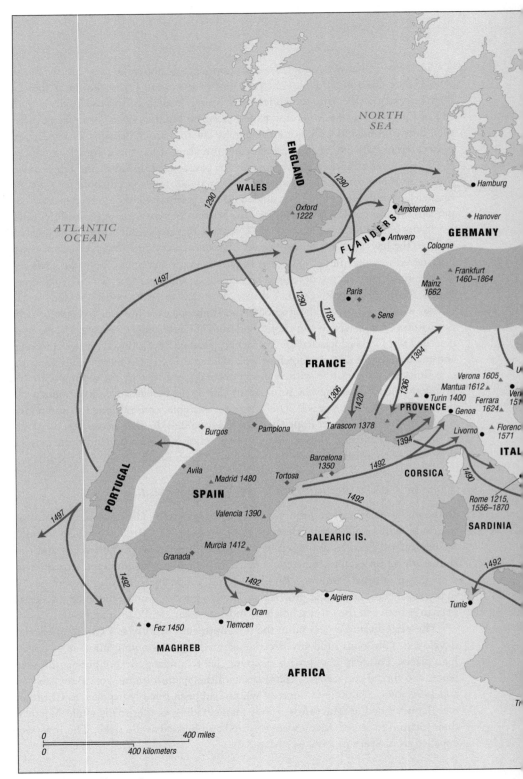

NORTH SEA

ENGLAND
WALES
Oxford 1222
1290
1290

ATLANTIC OCEAN

1497

Hamburg
Amsterdam
Hanover
Antwerp
Cologne
GERMANY
Frankfurt 1460–1864
Mainz 1662

FLANDERS

1290
1182
Paris
Sens

FRANCE

1394

1306
1420
1306

Verona 1605
Mantua 1612
Turin 1400
Ferrara 1624
PROVENCE
Genoa
Tarascon 1378
1394
Livorno
Florenc 1571
ITAL

Burgos
Pamplona
Avila
Madrid 1480
Tortosa
Barcelona 1350
1492
CORSICA
1490

PORTUGAL

SPAIN
Valencia 1390
Murcia 1412
Granada

1492
BALEARIC IS.
Rome 1215, 1556–1870
SARDINIA

1497

1492

1492

1492

1492
Algiers
Oran
Tlemcen
Fez 1450

Tunis

MAGHREB

AFRICA

0   400 miles
0   400 kilometers

94

Map 3.2 Jews in Christian Europe.

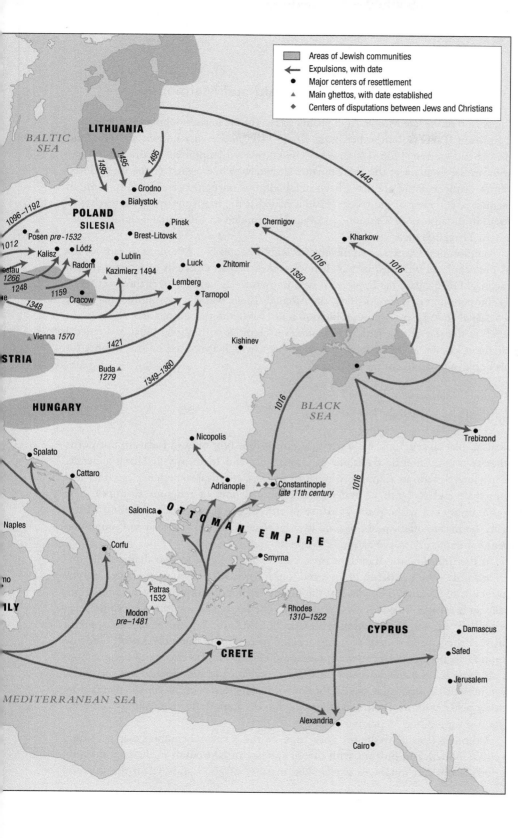

Areas of Jewish communities
Expulsions, with date
Major centers of resettlement
Main ghettos, with date established
Centers of disputations between Jews and Christians

BALTIC
SEA

LITHUANIA

1495
1495
1495

• Grodno
• Bialystok

1096–1192

POLAND
SILESIA

• Posen *pre-1532*

1012

• Pinsk
• Brest-Litovsk

• Chernigov

• Kharkow

• Kalisz
• Lódź
• Radom
• Lublin
Kazimierz 1494

eslau
1266
1248
1159
Cracow

• Luck
Lemberg
• Tarnopol

• Zhitomir

1016

1016

1348

1350

1421

Vienna *1570*

1349–1360

STRIA

Buda ▲
1279

• Kishinev

HUNGARY

1016

BLACK
SEA

• Trebizond

• Nicopolis

• Spalato

• Cattaro

Adrianople

Constantinople
late 11th century

1016

Naples

Salonica

OTTOMAN EMPIRE

• Corfu

• Smyrna

Patras
1532

Modon
pre-1481

Rhodes
1310–1522

CYPRUS

• Damascus

• Safed

• Jerusalem

ILY

no

CRETE

• Alexandria

Cairo •

MEDITERRANEAN SEA

95

Two Great Medieval Scholars: Rashi and Maimonides

The period of the late Middle Ages produced two of the greatest scholars in the history of Judaism: Rabbi Solomon ben Isaac (1040–1105), otherwise known as Rashi, and Moses ben Maimon (1135–1204), otherwise known as Maimonides. Rashi's commentaries on the Gemara of the Babylonian Talmud, which appeared in the first printed edition of the Talmud and have been in all editions since, are considered to form an essential component of the work. Rashi is hailed as the most unsurpassable teacher of Torah in the history of Talmudic Judaism. He founded an influential Talmudic academy in Troyes, France.

Maimonides, known as Rambam (for Rabbi Moses ben Maimon), is famous for his philosophical writings, in which he uses Aristotelian concepts to explain Jewish teaching. His *Guide of the Perplexed* is well known today, and for over three centuries his compendium of Talmudic law, the *Mishnah Torah*, was the most influential guide to *halakhah* in Judaism. Although Judaism is not a religion that emphasizes *dogma* (right belief) as the test of true faith, Maimonides is credited with giving Judaism a creedal statement known as the *Thirteen Articles of Faith* (which are found on the website for this book; www.oup.com/us/esposito).

> "If there is no peace, then there is really nothing, because peace is the equivalent of all other blessings put together."
>
> —Rashi

Kabbalah—Jewish Mysticism

Judaism, like all religions, has a mystical dimension. Not only in Judaism, but in the other two monotheistic traditions of Christianity and Islam, mystics have generally been viewed with an element of mistrust because mystical experience is direct and immediate and so tends to undermine traditional lines of religious authority. The mystic finds God without the guidance of either a priest or a teacher (rabbi). Moreover, the mystic often speaks of God in ways that are unconventional and sometimes seem contradictory to the nature of prophetic monotheism.

In the monotheistic traditions mysticism expresses itself in two dramatically different forms—the mysticism of love and union (the divine–human marriage) and the mysticism of identity. The place of the mystic in monotheism has always been especially ambivalent for the mystics of identity. The mystics of identity sometimes seem to say they are not just in union with God but *are* God. Whenever mystics speak in this way they are in danger of being accused of confusing themselves with God and claiming to be God. Any such representation would be heretical and blasphemous in all three biblical religions and thus unacceptable. And yet, despite this seemingly ever-present danger, each of the monotheistic religions has chosen to maintain an uneasy peace with its mystics, neither denying the importance and validity of mysticism nor suppressing its practice.

Although Jewish mysticism goes back to the ancient beginnings, it became a decisive influence in Judaism with the emergence of **Kabbalah** in the late medieval period. Kabbalism sought to explain the mystery of good and evil in the universe

> "I believe with perfect faith that the Creator, blessed be Your name, is not a body, and that You are free from all the accidents of matter, and that You have not any form whatsoever."
>
> —Maimonides' Third Principle of Faith

Kabbalah: Jewish mystical tradition

precisely at a time of intensifying persecution and pogroms. Jews could not help but seek an understanding of God that could sustain them through a new period of suffering.

The most important Kabbalistic work is the **Zohar** (Book of Splendor). According to Kabbalistic teaching, there was a time when God manifested himself in the world, allowing his *Shekinah* ("divine presence") to be perceived in all things. However, because of the fall of Adam, evil entered the world and the divine presence has been exiled from its unity with God as the infinite (*En Sof*). Humans were created for *deve-kut* ("communion") with God, but this relationship was destroyed by Adam's sin and must be reestablished through mystical contemplation (*kavanah*) of the divine through prayer and the devout performance of the requirements of *halakhah*. The reunion of all with the infinite will bring about nothing less than the ingathering of all Jews from exile to enjoy the messianic kingdom to come.

The Kabbalistic tradition comprises a profound mystical variation on the theme of exile and return. It can be seen as a powerful religious response to the overwhelming tragedy of persecution and expulsion that marked Jewish life in Europe in the late Middle Ages and beyond. It explained the age of darkness in which Jews lived in exile and offered them a hope of transcending that darkness with a future ingathering of all Jews.

Zohar: "Book of Splendor," the most important Kabbalistic work

Hasidism

The mystical impulse of Kabbalism was given further embodiment in the Hasidic movement. **Hasidism** came into its own in eastern Europe at the beginning of the eighteenth century largely in response to the region's endemic pogroms. A *hasid* is a pious one, whose life is marked by great devotion. With Hasidism, piety took on a new intensity of meaning.

Hasidism: form of Judaism strongly rooted in mysticism

The Hasidic movement emerged in Poland with the activities of Israel ben Eliezer, who was called *the Besht* by his followers. This title was a shortened form of Ba'al Shem Tov, or "Master of the Good Name," where the "good name" was understood to be the name of God. The Besht was an ecstatic healer who worked miracles using magic, amulets, and spells. He taught that joy is the appropriate response to the world no matter how much suffering Jews experience.

In fact, although Hasidism emerged in an era of pogrom and immense suffering in eastern Europe, the Hasidim say there is no greater sin than melancholy, or sadness (*atzut*). Indeed they argue that sadness, which stems from ignorance of the pervasive presence of God in all things, is the root of all sin. According to the Besht, God hides himself in his creation. Therefore, there is no distance between God and humanity for those who have the eyes to see. And once you do see, there can be no sadness but only *simhah*—deep, pervasive, passionate joy and celebration.

The Besht was a charismatic figure whose followers hung on his every word and gesture. Their prayer circles were characterized by ecstatic singing and dancing, and they looked forward to deeply moving spiritual talks by the Besht around the Sabbath

Tzaddik: in the Hasidic
tradition, a "righteous
man"—a religious leader
who is as influential as a
rabbi is in a traditional
Talmudic community

dinner table. The Besht became a model for the Hasidic notion of the **Tzaddik**, or "righteous man." The Tzaddik's authority in each Hasidic community was every bit as powerful as that of the rabbi in a traditional Talmudic community. For the Hasidim, the Tzaddik was no ordinary person but one especially chosen by God as a direct link between heaven and earth, who could intervene on behalf of the faithful and literally change the mind of God. Like the rabbis, the Tzaddik was a religious virtuoso; however, his virtuosity was of mystical piety and devotion, not of Talmudic scholarship. His holiness was said to be spontaneously contagious; just being near him, the Hasidim could catch his piety as a spark to light their own.

Hasidic Judaism offered a way to reach God other than Talmudic study: namely, devotion and prayer, which were within the reach of every sincere Jew. What was most extraordinary about Hasidic mysticism was, and is, its communal nature. One cannot achieve this state of joy and selflessness by going off alone to a mountaintop but only by total immersion in the community life of the Hasidim, organized around the festive worship made possible by the presence of the Tzaddik. It is this linking of deep mystical spirituality with community life that made Hasidism such a powerful force for renewal. In the nineteenth century, Hasidism moved toward reconciliation with Rabbinic Judaism by incorporating more emphasis on the study of Talmud and was eventually accepted by the rabbis who had originally rejected it.

Having surveyed premodern Judaism, we are now in a position to look at the emergence of modern forms and to understand better how they are both like pre-modern forms of Judaism and different from them.

Judaism and Modernity (1729–1967 CE)

The Emergence of Modern Religious Forms of Judaism

Reform Judaism

From the early days of Rabbinic Judaism, between the second and fifth centuries, until the French Revolution in 1789, Jews in Europe lived as a rejected minority in a world dominated by Christians. With Enlightenment secularization, the categories of human self-understanding underwent radical revision. Enlightened Europeans were secular universalists who defined their humanity not in terms of religious myths, which they believed created divisiveness, but in terms of reason, which they held to be a capacity found universally in human beings. The ideal of this new orientation was to replace the categories of "Jew" and "Christian" with a single category: "rational human being."

For the first time in almost 2,000 years, the dominant culture looked at Jews as rational beings, equal to all other human beings, and Jews were invited to participate as citizens alongside all other individuals in the modern capitalist nation-states (see Map 3.3). This message of inclusion was widely accepted by the Jews of western Europe.

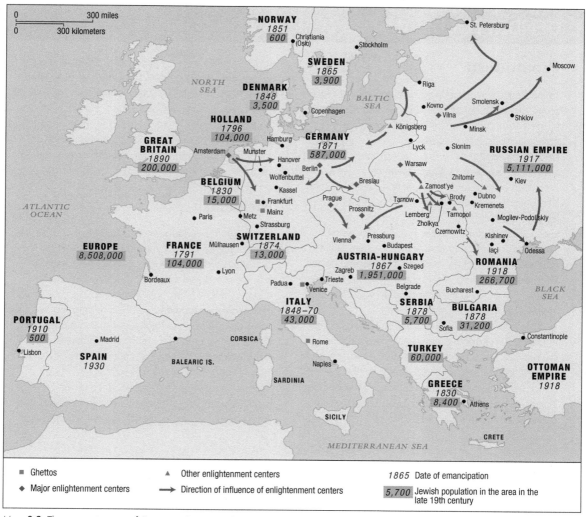

Map 3.3 The emancipation of European Jewry, 1789–1918.

It seemed that a new day was dawning. One of the leading Enlightenment scholars of the eighteenth century, Gotthold Lessing (1729–81), a gentile, wrote impassioned works proclaiming the humanity of Jews and of Muslims and arguing for their acceptance in society. Lessing befriended Moses Mendelssohn (1729–86), who became the leading figure in the Jewish Haskalah, or Enlightenment, movement, the eventual source of Reform Judaism, the first "modern" form of Judaism.

Like Hellenistic Judaism in the first century, the Haskalah movement favored partial assimilation into the gentile world, trying to show that in the 1800s, one could be an enlightened citizen of the secular world and a Jew at the same time. This required

GENDER FOCUS: Women in Judaism

Premodern

Talmudic Judaism shares with the emerging Judaism of the ancient biblical period a common assumption of premodern urban societies, transposed into a monotheistic frame of reference. Specifically, it was long assumed that there is a sacred natural order of the world, revealed by God, in which maleness is the normative pattern for full humanity. Indeed, women (like animals and slaves) are the property of men. A father could sell his daughter as payment for a debt (Exodus 21:7), for instance. Basically, a woman belonged to her father until she was given to the man who married her, to whom she then belonged. Women had no role in the public worship in the temple, but at the same time women were honored as mothers and the mainstay of the family.

The biblical attitude toward women was continued in premodern Rabbinic Judaism. However, during the biblical period certain exceptional women were revered for their wisdom and their gifts of prophecy: Miriam (the sister of Moses), Deborah (one of the judges of Israel), and Huldah (a prophetess during the reign of Josiah). Both Rabbinic and later Hasidic traditions also present models of women who were exceptions, noted for their learning and piety. Beruriah, the wife of Rabbi Meir, was noted for her skill as a Talmudic scholar, and Oudil, the daughter of the Ba'al Shem Tov, was praised for her wisdom and joyous piety. Nevertheless, such women were not the norm. They remained the exception that proved the rule.

Modern

Modern forms of Judaism tend to demythologize traditional Jewish gender roles as inessential historical accretions that may even contradict fundamental insights of Judaism concerning justice and human dignity. Thus, it is probably fair to say that the greatest equality for women has been among the secular forms of Judaism, especially Jewish socialism and Zionism, and among the most secular forms of religious Judaism—Reform first, then Conservative, and least among the Orthodox.

The Declaration of Independence of the State of Israel, drawing on the nation's secular socialist and Zionist roots, asserts complete equality of men and

the leaders of the Reform movement to answer a question that all modern forms of Judaism (including Orthodoxy) have confronted: How can I be both a Jew and a citizen of a secular state? It had been pointless to ask this question earlier, when secular states did not exist and Christian states offered Jews no possibility of citizenship.

Reform Judaism and all other forms of modern Judaism, however, have had to make a decision about how to relate to the larger secular society. Embracing the Enlightenment ideal of religion within the "limits of reason," the leaders of the Reform movement defined the essence of Judaism as a rational-ethical system rooted in the prophetic-ethical ideal of justice—an ethic that was Judaism's gift to humanity. Like their first-century Hellenistic counterparts, they did not think that this ethic was for Jews alone but rather that Judaism was its source and purest form. This universal rational ethic was the essence of Judaism; all other aspects of Judaism were open to negotiation.

women in social and political rights. The Equal Rights for Women law of 1951 guarantees women the same rights enjoyed by men to own property and to make decisions on behalf of their children. Among the explicitly religious forms of Judaism, the Reform movement has led the way. It was not until the 1970s that women began to be ordained (although one private ordination is said to have occurred in 1935 in a German Reform congregation).

Today it is not uncommon, in both Reform and Conservative synagogues in America, for a young woman to celebrate her bat mitzvah as a parallel rite to a brother's bar mitzvah. Nor is it unusual for women to read the Torah scrolls at a Sabbath service. And it is even becoming more common for women cantors to chant such services and for women rabbis to conduct them. All of this was unthinkable in premodern Judaism. And it remains unthinkable among the ultra-Orthodox.

Today in both Reform and Conservative Judaism, women are ordained to the rabbinate. Here Barbara Aiello, the first female rabbi in Italy, lights Hanukkah candles.

As Reform Judaism developed, it showed a remarkable openness to secular society. For instance, Jews could use the vernacular instead of Hebrew in worship; thus synagogue prayers and sermons could be spoken in the local language (German, French, English, etc.). As the movement developed in the late nineteenth century, it was also prepared to abandon the observance of kosher laws, restricting the foods Jews can eat, and other "historical accretions" as inessential to being Jewish. Indeed, it rejected the Talmud as revelation, seeing it instead as simply a human historical tradition. And it rejected belief in a literal coming of the messiah, replacing it with a belief in a messianic age that could easily be identified with the goal of the modern age of scientific and rational progress. Finally, it renounced any desire to return to the land of Israel, insisting that Jews were not a people tied to a specific land but a "religious community."

Among enlightened Jews, secular learning not only was permitted but took precedence. For instance, in deciding what is and what is not essential to Judaism, Reform

Judaism argued not from the "revealed will of God," as had premodern Judaism, but from the history of the development of Judaism as a religion. Thus "history" and "Judaism," not "God" and "Torah," became the defining categories. Religious disputes were to be settled primarily by appeal to the developmental history of Judaism. After all, what history reveals, Reform Jews argued, is that Judaism is a religion not of eternal, unchanging truths but of constant change. From their perspective, Reform Judaism is the true Judaism for the modern world and the logical successor, in the authentic unfolding of the historical tradition, to premodern Rabbinic Judaism.

Orthodox Judaism

To call Orthodox Judaism a modern form of Judaism may seem contradictory, for orthodoxy claims that it continues the ancient tradition of premodern Rabbinic Judaism. The issue between Reform and Orthodox Jews was whether, as Reform Jews held, God was acting through an ever-changing history, progressing toward an age of messianic freedom, or whether the Orthodox were correct in their view that God revealed himself only in the eternal, unchanging covenant given at Sinai. This reflects the choice modernization puts to all religions—whether to embrace historical change or reject it out of faithfulness to a view of premodern unchanging fundamental truths and practices.

Orthodox Jews wanted to present their choice of orthodoxy as if it were no choice. But clearly, the very appearance of Reform Judaism meant that one could no longer just be a Jew; one had to choose to be a Jew of a certain kind. In agreeing that it was necessary to choose, Orthodoxy gave evidence that it too was a Judaism of the modern period. From now on, like Reform Judaism, it would have to think of itself as one religious community alongside others. Premodern Rabbinic Jews had no such dilemma, for there was no "Judaism" to choose, only God, Torah, and Israel, the givens of one's birth into the chosen people.

Orthodoxy became, in many ways, the mirror image of Reform Judaism, for mirror images reverse the original that they reflect. Thus if Reform Jews prayed in the vernacular, the Orthodox insisted that all prayers be in Hebrew. If Reform Jews insisted on historical change, the Orthodox insisted on eternal unchanging truth. If Reform Jews decided issues of religious practice on the basis of history, the Orthodox decided them on the basis of the eternal word of God given in the Torah and the Talmud. If Reform Jews abandoned literal messianic beliefs, the Orthodox reaffirmed them. If Reform Jews dismissed the Talmudic requirements (*halakhah*) as historical accretions, the Orthodox insisted on continued observance of the requirements of the dual Torah (the written Torah and the oral Torah). And if Reform Jews abandoned any ambition to return to the land of Israel, the Orthodox prayed "next year in Jerusalem" while awaiting the deliverance of the messiah.

Orthodoxy's first great intellectual defender, Samson Raphael Hirsch (1808–88), sought to show that one can live as a Jew in a secular nation-state and remain fully Orthodox. Therefore, above all, what makes Orthodoxy a modern Judaism is that, like Reform Judaism, it divides the world into the religious and the secular, separating religion and politics in a way that allows Orthodox Jews to be both Jews and citizens of a secular nation-state.

Conservative Judaism

Once the lines had been drawn between the first two modern ways of being Jewish, it was perhaps inevitable that a third option would emerge, seeking a compromise. That option was Conservative Judaism. Conservative Jews saw Jewish life as the life of a historically ethnic people that included but was not limited to the religious dimension. Conservative Judaism arose among Jews who were deeply committed to the Orthodox way of life yet sympathetic to the "modern" intellectual worldview of Reform Judaism.

The message of the leaders of Conservative Judaism was "Think whatever you like, but do what the law requires." This position puts the emphasis on orthopraxy (right practice) as opposed to orthodoxy (right belief). Conservative Judaism, as the third option, is largely an American phenomenon and is the most widely embraced form of Judaism practiced in the United States.

In addition to the three main strands of modern Judaism there is another movement, known as Reconstructionism, founded in America in the 1930s by Mordecai Kaplan (1881–1983). Kaplan cast his understanding of Judaism in almost completely secular terms drawn from the modern social and historical sciences. Kaplan defined Judaism as the religion of Jewish civilization, where "religion" was understood not in supernatural terms but as the embodiment of the ideals and group identity of a culture.

The Emergence of Secular Forms of Judaism

The dawning of the age of Enlightenment created an optimistic mood among Jews. But that mood did not last, for the promise of inclusion for Jews turned out to be false. The hidden premise of the new offer became apparent in the aftermath of the French Revolution, which had offered full citizenship to Jews. The offer, however, gave *everything to Jews as individuals and nothing to the Jews as a people.* To be a citizen in the new secular society, one had to trade one's religious identity for a secular or nonreligious one.

The ideals of the Enlightenment were genuine enough, but they quickly crashed on the rocks of the intractability of human prejudice. As more and more Jews were "secularized" in Europe, either abandoning or minimizing their Judaism, they entered into the political and economic life of their respective countries. As they achieved success, a backlash occurred. Throughout Europe, non-Jews began to fear that the Jews were taking over "their" society.

By the end of the nineteenth century a secular, supposedly scientific, definition had come to replace the old religious definition of the Jews in European society. The Jews became defined as a race—an inferior race that had a biologically corrupting influence on society. With the introduction of the language of race, all the old Christian stereotypes of Jews as a rejected people were resurrected in a new guise. Theoretically, at least, the Jews as a religious people could be converted—hence, "the

Jewish problem" could be solved. But race is perceived as a biologically unchangeable fact; people cannot convert from one race to another. Moreover, the advocates of the "scientific" theory of race viewed any attempt at assimilation through intermarriage as racial pollution. In the 1930s the Nazi Party in Germany would begin to exploit this new kind of prejudice against "the Jewish race" to devastating effect.

In the United States, Jews fared better than in Europe. America was forged as a nation of many peoples, fleeing religious intolerance in England and on the continent. Anti-Semitism and other forms of religious bigotry were not absent from America's formative history, but Jews in America never experienced pogroms and mass expulsions. American individualism allowed more space for diverse ethnic and religious communal identities.

Jewish immigrants to the United States came in two waves. The first and more modest wave, dating from 1654, consisted of seekers of religious freedom, Jews of Spanish or Portuguese extraction, known as **Sephardic** Jews. The second and much larger wave began in the nineteenth century among the **Ashkenazi**, Jews of eastern Europe who were fleeing persecution and pogrom. By the beginning of World War II, approximately a third of the world's Jews lived in the United States. After World War II, twice as many Jews lived in the United States as in all of Europe.

While Jews in America were being integrated into society, in the late 1800s and early 1900s the Jews of western Europe were once more being persecuted. Most of the Jews of eastern Europe never did sense that they had been invited to join a new Enlightenment order of equality and inclusion. On the contrary, they experienced an increase in persecutions and pogroms. The challenge was to devise a strategy for surviving in societies that were replacing religious anti-Judaism with secular anti-Semitism. And it was among the more fully assimilated and secularized Jews that the new responses emerged, responses that would form a bridge from the modern forms of Judaism (Reform, Orthodox, and Conservative) to the postmodern and postcolonial Judaism of Holocaust and Redemption. These new secular forms of Judaism were Jewish socialism, Yiddish (ethnic) Judaism, and Zionism. Each one offered a distinct way of being Jewish that was capable of combining in interesting and powerful ways with the others in order to set the stage for the emergence of the Judaism of Holocaust and Redemption.

Sephardic: Jews whose traditions originated in Spain or Portugal

Ashkenazi: Jews whose traditions originated in central and eastern Europe

Jewish Socialism

Some of the strongest currents of Jewish socialism came out of eastern Europe, where secularized Jews saw in socialism another way of resolving the tension between being Jewish and being modern. As noted in Chapter 1, socialism, especially the later "scientific" socialism of Karl Marx, offered an essentially secularized version of the Jewish and Christian myths of history. It was a view of history as a story of exile and return, in which human beings begin in paradise (primitive communism), only to be expelled from the garden into a world of selfishness and sin (class conflict). Socialism, however, promises an eventual transformation into a future global, classless, society in which suffering and injustice will be overcome (including anti-Semitism) and all will live in perfect harmony—a vision very much like that of the messianic kingdom of God. Perhaps this is no coincidence, given that Karl Marx, whose father was a convert to Christianity, was the grandson of a rabbi.

Like Reform Jews, the Jewish socialists did not need to regard their message as exclusive to Judaism. For them it was enough to see Judaism as the unique contributor of the ideal of social justice to an international ethic for the whole human race. However, unlike their Reform counterparts, Jewish socialists no longer represented themselves as "religious"—for religion belonged to the prescientific age that was passing away. The pivotal date for Jewish socialism is usually said to be 1897, the year of the formation of the Bund, or Jewish Worker's Union, in Poland. Many secular Jews joined the socialist movement but rejected all connections with Judaism. They thought of themselves as purely secular, nonreligious persons. Some even vigorously disavowed their Jewish roots, going so far as to contribute to existing currents of anti-Semitism.

Yiddish Ethnic Judaism

Other Jewish socialists, however, wished to retain and affirm their ties to the history of the Jewish people. And so they turned to ethnicity as the key to Jewish identity— an ethnicity that was primarily identified with speaking the Yiddish language. Even secular Jews who no longer used or knew Hebrew knew Yiddish, an amalgam of Hebrew and German that developed from about the eleventh century and was the common language of European Jews. The focus on Yiddish language, and especially Yiddish literature, which often echoes Talmudic and biblical stories, gave secular Jews a way to identify with Judaism without being "religious" and to draw on the wisdom of the tradition. As the language of working-class Jews, Yiddish gave Jews a deep sense of "ethnicity," of being bound together in a common historical tradition that also offered a unique identity. That ethnicity could easily be tapped by Jewish socialists to mobilize Jews—that is, to organize them for the workers' revolution that was part of the Marxian scheme of history.

The Origins of Zionism

Zionism was born out of disenchantment with modernity and its Enlightenment promises. Unlike Jewish socialism, Zionism did not hold out much hope for a future in which Jews would be accepted as equals in society. In the Zionist view, the only viable solution for Jews in light of the long history of rejection, first by Christendom and then by modern secular society, was to have a state of their own where they could protect themselves.

Zion is a biblical term used to refer to the city of David—Jerusalem. The word *Zionism*, coined in 1893, represents a longing virtually as old as Judaism itself: to return from exile, home to Zion. In premodern Rabbinic Judaism, this longing was expressed in a messianic belief that someday God would send a messiah and

Theodor Herzl, founder of the Zionist movement to create a Jewish state.

reestablish a homeland for his people in the land of Israel. When Zionism appeared at the end of the nineteenth century, this secular movement to organize Jews for the creation of a homeland in Palestine was vehemently rejected by the Orthodox and ultra-Orthodox as blasphemy. Reform Jews, having defined themselves as a religious community rather than as a "people," showed little interest in returning to the Middle East. In truth, Zionism did not come into its own until after the Holocaust, when it seemed clear to Jews everywhere that they could never count on being accepted as equals in Europe, and that the only protection available to them would be in their own homeland—their own state.

A pivotal event in the development of secular (political) Zionism was the Dreyfus affair in France. This trial of a Jewish army officer on charges of treason had a profound influence on a young Jewish journalist, Theodor Herzl (1860–1904). The outcome of the trial—Dreyfus's conviction, despite being innocent—convinced Herzl that assimilation would never be a feasible option for Jews. In 1896 he wrote *The Jewish State*, in which he rejected assimilation and proposed the creation of a Jewish homeland. Thus was born a movement that was destined to change the future of Judaism: secular political Zionism. Herzl convened the First Zionist Congress in Basel, Switzerland, in 1897, the same year as the formation of the Jewish socialist Bund in Poland. At this conference the World Zionist Organization was founded.

"Distress binds us together and, thus united, we suddenly discover our strength. . . . Let sovereignty be granted us over a portion of the globe large enough to satisfy the rightful requirements of a nation; the rest we shall manage for ourselves."

—Theodor Herzl on Zionism

Herzl's Dream and Its Ramifications

Theodor Herzl died in 1904, but not his dream. He left behind a thriving and committed body of political Zionists, the World Zionist Organization. In 1911 this organization began a modest but persistent program of colonizing areas in Palestine, which was then under British colonial control. In 1917, as a result of Zionist efforts, the British foreign secretary, Lord James Balfour, wrote the letter now known as the Balfour Declaration, pledging Britain's support for a Jewish national home in Palestine. France, Italy, and the United States endorsed the idea.

Zionism sought continuity in the idea of the Jews as a historical people. Zionists reappropriated the biblical stories of the origins of Israel as part of their story, but the biblical narratives were to serve not as religious stories of God's actions in history but as "secular" stories of the Jewish people's struggles to achieve and preserve their national identity. The Zionists reacted to what they perceived as the failure (after almost 2,000 years) of the Rabbinic strategy of accommodation to the surrounding non-Jewish world and to the more recent Reform strategy of partial assimilation. They were not content to wait to be emancipated by others (whether God or modern gentiles). They were looking for Jewish heroes who were prepared to emancipate themselves. Thus they retold the stories of Moses and David as stories of nation builders and militant revolutionary political leaders.

For the Zionists, the interesting stories were the marginal ones of the Maccabean revolts of the second century BCE and those of the Maccabees' successors, the Zealots, who would rather kill themselves (as they did at Masada in 73 CE) than let the fight for their land end in surrender. The Zionists were looking for militant heroes who could serve as prototypes for a new kind of Jew, one prepared to fight to the last against all odds. This hero, they imagined, was the kind of Jew who would reestablish a homeland in Israel.

And yet, while calling for a new kind of Jew, Zionism was repeating the formative pattern of Judaism, telling a story of exile and return—a people who originated in the land of Israel, were forcibly dispersed for almost 2,000 years, and now sought to return.

An aerial view of Masada, where first-century Jews who had resisted Rome chose suicide rather than surrender. The defenders of Masada were an important symbol of courage and resistance to Zionists.

Some Sabras, secular Jews who led the Zionist movement to create an Israeli state, stand guard over their fields on a kibbutz in Israel in the early days of the new nation.

CONTRASTING RELIGIOUS VISIONS

As the following contrasting visions indicate, every religious tradition is capable of generating both visions that encourage peace and understanding and visions that encourage conflict and violence.

Abraham Joshua Heschel, 1907–72

On June 16, 1963, Rabbi Abraham Joshua Heschel sent a telegram to the president of the United States, John F. Kennedy. Heschel and other religious leaders were scheduled to meet with the president the next day to discuss race relations and civil rights in America. The rabbi proposed that the president declare a state of "moral emergency" to aid black Americans. "We forfeit the right to worship God as long as we continue to humiliate negroes. . . . Let religious leaders donate one month's salary toward a fund for negro housing and education. . . . The hour calls for high moral grandeur and spiritual audacity."

Abraham Joshua Heschel, 1907–72, a great Hasidic Jewish scholar and rabbi who marched with Martin Luther King Jr. at Selma and championed the way of nonviolence.

Abraham Joshua Heschel was born in Warsaw, Poland, on January 11, 1907. He was the son of a Hasidic rebbe and a long line of distinguished Hasidic teachers who were deeply steeped in Jewish mysticism. Heschel was a child prodigy. By age fourteen, he had mastered the Talmud and was himself writing Talmudic commentaries. As a young university student he was expelled from Germany by the Nazis and fled back to Poland and then to America, by way of England, shortly before the invasion of Poland. He taught first at Hebrew Union College in Cincinnati and then, for most of his career, at the Jewish Theological Seminary in New York. He is the author of numerous books that have deeply influenced modern Judaism, including *Man Is Not Alone*, *The Sabbath*, *God in Search of Man*, and *Man's Quest for God*.

Heschel's life demonstrates the capacity of Orthodox Judaism to embrace the pluralism of the modern world. As a great Jewish scholar and Hasidic rabbi, Heschel was the leading Jewish voice responding to social injustices in America during the civil rights/Vietnam War era of the 1950s and 1960s. An advocate of nonviolent civil disobedience, Heschel marched with Martin Luther King Jr. from Selma to Montgomery, Alabama, in the spring of 1965 in defense of civil rights for black Americans. "Any god who is mine but not yours, any god concerned with

Moreover, like Jewish socialism, Zionism offered secular Jews a powerful secular version of the goal of history. In the Zionist vision, however, the Jewish people were not incidental but essential. All in all, they made much more comprehensive and creative use of the stories of the biblical past than did the Yiddish-speaking Jewish socialists.

Like Jewish socialism, Zionism created a new way for secular Jews to be Jewish, reappropriating the tradition through story, language (which for Zionists was the recovery and reconstruction of Hebrew as a modern language), and social organization. While before World War II Jewish socialism had more adherents than Zionism, it was later eclipsed by a Zionism that absorbed and transformed its vision. After the Holocaust and the destruction of nearly a third of the world's Jews, the validity and the urgency of the

me but not with you," Heschel asserted, is an "idol," or false god. To segregate the races, he insisted, is nothing short of "segregating God."

Heschel showed himself to be a revolutionary not only in his advocacy for social justice for all peoples but in his openness to other religions, working closely with Christians and Buddhists to bring about social justice. Holiness, he insisted, is not to be limited to those of any one religion, not even Judaism. Holiness is defined by the intention of the heart and the righteousness of the deed.

Meir Kahane, 1932–90

Meir Kahane was born in Brooklyn, New York, on August 1, 1932. The son of a rabbi deeply involved in the Zionist movement, he too became a rabbi. In 1968 he founded the JDL, or Jewish Defense League. Kahane was no advocate for nonviolence. On the contrary, he argued that Jews cannot depend on others to defend them and need to learn to protect themselves, using violence if necessary.

Kahane's life illustrates the insistence of ultra-Orthodoxy that there can only be "one way" for all Jews, a way that protects them from pollution by the secular world and all religious diversity. In 1971 he moved to Israel and founded the anti-Arab Kach Party, which called for the forcible removal of all Arabs. This party attracted a strong following among the Gush Emunim and other religious Zionists. In 1984 Kahane was elected to the Knesset, but his party was banned before the next election, in 1988, on the grounds that Kach incited racism. Kahane was assassinated by an Egyptian Muslim radical in New York City on November 5, 1990, after a speech urging all American Jews to return to Israel to protect the land from the Arabs.

Kahane was an advocate of a messianic Zionism that was violently apocalyptic, expecting the messiah to come soon and lead the Jews in driving all Arabs out of Israel. For Kahane, any act that elevated Jews and humiliated Arabs and all other enemies of the Jews was viewed as sanctifying God's name and hastening the coming of the messiah.

In 1994 the Kach Party and its offshoot, Kahane Chai, were designated terrorist organizations by both the Israeli government and the U.S. government. Then, in 1995, another Kahane admirer, Yigal Amir, assassinated the prime minister of Israel, Yitzhak Rabin, to put a stop to his attempts to make peace with the Palestinians.

Quotations from: Abraham Joshua Heschel, *Moral Grandeur and Spiritual Audacity* (essays edited by Susannah Heschel) (New York: Farrar, Straus and Giroux, 1996).

Zionist message seemed self-evident to the overwhelming majority of Jews, both religious and secular. If they were to survive, Jews must have their own national homeland.

Zionism shaped a nation and turned a utopian dream into a reality—the state of Israel. Jewish ethnic socialism and Zionism together represented a powerful, if ambivalent, rejection of the modern era and its ideal of assimilation as defined by the Enlightenment. It was the amalgamation of these ways of thinking that made a natural bridge to the Judaism of Holocaust and Redemption, for without the socialist-Zionist revolution, there would be no state of Israel. And without the state of Israel, there would be only Holocaust and no sense of redemption—no sense of rescue from the forces of slavery and death similar to their ancient deliverance from slavery in Egypt into the "land of promise."

Judaism and Postmodern Trends in a Postcolonial World (1967–)

Challenges to Jewish Faith After the Holocaust

In 1933 Adolf Hitler and the Nazi Party came to power in Germany. By 1939 they had drawn Europe into World War II, a six-year war of expansion that was meant to give additional *Lebensraum* ("living space") to what the Nazis considered to be the superior Aryan race of Germany. Near the end, however, when Germany was losing badly and soldiers and supplies were desperately needed at the front, trains were diverted to the task of transporting Jews to the death camps. Hitler was more desperate to rid the world of Jews than he was to win the war.

The **Holocaust** was a singular event in human history that brought the modern era of progress to an end in mass death. *Holocaust* (which means "burnt sacrifice") is the name given to the attempt by Nazi Germany to eliminate an entire people, the Jews. Unlike the millions of others who died on the battlefronts of World War II, the Jews were not military combatants (see Map 3.4). The Jews of Germany were not enemies of Germany, but citizens. There was no military or territorial advantage to be had by systematically killing them. They were marked for death simply because they existed. Germans, defeated and humiliated in World War I (1914–18) and suffering from extreme economic depression as a result of war reparations, chose not to blame these troubles on the aggressive military actions of their government during the war. Instead, they said, "The Jews are our misfortune"—they are to blame. The Nazis rose to power partly by portraying the Jews as a racial pollutant or a diseased growth on the healthy body of the German people that had to be surgically cut out if the nation was to be restored to health and greatness.

When the Nazi Party came to power, the Jews were stripped of their citizenship and all their legal rights; their homes and businesses were appropriated; and they were herded into boxcars that delivered them to an elaborate system of death camps, where they were either worked to death as slaves or murdered in specially designed gas chambers made to order for mass killings. At the most infamous of the camps, Auschwitz, in Poland, it is estimated that 2 million Jews were executed.

One has to ask: Why the Jews? Blaming a scapegoat for misfortune is not unusual in history, but what induced the Nazis to pick the Jews for this role? The answer takes us, in large part, to the story of the beginnings of Christianity (which we will discuss further in Chapter 4). As a Jewish sect that came to be dominated by non-Jews, gentile Christians saw themselves as having superseded and replaced the Jews as God's chosen people. The establishment of Christianity as the dominant religion of the Roman Empire led to both legal discrimination and popular discrimination that often was expressed in violence against Jews as "the children of the devil"—a people

Holocaust: the attempt by Nazi Germany to exterminate the Jewish people

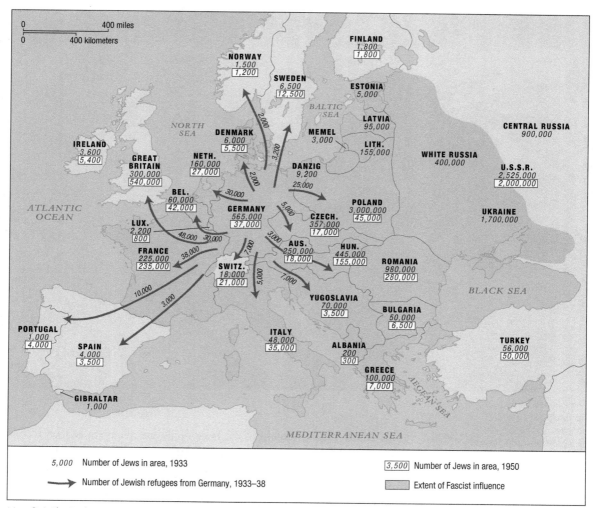

Map 3.4 The Holocaust.

most Christians believed had been rejected by God for their role in the "killing of Jesus, the Son of God."

Moreover, the "negative witness" theory suggested by St. Augustine portrayed the Jews as condemned to wander the earth without a home, their misery supposedly offering negative proof of the truth of Christianity. From the time of this early theologian (354–430) forward, through the Middle Ages and into the modern period, Jews were the scapegoats, blamed for whatever misfortunes occurred in Western civilization. Indeed, Hitler played on popular Christian anti-Jewish sentiments to rise to the position of chancellor of Germany. Later, neither the Catholic nor the Protestant churches of Germany

The Nazis rounded up European Jews and sent them to the death camps in boxcars. These Jewish prisoners, some of them children, were photographed at the infamous Auschwitz death camp.

officially protested the Nazi treatment of the Jews—only the treatment of Jewish converts to Christianity. It took more than Christian anti-Judaism to make the Holocaust possible; for instance, the rise of secular racial theory and scientific-bureaucratic forms of social control played an important part. Nevertheless, it is hard to imagine the Holocaust occurring without the significant contribution of Christian anti-Semitism.

The Holocaust deeply challenges the Jewish faith orientation promoted in the stories of the Exodus and exile traditions. If these stories promised a God who would always be with the people of the covenant, guiding and protecting them, then the Holocaust seemed to prove this promise a lie. Many Jews felt that God had failed to keep his promises.

After the Holocaust, some of the most Orthodox of Jews wanted to treat the Holocaust as a tragedy of the same type as the fall of the first and second temples, where these tragedies had been explained as due to a failure to keep the covenant. In fact, they proposed that the best way to remember the Holocaust was to include it in the period of fasting and mourning of Tisha B'Av. But to many other Jews, both secular and religious, this seemed wholly inappropriate. For the main victims of the Holocaust were not the most liberal and secularized Jews but rather the most orthodox and observant population in Jewry, the Jews of eastern Europe. Moreover, for many Jews the scope of the tragedy was so great that the argument of "failure to keep the covenant" faithfully enough seemed inadequate to explain it.

How does one commemorate such an event? And how, after the Holocaust, could Jews go on believing the promises of God to guide and protect them on their journey through time? Indeed, a generation after the Holocaust there emerged a number of important authors who offered suggestions on how Jews should respond to the Holocaust.

One author, Richard Rubenstein, says that God died at Auschwitz, and Jews will have to go on with their stories and their rituals without God. Emil Fackenheim argues that, on the contrary, God is still present in history. He justifies this view by suggesting that it is as if Jews had heard a silent yet commanding voice from Auschwitz, giving them a new commandment, a 614th commandment to be added to the 613 in the Torah. This commandment demands that Jews remain Jewish lest they allow Judaism to die, thus giving Hitler a posthumous victory.

Elie Wiesel, the Nobel Prize–winning author and himself an Auschwitz survivor, sees it somewhat differently.[2] Only the Jew knows, says Wiesel, that one can have the *chutzpah* (audacity) to argue with God as long as it is in defense of God's creation—as Abraham argued with God over the fate of the innocent at Sodom (Genesis 18:22–33). Indeed, a Jew has the right to put God on trial and find him guilty of abandoning the Jews during the Holocaust.

Another major Holocaust scholar, Irving Greenberg, argues that after Auschwitz, Jews can only live a "momentary faith"—tossed back and forth between the stories of the Exodus and the stories of the Holocaust. In one moment a Jew might believe

TEACHINGS OF RELIGIOUS WISDOM:
The 614th Commandment

The post-Holocaust Jewish scholar Emil Fackenheim, himself a survivor of the Holocaust, argues that Jews must not give in to despair and abandon their faith after the atrocities of the Holocaust. God, he says, speaks even from Auschwitz and gives Jews a new commandment to be added to the 613 he gave at Sinai.

Jews are forbidden to hand Hitler posthumous victories. They are commanded to survive as Jews, lest the Jewish people perish. They are commanded to remember the victims of Auschwitz lest their memory perish. They are forbidden to despair of man and his world, and to escape into either cynicism or otherworldliness, lest they cooperate in delivering the world over to the forces of Auschwitz. Finally, they are forbidden to despair of the God of Israel, lest Judaism perish. . . . A Jew may not respond to Hitler's attempt to destroy Judaism by himself cooperating in its destruction. In ancient times, the unthinkable Jewish sin was idolatry. Today, it is to respond to Hitler by doing his work.

Source: Emil L. Fackenheim, *God's Presence in History* (Northvale, NJ, and Jerusalem: Jason Aronson, 1997), p. 84.

in the promises of Sinai, only in the next moment to have them clouded over by memories of the smokestacks of Auschwitz. Like Wiesel, Greenberg argues that Jews can no longer be required to embrace the covenant, and yet they do so freely. Greenberg observes that this embrace takes on a wide variety of forms, from the extremely orthodox to the extremely secular. And after Auschwitz, he insists, all Jews are obligated to accept each other as Jews, accepting contemporary Jewish pluralism as an authentic covenantal pluralism. For Jews to turn their backs on other Jews, as some of the ultra-Orthodox in the state of Israel do when they refuse to acknowledge the Jewishness of non-Orthodox Jews, is another way of granting Hitler a posthumous victory. What has changed after Auschwitz, says Greenberg, is that Jews are free to observe or not to observe the covenant; they are not, however, free to reject Jews who exercise this freedom.

Post-Holocaust Judaism offers an alternative to the "one way" of ultra-Orthodoxy. This is a postmodern form of Judaism, in which there is not one single way to truth and to faithfulness but many. Covenantal pluralism is affirmed insofar as great diversity in thought *and* practice, both secular and religious, is allowed. Only one practice is not negotiable: the obligation of post-Holocaust Jews to accept one another in their diversity. Both ultra-Orthodoxy and the Judaism of Holocaust and Redemption seek a way out of what they see as the spiritual poverty of a modernism that made the Holocaust possible. The choice they offer to all Jews is either withdrawal from or involvement in the modern world, either back to what they view as premodern uniformity or forward to a new age of postmodern Jewish pluralism.

Finally, the post-Holocaust Jewish scholar Marc Ellis insists that Israeli Jews must never use the suffering of Jews in the Holocaust as an excuse for the oppression of their Palestinian neighbors. They must remember that the covenant relation of the Jews to the land includes the demands to ensure justice for all and to show compassion to the stranger. Not only must Jews accept other Jews in their diversity, they must accept their Christian and Muslim Palestinian neighbors in Israel in an environment of justice and peace for all. Such a task is not easy when extremists on all sides seek to undermine genuine efforts at compromise and cooperation, and yet many in the state of Israel continue the struggle to find that middle ground.

Challenges to Jewish Existence After the Holocaust

This new Judaism of Holocaust and Redemption, which has proven very attractive to American Judaism, Israeli Judaism, and Israeli nationalism, has a postmodern and postcolonial orientation. It attempts to find unity in the diversity of religious and secular Jews. Even its new "holy days" (or "holidays") display characteristics of both the holy and the secular. Indeed, two days that seem to be entering the Jewish calendar are recollections of seemingly secular events—*Yom Hashoah* (Day of Desolation), recalling the Holocaust, and *Yom Ha'atzmaut* (Independence Day), celebrating the founding of the modern state of Israel.

TALES OF SPIRITUAL TRANSFORMATION

The Nobel Prize–winning author Elie Wiesel, a survivor of Auschwitz, remembers an event that took place while he was a prisoner there. His tale shows that not even consignment to the death camps of the Holocaust could destroy Jewish faith.

The Jewish festival of the giving of the Torah by God to Moses, *Simhath Torah*, arrived. However, there was no Torah in the camp that Jews could use to ritually carry in celebration. Indeed, during this celebration Hasidic Jews pick up the Torah and literally dance with it to express their joy. So an old man looks around for a substitute to use for the Torah celebration. He sees a young boy and asks him,

"Do you remember what you learned in heder (Torah school)?" "Yes I do," replied the boy. "Really," said the man, "you really remember Sh'ma Yisrael" (the confession of faith in the oneness of God). "I remember much more," said the boy. "Sh'ma Yisrael is enough," said the man. And he lifted the boy, clasped him in his arms and began dancing with him—as though *he* were the Torah. And all joined in. They all sang and danced and cried. They wept, but they sang with fervor—never before had Jews celebrated *Simhath Torah* with such fervor.

Source: Elie Wiesel, *A Jew Today* (New York: Random House, 1978), p. 146.

The impact of the Holocaust on Jewish consciousness cannot be overstated. During the Holocaust the Nazis nearly succeeded in their goal of eliminating Jews from the face of the earth. Nearly a third of all Jews died in the Holocaust; nearly two-thirds of the Jews of Europe died. The eastern European Jewish communities were hit the hardest. Ninety percent of these Jews and more than 80 percent of all the rabbis, Talmudic scholars, and Talmudic students then alive were murdered.

Jews might have despaired after the devastation of the Holocaust, but the founding of the state of Israel by the United Nations in 1948 gave them hope. The counterbalancing of the Holocaust and the founding of the state of Israel fits the great formative story of Jewish existence—exile and return. After 2,000 years without a homeland, many Jews experienced the ability to return to Israel as a Jewish state as a miraculous act of divine redemption akin to the return to the land of promise after slavery in Egypt or after exile in Babylon. That redemption makes it possible for Jews to remember the Holocaust without despairing.

The history of the establishment of the modern state of Israel is complex. We will just note that in 1947, as a member of the newly formed United Nations, Britain asked the General Assembly to establish a special committee on Palestine. The report of this committee, UNSCOP, led to a resolution to divide Palestine into two states—one Jewish and the other Arab (see Map 3.5). The state of Israel was established on May 14, 1948, the date on which Great Britain gave up official control of the area. Within a year Israel would be admitted to the United Nations.

The Arab states, however, refused to accept the UN partition plan, and on May 15, 1948, the armies of seven Arab states invaded the newly formed nation and the war for independence was under way. The war was fought in two phases,

Map 3.5 The creation of the state of Israel.

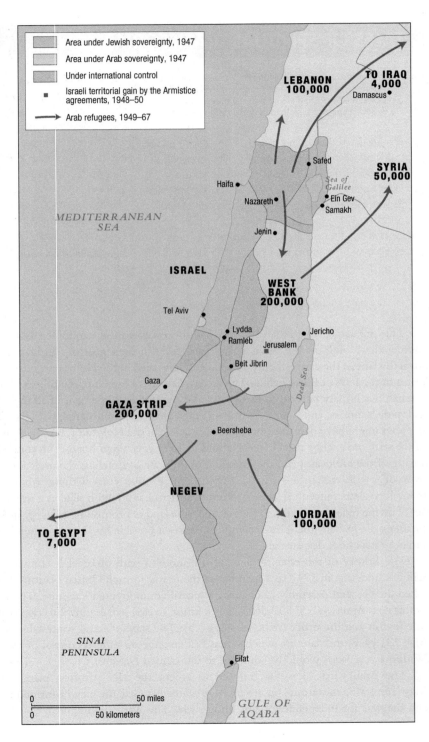

Area under Jewish sovereignty, 1947

Area under Arab sovereignty, 1947

Under international control

▪ Israeli territorial gain by the Armistice agreements, 1948–50

→ Arab refugees, 1949–67

LEBANON
100,000

TO IRAQ
4,000

Damascus

Safed

Sea of
Galilee

SYRIA
50,000

Haifa

Nazareth

Eín Gev

Samakh

Jenin

ISRAEL

WEST
BANK
200,000

MEDITERRANEAN
SEA

Tel Aviv

Lydda

Ramleb

Jericho

Jerusalem

Beit Jibrin

Dead Sea

Gaza

GAZA STRIP
200,000

Beersheba

NEGEV

JORDAN
100,000

TO EGYPT
7,000

SINAI
PENINSULA

Eilat

0   50 miles

0   50 kilometers

GULF OF
AQABA

with an intervening cease-fire, and ended in the defeat of the Arab forces and an armistice with the Egyptians in February 1949. Relations with neighboring Arab states remained tense throughout the decades that followed, flaring again into the wars of 1967 and 1973.

It is hard to overstate the impact of the 1967 war on Judaism. In June of that year, the state of Israel was seriously threatened by four predominantly Muslim nations: Egypt, Jordan, Syria, and Iraq. Israeli forces were overwhelmingly outnumbered. Israel perceived itself to be alone, without allies and doomed to what many feared would be a second holocaust. Israeli armed forces, under the leadership of General Yitzhak Rabin, staged a surprise air attack on the morning of June 5. In a brilliant series of military moves, Israel routed the combined Arab forces in a war that was over in six days.

At the end of the war, Israel occupied territory formerly under the control of the Egyptians and the Syrians—from the Suez Canal to the Golan Heights. In the process Israel had taken control of the entire area west of the Jordan River, including the Old City of Jerusalem (on June 7), recovering one of the holiest places for all Jews, the Western Wall of the second temple (destroyed by the Romans in 70 CE), which had been under Jordanian control (see Map 3.6). As the dust of the Six-Day War settled, Jews both in the land of Israel and in Diaspora were overwhelmed with a sense of awe at their seemingly miraculous deliverance. Even among the most secular or nonreligious Jews, many could not help but see the redemptive hand of God in these events.

In response a newly formed Palestinian Liberation Organization began a long and systematic policy of guerrilla warfare against Israel.

Leon Greenman, a Jewish survivor of Auschwitz, displays his Auschwitz serial number tattoo after addressing an Anti-Nazi League meeting in Brighton, England.

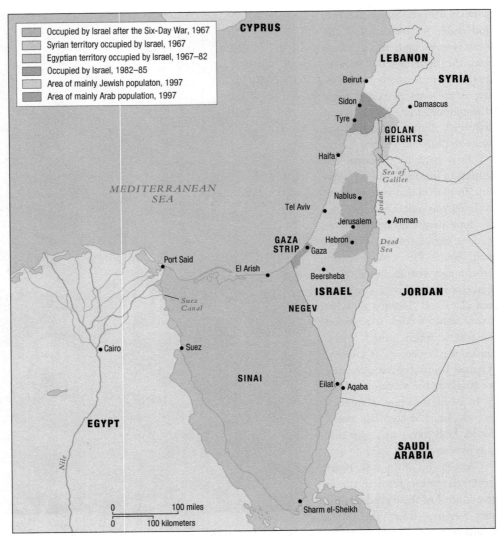

Map 3.6 *Arab–Israeli conflict from 1967.*

For many Jews the 1967 war was the turning point. From that time forward the meaningful connection between the Holocaust and the founding of the state of Israel could not be ignored. The two events became indissolubly linked in Jewish minds, and the days of remembrance of these two events became ever more prominent in the Jewish calendar.

The Yom Kippur War of 1973 was less decisive than the 1967 war in military terms, but it sparked a resurgence of religious Zionism. On October 6, 1973, the

Egyptian army penetrated the Israeli-occupied territory of the Sinai peninsula, while the Syrians invaded the Golan Heights. The surprise attack occurred on Yom Kippur, one of the holiest days in the Jewish calendar. Although caught off guard, Israel rallied and successfully rebuffed its attackers, but the event undermined confidence in the leadership of the Labor Party. Thus the ground was prepared for the rise of the conservative Likud Party, with the election of Menachem Begin as prime minister in 1977. Another result was increased political influence from religious Zionists like the Gush Emunim.

The Gush Emunim were committed to the notion that none of the occupied territories from the 1967 War were to be given back in any peace agreement after the 1973 war. Believing strongly that the Jews were chosen by God to inherit this land, they were no more inclined to share it with their Palestinian neighbors than many Christian and Muslim Palestinians were to share it with the Jews. Consequently, the Gush Emunim began an intensive program of establishing settlements in the occupied territory, an activity that was not authorized by the Israeli government. When Menachem Begin came to power, however, he supported the settlements. In this fashion, religious Zionism began to play an important role in Israeli public policy.

Youths celebrate the founding of the modern state of Israel at the Western Wall, waving an Israeli flag. The new state has deep religious significance for many Jews, who see it as a sign of God's saving activity after the near annihilation of European Jews in the Holocaust.

The signing of the Camp David Peace Accord on March 26, 1979. U.S. President Jimmy Carter (center) is flanked by President Anwar Sadat of Egypt on his right and Israeli premier Menachem Begin on his left.

While the settlements were in their infancy, however, Begin signed a peace treaty with the president of Egypt, Anwar Sadat. This agreement, signed at Camp David in 1979 with the encouragement of U.S. president Jimmy Carter, called for Israel to return occupied territory in the Sinai. Unfortunately, this provoked militant fundamentalists, like the Gush Emunim, to engage in terrorist tactics against their Palestinian counterparts.

The existence of the state of Israel represents for many Jews a redemption from 2,000 years of powerlessness, persecution, and exile. The state of Israel represents, for Jews, a new age of politics, power, and a capacity for self-defense in a world that has often been bent on subjugating or destroying them. Today, Jews continue to struggle to find a way to live constructively with their own diversity in the Diaspora. And they struggle as well to maintain the autonomy of the state of Israel, while seeking a just and lasting peace in the Middle East.

Conclusion

Jacob was left alone; and a man (a stranger) wrestled with him until daybreak. . . . Then he said, "Let me go, for the day is breaking." But Jacob said, "I will not let you go, unless you bless me." So he said to him, . . . "you shall no longer be called Jacob, but Israel, for you have striven with God and with humans, and have prevailed." . . . So Jacob called the place Peniel, saying, "For I have seen God face to face and yet my life is preserved."

—NRSV, Genesis 32:24–30

What we learn from the study of the diverse ways of being Jewish is that religion can either reject the secular or accommodate it. What form shall the life of the people Israel take in the modern world? That is the issue being debated among Jews as they move into the future. Those like the ultra-Orthodox, who reject the secular, see religion as being about a sacred, eternal, and unchangeable way of life that must not be profaned by accommodation with the world. Consequently, they are segregationists. All modern and postmodern/post-Holocaust religious forms of Judaism, by contrast, see the holy and the secular less as opposites than as complementary, and they tend to see historical change as the medium through which God reveals himself in time.

The modernist forms of Judaism (Reform, Conservative, and Orthodox) tend to regard diversity as competition in which one is "more right" than the others although all are Jews. The postmodern Judaism of Holocaust and Redemption envisions the diverse forms of Judaism as equal and mutually supporting. To the ultra-Orthodox, by contrast, diversity is apostasy, and segregation from the non-Jewish modern world and from all forms of Judaism that compromise with that world is the only path to being the true Israel or covenant people.

For Yiddish ethnicists, socialists, and Zionists, meaning is to be found not in the God of history but in the history itself. Such "secular" Jews are not "religious" in the traditional sense of biblical theism, but they do display one type of religious behavior commonly found in the history of religions—reverence for the ways of the ancestors, ways that are held sacred.

The strength of the modern/postmodern forms of Judaism is in their ability to adapt Jewish life to new environments and situations. The strength of the Orthodox and ultra-Orthodox is in challenging those who would adapt not to sacrifice the heart of Jewish religious existence as a people—God, Torah, and Israel. They would argue that history and Jewish ethnicity are not an adequate substitute.

The adventure continues as Jews everywhere wrestle with each other and with the world around them over what it means to be a Jew—especially in the state of Israel, where there can be no peace unless accommodation both among Jews and with their Christian and Muslim neighbors is found. And yet the very struggle of Jews everywhere, whether secular or religious, among themselves and with the non-Jewish world around them, is very Jewish. We need only recall the story of how Jacob's name was changed to Israel (Genesis 32:23–32): Jacob wrestled with the stranger who would not tell Jacob his name but instead blessed Jacob and changed Jacob's name to Israel, meaning "he who has wrestled with God and human beings and prevails." Throughout history, the drama of Judaism has been to wrestle with God and the stranger. Today, whether secular or religious, Jews are still deeply shaped by the stories of Israel, they still wrestle with the stranger, and they still prevail.

Discussion Questions

1. What does it mean to say that Judaism is a form of the "myth of history"? Give examples from both the biblical and postbiblical periods.

2. At what point in biblical history did the fundamental pattern of Jewish experience emerge, and what shape did it take? Give two examples from the history of Judaism, one secular and one religious.

3. What is the Talmud, and what is its significance for the religion of Judaism?

4. Compare and contrast Enlightenment Judaism (Haskalah) and Hasidic Judaism.

5. Whom would you nominate as the three most important post-biblical figures in the history of Judaism, and why?

6. In what ways have secular forms of Judaism transformed the shape of contemporary religious forms of Judaism? Give examples and explain.

7. How does the history of anti-Judaism in Western Christianity and Western civilization relate to the Holocaust?

8. What was the impact of the Holocaust on the shape of modern and postmodern forms of Jewish life, religious and secular?

9. What is the Judaism of Holocaust and Redemption, and how does it relate to modern and premodern forms of Judaism? Also, why might it be seen as the alternative to ultra-Orthodoxy?

10. Is Zionism a secular form of Judaism or a religious form, or both? Explain, with historical examples.

Key Terms

Ashkenazi	Hasidism	synagogue
bar mitzvah	Holocaust	Talmud
bat mitzvah	Israel	Tanak
circumcision	Kabbalah	Tannaim
covenant	kosher	temple
Diaspora	Marranos	Tisha B'Av
dual Torah	Mishnah	Tzaddik
Gemara	*mitzvot*	Zionism
gentile	Rabbinic	*Zohar*
halakhah	Sephardic	
haredim	*Shema*	

Suggested Readings

Fasching, Darrell J. *Narrative Theology After Auschwitz: From Alienation to Ethics* (Minneapolis: Fortress Press, 1992).

Greenberg, Irving. *The Jewish Way* (New York: Summit Books, 1988).

———. *For the Sake of Heaven and Earth: The New Encounter Between Judaism and Christianity* (New York: Jewish Publication Society of America, 2004).

Isaacs, Ronald H., and Kerry M. Olitzky, eds. *Critical Documents of Jewish History: A Source Book* (London: Jason Aronson, 1995).

Johnson, Paul. *A History of the Jews* (New York: Harper & Row, 1987).

Keppel, Gilles. *The Revenge of God: The Resurgence of Islam, Christianity, and Judaism in the Modern World* (University Park: Pennsylvania State University Press, 1991, 1994).

Lawrence, Bruce B. *Defenders of God: The Fundamentalist Revolt Against the Modern Age* (Columbia: University of South Carolina Press, 1995).

Neusner, Jacob. *The Death and Birth of Judaism* (New York: Basic Books, 1987).

———. *Self-fulfilling Prophecy: Exile and Return in the History of Judaism* (Boston: Beacon Press, 1987).

Rubenstein, Richard. *The Cunning of History: The Holocaust and the American Future* (New York: Harper & Row, 1975).

Schwartz, Barry. *Judaism's Great Debates: Timeless Controversies from Abraham to Herzl* (Lincoln: University of Nebraska Press, 2012).

Notes

1. Jacob Neusner, *The Death and Birth of Judaism* (New York: Basic Books, 1987), p. 116.
2. Elie Wiesel, *A Jew Today* (New York: Random House, 1978), p. 146.

Additional Resources

The Story of the Jews with Simon Schama (2013, television series). Available online, this five-part series traces 3,000 years of Jewish history from biblical origins to post-Holocaust Judaism and the state of Israel.

The Chosen (1981, feature film). Set in 1940s Brooklyn and based on a novel by Chaim Potok (published in 1967 by Simon & Schuster), this film presents the story of two young men, one from an ultra-Orthodox Hasidic family and the other from a more "modern" Orthodox family at the time of the Zionist struggle of Israel for statehood. A dramatic examination of the conflict between different ways of Jewish life and thought responding to the "modern" world at a critical moment in Jewish history. Color, 107 minutes, dir. Jeremy Kagan.

Genocide (1981, documentary). Academy Award–winning documentary on the Holocaust narrated by Elizabeth Taylor and Orson Welles. An Arnold Schwartzman production available from the Simon Wiesenthal Center (http://bit.ly/2i8SweK).

CHRISTIAN DIVERSITY 4

and the Road to Modernity

Overview

Somewhere in Africa, villagers gather to dance and sing tribal chants in praise of the risen **Christ**. In rural India, a small group of Christians, virtually indistinguishable from their Hindu neighbors, gathers to pray and offer flower petals before a statue of Jesus. And in an unadorned room in England, Quakers sit in silent prayer, waiting for the Holy Spirit to inspire one of them to speak a message to the rest. Elsewhere, in a small village in Latin America, peasants sit in a circle on a hillside, studying the Gospel of Luke and preparing to share bread and wine as the body and blood of Christ. In a small storefront church in the American Midwest, a small group of **Pentecostal** Christians, their arms stretched toward heaven, pray in tongues—their own unique spiritual language. Meanwhile in Rome, the pope, leader of the largest Christian denomination in the world, the Roman **Catholic** Church, processes into the great Cathedral of St. Peter escorted by a long line of men in flowing robes.

Despite their incredible diversity, all these believers are Christians engaged in Christian prayer and worship. The challenge before us is to understand the unity and diversity among Christians, especially in the contemporary world. This chapter provides an overview of the history of the process of modernization and globalization that began in Western culture in an ambivalent relationship with Christianity. This overview will also help us to better understand the reaction of other religions to modernization. ○ ● ○

Christ: title Christians apply to Jesus of Nazareth; from the Greek translation of the Hebrew word meaning "anointed one" or "messiah"

Pentecostal: churches that emphasize possession by the Holy Spirit and speaking in tongues

Catholic: churches that define their Christian authenticity through apostolic succession from the apostle Peter

◀ An artist's rendition of the image on the Holy Shroud or burial cloth, which popular piety understands to be the image of the body, including the face, of Jesus.

Photo of the actual face on the shroud that popular piety believes is that of Jesus. Kept in the Cathedral in Turin, carbon dating of the cloth itself suggests origins in the fourteenth or fifteenth century, but how the physiologically correct image got on the cloth has so far defied scientific explanations. Consequently, many faithful see it as a miracle. The Roman Catholic Church has not declared its authenticity but sees it as a reminder of Christ and encourages its role in popular devotion.

Overview: The Beliefs of Christians

Like Jews and Muslims, Christians believe that there is but one God, the God who made all things and rules over history. This God is the highest reality, and to act in harmony with the will of this God is the highest goal of life. Christians are unique, however, in believing that God is one God yet three persons (Father, Son, and Holy Spirit) and that the reality of this God is uniquely revealed in the life and person of Jesus of Nazareth. Christians believe that the eternal Word of God was united to humanity through the person of Jesus, who suffered and died on the cross for the sins of the world. They believe that Jesus was raised from the dead three days later and after forty days ascended to heaven, where he will reign until he comes again at the end of time to judge the living and the dead at the final resurrection.

Like Jews and Muslims, Christians believe that the gravest problem in human life is sin—the failure to live in harmony with the will of God. Sin has two dimensions: idolatry and injustice. Idolatry is more than worshipping the images of false deities; it is treating anything that is not God as if it were more important than God. Idolaters shift the focus from God to their own selfish desires like wealth and power, which leads to injustice. However, Christians differ from Jews and Muslims in their view of sin and how it is to be overcome. Most Christians define *sin* in terms of the concept of **original sin**, which says that the will to do good in all people was corrupted by Adam and Eve, the first human beings. Through their disobedience to God's will, Adam and Eve brought sin and death into the world. Thus, most Christians believe that while human beings were created good, their good will (the desire to do what is good) was corrupted by the inherited consequences of the sin of Adam and Eve. Out of compassion for humanity, God chose to send a savior, Jesus Christ, to redeem them by dying in reparation for their past sins and restoring human nature (re-creating a good will in them). In doing so, God united his divine nature to human nature, healing its flaws. With a good will restored, obedience to the will of God becomes possible and human destiny is returned to its true goal of eternal life with God.

The primary means for Christians to overcome sin and live in harmony with the will of God is to die to self spiritually and be reborn through faith in Christ. The Christian who has undergone this conversion experience believes he or she has become "born again," free to obey the word of God. Christians believe that during their earthly lives they are called to help bring about the **Kingdom of God** (or **Kingdom of Heaven**)—the beginning of a new creation of love, compassion, and justice in which death will finally be overcome, even as Jesus overcame death on the cross.

For centuries, Christians have sought to establish this Kingdom of God. This goal has forced Christians to try to understand the relationship between the church and the world and how their faith and way of life relates to the non-Christian world around them. Both Catholic Christianity, which took definitive shape in the early and medieval church, and the sixteenth-century **Protestant** movement to reform Catholicism have struggled with this question down to the present day.

It would be misleading, however, to think that all Christians in all times and places would agree with this explanation. Like all religions, Christianity has taken many forms and been many things to many people. Today Christianity is the largest religion in the world. With over 2.3 billion adherents, of whom about 1.1 billion are Roman Catholic, Christians represent about one-third of the world's population. Approximately 37 percent of Christians are Protestant, and 12 percent are either Greek or Russian Orthodox. Other minority Christian communities make up 1 percent of the global Christian population. Our primary task in this chapter is twofold: (1) to understand Christianity in all its diversity and (2) to appreciate the role that this religion has played in the development of modern society. So, here we will focus not just on religion but also on the emergence of the modern world out of the ancient world. This chapter will explore the way Christianity has influenced (and been influenced by) the social, political, and intellectual history of modernization as it emerged in the West.

As with other religions in the modern world, pluralism presents a challenge. Some Christians, who identify as **fundamentalists**, believe there should not be diversity among Christians and blame modernization for this development. They

original sin: sin of Adam and Eve, who disobeyed God when they ate the fruit of the tree of knowledge of good and evil. This sin was said to weaken the will to do good of all humans born after them

Kingdom of God/ Kingdom of Heaven: occurs whenever humans live in accord with the will of God

Protestant: churches that emphasize direct personal relationship with God in Christ (rather than through the mediation of the Church established by apostolic succession) as necessary for salvation

fundamentalist: the most conservative wing of Evangelical Protestants, who believe modern science threatens Gospel truths

modernist: the liberal wing of the Evangelical movement of the early twentieth century that embraced modern science and progress as promoting the goals of the Kingdom of God on earth.

Gospel: literally "good news"; refers to Jesus' message of salvation in the New Testament

have argued that the alliance of Christianity with the modern scientific and secular worldview is a mistake that could be corrected by returning to the pre-modern "fundamentals" of the faith. Others (**modernists**) have argued that the historical evidence shows there has always been diversity within Christianity. For them modernization is itself evidence of the power of the Christian **Gospel** to transform the world. In their view, Christians should embrace modernization as the path to human dignity and liberation.

Because the Christianity of yesterday helped shape the modern world, to understand the latter we need also to understand the former. We shall begin with the Protestant encounter with modernity and then look at Catholicism's struggle with the modern world. Then, to see how things came to be the way they are today, we shall return to the beginning in the first century and journey forward.

In the confrontation with modernity, both Catholics and Protestants responded to the scientific revolution in human thought that became obvious in the nineteenth

Christianity Timeline

31 CE	Crucifixion of Jesus of Nazareth
48–60	Letters of Paul of Tarsus
70	Fall of the Jewish temple in Jerusalem to the Romans; Gospel of Mark written
80–100	Gospels of Matthew, Luke, and John written
313	Edict of Milan by Constantine permitting Christianity in Roman Empire
325	Council of Nicaea declares Word of God to be same as (*homoousios*) God
380	Christianity declared the official religion of the Roman Empire by Emperor Theodosius
451	Council of Chalcedon, doctrine of two natures in the one person of Christ
500s	Development of Benedictine monasticism in the West
590–604	Pontificate of Gregory the Great, first great pope of the Middle Ages
732	Muslim invasion of Europe stopped at Tours by Charles Martel
800	Coronation of Charlemagne
1054	Schism between Eastern Orthodox and Western Roman Catholic Christianity
1095	First Crusade against Muslims and mass violence against Jews
1184	Inauguration of church inquisitions by Pope Lucius III
1198–1216	Pontificate of Innocent III, most powerful pope in history
1224–1274	St. Thomas Aquinas, greatest theologian of Middle Ages
1414	Council of Constance—papal decadence and the declaration of conciliar rule in the church
1453	Fall of Constantinople to the Muslim Ottoman Turks, end of Roman Empire
1517	Luther's Ninety-five Theses posted on church door at Wittenberg, beginning of Protestant Reformation
1545–1563	Council of Trent, Catholic Counter-Reformation

century. This revolution was precipitated by the emergence of new academic disciplines.

The first wave had been created by the natural sciences. Copernicus had outraged the European world when he suggested in 1543 CE that the earth was not the center of the universe. Later, geologists had concluded that the earth was far older than had been calculated by anyone who used the Bible as a guide. Then in 1859 Charles Darwin published *On the Origin of Species*, rendering completely implausible the biblical account according to which human beings appeared on earth on the sixth day of creation. Darwin claimed that evolution had been proceeding for many hundreds of thousands of years and was the result of a struggle between members of the various species culminating in the survival of the fittest.

The social sciences delivered the second shock wave. Critical historiography (the study of the writing of history) showed that popular legends about the past often did not accurately describe events. Sociologists and anthropologists who studied

1555	Peace of Augsburg—first attempt to end religious wars of the Reformation
1648	Peace of Westphalia—end of religious wars, quest for religious tolerance
1703–1791	John Wesley, founder of Methodism
1768–1834	Friedrich Schleiermacher, father of modern theology
1791	First Amendment to U.S. Constitution, guaranteeing religious freedom for all
1813–1855	Søren Kierkegaard, Christian existentialism
1851	Karl Marx publishes *Communist Manifesto*
1859	Charles Darwin publishes *On the Origin of Species*
1869–1870	First Vatican Council
1910–1915	Publication of *The Fundamentals* begins fundamentalist/modernist controversy
1939–1945	World War II and the Holocaust
August 6, 1945	Atomic bomb dropped on Hiroshima, Japan, leading to end of World War II
1947	India achieves independence; Church of South India is formed
1950s, 1960s	Emergence of civil rights movement under Martin Luther King Jr.; Pope John XXIII and the Second Vatican Council
1970s–1990s	Religious resurgence of evangelical fundamentalism and emergence of liberation theology movements
2005	Death of Pope John Paul II and election of Pope Benedict XVI
2013	Pope Benedict XVI resigns (the first resignation since the thirteenth century) to permit the election of a new pope, which occurred on March 13, 2013, when Jorge Mario Bergoglio, an Argentinean Jesuit, became Pope Francis
2016	Pope Francis forbids any Catholic mission to the Jews, who are already God's elect

societies comparatively suggested that humanity had invented the gods. Modern human beings were now asked to think of both society and human identity as created by human choices rather than by divine actions and decisions, as claimed by traditional teachings.

This new awareness created a problem. The issue that came to divide modern Christianity was whether to reject the developments of modernity, accept these new ways of thinking and understanding, or strike some kind of compromise between these two positions. Paradoxically, although modernity appeared to be a threat to Christianity, it had been nurtured, in significant part, by Christianity itself.

Encounter with Modernity: The Fundamentalist–Modernist Controversy (1859–)

The Protestant Confrontation with Modernity

When the first followers of Jesus of Nazareth looked up into the night sky in the first century, they did not see what modernists did when they looked upward in the nineteenth century. For modernists saw a cosmos with stars and planets scattered in infinite space. They knew that the earth is not at the center of the universe but just one of the planets circumnavigating a star (the sun) in one of many galaxies. When individuals in the first century looked up they saw a world shaped not by modern scientific imagination but by the imagination of the ancient Greeks. They accepted the Greek view that the earth was at the center of seven spheres. The higher spheres of the stars and the planets embodied spiritual beings that governed the universe. Everything above the moon, they believed, belonged to the realm of the spiritual and eternal, and everything below the moon belonged to the realm of the physical and temporal. The Greeks thought that the souls of all humans originated in the spiritual realm and had descended into the material realm. But the spiritual goal, each individual's hope of salvation, was to return to the spiritual realm above, beyond time, decay, and death.

In addition to the legacy of the Greeks, the worldview of the first Christians owed a debt to the Hebraic tradition of ancient Israel. This tradition held that creation is a story unfolding in time: In the beginning God spoke, and the story began. The story has many dramatic ups and downs, but at last God will bring the present world to an end, judge it, and transform it into a new creation. Today "modern" believers wrestle with the question of whether being a Christian requires adherence to the ancient worldview or can accommodate changing worldviews, including the modern scientific one.

The nineteenth century marked a critical turning point in the history of Christianity, as it sought to coexist with an increasingly "modern" secular and scientific world whose views challenged many of the fundamental truths and practices of Christians.

The central issue in modern Christianity has been the struggle between modernism and fundamentalism. Indeed, the term *fundamentalism* originated in reaction to American Protestant encounters with *modernism*.

By the end of the nineteenth century, higher education in America was increasingly secular and scientific. Each academic discipline developed its own rational and empirical standards that made no direct appeal to the Bible or Christian beliefs. In this context, Charles Darwin's theories on the biological evolution of humanity from lower primates challenged popular Christian beliefs. At the same time, new scholarship, which looked on the Bible as a historical, humanly created document, also challenged many pious beliefs about its teachings.

The challenges stemming from Darwinism and biblical criticism elicited two opposing responses: the modernism of liberal Christian **evangelicals** on the one hand and the fundamentalism of conservative Christian evangelicals on the other. Liberal evangelicals developed a new theology to show how modernism and Christianity were compatible. They saw God at work in evolution and in history and embraced a "Social Gospel" focused on making this world into the Kingdom of God. By the end of World War I, liberal evangelical Christianity dominated the northern Protestant churches. However, in the eyes of fundamentalist evangelicals, the attempt to adapt Christianity to the modern world was doomed to failure. What one ended up with was a Christianity emptied of everything that made it Christian and filled with everything that was secular and modern.

In a series of twelve paperback books entitled *The Fundamentals*, published between 1910 and 1915, champions of the fundamentalist movement spoke in defense of Bible-based religion and against the apostasy or betrayal, as they perceived it, of modernism. Convinced that liberal theology and Darwinism were undermining American civilization, they took their stand on the inerrancy of the Bible, pure and simple. If you did not share this belief, the fundamentalists did not consider you to be a true Christian.

The development of two opposing forms of evangelical Christianity was paradoxical. Evangelical Christianity had originated, in Europe, as a strategy for transcending the theological disputes and religious wars that occurred in the aftermath of the Protestant Reformation. These original evangelicals believed that a true Christian was identified not by acceptance of the right doctrines but by being "born again"—an emotional transformation undergone through a spiritual surrender to Christ that enabled Christians to accept each other, despite disagreements over fundamental beliefs.

The Catholic Confrontation with Modernity

In 1864 Pope Pius IX issued a Syllabus of Errors listing eighty "modern" teachings that challenged the church's control of knowledge and politics and admonished Catholics to reject them. In 1869 Pius IX called the First Vatican Council of cardinals and bishops to shore up the teachings of the church against the threat of modernism. In 1870 the papacy was besieged not only by modern ideas but threatened by modern secular politics when a newly unified Italy seized most of the Papal estates.

Thus Vatican I, as the council is now known, was in session precisely at the time when the intellectual and political authority of the papacy was most vulnerable. In

evangelical: Christian movements that emphasize the emotional power of conversion as a personal spiritual transformation through surrender to Christ

"If thou lovest God and all mankind, I ask no more: 'give me thine hand.'"

—John Wesley

Pope John XXIII, who opened the doors of the Roman Catholic Church to modernity by calling the Second Vatican Council, in a portrait from 1963.

1870, at the insistence of Pius IX, Vatican I declared the pope to be infallible. This meant that a pope's official declarations on faith and morals could not be altered, even with the consent of the church, including any future councils.

There is a striking similarity between Protestant and Catholic anti-modernist responses. Both attempted to prevent modernization and historical change from entering the church by an appeal to an infallible or inerrant authority that they believed was higher than scientific and secular authority. However, each responded by appealing to a different form of authority. For Protestants it was the Bible itself; for Roman Catholics it was the pope, as the final authority on how the Bible was to be interpreted.

It is all the more remarkable, therefore, that almost a century later a new pope would seek to reverse many of the decisions of Vatican I and come to terms with the modern world. When Pope John XXIII called the Second Vatican Council in 1962, he sought to reverse the more than four centuries of church attempts to reject the emerging modern world and also to heal the bad feelings generated by religious divisions within Christianity and in its relations with other religions.

The Second Vatican Council's meetings lasted from 1962 to 1965. John XXIII did not live to see them completed, but in his brief papacy (1958–63) he unleashed a spirit that transformed the Catholic Church from a world-shunning institution into one that was open to the modern world. In the decades since Vatican II, Catholics have wrestled with their future, with some wanting to return to the fundamentals of the Catholicism of Vatican I, and others wanting to modernize.

Our task now is to return to the beginning of Christianity and focus particularly on the roles it has played in the emergence of modernity in Europe and the promotion of European colonialism. Then we will further trace the new developments coming out of African and Asian Protestantism and Vatican II Catholicism. Finally, we will consider how these trends lead to a post-European diaspora form of Christianity open to religious pluralism in an age of globalization.

Premodern Christianity: The Formative Era (31–451 CE)

The New Testament and the Life of Jesus

Christianity begins in the first century with the life and teachings of Jesus of Nazareth as communicated in the Gospels of the New Testament. Being a Jew, Jesus participated in a religious tradition that went back 2,000 years before his time. This is acknowledged in the Christian Bible, which is made up of two parts. What Christians call the Old Testament is basically an adoption of the Pharisaic and Hellenistic Jewish collections of sacred writings that have been the official scriptures of Judaism since the end of the first century of the common era (CE). The scriptural writings of Christians, called the New Testament, did not assume the form of the twenty-seven books we have now until 367 CE—more than 300 years after the death of Jesus. During those centuries many stories were in circulation about the life and sayings of Jesus (e.g., other gospels such as the *Gospel of Thomas* and the *Acts of John*).

The tradition did not settle on a single story of Jesus for its Bible but actually included four distinct yet overlapping stories—the Gospels of Matthew, Mark, Luke, and John. To these were appended letters by the apostle Paul and others, a short history of the early church (the Acts of the Apostles), and a vision of the end of time (the book of Revelation). Christians believe that these scriptures show that Jesus of Nazareth is the Christ—the anointed one, or messiah—whose coming was foretold by the Hebrew prophets.

According to tradition, the Gospels were written by disciples (or disciples of disciples) of Jesus. Modern scholars believe Mark was written first (c. 70 CE), then Matthew and Luke used this Gospel and added further details. John was probably written last (c. 90 CE). Taking advantage of historical and archaeological findings that shed additional light on the biblical period, modern scholars do not believe any Gospel had a single author. Rather, each one began in shared oral traditions as told in different communities of believers after Jesus' death on the cross and attested resurrection. These traditions were eventually written down and edited to place the sayings of Jesus in the context of different remembered events from Jesus' life. All forms of Christianity share a common reverence for these stories of Jesus as they are found in the New Testament.

Christians in every culture tend to imagine the birth of Christ in terms of their own culture, as in this Chinese painting.

The Stories of Jesus

The stories of Jesus portray him as the embodied revelation of God. Jesus was born roughly at the beginning of the first century and grew up in Nazareth in ancient Palestine, then under Roman rule (see Map 4.1). Little is known of his youth, but according to the Gospel stories he was raised by Joseph, a carpenter, and his wife, Mary, the child's mother. The birth of Jesus was said to have been miraculous, for Mary became pregnant through the power of God as announced by an angel rather than through marital relations with Joseph.

Around the age of thirty, Jesus had a traumatic experience when his relative, John the Baptist, was arrested on orders from Herod (the ruler of Galilee) and eventually beheaded. Soon after John's arrest Jesus began teaching the very message that had gotten John in trouble with Herod—"Repent, for the kingdom of heaven is at hand" (Matthew 4:17).

While his family and friends at first thought he had gone mad, Jesus soon attracted followers who thought otherwise and called him rabbi, which means "teacher." The power of the Christian story is especially revealed in the Sermon on the Mount (Matthew 5–7), with its message of loving all, even your enemies.

In addition to preaching repentance and love, according to the scriptures, Jesus began working miracles—healing the sick (Mark 1:40–45; Matthew 9:18–22), walking on water (Mark 6:45–52; John 6:16–21), casting out evil spirits (Mark 1:23–28; Matthew 8:28–34), and miraculously multiplying a few loaves and fishes to feed a multitude, a story recounted in all four Gospels. As the fame of Jesus spread, some of the Sadducees and Pharisees (see Chapter 3), according to the stories, grew jealous of him and began to plot his demise. They had him handed over to the Romans who had heard some call him "messiah." While the Gospels typically make it appear as if the Jews, not the Romans, are the cause of Jesus' crucifixion, historians have pointed out that only the Romans had that power. Moreover, for the Romans the term *messiah* was associated with their enemies the Zealots. A militaristic sect of Judaism that engaged in guerrilla warfare against the Roman legions, the Zealots openly announced their expectation that God would send a messiah, a political revolutionary who would overthrow the Roman Empire. Historically, the reason the Romans condemned Jesus to be crucified—nailed to a wooden cross and left to die—was that they thought of him as an enemy of the state.

Whatever the political facts, the followers of Jesus came to find deep spiritual meaning in the Crucifixion. What is striking about Mark's account (15:34) of the event (found also in Matthew 27:46) is the bleakness of Jesus' final words: "My God, my God, why have you forsaken me?" This is very different from the final words of Jesus reported in other Gospels: "Father, into your hands I commend my spirit" (Luke 23:46) and "It is finished" (John 19:30). Mark presents a Jesus with whom even a hearer in the depths of despair can identify. And yet the Gospels do not allow despair to be the final word. For they offer the hope that just as Jesus was raised from the dead, so may be those who have faith in him.

As the story continues (John 20), some of the disciples came to Jesus' grave after three days, only to find an empty tomb. Later, Jesus appeared among them, displaying

"Love your enemies and pray for those who persecute you, so you may be children of your Father in heaven; for he makes his sun rise on the evil and on the good, and sends rain on the righteous and on the unrighteous."

—NRSV, Matthew 5:44–45

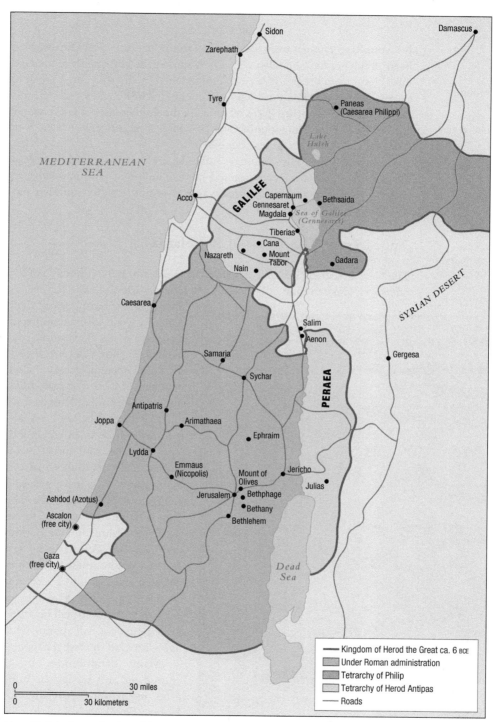

MEDITERRANEAN
SEA

Sidon

Damascus

Zarephath

Tyre

Paneas
(Caesarea Philippi)

Lake
Huleh

GALILEE

Acco

Capernaum
Gennesaret
Magdala

Bethsaida

Sea of Galilee
(Gennesaret)

Tiberias

Cana

Nazareth

Mount
Tabor

Gadara

Nain

SYRIAN DESERT

Caesarea

Salim

Aenon

Samaria

PERAEA

Gergesa

Sychar

Antipatris

Joppa

Arimathaea

Ephraim

Lydda

Emmaus
(Nicopolis)

Mount of
Olives

Jericho

Jerusalem

Bethphage

Julias

Ashdod (Azotus)

Bethany

Ascalon
(free city)

Bethlehem

Gaza
(free city)

Dead
Sea

	Kingdom of Herod the Great ca. 6 BCE
	Under Roman administration
	Tetrarchy of Philip
	Tetrarchy of Herod Antipas
	Roads

0   30 miles

0   30 kilometers

Map 4.1 Palestine at the time of Jesus.

his wounds to prove it truly was he, risen from the dead. Now the disciples, who had been afraid, began to be filled with a new spirit—the Holy Spirit of the God who had raised Jesus from the dead (Acts 2). Emboldened by this spirit they began to proclaim the message of the risen Lord who had conquered death and would return very soon. At this **Second Coming**, Jesus would raise the dead, judge the heavens and the earth, and inaugurate the Kingdom of God, in which all injustice would be overcome and suffering and death would be no more.

In a world filled with injustice, suffering, and death under the oppressive rule of the Romans, such a message inspired hope. The life of Jesus presented people with a story of suffering and tragedy that was real yet not final, for suffering and death are overcome in the resurrection.

Second Coming: belief that Jesus will return at the end of time to establish a new heaven and a new earth

Apocalypse: The Book of Revelation

The New Testament not only describes the life, death, and resurrection of Jesus but also offers a vivid description of how Jesus will return as Messiah. The *Apocalypse* or *Book of Revelation* is the last book of the New Testament (*Apocalypsis*, a transliteration of the Greek word for "revelation," leads to the familiar English title, *Apocalypse*). According to the opening chapter it is written by a man named John who had visions given to him on the island of Patmos.

Illustration of Jesus healing a leper from a biblical manuscript found at Mount Athos Monastery in Greece.

The plot of the book reveals that God is bringing time to an end in a final resurrection of the dead and a final judgment, and the churches must remain faithful and be prepared. First there will be a reign of 1,000 years of peace. Then there will be a great battle between the forces of good (led by the Messiah) and the forces of evil (led by Satan). After a battle against Satan and his minions, these forces of evil will be defeated and cast into a lake of fire. Then all suffering, death, and injustice will be destroyed; the dead will be raised; and the New Jerusalem will appear, where all will live with God in eternal happiness.

Many communities in the early church did not accept the book as genuine revelation, especially among the Eastern Greek-speaking churches. Eventually the Latin churches of European

Christianity accepted it, but even as late as the Protestant Reformation in the sixteenth century, Luther questioned whether it really belonged. The Book of Revelation has struck both fear and hope in the hearts of its readers over the centuries as they have puzzled over the possible meanings of its mysterious symbolism and whether it is to be read literally or symbolically. In the New Testament itself, Jesus is quoted as saying that no one knows the day or hour of the coming end of time, not even he, only his Father in heaven (Matthew 24:36). Despite this, the book's vivid and often violent descriptions of signs of the coming end of the world have led many Christians in later centuries to believe its descriptions suggested the end was coming in their own time.

God and Satan: Zoroastrianism and the Biblical Tradition

In the early biblical tradition, Satan, as we see in the Book of Job (chapters 1 and 2), is a member of God's court who acts as an *adversary* (the meaning of the word *satan*), and who can do nothing without God's permission. God gives Satan permission to send misfortune into Job's life but forbids him from taking his life. God does this to test Job's faithfulness but in the end rewards Job for remaining faithful. By the time of the emergence of Christianity in the first century, a new popular mythology of evil asserted that Satan, acting in rebellion, seeks to defeat God and God's intentions for salvation. In the Christian Gospels, Satan is portrayed as the enemy of the Kingdom of God or Kingdom of Heaven. He tempts Jesus (Matthew 4:1–11) and incites his enemies. Jesus, himself, is portrayed as an exorcist who can cast out those demons who serve the Devil's purposes.

The imagery of Zoroastrianism seems to inspire these new biblical accounts of the nature of evil. Zoroastrianism emerged as a religious phenomenon in Persia in the time approximately parallel to that between Moses in the thirteenth century BCE and the Babylonian Exile in the sixth century BCE. These Persian teachings are attributed to a prophet/teacher known as Zoroaster or

Zarathustra. The revelations given to Zarathustra are contained in scriptures called Gathas, which also contain other later materials from the Zoroastrian tradition offered by the *magi*—its hereditary priestly caste (reference to the magi is found in the birth story of Jesus in the Gospel of Matthew 2:1–12).

The complete book of Zoroastrianism is known as the Avesta and includes the Gathas, as well as the rituals and laws of the Zoroastrian tradition. The Gathas reveal the wisdom and benevolent power of Ahura Mazda, the "Wise Lord." The beneficent power of Ahura Mazda is opposed by another power, that of Angra Mainyu. If the first represents the highest power of Good in the universe, the latter represents the opposing power of Evil. Zoroastrians saw the universe as a struggle in time between Good and Evil—the holy spirit and the evil spirit—which will end with the final victory of Good over Evil at the end of time. As Zoroastrian cosmogony developed, human history was said to be predetermined to last 12,000 years. Zoroastrians developed a view of final judgment for each person leading to either a heavenly existence or punishment in a hell-like state until the end of time, when evil will be overcome and all will

continued

God and Satan: Zoroastrianism and the Biblical Tradition *continued*

be redeemed. This struggle between good and evil culminates in the final 3,000 years in which a savior figure is born for each thousand-year period, ending finally in the resurrection of the dead, the exile of Evil, and the creation of a new world and eternal life.

Zoroastrianism was eventually challenged in Persia by the seventh century CE emergence and spread of Islam. Islamic persecution of Zoroastrians followed, and many sought refuge in other lands. Today, the total world population of Zoroastrians is very small, estimated at about 200,000.

Joyful Iranian Zoroastrians celebrate the ancient midwinter Sadeh festival around a ritual fire near Tehran in January 2012.

Christianity's Emergence from Judaism

Jesus was born a Jew, lived as a Jew, and died as a Jew. His gentile (non-Jewish) followers, however, thought that Jews did not understand his message. As a consequence, what began as a way of understanding Judaism was embraced almost exclusively by gentiles, who thought of themselves as practicing a new and improved faith—Christianity. These gentile Christians came to teach what scholars call the myth of supersession—that God had rejected the Jews and chosen gentiles instead. It was a myth that would endure until the twentieth century.

Christianity, in fact, began as a Jewish sectarian movement. After 2,000 years of biblical history, especially after the Babylonian exile (586–538 BCE), a variety of movements (discussed in Chapter 3) developed in Judaism. There was no agreement on a common set of sacred writings among them. Only at the end of the first century of the common era did the Hebrew Bible as we know it come into existence, largely owing to the influence of the Pharisees and the Hellenists. At the beginning of the century, however, these groups and others were engaged in an ongoing argument about the right way of life for the people of Israel. Each movement saw itself as the correct model and all others as deviant. The result was a diverse set of sectarian movements, each proclaiming a message something like this: "We are the true Israel (i.e., the true Jews); you are not. The end of the world is at hand when God will come to judge the heaven and the earth. Jews who have strayed, who are thus no better than pagans, must repent and be ritually immersed. Then they will become true Israel again—true Jews who live the way we do." Until this time, the baptismal rite of ritual immersion and purification had been required only of non-Jewish converts to Judaism (along with circumcision for males).

Essential to the emergence of Christianity from Judaism is the preaching and teaching of Paul of Tarsus, a Pharisee and Hellenistic Jew. Without Paul, Christianity would not be the religion we are familiar with today. Paul of Tarsus at first treated the movement that began with the rabbi Jesus as a heretical form of Judaism, and he persecuted its followers. Yet he eventually came to argue that Christianity was not really a heresy but a way for gentiles to share in the promises made by God to the Jews. Paul, who came to be known as an apostle of Jesus, was not one of the original twelve apostles selected by Jesus and never met Jesus before his crucifixion. He came to know Jesus as the risen Lord after an extraordinary encounter on the road to Damascus, an experience that led him to change his message. Paul became the first great missionary of the Christian movement, and we know of Paul's thoughts and actions primarily from his letters to the churches that he founded in places like the ancient Greek cities of Corinth and Ephesus. These letters form approximately one-fourth of the New Testament.

Throughout history the Crucifixion has captured the imagination of great artists such as Matthias Grünewald, creator of this sixteenth-century altarpiece now in Isenheim, Germany.

Paul was born in what today is Turkey and educated in Jerusalem. Hellenistic Jews were very successful missionaries to the gentiles in first-century Judaism. They presented Judaism as open to Greek patterns of thought and behavior. When Paul became a convert to the Nazarene movement, as a Hellenistic Jew he continued this Hellenistic missionary activity but with a new twist: He argued that the task of the followers of Jesus was to bring the gentiles into Judaism as a "wild olive branch" grafted onto a cultivated olive tree of Judaism (Romans 11:16–18). Through Jesus, Paul taught, the gentiles were now called to share with the Jews in the promises made to Abraham (Ephesians 2:11–22). After the fall of the Jewish temple in Jerusalem (ca. 70 CE), this teaching was ignored in favor of the anti-Jewish view that gentile Christians supersede or take the place of the Jews as God's chosen people. Tradition says that Paul was martyred in Rome, probably around the year 60 CE.

The Fall of the Temple

First-century Judaism changed dramatically in the year 70 CE, when the Romans marched into Jerusalem, burned down the temple, and drove the Jews out of their holy city. In the aftermath of the fall of the temple, two movements emerged to shape Western religious history: the Pharisaic movement, which became Rabbinic Judaism, and the Nazarene movement (followers of Jesus of Nazareth), which became gentile Christianity.

The Pharisees survived the destruction of the temple because they were able to provide flexible Jewish leadership under dramatically new conditions. Unlike Pharisaic Judaism, the Nazarene movement never had a large following among Jews. Its greatest success was a missionary movement for the conversion of gentiles. The Nazarenes were an apocalyptic movement, believing that the end of time was at hand and that their special mission was to convert the gentiles before the final judgment. In this they were inspired by the prophecies of Isaiah that in the last days all nations would be gathered into Jerusalem (Isaiah 66:18–20).

A critical issue for the Nazarenes was the status of new gentile converts. This was taken up around the year 48 at a meeting in Jerusalem. The Christian tradition refers to this meeting as the first church council or the "Council of Jerusalem." The conservatives from Jerusalem argued that gentile converts had to be circumcised and obey the whole Mosaic law, as required of other Jews. Paul of Tarsus came to this meeting from Antioch, where he and other Hellenistic Jews were converting large numbers of gentiles. He argued that gentiles should be exempt from the requirement of circumcision and from most of the ritual obligations, focusing instead on obeying the moral commandments of the Mosaic covenant. The faction led by Paul won the argument, and a letter urging these changes went out to all the mission communities (Acts 15:19–21).

This ruling was decisive for the growth of the Nazarene movement among gentiles. Many gentiles who were attracted to Jewish monotheism but reluctant to embrace circumcision and kosher food restrictions then flooded into the movement.

By the second century Jewish-born persons made up a smaller and smaller proportion of the total membership. And as the leadership fell increasingly into the hands of gentiles, the movement lost its sense of identity as a Jewish movement and began to take on a separate identity as a new religion—Christianity.

The Origins of Christian Anti-Jewish Sentiment

We are now in a position to discuss a problem that has plagued the relationship between Jews and Christians throughout the history of Western civilization. The New Testament reflects the context of the Jewish sectarian arguments that had been going on in the first century, in which groups like the Zealots, the Essenes, and the Nazarenes disagreed with each other about who were the "true" Israel, each saying: "We, not you, are the true Israel, the true Jews. Therefore repent, be baptized, and become Jews the way we are, for the end of time and God's judgment are at hand."

These first-century Jewish sectarian arguments were incorporated into the sacred writings of Christianity found in the New Testament. However, when these statements were read and repeated by the leaders of the "Christian" movement in the

TEACHINGS OF RELIGIOUS WISDOM: Paul on Faith, Hope, and Love

With the possible exception of Jesus' Sermon on the Mount, no teaching of Christianity is better known than the apostle Paul's teaching on faith, hope, and love from his letter to the Corinthians (1 Corinthians 13:1–13, New American Bible*). These three—faith, hope, and love—came to be known as the "three cardinal virtues" of Christianity.

If I speak in human and angelic tongues but do not have love, I am a resounding gong or a clashing cymbal. And if I have the gift of prophecy and comprehend all mysteries and all knowledge; if I have all faith so as to move mountains but do not have love, I am nothing. If I give away everything I own, and if I hand my body over so that I may boast but do not have love, I gain nothing.

Love is patient, love is kind. It is not jealous, (love) is not pompous, it is not inflated, it is not rude, it does not seek its own interests, it is not quick-tempered, it does not brood over injury, it does not rejoice over wrongdoing but rejoices with the truth. It bears all things, believes all things, hopes all things, endures all things.

Love never fails. If there are prophecies, they will be brought to nothing; if tongues, they will cease; if knowledge, it will be brought to nothing. For we know partially and we prophesy partially, but when the perfect comes, the partial will pass away. When I was a child, I used to talk as a child, think as a child, reason as a child; when I became a man, I put aside childish things. At present we see indistinctly, as in a mirror, but then face to face. At present I know partially; then I shall know fully, as I am fully known. So faith, hope, love remain, these three; but the greatest of these is love.

second and later centuries, they were no longer seen as exhortations from one Jewish group to another. Now gentiles who had come to identify themselves as Christians saw themselves as the "true Israel" and took up the refrain: "We are the true Israel; you are not." Thus was born the Christian myth of supersession, or divine rejection. Christians now argued: "We Christians have replaced you Jews as God's chosen people. Because you did not recognize Jesus as messiah and had him crucified, God has rejected you and chosen us to supersede you."

In Christianity the teaching of supersession took an especially violent turn. It was disastrously extended to include the claim that not only had God rejected the Jews for all time, but it was the Christian duty to punish them. This view contributed to the persecution of Jews throughout much of Western history. It was not until the time of Vatican II (1962–5) that a commission created by Pope John XXIII condemned the teachings of supersession and divine rejection of the Jews and affirmed Paul's view, that gentiles are like a wild olive branch grafted onto the tree of Judaism to share in God's promises to Abraham. By the end of the twentieth century, most Protestant churches had renounced the teachings of supersession as well.

About the time of the fiftieth anniversary of Vatican II on December 3, 2015, a major statement of Orthodox Jewish leaders from around the world noted the dramatic change in Christian religious teachings and declared Jews ought to welcome this change with a new and more positive account of the relationship between the two religious communities. The separation between the two communities, they declared, is willed by God, to be a separation not between "enemies" but between "partners" sharing a common "covenantal mission" to further "the survival and welfare of humanity."

> "We all with one accord teach . . . the same Christ, Son, Lord, Only-begotten, recognized in two natures, without confusion, without change, without division, without separation; the distinction of natures being in no way annulled by the union . . . coming together to form one person."
>
> —Church Council of Chalcedon

Jesus as Son of God

In the first four centuries after the time of Jesus, Christians struggled to formulate an authoritative understanding, or dogma, of who Jesus is and what his significance is. The essential problem was how to translate an essentially Jewish message about a coming "messiah" into terms non-Jews could understand. These missionaries did not want pagans to confuse Christian claims about Jesus being **Son of God** with pagan myths in which divine beings come down to earth in humanlike bodies. The challenge for missionaries to the gentiles was to speak about the being and meaning of Jesus of Nazareth, the Son of God, without claiming either too little (that Jesus was just a good man) or too much (that Jesus was not really human but rather a supernatural being like the gods of pagan mythology). For about 300 years, Christians debated the various possible ways of thinking and speaking about Jesus and held several church councils. By the time the argument was settled, both extremes had been deemed **heresy**.

The most important councils were those of Nicaea in 325 and Chalcedon in 451. Some argued that Jesus was a divine being who only appeared to be human. Some argued that Jesus had a human body and a divine mind. Still others said that although his mind too was human, he had a divine will. Such views made Jesus a

Son of God: title applied to Jesus of Nazareth. According to the Gospel of Luke 3:38 Jesus is "son of Adam, Son of God"

heresy: negative term in Christianity for choosing to believe in doctrines viewed as erroneous by those who saw themselves as the more "catholic" or "universal"

kind of half-man and half-god, not unlike other characters in pagan mythology. The Council of Chalcedon rejected all such views, insisting that Jesus had a human body and a human mind and will, with a birth and a death like every other person. Jesus' humanity differed from that of others in only one way—he was without sin. Moreover, in this man Jesus, God was wholly present. The formula arrived at to reconcile the apparent paradox was that in the "one person" of Jesus there were "two natures" (divine and human) united "without confusion" or mixture. That is, in the person of Jesus divinity and humanity were united yet completely distinct.

Two beliefs had to be held together in this formula, that of Nicaea—that the Word through which all things were created was the "same as" (**homoousios**) God (i.e., eternal)—and that of Chalcedon—that the man Jesus was a mortal human being to whom was united that eternal Word (which had existed before its incarnation in the man Jesus). If the Word was not eternal, it could not confer eternity; and if Jesus was not mortal, his resurrection offered no hope to other mortals. This formula was meant to combat Gnostic Christian views, eventually declared heretical, to the effect that Jesus was a divine being (i.e., pure spirit)—a god who only appeared to be a "flesh and blood" human being and therefore could not really have died on the cross, nor would it have been necessary for him to arise from the dead.

> **homoousios:** Greek term for the belief that the Word of God through which all things were created is "the same as" God

The formula of two natures in one person developed at Chalcedon was complemented by another unique doctrine or belief of Christians—the belief in a triune (three in one) God, which had been affirmed at the Council of Constantinople in 381. The doctrine of the **Trinity** asserts that God is one essence but three persons. The formula "three persons in one God: Father, Son, and Holy Spirit" is symbolic and not really about mathematics. It means that God, the creator of the universe, can at the same time be present in the life of Jesus and in all things in the world through God's Word and Spirit without ceasing to be transcendent or beyond the universe. The doctrine of the Trinity is meant to explain that God is *in* all things without accepting the pantheistic notion that God *is* all things.

> **Trinity:** God as Father, Son, and Holy Spirit; God is not many gods but one God in three persons

Jews and Muslims, with their theology of a prophetic monotheism, according to which God is one and not three, have typically misunderstood the meaning of the doctrine of the Trinity. But then so have many Christians. Nevertheless, the intent of both the **"two natures, one person"** doctrine, concerning Jesus, and the doctrine of the Trinity, concerning God, is to affirm the uniqueness of a God who is both present in and transcendent to the cosmos. This is the true God who has no equals—the God of Abraham who is affirmed by Jews and Muslims.

> **two natures, one person:** doctrine that in the one person of Jesus are two natures (divine and human) coexisting in unity but without mixture

Constantinianism: The Marriage of Christianity and Empire

Perhaps the single most important political event in the history of Christianity was the conversion of the Roman emperor Constantine, the first monarch to champion the rights of Christians. Constantine, who issued the Edict of Milan in 313, was baptized on his deathbed. With this edict, Christianity went from being an often-persecuted religion to a permitted (and eventually the favored) religion in the empire.

Constantinian: under the first Christian Roman emperor, Constantine and through the Emperor Theodosius, the view that the emperor rules over both the church and the state, calls church councils and protects the church as the official religion of the Roman Empire

Up until this point, many Christians had tended to look at Roman civilization, with its imperialism and colonial domination of foreign territories, as the work of the devil. After Constantine, Christians began to see Roman imperialism as a good thing, as a way of spreading the Gospel throughout the world. The **Constantinian** vision achieved the status of official political policy in 380, when Christianity became the official religion of the Roman Empire under Emperor Theodosius. Within ten years, pagan worship was declared illegal and all pagan temples were closed. Only Judaism was permitted as an alternative to Christianity, and it existed under severe legal restrictions, with Jews losing many of the freedoms they had had under pagan Rome.

The Greek-speaking churches of the East took Constantine's relationship to the church as a model of how things should be. There were four great centers of Orthodoxy: Constantinople, Alexandria (Egypt), Antioch (Syria), and Jerusalem, each ruled by a patriarch. In the Eastern Byzantine part of the Roman Empire, centered in Constantinople, church and state existed symbiotically. The Christian emperor called church councils and even appointed the bishops. The emperor ruled over both church and state in the name of Christ.

However, the pattern of Western civilization that shaped the road to modernity was not that of Orthodox Christianity from the East but an important modification of it that put church and empire in a precarious relationship. The Constantinian model thrived in Byzantium until the fifteenth century. In the West, Roman political rule collapsed after the time of Theodosius. The political vacuum created by the absence

The Constantinian unification of church and state is illustrated in this Roman mosaic showing the Roman emperor at the center as the unifying ruler of both the state (on his right) and the church (on his left).

of an emperor in the West allowed the bishops of the Latin-speaking churches to assume much greater independence. The idea of separation between church and state developed. The bishop of Rome's power and authority grew as secular Roman political power and authority collapsed, leading to the idea of the primacy of the bishop of Rome as *pope* (father) over all other bishops.

Augustine, Architect of Western Christianity

From the fifth century through the emergence of modernity, the West has been deeply influenced by the theological thought of Augustine of Hippo, whom Christians typically refer to as St. Augustine. After Jesus and the apostle Paul, probably no other individual in history is more responsible for the shape of Western Christianity. Augustine's vision shaped the development of Roman Catholicism from the fifth through the twelfth centuries. Then he was eclipsed by Thomas Aquinas, only to be recovered by the Protestant reformers Luther and Calvin in the sixteenth century, who drew heavily on Augustine's writings.

Constantine died in 337. Augustine, who was born in 354 and died in 430, lived through the time of Theodosius and witnessed firsthand the transformation of the Roman Empire from a pagan empire into a Christian one in 380. This stunning transformation could not fail to impress contemporary observers, who could not believe that the pagan Roman Empire had become Christian through mere chance. They concluded instead that God intended to use the Roman Empire to provide the political unity and stability needed to spread the Gospel to the ends of the earth.

For centuries, Christians have turned to Augustine's spiritual autobiography, *The Confessions* (400), as a model of conversion and piety. Rulers of church and state have also long turned to his book *The City of God* (423) as a model for the political order. Indeed, Charlemagne, who on December 25, 800, became the first Holy Roman emperor, is said to have slept with a copy of *The City of God* under his pillow. The influence of *The Confessions* and *The City of God* on the history of European Christianity and European society is so vast that it is almost impossible to calculate.

The Confessions: *Faith, Reason, and the Quest for Wisdom*

A key turning point in Augustine's life, as he relates it, was the awakening of his mind and heart to a passion for wisdom when he was nineteen years old. Before that event, the young man had devoted himself to fulfilling selfish desires (*cupiditas*) for wealth, fame, power, and sexual pleasure. About the time Augustine was completing his studies in Carthage in Africa, he came across a book entitled *Hortensius*, by the pagan Roman author Cicero. This book, says Augustine, set him on fire with a new kind of desire (*caritas*)—the selfless desire for wisdom.

Augustine resolved to follow his doubts and questions wherever they might lead him. Augustine doesn't say that *Hortensius* changed his thinking but, rather, that it "altered my way of feeling . . . and gave me different ambitions and desires" (III, 4). Augustine's wording here is very important. His experience changed his feelings and desires, which

"I was not encouraged by this work of Cicero's to join this or that sect; instead I was urged on and inflamed with a passionate zeal to love and seek and obtain and embrace and hold fast wisdom itself, whatever it might be."

—Augustine, *Confessions,* Book III

in turn changed his thinking and eventually led to his full conversion. Christianity is a religion of the transformation of the heart as the symbolic location of the emotions. In the first century, Jesus had called his hearers to undergo a change of heart, and virtually every great reform and renewal movement in Christian history has returned to this theme.

Augustine's story of his conversion became a model for understanding the relationship between faith and reason. Theology, he said, is "faith seeking understanding." Some interpretations to the contrary, this does not mean "you first have to believe to be able to understand." Rather, you will be led to deeper understanding if you have faith and trust that God is working, through your doubts, to lead you to deeper understanding. In his *Confessions* Augustine says that only after his full conversion did he come to realize that when he had the faith to doubt, he already had an implicit faith in Christ, who was leading him to find true wisdom.

The City of God: *Augustine's Tale of Two Cities*

In the same way that *The Confessions* provided a model for faith and reason, *The City of God* provided a model for church and state. The meaning of history is unraveled for Augustine by a symbolic reading of the biblical stories as a history of two cities that exist side by side in history—the human city and the city of God. These two cities are guided by two different loves, *cupiditas* (selfish love) and *caritas* (selfless love). (These, of course, are the same two loves Augustine saw at war in his own life in his *Confessions*.) Augustine's formulation of the appropriate relationship of these cities provided the decisive model of relations between church and state, religion and politics, and sacred and secular for most of Western history.

For Augustine the story of the human city was the story of the history of civilizations going through endless cycles of progress and decline—a story without any clear purpose or meaning. But hidden within that history was another story—that of the city of God. This story, which is revealed in the Bible, has a clear purpose and direction. It is the story of a journey with God through time toward a final resurrection and eternal life for all who belong to the city of God. The city of God, however, was not the same as the church. In Augustine's view, some within the institution were not faithful believers while others outside of it were. Only at the final judgment will human beings come to know who truly belongs to the city of God.

In defining the relationship between the two cities Augustine argues that both state and church exist through God's will to serve God's purposes. God uses the state to establish the peace necessary for the spread of the Gospel by the church. In the journey through history each entity should serve the other. The state should be subject to the church in spiritual matters, and the church should be subject to the state in earthly matters. Neither should seek to dominate the other. However, in actual history the sides could never fully agree on where to draw the line between earthly matters and spiritual matters. Indeed, throughout most of Western history both popes and emperors maneuvered to upset the balance between the two by trying to dictate to the other.

The **Augustinian** vision is not yet the modern one that insists on a secular, or nonreligious, state that promotes religious pluralism and "freedom of religion."

Augustinian: views of St. Augustine emphasizing the separation of church and state, pope and emperor, rather than a Constantinian unity of authority over both in the emperor

On the contrary, he assumes that the two powers will work together to achieve a worldwide Christian civilization. Since the time of Augustine, most Christians have assumed that the task of Christianity is to transform every society into a "Christian society" comprising two branches: church and state. This pattern continued even after the Holy Roman Empire collapsed and the Protestant Reformation helped usher in the modern era. In more recent times, modern European culture replaced Roman civilization as the political order thought to be willed by God for the purpose of spreading Christianity around the world. Only gradually, after the religious wars the Protestant Reformation provoked, did Christians begin to explore an alternative—the modern idea of a secular, or nonreligious, state as the guarantor of freedom to worship in a religiously pluralistic world. We will return to this observation when we discuss modernization.

The Eastern Orthodox Churches

While our main emphasis is on Latin (Western) Christianity, because that is the form of Christianity that fostered the emergence of modernity, the Eastern churches have great historical and cultural significance. The earliest churches of Christianity were in communities that spoke Greek, not Latin. By the fourth and fifth centuries the Latin-speaking churches grew in number and influence to rival the Orthodox. The Greek churches did not accept the central authority of one bishop that the Roman churches affirmed. All the bishops answered to the emperor, but internally these churches were conciliar, placing ultimate authority not in a single bishop (a pope) but in church councils as meetings of all the bishops. The fifteenth-century Council of Constance, as we will see, tried to reassert a conciliar view of the church in the West.

Eastern Orthodox Christianity was distinctive for its mystical emphasis: Christ became human, it is said, so that humans could become divinized and share mystically in the eternal life of God—a process known as *theosis*. Orthodoxy is also distinctive for its understanding of sin as ignorance rather than as corruption of the will through original sin as put forward in Latin-Augustinian Christianity. For the Orthodox churches, Christ is the great teacher who comes to dispel human ignorance of oneness with God and to restore humans to mystical unity with the creator. The emphasis is not on Christ as the lord of History but on the cosmic Christ through whom all things are created, held together, and brought to fulfillment. From the beginning there was tension between the Eastern and Western churches, but a formal split did not occur until 1054.

This fifteenth-century miniature painting by Nicola Polani depicts Augustine writing *The City of God*.

Premodern Christianity:
The Classical Era (451–1517 CE)

Less than a century after the time of Augustine of Hippo, the Roman Empire and its civilization collapsed in the West. Over several centuries Europe was invaded by tribes from the north; and as tribal leaders upgraded themselves into lords of their domains, feudalism began to take shape. The feudal system was a network of loyalties established between a landholder (a king or a nobleman) and those who served him and his estates. It was a hierarchical arrangement, with the nobility on the top, subordinates (called vassals) in the middle, and serfs and slaves at the bottom. The nobles were members of either a secular warrior aristocracy or the religious aristocracy, for the church was a major landholder and church officials (bishops) too could be feudal lords.

The Middle Ages roughly span the sixth through the fourteenth centuries. It was a world without printing presses, and so the few existing books were handwritten. Only the elite among the clergy and the nobility could read, in any event. The average Christian got his or her religious view of life from sermons delivered by priests and from images depicted in the stained glass windows and on the walls of the churches and cathedrals. During this period, the church carried civilization forward into Europe, accomplishing this primarily through the spread of Christian monasteries. It was monasticism that provided the bridge of civilization between the ancient world and the modern world, bringing technological development and the light of learning to a European period that has been otherwise described as the Dark Ages.

Before the printing press was invented, all books were written by hand. Depicted is a medieval monk transcribing a text at his desk.

Monasticism was the first serious reform movement in the church. Once Christianity became the official religion of the Roman Empire, many who became Christians did so for reasons of expediency rather than piety. By the late third century, members of the Eastern (Greek) churches who wanted to lead an exemplary Christian life often felt they had to separate themselves from the corrupt world around them, moving into the desert to live simply, with much time for prayer. Gregory I, the first medieval pope, was born to aristocracy but abandoned his privileges to become a monk in the desert.

By the late fourth century, monastic communities had spread to the Western (Latin) churches. Whenever Christianity tended to grow corrupt with worldly power and success, it was monasticism that provided reform movements to call the church back to its spiritual mission. It was the beginning of a pattern. Whereas Greek Orthodox monasticism was supported by church and state, the Latin communities were set up according to the model of Benedict of Nursia (480–543). These were self-supporting communities of work and prayer under the leadership of an abbot. In the ancient world work was viewed as a task for slaves, but Benedict taught that "to work is to pray" and integrated physical labor into the daily schedule of group prayer and private devotions. The Benedictine monasteries preserved and developed not only spiritual knowledge but also ancient learning and technology. The Benedictines were the great engineers of the Middle Ages, developing impressive waterwheel and windmill technologies to improve the monks' productivity. The goal was to make work more efficient so that there would be more time for prayer. Thus, the monasteries brought to the West not only spiritual renewal but also intellectual and technological advances, making profound contributions to the full flowering of technological civilization in the modern period.

> "Idleness is the enemy of the soul; and there-fore the brethren ought to be employed in manual labor at certain times, at others, in devout reading."
> —*The Holy Rule of St. Benedict*, chapter 48.
>
> SOURCE: Rev. Boniface Verheyen, OSB, trans. *The Holy Rule of St. Benedict*, 1949 edition.

The Medieval Worldview: Sacraments and Festivals

In the medieval world, life on earth was seen as a test and a place of waiting to enter one's true home in heaven. Christians believed that when they died their souls would be separated from their bodies and would come before God for individual judgment. When at some future time the world would end, Jesus would return to raise the bodies of the dead and unite them with their souls. Those who had been faithful and good would be rewarded for all eternity in heaven, enjoying the "beatific vision" or presence of God; the rest would be doomed to eternal punishment in hell.

The church was God's gift to this world to help Christians prepare for their final judgment. The church was founded by Jesus Christ, who had passed on leadership of the church to his chief apostle, Peter (Matthew 16:18). This apostolic succession was continued by the popes, who were seen as the direct successors of Peter, guaranteeing that the church would be divinely guided because the pope speaks with the authority of Christ on earth. The Catholic Church claimed that apostolic succession proved that it alone was the one true church and that its task was to confer God's guiding and protecting grace upon all believers through the sacraments.

Sacraments

Through the descending hierarchy of the pope, the bishops, and the lower clergy, as Christ's priesthood, the **grace** of God was conferred on humankind, mediated to every Christian through seven **sacraments**: baptism, confirmation, Holy Eucharist (communion), marriage, ordination (holy orders), confession, and extreme unction. These sacraments were taken to be the outward and visible signs of God's inward, invisible grace (forgiveness and assistance), helping Christians grow spiritually and morally toward holiness or saintliness. Because the sacraments could be administered only by ordained clergy, every Christian was dependent on the priests and bishops of the church, under the rule of the pope, to be in a right relationship to God.

> **grace:** the idea of unmerited divine love and assistance given to humans

> **sacraments:** ritual materials and actions (such as pouring water over an infant at baptism), usually through mediation of ordained clergy, said to impart the grace of God to Christians

RITUALS AND RITES: Festivals

If the sacraments carried Christians from cradle to grave, the annual cycle of religious festivals carried them through the seasons of the year. and created for them a world of stories in which to dwell. The early church saw itself as living in the time between Easter and the advent, or "Second Coming" (Parousia) of Jesus Christ to raise the dead and judge the heavens and the earth. By the Middle Ages a church calendar had developed to immerse the faithful in a cycle of festivals and stories that reminded Christians of their origin and destiny. The church year began with Advent, whose stories evoke hope for the Second Coming. Next, Christmas and Epiphany were festival seasons designed to celebrate the stories of the birth of Jesus, the visit of the wise men from the East, and the baptism of Jesus. (No one knew the date on which Jesus was born; December 25 was chosen to compete with a popular pagan festival honoring the sun god.)

Children reenacting the nativity story.

The season of Christmas/Epiphany is followed by Lent, a time of penitence, fasting, and prayer in preparation for Easter. Its stories recall the temptations, healings, and teachings of Jesus. Lent culminates in Holy Week, in which the stories of Jesus' trial and death are recalled. In the Easter season, the church retells the stories of the resurrection and the subsequent appearances of Jesus to his disciples. The final season of the church year, Pentecost, recalls the descent of the Holy Spirit upon the apostles and the birth and growth of the church. After Pentecost, of course, comes Advent again and a new year of hope and expectation. Thus, for many centuries the cycle of festivals has allowed Christians to dwell in a world of stories that tie and bind them into the great cosmic drama in which God is bringing salvation to the whole world.

Medieval Christians were grounded in the sacraments and oriented by the festivals. They also sought divine aid through prayers to the saints and angels in heaven. That is, they prayed that exemplary Christians (saints) who had died and other spiritual beings, known as angels, would present their petitions to God in heaven. This was, after all, how things got done in medieval feudal society. If you wanted a favor from a member of the nobility or the king, it was best to ask someone at court to intercede for you. Hierarchies of saints and angels were believed to exist in heaven and to work in a similar fashion. On the other hand, it was believed that the angels who rebelled against God (Satan and his minions) exercised an evil influence over human beings that must be resisted through the power of prayer and the sacraments.

In this medieval worldview, we see the full integration of the biblical worldview of life, death, and resurrection of the body with the Greek metaphysical worldview of the cosmos as a hierarchical order. It forms the essence of the Catholic worldview. Lacking the historical consciousness that came after the Renaissance, medieval Christians thought this amalgamated worldview was exactly what Jesus had proclaimed in the Gospels.

rone des haultes œuures du noble Charlemaine roy de fran

De plusieurs batailles que Charlemaine eut alencontre

A depiction of the coronation of Charlemagne as the first Holy Roman Emperor by Pope Leo III on Christmas Day in the year 800 CE.

The Two Cities Revisited

Throughout the Middle Ages there was a struggle between the two cities that Augustine had described. From the time of the Holy Roman Emperor Charlemagne (800–14), the emperors sought to dominate the church and the popes sought to dominate the state. A turning point in the development of the power of the papacy was its emulation of a monastic model of church discipline that originated in France. Because Benedictine monasticism had a strong work ethic, many monasteries became great centers of wealth, which in turn led to abuses. In 910 a new reform movement swept through monasticism, and a new monastery was founded at Cluny, in east central France. The Cluny reforms aimed at spiritual renewal and reorganization.

In addition to their emphasis on spirituality, the Cluniac monasteries provided an important organizational model for the development of colonialism, first adopted by the church and later emulated by such secular institutions of modernity as the multinational corporation. Whereas each Benedictine monastery was a world unto itself, under its own abbot, all the Cluniac monasteries, regardless of location, were answerable to a central command—the monastic headquarters in Cluny. Under Pope Gregory VII (1073–85), Rome adopted this new form of organization, thus imposing papal authority, centered in Rome, over all the bishops in the church.

RITUALS AND RITES: The Seven Sacraments and the Life Cycle

The word *sacrament* comes from a Latin translation of the Greek word for "mystery," a term borrowed from first-century pagan cults known as mystery religions, whose rituals were performed in the hope of achieving immortality.

With the coming of the Protestant Reformation in the sixteenth century, only baptism and communion retained the status of sacraments. The other five rituals were rejected by Protestants on the ground that they could not be found as such in the New Testament. However, many of these "rejected" practices are observed in some Protestant denominations as rituals but not as sacraments in the full sense.

Baptism

The early Christians followed the Jewish practice of ritual immersion for new gentile converts in which the person's whole body was submerged in a river, lake, or special pool. For Christians, however, full submersion was seen as participation in Christ's death in the tomb; the emergence of the body from the water was equated with Christ's resurrection and departure from the tomb. The submersion was accompanied by the words "I baptize you in the name of the Father, the Son, and the Holy Spirit." As the practice of infant baptism developed in later generations, pouring of water over the baby's forehead was adopted as an alternative. Both types of baptism are still performed today.

This ritual is believed to flood the soul with divine grace (divine love, forgiveness, and assistance), erasing all stain of original sin. Baptism changed one's destiny from death to eternal life.

Communion

Equal in sacramental importance was the Eucharist, or Holy Communion. This practice seems to have been an adaptation of the Jewish blessing of the bread and wine at meals, especially as it was practiced at Passover, the Jewish remembrance of the people's deliverance by God from slavery in Egypt. In the Gospels, at Jesus' last Passover, he broke the bread, blessed it, and said, "This is my body." He blessed the wine, too, and told his disciples, "This is the cup of my blood, shed for you and for many for the forgiveness of sins." By eating the bread and drinking the wine consecrated by a priest or minister who represents Jesus, Christians believe they are partaking of the body and blood of Jesus (for some literally, for others spiritually), who died for their sins on the cross and brought them to eternal life. Both baptism and communion were established well before the Middle Ages.

Confirmation

The first converts to Christianity were adults who made a conscious decision to be baptized and to follow Christ. As the practice of infant baptism developed, so did a controversy over whether this was appropriate, since the infant was too young to make a conscious choice. Infant baptism, it was decided, signifies that God is choosing the child

Anglican Bishop Desmond Tutu, a Nobel Peace Prize winner, gives children communion during mass in Saint-Barnabas Church in South Africa.

rather than that the child is choosing God. At some point, however, a young Christian was expected to make a conscious choice to live for Christ. In the ritual of confirmation, young people at about the age of thirteen demonstrated their knowledge of the faith, were anointed on the forehead with oil, and made a public declaration of commitment to Christ. Thus, young adults were *confirmed* in the faith, accepting responsibility for the commitment made for them by the Christian community at baptism.

Marriage

During the Middle Ages, marriage was transformed from a civil proceeding into a sacrament. The union between a man and a woman came to be compared to the union between Christ and the church. As such it became more than a union between the couple for the purpose of raising a family. It became a ritual for uniting the spouses to each other in Christ. The husband and wife promised to love and care for each other as Christ loved and cared for his church.

Holy Orders

In the Middle Ages, a ritual also developed for inducting men into the priesthood. Bishops, Christ's representatives in the community of the faithful, ordained others, priests, to assist them in their pastoral work. In the ritual of ordination, bishops anointed the new priests' hands with oil to symbolize their sacred role in conferring the grace of God upon their parishioners through the administration of the sacraments. Bishops themselves were consecrated to their new office by the laying on of hands by other bishops.

Until the late Middle Ages, ordained priests could also be married. In the Western church, later reforms established the requirement that priests remain unmarried, or celibate. From this point on a man had to choose between the sacrament of marriage and that of ordination. In the Eastern church priests have always been allowed to marry, but bishops must be celibate.

Confession and Extreme Unction/Anointing of the Sick

Two additional sacraments were developed during the Middle Ages: confession, to mediate God's forgiveness for sin, and extreme unction (anointing of the sick), to confer God's power of healing in times of illness. In the early church it was common for people to put off baptism until death was near, for fear that sins committed after baptism could not then be washed away. To encourage baptism in infancy, the church developed a sacrament for the forgiveness of sins: The penitent would confess his or her sins and express true sorrow for them to a priest, who would then absolve the person, that is, forgive their sins in the name of Christ, thereby reconciling the sinner with God. The priest would also assign an appropriate penance for the absolved sinner to complete in reparation for his or her sins; for example, to repeat certain prayers or make a pilgrimage to a sacred place and resolve not to fall into sin again.

Closely associated with the practice of confession was the anointing of the sick with oil. In cases of serious illness, a priest would be called to anoint the Christian with oil in hopes of mediating God's grace to heal the person. Since this ritual of healing was administered to a person who was near death, it was called "extreme unction" and came to be thought of as the sacrament of those in danger of dying.

"Christ has no
body now but
yours. . . . Yours are
the feet with which
he walks to do good.
Yours are the hands
through which he
blesses all the world."

—St. Teresa of Avila

The height of papal power occurred under Pope Innocent III (1198–1216), who forced the kings of England and France into submission, authorized the Fourth Crusade, and launched an immensely punitive inquisition against all heretics without interference from civil authorities. Innocent actually had both absolute spiritual power over the church and temporal political power over the state, to which the papacy had long aspired.

The Promise and Threat of Christian Mysticism

Christianity has a long tradition of mysticism; that is, beliefs and practices thought to lead to a direct and immediate experience of God in Christ. Christian mysticism expresses itself in two dramatically different forms—the mysticism of love and union (the divine–human marriage) and the mysticism of identity. The former is exemplified by Spanish mystics of the sixteenth century, Teresa of Avila and her student, John of the Cross; the latter by the German mystic Meister Eckhart. Unlike early Christian theology, Christian mysticism has for centuries been enriched by the contributions of women: Teresa of Avila, Catherine of Siena, Therese of Lisieux, and Julian of Norwich, to name a few. In part this is because mystical experience is viewed as a gift from God that cannot be institutionally controlled. Consequently, it unleashes a powerful impulse toward equality. The mystical experience is accessible to male and female without distinction—all are equally in the image of the God without image.

As with the Jewish tradition, mysticism in Christianity has been viewed ambivalently. This is because some mystics seem to speak as if they are not just in union with God but, in some sense, *are* God, as sometimes seems to be the case for the mysticism of identity. Yet despite this strain of what some consider to be blasphemy, Christianity has continued to affirm the validity and importance of mysticism.

Christianity, Judaism, Islam: Crusades and Inquisition

Islam, which emerged from the Arabian desert in the early 600s, grew within the span of a century into a civilization larger than the Roman Empire had been. For a time the Muslims seemed poised to proceed east of Spain to conquer most of Europe. But Charles Martel, whose initiative led to the formation of the Carolingian dynasty and the Holy Roman Empire, turned the Muslims back at Tours in 732. Europe remained Christian, but its holy sites, in Palestine, were in the hands of Muslims.

The Crusades were meant to change that. There were four main Crusades, in 1095, 1147, 1189, and 1202. Armies were organized to march to the Holy Land (Jerusalem and surrounding territories) and free it from the Muslims. But as the crusading armies marched through Europe they unleashed devastating violence on the Jewish communities they encountered along the way. Fed by ancient Christian stereotypes of Jews as a "rejected people," the Crusaders killed an estimated 10,000 Jews in Germany alone during the First Crusade.

As the Crusaders advanced toward Jerusalem, considerable violence was done even to Orthodox Christians, whom papal troops considered semi-heretics. The Muslims were the Crusaders' primary targets, however, for they held the Holy Land in their possession and threatened the Eastern church, whose main center was Constantinople. Thus the Crusades were ostensibly for the purpose of driving back the Muslims, reclaiming Jerusalem, and reuniting the Eastern and Western branches of the church. Pope Urban II, who preached the First Crusade, promised that all soldiers who participated would have their sins forgiven and would enter heaven. In addition, Crusaders were promised that they could keep the lands they conquered. The Crusaders laid siege to Jerusalem in June 1099, and the city fell on July 15. Muslim men, women, and children lost their lives in a bloody massacre.

The Crusades brought dramatic changes to Christendom, opening up new trade routes and fostering interactions between cultures, all of which stimulated economies. As a result of their

This fourteenth-century manuscript painting depicts the Crusaders at the gates of Jerusalem.

exposure to new ideas and attitudes and new religious beliefs and practices, some Europeans embraced new forms of ancient "heretical" beliefs. For example, a religious movement known as the Cathari or Albigensians took root in southern France and began to spread. The Cathari believed in reincarnation, and their goal was to liberate the spirit from the evil of a fleshly body. This led Pope Lucius III (1184) to initiate the Inquisition, an effort to stamp out heresy. The Fourth Lateran Council in 1215 authorized the punishment of all heretics by the state and also prescribed distinctive dress for Jews and Muslims (e.g., pointed hats or yellow badges) and restricted Jews to living in ghettos. Soon, inquisitions under church auspices would become infamous for their cruelty.

There were positive consequences of the Crusades as well. Most of the Greek philosopher Aristotle's work, lost to the West, had been preserved by Islamic scholars. The rediscovery of Aristotle led to new and controversial ways of thinking in the new scholar-organized universities of Europe in the twelfth and thirteenth centuries. And for a brief time Jewish, Muslim, and Christian philosophers, such as Maimonides

(1135–1204), Averroes (Ibn Rushd, 1126–98), and Thomas Aquinas (1224–74), all used a common philosophical language to learn from one another's traditions, even if only, in the end, so that each could argue for the superiority of his own.

Christianity and Modernity (1517–1962)

The Early Roots of Modernity

By the year 1500, Europe had been transformed from feudal territories into a network of significant urban centers. In these cities, incorporation, a form of legal agreement that gave citizens the right of self-governance in exchange for taxes paid to the nobility, facilitated the emergence of individualism, an independent economy, and democratic self-governance. With increased craftsmanship and trade, corporate charters were also granted to the new "craft guilds" or "universities," as all guilds (not just educational ones) were called. These corporations mark the beginnings of the secularization of social institutions. Indeed, one of the defining characteristics of modernization is the existence of self-governing institutions that operate independent of direct religious authority (pope and bishops) and also of traditional medieval political authority (kings and lords). Education, too, declared its independence from the monasteries and cathedral schools, as scholars formed their own universities. It was in these scholarly guilds or institutions of learning that intellectual secularization first appeared, as scholars began to think about their subject matters with a sense of independence from direct church authority. These changes facilitated the development of the institutional and intellectual diversity characteristic of modern secular societies. In this environment three trends converged to shape the modern West: the millennialism of historical progress, the *via moderna* of autonomous reason, and the *devotio moderna* of emotional transformation.

Millennialism: History as Progress

One strand of modernity had its roots in the apocalyptic visions of Joachim of Fiore (1132–1202), a monk and abbot from Italy whose vision of history deeply influenced the modern age. Joachim's "everlasting Gospel" suggested that history can be divided into three ages corresponding to the three persons of the Trinity: the age of the Father (beginning with Abraham), which was superseded by the age of the Son (beginning with Christ), which would in turn be replaced by a third and final age, that of the Holy Spirit. Joachim thought of himself as living at the beginning of the millennium, the final age of the Spirit, in which there would no longer be any need for the institutional church and its clergy—nor for any other institution, including the state. Joachim, a mystic, expected the Holy Spirit to inspire harmony between all individuals, rendering existing institutions superfluous. This third age, which Joachim believed was predicted in the Book of Revelation, would be the beginning of the Kingdom of God on earth, an age of perfect harmony that was destined to last a millennium—that is, a thousand years.

Joachim's version of the myth of history as proceeding through three ages shaped the modern view of history as a story of progress. History was seen as moving forward from the ancient period through the medieval, culminating in the modern age. For Joachim the third age was identified with the triumph of mysticism over the institutional church. But his three ages became increasingly secularized in the eighteenth century, during the Enlightenment in western Europe. As a result, while the three-age model persisted, the Holy Spirit was no longer identified as the force behind the millennium. For instance, Gotthold Lessing, the great Enlightenment scholar, held that the education of the human race passed through three phases: childhood, adolescence, and adulthood. The last, or third age, he identified with the Age of Enlightenment, in which the autonomy of reason (instead of the Holy Spirit) would lead to a natural and rational harmony among human beings.

The *Via Moderna* and *Devotio Moderna*

According to Thomas Aquinas, the greatest of the late medieval theologians and also generally regarded as the most influential Roman Catholic theologian, faith complements and completes reason. For Aquinas the Prime Mover known through Greek philosophy is the same as the God of the Bible. One can have some knowledge of God through reason, independent of faith, but scripture enriches this knowledge immeasurably. Faith and reason, rightly used, can never contradict each other. However, the generation of theologians that followed Aquinas, known as nominalists, radically disagreed with him. William of Ockham (1287–1347) and other nominalists rejected this view as "ancient" (they called it the *via antiqua*) and outmoded. Describing instead a *via moderna,* or modern way, these later theologians argued that reason was of little help in discerning the will of God.

This "modern way" thus secularized the world by separating faith and reason. The only way to know God's will is through faith (emotional trust in God) and a fervent reading of scriptures as the revealed word of God (the *devotio moderna*). The only way to know the world God has created is through rational empirical investigation of the world God has actually created. Thus, when it comes to knowledge of the world, faith requires the secular *via moderna* of rational inquiry. And when it comes to knowledge of God, only revelation understood through "faith alone" will do. Protestantism and modernity are like two sides of the same coin, arising out of the *via moderna* and *devotio moderna* of late medieval theology to flourish in the Renaissance and the Reformation. Therefore, unlike all other religious traditions, Protestantism did not, at first, experience modernization as the intrusion of an outside force but rather as a form of experience nurtured from within. It was only as modernization and secularization took on lives of their own, independent of the Protestant Reformation, that they began to appear threatening.

The Renaissance and the Reformation developed together. The intent of the first Renaissance humanist thinkers was to recover the pre-Christian wisdom of the ancient world of Greece and Rome. These humanists represented the new independent scholarship of what came to be called "the humanities," focusing on history, classical pre-Christian philosophy, literature, and poetry. Similarly, the Reformation sought to reach back into antiquity and recover the original New Testament Christian vision as it existed before medieval theologians integrated it with Greek metaphysics. The spread of these modern ideas was greatly facilitated by a new technology, the printing press, in the 1450s. A growing number of people became literate. The printing press also greatly accelerated the development of national identities by promoting a common language and shared ideas within a geographic area.

The initiator of the Protestant Reformation was the German Augustinian monk Martin Luther (1483–1546), who embraced the new, modern way of thinking. While Luther thought that reason could be useful in secular matters, when it came to matters of faith, Luther called reason a "whore" that could not be trusted to lead one to God. Knowledge of God, rather, can be obtained only through faith and scripture undistorted by reason. "By faith alone," in fact, became the central doctrine of the Protestant Reformation, also embraced by the second major figure of the movement, John Calvin (1509–64).

In this portrait of Martin Luther, by the sixteenth-century painter and eyewitness Lucas Cranach the Elder, the fiery reformer, once an Augustinian monk, appears peaceful and contemplative.

IN SILENCIO ET SPE ERIT   M   L   FORTITVDO VESTRA

The Renaissance and the Reformation fostered a new individualism in the cities, encouraging people to have a sense of personal dignity and equality. This way of thinking could not be sustained without a shift from the medieval hierarchical view of authority to a more democratic view. Knowledge through empirical inquiry and political authority based on the consent of the governed define modernization. It is the encounter with these modern notions of knowledge and power that has, in more recent times, caused anxiety in traditional or premodern societies around the globe. Such societies, like those of premodern Europe, typically are imbued with a sense of sacred, cosmic hierarchical order in which those in power ruled with sacred authority from above. Protestantism, on the other hand, was part of the revolutionary shift away from divinely decreed hierarchies toward individuality, equality, and dignity.

Devotio Moderna and the Protestant Reformation

The *devotio moderna* is exemplified in Martin Luther's emotional experience of being "born again." Luther grew up in a medieval Catholic world in transition toward the modern world of the Renaissance. He began to train in law as a young man, but after nearly getting hit by lightning he abandoned that path, became an Augustinian monk, and was ordained as a priest. His quest for moral and spiritual perfection drove him to feel anxious and hopeless. He felt that he could never live up to what God expected of him. Then, somewhere between 1511 and 1516, he had a powerful spiritual experience. While studying Paul's letter to the Romans, he suddenly came to see the meaning of the phrase often translated as "The just shall live by faith" (Romans 1:17).

What Luther came to realize, he said, was that he was acceptable before God with all his imperfections, as long as he had faith in Christ, who had died for his sins. Salvation is a gift of grace. All sinners need to do is have faith; because of that faith, God will treat sinners as if they were saints, free of sin. With this realization, Luther said he was overcome by a liberating experience of being in the presence of a forgiving and compassionate God.

Luther also realized that justification (i.e., being considered to be just and good) before this God was not through a person's works but by God's grace. One cannot will faith; it is received as a gift from God. So salvation is by faith through grace— faith alone understood through scripture alone—not, as the Catholic Church had insisted, through grace *and* works, faith *and* reason, scripture *and* (hierarchical) tradition. This understanding of **justification by faith** is the cornerstone of the Protestant Reformation.

justification by faith: doctrine that humans are saved by faith as a gift from God rather than through their own will and works of obedience

In 1516, Pope Leo X authorized the selling of indulgences to raise funds to rebuild the Cathedral of St. Peter in Rome. Indulgences were a promise from the pope that the sins of generous donors would be wiped away so that after death, they would avoid being punished for their sins. For Luther, this was the last straw. Salvation was not to be purchased, since it comes by grace and faith alone. On October 31, 1517, Luther posted *Ninety-five Theses Against the Sale of Indulgences* on the church door of Wittenberg Castle, calling for public debate. That event marks the beginning of the Reformation.

Luther's challenge was how to reform a corrupted church tradition. His solution was to criticize the tradition by raising faith and scriptures to a higher level of authority than church tradition, using scripture itself to judge and reform the tradition. This option was not available to Christians before the canon, or list of books in the New Testament, had been agreed on (after 387). It was the Catholic tradition that picked the scriptures and created the Christian Bible, as Catholics would say, "under the guidance of the Holy Spirit." Without the success of Catholicism, Protestantism's "faith alone, scriptures alone" would not have been possible, and without the failures of Catholicism, Protestant reform would not have been necessary.

"Thereupon I felt myself to be reborn and to have gone through open doors into paradise. The whole of scripture took on a new meaning."

—Martin Luther

Luther started out protesting abuses in the church, but he quickly moved on to challenge the entire mediating role of the church, the sacraments, and the papacy. He did not start out to create a new form of Christianity, only to reform the existing tradition. But events soon turned a reformation into a revolution, and Protestant Christianity was born in a radical break with the ancient, medieval way. In addition to the ancient Catholic way of faith *and* reason, scripture *and* tradition, guided by papal authority, there would be the new, modern Protestant way of faith alone, through scripture alone, and the individual alone before his or her God.

Calvin and the Protestant Ethic

From the beginning, Protestantism was part of the revolutionary shift away from sacred hierarchy toward secular rationality, individuality, and equality. In this, Protestantism, in conjunction with Renaissance humanism, laid the groundwork for the emergence in the West of the ideas of human dignity and human rights. And yet, in the relation of Christianity to the state and to society, the basic assumptions of the Constantinian/Augustinian visions of the unity of church and state remained operative, at least for the major strands of the Protestant Reformation. The state should be a Christian state, only now that meant Protestant.

Next to Luther, John Calvin was the greatest of the reformers. Coming from France, Calvin transformed the city of Geneva, Switzerland, into a model for Protestant civilization. Arguing that human sinfulness requires that all power be limited, he created a Christian democratic republic with a separation of powers among its representative bodies. This institutional strategy served as a model for later secular democracies.

Protestant ethic: sociologist Max Weber's observation that Calvinist beliefs about the holiness of work contributed to accumulation of wealth and facilitated the growth of capitalism

The Protestant work ethic associated with Calvinism represents the secularization of the Benedictine motto "to work is to pray." Indeed, a major teaching of Luther and Calvin is the idea that work in the world (whether as a shoemaker or doctor, etc.) is as holy a task as praying in a monastery—indeed, a holier task. What makes work holy is not where it is done but doing it as a result of God's call. The **Protestant ethic** demanded that one live simply and work hard: "earn all you can, save all you can" to be able to "give all you can" for the greater glory of God. The early twentieth-century sociologist Max Weber suggested that this ethic helped to fuel the emergence of capitalism in Europe by encouraging both hard work, which allowed individuals to prosper, and savings, which were needed for investment. In Europe and North America, it was Calvin's rather than Luther's vision of Protestant civilization that most influenced the future, not only of democracy but also of Western capitalism and colonialism.

Other Reform Movements

If the *via moderna* split faith and reason apart and confined reason to the secular parts of life, the *devotio moderna* of mystical piety restricted faith to the domain of spiritual emotions. By the fourteenth and fifteenth centuries, a new kind of "this-worldly" mysticism—the *devotio moderna*—was creating popular pietistic movements for spiritual renewal that emerged without official church approval. These grassroots movements focused on personal piety founded on intense, emotionally transformative religious experiences. The experiences fostered a new, democratic spirit by emphasizing the equality of all before God and the spiritual benefits to be obtained from living simply. They were typically critical of the medieval Catholic Church, its wealth and its hierarchical order.

The Anabaptist Rebellion Against Both Church and State

We have described the Lutheran and Calvinist center of the Protestant Reformation. However, there were other branches as well. At one extreme were the radical reformers, and on the other the Anglicans. The radical reformers, especially the Anabaptists, have deep roots in the mystical and millennial grassroots movements of the late Middle Ages.

The Anabaptists were Christians who denied baptism to infants because the practice is not mentioned in the New Testament. They believed that only those who freely choose to join the church should be baptized. These views alienated Anabaptists from the Protestantism of Luther and Calvin, and Catholicism, and led to their persecution by both traditions. By 1535 over 50,000 Anabaptists had been martyred.

Interestingly, the pacifist strands of this movement stand out in the history of Christianity because the Anabaptists do attempt to break with the Constantinian vision of a Christian civilization, rejecting both the authority of the hierarchical church and the authority of the state. Pacifist Anabaptists refused any role in public service on the grounds that the state condones killing and that taking an oath of office goes against one of Jesus' statements in the Sermon on the Mount: "No one can serve two masters" (Matthew 6:24). The Hutterites, the Mennonites, and the Amish are all products of the Anabaptist branch of the Reformation. The most pious of their twentieth-century descendants among the Amish are distinctive for refusing to compromise their principles by taking advantage of modern conveniences such as electricity and motor vehicle transportation.

The Anglican Reformation and the Puritan Revolt

At the other extreme, the English Reformation was initiated by the state rather than by Christians in the churches. English monarchs initially championed Catholicism, describing Luther's views as "heretical." Indeed, Pope Leo X conferred the title "Defender of the Faith" on King Henry VIII. Problems arose, however, when Henry, who had no male heir to the throne, wanted to divorce his first wife and remarry in hopes of fathering a son. Pope Clement VII refused to give his permission to divorce. So in 1534, Henry VIII nationalized the church, making himself the head of what was now the Church of England; the archbishop of Canterbury obligingly declared his marriage invalid. Nevertheless, apart from breaking with the papacy, the English church remained essentially Catholic, and Henry continued to oppose and often punish those he considered to be heretics. Only after Henry's death were Protestant reformers safe in England.

As Protestants made inroads in Britain, the Church of England's doctrine did not seem pure enough for the Puritans, Calvinist radicals who were intent on returning to a New Testament Christianity free from all "popery." After a short period of dominance under their military leader, Oliver Cromwell, Puritans became persecuted.

The struggle to keep the premodern traditions pure is difficult. But note that this Amish woman is using in-line skates while pushing a baby stroller to reach her destination faster without utilizing gas or electricity.

Puritanism was a diverse and fragmented movement that had splintered into Congregationalists, Presbyterians (who prevailed in Scotland), Separatists, and Nonconformists, including Baptists. All rejected the thirty-nine Articles of Religion, the official statement of doctrine of the Church of England. In 1620, 101 Pilgrims sailed for North America. Over 40,000 Pilgrims fled England in the next two decades, bringing to the new colonies their propensity for sectarian diversity.

The Catholic Counter-Reformation

The Council of Trent was a series of meetings held in Italy between 1545 and 1563 for the purpose of responding to the reformers. The council reinforced the absolute power of the pope and made the medieval theology of Thomas Aquinas normative for the Catholic Church. It affirmed that the Catholic "tradition" was equal in authority to scripture and that Latin should remain the language of the Bible and of worship. It also retained the seven sacraments (which Protestantism had reduced to two, baptism and communion) and the importance of the saints, relics, and indulgences. Indeed, the buying and selling of indulgences was not even discussed. At the conclusion of the meetings of the Council of Trent, Pope Pius IV declared that there was "no salvation outside the Catholic faith."

Religious Diversity: Church and State in War and Peace

The Reformation led to political divisions and even open warfare between European Catholics and Protestants. Like Catholics, all Protestants (except the Anabaptists) assumed that the goal of Christianity was a Christian civilization. For the most part, however, neither side considered the other side Christian. Each tended to think the other was doing the work of the devil. Consequently, Christians resorted to warfare to settle whose religion would shape the public order. In Germany, a series of wars between Protestants and Catholics ended in the Peace of Augsburg in 1555, with its compromise statement "*cuius regio, eius religio*" (the religion of the ruler shall be the religion of the land). As a consequence, the splintering of the church seemed to match the splintering of Europe into nation-states. Another series of battles, known as the Thirty Years War, engulfed most of Europe but was brought to a conclusion with the Peace of Westphalia in 1648. This was a general settlement that reestablished the conditions of the Peace of Augsburg, with additional protections for religious minorities and encouragement of religious toleration (see Map 4.2).

The Protestant Reformation led not to a new sense of unity but to a chaotic diversity, especially as more people learned to read and interpret the Bible for themselves. The result, after much bloodshed, was the gradual transformation of both Protestantism and Catholicism into denominational religions. Whereas in medieval Catholicism and the early sectarian movements of Protestantism, each group had seen itself as the sole repository of truth, to which all in society should conform, denominational religions accept the establishment of religiously diverse communities, each expressing the private views of their adherents.

With the emergence of denominationalism, Christianity was on a path leading to a new relationship to the public and political order of society. The state as a secular and neutral political institution that favored no one religion emerged to become the normative model for the modern Western world. Paradoxically, this development continued to coexist with the assumption by many Christians that the task of Christianity was to Christianize the world. Consequently, as Europe's public order was becoming increasingly secular, European Christians were setting out to Christianize the world in concert with Western colonialism's political and economic attempts at global conquest.

Enlightenment Rationalism and Christian Pietism

Pietism and rationalism, two responses to the doctrinal, social, and political divisions created by the Reformation, were rooted in the split between faith and reason that we have already described. And both contributed to the development of Western notions of universal human rights.

Rationalism

The rise of modern science and technology was dramatic. Science came to express certainty. The more public and certain scientific knowledge appeared to be, the more private and uncertain religious knowledge seemed to be. As science developed, scientists came to believe that they had less and less need to bring God into their explanations.

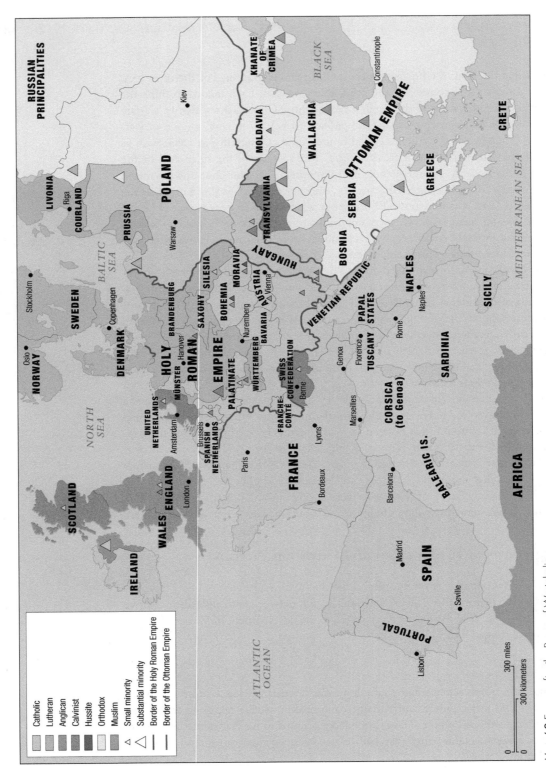

Map 4.2 Europe after the Peace of Westphalia.

Legend:
- Catholic
- Lutheran
- Anglican
- Calvinist
- Hussite
- Orthodox
- Muslim
- △ Small minority
- ◁ Substantial minority
- Border of the Holy Roman Empire
- Border of the Ottoman Empire

RUSSIAN PRINCIPALITIES

KHANATE OF CRIMEA

BLACK SEA

Kiev

Constantinople

WALLACHIA

MOLDAVIA

OTTOMAN EMPIRE

SERBIA

GREECE

CRETE

LIVONIA

Riga

COURLAND

PRUSSIA

POLAND

Warsaw

TRANSYLVANIA

HUNGARY

BOSNIA

MEDITERRANEAN SEA

BALTIC SEA

Stockholm

SWEDEN

NORWAY

Oslo

Copenhagen

DENMARK

BRANDENBURG

Hanover

SAXONY

SILESIA

MORAVIA

BOHEMIA

Nuremberg

AUSTRIA

Vienna

VENETIAN REPUBLIC

PAPAL STATES

NAPLES

Naples

SICILY

NORTH SEA

MÜNSTER

HOLY ROMAN EMPIRE

BAVARIA

WÜRTTEMBERG

PALATINATE

SWISS CONFEDERATION

FRANCHE-COMTÉ

Berne

Genoa

Florence

TUSCANY

Rome

SARDINIA

UNITED NETHERLANDS

Amsterdam

Brussels

SPANISH NETHERLANDS

Paris

Lyons

Marseilles

CORSICA (to Genoa)

FRANCE

Bordeaux

Barcelona

BALEARIC IS.

AFRICA

SCOTLAND

IRELAND

WALES

ENGLAND

London

ATLANTIC OCEAN

SPAIN

Madrid

Seville

PORTUGAL

Lisbon

0   300 miles
0   300 kilometers

During this period, the Enlightenment, human beings saw themselves as entering the adulthood of the human race. People no longer needed to be told what to believe. The Enlightenment was built on four key concepts:

1. use of one's own reason,
2. freedom from tradition through the rational critique of the past,
3. a view of nature as a finely tuned machine whose mechanisms can be rationally understood, and
4. the belief that history is guided by hidden laws of progress.

The power of reason was assumed to be capable of freeing human beings from the irrationality of the past (including the irrationality of religion), of discovering how the universe really works, and of introducing a golden age of progress.

deism: enlightenment view that God created the world as a watchmaker does a watch, leaving it to run without interference

Enlightenment rationalism fostered the emergence of **deism**, which likened the world to a clock and God to a divine clockmaker. Just as a clockmaker makes a perfect machine that runs on its own without assistance from its maker, so God, as creator, does not actively guide or influence events in the world.

The Enlightenment promised to overcome the divisions among human beings that had generated the religious wars of the Reformation by reducing religion to its rational elements. By eliminating the emotion-laden "superstitions" of traditional religions, rationalists believed they would create a more tolerant and harmonious world. Such an enlightened deism was characteristic of denominations such as the Unitarians and the Universalists. and played an important role in championing universal rights, stressing the fundamental unity of the human race. And indeed, in England and elsewhere laws of toleration began to be passed.

Pietism

What was missing in the clockwork universe of deism was warmth or emotion. The alternative to the cold rationality of both Enlightenment rationalism and Protestant rationalism was supplied by Pietism, a new movement that gave rise to evangelical Christianity. In their attempts to unite people of faith, who had been divided since the Protestant Reformation, the Pietists explored the emotional aspects of religion. Indeed, Pietism was a movement to recover the *devotio moderna* of the late medieval and Reformation periods.

Pietists sought to transcend religious differences by minimizing the role of sectarian dogma, which seemed to divide Christians, and maximizing the potentially unifying role of religious emotion. The true test of Christian faith, Pietists argued, is found not so much in dogma as in a changed heart. Thus the goal of evangelical piety was, in the beginning, antisectarian and anti-dogmatic. One of its greatest representatives, John Wesley (1703–91), believed passionately that doctrinal differences should not separate Christians and that the deep emotion of faith was the way to Christian unity.

John Wesley, the founder of Methodism, often preached to the men, women, and children of the new working class during the Industrial Revolution.

"If she have the necessary gifts and feels herself called by the Spirit to preach, there is not a single word in the whole book of God to restrain her, but many, very many, to urge and encourage her. God says she *shall* do so."

—Evangelical preacher Catherine Booth, cofounder of the Salvation Army

The first wave of Pietism came in the seventeenth century. It included such groups as the Moravians and the Quakers. The most far-reaching expression of Pietism in the eighteenth century was the Methodist movement begun by John Wesley, who was deeply influenced by the Moravians as well as by Catholic and Anglican mystics. Wesley, whose conversion had "strangely warmed" his heart, rejected some of Calvin's ideas and questioned the doctrine of original sin by emphasizing freedom of choice, suggesting that humans were capable of achieving spiritual and moral perfection.

Wesley's message was aimed primarily at the new working class created by the Industrial Revolution. Factory owners did not always pay fair wages, and working conditions and hours were often inhumane. The Methodist movement was one of the first constructive responses of Christianity to these changing conditions. Methodist communities were committed to a morality of perfecting both self and society. Mystical piety is a great equalizer in social experience because it is contagious and can overtake anyone, without regard to social status, race, gender, or creed.

Methodism's most striking accomplishments include leading roles in the abolition of slavery in England (1833) and in introducing women into the ministry. Both exemplify the importance of evangelical piety in the development of the modern commitment to human dignity, equality, and rights.

The power of the Methodist and other evangelical movements tapped a long Christian tradition of combining a simple regimen of prayer and devotion with life in small communities of discipline and mutual encouragement oriented toward improving the world. This formula fueled the monastic movement and the same spirit was carried forward in Calvinism and transferred to evangelical Christianity, primarily (but not exclusively) through Methodism. In these Protestant formulations, it would be spread around the world in the missions of the nineteenth century. Thus, paradoxically, the Augustinian vision of a mission to Christianize the world that had led to such terrible consequences as the Inquisition and the excesses of the Crusades also afforded a model for promoting human dignity and equality. The arrogant side of Western colonialism brought with it the seeds of its own demise as it spread around the world.

Nineteenth-Century Romanticism and Existentialism

The rationalism and pietism of the Enlightenment shared a faith in the progress of the human race. Drawing on the myth of the three ages as formulated by Joachim of Fiore in the thirteenth century, members of these groups shared a millennial belief that they lived in the final age of history, when people would throw off the authoritarianism of past tradition and institutions and, instead, be guided by an inner light that would bring with it progress and harmony. For this to come about, the rationalists relied on the *via moderna* of the cool light of reason. For the Pietists it was the *devotio moderna*— the warm emotional light of spiritual illumination that comes from being born again. Thus both share the millennial mysticism of Joachim of Fiore that has driven the modern spirit of progress. But the progress and harmony they expected from piety and from reason did not come.

The French Revolution in the Wake of the Failure of Reason

At the end of the eighteenth century economic conditions grew very bad in France, and they were not helped by the extravagance of the court of King Louis XVI. This led to the French Revolution, which began in 1789. In addition to replacing the government, the new leaders created a revolutionary, deistic religion featuring a "Cult of Reason" and later a "Cult of the Supreme Being." The churches were transformed into "Temples of Reason," and statues of the Virgin Mary were replaced by icons of "nature goddesses" and "the goddess of reason." Louis and his wife, Marie Antoinette, were executed in 1793, and in the Reign of Terror that followed, thousands of clergy and nobility were arrested and beheaded.

The bloody events of the 1790s brought about considerable disillusionment with reason. Reason had been embraced at the beginning of the Enlightenment as the way of avoiding fanaticism, dogmatism, violence, and intolerance. And yet in the French Revolution reason had shown itself to be fanatical, dogmatic, violent, and intolerant. Weary of the violence of urban life, people longed for the simplicity of nature uncorrupted by civilization. With the failure of reason, many people turned to emotion as the foundation for renewal of life. If the Enlightenment was rationalistic and mechanistic, the Romantic period that followed was emotional and organic. If the Enlightenment had sought to escape the suffocation of past tradition and enter a bright new future of scientific advances, Romanticism sought to return to the organic, familial, and emotional connections of traditional agricultural or village society. An ambivalent struggle between these alternative visions is still very much a part of our contemporary culture.

From Reason to Emotion: The Romantic Alternative to Enlightenment Rationalism

Friedrich Schleiermacher (1768–1834), considered to be the father of modern Christian theology, offered the Romantic solution to the problems of rationalism, suggesting that knowledge of God comes to people not through reason (the *via moderna*) but rather through emotion (the *devotio moderna*). Consequently, knowledge of God can coexist with scientific knowledge of the world: There is no conflict because the outer, secular, public sphere of reason is separate from the inner, private sphere of faith.

"The sum total of religion is to feel that, in the highest unity, all that moves us in feeling is one; . . . that is to say, that our being and living is a being and living in and through God."

—Schleiermacher

GENDER FOCUS: Women in Christianity

Christianity (like Judaism, Islam, and the religions of Asia) arose in patriarchal (male-dominated) societies. Historically, women have played the greatest roles in forms of Christianity that valued direct and immediate religious experience (mystical piety) as more authoritative than the institutional authority of the bishops. Thus in the early church women played a greater role in Gnostic (mystical and otherworldly) and Montanist (apocalyptic and ecstatic) Christian movements than in Catholicism, which was institutionally hierarchical. And yet there were always some women who were exceptions to the rule. According to the letters of Paul, women had leadership roles in some of the early Christian communities. As the early church became institutionalized, however, prevailing customs of male dominance seemed to reassert themselves, and the pattern of excluding women from roles as priests and bishops took hold.

During the Middle Ages women found ways to exercise autonomy and independence by founding female monastic orders. With the Protestant Reformation, however, even that option was taken from them, and women were largely confined to the home and child rearing. This began to change in the nineteenth century, when the evangelical missionary movements with deep roots in the mystical traditions of piety (*devotio moderna*) offered new opportunities for women in leadership roles. Including women in these missions played an important part in the political development of the women's movement for independence and the right to vote. Also, among the more unusual forms of Christianity, with mystical or Gnostic roots, women founded new traditions. For example, the Shakers, the Unity School of Christianity, and Christian Science were begun by Ann Lee, Emma Curtis Hopkins, and Mary Baker Eddy, respectively.

Another major source of women's autonomy was the *via moderna* as expressed in the denominations influenced by Enlightenment secularization and

A civil rights activist who marched with Martin Luther King Jr. in Selma, Barbara Harris was ordained a bishop in the Episcopal Church in 1980.

rationalism. Consequently, in the nineteenth century women began to be ordained in some Protestant denominations. The Congregationalists led the way in 1853. They were followed by the Universalists, the Unitarians, and other denominations. The mainline Protestant churches (e.g., Methodist, Presbyterian, Episcopal, and Lutheran) did not follow suit until the twentieth century. The Roman Catholic and the Orthodox churches still do not ordain women, arguing that the maleness of Jesus and the apostles reveals the divine intent for an all-male priesthood.

The last four decades of the twentieth century saw the rise of a theologically based feminism. The issue that divides feminists and fundamentalists is whether God created a sacred natural order in which men's and women's roles are eternally defined. Fundamentalists say yes, feminists say no. Feminists say that fundamentalists confuse the cultural attitudes and common practices of premodern societies with the will of God. Fundamentalists turn this argument around, saying that feminists and other liberation advocates confuse the cultural attitudes and common practices of modern societies with the will of God.

Moreover, Schleiermacher disputed the opinion of some Christians that the affirmation of faith in the resurrection of Jesus Christ depends on historical proof. When a person does not believe in the resurrection one day and then confesses such faith the next day, the theologian argued, the altered conviction was not the result of that person's having learned a new historical fact but of that person's having had a transformative emotional experience. This emphasis on transformative emotion places Schleiermacher directly in the tradition of the *devotio moderna* and evangelical Pietism.

> "To have a self, to be a self, is the greatest concession made to man, but at the same time it is eternity's demand upon him."
> —Kierkegaard

Kierkegaard and the Existentialist Response to Cultural Relativism

Another important development in modern Christianity was existentialism, marking the start of the postmodern exploration of the implications of cultural relativism. Existentialism was responding to the new thinking that accompanied advances in historical and social scientific consciousness. The results of both historical and ethnographic studies made people aware that various cultures interpreted "human nature" differently. Cultural relativism entails the acknowledgment and examination of these differences.

According to the existentialists, one is not born with an essential human nature. Rather, the core insight of existentialism is that "existence precedes essence." When you plant an acorn, you know you will get an oak tree. The essence of the tree is there from its beginnings. But when a human child is conceived, biology is not definitive because human freedom enters into the equation. No one can predict who or what that child will become. The life task of a human being is to create a self through his or her choices.

Søren Kierkegaard (1813–55) invented what came to be called Christian existentialism. Kierkegaard argued that if we have no essential human nature, each person must make a "leap of faith" inspired by faith in Christ to trust God to help him or her construct an identity as a loving and compassionate human being. Like Schleiermacher, Kierkegaard wrote that such faith depends neither on logical reasoning nor on historical proof but on a personal choice driven by powerful divinely inspired emotions that lead one to make the leap of faith.

Christian faith is proved not by scientific and/or historical facts, nor by metaphysical arguments, but by the emotional, moral, and spiritual transformation of the individual. In making this argument, Friedrich Schleiermacher became the founder of modern Protestant theology.

From the Holocaust to Hiroshima: The Global Collapse of the Modern Myth of History as Progress

The existentialist response to the social sciences and cultural relativism led some philosophers, such as Friedrich Nietzsche (1844–1900), to conclusions quite the opposite of Kierkegaard's—namely, that history and ethnography show "God" to have been a human invention. This God, Nietzsche claimed, is now dead, a circumstance that obliges us to invent our identities without God.

For Nietzsche, the modern world, rooted in science and evolution, was incompatible with belief in the biblical God. As Nietzsche saw it, European Christians who acted as if Christianity and modernity were compatible would one day realize that in embracing modernity they had killed God. Recalling the argument between fundamentalists and modernists at the beginning of this chapter, we can now see that Nietzsche and fundamentalists shared at least one conviction—that belief in God is incompatible with modernity. But for fundamentalists this meant that Darwin's theories had to be rejected, whereas for Nietzsche it meant belief in God had to be rejected.

Nietzsche, having rejected the God of the Bible, believed that history is guided by a struggle for existence that takes the form of a "will to power." Nietzsche argued that biblical morality teaches "weak values" such as forgiveness and pity that ultimately lead to resentment against persons who are strong and courageous. The future, he believed, should belong to those superior and creative aristocratic individuals who had the courage to "transvalue all values" and to make their own morality.

Little more than half a century after Nietzsche announced the death of God, the Nazis embraced their own distorted vision of Nietzsche's will to power. Nietzsche might have been surprised by the number of churchgoers who showed themselves quite willing to abandon their weak values of compassion in exchange for the Nazi ideals of elitism and the will to power. Between 1933 and 1945, Hitler and the Nazi Party ruled Germany and drew Europe and America into World War II (1939–45).

One of the key factors in Hitler's rise to power was his successful appeal to anti-Semitism in German and Austrian culture. Hitler was able to achieve power, in large part, by appealing to long-standing prejudice against the Jews created by the churches over the centuries. By the time of the Middle Ages, Christians viewed Jews as deserving to suffer for rejecting and crucifying the messiah, the Son of God. Consequently, the Nazis were able to strip the Jews of their citizenship, confiscate their property, and send them to concentration camps with very little serious resistance from the churches and often with their assistance. Over 6 million European Jews are estimated to have been killed, mostly in the gas chambers of the Nazi concentration camps.

> "Being a Christian is less about cautiously avoiding sin than about courageously and actively doing God's will."
>
> —Dietrich Bonhoeffer

Although the Christian churches might have been a powerful force against the Nazi attempt to exterminate the Jews, they were not. In Germany, by some estimates, only 20 percent of the Protestant churches resisted Hitler and the Nazi message. And Pope Pius XI signed an agreement with Hitler in hopes of protecting the autonomy of the German Catholic churches.

Christians in Denmark were one notable exception, and most of Denmark's Jews survived because of collective resistance by church and state. Le Chambon sur Lignon in France is another such exception: This small village of mostly French Protestants saved over 5,000 Jewish lives. Wherever the churches led resistance to the Nazis, Jewish lives were saved. Unfortunately, that did not happen often.

Reflection on the lessons of the Holocaust brought unprecedented change to Christianity in the last decades of the twentieth century. Since Vatican II and in response to the Holocaust, not only the Catholic Church but also the main Protestant denominations have sought to replace the myth of supersession (which held that the Jews were a rejected people) with an affirmation that the Jewish covenant is an authentic covenant with God—one that exists both prior to and apart from the Christian covenant. This public acknowledgment of the Jewish people as chosen by God and of the religion of Judaism as a valid expression of monotheism is unprecedented in the history of Christianity.

The horrors of World War II made Nietzsche's claim that God was dead seem more plausible. The killing of millions on the battlefields and in the camps, achieved by means of science and technology, represented the death of what "God" had become for many in Western civilization, namely, the "God of progress." People had good reasons to question whether modernity and "progress" were truly worthy human ideals.

Finally, with the dropping of the atomic bomb by the United States on Hiroshima, Japan, at the end of World War II and the accumulation of nuclear weapons by the USSR and the United States in the second half of the twentieth century, a turning point may have emerged. The possibility of a nuclear war that would destroy the planet made belief in the progress of history and a better future through science and technology seem far from inevitable. As the world moves beyond its modernist phase, many Christians are beginning to explore the possibility of separating the church's message from the myth of history as progress and from the assumptions of the cultural superiority of the West that reinforced colonialism.

"The madman jumped into their midst and pierced them with his eyes. 'Whither is God?' he cried; 'I will tell you. *We have killed him—* you and I. All of us are his murderers.'"

—Friedrich Nietzsche, "The Parable of the Madman"

SOURCE: Friedrich Nietzsche, *The Gay Science* (1882, 1887) para. 125; Walter Kaufmann, ed. (New York: Vintage, 1974), pp. 181–2.

Christianity and Postmodern Trends in a Postcolonial World (1962–)

From Colonial to Postcolonial Christianity

For most of its history Christianity has been predominantly a European religion. In 1600 the overwhelming majority of Christians in the world lived in Europe. However, the invention of the modern three-masted sailing ship (ca. 1500) unleashed massive changes that began when the countries of Europe acquired their first colonies. Colonial expansion was accompanied by worldwide missionary activity, led first by Catholic countries such as Portugal and Spain and later by countries with new Protestant centers of power, especially England. By 1900 only half of all the Christians in the world lived in Europe. By the end of the twentieth century the majority of the world's Christians resided in Latin America, Africa, and Asia. Thus, postcolonial Christianity is decisively non-European.

Even as church membership was waning in Europe, it was planting the seeds of its possible transformation and renewal in postcolonial forms elsewhere in the world. On the one hand, while birthrates among Christians declined in Europe, the number of children born to Christians elsewhere increased dramatically. On the other hand, the secularization of Europe led to a large decline in the practice of Christianity there. Paradoxically, at the same time, through European colonial expansion, Protestant evangelical Christians engaged in a massive missionary enterprise whose aim was the Christianization of every part of the world touched by colonization (see Map 1.3 in Chapter 1). This plan was justified by the assumption that European political and economic colonization was part of God's plan to spread the Gospel to the very ends of the earth.

The feeling of the superiority and global destiny of European civilization that accompanied colonialism communicated itself through an attitude of paternalism. At first many in the premodern cultures were impressed with the wonders of Western science and technology. Before long, however, indigenous peoples came to feel demeaned and diminished by the Westerners' attitude toward them.

In former colonial areas, whether in Africa, Asia, or the Americas, resentment against western Europeans inevitably led to a political backlash that typically coalesced around liberation movements. Activists called for rejection of some Western values, such as capitalism and individualism, in favor of political and economic independence and restoration of traditional values and customs. Yet other values espoused by the West, such as dignity and equality, ironically lent support to these indigenous liberation movements. We see this paradox, for example, in Gandhi's campaign to liberate India from English colonial domination, which appealed both to Hindu values and to modern Western values in just this way.

If colonialism brought modernity to the non-European world, the rejection of Western colonialism can be said to mark the beginnings of postcolonial and postmodern trends in Christianity. It is among postcolonial Christians that we might find the beginnings of a new postcolonial and non-Eurocentric form of Christianity, more open to coexistence with other religions and cultures.

Africa

For models of Christianity that break with both the premodern and modern Eurocentric visions of a "Christian civilization," one must look primarily to the African and Asian churches, where we see the emergence of a possible "diaspora" model of Christianity. A diaspora religion is one whose adherents are "dispersed" as minority communities among many nations and cultures, yet having a powerful transformative influence on these cultures. They aspire to be what the Gospel calls "the salt of the earth," bringing out the true flavor of everything around them.

At the beginning of the twentieth century there were scarcely any Christians in Africa. At the end of the century it was the fastest-growing geographic area for Christianity, and more than a fifth of the world's Christians can be found there today. Almost half of the population of Africa is now Christian, with Islam a close second.

There is a **liberation theology** in Africa, but, as the leadership of retired Anglican bishop Desmond Tutu in South Africa illustrates, it is less on the model of Marxist

liberation theology: emerged in Latin America in the twentieth century; the goal was to show that the Gospel was more radical than Marxism in its promotion of peace and justice for the poor.

In Africa and everywhere around the world, entry into the Christian faith is through the ritual of baptism, as shown here in Mozambique.

theory used by some Christians in Europe and South America in the twentieth century, and more on the model of Martin Luther King Jr.'s nonviolent civil rights movement in the United States. In the twenty-first century, African Christianity could be a major contributor to the development of a postcolonial Christianity. However, in Africa, Christianity's success tempts believers to envision a "Christian Africa" rather than a diaspora church serving a pluralist society.

India

European colonialism moved into Africa and Asia simultaneously. The British went into Ceylon (Sri Lanka), India, Burma (Myanmar), Malaysia, Singapore, Hong Kong, and various Pacific islands (also Australia and New Zealand). The French expanded into the Indochina peninsula, including Laos and Cambodia. The spread of Christianity that accompanied this colonial expansion was driven by the same Augustinian sense of the providential link between the expansion of European civilization and the spread of the Gospel.

In Asia, Christianity is a distinct minority presence and seems unlikely ever to become the dominant religion of civilizational order. Asia's contribution to the development of a postcolonial Christianity may well be the creation of a diaspora model of Christianity, one that will transcend traditional Western civilizational and denominational boundaries and be open to creative coexistence with other religions and cultures. Once India had won its independence from British colonial rule in 1947, there was increasing pressure on the churches in India to become less European and more Indian. In response, Indian Christians began to move beyond European denominational Christianity.

In 1947 Anglicans merged with Methodists and other Protestant bodies to form the Church of South India. Much later, the Protestant Church of North India was founded and also a Protestant Church of Pakistan (1970). With these changes there was also a shift of emphasis from conversion to dialogue, with the goal of showing the compatibility of Hinduism and Christianity. Christians have had to learn how to live as a diaspora religion in a largely Hindu culture, renewing efforts to indigenize Christianity with the appearance of Christian ashrams (both Protestant and Catholic) and **syncretistic** trends resulting in Hinduized forms of Christian worship.

syncretistic: identification of the gods of one religion with the gods of another

China and Japan

China did not welcome nineteenth-century missionizing, and after the Communist revolution of 1949 Christians were often persecuted. Today Christianity represents less than 4 percent of the population. Their presence is permitted so long as it appears indigenous and not the result of "foreign" missionaries. Government persecution seems to be focused on those Christian movements that advocate unpatriotic political issues, such as human rights, that threaten the Confucian ethos of Chinese society.

The Japanese experience is similar to that of China. In the sixteenth century, the Jesuits made converts in Japan but they were later persecuted. When missionaries returned in the mid-nineteenth century they found a thriving community of "hidden Christians" at Nagasaki. These believers were considered by Japanese rulers to be unpatriotic and subversive. Very quickly, Japanese Christians moved to assert their independence from Western forms of Christianity and to develop indigenous forms.

Korea

Korea is the great success story of Christian missionary activity in Asia. A Catholic presence in Korea goes back to the eighteenth century. Protestant missionaries came in the 1870s, but significant growth did not occur until Korea began signing trade agreements with the West in the 1880s. Korean interest in Christianity mounted after the Japanese victory over China in 1895, which Koreans rightly felt was threatening to their own autonomy. Christianity became identified not only with modernization and Westernization but also with anti-Japanese sentiments, which increased in 1910, when Japan annexed Korea.

After World War II, the victorious Allies divided the country into North and South Korea, and civil war followed (1950–53). Communists in North Korea have driven out Christians there. South Korea has the highest percentage of Christians of any nation in Asia except for the Philippines. Nowhere else in Asia has Christianity played as strong a role in public life as it has in South Korea, whose first two presidents were Christians. Since the 1970s a highly political liberation theology similar to that developed in Latin America, known as *minjung* or "the people's" theology, has emerged. And as in Africa and India, Korea too developed its own indigenous forms of Christianity, the most famous of which is the Unification Church of Sun Myung Moon, who is heralded by his followers as a new messiah—in this case an Asian messiah.

Given that the majority of Christians in the world are now non-European, it is likely that much of postcolonial Christianity will draw on the experiences of the various "mission churches" of Asia. The question remains whether the dominant model will be an African/South Korean model, aspiring against the odds to Christianize the continent, or an Indian model of minority diaspora churches, creatively reacting to the consequences of globalization and a world that is religiously diverse.

The United States

Although there were early Spanish and French settlements, the United States is primarily a result of colonization by the British. Indeed, it was a revolt against British colonialism by the citizens of its colonies that led to the Declaration of Independence in 1776 and later to the Constitution of the United States of America as the foundation for a new nation in 1787.

The citizens of the thirteen colonies that became the United States of America were largely but not exclusively refugees from the political intolerance toward sectarian religious minorities experienced in Europe. At first the European pattern of sectarian rivalry continued in the New World, but it soon became clear to the colonists that the uniqueness of America as an alternative to Europe had to lie in toleration of diversity. Consequently, the very first amendment to the U.S. Constitution declares: "Congress shall make no law respecting an establishment of religion, or prohibiting the free exercise thereof." These words guarantee religious freedom to all Americans by forbidding the government to name any religion as the state religion. This amendment, which became effective in 1791, created a major break with the Constantinian and Augustinian models of Christian civilization and opened the door to diaspora models of Christianity in the U.S. It was, however, a legal transformation that took on cultural embodiment only as non-Christian populations in America began to grow.

Gradually, diverse religious communities in North America came to think of the church as an invisible reality embracing all Protestants, and denominations as voluntary associations that one joined according to one's preferred style of being Protestant. But this new perspective was, at first, developed around the notion of America as a Protestant nation. Therefore, it was very traumatic when, beginning in the latter half of the nineteenth century, Catholic and Jewish immigrants poured into the

TALES OF SPIRITUAL TRANSFORMATION: Martin Luther King Jr.'s Kitchen Experience

Martin Luther King Jr. transformed the social and political landscape of America in the 1950s and 1960s by leading a movement of nonviolent protest against the practices of racial segregation in American life. The "civil rights movement," as it came to be known, led to equal rights under the law for people of all races and opened the way for the election of the first black president of the United States in 2008.

During the civil rights movement, King's life was threatened on a regular basis. There was a defining religious experience that lay behind his courage to continue despite these threats. King came home late from a bus boycott meeting when the movement was just beginning in Montgomery, Alabama. He was sitting in his kitchen when the phone rang. A voice said: "Nigger . . . we are tired of you and your mess now, and if you are not out of this town in three days, we're going to blow your brains out and blow up your house." Although he had received dozens of such calls before, this one got to him. Fear gripped him and he could not sleep, so he went to the kitchen for a cup of coffee. James Cone records King's telling of what happened.

> Something said to me, you can't call on daddy now; he's in Atlanta, a hundred seventy-five miles away. . . . You've got to call on that something, on that person that your daddy used to tell you about, that power that can make a way out of no way. And I discovered then that religion had to become real to me and I had to know God for myself. And I bowed down over that cup of coffee. I never will forget it. Oh yes, I prayed a prayer. And I prayed out loud that night. I said, "Lord, I'm down here trying to do what's right. I think I'm right. I think the cause that we represent is right. But Lord, I must confess that I'm faltering, I'm losing my courage and I can't let the people see me like this because if they see me weak and losing my courage they will begin to get weak." . . . Almost out of nowhere I heard a voice . . . "Martin Luther, stand up for righteousness. Stand up for justice. Stand up for truth. And lo, I will be with you, even until the end of the world." After that experience . . . I was ready to face anything. (James Cone, *Martin and Malcolm and America: A Dream or a Nightmare* [Maryknoll, NY: Orbis Books, 1991], 124–25).

Three days later King's home was bombed. Fortunately no one was hurt. While some gathered with guns seeking to protect him, he urged them to remain nonviolent, and he reminded them that no matter what happened, God would be with them in their struggle.

United States and tipped the balance away from a Protestant dominance. This led to a strong reaction of anti-Catholicism and anti-Judaism/anti-Semitism, which did not abate until the last half of the twentieth century, when Protestant, Catholic, and Jew came to be seen as acceptable alternatives within the North American denominational pattern. In the twenty-first century, the modern equilibrium is being further challenged by influxes of immigrants from Asia and the Middle East.

Consequently, the decision of whether to be a Christian civilization or adopt a diaspora model of Christian life is playing itself out not only in the developing world but in North America as well. While Fundamentalist movements want to create a public order

Not all Christian houses of worship in America have that New England look. This adobe mission church is in Taos, New Mexico.

focused on creating a "Christian America," a North American form of liberation theology seems to be embracing a diaspora model of Christianity. The liberation movement sees itself as one force among many, seeking social justice for all in a pluralist society.

North American liberation theology is shaped primarily by the civil rights movement, initiated by the Reverend Martin Luther King Jr., perhaps the most important figure for understanding postmodern Christianity in an age of globalization. King championed a diaspora model of Christianity in American social and political life. He was open to the wisdom of other religions, for he believed that God spoke to humanity in every time and in every culture. Indeed, he drew on the principles of nonviolence and civil disobedience, first perfected by the great Hindu leader Mohandas K. Gandhi, to bring about a nonviolent racial revolution in the United States. Moreover, he worked to bring an end to the war in Vietnam that was raging in the 1960s by participating in a cooperative nonviolent protest movement with Jewish and Buddhist leaders such as Abraham Joshua Heschel and Thich Nhat Hanh.

Dr. King and the Southern Christian Leadership Conference, which he founded in 1957, were at the forefront of the efforts to end racism in the U.S. In 1963,

CONTRASTING RELIGIOUS VISIONS

As the following contrasting visions indicate, every religious tradition is capable of generating both visions that encourage peace and understanding and visions that encourage conflict and violence.

Martin Luther King Jr. transformed the social landscape of American society by integrating the Sermon on the Mount with Gandhi's techniques of nonviolence to further racial and social justice in the United States.

Martin Luther King Jr.—the Gospel of Divine Mercy

Martin Luther King Jr. lived and died by Jesus' teachings from the Sermon on the Mount, found in the Gospel of Matthew (chapters 5–7). Here Jesus tells his hearers to love their enemies, do good to those who persecute them, and, when struck, turn the other cheek. God's love, like the rain, says Jesus, falls on the just and the unjust alike.

For centuries Christians were inspired by these teachings yet sought ways to avoid having to put them into practice. It was typically argued that "in the real world" to love your enemies while "turning the other cheek" was the equivalent of turning the world over to the rule of those who were most violent and unjust, which would be disastrous. So early Christian theologians like Augustine of Hippo developed the idea of "just war" or the just use of violence to protect the weak and the innocent. It was King's study of Gandhi's philosophy of nonviolence that enabled him to see that there was another alternative—nonviolent resistance to evil.

King argued that you do not simply hand the world over to those who are most violent. On the contrary, you create a mass movement of nonviolent noncooperation that brings society to a standstill until your enemy consents to compromise and begins to act more justly. This was the strategy King used to

Time magazine named Martin Luther King Jr. "Man of the Year"—the first black American ever so designated. In June 1964 the Civil Rights Act was passed, and in December King became the youngest person ever to win the Nobel Peace Prize. Then in the spring of 1965, King, accompanied by Rabbi Joshua Heschel and others, led a successful march from Selma to Montgomery, Alabama, to emphasize the need for laws to protect the right to vote for all blacks. He compared it to Gandhi's march to the sea, in India, to protest the unjust Salt Act tax. It was, indeed, a turning point, for on August 6, 1965, the Voting Rights Act was signed by President Lyndon Johnson. On April 4, 1968, at the age of thirty-nine, King was assassinated by a sniper in Memphis, Tennessee, but the civil rights movement went on to transform America to the extent that in 2008 the United States elected its first black President, Barack Obama.

organize a bus boycott in Montgomery, Alabama, in 1955 and 1956.

Tim LaHaye and Jerry B. Jenkins: *Left Behind*—the Gospel of Divine Judgment

Reportedly, more than 65 million books in the *Left Behind* series have been sold, and a children's series has sold more than 10 million copies. In addition there are a variety of related materials—movies, clothes, games, music, and so on. The series of novels on the coming end of the world is the core of a religious media sensation in contemporary American life and culture. In an interview for the television news program *60 Minutes*, the books' authors, Tim LaHaye and Jerry B. Jenkins, insisted that according to the Bible, when Jesus comes to judge the earth at the end of time he will not forgive his enemies. On the contrary, he will come to slay God's enemies in a final battle between believers and unbelievers, in which all believers will be "raptured" (lifted up into heaven) and all nonbelievers will be "left behind."

Martin Luther King Jr. put the emphasis on the Jesus of the Sermon on the Mount, who emphasizes

Not all Christians have embraced Martin Luther King Jr.'s nonviolent Christian message. In their best-selling "Left Behind" book series, Tim LaHaye and Jerry B. Jenkins portray the violence and terror of the God who comes to destroy his enemies at the end of time.

that God loves the "just and the unjust" alike, while for the authors of the *Left Behind* series, the Gospel's final message is not God's love for his enemies as found in Jesus' Sermon on the Mount but the violence and terror of the God who comes to destroy his enemies, which they believe can be found in the book of Revelation.

Conclusion: The Challenge of Religious Pluralism

A significant gulf divides the fundamentalist and postmodern ways of affirming Christian faith. Modern Christians tended to privatize religion and segregate personal piety from public life. Religion is a personal and family matter: public life should be secular and therefore free of religion. Neither fundamentalist nor postmodern Christians are willing to accept that model. Both insist that their faith should affect public life. The question is how to do this in an age of global pluralism, for the form that public faith takes in each is very different. Fundamentalism champions either a Constantinian or an

Augustinian vision of a global Christian civilization. Postmodern, postcolonial Christianity affirms a pluralistic world and a diaspora model of Christianity, as the "salt of the earth." Only a little salt is needed to flavor the whole society. Consequently, diaspora Christians seek to cooperate with others, religious and nonreligious, in achieving a compassionate social order with justice for all. We should not expect that all Christians will eventually agree with this view. More likely, as in the past, there will be diverse expressions of Christianity in diverse social, historical, and political circumstances.

Discussion Questions

1. What were the issues that were resolved by the development of the doctrine of "two natures in one person" (Council of Chalcedon) and of the Trinitarian nature of God (Council of Constantinople)? Do these doctrines put Christianity into fundamental disagreement with the prophetic monotheism of Judaism and Islam? Explain.

2. What is original sin, and why does it lead to the need to expect a savior? Is original sin a universal belief among Christians? Explain.

3. Why are Jesus, Paul, and Augustine often thought to be the three most important figures in the history of Western Christianity?

4. It can be argued that Eastern Christianity, Western Christianity, and postcolonial Christianity offer three different models for understanding the relationship between church and state and the relation of Christianity to the non-Christian world: a Constantinian model, an Augustinian model, and a diaspora model. Explain these models, and identify their strengths and weaknesses.

5. The idea of "modernity" is deeply rooted in the Christian version of the myth of history as it was interpreted by Joachim of Fiore. Explain how this is so. Give examples.

6. What is secularization, and how is it related to the history of Christianity?

7. How did Luther's understanding of Christianity differ from that of the medieval church? What was the political and religious significance of this difference?

8. How did the emergence of Protestantism contribute to the development of the secular nation-state?

9. How did Western colonialism contribute to the emergence of a post-European or postcolonial Christianity? Define and explain.

10. What are the issues that separate premodern from modern and postmodern Christianity, and how do they illustrate the fundamentalist–modernist debate?

Key Terms

Augustinian	Constantinian	fundamentalist
Catholic	deism	Gospel
Christ	evangelical	grace

heresy	original sin	Son of God
homoousios	Pentecostal	syncretistic
justification by faith	Protestant	Trinity
Kingdom of God	Protestant ethic	two natures, one
liberation theology	sacraments	person
modernist	Second Coming	

Suggested Readings

Bettenson, Henry, and Chris Maunder, eds. *Documents of the Christian Church*, 4th ed. (New York: Oxford University Press, 2011).

Fasching, Darrell J. *The Coming of the Millennium* (New York: Authors Choice Press, 1996, 2000).

Johnson, Paul. *A History of Christianity* (New York: Atheneum, 1976, 1979).

Keppel, Gilles. *The Revenge of God: The Resurgence of Islam, Christianity and Judaism in the Modern World* (University Park: Pennsylvania State University Press, 1991, 1994).

Lawrence, Bruce B. *Defenders of God: The Fundamentalist Revolt Against the Modern Age* (Columbia: University of South Carolina Press, 1995).

Littell, Franklin. *The Crucifixion of the Jews* (New York: Harper & Row, 1975).

Marsden, George M. *Understanding Fundamentalism and Evangelicalism* (Grand Rapids, MI: William B. Eerdmans, 1991).

McManners, John, ed. *The Oxford Illustrated History of Christianity* (New York: Oxford University Press, 2001).

Roof, Wade Clark, and William McKinney. *American Mainline Religion* (New Brunswick, NJ: Rutgers University Press, 1987).

Ruether, Rosemary. *Faith and Fratricide* (New York: Seabury Press, 1974).

———. *Liberation Theology* (New York: Paulist Press, 1972).

Stendahl, Krister. *Paul Among Jews and Gentiles* (Philadelphia: Fortress Press, 1976).

Tillich, Paul. *A History of Christian Thought*, Vols. 1 and 2 (New York: Harper & Row, 1967, 1968).

Von Campenhausen, Hans. *The Formation of the Christian Bible* (Mifflintown, PA: Sigler Press, 1997).

Additional Resources

From Jesus to Christ: The First Christians. This four-hour PBS video series traces Christianity from Jesus to Constantine. The entire series can be watched online at http://www.pbs.org/wgbh/pages/frontline/shows/religion/watch/. Includes timelines, study guides, etc.

A History of Christianity: The First Three Thousand Years, by Oxford historian Diarmaid MacCulloch. DVD available from PBS. Episode 1: The First Christianity; Episode 2: Catholicism: The Unpredictable Rise of Rome; Episode 3: Orthodoxy: From Empire to Empire; Episode 4: Reformation: The Individual Before God; Episode 5: Protestantism: The Evangelical Explosion; Episode 6: God in the Dock.

The Longest Hatred. A documentary on anti-Semitism in Christianity and Islam. Two videos, total of 150 minutes (Copyright Thames Television 1993 and WGBH Boston 1993).

ISLAM

5

The Many Faces of the Muslim Experience

Overview

Allahu Akbar. . . . There is no God but God. Come to prayer." Five times each day, Muslims throughout the world are called to prayer.

The images and realities of Islam and of Muslims across the world are multiple, diverse, and sometimes contradictory. Although poor villagers and wealthy urban professionals from Nigeria, Egypt, and Saudi Arabia to Afghanistan, Pakistan, and Indonesia assemble peacefully for prayer, violent Islamic extremists attack Muslims in Iraq, Afghanistan, Nigeria, and Pakistan. On the streets of Cairo, Geneva, Kuala Lumpur, and Jakarta, some Muslim women appear in stylish Islamic dress or Western fashions, while others wear dresses and veils that cover their hair and bodies.

Although in many Muslim societies the status of women is undermined by patriarchal cultures and reflects serious inequality, there are also significant indications of change. For example, in the United Arab Emirates, as in Iran, the majority of university students are women. Educated Muslim women in some sex-segregated countries (such as Saudi Arabia) are not visible in the workplace, but in other countries they work as engineers, doctors, scientists, teachers, and lawyers alongside their male colleagues. In contrast to those in many Muslim countries, Muslim women in America are as educated and earn as much as American Muslim men. Parenthetically, among religious groups in America, Muslims represent the second highest levels of education, after Jews.

◀ Adherents of the Sufi Naqshbandi order at the Islamic Institute in Cairo, one of the major mystical orders in Islam.

Islam Timeline

ca. 570	Birth of Muhammad
610	Muhammad receives first revelation, commemorated as "Night of Power and Excellence"
620	Muhammad's Night Journey to Jerusalem
622	Emigration (*hijra*) of the Muslim community from Mecca to Medina; first year of the Muslim lunar calendar
632	Muhammad's final pilgrimage to Mecca, farewell sermon, and death
632–661	Rule of the Four Rightly Guided Caliphs, formative period for Sunnis
638	Muslim conquest of Jerusalem
661–750	Umayyad Empire
680	Martyrdom of Husayn and his followers at Karbala, Iraq
750–1258	Abbasid Empire: height of Islamic civilization, patronage of art and culture, development of Islamic law, and rising trade, agriculture, industry, and commerce
756–1492	Andalusia (Muslim Spain): period of interfaith coexistence of Muslims, Christians, and Jews
8th–9th c.	Formation of major Sunni law schools
1000–1492	Christian reconquest of Muslim-ruled territories in Spain, Sicily, and Italy
1095–1453	Crusades
12th c.	Rise of Sufi orders
1187	Saladin and Muslim forces reconquer Jerusalem
1281–1924	Ottoman Empire (Middle East, North Africa, and portions of Eastern Europe)
1453	Fall of Constantinople/Istanbul, capital of former Byzantine Empire, to Ottomans
1483–1857	Mughal Empire (South Asia)
1501–1722	Safavid Empire (Iran)
1876–1938	Muhammad Iqbal, Islamic modernist and ideologue for foundation of Pakistan
1897–1975	Elijah Muhammad, leader of the Nation of Islam in the United States
1903–1979	Mawlana Abul Ala Mawdudi, founder of the *Jamaat-i-Islami* in India/Pakistan
1906–1949	Hassan al-Banna, founder of the Muslim Brotherhood in Egypt
1906–1966	Sayyid Qutb, radical, militant ideologue of the Muslim Brotherhood in 1950s and 1960s
1975	Wallace D. Muhammad (name later changed to Warith Deen Muhammad) succeeds his father, Elijah Muhammad, and progressively brings his followers into conformity with mainstream Sunni Islam
1979	Iranian Revolution and foundation of Iranian Islamic Republic under leadership of Ayatollah Khomeini; seizure of the Grand Mosque in Mecca by Muslim militants; Soviet Union invades Afghanistan
1990	FIS (Islamic Salvation Front) wins Algerian municipal and regional elections
1993	Bombing of World Trade Center in New York City by Muslim militants
1995	Welfare (Refah) party wins parliamentary elections; Dr. Necmettin Erbakan becomes Turkey's first Islamist prime minister
September 11, 2001	Terrorist attacks against the World Trade Center in New York City and the Pentagon in Washington, DC; sparks U.S.-led war against global terrorism and the hunt for Osama bin Laden and al-Qaeda

2003	U.S.-led invasion of Iraq and overthrow of Saddam Hussein; Iran's Shirin Ebadi becomes first Muslim woman to win Nobel Prize for Peace
2004	French Parliament bans Muslim headscarf in schools and public places; terrorist train attack by Muslim militants in Madrid, Spain
2006	Hamas landslide victory in Palestinian elections; Bangladeshi Muslim economist Muhammad Yunus and his Grameen Bank win the Nobel Peace Prize
2007	Turkey reelects Prime Minister Erdogan and Justice and Development Party in parliamentary elections; Declaration on Muslim-Christian relations signed by some 138 Muslim religious leaders and authorities
2009	Popular protests in Iran following controversial presidential elections marred by corruption; Nicknamed the "Twitter Revolution" because of its use of social networking tools to organize nonviolent protests
2011	Reelection of Erdogan in Turkey; Beginning of the "Arab Spring," sparked in Tunisia and Egypt, a series of nonviolent protests calling for greater levels of democracy, freedom, and an end to government corruption
2011	Osama bin Laden, the founder and head of the Islamist militant group al-Qaeda, killed in Pakistan by American military
2011	Ennahda (the Renaissance Party), in Tunisia's first democratic election, wins a plurality of votes in the Constituent Assembly
2012	In first open democratic elections in Egypt, the Muslim Brotherhood wins a majority of the vote in the parliamentary election to the People's Assembly, and the Brotherhood's Mohammed Morsi is elected president
July 30, 2013	After widespread antigovernment demonstrations, Mohammed Morsi is overthrown in a military-led coup
August 14, 2013	Egyptian security forces use lethal force, killing more than 625 and injuring thousands. The interim government moved quickly to declare the Muslim Brotherhood a terrorist organization and attempted to totally suppress it, using mass arrests and military trials that drew sharp criticism from major international human rights organizations. The government cracked down and arrested foreign journalists and Egyptian critics and democracy activists.
January 27, 2014	Tunisian Assembly passes new constitution
March 24, 2014	An Egyptian court sentences 529 members of the outlawed Muslim Brotherhood to death, the largest mass death sentence in modern Egyptian history
2014	Malala Yousafzai of Pakistan awarded Nobel Prize for Peace
2015	National Dialogue Quartet awarded Nobel Prize; Aziz Sancar of Turkey awarded Nobel Prize for Chemistry
2015	Islamic Declaration on Global Climate Change in response to Pope Francis's encyclical, *Laudato si'*
2015–2016	Muslim extremists' terrorist attacks, including operations in Paris, Brussels, Nice, and San Bernardino, CA
2016	Recent and current Muslim women presidents: Atifete Jahjaga (Kosovo) and Bibi Ameenah Firdaus Gurib-Fakim (Mauritius)
January 2016	The Marrakesh Declaration on the Rights of Religious Minorities in Predominantly Muslim Majority Communities—250 Muslim religious leaders, heads of state, and scholars defend the rights of religious minorities in predominantly Muslim countries

Islamic associations in the poor neighborhoods of Cairo and Algiers, Beirut and Mindanao provide families who cannot afford state services or who live under governments that do not provide adequate social services with inexpensive and efficient educational, legal, and medical social services. Many mainstream Muslims have worked for democratic reforms, turning to the ballot box when given the opportunity. Members of Islamic organizations have been elected to parliaments in Turkey, Algeria, Jordan, Egypt, Kuwait, Yemen, Pakistan, Thailand, and Malaysia. They have been elected prime minister of Turkey and served as president of Indonesia and Turkey and in cabinet-level positions in many countries. Others have been elected officials in professional associations of doctors, lawyers, engineers, journalists, and teachers. At the same time, the terrorist attacks of 9/11 signaled a new era of global terror from the Middle East to South Asia, Russia, Europe, the United States, and beyond.

Islam: submission or surrender to God

Muslim: one who follows Islam

This chapter will look at the history and heritage of **Islam** and impact on **Muslim** societies and world events today. It will explore the challenges and struggles within the global Muslim community in defining the meaning of Islam for modern and postmodern life.

The study of Islam and Muslim societies requires a bridging of the gap between religion, history, politics, and culture. Let us begin by briefly discussing what Islam is and where the Islamic world is.

ummah: Muslim community of believers

The word *islam* means "submission" or "surrender." A Muslim is one who submits, who seeks to actualize God's will. The Muslim community (***ummah***) is a transnational community of believers, ordained and guided by God, whose mission is to spread and institutionalize an Islamic Order, to create a socially just society: "You

Mecca is the holiest city of Islam: the birthplace of the Prophet Muhammad, where the earliest revelations occurred and toward which Muslims turn in prayer five times each day. Muslims on pilgrimage gather near Mecca's Grand Mosque following Friday dawn prayers.

are the best community ever brought forth for mankind, enjoining what is good and forbidding evil" (Q. 3:110).

Islam belongs to the Abrahamic family of monotheistic faiths. Like Jews and Christians, Muslims view themselves as the children of Abraham, as proclaimed in each of their sacred scriptures: the Old and New Testaments and the Quran. Despite significant differences, Judaism, Christianity, and Islam share a belief in one God, the creator, sustainer, and ruler of the universe who is beyond ordinary experience. And all three religions believe in angels, Satan, prophets, revelation, moral responsibility and accountability, divine judgment, and reward or punishment. Yet while Jews and Christians claim descent from Abraham and his wife, Sarah, through their son Isaac, Muslims trace their religious roots back to Abraham (Ibrahim) through Ismail, his firstborn son by Hagar, Sarah's Egyptian servant.

Today, Islam is the world's second-largest religion. Its 1.5 billion followers can be found in some fifty-seven predominantly Muslim countries, extending from North Africa to Southeast Asia (see Map 5.1). Although Islam is often associated with the

> "Say: He is Allah, the One and only; Allah, the Eternal. He did not beget, nor is He begotten; And there is none like Him."
>
> —Quran, 112

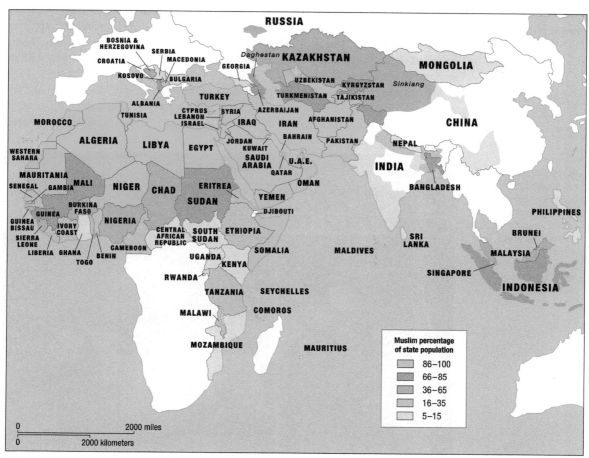

Map 5.1 The Muslim world.

Arabs, they constitute only about 20 percent of the worldwide Muslim community. In fact, the vast majority of Muslims live in Asia and Africa: Indonesia, Bangladesh, Pakistan, India, and Nigeria. In recent years, Islam has become a significant presence in the West as the second- or third-largest religion in Europe (in particular, France, Germany, and England) and in North America. Today the capitols or major cities of Islam are not only traditional strongholds like Cairo, Damascus, Baghdad, Mecca, Islamabad, and Kuala Lumpur, but also London, Paris, Marseilles, Brussels, New York, Detroit, and Los Angeles.

In contrast to the modern secular belief in the separation of church and state, Islam for many Muslims represents a comprehensive worldview in which religion and society, faith and power, are more closely bound. Throughout much of history, to be a Muslim was not simply to belong to a faith community but to live in an Islamic community or state, governed (in theory if not always in practice) by Islamic law. Historically, Islam has significantly informed politics and society, giving rise to vast Islamic empires and states as well as Islamic civilization.

Quran: Muslim scripture

From Islam's origins to the present, Muslims have been engaged in a continuous process of understanding and interpreting the word of God (**Quran**) and applying Islamic practices to their lives. Thus, while it is correct to say that there is one Islam, revealed in the Quran and the traditions of the Prophet, there have been many interpretations of Islam: some complementing each other, and others in conflict.

Muslims today, like other people of faith, struggle with the relationship of their religious tradition to modernity and postmodernity. How does a faith revealing a God-centered universe speak to a modern, post-Enlightenment, human-centered

Muslim dietary law, like Judaism's kosher law, requires the ritual slaughter of animals permitted to be eaten. Today across America, *halal* butcher shops may be found, providing these religiously prepared meats for their Muslim customers.

secular world that emphasizes reason and science? Like Judaism and Christianity, Islam contends with questions about a range of social, cultural, and scientific issues. The questions are many: What is the relationship of Islam to secularization? Should Islam today be restricted to personal life, or should it be integral to the state, law, and society? Is Islam compatible with modern forms of political participation? In the twenty-first century, what should be the Islamic positions on treatment of religious minorities, non-Muslims, and women?

Encounter with Modernity: The Challenge of Western Colonialism

Throughout history, Muslims believed that the early and rapid expansion of Islam and Islamic empires and their success and power were signs of God's guidance of and pleasure with the Islamic community. Yet the Islamic world has witnessed upheaval and renewal since the nineteenth century as Muslims absorbed the impact of European colonialism, which challenged Muslim historical self-understanding and pride and in many cases self-governance.

By the nineteenth century, Europeans had colonized many Muslim areas: the French in North, West, and Equatorial Africa and the Levant (Lebanon and Syria); the British in Palestine, Transjordan, Iraq, the Arabian Gulf, and the Indian subcontinent; and in Southeast Asia, the British in Malaya (Malaysia, Singapore, and Brunei) and the Dutch in Indonesia.

Muslims found themselves on the defensive against a European imperialism that threatened their political, religious, and cultural identity and challenged time-honored beliefs and practices. Muslim responses to colonialism and Western culture and ideas varied from rejection and confrontation to admiration and imitation.

While many conservative religious leaders resisted any significant change and new Western-oriented elites opted for a Western secular approach, Islamic modernist reformers sought a middle path that would restore their debilitated community by bridging the gap between their heritage and modernity. These reformers emphasized the compatibility of Islam with reason, modern science, and technology, reminding Muslims of the development of Islamic civilization and its contributions to philosophy, science, medicine, mathematics, and architecture. Reformers championed the need for **ijtihad**, the reinterpretation of Islamic law to meet the needs of the modern world. However, they neither produced a systematic reinterpretation of Islam nor developed effective organizations and institutions to promote their reformist message. These two failures led to the emergence of modern Islamic activist organizations (sometimes referred to as fundamentalist movements), such as the Muslim Brotherhood in the Middle East and *Jamaat-i-Islami* (the Islamic Society) in South Asia. Both these organizations criticized Islamic reformers for Westernizing Islam. In particular,

ijtihad: interpretation or independent reasoning in Islamic law

they condemned those Muslim countries that uncritically adopted Western models of development. Islam, they insisted, is a comprehensive way of life that offers an alternative path to Western social order, including capitalism, communism, and socialism. These activist movements and their many offshoots, from mainstream social and political organizations to radical revolutionary groups, continue to be major forces today.

During the post–World War II era, most of the Muslim world regained its independence. However, the boundaries of modern nation-states (such as Lebanon, Syria, Sudan, Jordan, Iraq, Kuwait, Malaysia, and Pakistan) were arbitrarily drawn by the European colonizers. Indeed, many Muslim rulers were appointed by colonial governments; others, often military officers or former officers, simply seized power. As a result, instead of elected governments, much of the Muslim world received a legacy of autocratic rulers (kings, military and ex-military) not of their choosing.

The political legitimacy of rulers and issues of national identity have plagued many of these nations to this day. Their governments have relied for control and stability on internal security forces rather than elections. Because the West provided the models for development, it was widely supposed that modernization and progress would depend on Westernization and secularization. Iran's Islamic revolution of 1979–80 shattered this assumption.

The Islamic Resurgence

The Iranian revolution signaled the resurgence of Islam in Muslim politics. Although the revolution drew attention to the reassertion of Islam in politics and society, Islam had already become a major factor in Muslim politics for more than a decade before 1979 in Egypt, Libya, and Pakistan. The crushing military defeat of combined Arab forces in the Six-Day War with Israel of 1967 and the consequent loss to Israel of major territories (especially Jerusalem, the third-holiest city of Islam) became "*the disaster*" in Muslim consciousness.

Despite national independence, most Muslim countries had remained politically and economically weak, underdeveloped, and dependent on the West. What went wrong? To regain past power and glory, many Muslims believed that they must return to the straight path of Islam. The 1973 Arab oil embargo and the later Islamic revolution in Iran reinforced the belief that Muslim economic and political power could be attributed to the resurgence of Islam in contemporary Muslim politics and society.

During the late 1960s and 1970s, Islam enjoyed a higher profile in personal and public life, demonstrated by greater religious observance and Islamic dress as well as the growth of Islamic political and social organizations and institutions. In addition, governments in Egypt, Libya, Sudan, and Pakistan as well as their opposition political parties turned to Islam in politics during the 1970s and 1980s to enhance their legitimacy and mobilize popular support. At the same time, Islamic activist organizations grew in number and size throughout the Muslim world. Alongside Islamic organizations such as the Muslim Brotherhoods of Egypt, Syria, Jordan, and Sudan, there were violent revolutionary organizations with names like Jund Allah (Army of God), Hezbollah (the Party of God), and Islamic Jihad.

Yet, by the late 1980s and 1990s, a quiet (nonviolent) revolution had also occurred. From North Africa to Southeast Asia, Islam was playing an increasingly important role in the socioeconomic and political life of society. In the twenty-first century, Islamic activists and parties are a significant factor in electoral politics in Egypt, Algeria, Morocco, Sudan, Lebanon, Jordan, Turkey, Palestine, Pakistan, Malaysia, and Indonesia. Many authoritarian rulers have experienced the power of religion in Muslim politics through ballots of Islamic supporters as well as bullets of the more radical groups.

Islam in the West

In the twenty-first century, Islam is the fastest-growing religion in North America and in Europe; the second-largest religion in France, Holland, Belgium, and Germany; and the third-largest in Britain and the United States. Even without increases in Muslim immigration and conversions to Islam, by mid-century projected Muslim birthrates will result in Islam's replacing Judaism as the second-largest religion in the United States.

Muslims in the United States, like other religious or ethnic minorities before them, face many questions about their faith and identity: Are they Muslims in America or American Muslims? Can Muslims become part of a pluralistic American society without sacrificing or losing their identity? Can people be Muslims in a non-Muslim state that is not governed by Islamic law? Can the U.S. legal system accommodate particular Muslim religious and cultural differences?

While some in the West speak of a post-Christian society, for many Muslims, the concept of a post-Islamic society is not relevant. For them, the debate is not over whether religion has a place and role in society, but rather what kind of Islam or Islamic presence should exist. Understanding Islam today requires an appreciation of the full spectrum of Muslim responses to the modern world, ranging from those who view Islam as a personal faith to others who wish to see it implemented more formally in state and society.

Throughout the ages, when Muslims have sought to define or redefine their lives, the starting point has always been an understanding of the past. To understand Islam's present and future, we must learn about the history and development of Islam and the Muslim community.

Premodern Islam: The Formative Era

For Muslims, the formative period is the time of the Prophet Muhammad, a period that included the revelation of the Quran and Muhammad's founding of the first community. It is often seen as the time of the purest and most authentic Islamic community, a society that was to be emulated by future generations, and a model to return to for inspiration and guidance. Because of the remarkable success of Muhammad and the early Muslim community in spreading the faith of Islam and the rule of Muslims, an idealized memory of Islamic history and of Muslim rule became the model for success, serving as a common reference point for later generations of reformers.

At the core of Muslim belief and faith are the messenger and the message. As Christians look to Jesus and the New Testament and Jews look to Moses and the Torah, Muslims regard Muhammad and the Quran as the final, perfect, and complete revelation of God's will for humankind.

Allah: God

The foundations of Islam are belief in God (**Allah**, Arabic for "The God") and in God's messenger, Muhammad. Though God is beyond our ordinary experience, or transcendent, Islam teaches that he can be known directly through his messengers and revelations. Thus, Muhammad and the Quran, the final messenger and the message/ revelation, are key in the formation and development of the Islamic tradition, its beliefs, laws, rituals, and social practices. Learning more about the messenger and the message will increase our understanding of Islam today and our insights about the sources Muslims use to guide their lives in the twenty-first century.

Muhammad's Early Life

Few observers in the sixth century would have predicted that Muhammad ibn Abdullah and his birthplace in central Arabia would come to play pivotal roles in world history and world religions. They could not have imagined the future impact of an orphan raised in a vast desert region marked by tribal warfare and bounded by two great imperial powers, the Eastern Roman (or Byzantine) Empire and the Persian (Sassanid) Empire. And yet the message Muhammad brought from God and the force of his personality would transform Arabia and have a significant impact on much of the world.

Pre-Islamic Arabian society and religion were tribal in structure and organization. Individuals lived in extended families; several related families constituted a clan; a cluster of several clans comprised a tribe. Al Ilah (Allah) was seen as the high god over a pantheon of tribal gods and goddesses who were believed to be directly active in everyday life. Each city or town had its divine patron/protectors and shrine. These tribal gods and goddesses were respected and feared focal points of sacrifice, prayer, and pilgrimage. The tribal polytheism of Arabia was embodied in a cube-shaped building that housed the idols of 360 tribal gods and was a center of pilgrimage. Located in the ancient city of Mecca, this cube, *Kaaba*, would be rededicated to Allah in the seventh century.

Tribal polytheism was little concerned with an afterlife, divine judgment, or reward or punishment after death. Individual identity and rights were subordinated to tribal and family identity, authority, and law. The key virtue, "manliness," included loyalty to family and protection of its members, bravery in battle, hospitality, and honor. There was little sense of moral responsibility and accountability beyond tribal and family honor. This era, in which justice was guaranteed and administered not by God but by the threat of retaliation by family or tribe, is referred to as the period of ignorance (*jahiliyya*) before Islam.

Forms of monotheism did exist in Arabia; both Arab Christian and Jewish communities had long resided in the region. The Quran also speaks of Arab monotheists, *hanifs*, descendants of Ibrahim (Abraham). In addition, Arab traders would have encountered Judaism and Christianity, since Jewish and Christian merchants regularly came to Mecca, a major center for trade as well as pilgrimage. However, monotheism's most powerful appeal to the Arabs came only when the Prophet Muhammad received his revelation from Allah.

Both in his lifetime and throughout Muslim history, Muhammad ibn Abdullah has served as the ideal model for Muslim life. He is viewed as the last or final prophet, who brought the final revelation of God. Thus, the Prophet and his example, or *Sunnah*, are central to Islam and Muslim belief and practice. Muhammad is not only the ideal political leader, statesman, merchant, judge, soldier, and diplomat but also the ideal husband, father, and friend. Muslims look to his example for guidance in all aspects of life: eating; fasting; praying; the treatment of a spouse, parents, and children; the creation of contracts; the waging of war; and the conduct of diplomacy.

There is little information about Muhammad's life before his "call" to be God's messenger. The portrait of his childhood and youth is drawn from early Muslim writers, legend, and Muslim belief. Muhammad ibn Abdullah was born in 570 into the ruling tribe of Mecca, the Quraysh. Orphaned at an early age, Muhammad was among the tribe's "poorer cousins," raised by an uncle and later employed in Mecca's thriving caravan business. Muhammad had one wife, Khadija, for twenty-eight years, until her death. Much is recorded about Muhammad's relationship with Khadija, who was his closest confidante and strongest supporter. The couple had six children, two sons who died in infancy and four daughters. After Khadija's death, Muhammad married other women, all but one of them widows.

By the age of thirty, Muhammad had become a prominent member of Meccan society. Known for his business skill, he was nicknamed al-Amin, the trustworthy. Reflective by temperament, Muhammad would often retreat to the solitude of Mount Hira to contemplate his life and society. Here during the month of Ramadan in 610, on a night Muslims commemorate as the Night of Power and Excellence, the forty-year-old Muhammad became the messenger of God. He received the first message, or divine revelation, from a figure identified by later tradition as the angel Gabriel: "Recite in the name of your Lord who has created, / Created man out of a germ cell. / Recite, for your Lord is the most generous One, / Who has taught by the pen, / Taught man what he did not know."

Muhammad became a link in a long series of biblical prophets. Like Moses, who had received the Torah on Mount Sinai, Muhammad received the first of God's revelations on Mount Hira: "It is He who sent down to you the Book with the truth, confirming what went before it: and He sent down the Torah and the Injil ["Evangel," "Gospel"] before as a guidance to the people" (Q. 3:3). Also, like Amos and Jeremiah

jahiliyya: unbelief; ignorance; used to describe pre-Islamic era

before him, Muhammad served as a "warner" from God who admonished his hearers to repent and obey God, for the final judgment was near:

> Say: "O Men I am only a warner." Those who believe, and do deeds of righteousness—theirs shall be forgiveness and generous provision. And those who strive against our signs to avoid them—they shall be inhabitants of Hell. (Q. 22:49–50)

Muhammad continued to receive revelations for more than two decades (610–32); together these revelations constitute the text of the Quran (literally, "the recitation or reading").

The first ten years of Muhammad's preaching were difficult. At first he revealed his religious experience to his wife and close friends only. When he finally began to preach God's message, which was critical of the status quo, he encountered the anger of Mecca's powerful political and commercial leaders. In the name of Allah, the one true God, Muhammad increasingly denounced polytheism and thus threatened the livelihood of those who profited enormously from the annual pilgrimage to Mecca. Equally problematic, Muhammad preached a message that strongly condemned the socioeconomic inequities of his time. The Prophet denounced the exploitation of the poor, orphans, and widows as well as prevailing business practices such as false contracts and usury (lending money at very high rates of interest). Muhammad called all true believers to join the community of God, a universal community that transcended tribal bonds and authority and was led by Muhammad, not by the Quraysh.

As Muhammad continued to preach, his situation in Mecca became more difficult. After ten years of rejection and persecution in Mecca, Muhammad and his followers migrated to Yathrib, renamed Medina ("city" of the prophet) in 622. Invited to serve as arbiter or judge for Muslim and non-Muslim alike, Muhammad became the political and religious leader of the community. Medina proved a new beginning, as the Muslim community prospered and grew.

After the *Hijra*

hijra: migration of Muhammad from Mecca to Medina; marks first year in Muslim lunar calendar

The emigration (*hijra*) from Mecca to Medina in 622 was a turning point in Muhammad's life and in Islamic history. The central significance of *hijra* and the birth of the Islamic community (the *ummah*) led to Muslims dating their calendar not from the birth of the Prophet or from the first revelation but from the creation of the Islamic community at Medina. Thus, 622 CE became 1 AH, "after the *hijra*."

tawhid: oneness of God; monotheism

Muhammad did not intend to create a new religion; rather, he was a prophet and reformer. His message proclaimed an absolute monotheism, the unity (**tawhid**), or oneness, of God and God's final revelation. Polytheism and idolatry were to be condemned and suppressed. Islam was to be a corrective to Arabian polytheism, and,

Muslims believe, the distortions of God's original revelation to Moses and Jesus by the authors/editors of the Bible that had occurred over time. Muhammad called all to repentance, to turn away from the path of unbelief and false practice and toward the straight path (**sharia**) of God. Thus, Muhammad (the last, or "seal," of the prophets; Q. 33:40) and the Quran (the complete, uncorrupted revelation) were a restoration of the true faith and message of God.

sharia: Islamic law

Muhammad taught that submission (*islam*) to God was both an individual and a community obligation. Tribal identity must be replaced by identification with Islam, now the primary source of community solidarity. This belief was reinforced by the Quran's emphasis on social justice and social welfare, in particular protection of women, orphans, and the poor. Muhammad rejected or reformed some rituals and introduced others. Importantly, he reinterpreted the pre-Islamic Arabian pilgrimage to the Kaaba at Mecca. The Kaaba was cleansed of its 360 tribal idols and rededicated to Allah. Pilgrimage to the Kaaba in Mecca, like prayer five times each day, became one of the Five Pillars, or required practices, of Islam.

While Muhammad led the community at Medina, he, in light of continuing revelations, forged its identity, consolidated its political base, and established its basic religious law and practice.

The courtyard of the Mosque of the Prophet in Medina, the first mosque in Islam, is among the most sacred sites in Islam. The original structure has been rebuilt and expanded several times.

Muhammad skillfully employed both force and diplomacy to defeat the Meccans and then to unite the tribes of Arabia under the banner of Islam. In 624 Muhammad and his followers successfully engaged and defeated the far larger Meccan forces at the Battle of Badr. For Muslims, then and now, this battle has special significance, a "miraculous" victory in which the forces of Allah and monotheism were pitted against those of Meccan polytheism. Yet despite overwhelming odds, the army of God vanquished the unbelievers. The Quran itself tells of God's assistance (Q. 8:42ff., 3:123) in securing the victory. The Battle of Badr became a symbol of divine favor and intervention remembered and invoked throughout history.

After a three-year series of battles, a truce was struck. However, in 630, Muhammad, charging that the Meccans had broken the truce, led an army of 10,000 on a march to Mecca. The Meccans surrendered without a fight. Muhammad proved magnanimous in victory, rejecting vengeance and plunder and instead granting amnesty to his former enemies. The majority of the Meccans converted to Islam, accepted Muhammad's leadership, and became part of the Islamic community.

People of the Book: those possessing a revelation or scripture from God; refers particularly to Jews and Christians

In his early preaching, Muhammad had looked to Jews and Christians as natural allies. As "**People of the Book**" who had received prophets and revelation, they had much in common with Muslims. He anticipated the acceptance of Islam by the Jews of Medina, and initially presented himself as a prophetic reformer reestablishing the religion of Abraham. However, the Jewish tribes of Medina, who had lived there a long time and had political ties with the Quraysh of Mecca, did not accept the reformer's message. While the majority of tribes converted to Islam, Medina's three Jewish tribes (comprising half the population of Medina) did not. Until that time, Muslims had faced Jerusalem to pray and, like the Jews, fasted on the tenth day of the lunar month. However, when the Jews rejected Muhammad's claims, Muhammad received a revelation and changed the direction of prayer from Jerusalem to Mecca. Thereafter, Islam was presented as a distinct religious alternative to Judaism.

Muhammad next set forth the Charter (or Constitution) of Medina, which described the rights and duties of all citizens and the relationship of the Muslim community to other communities. Jews were recognized as a separate community, politically allied to the Muslims but retaining internal religious and cultural autonomy. However, political loyalty and allegiance were expected. The Jews' denial of Muhammad's prophethood and message and their political ties with the Meccans became a source of conflict. The Quran accuses some Jewish tribes of regularly breaking treaties: "Why is it that whenever they make pacts, a group among them casts it aside unilaterally?" (Q. 2:100). Muslim perception of intrigue, rejection, and betrayal by the Jewish tribes led first to exile and later to warfare. After the Battle of the Ditch in 627, the Jews of the Banu Qurayza, a Jewish tribe who lived in Yathrib, were denounced as traitors who had consorted with the Meccans. In the end, Muhammad moved to crush the remaining Jews in Medina.

"In matters of faith, He has laid down for you the same commandment that He gave Noah, which We have revealed to you [Muhammad] and which We enjoined on Abraham and Moses and Jesus: 'Uphold the faith and do not divide into factions within it.'"

—Quran 42:13

Muhammad's use of warfare was in keeping both with Arab custom and the Hebrew prophets' belief (Exodus 14:14, Deuteronomy 20:4, and 2 Kings

10:25–31) in the conquest and the punishment of "enemies of God." Both believed that God had sanctioned battle with the enemies of the Lord. However, it is important to note that the motivation for Muhammad's actions was political rather than racial or theological, a fact often overlooked by critics of Islam as well as militant Muslims.

In 632, Muhammad led the pilgrimage to Mecca. There the sixty-two-year-old leader delivered a farewell sermon in which he emphasized:

> Know ye that every Muslim is a brother unto every other Muslim, and that ye are now one brotherhood. It is not legitimate for any one of you, therefore, to appropriate unto himself anything that belongs to his brother unless it is willingly given him by that brother.[1]

This event continues to be remembered and commemorated each year by millions of Muslims who make the annual pilgrimage to Mecca.

The Message of the Quran

Muslims believe that the Quran is the eternal, uncreated, literal, and final word of God revealed to Muhammad as guidance for humankind (Q. 2:185). Thus, for Muslims, Islam is not a new religion but rather the oldest, for it represents the "original" as well as the final revelation of God to Abraham, Moses, Jesus, and Muhammad.

The Prophet Muhammad is seen as an intermediary who received God's message and then communicated it over a period of twenty-two years. The text of the Quran is about four-fifths the length of the New Testament. The Muslim scripture consists of 114 chapters (**surahs**) of 6,000 verses, arranged by length, not chronology.

surahs: chapters of the Quran

The God (Allah) of the Quran is seen as the creator, sustainer, ruler, and judge of humankind. He is merciful and just, the all-knowing and all-powerful, the lord and ruler of the universe. The Quran teaches that God's revelation has occurred in several forms: in nature, in history, and in scripture. God's existence can be known through nature, which points to or contains the "signs" of its creator and sustainer (Q. 3:26–27). Human history also contains clear examples and lessons of God's sovereignty and intervention (Q. 30:2–9). And finally, God's will for humankind has been revealed through a long line of prophets and messengers: "Indeed We sent forth among every nation a Messenger saying: 'Serve your God and shun false gods'" (Q. 16:36).

Muslims believe that the Quran, like the Torah and the Evangel (Gospel), is taken from an Arabic tablet, the source of all scriptures, preexisting with God in heaven. From it, the teachings of the three Abrahamic faiths (Judaism, Christianity, and Islam)

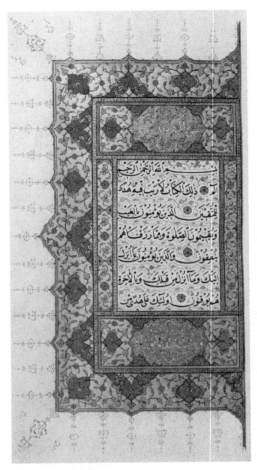

God's word, as revealed in the Quran, is the final and complete revelation. It provides the primary and ultimate source of guidance, the basis for belief and practice in Islam. Study, memorization, recitation, and copying of the Quran have been central acts of piety. The noble art of copying the Quran has produced a rich tradition of calligraphy. This manuscript page provides a beautiful example.

were revealed at different stages in history. Indeed, many Muslims take their names from the biblical prophets, who also are named in the Quran Ibrahim (Abraham), Musa (Moses), Sulayman (Solomon), Dawud (David), Yahya (John), Maryam (Mary), and Issa (Jesus). Mary, the mother of Jesus, is cited more often in the Quran than in the entire New Testament.

Because Arabic is the language of the Quran, all Muslims memorize, recite, and pray the Quran in Arabic, whether they understand it fully or not. Much as the Roman Catholic Mass until the middle of the twentieth century was always said in Latin, Arabic is viewed as the sacred language of Islam; indeed, it is regarded as the language of God. Whatever their local language, Muslims pray in Arabic five times each day.

Because the Quran is regarded as God's sacred Word, it is handled with reverence. Memorization of the entire text of the Quran is a time-honored act of piety. For many Muslims the clearest evidence of the Quran's power and uniqueness is its impact on its hearers; indeed, many have been moved to conversion after hearing the beauty of a Quranic recitation. Recitation or chanting of the Quran is a major art form as well as an act of worship. Muslims gather in stadiums and auditoriums around the world to attend international Quran recitation competitions. To win an international competition can be a source of great national pride.

A Golden Age of Expansion, Conquest, and Creativity

The rule of Muhammad and his first four successors, or **caliphs**, is seen by Sunni Muslims as the formative period of Muslim faith and history. After God sent down his final and complete revelation for humankind through his last prophet, the Islamic community/state was created, and the primary sources of Islamic law, the Quran and **Sunnah** of the Prophet, originated. Both reformers and Islamic revivalists today look to this period as the reference point for divine guidance and historical validation. Muslims believe that the revealed message of the Quran and the example of the Prophet and his successors were corroborated in history after "miraculous" victories at Badr and elsewhere, by the spread of Islam as a faith as well as its phenomenal geographic and political expansion, which produced Islamic Empires.

Muhammad united the tribes of Arabia under the banner of Islam through preaching, diplomacy, and force. During the century after his death, the period of the four Rightly Guided Caliphs, Muslim armies spread the faith and rule of Islam, inspired by their faith and material (bounty from richer societies) and spiritual rewards (paradise for those who died and were remembered as martyrs). These highly motivated armies overran the Byzantine and Persian empires, which had already been greatly weakened by internal strife and constant warfare between them.

Christendom experienced the early expansion of Islam as a threat to its religious and political hegemony. Muslim rule, and with it the message of Islam, quickly spread from the Byzantine and Persian empires to Syria, Iraq, and Egypt and then swept across North Africa and into Europe, where Muslims ruled Spain and the Mediterranean from Sicily to Anatolia (see Map 5.2).

For non-Muslim populations in Byzantium and Persia, who had been subjugated by foreign rulers, Islamic rule meant an exchange of rulers rather than a loss of independence. Many in Byzantium willingly exchanged Greco-Roman rule for that of the Arabs with whom they had closer linguistic and cultural affinities and to whom they paid lower taxes. Upon declaration of their allegiance to the Islamic state and payment of a tax, these "protected" (***dhimmi***) peoples could practice their faith and be governed by their religious leaders and law in matters of faith and private life.

caliph: successor of Muhammad as political and military leader of the Muslim community

Sunnah: example set by Muhammad of living the principles of the Quran

dhimmi: "protected"; refers to non-Muslim peoples who were granted religious freedom under Muslim rule in exchange for payment of a tax

Because Muslims believe that the Quran is God's Word or revelation, from an early age children are taught to recite the Quran.

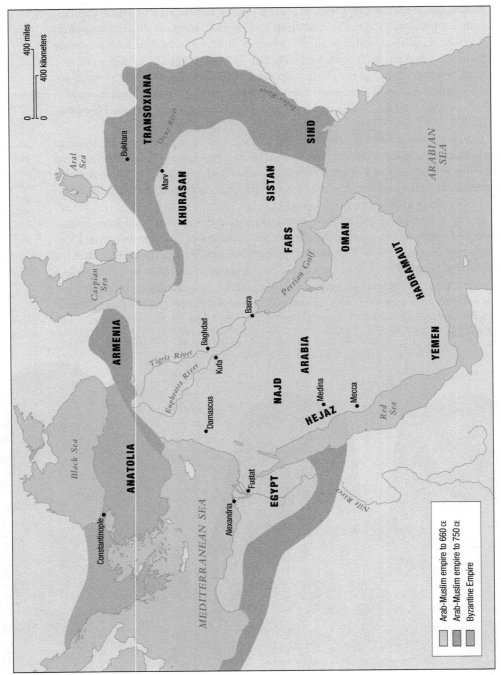

Map 5.2 The Muslim Empire to 750 CE.

Arab-Muslim empire to 660 CE
Arab-Muslim empire to 750 CE
Byzantine Empire

Islam proved more tolerant than imperial Christianity, providing greater religious freedom for Jews and indigenous Christians. Under Muslim rule, most local or indigenous Christian communities, persecuted by the "foreign" Christian orthodoxy of their rulers, could practice their faith.

The rapid spread of imperial Islam produced a vibrant Islamic civilization that flourished from the ninth to the twelfth centuries. Urban cultural centers emerged in Cairo, Baghdad, Cordova, Palermo, and Nishapur. With significant assistance from Christian and Jewish subjects, Muslims collected the great books of science, medicine, and philosophy from the West and the East and translated them into Arabic. The age of translation was followed by a period of great creativity as a new generation of Muslim thinkers and scientists made their own contributions to learning in philosophy, medicine, chemistry, astronomy, algebra, optics, art, and architecture. Towering intellectual giants dominated this period: al-Farabi (d. 950), Ibn Sina (known as Avicenna, 980–1037), Ibn Rushd (known as Averroes, d. 1198), al-Biruni (973–1048), and al-Ghazali (d. 1111).

In later centuries, Europeans, emerging from the Dark Ages, turned to Muslim centers of learning to regain their lost heritage and to learn from Muslim advances. Many of the great medieval Christian philosophers and theologians (Albert the Great, Thomas Aquinas, Abelard, Roger Bacon, Duns Scotus) acknowledged their intellectual debt to their Muslim predecessors.

The failures and reforms of Muslim societies today, as in the recent past, are often measured against this history, at times romanticized, of an earlier period of brilliant success.

Diversity, Division, and Dissent

The accomplishments of Islam's early history were also marked by division. During Muhammad's lifetime, the community had been united by his prophetic claims, charismatic leadership skills, and the divine revelations he continued to receive. However, Muhammad's death led to crises, dissent, and civil wars.

Given the pivotal role of Muhammad in the life of the community, his death in 632 was a traumatic event. What was the community to do? Who was to lead? These questions were to threaten the community's survival.

Muhammad's senior followers, known as the *Companions* of the Prophet, moved quickly to reassure the community. In proclaiming Muhammad's death to the faithful, the Companion Abu Bakr declared: "Muslims! If any of you has worshipped Muhammad, let me tell you that Muhammad is dead. But if you worship God, then know that God is living and will never die." The Companions selected Abu Bakr as caliph (*khalifah*, "successor or deputy"). As caliph, he was not a prophet but rather Muhammad's successor as political and military head of the community.

This next stage in the history of the Muslim community, the Caliphate (632–1258), has traditionally been divided into three periods: the time of the Rightly Guided Caliphs

This enameled glass mosque lamp, made in the early 1300s, was dedicated to a Muslim ruler. Quotations from the Quran decorate the lamp.

(632–61), followed by the Umayyad (661–750) and Abbasid (750–1258) dynasties. During these centuries a vast empire was created, with successive capitols at Medina, Kufa, Damascus, and Baghdad, resulting in a politically and militarily powerful and culturally brilliant Islamic civilization. However, it was the earliest period, that of the Rightly Guided Caliphs, that was to become the example for later generations of believers.

Abu Bakr (632–34), the first successor of Muhammad, was tested almost immediately when some Arab tribes attempted to declare their independence from the community. Abu Bakr crushed the tribal revolt, consolidated Muslim rule over the Arabian Peninsula, and preserved the religiously based unity of the Islamic-community state.

Abu Bakr's successor, Umar ibn al-Khattab (634–44), initiated a period of expansion and conquest. During the reign of the third caliph, Uthman ibn Affan (644–56), from the Umayyad clan, tribal factionalism resurfaced with a series of rebellions that would plague the Islamic community's development.

A second crisis of leadership, with repercussions down through the centuries, occurred when civil war broke out during the reign of the fourth caliph, Ali. Although in 632 the majority of the community had supported the selection of Abu Bakr as caliph, a minority dissented, believing that leadership should stay in the family of the Prophet and thus pass to its senior male member, Ali, instead of Abu Bakr. In addition to being Muhammad's cousin, Ali was the Prophet's son-in-law, having married Fatima, a daughter of Muhammad and Khadija. Shortly after Ali's accession to power, a group that included Muhammad's widow, Aisha, the daughter of Abu Bakr, challenged his authority. This was followed by the rebellion of Muawiya, the governor of Syria. Arbitration proved inconclusive but did lead to two results that have had a profound impact on the history of Islam.

First, a group of Ali's followers, the Kharajites (those who "go out," or secede), broke away. The Kharajites held both Ali and Muawiya to be unbelievers whose revolt against God was punishable by death. Second, after Ali was assassinated by a group of Kharajites, Muawiya then seized power in Syria and established the Umayyad dynasty (661–750).

The Umayyad dynasty was responsible for the rapid spread of Islam and the emergence of imperial Islam, with its capital in Damascus. However, opposition to what later Muslim historians would characterize as impious Umayyad caliphs also resulted in important reform movements. Some movements, such as the Kharajites and the Shiah, were revolutionary, while others led to the development of Islamic law and mysticism (Sufism).

The Kharajites, who had broken with Ali, emerged as revolutionaries who, although unsuccessful in their own times, continue to inspire contemporary radical groups. The Kharajites interpreted the Quran and the Sunnah literally and sought to impose their beliefs on others. They viewed the world as divided into Muslims, defined as those who agreed with the Kharajites, and infidels, those who differed with the Kharajites and were thus the enemies of God and to be fought and killed.

Like extremist Muslim groups today, the Kharajites, claiming to follow the letter of the Quran and the example of the Prophet, adopted their own interpretation of Islam. Seeing themselves as God's righteous army, they believed that violence was obligatory in their battle against the usurpers of God's rule. Other Muslims who committed an action contrary to the letter of the law (as interpreted or understood by the Kharajites) were guilty of grave sin. According to the Kharajites, they were apostates and thus had committed treason against the Islamic community-state. If they did not repent, they were to be fought against and killed. Many of the components of this early Islamic worldview may be found in twentieth- and twenty-first-century Muslim extremist writings, including those of the Muslim Brotherhood's Sayyid Qutb, who will be discussed in the Radical Islam section, and in the ideology of groups such as al-Qaeda and ISIS.

The Origins of the Sunni–Shiah Split

A second major revolutionary movement spawned by opposition to Umayyad rule was the rebellion by the followers of the fourth caliph, Ali. The results of this violent disagreement would lead to the two major branches of Islam, the communities of the **Sunni** majority and the **Shiah**, or Shii, minority.

The followers (*shiah*, "partisans") of Ali had been thwarted twice: when Muhammad's cousin was not appointed as the first caliph, and later when Muawiya seized the caliphate from Ali, the Prophet's fourth successor. In 680, when the Umayyad ruler Yazid, the son of Muawiya, came to power, Husayn, the son of Ali, was persuaded by a group of Ali's followers in Kufa (a city in modern Iraq) to lead a rebellion. However, the support promised to Husayn did not materialize. Husayn and his army were slaughtered by the Umayyad army at the city of Karbala (also in modern Iraq).

The memory of Karbala and the "martyrdom" of Husayn resulted in a Shii worldview, a paradigm of suffering, oppression, and protest against injustice. The mentality encouraged by this paradigm was reinforced by the Shiis' minority status and discrimination against them through the centuries. It sustained the community throughout history and, as Iran is a majority-Shiah state, became a major source of inspiration during Iran's "Islamic" revolution of 1978–79.

Sunni Muslims constitute 85 percent and Shiah approximately 15 percent of the global Islamic community. Although united in their common confession of faith in God, the Quran, and the Prophet Muhammad, their notions of leadership and history differ. The reality of the dynastic Umayyad and Abbasid caliphates notwithstanding, in Sunni Islam, the caliph ideally is the selected or elected successor of the Prophet. However, he serves only as the political and military leader of the community. He is not a prophet. By contrast, in Shiah Islam, the **imam**, or leader, is not selected from among the members of the community but must be a direct descendant of the

Sunni: Muslims who accept the Sunnah and the historic succession of the Caliphs

Shiah: followers of Ali, the cousin and son-in-law of Muhammad

imam: in Sunni Islam, the prayer leader and one who delivers the Friday sermon; in Shia Islam, refers to Ali's descendants, who are believed to be the legitimate leaders (not the Sunni caliphs) of the global Muslim community or *ummah*

The Blue Mosque, Shrine of Ali bin Thabit, cousin and son-in-law of Prophet Muhammad. Ali was the fourth caliph of Sunni Islam and the first imam of Shiah Islam. Built in the fifteenth century, the mosque has survived countless wars in near perfect condition. While some believe that it houses the tomb of Ali, most believe that he is buried in the Imam Ali Mosque in Najaf, Iraq.

Prophet's family. Moreover, he is both the religious and the political leader of the community. Though not a prophet, he is the divinely inspired, sinless, infallible, and final authoritative interpreter of God's will as formulated in Islamic law.

Sunnis and Shiah also developed differing interpretations of history. For Sunni, the early success of Islam and the power of its rulers were signs of God's rewards to a faithful community and historical validation of Muslim belief and claims. In contrast, the Shiah saw the same events as the illegitimate usurpation of power by Sunni rulers. For the Shiah, therefore, history is the theater for the struggle of a minority community, righteous but historically disinherited and oppressed, that must restore God's rule on earth under his imam. The early centuries of Islamic history would witness ongoing struggles between Sunnis and Shiah but also the remarkable development of religious thought (Islamic law, theology, and mysticism), institutions, traditions, and civilization.

Premodern Islam: The Classical Era

A critical issue faced by all religious believers today is the continuity of current religious belief and practice with centuries-old sacred traditions. So, too, Islamic tradition and heritage are used to justify contemporary beliefs and practices and as the basis for Islamic reform.

Law and Mysticism: The Exterior and Interior Paths to God

Dissatisfaction with Umayyad rule, in which wealth led to abuse of power and corruption, resulted in the development of two non-revolutionary reform movements: the *ulama* (religious scholars, or learned ones), with their Islamic law, and the Sufis, whose Islamic mysticism we shall discuss later.

In contrast to Christianity's emphasis on doctrine or theology, Islam, like Judaism, places primary emphasis on religious observance of and obedience to God's law. Muslims are commanded by the Quran to struggle (the literal word for struggle is *jihad*) in the path (*sharia*) of God, to realize, spread, and defend God's message and community. The faithful are to function as God's representatives on earth, promoting good and prohibiting evil (Q. 3:104, 3:110). All Muslims are responsible as individuals and as a community for the creation of the good society. Despite vast cultural differences, Islamic law is both an idealized blueprint and a moral compass that has provided a source of guidance and a code of behavior for Muslims throughout the ages.

Islamic law developed during the Umayyad dynasty in the eighth and ninth centuries as a response to religious as well as political concerns. Legal experts developed and standardized the law, with a view to limiting the power of the caliph or his appointed judges. Islamic law continued to flourish during the tenth century under the Abbasid caliphs, who overthrew the Umayyads and legitimated their revolution by becoming the patrons of Islam and Islamic law. It is important to note that Islamic law did not develop primarily from the practice of courts or from government decrees but through the interpretation of scholars. In Sunni Islam, the *ulama* based a religious blueprint on four official sources of Islamic law: the Quran, the Sunnah, *qiyas*, and *ijma*.

The primary material sources of Islamic law are the Quran and Sunnah (example) of the Prophet. The Quran contains eighty prescriptions that would qualify as law in the strict sense of the term; the majority of Quranic texts provide general principles and values, reflecting what the aims and aspirations of Muslims should be.

The second source of law is the Sunnah, which comes from the Quran, early biographies, and especially prophetic traditions. The Sunnah consists of hundreds of thousands of narrative stories or reports (**hadith**) about what the Prophet said and did, and seemingly addresses every situation. The centrality of the Prophetic traditions cannot be overestimated: "They are associated with the person who is 'alive' here and now and who is as revered and loved by all Muslims now as he was fourteen centuries ago."[2]

The third source of law is analogical reasoning (*qiyas*). When confronted by a question or issue not addressed specifically in the Quran or Sunnah, jurists looked for similar or analogous portions of scripture to identify principles that could be applied to a new case. For example, there is no specific text dealing with the use of mind-altering

ulama: religious scholars

jihad: the struggle to be a good Muslim, to follow God's will; armed struggle in defense of Islam or the Muslim community; offensive warfare by Muslim leaders to spread their rule or by Muslim terrorists to legitimate their actions

"Goodness is not turning your faces towards the East or West; goodness is to believe in Allah, the Last Day, angels, and the Book, and the prophets; to spend money, out of love for Him, for your kin, for orphans, for the needy, for the wayfarer, for those who ask, and for the freeing of slaves; to be steadfast in prayer, and pay the alms tax regularly; to fulfill contracts you have made; and to be firm and patient, in pain (or suffering) and adversity, and throughout all periods of panic. Those are truthful and God-fearing people."

—Quran 2:177

hadith: narrative report of Muhammad's sayings and action

qiyas: legal term for analogical reasoning

drugs, but from *qiyas*, jurists can justify the condemnation of such substances on the basis of sacred texts that plainly forbid the consumption of alcohol.

Finally, consensus (*ijma*) is based on a statement traditionally attributed to the Prophet: "My community will never agree on an error." In reality, consensus has generally amounted to acceptance of or agreement on an issue from the majority of religious scholars who represented religious authority.

The two main divisions of Islamic law concern a Muslim's duties to God (*ibadat*), which consist of obligatory religious practices such as the Five Pillars of Islam, and social transactions or duties to others (*muamalat*), which include regulations governing public life, from contract and international law to laws on marriage, divorce, and inheritance.

Islamic law is a source of unity and guidance, but individual jurists and legal scholars from diverse social backgrounds and cultural contexts have differed in their interpretation of texts, in their personal opinions, and in their notions of equity and public welfare. Diversity and disagreement in Islamic law are reflected in the acceptance of different law schools and the validity of their divergent opinions.

We see these differences in official legal opinions or interpretations (*fatwas*) of Muslim jurists (*muftis*) who advised judges and litigants in the past and in recent times. In the Gulf War of 1991, some muftis supported Iraq, and others supported a U.S.-led coalition that included troops from Egypt, Kuwait, and Saudi Arabia. Similarly, sharp differences have existed among religious leaders over the religious legitimacy or illegitimacy of suicide bombing in Israel-Palestine. But however different and contentious interpretations of Islamic law have been throughout Islamic history, the Five Pillars of Islam unite all Muslims in their worship and following of God.

The Five Pillars of Islam

If God, the Quran, and the Prophet Muhammad unite all Muslims in their common belief, the Five Pillars of Islam provide a unity of practice:

1. *The Declaration of Faith.* A Muslim is one who bears witness that "There is no God but the God and Muhammad is the messenger of God." One need only make this simple statement, known as the ***shahadah***, to become a Muslim.

2. *Prayer.* Five times a day, Muslims throughout the world are called to worship God. In many cities of the world, this call comes from the ***muezzin*** from atop the tower (minaret) of the mosque.

   Prayer (***salat***) is preceded by a series of ablutions to cleanse the body and to symbolize the purity of mind and body required for worshipping God. Facing the holy city of Mecca, Muslims recall the revelation of the Quran

---

Margin glossary:

ijma: in Islamic law, consensus

ibadat: worship, ritual obligations

muamalat: social interactions

fatwa: legal opinion or interpretation from a Muslim legal expert (*mufti*)

mufti: legal expert who issues *fatwas* to judges and litigants

"Recite what has been revealed to you of the Book and perform prayer regularly: for prayer restrains from shameful and unjust deeds. Allah's remembrance is the greatest (thing in life) and Allah knows what you do."
—Quran 29:45

shahadah: Muslim declaration of faith

muezzin: one who issues the call to prayer from the minaret of a mosque

salat: prayer performed five times each day

These Uzbek Muslims, like fellow believers across the world, perform their prayers five times each day.

and reinforce a sense of belonging to a single, worldwide community of believers. Muslims may pray in any appropriate place wherever they happen to be. They may do so as individuals or in a group. For Muslims, *salat* is an act of worship and adoration of God and remembrance of his word, not one of request or petition.

On Friday, the noon prayer is a congregational prayer that usually takes place in a **mosque** (*masjid*, "place of prostration"). A special feature of the Friday prayer is a sermon (*khutba*), preached from a pulpit (*minbar*). Since there is no priesthood in Islam, any Muslim may lead the prayer. In many communities, larger mosques do have an imam who leads the prayer and is paid to look after the mosque.

3. *Almsgiving.* The third pillar of Islam is the *zakat*, almsgiving. As all Muslims share equally in their obligation to worship God, so too do they look after the social welfare of their community. This is accomplished through an annual contribution of 2.5 percent of one's accumulated wealth and assets, not just on income. *Zakat* is not charity, since almsgiving is

mosque: a building used for public and community worship

khutba: sermon delivered in a mosque on Fridays

minbar: mosque pulpit from which *khutba* is preached

zakat: almsgiving

A muezzin calling the faithful to prayer in the city of Kashgar in western China.

Muslims are required to abstain from food and drink from dawn to dusk during the month of Ramadan. At dusk each day during Ramadan, families gather to break the fast and share a meal. This practice is called "breakfast."

"Alms are for the poor, the needy, and those employed to administer the (funds); for those whose hearts are bound together; as well as for freeing slaves and [repaying] debts; spending in the cause of Allah and for the wayfarer: thus Allah commands, and Allah is All-Knowing and Wise."
—Quran 9:60

Ramadan: ninth month of Muslim calendar, during which Muslims fast

hajj: annual pilgrimage to Mecca, in which all adult Muslims are expected to participate at least once if physically and financially able to do so

seen as a duty imposed by God. Just as the Quran condemns economic exploitation, it warns against those who accumulate wealth and fail to assist others (Q. 3:180). Those who have benefited from God's bounty, who have received their wealth as a trust from God, are required to look after the needs of the less fortunate members of the Muslim community.

4. *The Fast of Ramadan*. Muslims are required to fast during **Ramadan**, the ninth month of Islam's lunar calendar. From dawn to dusk, all healthy Muslims must abstain from food, drink, and sex. The primary emphasis is less on abstinence than on spiritual self-discipline, reflection, and the performance of good works.

The fast is broken at the end of the day by a light meal. In the evening, families exchange visits and share foods and sweets that are served only at this time of the year. The month of Ramadan comes to an end with a three-day celebration, the Feast of the Breaking of the Fast (Id al-Fitr), one of the great religious holy days and holidays of the Muslim calendar.

5. *Pilgrimage to Mecca*. The pilgrimage season follows Ramadan. Every adult Muslim who is physically and financially able is expected to perform the pilgrimage (*hajj*) to Mecca in Saudi Arabia at least once in his or her lifetime. Just as Muslims are united five times each day as they face Mecca in worship, each year almost 2 million Muslims from every part of the globe make the physical journey to this spiritual center of Islam, where they again experience the unity, breadth, and diversity of the Islamic community. Pilgrims wear white garments, symbolizing for everyone, rich and poor alike, the unity

The pilgrimage to Mecca is one of the Five Pillars of Islam. All Muslims, health and wealth permitting, are expected to make the pilgrimage at least once in their lifetime.

The Kaaba. The pilgrimage (*hajj*) to Mecca, one of the Five Pillars of Islam, takes place during the first ten days of the twelfth month of the lunar calendar. The focus of the pilgrimage is the Kaaba, "the cube," also known as the House of God, which tradition says was built by Abraham and his son Ismail. Pilgrims circumambulate the Kaaba, located within the Great Mosque of Mecca. This is a ritual act that many believe symbolizes the angels' circling of God's throne in heaven.

and equality of all believers before God. Men and women worship together. There is no segregation of the sexes.

When the pilgrims reach Mecca, they proceed to the Grand Mosque that houses the Kaaba. There they pray at the spot where Abraham, the patriarch and father of monotheism, stood, and they circumambulate the Kaaba seven times. Another part of the *hajj* is a visit to the Plain of Arafat, the site of Muhammad's last sermon, where pilgrims seek God's forgiveness for their sins and for those of all Muslims throughout the world.

Those who have made the *hajj* often use the honorific title *hajj*. Many, as demonstrated by this house in Jerusalem, decorate the facade with illustrations to show that the owner has been to Mecca.

The pilgrimage ends with the celebration of the Feast of Sacrifice (Id al-Adha). The "great feast" commemorates God's testing of Abraham by commanding him to sacrifice his son Ismail (in the Jewish and Christian traditions it is Isaac who is put at risk). Commemorating God's final permission to Abraham to substitute a ram for his son, Muslims sacrifice animals (sheep, goats, cattle) not only in Mecca but across the Muslim world. While some of the meat is consumed, most is distributed to the poor. The three-day Feast of Sacrifice is a time for rejoicing, prayer, and visiting with family and friends.

Women and Muslim Family Law

If many Muslims speak of Islam as liberating women, others in the West as in Muslim countries decry the continuing marginalization and oppression of women. The position of Muslim women must be viewed within the dual historical context of the development of Islamic law and the politics and culture of their societies. Islamic law itself

"For Muslim men and women—for believing men and women, for devout men and women, for true men and women, for men and women who are patient and constant, for men and women who humble themselves, for men and women who give in Charity, for men and women who fast (and deny themselves), for men and women who guard their chastity, and for men and women who engage much in Allah's praise—for them has Allah prepared forgiveness and great reward."

—Quran 33:35

reflects both the Quranic concern for the rights and protection of women and the family and the traditions of the patriarchal, male-dominated society within which Islamic law was developed.

The Quran introduced reforms affecting the status of women both through new regulations and by teachings that led to the modification of prevailing customs. The Quran recognized a woman's rights to contract marriage, to receive and keep her dowry, and to own and inherit property. No equivalent rights existed in Christianity or in Judaism during or long after the lifetime of the Prophet. In fact, women in the West did not gain inheritance rights until the nineteenth century.

As the Five Pillars are the core of a Muslim's duty to worship God (*ibadat*), family law is central to Islam's social laws (*muamalat*). Because of the centrality of the community in Islam and the role of the family as the basic unit of society, family law has enjoyed pride of place in the development of Islamic law and in its implementation throughout history. Similarly, though the emergence of modern Muslim states has often seen the adoption of Western-oriented civil and commercial laws or legal systems, in most countries Muslim family law has remained in force. While in some countries family law has been reformed rather than replaced, often this reform has generated considerable debate. In the 1980s, the resurgence of Islam was often accompanied by attempts to return to the use of classical or medieval family law and to reverse modern reforms. Thus today, as in the past, the subject of women and the family remains an extremely sensitive subject in Muslim societies.

The status of women and the family in Muslim family law is the product of many factors: traditional Arab culture, Quranic reforms, foreign ideas and values assimilated from conquered peoples, and the interpretation of male jurists in a patriarchal society. Regulations developed in the early centuries of Islamic history regarding marriage,

Jihad: The Struggle for God

Jihad, "to strive or struggle," is sometimes referred to as the sixth pillar of Islam, although it has no such official status. In its most general meaning, *jihad* refers to the obligation incumbent on all Muslims, as individuals and as a community, to exert themselves to realize God's will, to lead a virtuous life, to fulfill the universal mission of Islam, and to spread the Islamic community through converting others. Thus, today it can be used to describe the personal struggle to uphold the Five Pillars and follow the example of the Prophet. In our times, the term is used to describe the struggle for educational or social reform—to establish good schools, to clean up a neighborhood, to fight drugs, or to work for social justice. However, it also includes the struggle for or defense of Islam, or holy war. Although *jihad* is not supposed to include aggressive warfare, this tactic has been invoked by early extremists such as the Kharajites, by rulers to justify their wars of conquest and expansion, and by contemporary extremists such as Osama bin Laden and ISIS as well as other militant organizations in Lebanon, the Persian Gulf, and Indonesia.

divorce, inheritance, and bequests have guided Muslim societies, determining attitudes toward women and the family.

The Quran teaches that men and women are equal before God in terms of their religious and moral obligations and rewards (Q. 33:35). However, husbands and wives are seen as fulfilling complementary roles, based on differing characteristics, capacities, and dispositions and their traditional roles in the patriarchal family. Men function in the public sphere, and are responsible for the financial support and protection of the family.

A woman's primary role is that of wife and mother; she is responsible for the management of the household, raising her children and supervising their religious/moral training. In light of women's more sheltered and protected status and men's greater experience in public life and broader responsibilities, the Quran (and Islamic law) teaches that wives are subordinate to husbands (Q. 2:228), and in Islamic law the testimony of one man is worth that of two women. Similarly, because men in a patriarchal system were responsible for the economic well-being of all women and other dependents in the extended family, the male portion of inheritance was twice that of a female.

Marriage is a primary institution in Islam, regarded as incumbent upon all Muslims. It is a civil contract or covenant, not a sacrament. It safeguards chastity and the growth and stability of the family, legalizing sexual intercourse and the procreation of children. Reflecting the centrality of the family and the identity and role of individual family members, marriage is not simply an agreement between two people but between two families. Thus, marriages arranged by the two families or by a guardian are traditional, although the majority of jurists agreed that a woman should not be forced to marry a man against her will.

Many non-Muslims are unaware of Quranic reforms affecting women or the differing interpretations of a Quranic text. For example, many equate Islam with polygamy or, more accurately, polygyny. Although the Quran explicitly permits a man to marry four wives, the same verse (Q. 43) notes that if all cannot be supported and treated equally, then only one is permitted. The purpose of this provision was not to discourage all men from practicing monogamy but to afford protection to unmarried women as well as to regulate the rights of men. Islamic modernists in recent years have used this same spirit and another verse ("You are never able to be fair and just between women if that is your ardent desire," Q. 4:129) to argue that the Quranic ideal is monogamy and that plural marriages should be restricted or eliminated. In particular, they note that the original revelation was given to a premodern community in which losses in battle left many widows who needed protection. More important, many maintain that the demands of modern life make it extraordinarily difficult for any man to provide equally for more than one wife, especially in terms of time and affection.

Islamic law, reflecting the spirit of the Quran (Q. 4:35) and a saying of the Prophet ("of all the permitted things divorce is the most abominable"), regards divorce as permissible but reprehensible. One authoritative legal manual calls divorce "a dangerous and disapproved procedure . . . nor is its propriety at all admitted, but on the ground of urgency of relief from an unsuitable wife."[3] Islamic law itself, as if to underscore the seriousness of divorce, prescribes that a man must pronounce the words or formula of divorce three separate times to make it irrevocable.

The strong influence of custom can be seen in the more limited rights of divorce accorded women. For example, in contrast to men, women had to go to court and present grounds for divorce. In addition, women seeking divorce were limited to charges like physical abuse, abandonment, and failure to provide adequate maintenance. Beginning in the 1920s, some Muslim governments relaxed these and other legal restrictions on women.

Historically, divorce rather than polygamy has proved to be the more serious social problem in Muslim societies, as a woman's Quranic and legal rights to contract and dissolve her own marriage, to receive and control her dowry, or to inherit often disappeared under the pressures of entrenched patriarchal societies. Thus custom tended to prevail over Islamic law as well as the Quran.

A well-known example of the interaction of custom and scripture is the veiling and seclusion (***purdah***) of women. These customs, assimilated by Islamic practice from the conquered Persian and Byzantine empires, have been viewed by many (though certainly not all) as appropriate expressions of Quranic principles and values. The Quran does not stipulate the veiling and seclusion of women, although it does say that the wives of the Prophet should speak to men from behind a partition. It tells women to dress and behave modestly (Q. 24:30–31), but the admonition applies to men, as well.

Veiling and seclusion have varied considerably across Muslim societies and in different historical periods. Originally veiling had been meant to protect women in upper-class urban surroundings, where they enjoyed mobility and opportunities to socialize. Village and rural women were slower to adopt the measure, which interfered with their ability to work in the fields.

Over the centuries, as the practices of veiling and seclusion spread, there were negative effects on the status of women. The institution of *purdah* cut off many women's access to the mosque, the social and educational center of the community. This isolation further lowered their status. Poorer women were often restricted to small houses with limited social contacts. The twentieth-century Muhammad al-Ghazali (d. 1996) said: "Ninety percent of our women do not pray at all; nor do they know of the other duties of Islam other than their names."[4]

Although debate rages today in many Muslim societies about the status and character of "the Muslim woman," with greater opportunities for women's education and employment have come calls to reform the inequities of some Muslim laws that affect women only. Modernizing governments since the 1920s have reformed Muslim family laws in marriage, divorce, and inheritance.

Reforms included measures that restricted a male's right to unilaterally divorce his wife as well as to practice polygyny. In fact, a wife was permitted to specify in her marriage contract that a husband must obtain her permission before taking another

purdah: seclusion of women from men who are not relatives

wife. A wife's grounds for divorce were increased, as well. These reforms were partial and were imposed from above through legislation. They were often resisted or reluctantly accepted by the *ulama*. However, with the more recent resurgence of Islam, more conservative or traditional religious forces have rejected family law reforms as Western inspired, calling instead for a return to classical Islamic laws and seeking again to limit and control women's role in society.

The Interior Path of Love: Islamic Mysticism

Alongside the path of law (*sharia*) is the interior path or way (*tariqa*) of Sufi mysticism, a major popular religious movement within Sunni and Shii Islam. Whereas the *sharia* described the duties and rights that order the individual and community, Sufism offered an esoteric path or spiritual discipline. The Sufi method sought not only to follow God but also to experience God's presence.

Islamic mysticism, like Islamic law, began as a reform movement. Having successfully united the tribes of Arabia and conquered the Byzantine and Persian empires, the *ummah* entered a new phase in its development. In its capital, Damascus, the Umayyad caliphs established an imperial court characterized by material luxuries. Pious Muslims increasingly saw these changes as evidence that God and submission to his will were being replaced in the courts of dynastic rulers by concerns for power and wealth. To counter this trend, critics began to study the Quran, the traditions of the Prophet, and the performance of religious duties, re-emphasizing the centrality of God over worship of the material world and its rewards.

The term **Sufism** comes from the coarse woolen garment (*suf*, "wool") worn by many of these early ascetics. The reformers did not reject the world so much as dependence on the things of this world. Desiring a more faithful return to the purity and simplicity of the Prophet's time, Sufi men and women practiced self-denial and good works. The **Sufis** were known for detachment from the material world, repentance for sins, fear of God and the Last Judgment, and selfless devotion to the fulfillment of God's will.

Sufism: Islamic mysticism

Sufis: Muslim mystics

Early emphasis on ascetic detachment and meditation was complemented by the fusion of asceticism with an undying devotional love of God as exemplified by Rabia al-Adawiyya (d. 801). This joining of the ascetic with the ecstatic permanently influenced the nature and future development of Sufism. An attractive woman, Rabia declined offers of marriage, not willing to permit anyone or anything to distract her from total commitment to God. Nothing captures better her selfless devotion than the following words attributed to her:

> O my Lord, if I worship Thee from fear of Hell, burn me in hell, and if I worship Thee in hope of Paradise, exclude me thence, but if I worship Thee for Thine own sake, then withhold not from me Thine Eternal Beauty.[5]

Turkish Sufi order (Mawlawi *tariqah*), founded by Jalal al-Din Rumi (d. 1273), one of the most famous Sufi mystics. These men are popularly known as *whirling dervishes* because of one of their meditation rituals, a dance in which they revolve to the music of Sufi songs.

Over the years, a variety of ascetic and ritual practices were adopted as part of the mystic way, including fasting, poverty, silence, and celibacy. Among the Sufi techniques to experience the presence of God are rhythmic repetition of God's name, breathing exercises that focus consciousness on God, and the use of music and dance to show devotion to God and Muhammad. The best-known use of dance is that of Turkey's whirling dervishes, who circle their master to imitate the divinely ordained motions of the universe.

One popular practice of Sufism is the veneration of Muhammad and Sufi saints as intermediaries between God and humanity. Despite the official Islamic belief that Muhammad was only a human being and did not work miracles, over the centuries stories arose of the Prophet's extraordinary powers. In Sufism these stories were extended to Sufi saints, called the friends (**wali**) or protégés of God, who are said to perform such miracles as curing the sick, multiplying food, and reading minds. The burial sites or mausoleums of Sufi masters became religious sanctuaries visited by pilgrims.

wali: Sufi term referring to a saint

Though Sufi spirituality complemented the more ritual and legalistic orientation of the *ulama* and the *sharia*, the relationship between the two was often tense. The *ulama* tended to regard Sufi masters and the mystic way as a challenge to their authority and their interpretation of Islam. Sufis tended to regard the *ulama's* legalistic approach to Islam as lesser, incomplete, and subordinate to the Sufi way.

The majority of the *ulama* reacted to these challenges to their authority and worldview by condemning Islamic mysticism in the name of Islamic orthodoxy. At this critical juncture a prominent Islamic scholar, Muhammad al-Ghazali (1058–1111), emerged to reconcile the tensions.

Al-Ghazali spent many years practicing and studying Sufism in Arabia and Palestine. His great work, *The Revivification of the Religious Sciences*, argued that law, theology, and mysticism were neither incompatible nor inconsistent with one another. This reassured the *ulama* about the orthodoxy of Sufism. In al-Ghazali's great synthesis, law and theology were presented in terms that the *ulama* could accept, but they were grounded in religious experience and interior devotion (Sufism). Al-Ghazali reconciled the *ulama* and the Sufis, earning him the title "Renewer (*mujaddid*) of Islam." While the tension between many of the *ulama* and Sufism continued, Sufism in the twelfth century and later swept across much of the Islamic world. Sufi orders became the great missionaries of Islam, and Sufism became integral to everyday popular religious practice and spirituality.

In modern times, some religious conservatives and reformers have remained critics of Sufism, despite its widespread popularity, and extremists like ISIS have destroyed historic Sufi shrines.

The many faces of contemporary Islam include not only the more visible reassertion of Islam in Muslim politics but also the revitalization of Muslim piety and spirituality. These adherents of the Sufi Naqshbandi order at the Islamic Institute in Cairo represent one of the major mystical orders in Islam. Not only did they play an important role in reformist and anticolonialist movements throughout the Islamic world in the past, they also do so today.

Islam and the State

As we have seen, the early success of Islamic empires influenced the development of Islamic law and mysticism. From Muhammad's establishment of the first Muslim community at Medina in 622 CE, the soldiers, traders, and Sufis of Islam spread God's word and rule, creating a vast region of Islam (*dar al-Islam*). The caliphate, with its centralized Islamic empires, the Umayyad (661–750) and Abbasid (750–1250) dynasties, was followed by Muslim sultanates extending from Timbuktu in Africa to Mindanao in Southeast Asia. During this period great Muslim empires also emerged: the Ottoman in the Middle East (1281–1924), the Safavid (1501–1722) in Iran, and the Mughal (1483–1857) in South Asia.

mujaddid: "renewer"; one who comes to restore and revitalize Islamic community and practice

dar al-Islam: territory controlled and ruled by Muslims

However different these empires and sultanate states were, Islam constituted the basis of their political and social life. Religion informed the state's political, legal, educational, and social institutions. The *caliph* or *sultan*, as head of state, was seen as the political successor of Muhammad. Though not a prophet, he was the protector of the faith who was to implement Islamic law and to spread Islamic rule. The *ulama* were the guardians of religion, its interpreters, and as such often served as advisers to *caliphs* and *sultans*. Although not an ordained clergy, they were a major intellectual and social force in society. They played a primary role in the state's religious, legal, educational, and social service institutions. The *ulama* were theologians and legal experts, responsible for the application of the law and the administration of *sharia* courts. They ran the schools and universities that trained those who aspired to public as well as religious office. They administered funds for a range of services, from the construction and maintenance of mosques, schools, student hostels, and hospitals to roads and bridges. In time, they came to constitute a religious establishment alongside and often dependent on the political establishment. Indeed, in many empires the ruler appointed a senior religious leader, *Shaykh-al-Islam*, as head of religious affairs, a post that still exists in many Muslim countries today.

In an Islamic state, citizenship was also based on religious affiliation. Muslims were full citizens, enjoying all the rights and duties of this position. As discussed earlier, Jews and Christians, as People of the Book, were also citizens, but they had the status of protected people (*dhimmi*). Islam also informed the international relations of the state. The spread of Islam as a faith and a religiopolitical system was legitimated by the Quran and by the teaching and example of Muhammad. Conquest and diplomacy, force, persuasion, preaching, and alliances were its means.

The obligation to strive (*jihad*) to realize God's will included *jihad* as an armed struggle to defend Islam or the community and to spread Muslim rule. As such, *jihad* became part of Islam's doctrine of war and peace. As Islamic empires spread,

Sheikh Lotf Allah Mosque in Isfahan, Iran, completed in 1618, is one of the architectural masterpieces of Safavid Iranian architecture.

The Taj Mahal, the mausoleum built (1631–47) by the grief-stricken emperor Shah Jahan for his beloved wife Mumtaz Mahal, who died in childbirth. Situated in a forty-two-acre garden, it is flanked by two perfectly proportioned mosque complexes. This crowning achievement, a landmark of world architecture, symbolizes the wealth and splendor of the Mughal Empire. The project brought together craftsmen and calligraphers from the Islamic world who worked with Muslim and Hindu craftsmen from the empire.

non-Muslims could pick one of three options: to convert to Islam, to become "protected people" (*dhimmi*) and pay a poll tax, or to become enemies to be fought.

For the believer, the role of Islam in state and society reflected the continuum of Muslim rule, power, and success from the time of the Prophet Muhammad to the dawn of European colonialism. This continuity of an Islamic ideology and system reinforced the purpose and mission of a divinely guided community. As a result, Sunni Muslim history contains the belief that following the Islamic community's divine mandate to spread God's guidance and governance will lead to prosperity and power in this life as well as the promise of eternal life in heaven.

The rapid spread of Islam as a dynamic faith and imperial power was regarded as a theological and political threat to Christendom, epitomized by the launching of the Crusades.

Islam and the West (Christendom): The Crusades

Despite common religious roots and instances of cooperation, the history of Islam and Western Christendom has been marked more by confrontation than by peaceful coexistence. For the Christian West, Islam is seen as the religion of the sword; for many Muslims, the Christian West was epitomized first by the Crusades and centuries later by European colonialism.

Unlike Judaism or any other world religion, Islam constituted an effective theological and political challenge to Christendom and its ambitions. From the seventh to the eleventh centuries, Muslim armies overran the Byzantine Empire, Spain, and the Mediterranean, from Sicily to Anatolia. At the same time, Islam challenged Christian religious authority. Appropriating Christianity's insistence that the New Testament describes a new covenant and revelation superseding that of the Jews, Muslims now claimed that God, due to the corruption of the original revelations to Jews and Christians (for example, the Christian doctrine that Jesus was in fact the Son of God, the second person of the Trinity), had sent down His final and complete revelation, the Quran, to Muhammad. Muslims, like Christians before them, now also claimed to have a divinely mandated universal mission to call all to Islam. Christianity and Islam, theologically and politically, were on a collision course.

By the eleventh century, Christendom's response to Islam was twofold: the struggle to reconquer Andalusian Spain (1000–1492), where the coexistence of Muslims, Christians, and Jews had produced a vibrant culture, and the undertaking of the Crusades (1095–1453).

Jerusalem had been taken by Arab armies in 638. Thereafter, for five centuries, Muslims lived in peaceful coexistence with Christians and with Jews. Although banned by Christian rulers, Jews were permitted by Muslims to return to live and worship in

Courtyard of the Lions, Alhambra Palace, the fourteenth-century residence of the Nasrid dynasty in Granada, Spain, one of the remarkable monuments remaining from the several centuries of Muslim rule in Andalusia, when Muslims, Jews, and Christians coexisted and produced a high culture.

Jerusalem. However, in the eleventh century political events that pitted Christendom against Islam began a period of distrust that continues to the current day.

In 1071, the Byzantine emperor Alexius I, whose army had been decisively defeated by a Seljuq (Abbasid) army, feared that all Asia Minor would be overrun. He called on other Christian rulers and the pope to come to the aid of his capital, Constantinople, by undertaking a "pilgrimage," or crusade, to free Jerusalem and its surrounding area from Muslim rule. For the leader of the Western church, Pope Urban II, Jerusalem provided an opportunity to gain recognition of papal authority. In addition, Christian rulers, knights, and merchants were driven by the promise of booty as well as potential trade and banking opportunities if a Latin kingdom was established in the Middle East. This enthusiastic response to Alexius united Christendom in a holy war against the "infidel," ostensibly to liberate Jerusalem.

Few events have had a more shattering effect on Muslim–Christian relations than the Crusades. Western perceptions of the Crusades are shaped by three myths:

- Muslims were the protagonists
- Christendom triumphed
- the sole purpose of the Crusades was to liberate Jerusalem.

In fact, the Crusades were launched by Urban II and Christian rulers for political and economic (as well as religious) reasons. Moreover, on balance the Muslims prevailed.

For Muslims, the collective memory of the Crusades lives on as an example of the aggression and imperialism of the Christian West and a reminder of Christianity's early hostility toward Islam. While Muslims remember July 15, 1099, when the Christian crusaders conquered Jerusalem and massacred all its Jewish and Muslim inhabitants, as an episode of horrific violence, European Christian monks hailed it as the greatest event in world history since the crucifixion of Christ. Muslims contrast that massacre with the later actions of Salah al-Din (Saladin), the great Muslim general, who, in reconquering Jerusalem in 1187, spared noncombatants.

By the fifteenth century the Crusades ended. They had failed in their supposed aim to unite Christendom and turn back Muslim armies. Amid a bitterly divided Christendom, the Byzantine capital, Constantinople, fell in 1453 to Muslim armies, was renamed Istanbul, and became the seat of the Ottoman Empire. For Muslim–Christian relations, what actually happened in the Crusades is less important than how the period has been remembered. Each community (Islam and Christianity) sees the other as militant holy warriors, determined to conquer, convert, or eradicate the other, and thus an enemy of God—an obstacle and threat to the realization of God's will. This bitter history continued through the era of European colonialism and shaped the superpower rivalry that began in the twentieth century.

Understanding Islam today requires an appreciation of key historical events from the eighteenth to the twentieth centuries as well as of the causes and nature of pre-modern and modern reform movements. Sacred texts and long-held religious beliefs, combined with the specific sociopolitical contexts of Muslim communities, have been critical factors in producing a diversity of Muslim experiences and interpretations of Islam.

Premodern Revivalist Movements

From the eighteenth to the twentieth centuries, the Islamic world witnessed a period of upheaval and renewal. In many countries Muslim societies, already threatened by European colonialism, failed and declined for internal reasons. Such crises sparked responses from religious social/political revivalist movements across the Islamic world. Though their political and socioeconomic conditions varied, all revivalist movements were concerned about religious, political, and social disintegration, and all were convinced that the solution lay in a renewal of the Islamic way of life.

Islamic revivalist movements draw on a long tradition of revival and reform. Islamic revival and reform involve a call for a return to the fundamentals, the Quran and Sunnah, and the right to interpret (*ijtihad*, or use of independent judgment) these primary sources of Islam.

In the eighteenth and nineteenth centuries, this belief took on popular religious forms. While such Islamic revivalists claimed to return to the original teachings of the Quran and the Prophet Muhammad, in fact each one produced new religious interpretations and cultural syntheses. The Wahhabi movement in Arabia and the Mahdiyya in Africa are perhaps the best known of the post-medieval revivalists. Each exerted a formative influence on modern Muslim states: the Wahhabi in what is now Saudi Arabia and Qatar and the Mahdist in Sudan.

Geometric design plays a major role in Islamic art. Artists use circles, triangles, hexagons, and squares to create ornate patterns to express and reinforce the unity of the Islamic world vision. This striking illustration comes from a Moroccan Quran tablet.

A religious leader, Muhammad ibn Abd al-Wahhab (1703–92), and a local tribal chief, Muhammad ibn Saud (d. 1765), joined forces to produce a united, militant religiopolitical movement. Abd al-Wahhab was dismayed by the condition of his society, which he saw as having degenerated to that of pre-Islamic Arabia, a period of ignorance (*jahiliyya*) of Islam. He was appalled by such popular religious practices as the veneration of Sufi saints, which he believed compromised the unity or oneness of God, and he was very critical of the Islamic community in Arabia, which had fallen back into tribalism and tribal warfare. He condemned some devotional rituals as idolatry, the worst sin in Islam, and dismissed others as pagan superstitions. Abd al-Wahhab wished to purify Islam from all foreign un-Islamic practices.

The Wahhabi movement waged a rigorous holy war to subdue and unite the tribes of Arabia. Muslims who did not go along were declared enemies of God who must be fought. Unlike other revivalist movements, the Wahhabi chose to completely suppress rather than merely reform Sufism.

The Mahdi of the Sudan, on the other hand, was a charismatic Sufi leader who initiated a militant reformist religiopolitical movement. The founder of the Mahdiyya order, whose name was Muhammad Ahmad, proclaimed himself *Mahdi* ("divinely guided one") in 1881. Thus, he went beyond most other revivalist reformers who claimed the right to interpret Islam and instead said that he was a divinely appointed representative of God.

The Mahdi established an Islamic community by uniting his followers. He also justified waging holy war against other Muslims, declaring Sudan's Ottoman Muslim rulers to be infidels. During this period, Sufism was reformed, and alcohol, prostitution, gambling, and music were outlawed. After a four-year struggle, Mahdist forces overcame Egyptian forces of the Ottoman Empire, and an Islamic state was established in Khartoum in 1885.

> *Mahdi*: "divinely guided one" who is expected to appear at the end of time to usher in a perfect Islamic society of peace and social justice

Islam and Modernity

By the nineteenth century, the decline of Muslim societies made them vulnerable to European imperialism, which ultimately did much to shape the modern Muslim world politically, economically, religiously, and culturally. When Europe overpowered North Africa, the Middle East, South Asia, and Southeast Asia in the nineteenth century, reducing most Muslim societies to colonies, many Muslims experienced these defeats as a religious crisis as well as political and cultural setbacks.

Colonialism brought European armies and Christian missionaries, who attributed their conquests not only to their military and economic power, but also to the superiority of Western civilization and the truth inherent in Christianity. The French spoke of a "mission to civilize" and the British of "the white man's burden." Thus, the missionaries who accompanied the armies of bureaucrats, soldiers, traders, and teachers were quick to spread the message of the superiority of Christian religion and civilization.

Muslim responses to Europe's political/religious dominance varied, ranging from resistance or warfare in "defense of Islam" to accommodation to (and selective assimilation of) Western institutions and values. Some advocated following the example of the Prophet Muhammad, who in the face of persecution in Mecca chose to emigrate from Mecca to Medina and later to fight. However, the military defense of Islam and Muslim territory was futile against the large, modernized weapons of superior European forces. Emigration to a "safe, independent" Muslim territory was impossible for most.

Many Muslim rulers were attracted to what they believed were the sources of European power and success: Western knowledge, science, and technology. Their goal was development of modernized societies with modern militaries. Students were sent to study in the West, and political, economic, and educational institutions, based on European models, were created in many parts of the Muslim world. As a result, a modern Muslim elite quickly emerged.

These elites, intellectually and culturally influenced by the West, regarded the traditional Muslim religious establishment as relics of the past, incapable of responding to the demands of modern society. Most advocated a Western secular model of development, and the adoption or adaptation of Western political, legal, economic, educational, and social institutions.

Islamic Modernism

In the late nineteenth and early twentieth centuries, Islamic reformers sought to bridge the gap between conservative religious leaders and modernizing secular elites. Reformers developed an Islamic rationale for the reinterpretation of Islamic doctrine and law and the adaptation of modern ideas, science, technology, and institutions. Declaring Islam to be a religion of reason, science, and progress, reformers called on Muslims to reclaim the beliefs, attitudes, and values that had previously contributed to powerful Islamic empires and flourishing Islamic civilizations.

Islamic modernism challenged both the leadership and doctrines of the conservative religious establishments, rejecting blind acceptance of the authority of the past. Many of these reformers were not traditionally trained religious scholars but modern educated "laymen" who claimed the right to interpret and reinterpret Islam. They repudiated the authority of the *ulama* as the sole "keepers of Islam" as well as the tradition that the *ulama's* legal doctrines and interpretations were binding.

The rationale of Islamic modernism was based on a two-part understanding of Islamic law. Reformers distinguished between Islamic laws that consisted of divinely revealed and unchanging laws and values and those laws that were the product of human reason and custom, developed to meet specific social and historical needs. Thus, modernists distinguished between the unchanging laws of God (such as those governing prayer, fasting, and pilgrimage) and social legislation or regulations that were capable of change.

Islamic modernism remained primarily attractive to the intellectual elite. It provided the precedent for adapting "modern" ideas and institutions (from the nation-state and parliamentary government to women's education), as well as the notion that those qualified to interpret Islam extended beyond the *ulama*. However, it failed to produce a systematic reinterpretation of Islam or to develop effective organizations to spread and implement its message. These shortcomings contributed to the emergence of revivalist activist organizations like the Muslim Brotherhood in Egypt and the Jamaat-i-Islami (Islamic Society) in South Asia.

Modern Islamic Revivalist Movements

The presence of Europe in the Muslim world and the seeming failure of reformers to block Western political and cultural influence led to two major Islamic revivalist movements in the Middle East and South Asia in the 1930s: the Muslim Brotherhood

(*Ikhwan al-Muslimin*) and Jamaat-i-Islami. Their trailblazers, Hassan al-Banna (1906–49) and Sayyid Qutb (1906–66) of the Brotherhood and Mawlana Abul Ala Mawdudi (1903–79) of the Jamaat have had an incalculable impact on the development of Islamic movements throughout the Muslim world to the present day. The worldviews of both movements are based on an interpretation of Islam that informed social and political activism. Their founders are the architects of contemporary Islamic revivalism, men whose ideas and methods have been studied and emulated by scholars and activists from the Sudan to Indonesia.

Hassan al-Banna established the Muslim Brotherhood in Egypt in 1928, and Mawlana Abul Ala Mawdudi, a journalist, organized the Jamaat-i-Islami in India in 1941. Both leaders combined traditional Islamic educational backgrounds with knowledge of modern Western thought. Believing that their societies were dominated by and dependent on the West, both al-Banna and Mawdudi posited an "Islamic alternative" to conservative religious leaders as well as to Western-oriented Islamic and secular modern elites. The *ulama* were regarded as outmoded, a religious class whose fossilized Islam and co-optation by governments held back the Islamic community. Modernists, on the other hand, were seen as having been influenced by blind or uncritical admiration for the West.

The Brotherhood and the Jamaat proclaimed Islam to be a self-sufficient, all-encompassing way of life, an ideological alternative to Western capitalism and Marxism. Joining thought to action, these movements provided Islamic responses to such issues as how best to respond to European colonialism and to revitalize the Muslim community. In contrast to Islamic modernists who justified adopting Western ideas and institutions because they were compatible with Islam, al-Banna and Mawdudi sought to produce new interpretations, using Islamic sources. For these men, the cultural influence of the West threatened the very identity and survival of the Muslim community and was far more dangerous in the long run than political intervention.

Though they opposed Westernization, the Brotherhood and the Jamaat were not against all forms of modernization. They provided modern educational and social welfare services, and used modern technology and mass communications to spread their message and mobilize popular support. That message, though rooted in Islamic sources, was created for a twentieth-century audience. It addressed the political and social problems of modernity as seen through their Muslim eyes and interpretations of Islam. Both organizations recruited followers from mosques, schools, universities, and society: students, workers, merchants, and young professionals, primarily city dwellers from the lower middle and middle classes. The goal was to produce a new generation of modern, educated, but Islamically oriented political and social leaders.

Al-Banna and Mawdudi advocated a process of reform rather than violent political revolution. To establish an Islamic state required first the Islamization of society through a gradual process of social change. Both the Brotherhood and the Jamaat maintained that Muslims should not look to Western systems such as capitalism or communism, and argued that faith in the West was misplaced. They observed that Western democracy had itself contributed to authoritarianism, economic exploitation,

RITUALS AND RITES: Ideological Origins of Contemporary Revivalism

Despite differences, Hassan al-Banna and Mawlana Mawdudi shared the following ideological worldview based on a historical tradition that has inspired and guided many contemporary reform movements.

1. Islam is a comprehensive way of life, a total, all-embracing ideology for personal and public life, for state and society.
2. The Quran, God's revelation, and the example (Sunnah) of the Prophet Muhammad are its foundations.
3. Islamic law (the *sharia*, the "path" of God), based on the Quran and Sunnah, is the sacred blueprint for Muslim life.
4. Faithfulness to the Muslim's vocation to reestablish God's sovereignty or rule through implementation of God's law results in success, power, and wealth of the Islamic

community (*ummah*) in this life as well as eternal reward in the next.

5. Muslim societies fail and become subservient to others because they have strayed from God's divinely revealed path, following the secular, materialistic ideologies and values of the West or of the East—capitalism or Marxism.
6. Restoration of Muslim pride, identity, power, and rule (the past glory of Islamic empires and civilization) requires a return to Islam, the reimplementation of God's law, and the acceptance of God's guidance for state and society.
7. Science and technology must be harnessed and used within an Islamically oriented and guided context to avoid the Westernization and secularization of Muslim society.

corruption, and social injustice. Further, they believed that Western secularism and its separation of religion and the state would be responsible for the ultimate downfall of the West. Finally, the Brotherhood maintained that years of Arab subservience to the West had not prevented the West from betraying Arabs by supporting Israeli occupation of Palestine.

Radical Islam

The Muslim Brotherhood had a confrontation with the Egyptian state in the late 1950s and 1960s that caused a group within the movement to become more militant and radicalized. The chief architect of this transformation, Sayyid Qutb, recast the ideological beliefs of Hassan al-Banna and Mawlana Mawdudi into a revolutionary call to arms.

A devout Muslim, Sayyid Qutb had memorized the Quran as a child. Like many young intellectuals of the time, he studied Western literature and grew up an admirer of the West. Qutb was a prolific writer and an active participant in contemporary literary and social debates.

In 1949, Qutb traveled to the United States to study educational organization. Although he had come to the United States out of admiration, Qutb's experiences convinced him that the sexual permissiveness, moral decadence, and anti-Arab bias, which he perceived in U.S. government and media support for Israel, had corrupted all of Western civilization. Shortly after his return to Egypt in 1951, Qutb joined the Muslim Brotherhood.

During the 1950s, Qutb emerged as a major voice of the Muslim Brotherhood, especially influential among the younger, more militant members. Government crackdown on the Brotherhood and Qutb's imprisonment (1954–64) and torture increased his radicalization. He took the ideas of al-Banna and Mawdudi to a militant radical revolutionary conclusion.

Qutb regarded Egypt and other Muslim authoritarian governments as repressive and anti-Islamic. Society was divided into two camps, the party of God and the party of Satan, those committed to the rule of God and those opposed to it. There was no middle ground between the forces of good and of evil. Qutb advocated a group of true Muslims within the broader, corrupted society. He further maintained that the creation of an Islamic system of government was a divine commandment. Given the authoritarianism of many regimes, Qutb concluded that government reform was impossible and *jihad* as armed struggle was the only way to implement a new Islamic order. Islam, he declared, stood on the brink of disaster, threatened by repressive anti-Islamic governments and the neocolonialism of the West and the East. Qutb went beyond his predecessors when he declared Muslim elites and governments as enemies of God, against whom all true believers should wage holy war. Many later radical groups, including al-Qaeda and ISIS, have adopted Qutb's critique of Muslim rulers as necessitating the violent overthrow of un-Islamic systems of government.

In 1966, Qutb and several other Muslim Brotherhood leaders were executed. The government attempted to purge and destroy the Brotherhood, not just Qutb and his followers. Thousands of Brothers were arrested and tortured, while others went underground or fled the country. Many concluded that the Brotherhood had been totally crushed, a prediction that was to prove false a decade later.

It is difficult to overstate the impact of Hassan al-Banna, Mawlana Mawdudi, and Sayyid Qutb on contemporary Islamic movements. Combining religiopolitical activism with social protest or reform, contemporary movements range from moderate groups that function with society to violent extremists and terrorists, from selective criticism of the West to rejection and attacks on all that the West stands for. Indeed, these movements reflect the multiple issues facing Muslims in their struggle to determine the relationship of Islam to modern state and society:

- countering Western political and cultural dominance
- dealing with the challenges of modernity to Islamic belief
- redefining Islam and its relevance to modern life and society
- addressing the clash of cultures not only between the West and the Muslim world but within Muslim societies over religious and national identity and development.

Islam and Postmodern Trends in a Postcolonial World

The Impact of the Islamic Resurgence

In recent years, the Muslim world has experienced a contemporary resurgence of Islam. New Islamic governments or republics were established in Iran, Sudan, and Afghanistan. Rulers, political parties, and opposition movements have used Islam to attract supporters. Islamic activists have led governments in Egypt, Turkey, and Tunisia, served in cabinets and in elected parliaments, and served as senior officials in professional associations. At the same time, a minority of militant extremist organizations, in Egypt, Algeria, Nigeria, Lebanon, the West Bank and Gaza, Pakistan, Afghanistan, and Indonesia have engaged in violence and terrorism to topple governments or achieve related goals. Extremists have left a legacy of kidnapping, hijacking, bombing, and murder from the Middle East to Southeast Asia, Europe, and the United States. Understanding this phenomenon requires an awareness of its roots. What were the causes and conditions that led to the contemporary resurgence of Islam?

Islam in Modern State and Society

A map of the modern Muslim world offers a visual explanation for the upheaval in Muslim societies. During the twentieth century, former Islamic empires and sultanates were replaced by modern nation-states, carved out by European colonial powers after World War I. By World War II, most of these newly designated states had won their independence, but the new rulers had been placed on their thrones by their former colonizers. Moreover, Westernized elites introduced or imposed European culture and values in many Muslim societies. As a result, issues of government legitimacy as well as national and cultural identity remained unresolved. During the Cold War, the stability of many rulers was due to their military and security forces and the support (financial and military) of Western or Soviet allies rather than widespread political participation and empowerment.

Once these modern nation-states had been created in the Muslim world, it was expected that they would generally follow a secular path of development. Outwardly, this seemed to be the general case. While Saudi Arabia proclaimed itself an Islamic state, most new nations adopted or adapted Western political, legal, social, economic, and educational institutions and values. Turkey, for example, under the leadership of Mustafa Kemal Atatürk, suppressed Islamic institutions, banned Islamic dress and Islamic law, and transplanted Western secular laws and institutions to create its own version of a secular state.

However, Egypt, Syria, Iraq, Pakistan, Malaysia, and Indonesia created what may be called "Muslim states." In these and most other countries in the Islamic world, the majority populations are Muslim, but Western-inspired institutions (such as parliaments, educational systems, and banks) have been generally adopted. Western dress, culture, and entertainment became pervasive among the wealthy and powerful in urban centers.

Throughout the first three-quarters of the twentieth century, progress and prosperity in Muslim societies were regarded as dependent on the degree to which Muslims and their societies were "modern." The degree of progress and success for individuals, cities, and governments was measured in terms of conformity to Western standards and values. Based on these criteria, Turkey, Tunisia, Egypt, Lebanon, and Iran were often seen as among the more modern, advanced, and "enlightened" (that is, Westernized and secular) countries. Saudi Arabia, the states of the Persian Gulf, Afghanistan, Bangladesh, and Pakistan were generally regarded as more traditional, religious, and thus "backward."

The Failure of Modernity and the Islamic Revival

The late 1960s and 1970s shattered the hopes of many who believed that national independence and Western-oriented development would usher in strong states and prosperous societies. The crises of many Muslim societies at this time proved a powerful catalyst for a religious resurgence and revival. The realities of many Muslim societies raised questions of national identity and the political legitimacy of rulers as well as of religious faith and meaning. Such pervasive conditions as poverty, illiteracy, failed economies, high unemployment, and unequal distribution of wealth could not be blamed entirely on Western influences.

The signs of these profound problems would not become fully appreciated in the West until the Iranian revolution of 1978–79. There were previews, however, during the preceding decade: the 1967 Arab–Israeli war, Malay–Chinese riots in Kuala Lumpur in 1969, the Pakistan–Bangladesh civil war of 1971, and Lebanon's civil war of the mid-1970s. Such catalytic events triggered a soul-searching reassessment among many Muslims.

Many saw the return of Islam as a domestic and international political force as signaling a return of God's guidance and favor. However, the fall of the Shah of Iran and an *ulama*-led revolution in that country were as threatening for many Sunni Muslim governments and elites (especially those in majority Shiah Gulf states like Iraq, Saudi Arabia, Bahrain, and Kuwait) as these events were to Western observers.

Perhaps the most significant symbolic event, which sparked Arab and Muslim dissatisfaction, was the 1967 Arab–Israeli war, the Six-Day War. Israel defeated the combined forces of Egypt, Syria, Iraq, and Jordan in a "preemptive" strike, which the Israeli government claimed was necessary to counter a planned Arab attack. The Arabs experienced a massive loss of territory: Sinai, Gaza, the West Bank, and in particular Jerusalem, the third-holiest city (after Mecca and Medina) of Islam. Muslim loss of Jerusalem in the 1967 war was a traumatic experience, which made Palestine and the Arab–Israeli conflict not just an Arab Muslim and Arab Christian issue but

The Dome of the Rock in Jerusalem, a major holy site and place of pilgrimage erected by the Umayyad caliph Abd al-Malik, was completed in 692. The famous shrine is built on the spot from which Muslims believe Muhammad ascended to God and then returned to the world. In this story, one of the grand themes of Islamic scholarship and popular piety, the Prophet, in the company of the angel Gabriel, was transported at night from the Kaaba in Mecca to Jerusalem. From there, he ascended to the heavens and the presence of God.

a worldwide Islamic issue. Many who asked what had gone wrong in their societies also wanted to know why Israel had been able to defeat the combined Arab forces. Were the weakness and failure of Muslim societies due to their faith? Was Islam incompatible with modernity and thus the cause of Arab backwardness and impotence? Had God abandoned the Muslims?

As we have seen, from the seventeenth to the nineteenth centuries, internal threats to Muslim societies were followed by the external threat of European colonialism. The mid-twentieth century, however, was a period of independence and Muslim self-rule. The failures of the "modern experiment" led many to a more authentic, indigenous alternative to modern nationalism and socialism. Despite significant differences from one country to the next, many Muslims worldwide sought an Islamic alternative to Western capitalism and Soviet Marxism. In this context, Islam became a rallying cry for political organization and mass mobilization.

The Religious Worldview of Contemporary Islamic Activism

Islamic activists shared the following beliefs or points of ideology:

1. Islam, a comprehensive way of life, is and must be integral to politics and society.
2. The failures of Muslim societies were caused by departing from the path of Islam and depending on Western secularism, which separates religion and politics.

3. Muslims must return to the Quran and the example of the Prophet Muhammad and reintroduce Islamic laws.

4. Modern development must be guided by Islamic values rather than those that would lead to Westernization and secularization of society.

As Islamic symbols, slogans, ideology, leaders, and organizations became prominent fixtures in Muslim politics, religion was increasingly used both by governments and by reform and opposition movements to enhance their legitimacy and to mobilize popular support. Islamic movements and organizations sprang up across the Muslim world. A variety of opposition movements appealed to Islam: In Iran Ayatollah Khomeini led the "Islamic revolution" of 1979–80; militants seized the Grand Mosque in Mecca in 1979, calling for the overthrow of the government; religious extremists assassinated Egyptian president Anwar Sadat in 1981. At the same time, Afghan freedom fighters (*mujahideen*, "holy warriors") in the late 1970s and early 1980s led a successful resistance movement against the Soviet Union's invasion and occupation.

The leadership of most Islamic organizations (particularly Sunni groups) was and remains outside the control of the *ulama*. Many leaders have degrees in modern science, medicine, law, engineering, computer science, and education. While the majority of Islamic organizations work within the system, a minority of violent extremists insists that Muslim rulers are anti-Islamic and that violence and revolution are the only way to liberate society and impose an Islamic way of life.

From the Periphery to Mainstream Politics and Society

The 1980s were dominated by fear of "radical Islamic fundamentalism," embodied in Iran's announced desire to export its "Islamic fundamentalist revolution" and the activities of clandestine extremist groups. Feeding these fears were disturbances by Shiah in Saudi Arabia, Kuwait, and Bahrain; Iran's strong backing of a Lebanese Shiah group, Hezbollah, which emerged in response to the Israeli invasion and occupation of Lebanon; and a series of hijackings, kidnappings, and bombings of Western embassies.

By the late 1980s and early 1990s, it was increasingly clear that a nonviolent "quiet revolution" had taken place in many parts of the Muslim world. Islamic revivalism and activism had in many contexts become institutionalized in mainstream society. Islamically inspired social and political activism produced schools, clinics and hospitals, and social service agencies, such as day care, legal aid, and youth centers. Private mosques were established alongside those controlled by governments, and financial institutions such as Islamic banks and insurance companies appeared. In addition, an alternative elite emerged consisting of modern-educated but Islamically (rather than secularly) oriented professionals. By the mid-1990s, Islamic activists could be found in the cabinets and parliaments of many countries and in the leadership of professional organizations.

The Road to 9/11

At the same time, radical extremist groups such as Egypt's *Gamaa Islamiyya* (Islamic Group) and Islamic Jihad attacked rulers, government institutions, military and security forces, foreign tourists, and Christian churches. Extremists were convicted in the United States and Europe for terrorist acts, such as the 1993 bombing of the World Trade Center in New York. Terrorist attacks increased throughout the decade. By the late 1990s, Osama bin Laden, the leader of al-Qaeda, was increasingly regarded as the "godfather" of global terrorism and a major funder of extremist groups. His involvement was suspected in the 1993 World Trade Center bombing, the killing of eighteen American soldiers in Somalia in 1993, and two bombings in Saudi Arabia—Riyadh in 1995, Dhahran in 1996. In February 1998, bin Laden and other militant leaders announced the creation of a transnational coalition of extremist groups, the World Islamic Front for Jihad Against Jews and Crusaders. His own organization, al-Qaeda, was linked to a series of terrorist acts: the truck bombing of American embassies in Kenya and Tanzania in August 1998 that killed 263 people and injured more than 5,000, followed in October 2000 by a suicide bombing attack against the USS *Cole*, which killed seventeen American sailors.

September 11, 2001, would prove to be a watershed, signaling the extent to which Muslim extremists had become a global threat, in particular emphasizing the role of Osama bin Laden and al-Qaeda in global terrorism.[6]

Bin Laden's message appealed to the feelings of many in the Arab and Muslim world. A sharp critic of American foreign policy toward the Muslim world, he denounced U.S. support for Israel and sanctions against Iraq, which he said had resulted in the deaths of hundreds of thousands of civilians. He dismissed as the "new crusades" the substantial American military presence and economic involvement in his native Saudi Arabia.[7]

Al-Qaeda represented a new global terrorism, associated at first with the Muslims who had gone to Afghanistan to fight the occupying Soviets in the 1980s, and reflected in acts of terrorism in Central, South, and Southeast Asia, often attributed to the influence of Saudi Arabia and Wahhabi Islam. Bin Laden and other terrorists transformed Islam's norms about the defense of Islam and Muslims under siege to legitimate the use of violence, warfare, and terrorism. Their theology of hate promotes a view

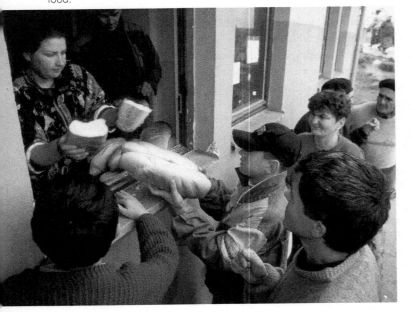

The ethnic warfare that accompanied the breakup of Yugoslavia had tragic effects in Bosnia, one of the oldest Muslim communities in Europe. Refugees of all ages, at Mihatovici, near Tuzla, line up to receive food.

CONTRASTING RELIGIOUS VISIONS

As the following contrasting visions indicate, every religious tradition is capable of generating both visions that encourage peace and understanding and visions that encourage conflict and violence.

Muhammad Iqbal (1876–1938)

Educated at Government College in Lahore, Pakistan, Iqbal studied in England and Germany, where he earned a law degree and a doctorate in philosophy. Iqbal's modern reinterpretation of Islam combined his Islamic heritage with Western philosophy. Both admirer and critic of the West, Iqbal acknowledged the West's dynamic spirit, intellectual tradition, and technology but was sharply critical of European colonialism as well as of the materialism and exploitation of capitalism, the atheism of Marxism, and the moral bankruptcy of secularism.

The Reconstruction of Religious Thought in Islam summarizes Iqbal's reformist vision. Like other Islamic modernists, Iqbal rejected much of medieval Islam as stagnant. He compared the need for Islamic reform to that confronting Christianity at the time of the Reformation. Iqbal emphasized the need to reclaim the vitality of early Islamic thought and practice, calling for a bold reinterpretation (*ijtihad*) of Islam. He attempted to develop alternative Islamic models for modern Muslim societies. Thus, for example, drawing on Islamic traditions, he sought to "rediscover" Islamic principles and values that would provide the basis for Islamic versions of Western concepts and institutions such as democracy and parliamentary government.

Osama bin Laden (1957–2011)

Born in Riyadh, Saudi Arabia, bin Laden received a degree in public administration in 1981 from King Abdul-Aziz University. A major turning point in bin Laden's adult life occurred in 1979, when the Soviets occupied Afghanistan. From 1979 to 1982, he used his financial resources to support the *jihadi* resistance against the Soviets, providing construction materials, building roads and airfields, and then moving to Afghanistan to set up his own camps and command Arab *mujahideen* forces, who became known as "Arab Afghans." He later created al-Qaeda, "the base," to organize and track the fighters and funds being channeled into the Afghan resistance.

Bin Laden's opposition to the American-led coalition in the Gulf War of 1991 placed him on a collision course with the Saudi government and the West. In 1994 the Saudi kingdom revoked bin Laden's citizenship and moved to freeze his assets because of his support for militant fundamentalist movements. Assuming a vocal leadership role in international terrorism, in 1996 bin Laden issued a Declaration of Jihad that called for the United States to be driven out of Arabia, the overthrow of the Saudi government, the liberation of Islam's holy sites of Mecca and Medina, and the support of revolutionary groups around the world. In 2000 he was among the founders of the World Islamic Front for Jihad Against Jews and Crusaders, an umbrella group of radical movements across the Muslim world, and issued a *fatwa* emphasizing the duty of all Muslims to kill U.S. citizens and their allies. Osama bin Laden was killed in Pakistan in 2011 by a U.S. military operation.

of a cosmic struggle between the armies of God and of Satan, the forces of good and evil, right and wrong, belief and unbelief: those who are not with them, Muslim or non-Muslim, are judged to be against them. These extremists "hijacked" the Islamic concept and institution of *jihad* in an attempt to lend legitimacy to their acts of violence and terror.

Globalization and Hijacking of *Jihad*

In recent years the word *jihad* has become familiar to Western ears. On the one hand, the term's primary Quranic religious and spiritual meanings became more widespread: *Jihad* was the "struggle" or effort to follow God's path, to lead a moral life, and to promote social justice. On the other hand, the idea of *jihad* as armed struggle has been widely used by resistance, liberation, and terrorist movements alike to legitimate their cause and recruit followers. Understanding the multiple meanings of *jihad* is critical to understanding Islam and Muslim politics today.

As we learned earlier in this chapter, the central importance of *jihad* is rooted in the Quran's command to "struggle or exert" oneself in the path of God. *Jihad* has several major meanings. First and foremost it refers to the moral struggle to be virtuous, to do good works. Depending on circumstances, it also can mean fighting injustice and oppression, spreading and defending Islam, and creating a just society through preaching, teaching, and, if necessary, armed struggle. These two broad meanings of *jihad*, nonviolent and violent, are contrasted in a well-known tradition that reports that when Muhammad returned from battle, he told his followers, "We return from the lesser jihad to the greater jihad." The greater *jihad* is the more difficult and more important struggle against one's ego, selfishness, greed, and evil.

Jihad as Armed Struggle

The earliest Quranic verses dealing with the right to engage in a "defensive," armed *jihad* were revealed shortly after the *hijra* (emigration) of Muhammad and his followers to Medina. At a time when they were fleeing from persecution in Mecca and forced to fight for their lives, Muhammad is told in the Quran: "Leave is given to those who fight because they were wronged—surely God is able to help them—who were expelled from their homes wrongfully for saying, 'Our Lord is God'" (Q. 22:39–40). The defensive nature of *jihad* is emphasized in 2:190, "And fight in the way of God with those who fight you, but aggress not: God loves not the aggressors."

The Quran and Islamic law provide detailed guidelines and regulations regarding the conduct of war: who is to fight and who is exempted (48:17, 9:91), when hostilities must cease (2:192), and how prisoners should be treated (47:4). Verses such as 2:294 emphasize that warfare and the response to violence and aggression must be proportional: "Whoever transgresses against you, respond in kind." From the earliest times, it was forbidden in Islam to kill noncombatants as well as women and children and monks and rabbis, who were promised immunity unless they took part in the fighting.

But what of those Quranic verses, sometimes referred to as the "sword verses," that call for killing unbelievers, such as, "When the sacred months have passed, slay the idolaters wherever you find them, and take them, and confine them, and lie in wait for them at every place of ambush" (9:5)? This is one of a number of Quranic verses that are cited by some critics to demonstrate the inherently violent nature of Islam, and selectively used (or abused) by some Muslim religious extremists to develop a theology of hate and intolerance and to legitimate unconditional warfare against unbelievers. The privileging of the sword verses dates back to the early centuries of Islam.

During the period of early Muslim expansion and conquest, many of the *ulama* (religious scholars) enjoyed royal patronage. They provided a rationale for caliphs to pursue their imperial dreams and, in the name of spreading Islam, to extend the boundaries of their empires. Classical jurists argued that the sword verses (9:5 and 9:123) abrogated, or canceled, the earlier verses that limited *jihad* to defensive war, thus permitting unprovoked military action in the cause of God. However, the full intent of the sword verse "When the sacred months have passed, slay the idolaters wherever you find them" is frequently distorted. First, the verse refers to the specific context: The early Muslims were being persecuted and attacked by their Meccan enemy. The term *idolaters* here refers to the Meccan polytheists, not to "unbelievers" in general (or, as extremists would hold, to Jews and Christians). Second, the tendency to quote the first part of the verse in isolation distorts the full intent of the passage, which is followed and qualified by: "But if they repent and fulfill their devotional obligations and pay the *zakat* [the charitable tax on Muslims], then let them go their way, for God is forgiving and kind" (9:5).

Bin Laden and other terrorists choose the selective militant interpretation of the so-called sword verses, ignore the criteria of Islamic law for a just *jihad*, and recognize no limits but their own. They reject the tenets of Islamic law regarding the goals and means of a valid *jihad*: that the use of violence must be proportional; that innocent civilians should not be targeted; and that *jihad* can be declared only by a ruler or head of state. Today, extremists legitimate their unholy wars in the name of Islam itself, bypassing the Quranic requirement that authorization for *jihad* be given by a nation's ruler.

While Al-Qaeda, like ISIS, has enjoyed support from a significant minority of Muslims and religious leaders, the majority of Muslims and major Islamic scholars and religious leaders have condemned such attacks as unjustified. For example, the Gallup Organization in 2005–8 surveyed some thirty-five predominantly Muslim countries (from Morocco and Pakistan to Indonesia) as part of its World Poll. The vast majority (93 percent) of all those polled said the 9/11 attacks were unjustified; 7 percent said the attacks were completely justified. The Islamic Research Council at al-Azhar University, regarded by many as the highest moral authority in Islam, and other prominent religious leaders issued authoritative declarations (*fatwas*) against bin Laden's and other terrorists' initiatives:

> Islam provides clear rules and ethical norms that forbid the killing of non-combatants, as well as women, children, and the elderly, and also forbids the

pursuit of the enemy in defeat, the execution of those who surrender, the infliction of harm on prisoners of war, and the destruction of property that is not being used in the hostilities.[8]

Suicide Bombing: War of the Fatwas

Few issues have been more contentious among religious authorities than suicide bombing. The issue of suicide bombing and the question of its legitimacy or illegitimacy crystallized in the Israeli–Palestinian conflict (1947–present). Amid escalating Israeli and Palestinian violence, some Palestinians and other Arabs argued that suicide bombers were committing not an act of suicide but one of self-sacrifice, the only option for resistance and retaliation against an enemy with overwhelming military power and foreign support.

Suicide attacks, especially those that target innocent civilians or noncombatants, precipitated a sharp debate among prominent religious authorities in the Muslim world. Sheikh Ahmad Yasin, the late religious leader and founder of Hamas, as well as many other Arab and Palestinian religious leaders have argued that suicide bombing is necessary and justified when faced with Israel's illegal occupation and overwhelming military power.

Although Yusuf Qaradawi, a prominent religious scholar and public figure, condemns acts of terrorism and suicide bombings, he has made a clear exception when it comes to the Palestinian–Israeli conflict. His strong opposition to Israeli occupation and policies led to early support for suicide bombing in Israel. Qaradawi was one of the first religious scholars to issue a *fatwa* that justified suicide bombings in Israel, based on the premise that Israelis were not civilians but combatants in a war of occupation waged against the Palestinians. In sharp contrast, Abdul-Aziz Al Al-Shaykh, the former Grand Mufti of Saudi Arabia, condemned all suicide bombing as un-Islamic and forbidden by Islam.

While a vocal minority supported bin Laden and al-Qaeda, the Gallup World Poll found that 91 percent of Muslims interviewed after the attacks of 9/11 believed that these acts were morally unjustified.

Post 9/11: Impact and Response

Despite the presence of major polling data showing that American Muslims are as educated, integrated, and diverse as other religious groups, the twenty-first century has been a trying time for the faith community. The 9/11 bombings in the United States and subsequent acts of terrorism globally were accompanied in the United States and Europe by an exponential growth of far-right politicians, political commentators, media personalities, and some religious leaders who conflated mainstream Islam with terrorism. They fed an increase in discrimination against Islam and Muslims ("Islamophobia"), resulting in widespread suspicion of mainstream Muslims, hate crimes, and the belief that Islam, not just Muslim extremism, is a threat.

At a 2004 UN conference, "Confronting Islamophobia: Education for Tolerance and Understanding," Secretary-General Kofi Annan addressed the international scope of this problem, warning, "When the world is compelled to coin a new term to take account of increasingly widespread bigotry—that is a sad and troubling development. Such is the case with 'Islamophobia.'"

A 2006 *Washington Post*/ABC News poll "found that nearly half of Americans—46%—have a negative view of Islam, seven percentage points higher than a few months after Sept. 11, 2001." In Europe, Islam was overwhelmingly singled out as the religion most prone to violence, with percentages of those who agreed with this ranging from 63 percent in Britain to 87 percent in France and 88 percent in the Netherlands.

If some blamed the religion of Islam for the growth of radicalism and the appeal of bin Laden and other terrorist leaders, others identified U.S. and European policies in the Muslim world—uncritical support for authoritarian regimes, Palestinian–Israeli policies, and the West's double standard in promoting democratization—as major catalysts. In the aftermath of the 9/11 attacks in the U.S. and subsequent attacks in Europe and beyond, anti-Islam and anti-Muslim greatly increased as the vast majority of Muslims were brushstroked by the vitriolic statements and acts of terrorism carried out by Osama bin Laden, al-Qaeda, and other terrorist organizations. As a result, many Muslims have been victims of religious and racial bias, discrimination, hate speech, violence, and the erosion of their civil liberties.

Events in August 2010 sparked a national public debate, revealing the depth of anti-Islam and anti-Muslim sentiment and attracting national and international attention. Park 51 was a plan to build an Islamic center in Manhattan, two blocks from the site of the World Trade Center. Modeled on the 92nd Street Y, a community center formerly operating as the New York Young Men's/Young Women's Hebrew Association, Park 51's facilities, which were approved by local government and community officials, were to include a prayer room. Yet after this quiet round of approvals, suddenly it became a national focal point for protests and demonstrations led by outside anti-Islam and Muslim activists, Robert Spencer and Pamela Geller, founders of Stop Islamization of America, who called it the "Ground Zero Mosque" even though it was not at Ground Zero. Lost in the "fog of war" was the fact that there had been a Muslim prayer room on the seventeenth floor of the World Trade Center's South Tower. On any given day, its users "might include financial analysts, carpenters, receptionists, secretaries and ironworkers." Both Islam itself, and Muslims who were American natives, immigrants who had earned citizenship, visitors conducting international business—the whole Muslim spectrum of nationality and race—were part of the life of the World Trade Center.

The protests, demonstrations, and vitriolic language had reached such a fever pitch that they led to a *Time* magazine cover story asking "Is America Islamophobic?"; the article reported a poll finding that 28 percent of voters did not believe that Muslims should be eligible to sit on the U.S. Supreme Court and that nearly one-third believed that Muslims should be barred from running for President.

Media, in particular social media, enabled bloggers and pundits to spread charged stereotypes and representations, and to organize and mobilize pockets of existing anti-Muslim prejudice. In the United States efforts to erect mosques have met with fierce backlash and charges that they are "command centers for terrorism." In many U.S. states, anti-*sharia* legislation has been introduced despite the fact that there has been no significant attempt to introduce *sharia* in America and that it is impossible to do so under the U.S. Constitution.

European Muslims

In Europe, anti-Muslim prejudice has been closely linked to the "War on Terror" and the anti-immigrant drumbeat about the impending demise of Europe's religious (Christian) identity and cultural heritage. Soon, critics warn, the continent will be transformed into "Eurabia," or in Great Britain, "Londonistan."

The institutionalization of anti-Muslim prejudice is illustrated by hijab and/or burqa and burkini bans in France, Germany, and Austria or turning women in burqas over to the local police in Belgium, or by survey responses about Muslims. In France, 68 percent of French citizens believed Muslims were "not well integrated into society," 55 percent said the "visibility of Islam is too large," and 60 percent were concerned about Muslim's refusal to integrate into French society.

Women join a demonstration organized by "Stand up to Racism" outside the French Embassy in London on August 26, 2016, against the burkini ban on French beaches.

In Germany, 79 percent of those surveyed said that Islam was "the most violent religion." In August 2016 the mayor of Cannes banned the wearing of burkinis (a stylish, full-bodied women's swimsuit) on beaches; other cities across France did the same. France's prime minister backed the ban, stating that the swimsuits were not compatible with French values and were based on the "enslavement of women." Women were issued fines, some citing them for not wearing an outfit that respected good morals and secularism. On August 26 France's top administrative court, in a decision that stunned many in France, overturned the burkini ban.

Far-right political parties, like the British National Party led by Nick Griffin, and the Netherland's Party for Freedom of Geert Wilders, espouse anti-immigrant and anti-immigration policies and fan the flames of Islamophobia with unbalanced and inaccurate narratives about Muslims and Islam. The BNP warns that Islam "presents one of the most deadly threats yet to the survival of our nation," and Wilders maintains that "the Koran is an evil book that calls for violence, murder, terrorism, war and submission. . . . We need to stop the Islamisation of the Netherlands. That means no more mosques, no more Islamic schools, no more imams."

In China, followers of traditional Islam (Gedimu, from the Arabic for "old," *qadim*) build communities around small central mosques. Muslim men meet here in Beijing for communal prayers in the central congregational mosque.

The net result of this xenophobic far-right extremism could be seen in the rhetoric, policies, and significant election performance of far-right political parties in Europe and Donald Trump in America, and in their common opposition to Muslim immigration, specifically to the tens of thousands of immigrant victims of Syria's brutal civil war—just a fraction of the 4.7 million refugees this war has created.

A Common Word Between Us and You

In sharp contrast, in a world in which some in the Muslim world and in the West speak of or even promote a clash of civilizations between them, a historic event occurred on October 11, 2007. In a dramatic and groundbreaking display of interreligious solidarity, 138 of the world's most senior Muslim leaders wrote a letter, "A Common Word Between Us and You," to the heads of all Christian churches. The letter's authors—Muslims from around the world and from both the Sunni and Shiah, Salafi and Sufi traditions—declared that with over half of the world's population consisting of Muslims and Christians, meaningful world peace can only come from peace and justice between the two largest global faiths, despite their differences. The letter, based on a close study of both the Bible and the Holy Quran, was an open invitation to Christians to unite with Muslims to cooperate in creating peace and understanding and defusing tensions, based on what is most essential to their respective faiths—the commandments of love, the shared belief of both Muslims and Christians in the principles of love of one God and love of neighbor.

Islam and the Arab Awakening: Between Authoritarianism and Pluralism

Beginning in late 2010, the "Arab Uprisings" or "Arab Spring" marked a potentially historic transition in the political makeup of many Muslim countries: Tunisia, Egypt, Libya, Syria, and Bahrain. A broad sector of society, eager for change and democratic reforms, made their voices heard and rebelled against decades-long authoritarian rule, reclaiming their dignity and national pride and insisting that they would decide the direction and the future of their countries. In Egypt and Tunisia, Islamist candidates and parties, though initially not among the leadership, swept into power in democratic post-uprising elections. If many voted for Islamists, many others were dismayed and feared Islamist rule would lead to increased religiosity in politics. Some asked, "Can the Islamists lead?"

The United States and European Union were equally challenged to work with Islamically oriented government leaders. The question of "how" Islam and democracy would be compatible had become even more real and relevant. However, the challenge to new governments to satisfy the expectations of diverse sectors of society, in particular to jump-start failed economies and address issues of high unemployment and now high expectations, was formidable. By 2013, the Arab Spring began to look like an Arab winter. Both the governments of Egypt and Tunisia struggled to govern and to deal with opposition critics and movements. The hardest hit was Egypt, where a nationwide anti-Morsi and anti-Brotherhood protest movement galvanized on June 30, around the anniversary of Morsi's troubled first year in power. Many demanded that Morsi resign or be driven from office, providing an excuse for a military-backed coup, with strong financial support from Saudi Arabia and the United Arab Emirates (UAE) and the return to authoritarianism under Egyptian army chief General Abdel Fattah el-Sisi.

Under el-Sisi, the military launched an operation against Muslim Brotherhood demonstrators, using lethal force that left thousands dead and thousands injured, the worst violence in modern Egyptian history. The interim government moved quickly to declare the Muslim Brotherhood a terrorist organization and attempted to totally suppress it, using mass arrests and military trials that drew sharp criticism and condemnation from major international human rights organizations. On March 24, 2014, an Egyptian court sentenced 529 members of the Muslim Brotherhood to death, the largest mass death sentence Egypt had seen in recent times.

Questions for Postmodern Times: Issues of Authority and Interpretation

For Muslims today, the issue of how much change is possible or permissible in Islam and what kinds of change are necessary is central to virtually all the questions they face regarding their faith and contemporary life: the relationship of Islam to the state, political participation or democratization, reform of Islamic law, promotion of religious and political pluralism, and the rights of women.

While all Muslims continue to affirm belief in God, Muhammad, and the Quran, Muslim interpretations of Islam today vary significantly. Some believe that Islam, like most faiths in the modern age, should be primarily a private matter; many others have struggled to implement Islam in public life as well. Although categories are not clear-cut and at times overlap, certain general Muslim attitudes toward change may be identified: secularist, conservative, traditionalist, Islamist (mainstream and extremist) and Muslim neo-modernist.

Like their counterparts in the West, secularists believe religion is a personal matter that should be excluded from politics and public life. Calling for the separation of religion and the state, they believe that Islam belongs in the mosque, not in politics, and that the mosque should solely be a place of prayer, not of political activism.

Conservatives emphasize following past tradition and are wary of significant change or innovation, regarded as deviation from Islam, the equivalent of Christian heresy. Represented by the majority (though certainly not all) of the *ulama* and their followers, conservatives continue to assert the primacy and adequacy of centuries-old Islamic law. Advocating the reimplementation of Islamic law through the adoption of past legal doctrine, they resist substantive change.

Traditionalists also believe in the centrality of tradition and classical Islamic law, but they also recognize that those Islamic laws and traditions, based primarily on human interpretation rather than a sacred text, can be reinterpreted, changed, or expanded in light of new social, economic, and political realities.

Islamic activists or Islamists represent a broad spectrum, from ultra-orthodox, literalist, and puritanical movements to more flexible and reform-minded believers, from those who hold mainstream political and social positions to militant extremists and terrorists. In the name of a return to the Quran and Sunnah, fundamentalist-oriented Islamists speak of purifying Muslim belief and practice by a rigorous and literalist embrace of the past, whereas more reformist Islamists and Muslim neo-modernists are prepared to interpret and reformulate Islamic belief and institutions. Muslim neo-modernists, despite some overlap with mainstream Islamists, are more open to substantive change. They distinguish more sharply between the principles and values of Islam's immutable revelation and certain historically and socially conditioned practices and institutions, which they believe can and should be subject to widespread change to meet contemporary circumstances. A dangerous Islamist terrorist minority nonetheless attempts to legitimate and impose their beliefs, recruit followers, and rule domestically and globally.

fiqh: "understanding"; human interpretation of divine law that produced Islamic law (*sharia*)

At the heart of reformist approaches to Islam is the relationship of the divine to the human in Islamic law. Thus reformers focus on the need to distinguish between the *sharia*, God's divinely revealed law, and Islamic law, much of which is the product of historically conditioned human understanding (*fiqh*). Reformers go further than conservatives or traditionalists in their acceptance of the degree and extent to which classical Islamic law may be reinterpreted or changed. They argue that just as early Muslim jurists applied the principles and values of Islam to the societies of the past, today a new reinterpretation or reconstruction of Islam is needed. But who has the authority to do this work?

As in the past, both the *ulama*, the religious scholars of Islam, and Muslim rulers continue to assert their right to protect, defend, and interpret Islam. The *ulama* persist in regarding themselves as the guardians of Islam and its only qualified interpreters. Many rulers combine their obligation to protect and promote Islam with the state's power to impose a certain "brand" of Islam.

Today, many reformers argue that it is not rulers or the religious scholars but the laity and parliaments that should be major actors in the process of change. While the *ulama* base their authority on their training in traditional Islamic disciplines, lay Muslims counter that they possess the legal, economic, and medical qualifications necessary to address contemporary issues and should be counted among the "experts" along with the *ulama*.

Islam in the West[9]

Muslims were long an invisible presence in the West. Those who came as immigrants wanted to fit in to their new societies, and live quietly in their adopted countries. Others wished to live apart, to avoid possible loss of identity or assimilation into a Western, non-Muslim society. Political events in the Muslim world reinforced a desire for a low profile in any country to which Muslims had relocated; in some cases Muslims found themselves on the defensive. Images and stereotypes from the past, of camels and harems, were replaced by modern impressions of violence and terrorism associated with the threat of militant "Islamic fundamentalism." The result has often been Muslim-bashing and what some have called *Islamophobia*: anti-Muslim bias, discrimination, and violence toward Muslims on the basis of their faith or race.

Today, Muslims in Europe and America no longer live primarily in clusters of immigrants; rather they are members of second- and third-generation communities, participating in professional and civic life. Yet many continue to face issues of faith and identity as a religious minority.

The Muslims of Western Europe

More than 44 million Muslims live in Europe. Because many, though certainly not all, wish to retain their religion, culture, and values, the presence and citizenship of Muslims in Western Europe, as in America, have made assimilation, integration and multi-culturalism an increasingly urgent and explosive issue.

In contrast to America, in Western Europe the Muslim presence is due in large part to immigration based on a vestigial colonial connection. After independence, many professionals and skilled laborers from former European colonies in Africa, South Asia, and the Arab world immigrated to Europe, seeking a better life. In the 1960s and 1970s, unskilled workers flooded into European countries whose growing economies welcomed cheap labor. In addition, from the 1970s onward, increasing numbers of Muslim students came to Europe, as they did to America, to study. While many returned home, others chose to stay for political or economic reasons. The largest Muslim population in Western Europe is in France, with 4.7 million Muslims (70 percent of whom come from North Africa), followed by Germany (4.3 million) and the United Kingdom (2.9 million). The Muslims of France, comprising almost 7.5 percent of the population, now exceed Protestants and Jews in number and are second only to France's Catholic community. There are grand mosques in Paris and Lyon and more than a thousand mosques and prayer rooms throughout the country. The majority of Germany's Muslims are of Turkish origin (63 percent); Britain's Muslims come primarily from the Indian subcontinent.

For many years, Islam and other religions were suppressed and persecuted in Albania by a communist regime that declared the state officially atheist in 1967. Many mosques in this Muslim majority country were closed or destroyed, and religious symbols were banned. In 1990 the ban was lifted, and this and other mosques were rededicated and opened.

The issue of Muslim identity has been particularly acute in France, where the government has taken a firm stand in favor of total assimilation or integration. The issue was symbolized in a celebrated case in which female Muslim students were banned from wearing headscarves in public schools. In February 2004, France's National Assembly ignored protests and criticism from around the world and voted 494–36 to approve the controversial ban. Although the new law was aimed primarily at Muslims wearing the *hijab*, other religious apparel (large Christian crucifixes and Jewish skullcaps, or *yarmulkes*) was included; violators face suspension or expulsion. The government argued that this law is needed not only to protect France's secular traditions but also to ward off rising Islamic fundamentalism. Controversy over Islamic dress continued in 2010, when France, along with Belgium, moved to ban the *niqab*, wearing of a full-face veil, in public places.

In all Islamic communities, mosques are the social and community centers. Here, at the end of the Ramadan fast, women prepare to pray in the mosque in Regent's Park, London.

Violence and terror in Libya, Iraq, and Syria by militants, ISIS in particular, have launched mass migrations to Western Europe. The influx of large numbers of refugees and their possible impact on jobs and the economy—as well as concerns over safety and security due to ISIS attacks in Paris, Brussels, and other European cities— has raised fears that anti-immigrant right-wing political parties and their leaders have exploited.

Islam in America

Islam is the fastest-growing religion in the United States. Many believe that in the first half of the twenty-first century, Islam will become the second-largest religion in America, after Christianity. The estimates of the number of American Muslims vary significantly, from 3 million to 7 million. Muslim Americans are racially diverse communities in the United States; two-thirds are foreign-born.[10] Most (60 percent) are South Asians from the Indian subcontinent, and 35 percent are indigenous African Americans. The majority are Sunni, but there is a strong Shiah minority. Racial, ethnic, and sectarian differences are reflected in the demographic composition and politics of some mosques, as well: Many houses of worship incorporate the diversity of Muslims in America, but the membership of others is drawn along ethnic or racial lines.

Muslims were present in America prior to the nineteenth century. Perhaps 20 percent of the African slaves brought to America from the sixteenth to the nineteenth centuries were Muslim. However, most were forced to convert to Christianity. It was

The Muslim community in America is a rich racial, ethnic, and cultural mosaic of indigenous believers, the majority of whom are African American, and immigrant Muslims. Thousands of Muslims from New York's varied ethnic communities pray next to Coney Island's landmark Parachute Jump to celebrate the Feast of Sacrifice (Id al-Adha). This major religious holiday commemorates God's command to Abraham to sacrifice his son Ismail.

not until the late nineteenth century that significant numbers of immigrant Arabs, mostly Christians with a smaller number of Muslims, arrived. After passage of the Immigration and Nationality Act of 1965, greater numbers of highly skilled Muslims migrated to America, many from the Middle East and South Asia (India, Pakistan, and Bangladesh). In contrast to Europe, which attracted large numbers of Muslims as immigrant laborers in the 1960s and 1970s, many who have come to America in recent decades have been well-educated professionals, intellectuals, and students.

The Transformation of "The Nation of Islam"

African American Islam emerged in the early twentieth century when a number of black Americans converted to Islam and established movements or communities. Islam's egalitarian ideal, in which all Muslims belong to a brotherhood of believers, transcending race and ethnic ties, proved attractive. The most prominent and lasting movement, the Nation of Islam, was associated with Elijah Muhammad (formerly Elijah Poole, 1897–1975).

Malcolm X (d. 1965), also known as El-Hajj Malik El-Shabazz, African American Muslim leader, civil and human rights advocate. An early disciple of Elijah Muhammad, chief minister of the Nation of Islam, he became one of its most prominent leaders and spokespersons. He withdrew from the Nation in 1964, becoming a follower of Sunni Islam. He was assassinated in 1965 by members of the Nation of Islam.

Elijah Muhammad had been a follower of Wallace D. Fard Muhammad, who preached a message of black liberation in Detroit in the early 1930s. After Fard mysteriously disappeared in 1934, Elijah Muhammad became the leader of the Nation of Islam. Adopting the title of the Honorable Elijah Muhammad, he claimed to be the messenger of God. Under his leadership, the Nation of Islam, popularly known as the Black Muslims, was transformed into a national movement. Elijah Muhammad preached black liberation and nationalism, black pride and identity, strength and self-sufficiency, black racial supremacy, and strong family values. The spirit and ethic of the Nation of Islam was embodied in the phrase "Do for self," a doctrine of economic independence that emphasized self-improvement and responsibility through hard work, discipline, thrift, and abstention from gambling, alcohol, drugs, and eating pork.

The Nation of Islam differed significantly from mainstream Islam in a number of basic beliefs. It claimed that Allah (God) was human—the black man named Wallace D. Fard—and that Elijah Muhammad (not the Prophet Muhammad) was the last messenger of God. The Nation taught black supremacy and black separatism, whereas Islam teaches the brotherhood of all believers in a community that transcends racial, tribal, and ethnic boundaries. The Nation did not subscribe to major tenets of the faith, such as the Five Pillars of Islam.

Three individuals epitomize the development and transformation of Elijah Muhammad's Black Muslim movement: Malcolm X, Wallace D. Muhammad (Warith Deen Muhammad), and Louis Farrakhan.

Malcolm X (1925–65), born Malcolm Little, exemplified the personal and religious transformation for which the Nation of Islam was noted. His experience of racism and prejudice led to his alienation from and rejection of American society. A prison sentence was the result of an early life of drugs and crime in the ghettos of Roxbury, Massachusetts, and later in New York's Harlem. During his incarceration (1946–52) he read widely in history, politics, and religion. Malcolm came to see Christianity as the "white man's religion" and to say that the white man's interpretation of the Bible has been "the greatest single ideological weapon for enslaving millions of nonwhite human beings."[11] In 1948 he formally turned to Elijah Muhammad and accepted the teachings of the Nation of Islam. Malcolm Little became Malcolm X.

A gifted speaker, dynamic and articulate, and a charismatic personality, Malcolm X rose quickly through the ranks of the Nation of Islam to national prominence in the 1950s and early 1960s. He organized many of the Nation's temples; started its newspaper, *Muhammad Speaks*; and recruited new members, including the boxer Cassius Clay, renamed Muhammad Ali.

However, Malcolm's increased involvement in domestic and international politics, and his contacts with Sunni Muslims in America and the Muslim world, gradually changed his religious/ideological worldview and put him increasingly at odds with Elijah Muhammad's teachings about self-sufficiency and separation from "white man's politics." Malcolm came to believe that "the Nation of Islam could be even a greater force in the American Black man's overall struggle if we engaged in more action."[12] Such statements made him a target for those within the Nation who were jealous of his prominence. As a result, he found himself increasingly marginalized.

In March 1964 Malcolm X left the Nation of Islam to start his own organization and a month later went on pilgrimage to Mecca where he underwent a second conversion—to mainstream Sunni Islam. The pilgrimage exposed the contradiction between the religious/separatist teachings of the Nation and those of the global Islamic community. Malcolm was especially affected by the Muslim emphasis, which he experienced firsthand during the hajj, on the equality of all believers.

During the 1960s, not only Malcolm X but also Elijah Muhammad's son, Wallace D. Muhammad, questioned the teachings and strategy of his father. In February 1975 Wallace succeeded his recently deceased father as supreme minister and, supported by his family and the Nation's leadership, he set about reforming the Nation's doctrines and organizational structure, integrating the Nation within the American Muslim community, the broader American society, and the global Islamic community.

The Nation and its teachings were brought into conformity with orthodox Sunni Islam, and the organization was renamed the World Community of al-Islam in the West (WCIW). Wallace Muhammad made the pilgrimage to Mecca and encouraged his followers to study Arabic to better understand Islam. The community now observed Islam's Five Pillars. Black separatist doctrines were dropped as the community proceeded to participate in the American political process. The equality of men and women believers was reaffirmed; women were given more responsible positions in the ministry of the community. In 1980, as if to signal his and the community's new religious identity and mission, Wallace changed his name to Warith Deen Muhammad and renamed the WCIW the American Muslim Mission.

The transformation of the Nation of Islam under Warith Deen Muhammad did not occur without dissent. Louis Farrakhan (born Louis Eugene Walcott, in 1933), a bitter foe of both Malcolm and Wallace, broke with Wallace in March 1978. Farrakhan retained the name and organizational structure of the Nation of Islam as well as its Black Nationalist and separatist doctrines. However, from 1986 onward, while using many of the political and economic teachings and programs of Elijah Muhammad, he moved the Nation closer to more orthodox Islamic practices.

Muhammad Ali, renowned heavyweight boxing champion of the world. Born Cassius Clay in 1942, he revealed in midcareer that he had become a member of the Nation of Islam and changed his name to Muhammad Ali. He became the most prominent and popular Muslim public figure in America and globally.

TALES OF SPIRITUAL TRANSFORMATION: Malcolm X

After leaving the Nation of Islam in March 1964, Malcolm X made the hajj, pilgrimage to Mecca. The experience transformed his life and changed his perspective on racism:

> There were tens of thousands of pilgrims, from all over the world. They were of all colors, from blue-eyed blondes to black-skinned Africans. But we were all participating in the same ritual, displaying a spirit of unity and brotherhood that my experiences in America had led me to believe never could exist between the white and the nonwhite.
>
> You may be shocked by these words coming from me. But on this pilgrimage, what I have seen, and experienced, has forced me to rearrange much of my thought patterns previously held, and to toss aside some of my previous conclusions. . . . During the past eleven days here in the Muslim world, I

have eaten from the same plate, drunk from the same glass, and slept in the same bed (or on the same rug)—while praying to the same God with fellow Muslims, whose eyes were the bluest of the blue, whose hair was the blondest of blond, and whose skin was the whitest of white. And in the words and in the actions and in the deeds of the "white" Muslims, I felt the same sincerity that I felt among the black African Muslims of Nigeria, Sudan, and Ghana.

> We are truly all the same—brothers. All praise is due to Allah, the Lord of the worlds.

He returned a Muslim rather than a Black Muslim, changing his name to El Hajj Malik El-Shabazz. On February 21, 1965, Malcolm Shabazz was assassinated as he spoke to an audience in New York.

While Farrakhan's militancy and anti-Semitic statements brought condemnation, the effectiveness of the Nation in fighting crime and drugs in African American communities and in rehabilitating prisoners earned praise. Though the Nation of Islam has far fewer members than Warith Deen Muhammad's American Muslim Mission, Farrakhan's persona and actions gave him a disproportionate amount of media visibility and recognition as the twentieth century drew to a close.

Issues of Adaptation and Change

Muslims in America have been challenged by a culture that, despite separation of church and state, retains a Judeo-Christian ethos in which Judeo-Christian values are regarded as integral to American identity and Jewish and Christian holidays are officially recognized holidays. The tendency of some in America, as in Europe, to contrast American "national culture" with Islamic values further complicates the process of Muslim assimilation. Finally, the American media's disproportionate coverage of violence and terrorism (as reflected in the maxim "If it bleeds, it leads") has unfairly projected the image of Islam as a particularly militant religion.

Islam in America provides many examples of significant change and reform. Both mosques and their leaders, or imams, have been transformed by the American experience. Because Friday is a workday and a school day in America, many Muslims are not able to attend the Friday congregational prayer. Therefore, for many, Sunday at mosques and Islamic centers is the day of congregational prayer, religious education ("Sunday school"), and socializing. Teaching materials and syllabi on Islam and Muslim life are available for the instruction of children and adults at mosques and in schools. Imams in America not only are responsible for the upkeep of mosques and leading of prayers, but often take on the duties of the clergy of other faiths, serving as counselors to military and as hospital and prison chaplains.

Today, American Muslims increasingly seek to empower themselves, participating in rather than simply reacting to life in America. The contemporary American Muslim community is increasingly more integrated educationally, economically, and socially and in many areas religiously. Muslim advocacy and public affairs organizations promote and lobby for Muslim rights and community interests.

Moreover, Muslim educational associations monitor textbooks and the teaching of Islam to ensure accuracy and objectivity. Public affairs organizations respond to misinformation in the media and to objectionable policies and actions by legislators and corporations. They reach out to religious leaders and communities, political leaders and policymakers, human rights organizations and relief agencies. Islamic information services develop and distribute films, videos, and publications on Islam and Muslims in America to further better understanding. Some communities have primary and secondary Islamic schools.

Like Catholic and Jewish communities before them, which created their own schools to safeguard and preserve the faith and identity of the younger generation, some Muslim communities have created Islamic schools that combine a standard academic curriculum with training in Arabic and Islamic studies.

Islam: Postmodern Challenges

Islam and Muslims today are again at an important crossroads. What does it mean to be a Muslim in an increasingly globalized and pluralistic world and society? How should Islam's sacred sources and heritage be interpreted to respond to issues of religious authority, secularism, the role of *sharia*, the rights of women and minorities, religious extremism, and terrorism?

Like the other Children of Abraham, their Jewish and Christian cousins, Muslims face questions of faith and identity in a rapidly changing world. As in all faiths, the unity of Islam embraces a diversity of interpretations and expressions, a source of dynamism and growth as well as contention and conflict. The challenge for all believers remains the pursuit in a diverse world of "the straight path, the way of God, to whom belongs all that is in the heavens and all that is on the earth" (Q. 42:52–53).

While the Quran and Sunnah of the Prophet Muhammad remain the basis of belief for all Muslims,

As in other world religions, in Islam marriage is solemnized in a religious ceremony. This Baghdad wedding is an occasion for great joy and celebration among the couple's family and friends.

vigorously debated questions have been raised in the areas of interpretation, authenticity, and application. Some Muslim scholars distinguish between the Meccan and Medinan *surahs* (chapters). The former are regarded as the earlier and more religiously binding; the latter are seen as primarily political, concerned with Muhammad's creation of the Medinan state and therefore not universally binding. Still other Muslim scholars say that whereas the eternal principles of the Quran are to be applied to changing sociopolitical contexts, rules that addressed conditions in past historical periods are not necessarily binding today.

Although the example (Sunnah) of the Prophet Muhammad has always been the standard in Islam, from earliest times Muslim scholars saw the need to examine critically the enormous number of prophetic traditions (*hadith*). A sector of modern Western scholarship questioned the authenticity of the hadith, maintaining that the bulk of the Prophetic traditions are fabrications written long after the death of the Prophet. Many Muslim scholars (and some non-Muslim scholars), while acknowledging issues of historicity and authenticity, have taken exception to this sweeping position. If many of the *ulama* continue to accept the authoritative collections of the past unquestioningly, other Muslim scholars have in fact become more critical in their approach and use of tradition (*hadith*) literature.

Contemporary Muslim debate over the role of Islam in politics and society reflects an array of questions: Is there one classical model or many possible models for the relationship of religion to political, social, and economic development? If a new Islamic synthesis is to be achieved that provides continuity with past tradition, how will this be accomplished? Will it be imposed from above by rulers and/or the *ulama* or legislated in populist fashion through a representative electoral process? These questions are reflected in the debate over the nature and role of Islamic law in Muslim societies.

Islamization of the Law

The implementation of *sharia*, where it has occurred, has not followed a fixed pattern or set interpretation even among those countries considered conservative or fundamentalist. For example, although women in Saudi Arabia cannot vote or hold public office, in Pakistan and Iran (despite other restraints) women vote, hold political office in parliaments and cabinets, teach in universities, and hold responsible professional positions. However, Islamization of law has underscored several problematic areas: the **hudud** (Quranically prescribed crimes and punishments for alcohol consumption, theft, fornication, adultery, and false witness), the status of non-Muslims and minorities, and the status of women. All potentially involve changes in Islamic law.

While some call for the reimplementation of the *hudud* punishments, other Muslims argue that harsh measures such as amputation for theft and stoning for adultery (not mentioned in the Quran) are, like stoning in the Old Testament or many corporal punishments practiced by governments in centuries past, no longer suitable. Among those who advocate imposition of the *hudud*, some want it introduced immediately and others say that it should be contingent on the creation of a just society in which people will not be driven to steal to survive. Some critics charge that while appropriate relative to the time they were introduced, *hudud* punishments are unnecessary in a modern context.

hudud: Quranically prescribed crimes and punishments adopted by some countries and advocated by some groups as evidence of the "Islamic" nature of their political rule and law

Women and Minorities

As we have seen, one result of contemporary Islamic revivalism has been a reexamination of the role of women in Islam. More conservative religious voices have advocated a return to veiling and sexual segregation as well as restrictions on women's education and employment. Muslim women are regarded as teachers of family faith and values, whose primary role as wives and mothers limits or prevents participation in public life. The imposition of reputed Islamic laws by some governments and the policies of some Islamist movements have reinforced fears of a retreat to the past. Among the prime examples have been the enforcement of veiling, closure of women's schools, restriction of women in the workplace, and extremist attacks and killings. In fact, the picture is far more complex.

Modern forms of Islamic dress have the practical advantage of enabling some women to assert their modesty and dignity while functioning in public life in societies where Western dress often symbolizes a more permissive lifestyle. It creates a

GENDER FOCUS: Women and Empowerment

Muslim women in the twentieth century had two clear choices: the modern Westernized lifestyle of an elite minority of women, or the more restrictive traditional "Islamic" lifestyle of the majority of women, who lived much as their grandmothers and great-grandmothers had lived. The social impact of the Islamic revival produced a third alternative that is both modern and firmly rooted in Islamic faith, identity, and values. Muslim women, modernists, and Islamists have argued on Islamic grounds for an expanded role for women in Muslim societies. Rejecting the idea that Islam itself is patriarchal and distinguishing between revelation and its interpretation by all-male *ulama* in patriarchal settings, Muslim women have reasserted the right to be primary participants in redefining their role in society. In many instances, this change has been symbolized by a return to the wearing of Islamic dress or the donning of a headscarf, or *hijab*. Initially prominent primarily among urban middle-class women, this new mode of dress has become more common among a broader sector of society. For many it is an attempt to combine religious belief and Islamic values of modesty with contemporary freedoms in education and employment, to pair a much-desired process of social change with indigenous Islamic values and ideals. The goal is a more authentic rather than simply Westernized modernization.

protected, private space of respectability in crowded urban environments. For some it is a sign of a specifically Islamic feminism that rejects what is regarded as the tendency of women in the West (and elite Westernized Muslim women) to go from being defined as restricted sexual objects in a male-dominated tradition to so-called

Queen Rania of Jordan (center) at prayer with other Muslim women.

free yet exploited sexual objects. Covering the body, it is argued, defines a woman and gender relations in society in terms of personality and talents rather than physical appearance.

New experiments by educated Muslim women to align their lives more closely to Islam have also resulted in more women "returning to the mosque." In the past, when women were restricted to the home and allowed only limited education, they did not participate in public prayer in mosques. While some attended the Friday congregational prayer, sitting separately from the men, it was more common for women to pray at home and to leave religious learning to men. Today in many Muslim countries and communities, particularly those that have been regarded as among the more modernized, women are forming and leading prayer and Quran study groups. To justify these public activities, women cite the examples of Muslim women in early Islam who fought and prayed alongside men and of women who were held in high repute for their knowledge and sanctity. Globally, Muslim women are writing and

Featured with Pope Francis, Sheikha Mozah, like many other monarchical wives in the Middle East, is a high-profile figure in Qatar's politics and society. She is chairperson of the Qatar Foundation for Education and a driving force behind Education City and Al Jazeera Children's Channel.

The Quran and Islamic tradition enjoin modesty, and thus everyone is required to wear modest dress. The diversity of attire found across the Muslim world is reflected in this group of young Muslim women in the United States. Though all are dressed modestly, some wear a headscarf (*hijab*) while others do not.

speaking out on women's issues. They draw on the writings not only of male scholars but also, and most importantly, on a growing number of women scholars who utilize an Islamic discourse to address issues ranging from dress to education, employment, and political participation.

While traditions remain strong and are forcefully defended by those who call for a return to veiling and segregation or seclusion of women, Muslim women have become catalysts for change. In the United Arab Emirates, as in Iran, the majority of university students are women. Women have increasingly empowered themselves by entering the professions, running for elective office, becoming students and scholars of Islam, and establishing women's professional organizations. Women's organizations such as Women Living Under Muslim Laws, based in Pakistan but international in membership; Musawah: Global Movement for Equality and Justice in the Muslim Family; and Malaysia's Sisters in Islam are active internationally in protecting and promoting the rights of Muslim women.

Islamic Reform

Islamic reformers face formidable challenges, including the discrediting of militant ideas and ideologies and the reform of those *madrasas* and universities that perpetuate a "theology of hate" and train so-called jihadists. An obstacle to reform efforts is the ultraconservatism of many (though not all) *ulama*, which hinders reform in the curriculum and training of religious scholars, leaders, and students.

For decades, quietly, persistently, and effectively, a group of reform-minded Muslims have articulated a variety of progressive, constructive Islamic frameworks for reform. These intellectual activists represent voices of reform from North Africa to Southeast Asia and from Europe to North America. They respond to the realities of many Muslim societies, the challenges of authoritarian regimes and secular elites, the dangers of religious extremism, and the burden of well-meaning but often-intransigent conservative religious scholars and leaders.

Islamic reform is a process not only of intellectual ferment and religious debate but also of religious and political unrest and violence. The lessons of the Protestant Reformation, the Catholic Counter-Reformation, and more recently Vatican II demonstrate that religious reformations take time and are often fraught with conflict and even danger. Generations of reformers, often a minority within

Indonesia has the largest Muslim population in the world. These women from the province of Aceh, contestants seeking to become Miss Indonesia, learn how to perfect the application of makeup.

TEACHINGS OF RELIGIOUS WISDOM: A Bosnian Prayer

Our Lord
Do not let success deceive us
Nor failure take us to despair!
Always remind us that failure is a temptation
That precedes success!
Our Lord
Teach us that tolerance is the highest degree of power
And the desire for revenge
The first sign of weakness! . . .
Our Lord

If we sin against people,
Give us the strength of apology
And if people sin against us,
Give us the strength of forgiveness!
Our Lord
If we forget Thee,
Do not forget us!

Source: A Bosnian Prayer cited by Mustafa Ceric, Grand Mufti of Bosnia-Herzegovina, in his "Judaism, Christianity, Islam: Hope or Fear of Our Times," in James L. Heft, ed., *Beyond Violence* (New York: Fordham University Press, 2004), pp. 54–55.

their communities, struggle today against many powerful forces, including conservative religious establishments, with their medieval paradigms; authoritarian regimes able to control or manipulate religion, education, and the media; and political and religious establishments that often see reformers as a threat to their power and privilege.

Conclusion

With 1.8 billion members—one-fourth of the world's population—the global Muslim community is second only to Christianity's 2.3 billion. Despite setbacks, for fifteen centuries Islam has proven vibrant and dynamic, growing spectacularly as a faith and empire from the time of the Prophet Muhammad. Islam's message and way of life have attracted followers of every race and culture, adapting to diverse cultures from Africa to Asia and Europe to America. Unity of faith has been accompanied by a diversity of expressions. In the twenty-first century, Islam is at a crossroads. Muslims face yet another watershed as they struggle to implement their faith and practice within the realities and challenges of contemporary life.

The struggle for reform is religious, intellectual, spiritual, and moral. But it must be a more rapid and widespread program of Islamic renewal that not only builds on past reform movements but also follows the lead of today's enlightened religious leaders and intellectuals by engaging in the process of reinterpretation (*ijtihad*) and reform.

The pace of reform has been slow in many countries and societies that are dominated by authoritarian regimes, entrenched elites, and a global politics in which

Western governments, despite their democratic principles and values, are often willing to support autocrats to protect their own national interests. The process has been compounded by the threat and attacks of Muslim extremists within Muslim countries and in the West.

In contrast to Christianity's centuries-long Protestant Reformation and Vatican II in Roman Catholicism, the forces of globalization and development today necessitate a more rapid process of change. While the trajectory of Islamic reform and its outcome remain uncertain, Muslims are challenged to exemplify the Quranic prescription that the Islamic community (*ummah*) pursue a just and middle (*wasat*) path: "Thus We have made you a just community, that you may witness to humanity" (2:143) as, like those before them, it seeks to follow "the straight path, the way of God, to whom belongs all that is in the heavens and all that is in the earth" (42:52–53).

Discussion Questions

1. Identify and describe the Five Pillars of Islam.

2. What are the differences between Sunnis, Shiah, and Sufis?

3. What is the difference between the *sharia* and *fiqh*? What impact have these aspects of Islam had on modern revivalism and reformism?

4. What are the origins of the Crusades? Explain their long-term effects on Muslim–Christian/Western relations.

5. Discuss the impact of European colonialism on the Muslim world. What are some of the ways in which Muslims responded to it?

6. What is *ijtihad*? Why is this concept at the heart of the question of the relationship between Islam and modernity?

7. Describe the different themes and techniques used for the revival and reform of Islam in the eighteenth century.

8. Discuss the basic tenets and significance of the Muslim Brotherhood and the Jamaat-i-Islami.

9. What are the causes and conditions that led to the contemporary resurgence of Islam?

10. How is Islam used both to support and to oppose the state? Give examples.

11. Describe the diverse meanings of *jihad*. How has the concept been used by different Islamic movements to justify their activities?

12. Discuss the origin and development of the Nation of Islam. Do African American Muslims differ from mainstream Muslims?

13. How has Islam affected or changed the status of women? How are women influenced by Islamic movements today? How are they influencing these movements?

14. What are some of the major issues facing Muslims living in non–Muslim-majority countries today, particularly in Europe and America?
15. Identify and discuss several key areas of Islamic reform.

Key Terms

Allah	*jahiliyya*	**Ramadan**
caliph	*jihad*	*salat*
dar al-Islam	*khutba*	*shahadah*
dhimmi	*Mahdi*	*sharia*
fatwa	*minbar*	**Shiah**
fiqh	**mosque**	**Sufi**
hadith	*muamalat*	**Sufism**
hajj	*muezzin*	**Sunnah**
hijra	*mufti*	**Sunni**
hudud	*mujaddid*	*surah*
ibadat	**Muslim**	*tawhid*
ijma	**People of the Book**	*ulama*
ijtihad	*purdah*	*ummah*
imam	*qiyas*	*wali*
Islam	**Quran**	*zakat*

Suggested Readings

Armstrong, Karen. *Islam: A Short History* (New York: Modern Library, 2002).
Brown, Jonathan. *Hadith: Muhammad's Legacy in the Medieval and Modern World* (Oxford: Oneworld Publications, 2009).
———. *Very Short Introduction: Muhammad* (Oxford: Oxford University Press, 2010).
Donohue, John, and John L. Esposito, eds. *Islam in Transition: Muslim Perspectives*, 2nd ed. (New York: Oxford University Press, 2006).
Esposito, John L. *The Future of Islam* (New York: Oxford University Press, 2010).
———, ed. *Islam: The Straight Path*, 4th rev. ed. (New York: Oxford University Press, 2010).
———. *The Islamic World: Past and Present*. 3 vols. (New York: Oxford University Press, 2004).
———, ed. *The Oxford History of Islam* (New York: Oxford University Press, 2000).
———. *Unholy War: Terror in the Name of Islam* (New York: Oxford University Press, 2000).
———. *What Everyone Needs to Know About Islam*, 2nd ed. (New York: Oxford University Press, 2011).
———with Dalia Mogahed. *Who Speaks for Islam? What a Billion Muslims Really Think* (New York: Gallup Press, 2008).
Lings, Martin. *What Is Sufism?* (London: I. B. Tauris, 1999).
Nasr, Seyyed Hossein. *The Heart of Islam: Enduring Values for Humanity* (San Francisco: Harper, 2002).

The Quran: A Modern English Version, trans. Majid Fakhry (Berkshire, UK: Garnet, 1996).

The Qur'an, trans. Haleem, M. A. S. Abdul (Oxford: Oxford University Press, 2008).

Ramadan, Tariq. *Western Muslims and the Future of Islam* (New York: Oxford University Press, 2005).

Sonn, Tamara. *A Brief History of Islam* (Malden, MA: Wiley-Blackwell, 2010).

Notes

1. Ibn Hisham, quoted in Philip K. Hitti, *History of the Arabs*, 9th ed. (New York: St. Martin's Press, 1966), p. 120. For the text within the context of a major biography of the Prophet Muhammad, see Ibn Ishaq, *The Life of Muhammad*, trans. A. Guillaume (London: Oxford University Press, 1955), p. 651.
2. Seyyed Hossein Nasr, *Muhammad: Man of God* (Chicago: Kazi Publications, 1995), p. 90.
3. *The Hedaya*, trans. Charles Hamilton, 2nd ed. (Lahore, Pakistan: Premier Books, 1957), p. 73.
4. As quoted in Reuben Levy, *The Social Structure of Islam* (Cambridge: Cambridge University Press, 1955), p. 126.
5. Margaret Smith, *Rabia the Mystic and Her Fellow-Saints in Islam* (Cambridge: Cambridge University Press, 1928), p. 30.
6. For perceptive discussions of Osama bin Laden, see A. Rashid, *Taliban: Militant Islam, Oil, and Fundamentalism in Central Asia* (New Haven, CT: Yale University Press, 2000), and J. K. Cooley, *Unholy Wars: Afghanistan, America and International Terrorism* (London: Pluto Press, 2000).
7. Osama bin Laden, "From Somalia to Afghanistan, March 1997," in *Messages to the World: The Statements of Osama Bin Laden*, ed. Bruce Lawrence (New York: Verso, 2005), 44–57.
8. *Al-Hayat*, November 5, 2001.
9. This section is adapted from John L. Esposito, *Islam: The Straight Path*, 3rd ed. (New York: Oxford University Press, 1998), and *Muslims on the Americanization Path* (New York: Oxford University Press, 1999).
10. http://en.wikipedia.org/wiki/Islam_in_the_United_States#cite_note-PewForum-60# cite_note-PewForum-60 (accessed May 14, 2011).
11. Malcolm X with Alex Haley. *The Autobiography of Malcolm X* (New York: Ballantine Books, 1973), pp. 241–242.
12. Quoted in Clifton E. Marsh, in *From Black Muslims to Muslims: The Transition from Separatism to Islam*, 1930–1980 (Metuchen, NJ: Scarecrow Press, 1984), p. 76.

Additional Resources

Oxford Islamic Studies Online (http://www.oxfordislamicstudies.com). A comprehensive scholarly resource for the study of Islam.

Oxford Bibliographies Online (http://oxfordbibliographies.com). Developed cooperatively with scholars and librarians worldwide, the "Islamic Studies" portal at this site is an excellent starting point for research and further understanding.

Islamicity (http://www.islamicity.com). This extensive site provides a nonsectarian, comprehensive, and holistic view of Islam and Muslims to a global audience.

CDs

Zain Bhika, *Allah Knows* (http://www.youtube.com/watch?v=RpjIsSdsT6A)
Michael Sells, *Approaching the Qur'an* (contains CD of Qur'an recitation)
Sami Yusuf, *Without You* (http://www.youtube.com/watch?v=7-ROGqpdRf8)

Films/DVDs

Cities of Light: The Rise and Fall of Islamic Spain (http://www.pbs.org/programs/citiesof light/)
Great World Religions: Islam (http://www.thegreatcourses.com/tgc/courses/course_detail.aspx?
   cid=6102)
Inside Islam: What a Billion Muslims Really Think (http://www.youtube.com/watch?v=
   FFDyDHSlTfc)
Islam: Empire of Faith (www.pbs.org/empires/islam)
Muhammad: Legacy of a Prophet (http://upf.tv/about-upf/our-work/shop/shop-muhammad-
   dvd.html)
National Geographic, *Inside Mecca* (https://www.youtube.com/watch?v=PWhPSk5pfHg)

HINDUISM, JAINISM, AND SIKHISM

6

South Asian Religions

Overview

"Namaskar." Millions of Hindus every day share this ancient Sanskrit greeting with each other as well as their gods. Whether they are in the ancient city of Varanasi (Benares) or a newly consecrated sanctuary in Minneapolis, Minnesota, this greeting gives clear indication that we are entering the religious domain of South Asian religions.

What immigrants from all over modern South Asia practice as Hinduism is much less varied than what their relatives back in their homeland observe. Ancient beliefs and practices continue to thrive today despite all the revisions and reforms introduced by colonial rule, independence, and the advent of science. In India and across the Hindu diaspora, there are newly built monasteries for traditional study (**mathas**) at the feet of recognized masters, or **gurus**. And there are also yoga centers in major cities like Mumbai that cater to India's new middle class, which resemble those found in London or Chicago. Add to these the Jain and Sikh temples, as well as the new sects that have arisen around charismatic gurus who combine classic doctrines with ideas from other Asian traditions or the West. Today there are also communities in which

matha: Hindu monastery

guru: a spiritual and cultural teacher, regarded by students as semidivine

◀ Brahmin priests worshipping an image of Vishnu, requesting divine blessings for their community.

261

very conservative priests memorize, recite, and pass down the earliest hymns and rituals, some dating back 3,000 years. And in the great centers such as Varanasi, hundreds of thousands of pilgrims each year make offerings and see the deities enshrined in their magnificent temples. In many villages across the Indian subcontinent, where 60 percent of the population still lives, ritual practices within families and in local temples remain vigorous.

In this chapter we will explore how Hinduism and the other South Asian religious traditions are unlike the monotheistic world religions. To start with, we need to understand what the term *Hinduism* does and does not mean.

Hinduism Timeline

ca. 3500–1600 BCE	Indus Valley civilization in northwestern South Asia
1500 BCE	Decline of major Indus cities; populations migrate east to Gangetic plain
1500–500 BCE	Formative period of Vedic civilization
900–400 BCE	Shramana period of wandering ascetics and composition of the first Upanishads
500 BCE	Lifetimes of Shakyamuni, the Buddha, and Mahavira, founder of Jainism
300–100 BCE	Texts of brahmanical orthodoxy formulated (e.g., *Laws of Manu*)
100 BCE–400 CE	Composition of devotional texts and epics *Ramayana* and *Mahabharata*
50 BCE–300 CE	Composition of the *Bhagavad Gita* and Patanjali's *Yoga Sutras*
100 CE–700 CE	Hindu traditions established along rim of Indian Ocean in Southeast Asia
320–647	Classical temple Hinduism established
500-ff.	Development of Advaita Vedanta school; textual expressions of Hindu tantrism as counterculture
788–820	Life of Shankara, exponent of Advaita Vedanta and creator of Hindu monasticism
800–1200	Six brahmanical schools established as divisions in elite philosophical Hinduism
1025–1137	Life of Ramanuja, philosophical defender of *bhakti* faith
1200–1757	Muslim rule of North India; Buddhism virtually extinguished in South Asia
1420–1550	Era of great devotional saints (e.g., Mirabai, Ravidas, Kabir, Chaitanya, Surdas)
1469–1539	Life of Nanak, the founder of the Sikh faith
1526–1707	Mughal dynasty; Muslim rulers move from ecumenical views to anti-Hindu, anti-Sikh policies
1708	Death of tenth guru, Gobind Singh; Sikh text *Adi Granth* declared guru of the community
1757–1857	British East India Company dominates Indian political life
1815	Christian missionaries present in most cities and towns of British India
1828	Founding of the Brahmo Sabha (later Brahmo Samaj) by Rammohan Roy
1830–1890	First Hindu texts reach North America, influence the Transcendentalists
1834–1886	Life of Ramakrishna, charismatic guru with ecumenical teaching

Defining Hinduism: Unity, Diversity, Localities

What we label "Hinduism" ranges from monotheism to polytheism to atheism; from nonviolent ethics to moral systems that require blood sacrifices to sustain the world; from critical, scholastic philosophical discussion to the cultivation of sublime, mystical, wordless inner experiences. "Hinduism" as we use the term indicates the variety of spiritual traditions originating in South Asia that comprise the third-largest world religion today. The term owes its origins to *Sindhu*, the Persian word for the

1858–	After uprising, British crown assumes direct rule over India; South Asian ethnic groups recruited for government service across British Empire spread Hinduism globally
1863–1902	Life of Swami Vivekananda, Ramakrishna's disciple, who led global Ramakrishna Mission
1875	Foundation of the Arya Samaj by Swami Dayananda Saraswati
1920–1948	M. K. Gandhi (1869–1948) leads civil disobedience campaigns, articulating ecumenical Hindu reformism influenced by Western culture
1923	Founding of the Rashtriya Svayamsevak Sangh (RSS), Hindu nationalist group
1940	Ashram established by Sathya Sai Baba, beginning of large global movement
1947	Independence of India from Britain; prime minister, J. Nehru, declares India a secular state
1948	Gandhi assassinated by Hindu extremist
1964	Vishva Hindu Parishad (VHP) founded to unite Hindu leaders and devotees worldwide
1964	International Society for Krishna Consciousness (ISKON) established by Bhaktivedanta (1896–1977)
1984	Sikh extremists occupy Golden Temple in Amritsar; armed removal by Indian army; assassination of the prime minister, Indira Gandhi
1987	Weekly Indian television series *Ramayana* inspires rising sentiments of Hindu nationalism
1992	Hindu agitation in Ayodhya culminates in destruction of Babri Mosque; Hindu–Muslim riots across South Asia
1995	The Swaminarayan Mandir opens in London, the largest traditionally built Hindu temple outside India
1998	The Bharatiya Janata Party (BJP), a Hindu nationalist political party, wins parliamentary majority for the first time; rules until 2004
2002	Hindu hooligans riot in BJP-led Gujarat state, killing 2,500 Muslims, looting Muslim businesses, and displacing 200,000
2004	BJP loses national parliamentary elections but retains control of ten states across India
2007	During Kumbha Mela, Hindu holy men stage demonstration against Ganges pollution
2011	Death of global Hindu teacher Sathya Sai Baba
2014	BJP wins national parliamentary elections, returns to power

great Indus River. Conquering Muslims used *Hindu* to designate people who lived east of the Indus, and later the British applied the term to the non-Muslim natives of the region.

A singular term for "Hinduism" was never in use in premodern South Asia, and it never stood for a single way of being religious. Some South Asian intellectuals and politicians in the last two centuries did adopt it to distinguish its beliefs from those of the Muslim and Christian. What is meant, or what should be meant, by "true Hinduism" has remained contested throughout history, especially in the modern and postcolonial eras.

Religion in South Asia has been the most pluralistic and least centrally organized in the world, a characteristic dating back at least a millennium. Hinduism itself incorporates differences at least as fundamental as those between Judaism, Islam, and Christianity. Therefore, it is only by distinguishing the various "Hindu" traditions from the more general and monolithic term *Hinduism* that we can compare this tradition with other world religions.

Though the great majority of Hindus live on the South Asian subcontinent, an important postcolonial development has been their global diaspora, which has made Hinduism a global faith today. The estimated number of Hindus had surpassed 800 million by the turn of the millennium; after Islam, it is the second-fastest-growing world religion. Today, India remains the heartland of Hinduism (see Map 6.1). The modern state of India has been a secular democracy since its inception in 1947. It has over eighteen major culture regions, whose ethnic groups speak over a thousand languages. While every region in South Asia has its distinctive religious history, the most profound differences are seen between the traditions of North and South India.

Among the other South Asian states, Nepal was until 2006 the world's only Hindu nation, with a large majority of its 30 million people identifying themselves as Hindu. Two Muslim nations, Pakistan and Bangladesh, contain Hindu minorities (3 percent and 16 percent, respectively). Fifteen percent of Buddhist Sri Lanka's population of 25 million is Hindu. Five to 10 percent of Malaysia's large population is Hindu. Small communities of Hindus are also found in Myanmar (Burma), Indonesia, Fiji, and the Caribbean.

In North America there are over 2.25 million Hindus, with immigrants far outnumbering converts, making Hinduism the fifth largest group. In the United States, as across Europe, Hindu temples serve as centers of religious teaching and ritual practice. The yoga and meditation traditions that involve training the body and mind have been the most influential vehicles for spreading Hinduism among non-Indian peoples.

This chapter surveys this diverse spiritual tradition of Hinduism and provides an overview of its two great independent traditions, Jainism and Sikhism. (Buddhism, the third great religion of South Asia, is the subject of the next chapter.) We begin with the earliest form of religious life shaped by the Vedas, texts that are among the oldest (3,500 years old) in human history. We next move through a succession of religious beliefs and practices that have found expression since then, flourishing without

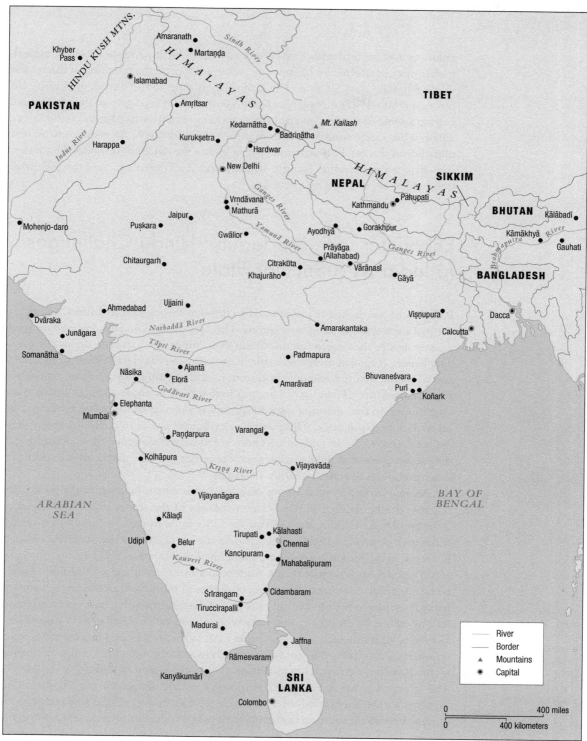

Map 6.1 India, with major cities and holy places.

HINDU KUSH MTNS.

Khyber
Pass

• Islamabad

PAKISTAN

Indus River

• Harappa

• Mohenjo-daro

HIMALAYAS

Amaranath
• Martaṇḍa

Sindh River

• Amṛitsar

Kedarnātha •
Kurukṣetra • Badrinātha
• Hardwar

Mt. Kailash ▲

TIBET

New Delhi

Ganges River

Vṛndāvana •
• Mathurā

Jaipur
Puṣkara •

Gwālior •

Yamunā River

Ayodhyā •

HIMALAYAS

NEPAL

Kathmandu •
Paśupati •

Gorakhpur •

SIKKIM

BHUTAN

Kālābadī •

Kāmākhyā •

Brahmaputra River

• Gauhati

Chitaurgarh •

Citrakūṭa •

Khajurāho •

Prāyāga
(Allahabad) •
Vārāṇasī •

Ganges River

BANGLADESH

• Gāyā

Ahmedabad •

Ujjaini •

Narbaddā River

Amarakantaka •

Viṣṇupura •

Dacca

Dvāraka •

Tāpti River

• Junāgara

Calcutta •

Somanātha •

Padmapura •

Nāsika •
Elorā •

• Ajantā

Amarāvatī •

Godāvari River

Bhuvaneśvara •
Purī •
• Koṇark

Elephanta •

Mumbai

Paṇḍarpura •

Varangal •

Kolhāpura •

Kṛṣṇa River

Vijayavāda •

ARABIAN
SEA

Vijayanāgara •

BAY OF
BENGAL

Kālaḍī •

Udipi •

Belur •

Tirupati •
• Kālahasti

Kancipuram •

Kauveri River

Śrīrangam •

Tiruccirapalli •

• Chennai

• Mahabalipuram

• Cidambaram

Madurai •

• Jaffna

Rāmesvaram •

Kanyākumāri •

SRI
LANKA

Colombo •

| River |
| Border |
| ▲ Mountains |
| ⊙ Capital |

0 ————— 400 miles
0 ————— 400 kilometers

265

priests or institutional authority. We finally focus on how these loosely connected traditions were affected by Islamic rule (1200–1780), and the founding of the separate world religion called Sikhism. The chapter then turns to the impact of British colonial rule (1800–1947) on religious life in South Asia. A final goal of this chapter is to convey a sense of modern and postcolonial change amid extraordinary continuities in religious life today, some of which date back three millennia. In addition to an array of traditions that can be described as falling within the circle of "orthodox Hinduism," this chapter also examines Jainism, which began 2,500 years ago; and the Sikh tradition, which began about 500 years ago.[1]

Encounter with Modernity: Hindu Challenges to India as a Secular State

Religion in South Asia has continued to develop throughout its history, preserving the past even amid striking innovations. This was possible, in part, because no single priestly group, theologian, or institution ever imposed a universal definition of the core beliefs. Regional diversities made this religious freedom even more pronounced, and in South Asia the religious imagination, and questing after spiritual experience, was extraordinary. There have been no heresy trials or inquisitions in South Asia's long history; in fact, debating spiritual truths was a regular feature of premodern court life and in society at large. This pattern of exuberant pluralism continues to the present, with the result that ancient traditions are preserved alongside those originating in the medieval era, and these threads weave together with the traditions introduced by nineteenth- and twentieth-century reformers.

Because of this diversity, those who led South Asia to independence from colonial rule firmly believed in the Western concept of the secular state. These leaders, including M. K. Gandhi, insisted that for India to be modern it should be a secular democracy, formally favoring no religion. In the last decades of the twentieth century, however, many Hindu citizens have questioned this stance.

In reacting to perceived threats from modern secularism and non-Hindus, Hindu revivalist groups have created new organizations to promote the religion. Among the many responses to British colonial rule, one of the most enduring has come from institutions calling for thoroughgoing reform of "Hindu-ness" (***Hindutva***) in national life and the reconstitution of India as a Hindu state. With roots among nineteenth-century reformers, this ideology began to be forcefully articulated in 1923 across the nation by the **Rashtriya Svayamsevak Sangh** ("National Union of [Hindu] Volunteers"). This group, known as the **RSS**, proposed a nativist definition of "Hinduism" as devotion to "Mother India." Members have worked in the political arena to promote candidates wishing to repeal the secular rule of law India instituted in 1947, when the

Hindutva: "Hinduness"; Hindu identity

Rashtriya Svayamsevak Sangh (RSS): "National Union of [Hindu] Volunteers"; group advocating "Hinduism" as devotion to "Mother India"

country gained independence from Great Britain. By 2014, RSS membership had grown to over 5 million.

It was only with the most recent incarnation of an RSS-allied political party, the **Bharatiya Janata Party (BJP)**, that Hindu nationalists finally found success in electoral politics across the nation. In the 1998 elections, the BJP became India's ruling party, a position it held until 2004. Campaigning on economic themes, the BJP won back control over the Indian Parliament again in the spring of 2014.

Bharatiya Janata Party: Hindu nationalist political party

The BJP, which is led mostly by high-caste politicians and appeals primarily to middle-class urbanites, rose in prominence as its leaders sought to symbolize the unity of a militant and revived Hindu India. The BJP and its allies also stoked popular resentment over government-sponsored affirmative action initiatives that set quotas for civil service hiring and admission to state colleges for the most disadvantaged, or "scheduled caste," members, a move aimed to break disproportionate high-caste control over the nation's governmental and educational institutions.

The most hard-line RSS policy is to provoke confrontations with South Asian Muslims by accusing the secular government of favoring them in its civil laws and of protecting medieval-era mosques that were purportedly built on North Indian sites sacred to Hindus. The first and most violent focus was on Ayodhya, where in 1528 the Mughal ruler Babar built a Muslim house of worship known as the Babri Mosque. Modern BJP partisans claim that the site was the birthplace of Rama, a human incarnation of the god Vishnu. Responding to the call made by many Hindu nationalist groups, thousands of volunteers converged on the site in December 1992. They attacked and subdued government troops protecting the site and then broke up the Babri Mosque with hammers, steel rods, and crowbars. In the aftermath, rioting broke out between Muslims and Hindus in other Indian towns and in Pakistan. Over 2,000 people perished.

The RSS- and BJP-led movements advocate paths to religious modernization found elsewhere in the world: They adopt the latest media technology to promote their message; they reject Enlightenment-inspired critiques of religious belief; and they insist that the secular political systems established in the colonial and postcolonial eras give way to a religious state. They have used the ancient idea of Mother India to express symbolically their sense of her being "raped" during Muslim, colonial, and postcolonial secular rule.

The appeal of the Hindu-India movement has shown persistent strength. Hindu nationalists have provided a focal point for political action by those involved in guru-oriented sects, with their emphasis on personal devotional enthusiasm (discussed later in this chapter), and for those middle-class Hindus now drawn to yoga centers of today (also discussed later), both of which offer different versions of "Hinduism." Nationalist politicians thus appeal to religious identity and arouse anti-Muslim sentiments to attract a large number of middle-class Hindus across the nation.[2] To better understand the significance of Hindu nationalism's challenge to modern secular India, we must go back to the beginning and trace the historical development of this tradition.

Bull seal, Harappa, ca. 1800 BCE. Although the meaning of the zebu bull symbol here is uncertain, this animal was later regarded as the vehicle of the great god Shiva.

Premodern Hinduism: The Formative Era

The Aryans and Religion in the Vedic Era

The story of ancient South Asian history used to involve an invasion of the subcontinent from the northwest by an aggressive, light-skinned people who called themselves Aryans. These Aryan warriors were imagined to have destroyed the cities of the Indus Valley, a civilization as ancient as those of Egypt and Mesopotamia. After forcing the dark-skinned inhabitants of the Indus Valley to flee to south India, the Aryan hordes moved east and subdued the tribes they encountered across the Gangetic plain. This version of history was used to explain the modern distribution of "north" and "south" India as separate linguistic and racial zones. In this telling, the Aryans were supposed to be a militarily and culturally superior people.

This view of history contained a racial assumption welcomed by early European scholars and by high-caste Hindus in the modern and postcolonial era. Then, when Sanskrit, the language of Hinduism's Vedic hymns, was discovered to be an Indo-European language and so related to most languages of Europe, it was also concluded that the ancestors of the modern Hindu elite were distantly kin to the British. Western archaeologists and the British colonial government supported such research and found this imagined history attractive. British imperial rulers, in particular, welcomed support for their view of modern Indians as superstitious and modern Hindu priests as corrupt, thereby justifying their presence.

Although migration in prehistory is accepted by objective historians, scholars now find no justification for understanding "Aryan" as a racial term, and they reject any suggestion that the ancient Aryans or their descendants were or are culturally superior to those living in south Asia before them. The ancient Indus Valley cities are now understood to have declined not through conquest but owing to regional climatic changes. There are also signs that the Indus Valley culture in fact contributed significantly to subsequent "Aryan" culture. Although "Aryan culture" had been adopted by most politically dominant groups in the region by 700 BCE, most of the religious beliefs and ritual practices of Hindus today are those recorded in texts that were composed *after* the original four Vedas, which we'll discuss more in this next section.

Vedic Religion

Vedas: collection of earliest Hindu hymns

Knowledge of early Indic religion comes from the four **Vedas**, a collection of over a thousand hymns addressed to the gods. The oldest is the *Rig Veda*. These hymns show no systematic ordering, or single mythological framework. It is likely that the Vedic hymns were collected and appreciated by only the most elite social groups of that earlier millennium (1500–500 BCE).

brahmin: highest caste, many serving as priests

Early Vedic religion was centered on fire sacrifices. The sacrifices were performed by a special, hereditary group of priests called *brahmins*, who chanted the Vedic

A brahmin priest in Nepal tends a sacrificial fire pit for his patrons.

hymns and orchestrated intricate rituals intended to gratify the numerous Aryan deities. Accompanied by chants, the brahmins placed grain, animal flesh, and clarified butter in a blazing fire, thereby transforming the offerings into fragrant smoke to nourish and please the gods. If kept happy, well fed, and strengthened through the offerings, the deities would sustain creation and ensure the prosperity of the sacrificers.

The language of the Vedic hymns, called Sanskrit, was thought to be divine in origin. The hymns were memorized by brahmin priests and taught to men in succeeding generations. The Vedas existed for over two millennia in oral form; the earliest extant written manuscripts, which date back only to the eleventh century of the common era, include annotations showing proper accents and supplying ritual contexts.

The major deities of the Vedic world, all male, were connected to sacrifice, martial conquest, mystical experience, and maintenance of moral order. Agni, the fire god, was essential for the successful ritual. Indra, the warrior deity, has the greatest number of hymns dedicated to him. It was Indra who subdued foreign gods, and it was Indra who was called on to lead the Aryan men into battle. The deity Soma was a divine presence dwelling within a psychoactive substance of the same name, which humans and deities drank before battle and at the end of major rituals. Another important deity, Varuna, was thought to enforce the moral order of the universe and to distribute punishment or reward. The hymns indicate that humans approached Varuna with personal petitions for forgiveness.

Death and afterlife in the early Vedic era were envisioned as alternative destinies. There was the possibility of becoming an ancestor and reaching a heavenly afterlife if one lived morally, but only if one's family, in the first year after one's death, performed special memorial rituals. Alternatively, those whose deeds were immoral or

"In your offspring you are born again; That, O Mortal, is your immortality."

—*Taittiriya Brahmana*

SOURCE: Quoted in Patrick Olivelle, *Samnyasa Upanishads* (New York: Oxford University Press, 1992), p. v.

whose families failed to do the proper rituals lost their individual identity and merely dissolved back into the earth.

Vedic religion was marked by faith in the power of the gods, ritual acts to influence them, and the spiritual resonance of Sanskrit words. The Aryans believed with absolute certainty in the primacy of their deities. By 100 CE, however, the dominant devotional tradition placed all the central deities of the earliest pantheon into lesser roles: Indra was now king of the minor heavenly hosts, Agni was confined to be a guardian of ritual, Soma was seen as the deity residing in the moon, and Varuna became the lord of the ocean. Similarly, the Vedic concept of the natural human order that the gods enforced was replaced by three dominant themes in subsequent Hinduism: reincarnation, the law of karma, and the concept of sacred duty.

Karma, Yoga, and the Quest for Liberation

Later Vedic hymns indicate that a very different spiritual orientation had entered the Aryan world. The practice of asceticism—involving retreat into the forest, silent introspection, and the cultivation of trance states—was likely the first indigenous pre-Vedic spiritual tradition absorbed into the dominant religion. A synthesis of this spirituality emerges in the **Upanishads**, the remarkable tracts that began to be appended to the Vedic hymns after 1000 BCE. The dialogues themselves and the name they are given—*upanishad* means "sitting near devotedly"—portray disciples learning at the feet of gurus who have gone beyond the Vedic sacrificial framework to adopt ascetic practices. These gurus developed new teachings and practices aimed at realizing the fundamental realities underlying all existence.

Upanishads: appendices to the Vedas that record Hindu mystical teachings

The central idea they introduced is that of **samsara**, "the world," in which all phenomena are really only secondary appearances. But blinded by illusion, humans act foolishly and thereby suffer from the pains of samsara. These last until humans realize that the underlying reality is everywhere the same, and it is the unchanging spirit (**Brahman**). This truth is stated concisely in the Chandogya Upanishad when the teacher states, "That [i.e., Brahman] thou art," or more directly, "You are divine." The individual soul (**atman**) dies and is reincarnated over and over again until it finds release from the cycle by realizing that it is nothing other than Brahman, the ultimate reality of the world, the universal spirit.[3]

samsara: "the world" of rebirth subject to the law of karma

Brahman: unchanging world spirit that arises at creation

atman: the soul, which transmigrates after death

An individual's destiny in samsara is determined by his or her actions (deeds and thoughts). Good deeds lead to good consequences, while bad deeds lead to evil consequences. This natural law, which operates throughout samsara and affects the destiny of the atman, is called **karma**, a complex term whose meaning is often oversimplified. Ultimately, through good deeds and specific yoga practices, the individual works toward realization of the highest truth and the achievement of **moksha**, release from further reincarnation. (All the world religions born in India, including Buddhism, Jainism, and Sikhism, accept the reality of samsara, but differ in their analysis of karma and the practices needed to achieve moksha.)

karma: "action"; effects of actions that condition a being's future

moksha: "release" from future rebirths and deaths; salvation

TEACHINGS OF RELIGIOUS WISDOM: A Maid Teaches a Holy Man How to Discern Rebirth Destiny

A certain holy man, well skilled in Brahmanical lore and who had spent his whole life in the study of the *Vedas* and other religious works, went on a journey. At the first town he entered he, . . . while resting himself [near a domicile], saw a funeral pass, . . . when, to his astonishment, he heard the mistress from within the house inquire from the maidservant as to whether the deceased had gone to heaven. Commanded to do so, the girl went out, and in a short time returned, giving an answer in the affirmative. A similar occurrence took place, but in this instance the maidservant's reply was in the negative. Lost in amazement, the sage demanded how she was able to make known the workings of karma which were to him, notwithstanding all his learning, inscrutable. The maid replied that it was an extremely easy task to ascertain the destination of departed souls . . . as it was only necessary to attend at the . . . place of cremation and listen to the opinion expressed regarding them by their neighbors. If ten of them concurred in speaking in praise of the deceased, it was almost certain that he had gone to a heavenly rebirth; if, on the contrary, they agreed in asserting that he was an evil-doer, it was equally sure that he went to a worse rebirth.

Source: A. K. Ramanujan, *Folktales from India* (New Delhi: Penguin Books India, 1993), p. 55.

Yoga

Yoga refers to various disciplined practices by which humans can realize their true spiritual essence, the atman within. First appearing in the late Upanishads, these practices were codified in a text, the **Yoga Sutras**, attributed to a sage named Patanjali (ca. 150 BCE). The yoga meditation tradition is for the highly advanced spiritual elite, for those attempting to escape *samsara* by ending, or "burning up," all past karma.

The *Yoga Sutras* assume that yoga can be performed properly only by individuals of high moral character, who have renounced most material possessions, live in simplicity (including vegetarianism), and study the teachings regarding the "inner reality." Practice begins first with postures designed to make the body flexible and to awaken its energies, then develops breath control to harness and enhance the body's primal energy. After focusing the mind on a single object for long periods, the *yogin*, or adept practitioner experiences increasingly refined states of consciousness as the mind is withdrawn from external sensation. These experiences culminate in a trance state (*samadhi*). It is in samadhi that the yogin develops awareness of the origin of consciousness itself: the life-giving, pure, and blissful atman.

The progressive practice of yoga weakens the power of ignorance and egotistic desire that naturally distort human consciousness. The ultimate goal in yoga meditation is to dwell for extended periods in trance, reaching the highest state, an awareness

yoga: "union"; practices that lead to union with the divine

Yoga Sutras: ancient text codifying yoga practices, attributed to Patanjali

"By austerity a man achieves goodness, and through goodness he takes hold of the mind. Through the mind he reaches the self, and reaching the self he comes to rest."

—*Maitreya Upanishad*

SOURCE: Patrick Olivelle, *Samnyasa Upanishads* (New York: Oxford University Press, 1992), p. 160.

Seeking to discern Brahman within themselves, ancient Hindu holy men practiced many forms of austerity, as shown in this Punjabi painting of yoga positions.

that is perfectly at one with the atman. The yogin who reaches this state is said to put an end to all past karma and to experience moksha. This yogin is thought to be omniscient and capable of supernormal feats, such as telepathy and clairvoyance. This enlightenment experience and the capacity to know others' tendencies and thoughts makes the yogic sage an ideal spiritual guide for other religious seekers.

The great majority of Hindus base their religious lives around the reality of karma. Although interpretations vary, Hindu karma doctrine asserts that all actions performed by an individual set into motion a cause that will lead to a moral effect in the present and/or future lifetimes. A natural mechanism functions to make the cosmos orderly and just. This has meant that inclinations to do good and avoid evil were backed up by the belief in karmic retribution for one's actions. Since old karma is coming to fruition constantly and new karma is being made continuously, it is—in most explications—incorrect to see karma doctrine as fatalism. Further, not all events in life are due to karma; Indic religious philosophies and medical theory have also recognized natural causalities as part of the human condition.

What is implicit in karma theory for typical human beings is that one's karma in daily life is in fact unknown. In practice, this uncertainty principle explains the Hindu tendency to turn to astrology for guidance at times of important decisions. As Indian society developed, other ideas were tied to karma, weaving tighter the socioreligious fabric of classical Hinduism.

OM

First appearing in the Upanishads, where it is described as the "seed sound" of all other sounds, OM (also written phonetically as AUM) is one of the most prominent symbols of Hinduism. Repeated as part of almost every mantra for offerings and meditation as well as written calligraphically on icons and other symbols, OM has become an ever-present symbol, often reflecting sectarian differences. Upandishadic interpretations developed in yoga, for example, where OM is seen as a symbol of cosmic origination and dissolution. OM's components also include all four states of consciousness in yoga theory, with A as waking, U as dreaming, M as dreamless sleep, and the syllable as a whole "the fourth." OM is the sound-form of atman-Brahman. Repeating OM is thus the key to meditation that leads to moksha. The written OM, shown in the title bar to this box, adorns all the major deities as represented in the popular art forms.

Sadhus have been a part of the Hindu tradition for three thousand years. Wandering Hindu ascetics today adhere to a variety of paths, from the bhakti devotional devotees to yogins seeking the divine without form.

Premodern Hinduism:
The Classical Era (180 BCE–900 CE)

The first great empire in South Asian history was that of the Mauryas (300–180 BCE), whose emperors helped to spread Buddhism and its ideal of compassion as a principle of just rule. As Buddhism expanded and thrived, it competed with early brahmin-led traditions.

Classical Hinduism, the product of response to Buddhism by the brahmin priests and spiritual teachers, synthesized aspects of this missionary faith while also embracing pre-Aryan deities and other indigenous Indic traditions. As a result, nonviolence and vegetarianism became ideals of high-caste religiosity, Hindu monasteries for training and meditation were begun, and a distinctive theistic dimension of Hinduism found

"This is the entire aim of yoga: rendering in personal experience of the Truth which universal nature had hidden in herself. . . . It is the conversion of the human soul into the divine soul and of natural life into divine living."

—Aurobindo Ghose

SOURCE: Stephen Hay, ed., *Sources of Indian Tradition*, 2nd ed., vol. 2 (New York: Columbia University Press, 1988), p. 155.

Marble statue of the saint Mahavira in meditation, enshrined in a Jain temple located in Jaisalmer, India.

increasingly popular acceptance. Classical Hinduism in North India reaches a mature synthesis in the Gupta dynasty (320–647 CE), when wealth and the cultural expressions of devotional Hinduism flowered in all the fine arts. This tradition was so compelling that by 1200 CE, Hinduism had slowly absorbed the Buddha within its panoply of gods and Buddhism had virtually disappeared from South Asia except for the Himalayan (Nepal) and Sri Lankan peripheries. Brahmin writers in the classical age composed Sanskrit literature that codified and disseminated expressions of this new synthesis in philosophy, theology, and law. These texts and leaders unified the subcontinent with one fundamental paradigm: An individual's place in society is defined in terms of karma.

Early Heterodox Indic Religions: Jainism and Buddhism

By 700 BCE, the religious movements of South Asia were especially diverse. Most were organized around brahmin teachers, who reinterpreted the Vedic sacrifice or sought new ascetic methods to experience ultimate reality. Most of these teachers taught that the Veda was sacred and formed the bedrock of all revelation. From this time onward, the traditions that adopt this view, and that accept the legitimacy of caste and brahmin priesthood, have been regarded by traditional scholars as "orthodox" Hindu schools.

But there were other charismatic teachers who formed organized Indic religions who did not accept the Veda, adopt the ideology of caste, or revere those born as brahmins. Indeed, they regarded brahmin ascetics as deluded. These heterodox religions—first Jainism and Buddhism in ancient times, and then Sikhism by 1520—became world religions in their own right. Significantly, each was founded by members of the warrior caste; each shaped a community of elite disciples who insured the movement's long-term survival; and each developed its own distinctive spiritual practices that won the loyalty of warriors and merchants. Buddhism is covered in the next chapter, and Sikhism later in this chapter. We now turn our attention to Jainism.

Jainism: The Tradition of Spiritual Conquerors

Among the many seekers who retreated to the forests of ancient north India were some totally committed to liberation from death and rebirth. Little is known about most of these wanderers; aside from the Upanishads, the only accounts that survive are those of the few successful religions that emerged in this era, Buddhism and Jainism. Found now in parts of India, as well as in small communities in East Africa, England, and North America, Jainism is a minor world religion, over 2500 years old, with between 5 to 8 million followers today.

Jain tradition records the existence of twenty-four sages who have realized the true nature of the world and discovered the only path to overcome human bondage in it. These sages are called Tirthankaras ("ford finders"), whose name refers to the shallow places where "fording," or crossing, a river is easiest. The last two Tirthankaras are Parsavanath (ca. 850 BCE) and Mahavira (599–527 BCE). The latter was influenced by the former, and both are revered for attaining release (moksha) from samsara by adopting a rigorous ascetic life.

While the Jain saints believed in samsara and moksha, their precise understanding of these is distinctive, compared to the other great Indic religions. This world, they agree, is based on the suffering in samsara; unlike Hindu and Buddhist philosophy, however, to Jains samsara is real in a material sense, and not an illusion. The Jains regard the only solution to samsara is to escape it, and their sages taught that only through non-action can individuals find true happiness. This non-action involves stopping any killing in any form, intentional or not. For Jains, "non-killing is the supreme path."

Like the Upanishadic teachers, Jains regard the soul as the repository of all deeds. Although in itself a pure, clear entity, the soul is caught in a karmic trap, tarnished due to killing (intentional or not) done in this and previous lives. It is this killing karma residue that corrupts spiritual awareness. Total nonviolence in thought, word, and deed dissolves this residue; noninterference in all worldly connections is the only way to end even subtle violence. The religious life of Jain householders seeks to limit new karma that might further darken the soul; the religious occupation of monks and nuns is more intensive, seeking to stop altogether making any new karma as well as rapidly burn up the residue of the old.

Purification of the soul by burning off the residue of past killing is the goal of all Jain practices. The householder majority undertake periodic fasts or periods of renunciation in pursuit of this goal. Others dedicate themselves to attain the highest goal of *samyak darshan*, "complete intuition" into the world's workings. All Jains seek to develop "detachment and forgiveness," a mind that cultivates self-control and renunciation.

Jains believe that to achieve moksha requires taking monastic vows. With community support, the elite undertake more austere fasting, meditation, and scripture study. These three practices cause past karma to ripen prematurely and end karma quickly.

After Mahavira's death, the Jain community spread, attracting the patronage of ancient Indic kings. But around 310 BCE, the community split due to differences in interpretations of the rules of asceticism, the role of women, and which texts were authoritative. Some moved south; they called themselves the Digambara ("Sky-clad") who require male monastic nakedness. This group believes the true texts were lost and so rely on treatises called the Prakaranas. Those who remained in the north called themselves the Svetambara ("white clad monks"). They held that their texts were the valid ones. In Svetambara Jainism, women are given a full spiritual place, and up until the present day, nuns far outnumber Svetambara monks. From antiquity until the modern era, these two groups developed in isolation. Despite some points of difference, they share many beliefs and practices, especially the view that only monastics can reach moksha.

We forgive all living beings
We seek pardon from all living beings
We are friendly toward all living beings
And we seek enmity from no one.

—Jain prayer

By the fifth century CE, Jains began building temples housing images of the Tirthankaras. These temples included shrines to some Indic gods as well. Jains viewed gods not as world creators or sustainers, but merely as powerful beings still bound by karma who are destined to return for future rebirth. From this time, Jains integrated their religious tradition in the wider Hindu society. For example, gods affecting worldly life could be worshipped by Jain householders, even in Hindu temples. While Jains also accepted caste hierarchy, they rejected the doctrine that brahmins were born as spiritually superior human beings.

Jainism thus found a niche in the religious pluralism of South Asia over the last millennium. Jain businessmen—who worked hard, consumed modestly, emphasized education, and were masters of accommodation—have been extremely successful in many enterprises and served as lavish patrons of their faith, securing its future.

The Reality of Karma and Caste

As we have seen, the idea of karma explains the destiny of every living being according to its moral past. Humans get what they deserve, although not necessarily in a single lifetime. This idea of karmic retribution had become widely accepted by the classical era, and brahmin social thinkers built on it to formulate the basis of the ideal Hindu society in a series of texts called the *Dharmashastras* (*Treatises on Dharma*). These texts, the most famous of which is known by the English title *The Laws of Manu*, make a series of arguments about karma while also describing practices and social policies designed to keep the world in order. They center on the policies needed to insure

dharma: "duty" determined by caste and gender

sacred social and cosmic order by extensively discussing **dharma** (holy duty).

The *Dharmashastras* assume that one's birth location reveals one's karma. They also argue that high-status birth gives one a higher spiritual nature, reflecting one's good karma past. Rebirth, then, is assumed to fall into regular patterns, and this natural process justifies seeing society as divided into groups with very separate natures and capacities. These groups have come to be called "castes" in English.

Hindu law codes became the basis of Indian law in the early classical period. They prescribed that those born into a caste should marry within that group. Such individuals were believed to have closely matching karma. If they married and had children within their group, reincarnation patterns should be clearly maintained. Each of the four main castes had its own traditional tasks: *Brahmins* were masters of the Vedic and ritual practice; *kshatriyas* were rulers and protectors of society; *vaishyas* specialized in artisanship and trade; and *shudras* performed the labor and menial tasks for those in the upper castes.

Each of these four main castes included hundreds of caste subgroups, which to this day vary regionally in their surnames and specific social functions. It is important to note that in antiquity as well as the present day, intercaste marriages, political events, and local history resulted in much more social flexibility than is prescribed in the brahmanical texts.

Each caste was thought to have a singular proper duty to perform in life; the term for this, *dharma*, is central throughout the subsequent history of Hinduism. The *Dharmashastra* texts argue that one must live according to one's place in the world, which has been assigned from all earlier lives. Only by doing so does one make the good karma needed to move "upward" in samsara. As one passage in *The Laws of Manu* (10:97) warns, "Better to do one's own dharma badly than another caste's dharma well." This also implied that women should always be subordinate to men.

Hindu religious law, therefore, does not see all human beings as having the same social and religious status or as being subject to the same legal standards. While religious views underlie this system of social inequality, Hindu social theorists argued that in the fullness of time samsara and its law of karmic retribution allow for cosmic justice, matching karmic past to social function. In the end, every soul will move upward through samsara to be reborn as a brahmin male and reach liberation. Individual freedom is sacrificed for harmony and for society's ultimate and eventual collective liberation.

Thus, in theory, the religious underpinning of the caste system has legitimated the social hierarchy. It preserves the purity and privileges of the highest castes and argues that society depends on brahmins: If they live in purity and use their ritual mastery to worship the gods properly, they ensure that divine grace will sustain a successful society. Consistent with this belief system, high-caste Hindus view their superior status as based upon exemplary actions in previous lives. As we shall see, this sanctioning of high-caste privilege had early critics among Buddhists and Jains and, later, among Sikhs as well.

Classical Hindu writers also prescribed other endeavors to realize the ideal Hindu life. We now consider how the individual was expected to fulfill his or her dharma.

The Four Stages and Four Aims of Life

Hindu texts describe four stages and four aims of life. These four stages are:

1. The student
2. The householder
3. The forest dweller
4. The homeless wanderer (*sadhu*).

The male student studies in the house of his teacher. What he studies depends on his caste and ability, but all were to memorize portions of Vedas as well as become proficient in archery, medicine, astrology, and music.

Upon completing the student phase, a man marries and becomes a householder. In this second stage of life, his duty is to perform the traditional rites and raise his children to continue his lineage. The *Dharmashastras* require women to subordinate themselves to men, although husbands are supposed to respect their wives and maintain happiness within the household. Marriage is treated as a sacrament, and divorce is not allowed.

A sadhu Hindu ascetic, coated in ash, consults a ritual text.

In the third stage, when a couple finds the household well handled by their male descendants, they become forest dwellers. They focus on spiritual matters by retreating to the forest, living only on wild foods and renouncing sex. Their chief concerns are rituals and meditation.

The fourth stage of life, the homeless wanderer (*sadhu*), begins when the forest dweller is close to moksha realization. Persons now wander alone; no rituals need be done, and they renounce all but what can be carried. Their remaining days are devoted to pilgrimages and to yoga practice.

Since individuals differ in their karma-determined capabilities according to caste and stage of life, the *Dharmashastras* also identified four aims of life:

1. Material gain/worldly success (*artha*)
2. Sensory pleasure (*kama*)
3. Fulfilment of duty (*dharma*)
4. Release from the cycle of birth and death (*moksha*)

The first aim, *artha*, is reflected in South Asian folk literature of animal stories and human parables. These stories impart instructions toward this goal in life, an indication that belief in karma can coexist for pious Hindus with an interest in material success.

The second aim, *kama*, was an acceptable goal for householders seeking to fulfill the duty of propagating the family line. Many in the West have heard of the *Kama Sutra*, which discusses sexual pleasure as well as many other ways to achieve satisfaction in life.

The third aim, *dharma*, we have already discussed. The other aims of life are justly pursued only if they remain consistent with one's caste and gender-appropriate duties.

The last of the four aims, *moksha*, is adopted by few, but the texts counsel that everyone should respect and support through almsgiving those who pursue this aim. Hindus still venerate the sadhu saints, who follow this path of spiritual wandering.

Epics and the Development of Classical Hinduism

For the majority of Hindus, theology, law, and the models for religious life are conveyed in the sacred stories and by characters of the great epics: the *Mahabharata* and the *Ramayana*. By the classical era, these two epics had been composed from oral sources that originated in accounts of early battles fought by warriors in the ancient Aryan clans.

The *Mahabharata* records a devastating feud between rival sides of a family as they vied for control of the northern plains, each one aided by supernatural allies. One side has usurped power from the other, but the rightful heir has no desire to shed the blood of his kin to take it back. This dilemma provides the moral element of the story. This rivalry ended in a war of immense carnage that in theological interpretation marks the onset of the current dark age, the **Kali Yuga**. The *Mahabharata* (especially its most famous portion, the ***Bhagavad Gita***) presents diverse and nuanced discussions of dharma, especially that pertaining to warriors, kin, and women. It also describes the role of divinity in human affairs. The epic reveals the many difficulties, paradoxes, and ambiguities that face those who wish to apply the religious ideals of the *Dharmashastra* to ambiguous real-life circumstances.

In the second great epic, the *Ramayana*, the underlying historical circumstance is the rivalry between one Aryan clan—symbolized by the hero Rama—and the non-Aryans of the south, portrayed as powerful demons subject to unbridled lust, immorality, and disrespect for Vedic sacrifices. Invoking the forces of nature and his animal allies, Rama defeats the demon Ravana who had kidnapped his wife Sita and returns home to establish a unified Hindu kingdom. The tale has provided groups across South (and Southeast) Asia a narrative to express their own views on ethnic relations, what makes a good king, gender relations, and the relationship between northerners and southerners. In fact, there is no single *Ramayana* today, for through its telling and retellings hundreds of groups have claimed their particular version as sacred and central to their own Hindu ideal.

Mainstream Hinduism and the Rise of Devotion to the Great Deities

Most of the deities who became the focus of Hindu devotional life by the classical age differed from those of the earliest Vedic hymns. An entirely new collection of Sanskrit texts, called ***puranas***, was composed to describe these great gods, specify their forms of worship, and celebrate the early saints who cultivated divine love for them. The purana stories recount examples of human incarnation, instances of divine omniscience, and episodes of grace. Heroes in these stories become models of exemplary devotional faith, or ***bhakti***.

All the puranas share an important assumption about humanity living in the Kali Yuga, the current and "dark" post-Vedic age. This era, said to have begun in 3102 BCE, is defined as the period of degeneration, in which human spiritual potential is declining. The puranas declare that the deities have extended their grace to humanity in return for their followers' unselfish devotion. While the ascetic practices of yoga do not end (and not all Hindus accepted Kali Yuga theory), this ideal of bhakti, the full commitment of heart and mind to devotional practice, became the predominant one for Hinduism from the classical era until the present day.

Hinduism's shift toward bhakti merges a new theology with the fundamental ideas of the formative era: samsara, karma, and moksha. The devotional tradition accepts the early model but builds on it by asserting that the great deities, such as Shiva, Vishnu, and Durga, have the power to reward devotion by altering the karma of the

Kali Yuga: the dark age in which the world is currently

Bhagavad Gita: Hindu scripture extolling the divinity of Krishna; part of the epic *Mahabharata*

puranas: popular texts extolling glories of Hindu deities

bhakti: devotionalism to a Hindu divinity

bhakta (devotee). By absorbing human karma, these deities can bring their grace to persons seeking moksha. This view is most dramatically expressed in the *Bhagavad Gita,* where the deity Krishna argues that desireless action is possible only through egoless bhakti faith and that the true suspension of all action (which produces additional karma) is impossible.

By the classical era, purana texts asserted the existence of 330 million deities. How could the theologians account for such incredible diversity? The bhakti saints and theologians argued that the existence of countless gods reflects the grace of the divine, since the overwhelming needs of a humanity comprising innumerable individual karmas could only be met by such an enormous number of gods. The challenge for each Hindu is to find and focus on the one deity whose form is most appropriate to his or her level of spiritual maturity.

In later Hinduism practice, each devotee chooses a personal deity to be at the center of his or her religious life, a focus for personal communion through an emotional relationship. Although most teachers (and families) believed that Hindus should respect all the great deities as well as lesser, local spirits, it was nonetheless essential for each person to establish a single divinity to venerate as a channel for grace. Among theologians, the terms and mechanisms of liberation vary; in many of the puranas, rebirth in one's chosen deity's heaven—not exit from samsara—is proclaimed as the highest human goal devotees need strive for.

The concept of "chosen deity" requires knowing extensively and loving selflessly that particular god. This meant making offerings (*puja*, to be discussed later in this chapter), meditating, and studying the purana stories.

Each of the great deities of Hinduism has come to be known through the purana texts, and theologians provide different explanations for how and why the divine beings have manifested themselves to save humanity from mundane dangers and to bestow ultimate liberation. In the following sections we'll examine the great deities in more detail, starting with Ganesh.

A linga, the image commonly used to worship Shiva.

Ganesh

Judged by the number of shrines and the universality of his image, the elephant-headed Ganesh is the tradition's most popular divinity. Most Hindus worship Ganesh not as a divinity who will help them achieve liberation but more to secure his aid in worldly life. With a potbelly and love of sweets signaling his sensual orientation, Ganesh, who is commonly honored with offerings at the start of most rituals and journeys, is regarded as the kind, "fix-it" god in the pantheon.

Shiva

Shaivite: devotee of Shiva

The **Shaivite**, or one whose chosen deity is Shiva, focuses on two beliefs: that Shiva's essence is found in all creative energies in this world, and that one can find one's own divine nature by dedicating bhakti practice to this lord. As described in the puranas, Shiva merges opposing sides of Hindu life: He is both the ideal ascetic revered by

Elephant-headed Ganesh, god of success, is found in every Hindu community. He is always worshipped first and before any major undertaking.

yogins, and the successful householder who marries the goddess Parvati and fathers the divine sons Ganesh and Kumar.

In Hindu legend, Shiva saves the world repeatedly and requites devotion with his grace. However, Shiva also has a wrathful side and will punish humans as well. The puranas attribute to Shiva the periodic cosmic upheavals that return the universe to a formless, empty resting state. The sectarian Shaivite theologians see the linking of world creation, fertility, and destruction as signifying Shiva's omnipresence, making him the supreme "Great God."

Vishnu and His Avataras, Rama and Krishna

Although they may respect Shiva, Vishnu devotees (**Vaishnavites**) believe that their chosen deity is the one who truly underlies all reality. Vishnu alone is mentioned in the Vedas. He alone begets the god Brahma, who then begins another cycle of creation.

The great theme of Vishnu theology is that of incarnation. The puranas dedicated to him recount many episodes in the earth's history when demons threatened creation. At these times, Vishnu assumed the form of whatever was

Bearing a mace, a discus, and a conch, Vishnu is represented as Lord of the Universe.

Vaishnavite: devotee of Vishnu

"O Mother! Thou art
    present in every
    form;
Thou art the universe
    and in its tiniest and
    most trifling things.
Wherever I go and
    wherever I look,
I see Thee, Mother,
    present in thy cosmic
    form.
The whole earth—
    earth, water, fire,
    air—
Are all thy forms, O
    Mother, the whole
    world of birth and
    death."

SOURCE: David Kinsley, *The
Sword and the Flute* (Berkeley:
University of California Press,
1975), p. 116.

shakti: innate, creative
force of this universe,
understood as feminine

shaktas: devotees of
Devi

needed to smash the threat. Some of these incarnations, or **avataras**, were animals and most were local heroes. The texts also suggest Vishnu's role in humanity's future liberation. One avatara, Kalki, is expected to come riding on a white horse to guide humanity as the Kali Yuga turns darker. Although the names and number of avataras varies, two of the most important and widely accepted are Rama and Krishna.

We have already encountered Rama, hero of the *Ramayana*, who slays the demon Ravana and reveals the ideal of proper filial obedience to parents, loyalty to brothers, and the exemplary conduct of Hindu kings. His alliance with the monkey leader Hanuman also signals the ideal of harmonizing the divine with the natural world. A second form of Rama is one dedicated to destroying any evil kings who would disturb brahmins or their rituals.

The most complex and multifaceted of the Vishnu avataras, Krishna is revered in many forms: the infant trickster god, whose every prank and every gesture reveal his underlying divinity; the child who as "the butter thief" also steals the hearts of the world's mothers and fathers; the brave youth who rescues villagers from the poison of evil serpent deities and from the cruel rains sent by the Vedic god Indra; and the divine paramour and consort of the female cowherds. Finally, Krishna is the mature guru who offers counsel about the necessity of serving the world according to one's dharma. Many of his sectarian devotees believe that Krishna is in fact the reality from which all the gods originate.

The Devis

As with human society, Hindus experienced the divine as divided into male and female beings; perhaps from a tradition originating among the pre-Aryan indigenous peoples, Hindus believe that goddesses are born of the earth, residing in mountains and rivers. Across South Asia, these are referred to as "Devi" in a generalized way, and with names specific to special incarnations that, like the male gods, arose to assist humans with their problems (e.g., drought), and especially with predations of powerful demons. Early Indian art depicts the fertile, creative power of the universe in scenes where a young woman touches a tree, her innate energy (*shakti*) causing it to burst into bloom. Those who predominantly worship goddesses are called *shaktas*, and theirs is the third general group among Hindu deity worshippers, alongside Vaishnavites and Shaivites.

The earth goddess may be addressed as Ambika ("Mother"), Sita ("[born of the]

Durga, riding her vehicle, the tiger, carries the weapons of the male gods.

The Dance of Shiva

One of the most lyrical and evocative symbols of Hinduism is that of Nataraja, Shiva as Lord of the Dance. The upper right hand holds the twin-sided drum, from which sacred sound emerges, counting time and originating sound's creative resonance. The opposite hand holds a flame; Shiva's holding a fire points to his being a refuge to followers in the fires of *samsara*. Fire also alludes to this deity's role as destroyer at the end of a great world era. Both hands move together in Shiva's great dance, ceaselessly integrating cosmic creation and destruction, including all the gods. Another hand shows the "fear-not" gesture, and the fourth points to his upraised foot, the place Hindu devotees touch most often in ritual. Shiva dances while treading on a demon who symbolizes delusion. Thus, to enter into the Dance of Shiva means to brave the circle of rebirth, transcend the limitations of time and apparent opposites, and join with the divine powers of the great deity whose grace and eternal energy can remove spiritual obstacles. Because the cosmos has become a manifestation of Shiva's power, a dance done simply for the purpose of his own entertainment, wherever individuals can cultivate artistic pleasure, they can find union with Shiva.

Shiva Nataraja, Lord of the Dance: twelfth-century bronze image from southern India.

tilled furrow"), or Sati ("the Virtuous"). All these forms draw on the creative, mothering female force. Another widespread and primordial sense of female divinity is that associated with destruction; this has been primarily in the form of the smallpox goddess, called Shitala or Ajima.

Yet other related female forms are the goddesses who destroy demons, Durga and Kali. Those needing to confront death to arrive at mature spirituality can make Kali their chosen deity. To visualize the dance of Kali means seeing that life is inevitably surrounded by death, and understanding that the gift of human life should not be wasted. Devotional communion with Durga and Kali requires bhaktas to offer them blood through animal sacrifice to secure their blessings.

Hindu theology also views the pantheon as balancing the unique powers of male and female. The cosmos, like the human species, is seen as created and sustained by the same combination of gender energies: the male shakta and the female shakti. Each is incomplete and even dangerous without the balancing influence of the other. Thus, most of the Hindu deities are married. We shall see later how tantric Hinduism carries the implications of this theology into individual yoga practice.

Premodern Hinduism: The Postclassical Era (900 CE–1500 CE)

The Formation of Major Hindu Schools of Thought

During the late classical era, the brahmin elite consolidated their philosophical positions. These texts became and have remained authoritative for the tradition. Every school's texts sought to explain the nature of the physical world, the boundaries of individuality, the basis for establishing human knowledge, and the means to liberation. All told, these texts and the epics comprise an extraordinarily large sacred literary tradition.

The orthodox schools formed in response to the heterodox, or nonstandard, schools of Buddhism and Jainism. Those discussed here came to dominate the Hindu intellectual tradition.

Sankhya

One of the oldest systematic philosophy schools to appear, the Sankhya school's ideas were especially important in subsequent Hindu thought. The Sankhya school (literally, "analysis") posits a dualistic universe of matter (*prakriti*) bonded in various combinations with spirit (*purusha*). Both matter and spirit are eternal, with an infinite number of purushas eternally distinct from one another.

Sankhya admits the reality of gods but denies the existence of a transcendent, personal God. The purpose of spiritual life is isolating purusha from prakriti. Sankhya's differentiation of spirit-matter combinations, which has informed Hindu culture to the present, is applied to the analysis of human personality, gender, species, the seasons, aesthetics, medicine, and even foods.

One typical use of Sankhya theory is to assess the spiritual status of human beings. All beings are combinations of three primary material qualities or "strands" that bind spirit to the material world: *sattva* (associated with purity, goodness, subtlety), *rajas* (passion, raw energy), and *tamas* (darkness, inertia, grossness). In the Sankhya view, too, even the gods are qualitatively similar to humans, different only by having more sattva. This school thereby sees the incarnation of divinities in human form as part of the universe's natural processes.

Advaita Vedanta

The Advaita Vedanta school is monistic; that is, it regards the singular reality of the universe as impersonal spirit. This view draws on the Upanishads' formula of Brahman = atman. This school of thought became the prevailing scholastic philosophy of South Asia after 500 CE, and it is most often emphasized by modern Hindu reformers. Advaita Vedanta's enduring central place among Hindu philosophies was due to the brilliance of the great philosopher **Shankara** (ca. 788–820). His commentaries and treatises received additional exposure through public debates with proponents of other schools.

Shankara argued that the apparent difference between the material and physical worlds is pure illusion (*maya*). Only study and yoga practice can enable a seeker to gain true knowledge.

Shankara admitted that one could in elementary and intermediate stages of spiritual development relate to Brahman as a personal divinity. with human characteristics (*saguna*) such as power and grace (**saguna Brahman**). But ultimately, moksha can be achieved only by going beyond this projection of a deity in terms of human characteristics to experience Brahman by merging one's own soul with **nirguna Brahman**, that reality "without characteristics."

Shankara also organized the first great network of Hindu monasteries (*mathas*) that supported male ascetics whose rule of conduct specified vegetarianism, dress in an ochre robe, use of a walking staff, and horizontal forehead markings. This monastic order grew, expanded, and survives to this day.

The Theology of Qualified Monism: Vishishta Advaita

While Shankara's monistic thought and practice appealed to intellectuals and ascetics, it was quite different from the religious experience of most devotees who revered the gods. It remained for later theologians, particularly **Ramanuja** (ca. 1025–1137), to link scholastic theology with popular theistic practice. Ramanuja argued that human beings could not really recognize the divine, except in the perceivable world. Why? Since Brahman pervades all reality, the religious path to moksha cannot and need not proceed beyond saguna Brahman. Like Shankara, Ramanuja wrote his own commentary on the Upanishads, but he reached a very different theistic conclusion about their ultimate spiritual truth. He emphasized Vishnu as the form of Brahman most effectively worshipped.

Ramanuja asserted that each individual is ultimately a fragment of Vishnu, wholly dependent on him, and that a perfect understanding of this could be realized only through intense devotion (*bhakti yoga*). This theology also holds that souls do not ultimately merge with Brahman, maintaining a "separate nondifference," even in moksha.

Tantric Hinduism

A major innovation of post–classical era Hinduism was **tantra**. Like the bhakti theology already mentioned, the tantric tradition built on earlier ideas and practices

Shankara: influential Hindu philosopher, advocating the impersonal ultimate reality

saguna Brahman: human form of the world spirit

nirguna Brahman: impersonal form of the world spirit

Ramanuja: Influential theologian who emphasized worship of Brahman as Vishnu

Shri Yantra, symbol of the goddess used in meditation.

tantra: esoteric practices leading to moksha

but advocated new forms of spiritual experience. The name *tantra* relates to weaving, in this case likely indicating the interweaving of teaching and texts. The emergence of tantra can be seen in both Hinduism and Buddhism, indicating how thoroughly these later traditions affected each other.

Tantric teachers accepted the Kali Yuga theory of a world in spiritual decline, and their texts typically begin by underscoring how the tantric path to liberation in this lifetime is suited for the Kali Yuga age. The assumption is that what worked for the Vedic sages is too subtle for today, and that what was prohibited to the seeker in the Vedic ages is precisely what is needed today for spiritual breakthrough. Tantric teachings are not given openly or universally, but are bestowed by teachers only to those deemed capable of practicing methods that, as we shall see, contradict the dharma-based morality of the upper castes. There are many tantric traditions, each deriving from an enlightened saint called a **siddha**, who discovered in an intensive personal quest a method of meditation and understanding that culminates in moksha. This personal lineage was passed down in small circles following specific beliefs and practices derived from the original master. The unorthodox practices and extraordinary experiences were thought to be dangerous for those unready for them; this made the siddha teachers wary of instructing unproven individuals and led them to prescribe dire penalties for any initiate who revealed anything about tantric practice to outsiders.

siddha: tantric saint

All the tantric paths are rooted in the ancient yoga traditions we have discussed. Tantric yoga regards the body as a microcosm of the universe; adepts believe that all bodily energies, if harnessed and focused, are capable of producing a transformative religious experience. What is distinctive in tantric yoga is that the primal energies of male and female are the essential focus. Thus, tantra incorporated the devotional worship of female deities in union with their consorts. Many tantric teachings prescribe the practice of ritualized sexual union during which both partners visualize themselves as divinities, cultivating in each other an enlightened awakening through the transformative energy that arises through their union. The goal is realization of the one universal blissful spirit that is beyond gender.

Tantric yoga entails mastering complex rituals and practices that invert caste-based status and gender hierarchy norms. Places of tantric practice include cremation grounds, the most polluted ritual sites; ritual implements include human bones and skulls. The sexual yoga and the use of forbidden foods (meat, fish, and alcohol that are otherwise unacceptable for high-caste groups) shocked orthodoxy, but they were deployed for the highly traditional goal of freeing the individual's mind to realize moksha.

While tantra was at first a "counterculture" juxtaposed against orthodox Hinduism, its influence slowly grew, even among the high castes. Later, tantric ideas shaped

The six centers of the tantric body, displayed in relation to a yogin.

Hindu life-cycle rites and temple ritualism, as priests who had delved into tantric practice revised ancient rituals, keeping the older outward practices and adding meaning for the general public as well as communicating inner truths for those attuned to esoteric tantric symbolisms.

The Early Islamic Era: Delhi Sultanate (1192–1525)

Soon after the conversion of central Asian and Turkic peoples to Islam in the first centuries after the death of the Prophet Muhammad (632 CE), Muslim converts came to South Asia, and the region began to absorb Islamic influences. Muslim traders enhanced transregional trade and settled in caravan and port towns. They built mosques and eventually brought religious scholars and clerical authorities to guide the slowly growing Islamic communities. The conquest of northern India by Ghuride armies from central Asia (1192) defeated the Hindu kings.

Over 500 years of Muslim rule in South Asia followed, an era of increasingly centralized government. In many areas, Muslims displaced kshatriyas as heads of regional states; in many other places, Hindu rulers continued as their vassals. The Delhi Sultanate included the northern sections of modern Pakistan and India, from the Indus to the Upper Ganges. In general, authorities of the sultanate did not attempt to regulate indigenous religion, and Hindu traditions continued. Indeed, the great bhakti saints who rose to prominence in this era have dominated the popular Hindu devotional imagination ever since.

Religion in the Mughal Era (1526–1707)

The great Mughal Empire that controlled northern and central India from 1526 until 1707 represented the second era of Muslim rule across much of South Asia. In its first century, Mughal rule was a prosperous and peaceful era in which Indo-Islamic culture flourished, especially in architecture and the fine arts. The Taj Mahal in Agra is the most famous among hundreds of magnificent buildings erected in this period. There was a significant rise in converts to Islam across North India during the Mughal dynasty.

The Rise of Sikhism

One of the principal bhakti saints, Guru Nanak (1469–1539), achieved unparalleled success as founder of the last great heterodox religion to originate in India, Sikhism. His disciples now number over 30 million, eclipsing the number of Jews in global population.

Guru Nanak was born before the beginning of Mughal rule. A member of the warrior caste, he was well-educated in the religious literatures of Sanskrit, Persian,

"In men of animal nature, Shakti sleeps, but for tantrics she is wide awake. He who serves shakti is the 'true worshipper.' Whoever knows the rapture of the soul's union with the ultimate is the true adept at lovemaking. All others are merely enjoyers of women."

—Kularnava Tantra V. 107–13

SOURCE: India Sinha, *Tantra: The Cult of Ecstasy* (London: Hamlyn, 1993), p. 144.

and Arabic. By the age of twenty-nine, Nanak was married, father of two children, and employed as a civil servant. In 1498, a three-day mystical religious experience changed his life. His first pronouncement after a long silence indicated the vision that he would pursue: "There is neither Hindu nor Muslim, so whose path shall I follow? I shall follow God's path. God is neither Hindu nor Muslim and the path that I follow is God's."[4]

For the next twenty years, Nanak wandered as a pilgrim. He was drawn to answer the paradoxical question of why, if God is one and indivisible, humanity should be divided into competing and very different faiths. Conveyed in poetry and song, his spiritual experiences and moral teachings were collected and recorded in the **Janam Sakhis**, the traditional stories about his life that include encounters with animals, rulers, commoners, and holy men—Hindu sadhus and Muslim Sufis alike. Legends concerning Nanak's life describe his travels throughout South Asia, his visits to Tibet and Mecca. Everywhere his spiritual understanding and supernormal powers are said to surpass those of all others. Sikh tradition holds that Nanak respected both Hindu and Islamic traditions, but that his mission was to correct the mistaken practices and beliefs of both, thereby revealing the full spiritual truth and the proper path to realize it.

When he returned home from his wandering at age fifty, Nanak set out to do just this. Back in the Punjab, he taught all who were interested and soon attracted many disciples, known as "Sikhs," who were drawn by the community whose rules and rituals he established. Convinced that the caste system was wrong, Nanak had all his disciples eat as one family from a common kitchen, without hierarchy; he also was insistent that women deserved respect and religious equality. Many across north India were drawn to the charismatic guru as well as the reformist community whose rules and rituals he established. Nanak continued to compose religious verse, with 974 hymns in total forming the core of the Sikh scriptures when they were compiled by his successor a half century later.

Many disparate Hindu groups joined this new community, which offered an indigenous monotheistic alternative to Islam. After designating a successor, Nanak died in 1539.

The Ten Gurus and the Development of the Sikh Community

After Nanak there were nine other gurus who managed the burgeoning Sikh communities across the region. The second and third gurus gathered the songs and sermons composed by Nanak, adding hymns of their own and those composed by Hindu saints and Muslim Sufis, to form the holy scripture called the **Adi Granth**. This text, containing over 7,000 hymns, remains the unique focus of Sikh worship to this day. The Adi Granth is organized in chronological order beginning with hymns composed by Nanak, then hymns composed by the other gurus, followed by the hymns of other saints. Each hymn came to have its own traditional tune for singing.

Janam Sakhis: traditional stories about the life and teachings of Guru Nanak

Of women we are born, of women conceived,

To a woman engaged, to woman married

Woman we befriend, by women is civilization continued. . . .

It is by woman that order is maintained

Then why call her evil from whom great men are born?[5]

—Sikh hymn

SOURCE: Patwant Singh, *The Sikhs* (New York: Doubleday, 1999), p. 27.

Adi Granth: scripture worshipped by Sikhs

The town of Amritsar ("Pool of Ambrosia") in India was built and became the center of the faith up to the present day. Its Golden Temple, set in a lake, is the crown jewel of Sikh architecture. Tradition holds that the site on which the Golden Temple stands was sanctified by a visit from Guru Nanak, who instructed his successors to develop the area into a great spiritual center that would radiate a message of love and peace to humanity. The tenth guru, Gobind Singh (1666–1708), declared that in the future, the guru of the Sikhs in spiritual matters would be the holy text itself, when the second name for it became the Guru Granth Sahib. From when this temple was opened in 1604, every day until the present this text has been taken out and its hymns chanted from dawn until dusk.

In the early years of Mughal rule, the Sikhs gained popularity and were welcomed at court. The emperor Akbar (1561–1605) found in the faith a tolerant monotheistic theology and regarded the followers as a disciplined moral community. Akbar's successors, however, felt distrustful about the Sikhs' growth and political influences. The fifth guru, Arjan (1581–1606), was tortured and martyred on the order of one emperor, and in 1669, when another Mughal ruler ordered all Hindu temples and schools demolished, Sikhs resisted, and many died defending their faith. It was in response to this growing persecution that the Sikh tradition came to emphasize training in martial skills and bravery in defending the community. A group called the **Khalsa** ("The Pure") was formed, a dedicated elite order of men and women ready to struggle and die if necessary in defense of the faith. Training camps in archery, swordsmanship, and cavalry fighting were established to empower men to perform this religious duty. The Khalsa, who adopted a strict lifestyle as guardians of the faith, marked themselves by their appearance: uncut hair (covered with a turban), short trousers, steel wristlet, comb, and sword. Sikhs in the Khalsa also adopted the names Singh ("lion") for men and Kaur ("princess") for women, to eliminate caste distinctions within the community.

Traditional image of Guru Nanak.

Khalsa: "The Pure"; Sikh organization for defense of the faith

In the Gurmukhī script, *Ek Onkar* is a combination of three letters: *Ek, Aum,* and *Kar,* which is a line drawn over the Om, signifying continuity, timelessness, and eternity.

Sikh Theology, Morality, and Spiritual Practices

Nanak's spiritual path contained elements found in both Hindu and Muslim traditions. As in Islam, Nanak taught that there is only one "God," who never walked the earth as a man (i.e., had not had an incarnation). Nanak also set his teaching firmly in the Hindu nirguna tradition, mystically affirming that

"Omkar
True name
Being who creates
Beyond fear and opposition
A form beyond time
Unborn, self-born
The guru's grace."
—Nanak

SOURCE: *Songs of the Saints of India*, p. 78.

this God is entirely beyond form and human categories. To specify this god, Nanak introduced the terms **Om-kara** ("Divine One") and **Sat Guru** ("True Teacher").

Anticipating reformers of colonial and postcolonial Hinduism, Sikhs deny that asceticism is necessary, asserting that householders are perfectly capable of realizing the highest goal of liberation. Similarly, they say that ritual acts and pilgrimages have no spiritual effect. In addition, they reject the authority of the Vedas and the innate sanctity of the brahmin caste. The Sikhs' non-Vedic orientation has caused high-caste Hindus to regard them as heterodox.

Residing in the human heart and communicating with those who live rightly and develop their spiritual faculties, Sat Guru freely bestows grace that ends individual karma and rebirth. In Sikh spiritual understanding, the human struggle involves rejecting ego-centered living and embracing the divine Sat Guru within. Revelation occurs through the effect of divine sound on one's consciousness. The Adi Granth is the center of their rituals and ceremonies. Therefore, Sikh religiosity is centered on listening to, and congregationally singing, the hymns composed by Nanak and other saints and sitting in the presence of the holy book, whose very words both reflect and impart this grace.

Rejecting caste norms while living among a Hindu majority, Sikhs affirm the social equality of all humanity, regardless of caste, race, creed, or gender. Women can join the Khalsa and, following the views of Nanak, Sikh women were emancipated from conformity to the gender practices of both Islam and Hinduism. They were not required to wear veils, widows could remarry, and women could be religious preachers and the political heads of administrative districts in the fledgling Sikh states in Punjab. All Sikhs are expected to refrain from drugs including tobacco and alcohol, and many do not eat meat. Community service is an important and expected expression of faith; hard work and attaining wealth is encouraged; onerous work undertaken for others is highly respected. Being fit and active in defense of the weak and oppressed is an important part of the Sikh lifestyle.

There is no priesthood or ordained ministry in Sikhism; men and women pray together. Sikhs have had to make accommodations yet establish separate boundaries through their rituals. To become a Sikh requires making a profession of belief, affirming the essentials of nirguna theology and the need for each individual to earn liberation:

There is one God, his name is truth eternal
He is the creator of all things, the all-pervading spirit
Fearless and without hatred, timeless and formless.
Beyond birth and death, he is self-enlightened.
He is known by the Guru's grace.[6]

Sikhs find their liberation in combining public and private worship with social action, earning an honest living, giving alms, and doing community service. The great sixth guru, Harogobind (1595–1644), established the Sikhs' main religious institution, the ***gurudwara***, based on the teachings and examples of Nanak. This architectural and

gurudwara: Sikh temple

The Golden Temple in Amritsar, Punjab. This great landmark for Sikhs worldwide, and the faith's chief pilgrimage center, was occupied in the early 1980s by militants seeking Punjab's secession from India.

institutional form provides a common focal point for Sikh devotion and a place for communal gathering. The gurudwara hall is typically plain and undecorated, completely lacking in images. At one end is a raised platform with a silk covering on which a copy of the Adi Granth is central. From dawn until dusk a learned member of the community reads and sings from the text; those Sikhs in attendance can join in to sing as they sit below the text on the floor that is covered with white cloth. Any time the text is opened in the gurudwara, a member of the community must sit by it, just as a human guru must have a disciple in attendance. There is no priesthood in Sikhism; anyone can give teachings or read the scripture. This sanctuary can also accommodate individuals coming for prayer or meditation at any time.

The gurudwaras also contain a common kitchen where community vegetarian meals are prepared for all who come and where all eat together. Thus, kitchen service reflects the moral teachings of Sikhism: the centrality of community, its egalitarian nature, and social action. Within India's Hindu caste society, the Sikh religious lifestyle and social norms were revolutionary, bringing all members together regardless of caste and station in life. Today, the serving of community meals for all needing to eat is a central practice. It is a form of service to the poor seen every day at the Golden Temple in Amritsar and in Sikh communities globally. Its spirit is reflected in the aphorism "Where there are Sikhs, there is no hunger."

Hinduism and Modernity

In the modern period, Hindu tradition continues, with global influences entering the South Asian experience. Although some South Asians vigorously preserve elements of premodern religious culture, others have adopted new beliefs and practices. Scientific ideas associated with the Enlightenment affected nearly everyone through education, technology, and medicine; the views and practices of Christian missionaries as well as the political practices of the modern state impacted almost everyone as well. Most important, the pattern of reform and synthesis that has kept this religion so flexible has continued, launching neo-Hindu teachers not only in South Asia, but worldwide. Classical and reformed types of Hinduism as well as political movements emphasizing religious identity have proven extremely successful. We turn now to this time of immense change and innovation.

Hinduism Under British Colonialism

The first Europeans known to have settled in South Asia in Mughal times were Roman Catholic missionaries, initially the Dominicans in the Portuguese colony of Goa by 1510 and, after 1540, the Jesuits, led by Francis Xavier. Early merchants also arrived by sea to trade for spices, silks, indigo, and cotton goods. Although they had competitors among early Dutch, Portuguese, and French traders, the British under the East India Company eventually were the most successful at establishing themselves permanently. As the Mughal Empire over its last fifty years slowly disintegrated and the region's "Hindu states" asserted their independence, civil disorder increased, causing trade and tax revenues to decline. In this unstable atmosphere, the British strengthened their trade missions with armed fortresses, and by 1730 military detachments were integral to the British mercantile presence. From these centers, the British were drawn into conflicts; when they defeated local rulers in battle, they made alliances and extended their command and control. South Asia soon became a patchwork of British territory and "princely states" that submitted to the British but were still ruled in their internal affairs by Hindu or Sikh royalty, or by Muslim sultans.

Modern scholarship on India and Hinduism originated in this context of Europeans seeking to learn about native peoples in order to tighten imperial control. British officials believed that it was their duty as white Europeans to spread "enlightened" civilization to the peoples of South Asia. This message was, in turn, repeated back in Europe to justify the expanding colonial enterprise that had begun with merchants.

British schools were established in South Asia to train young Indians to serve in the colonial bureaucracy. This new class of Indians made first contact with modern ideas from Europe, especially in political thought, the natural sciences, and Christianity. This process unfolded in the colonial urban centers, beginning with Calcutta. Knowing the English language and culture became the necessary path for any ambitious Indian subject living under British rule.

By 1813 missionaries had arrived from every major Christian denomination. Many challenged Hinduism on every front, from theology and ritual practices to morality and caste norms. Some Christian ministers suggested that the British triumph in India represented God's judging Hinduism to be an idolatrous and demoniac heresy. Many South Asians came to regard the missionaries as in league with the colonialists. Crude depictions of Hindus and Indian culture by the newcomers sparked resentments.

British Viceroy Lord Curzon (1859–1925) with a ruler of a princely state. British rule produced both crises and new opportunities for Hindu elites.

In 1857 widespread civil disturbances swept across British-held territories. During this period, called "the mutiny" by the British and regarded by many Indians as "the first war of independence," Indian troops and peasants gave vent to resentments over colonial law and administrative insensitivities, executing some British officers and murdering their families. Colonial troops and loyal mercenaries eventually put down the rebellion and brutal reprisals were taken against Indian citizens. When order had been restored, in 1858, the British parliament dissolved the company that had held the royal charter for trade with Asia and declared the Queen's direct rule. India became "the jewel in the crown" of the British Empire for the next ninety years.

Challenges and Responses to Colonialism

The early modern era thus presented individual Hindus and Hindu institutions with challenges that they shared with other colonized peoples across the globe. These challenges appeared simultaneously in several forms: the scientific worldview of the European Enlightenment, humanistic critiques of religion, racial theories of European superiority, and the triumphalist Gospel teachings of outspoken Christian missionaries.

The early Christian missionaries from Britain were largely Protestant. Some boldly challenged Hinduism at temples, denouncing images and practices as "idolatry." Most more quietly established churches, schools, and hospitals. As a result, the ideas of

Considered the "first war of independence" by Indian nationalists, the uprising in 1857 was provoked by alleged disrespect of Muslim and Hindu troops under British command.

nineteenth-century Protestantism had a distinct impact on Hindus, who sought to reform their own traditions. Protestant emphases that were significant among Hindu reformers included the use of historical and scientific methods in the search for core scriptures and doctrines, and criticism of ritual that was not consistent with these doctrines. Other Protestant perspectives were distrust of traditional priests as purveyors of superstition as well as spiritual individualism, whereby each person is responsible for his or her own spiritual destiny. Hindu reformers were further influenced by the Protestant linking of social uplift initiatives with religious reforms and the prestige of monotheism. In colonial India, too, new forms of "Protestant Hinduism" mobilized the colonized to protest against British imperialism.

Although most South Asians did not convert to Islam or Christianity, many regions in which Hindus lived were ruled by non-Hindus (Muslims and the European successors). This state of affairs was distressing because conquest by outsiders suggested that the power and grace of the Hindu deities had been eclipsed. Further, the economic dislocations due to imperialism in many instances undermined the traditional channels of financial support for Hindu scholars, activists, and temples.

The colonial government's political practice was to use religious identity as the basis for official dealings with "native constituencies." Thus, "Muslim," "Hindu," and "Sikh" communities were treated as politically defined identities. As a result, Hindus, Muslims, and Sikhs competed against one another for favorable treatment at the hands of the colonial government. Communal divides opened where none had existed. Since 1947, tensions between these groups defined by religion have resurfaced, sometimes tragically.

The nineteenth century saw a variety of Hindu responses to colonialism. The early influential leaders were mainly brahmins, the traditional priestly caste that had long emphasized literacy and education. Among this elite group, especially those in areas of most intense contact (Mumbai and Calcutta), the initial reaction to the British shifted from indifference to more engaged positions: either hostility or curiosity. We turn now to examine prominent examples among these Hindu responses.

The First Reformist Generation: Rammohan Roy, Brahmo Samaj, and the Tattvabodhini Sabha

The success of the colonial powers raised an uncomfortable question: How could the world-preserving great deities have allowed non-Hindus to overshadow Hindus and to defame Hindu society? Some Hindus gave an answer similar to that of other faiths struggling under colonialism: Revelation has not failed, but the community has lost true belief and practice. Therefore, the community needs to be reformed. The first to articulate this position for Hinduism was **Rammohan Roy** (1772–1833), who is regarded by many as "the father of modern India." Roy called for the reform of certain Hindu beliefs and practices prevalent across India, including superstition, caste discrimination, and the practice of widow immolation (*sati*). He argued for universal education in English so that Indians could study modern math, science, and medicine. Roy was equally outspoken in defending Hinduism against missionary attacks, drawing on his study of the Bible and rational analysis to critique Christian dogmas.

Christian missionaries possessed overwhelming confidence in their work, but converted relatively few. Muslim and Hindu leaders of South Asia often criticized missionary hypocrisy, but some adopted reforms due to their influence. This cartoon captures local resentment of missionary practices and their calls to "destroy your gods, burn your books, be converted . . ."

Rammohan Roy: pioneering religious figure who called for the reform of Hindu beliefs and practices

In 1828 Roy founded Brahmo Sabha, an organization to further his reformist views. In 1841 the name was changed to the Brahmo Samaj, whose official English title—"Fellowship of Believers in the One True God"—expresses its goal of uniting Hindus of all castes to proclaim a reformist, monotheistic ideology. The Brahmo Samaj's importance lies in its strong influence on subsequent generations of Hindu reformers and revivalists; their writings also reached America and Europe, among the first to describe Hinduism to the West.

The **Tattvabodhini Sabha** ("Truth-Propagating Society") was an influential group in Calcutta associated with Roy's teachings. Aimed at exploring and propagating the teachings of Vedantic Hinduism in light of enlightenment rationality, the group was funded by leading members of the rising middle class that was prospering under British rule. Its meetings attracted leading Hindu teachers and philosophers; their addresses were published in vernacular languages and circulated widely among the colonial-era native class: entrepreneurs, landed gentry, school teachers, journalists, a mixture of high castes and newly rich businessmen.

> **Tattvabodhini Sabha:** colonial Hindu sect in Calcutta that promoted adaptation to India's new economic and political realities

The Tattvabodhini Sabha's revivalism was influenced by their commitment to promote the "modern Hindu's" adaptation to India's new economic and political realities. Their publications merged these values—working hard, living honestly, saving rationally, and promoting altruism—with their view of Vedanta's message of the individual controlling personal desires. Along with Roy, they saw reformed Hinduism now being led by the "godly householder," not the premodern elite of world-renouncing ascetics. Instead of seeking to extirpate all human desire, Hindus should accept desire's power but guide it "according to *dharma*" (here, "justice") and for society's overall betterment. Like the ethos underlying the successful Protestant businessmen then leading the global spread of capitalism, this influential Hindu elite articulated a congruent view of human mission, though they built this on a very different metaphysical foundation.

More Strident and Sectarian: Dayananda and the Arya Samaj

> **Arya Samaj:** religious organization that redefined and defended reformed Hindu traditions

Similar in many respects to the Brahmo Samaj but centered in Bombay and Lahore, the **Arya Samaj** was founded in 1875 by the brahmin teacher Swami Dayananda (1824–83). Dayananda held the fundamentalist view that only the four Vedas were valid sources for true Hinduism and that they were in fact "infallible," containing all knowledge, even the root ideas of modern science. India, he famously proclaimed, "needed nothing from the West." For him, as for Roy, the essential Hindu theological idea was monotheism. Accordingly, he rejected post-Vedic scripture and saw later polytheism as the reason for Hinduism's decline. Dayananda tirelessly denounced practices such as child marriage, untouchability, and the subjugation of women. He composed his own simplified list of ethical norms and a description of properly reformed Vedic rituals. He also denounced Sikhism.

Numerous Dayananda Anglo-Vedic colleges and high schools continue the Arya Samaj revivalist tradition to the present day. Many of the current Bharatiya Janata party members and leaders have been influenced by the Arya Samaj.

Jain Reformism

Like other communities, Jains in the last century have revitalized their traditions and spread them globally through their communities and businesses. Jains today have emphasized how their doctrines are compatible with science; they have also focused on the virtues of vegetarianism and animal protection. Movements focusing on environmental health have been led by Jains; and in recent decades, some teachers have accepted Westerners into the Jain monastic community, especially in England and the United States. In 1975, to celebrate the 2,500th anniversary of the saint Mahavira, a new symbol was devised to represent the tradition. In 2010, the first Jain center in the United States was opened in Boston.

Sikh Reform and Resurgence

Through their resistance to the Mughals, the Sikhs eventually carved out their own kingdom in western India that lasted from 1799 until 1849, when it was absorbed into British India. After this, Sikh men were recruited into the colonial army, becoming renowned for their disciplined character and martial abilities. Sikhs also found success as civil servants, educators, and businessmen. Soon, Sikhs were serving across the British Empire, and on retirement many settled outside India, from Singapore and Hong Kong to England. These migrants brought their faith with them, making Sikhism a large global faith today.

Sikhs also responded to the religious challenges posed by South Asia's colonial situation and the aggressive Christian missionaries who appeared in the Punjab. One reformist group, known as the Nirakaris, emphasized ascetic values and fervent devotion to the Formless One (*nirankar*). Its founder, Baba Dayal (1783–1855), like some Hindu reformers, wanted to purify the faith of superstitions and any Hindu practices. Another Sikh reformist organization, the Singh Sabha (Lion Society), was formed in 1879 to advocate traditional values and implement social and educational programs to defend the faith. Centered in Amritsar, the Singh Sabha sponsored publications that encouraged religious pride among Sikh communities across India and abroad.

By 1920, calls for independence were rising across South Asia. Sikhs joined the movement due to the abuses of the British government in two areas: a national policy that placed Hindu caretakers in control of Sikh gurudwara, and the administrative decision to place control of the Golden Temple in the hands of a British Deputy Commissioner. A new Sikh political action group, the Akali Dal, was formed to address these problems. The Gurudwara Act of 1925 was successful in returning to a

परस्परोपग्रहो जीवानाम्

PARASPAROPAGRAHO JĪVĀNĀM

The pratīka: symbol of the Jaina faith, officially adopted during the 2,500th anniversary of Mahavira's nirvana (1975). The palm of the hand bears the word *ahimsa*; the svastika topped by three dots and the crescent represent the four destinies, the threefold path, and the abode of the liberated souls, respectively; the slogan below the figure of loka-akasa calls for the mutual assistance of all beings.

Ramakrishna Mission: influential Hindu missionary and reform organization founded by Swami Vivekananda

Different people call on [God] by different names: some as Allah, some as God, others as Krishna, Shiva, and Brahman. It is like the water in a lake. Some drink it at one place and call it "*jal,*" others at another place and call it "*pani,*" and still others at a third place and call it "water." The Hindus call it "jal," the Christians "water," and the Muslims "pani." But it is one and the same thing.

—Parable by Ramakrishna

Sikh committee the sole authority to manage the historic gurudwaras in the united Punjab, including the Golden Temple. The Akali Dal then joined Muslim and Hindu groups seeking the end of British rule, and they continue to pursue Sikh interests in postcolonial India.

Ramakrishna and Vivekananda: The First Global Hindu Mission

A brahmin like Roy and Dayananda but with a much more humble educational background, Ramakrishna (1834–86) was a charismatic guru who attracted reform-minded Hindus. His spiritual experiences included long periods of trance in which he reported being possessed in turn by Kali, Sita, Rama, Krishna, Muhammad, and Jesus. Ramakrishna's teaching emphasized that the entire universe is permeated by the paramount divine spirit, a reality that is called different names by the world's different people, but whose essence is one. In articulating this view, Ramakrishna was updating to a global scale the interfaith teaching of the classical Hindu school we have already discussed, that of Vedantic Hinduism.

Swami Vivekananda (1863–1902), Ramakrishna's foremost disciple, became a guru in his own right and presented this theology in a systematic manner. Vivekananda was the first great missionary representative of Hinduism on the global stage. His popularity grew through lectures on Hinduism across America and Europe. Most Westerners' first acquaintance with Hinduism is largely a product of the teachings of Vivekananda and his later followers.

Vivekananda organized the **Ramakrishna Mission**, whose institutions spread across India. The mission advocated reformist traditions and embraced a global ecumenical awareness. Its highly organized order of monks cultivated inner spiritual development through yoga, taught "the Gospel of Ramakrishna," and established educational institutions, hospitals, and hospices open to all. The Ramakrishna Mission became the first great global Hindu organization with a vision of ecumenical Hinduism as the savior of the world, not merely of India. The mission's disciples in the West now support its global reach. By 2016 it had published several hundred books and built retreat centers, libraries, and sanctuaries in major cities in seventeen countries.

The Work of Gandhi: Hindu Elements in Indian Nationalism

By the turn of the twentieth century, Britain's command over the subcontinent included a vast modern infrastructure (roads, railroads, telegraph) that supported increasing trade. The presence of Christian missions and the colonial government's bureaucracy had also expanded. Indian leaders and organizations seeking to strengthen and reform Hinduism were also multiplying through this period, and religious reformism and political activism frequently converged.

Mohandas K. Gandhi, a great political leader who merged European ideas with reformist Hindu teachings to lead India to independence.

The growing independence movement drew on religious identity and pride. An important player in the independence movement was the Indian National Congress, founded in 1880 in Bombay. Although dominated by brahmins and a few Muslims, who were mostly urban, English-educated lawyers, the Congress sought to speak for all Indians. While it proclaimed loyalty to the Raj, as the British colonial government was called, the Congress agitated nonviolently for greater economic development and the growth of self-rule. Thus, it gained acceptance as the party to communicate Indian needs to the colonial government.

The spiritual background motivating many of the Congress leaders was that of the reformists who sought to regenerate Indian culture (both Hindu and Islamic). Indeed, many were convinced that India had a spiritual message for the future of humanity. Such a sentiment was heightened by the two world wars, whose devastation suggested that neither science, European political systems, nor Christianity was to be triumphant in global history.

Mohandas K. Gandhi (1869–1948) became the most significant leader to guide South Asia to independence. Gandhi himself embodies the changes affecting South Asia as the era of globalism under colonialism was brought to an end. As a reformist Hindu who merged European and Indian cultures, Gandhi became one of the greatest world figures of the twentieth century.

On the national stage, Gandhi linked the Congress elite with the masses. Although some disagreed with his stands, he was a nationally venerated guru, an activist who wrote and acted creatively to reinterpret Hinduism in an ethical, this-worldly manner.

Mohandas K. Gandhi: iconic leader who inspired mass support and led India to independence by combining religious and political reforms

Gandhi went on hunger strikes to move British officials (or, at times, other Indian leaders) to reconsider their positions. The honorific *Mahatma* applied to his name, meaning "great-souled [one]," expresses the profound spiritual respect he garnered in his lifetime.

Carrying on the work of earlier reformers, Gandhi decried high-caste discrimination toward others, and he especially highlighted the brutal treatment of the "untouchable" lowest caste as a blight on Hinduism. He also extended the Hindu and Jain notion of **ahimsa** (nonviolence) to describe an entire way of life, what he called **satyagraha**, guided by this ideal. Through following ahimsa in all spheres, Gandhi argued, the modern Hindu could find the truth in humble daily work. It was a principle that could transform the individual and society, imbuing each with a spiritual center.

ahimsa: nonviolence

satyagraha: "grasping the truth"; Gandhi's central principle of disciplined nonviolence that reflects ethical truth

Gandhi's life work was crowned in 1947, when India finally gained its independence. However, celebration of this long-anticipated moment was shattered by the violence that accompanied it. The British allowed no time for the orderly implementation of their partition, which divided India, a new secular nation, from the new Muslim state of Pakistan. A civil war broke out in which an estimated 4 million people perished. Nearing the age of eighty, Gandhi traveled to many of these areas in an attempt to quell the chaos, but largely in vain. He was murdered in 1948 by a member of a fundamentalist Hindu group that had opposed partition and accused Gandhi of "concessions" to Muslims and the lowest castes.

Gandhi

M. K. Gandhi was born in a merchant family in the western region of Gujarat. As a young man he traveled to London to study law. While there he encountered for the first time the classical Hindu texts, all in English translations. He was introduced to them not by an Indian *guru* but through meetings at the Theosophical Society, a group of European mystics interested in the secret doctrines they felt were at the root of all world religions.

After becoming a lawyer, Gandhi settled in South Africa, then a British colony with a large Indian minority. He was soon drawn into political activism in opposition to the racist and discriminatory imperial practices directed toward South Asians as "coloreds." From experiences with protests and community organization, Gandhi developed his principle of *satyagraha*. This concept has roots in the Hindu and Jain doctrine of nonviolence (*ahimsa*) and in Christianity's injunctions to love one's enemy. Gandhi's work in South Africa among Indian immigrants drew the attention of Congress leaders in India, who urged him to return. He did so in 1915.

Although Gandhi always retained respect for British law and the moral ideals articulated in Western religions, back in India he abandoned Western dress for the humble loincloth of the Indian peasant. Gandhi's greatness as a political leader was likewise built on his connection with the Indian masses, a relationship that developed through his tours of the countryside, his involvement with peasant protests, his self-imposed poverty, and an effective organization (including a daily newspaper).

India in many respects abandoned Gandhi's concept of spiritually centered, small-scale development. Only in civil law has India continued to embrace Gandhi's vision, in its attempts to eradicate caste discrimination. Though challenged by Hindu nationalists, the modern state of India has still held to its fundamental identity as a secular—not Hindu—nation.

Hinduism and Postmodern Trends in a Postcolonial World

In India today, one can witness religious practices from the most ancient period; practice "laughing yoga" with young professionals in an urban park before going to work; and witness a demonstration organized by a Hindu fundamentalist group that wants to make their version of "Hinduism" the state religion. Because there is no single version of "Hinduism" on which to center our treatment of contemporary change, and there is no single institution or person in authority who can speak for all Hindus, we now focus on representative case studies that illustrate patterns of unity in the diversity of postmodern Hinduism.

The Persistence of Traditional Religious Understandings

Despite the progress of modernization, there has been a remarkable persistence of traditional beliefs and practices in postcolonial India. While no single school or theology is representative of "Hinduism," it is possible to trace broadly shared understandings among the traditions that have remained influential to the present.

The Presence of the Divine

Whatever specific doctrines or practices an individual Hindu follows, life entails more than satisfying the needs dictated by survival. A divine reality enfolds human reality, interpenetrating the material world and human experience. This occurs primarily through the soul (atman), which animates an embryo in the womb and energizes human life.

Hindu society is unique in its veneration of the sacred in the daily rhythms of life. Rituals honor the rising and setting sun; offerings are made at humble temples erected near stones or trees; and inhabitants revere rivers and mountains as well as animals such as elephants, snakes, monkeys, and (of course) cows. Devotees worship at shrines for the divine protectors of houses, families, artisans, and castes; farmers worship guardian deities of their fields. In some villages, a spirit medium cures those possessed by ghosts or demons through offerings and trance. And astrologers advise on how the distant deities who appear in the night sky can best be propitiated. Finally, at every key moment in a person's life—birth, coming of age, marriage, and death—the local brahmin is called on to perform rituals.

In urban areas where some of the older traditions are less prominent, brahmins can still be found performing such rites and also adapting Hindu practices to changing times. For example, since 2004, a regular service offered to all customers of Maruti Udyog cars, the most popular automotive brand in modern India, is to have a brahmin priest perform a puja for the vehicle's good fortune; Maruti Udyog showrooms also feature a line of automotive accessories that include dashboard statues of the Hindu gods.

This excursion into Hinduism as lived tradition today makes clear the immanence of spirit is respected and the gods live next door. It is the human task to find harmony with them and eventually to seek liberation from rebirth by finding the spirit in whatever guise one is most suited to discover. Even in modern cities and among individuals who are highly educated, the wish to connect with and worship the divine remains strong today.

Hindu Inclusivity Accommodates Wide-Ranging Sectarianism

Another distinctive characteristic of Hinduism today is the broad range of ideas about the sacred and the tendency for individuals to accept alternative or even opposing views. The coexistence of so many competing theologies and religious practices and even the toleration of nonbelievers have been based on two notions. First is the belief that a human understanding of the highest truth, whatever that is held to be, is never complete or perfect. Second is the expectation that as individuals learn and practice more deeply, they will see reality more clearly. From these twin perspectives, persons thought to hold false views are simply located on a lower rank in a hierarchy, not rejected. A wrongheaded person may be ignorant, immature, or incomplete, but not evil.

Muslim–Hindu relations continue to be important and contentious in modern India. Communal enmity on religious lines was rare after Islam won acceptance in South Asia (1000 CE), mainly because group identity developed predominantly according to caste, region, and political loyalties. Religious enmity is not an eternal, inevitable standpoint in South Asia or elsewhere; in the past, as today, it has been the product of a specific historical context, shaped by human actions and political policies.

Though Hindu nationalists have rejected this tolerant stance, even questioning the loyalty to India of Muslims and Christians, many still share the inclusivist religious attitude. It has encouraged new spiritual searches and the appearance of new religious sects that combine beliefs and practices from various traditions, including astrology, Buddhism, and "secular" traditions such as psychology.

Although Hindu groups accept others and acknowledge their value, many Hindus are indeed sectarian in their religious orientation. While the view "all the gods are one" is widely expressed, not everyone shares it. Adherence to the ecumenical strategy of inclusivity, of accepting the legitimacy of competing religious standpoints, does

A Hindu priest in Nepal offers *tika* powder, an essential part of the daily worship service for every god. The powder will later be used by the Brahmin priests to mark the foreheads of devotees.

not oblige one to abandon one's own sect's truth claims. Thus Hindu worldviews have held their primacy throughout modern times and into the postcolonial era; it has mainly been in reforming and modernizing their social institutions that Hindus have adopted non-Hindu ideas.

Contemporary Hindu Practices

What provides Hinduism with a measure of unity is not a single belief system, but a set of ritual actions that most individuals will observe. There is a common set of ritual actions that individuals can choose to connect with the divine, however they conceive it. There are also individuals whom most Hindus can consult with (ritualists, astrologers, gurus) to act on, and deepen, their beliefs. Beginning several thousand years ago, and continuing today, these have defined the Hindu life.

The Guru–Disciple Relationship

Dating from the time of the Upanishads, one central Hindu tradition has been the relationship connecting gurus and disciples. Just as Hindus perceive the divine in the world around them, they find spirit alive in its realization by those who reach moksha, achieve spiritual powers, and share their experiences for the benefit of humanity. Charismatic saintly gurus still hold a central place in both traditional and reformist Hinduism.

We have noted the lasting forms of organized Hinduism that emerged in the postclassical era. Then, as now, numerous spiritual teachers emerged in the traditional manner of undergoing long periods of training with independent gurus and then attracting their own disciples. Guru residences called **ashrams** sustain the community that performs rituals, meditates, and learns together under the guru's direction. Many Hindu guru-centered institutions last only as long as the charismatic teacher lives or only through his first generation of designated successors. Others continue, and in these cases we see the central Hindu notion of lineage; that is, the belief that today's teachers are connected to earlier gurus, back to the first enlightened sage in the line.

ashram: center of religious practice following a guru

The circle of disciples must master the guru's instructions on the key spiritual practices (meditation, worship, etc.), most often memorizing them through intensive repetition. They may also collect their guru's teachings, sometimes only in memory, sometimes through writing or even video. Eventually, the disciples are also designated as gurus by the teacher, usually once they have reached an advanced age, and so lineage continues. Accepting a guru entails assuming a new identity, which is symbolized in the widespread practice of receiving a new name. The true guru is the one who can open access to spiritual awakening, but the disciple can expect the guru's full grace and loving guidance only through the complete abandonment of ego.

Living with Karma: Rituals, Astrology, and Rebirth

The classical doctrines associated with karma, reincarnation, and liberation are the center of Hindu (and Buddhist) belief, regardless of the school one follows or one's focus on a particular chosen deity. Karma is thus the most important spiritual force in the universe, determining one's place in the cosmos. Because what one does in a particular incarnation influences future destiny, Hindu belief does not posit a fatalistic worldview. Non-karmic causes (natural forces, biological reactions, chance) also shape human life, so Hindus can say, like many Americans, "It was meant to be" as well as "Things just happen." Only enlightened saints are capable of knowing their karmic past and future; everyone else remains uncertain. For this reason, the practice of meritorious ritual is a sensible approach to living with karma, as is consultation with astrologers.

Along with karma, a person's destiny can be shaped by group actions. Husbands and wives worship together and act together in many ways. Marriage ritual ties couples for life and can include a vow to be reborn together in future incarnations (a popular motif in South Asian folklore). Entire families are thought to be shaped by the actions of elders.

Hindus today may explain their individual and collective destiny in terms of karma causality, but understandings about the workings of next-life destiny are anything but certain. For example, some individuals do indeed see everything in life as fated from earlier lifetimes. But most Hindus believe that their destiny today and in future lifetimes is also determined in significant part by their future moral actions and ritual acts. The puranas and guru parables often state that being human and being Hindu are rare incarnations in samsara and should not be wasted. People may be reborn as other beings inhabiting this world, into purgatories that receive evil human beings, or into heavenly realms created by each great deity as dwelling places reserved for good and devout devotees. Indeed, many Hindus today regard rebirth in heaven, not union with Brahman, as the highest destiny.

Gestures of Respect for the Divine

Respectful gestures and puja are the means by which many Hindus relate to the divine. Stylized greetings, prostrations, and circumambulation (walking around an icon or temple) are among the best-known ritual gestures.

Hindus greet each other by raising the joined palms to shoulder level and repeating *"Namaskara"*/*"Namaste"* ("salutation"/"greetings"), sometimes bowing. Some gurus teach that saluting other humans in this way is a theological statement: "I center my physical self in the atman located in my heart and salute your same holy center."

A Hindu astrologer. Astrology provides suggestions about when to act in the world, in harmony with the planetary gods and one's own karma.

Namaskara or *namaste*, the gesture of respectful greeting directed to the gods and humans.

The core gesture of namaskara can be multiplied into any number of prostrations, either with the knees touching the ground or fully prone. This gesture, too, is one humans may do to other humans by, for example, grasping the feet of the one honored, such as a guru, a priest, an elder in the family, a mother-in-law (for a daughter-in-law), a husband (for a wife), or parents (for children).

Another Hindu perception of the body involves the differentiation between its two sides: The right side is the pure side, so Hindus eat with the right hand; the left hand is used to wash after calls of nature and is regarded as impure. As an extension of this, the circumambulation of an icon or temple should be performed in a clockwise manner, keeping one's right side closest to the sacred object.

Puja

puja: ritual offering to a deity

The concept of **puja**, or homage, is also built on the assumption that humanity and the divine must maintain an intimate connection marked by respectful hierarchy. For humans, the great deities (such as Shiva, Durga, and Vishnu) are superiors. Puja involves all the expressions by which an inferior can welcome, show respect for, and entertain a distinguished guest. Ideally, all ritual acts express a faithful bhakta's submissive and adoring service to the divine.

To mark and purify any space and make it suitable for puja, cow dung is a necessary ground coating; offerings of cow's milk or butter are often made. The cow is sacred to Hindus; one ancient text suggests that all the divinities exist in the cow, and another sees the cow as an incarnation of the goddess Devi.

In doing puja, the bhakta seeks to please the deity as if the divine personage possessed five senses, and the offerings of puja can be classified accordingly: Incense pleases the sense of smell; flowers please the senses of sight and smell; foods gratify the taste; mantras and music please the hearing; cloth pleases the deity's sense of touch.

The inseparability of otherworldly and mundane blessings is seen in the full process involved in making a puja offering and then receiving back the remains, **prasad**. These substances carry a subtle infusion of divine blessing, turning all prasad into "medicine." Food can be eaten, flowers worn in the hair, incense smoke wafted around the body, and holy water sipped. Colored powders that decorate an icon are carefully collected, mixed with water, and used to mark the forehead with a *tilak*, a spot in the center of the forehead above the eyes. Families often share from the same plate the prasad returned from the common family puja.

prasad: remains of any substance used in a puja, believed to have healing properties

Hindus need never worship in public and may make all puja offerings to icons in a home shrine. In temples with priestly attendants, devotees usually place on the puja tray coins or uncooked rice to be taken by the priests. It is through the medium of puja that Hindu householders contribute to the subsistence of their priests and temples. Hindu temples can be humble thatched buildings sheltering crude stones with no resident priests or magnificent palaces built to house jeweled images attended by hosts of priests and other temple servants. Great temples may be surrounded by monasteries, music pavilions, pilgrim hostels, and sacred ponds; these are the pre-eminent centers of Hindu culture.

Hindu puja. Ritual is the means of expressing individual devotion and soliciting divine grace.

Through this adherence to orthopraxy, we can see how ritual traditions define the individual Hindu's passage through the circle of life, from birth to death. The rituals generate good karma, petition the gods for protection, and maintain the family in a state of ritual purity necessary for future pujas. We now survey the cycle of major festivals that mark the passage of the typical Hindu's day, month, and year. Here again, the unity of Hinduism is seen in the rituals that unite individuals, families, and communities to revere and petition the succession of deities.

RITUALS AND RITES: Hindu Life-Cycle Rituals

The *Dharmashastras* list over forty life-cycle rituals most observed today by families at the top of the caste hierarchy. We summarize the most popular contemporary practices briefly here, using terms and culture of northern India as representative.

Birth Rituals

Pregnant women are given empowered charms to protect the fetus and are made to stay within the family, isolated from demons and from sources of pollution. Despite the spilling of the mother's blood and bodily fluids, birth is a time of "happy pollution"; and for the period of the mother's recovery, the family abstains from puja and does not eat with outsiders.

Early Childhood Rituals

The ritual called *namkaran* serves to give an infant its formal name. Naming children after the deities is a common practice, and this can be done according to a parent's chosen deity, for the day on which the child is born, or simply for auspiciousness. The carefully noted birth time must be used to construct a horoscope, which will be kept for lifelong consultation. Before the first birthday, the final early childhood rite of first rice feeding introduces the baby to solid food.

Coming of Age

Boys and girls are led on different ritual paths emphasizing male dominance and female fertility. The rites marking adulthood for both sexes establish expectations and responsibilities of full Hindu personhood. Since the *Dharmashastra* forbids teaching Vedic verses to women, adult females are not assigned brahmanical rites but participate in their husbands' rituals.

Girls are initiated as women when they have their first menstruation. During this time, elder females in the family tell stories of the deities and instruct the girls on aspects of adult religious practice and the duties of Hindu women.

Boys of the top three castes are ceremonially given a sacred thread, after which they receive the first teachings from the family guru, including the rituals associated with the wearing of a multistranded thread (*janai*) over the left shoulder and right hip. (In modern times, this "wearing the thread" is maintained most consistently among brahmin families only.) Boys are also given their first mantra to memorize, the Rig Vedic Gayatri (3.62.10), to be repeated daily at the rising and setting of the sun:

Hindu and Sikh Festival Practice

Many Hindus today carry a small pocket almanac that organizes the Western, lunar, and solar succession of days. Why are these so popular? Since the year is punctuated by a succession of great and small festivals, some lasting only a day, others stretching over ten days, Hindus must harmonize personal, family, and business affairs with the religious celebrations.

Part of the reason for this elaborate festival agenda is that across South Asia, it is customary for each important deity to have a special day and procession that is the occasion for extraordinary acts of devotion. At these times, the god or goddess is more accessible to devotees and more inclined to extend grace to those who demonstrate their faith. During the Hindu festivals, legends and myths are retold by religious

We meditate on that excellent light of the divine sun
May he illumine our minds.

In adult initiation, boys become "twice-born" through this second birth into the knowledge of the Veda and Vedic ritual.

Householder

Marriage is usually arranged by the couple's families, although many young people today can veto a choice proposed for them. The relatives consult an astrologer to ensure that their characters and karmas are compatible.

Upon marriage, a Hindu woman leaves her home, often with a dowry, to live with her mother-in-law, shifting forever her ritual center to the husband's family line. (This pattern is less common today in the urban middle classes as well as among the rural population that is drawn to migrate to cities in search of jobs and education.)

Death

Death produces a state of pollution that for immediate kin endures for an entire year. When someone dies, the family wishes to perform all the rites to ensure that the soul will go to its best possible rebirth. However,

the death of a loved one also produces worry that the soul might be reincarnated as a dangerous or wandering ghost. This concern has given rise to the custom of cremating a corpse as soon as possible after death and before sundown. Carrying the body to the cremation site, the *ghat*, is men's work, with the eldest son lighting the pyre for the father and the youngest son doing so for the mother. The women, who stay at home during the cremation, must remove their ornaments and sweep the house, beginning to repurify the house polluted by death. The men who cremate must collect the burned remains so that the family can immerse them in a holy river.

After-Death Rites

Before the family may reestablish purity in their homes and resume social life, they must perform the first rites of feeding the departed soul, who is thought to wander as a ghost for up to one year. Here, Hindu tradition is preserved in the performance of the ancient Vedic rites: The mourners offer a puja of ritual rice ball offerings, to feed the soul and build up its strength to continue on its afterlife journey. Rites for parents and especially fathers are done yearly on the death anniversary.

scholars or enacted through live cultural performances. In many of the festivals, special foods, drinks, and decorations are made that appear at no other time. Some festivals are reserved for fasting, ascetic acts, or other penances.

The greatest festivals are immense spectacles, and arranging for the myriad cultural performances and sideshows requires the participation of thousands. Arrays of electric lights, clouds of incense, and blaring loudspeakers overload the devotees' senses. The gatherings can create a marvelous sense of community among *bhaktas*, drawing pilgrims from afar to witness and to seek blessings.

Pilgrimage Festivals

From earliest times, Hindus believed the mountains and rivers of the land bounded by the Himalayas and the oceans to be abodes of the deities and the places where

Hindus associated with large temples take out the images of the great gods yearly. The most dramatic of these outings is a large chariot, like this one in Puri, that is pulled by devotees (here in Madurai, Tamil Nadu, India) to earn merit.

RITUALS AND RITES: Major Festivals

Diwali

Across the north of India, the year begins with *Diwali*, the festival around the autumnal equinox that focuses on Lakshmi, goddess of wealth. On the main day families wear new clothes, sweep their houses clean, arrange a special altar with puja laid out for the goddess, and set up lights to guide her. On a subsequent day, brothers and sisters honor their kin ties, and individuals may do other special pujas to strengthen their health for the year ahead. Middle-class families now send "Diwali cards," akin to Christmas cards.

Sri Panchami

The festival of Sri Panchami is dedicated to Saraswati, the goddess of learning and the fine arts. Students, scholars, and artists all will flock to her temples. Some temples set up a whitewashed wall on which young children are to write their first letters, for traditional Hindu parents wait until this day to begin to teach their children to read and write.

Shiva Ratri

Shiva's Night, Shiva Ratri, is the end-of-winter festival, one of two festivals each year dedicated to Shiva. This festival emphasizes fasting and offerings to Shiva's phallic icon, the *linga*. In some localities, the festival connects with the god's control of the myriad ghosts and goblins that occupy the lower portions of the Hindu pantheon. It is also the time for ascetics to make offerings at Shiva's temples, which fill with thousands of sadhus and yogins who meditate, instruct devotees, receive donations, and demonstrate their powers.

Holi

Hinduism's "feast of love," or Holi, is the year's primary festival honoring Krishna in his guise as the playful trickster god. For the primary three or so days, all of society is at play. Normal caste and gender rules are suspended, and established hierarchies and expectations are inverted. Women may sing lewdly in public or douse male passersby with buckets of water, and public officials such as

Children enjoying Holi, the festival when humans join Krishna in living life as a divine sport.

policemen suffer usually playful pranks; in villages, an untouchable may be declared "headman" for the duration of the festival. On the last day, bonfires are lit to consume evil, commemorating Krishna's defeat of a female demon who sought his demise. Holi is now becoming an international commercial holiday, spread by Hindu immigrants and those who are eager to find a reason to throw a party.

Tij

Tij is the festival for women, who can act in imitation of Parvati, one incarnation of Devi, who fasted,

continued

RITUALS AND RITES: Major Festivals *continued*

meditated, and underwent purification in the hopes of winning the husband she deserved. For those already married, these actions are for the long life of one's spouse. During Tij, some women spend the night at a temple, where they sing devotional songs while fasting and listen to stories associated with Parvati and other exemplary women.

Dashara

In many places the largest yearly Hindu celebration, Dashara usually falls just before the first rice harvest. It has become the occasion for marking two separate divine events. For Rama bhaktas, this festival celebrates both Rama's birth and his victory over the demon Ravana; *Durga Puja* similarly enfolds the community in the goddess Durga's "Nine Nights" of struggle against the demon Mahisha. The "Victory Tenth Day" commemorates Durga's slaying of Mahisha. To imitate the goddess in her moment of triumph and to bathe her images in the blood offerings that she most loves, devotees perform animal sacrifices at her temples, beheading primarily goats, fowl, and water buffalo.

darshan: seeing the divine; making eye contact with a god, holy site, or guru

Pilgrims at the Amarnath Cave. Devotees worship the ice lingam of the great god Shiva found within this Himalayan hillside.

sages have realized the highest truths. From then until now, devotees have gone on pilgrimages to see these sacred persons and places (for **darshan**, viewing the divine). On their journeys today, Hindus do the rituals described for temples, make offerings and expressions of respect, and bring home treasured prasad.

The most dramatic among the Hindu sacred sites are located in the Himalayas, the world's highest mountain chain, where the very names of the snow-clad peaks reflect the perception of divine residence. According to one passage in the *Skanda Purana*, seeing any of the Himalayan peaks will transform one's karma: "As the dew is dried up by the morning sun, so is the bad karma of mankind by the sight of Himalayas."

Temples attract local devotees and distant pilgrims, who also are drawn to the darshan of the Himalayas.

Rivers are also focal areas for pilgrimage. The Ganges and its tributaries that flow down from the Himalayan glaciers all are associated with divinity. The Ganges is conceived as a goddess; and as such, many bathing rites are done along its banks, where devotees hope to draw on her capacity to "wash away" bad karma. Ganges water is seen as the best source for purifying a ritual space, so pilgrims collect it and store it for future ritual use. All rivers in South Asia are identified with the Ganges. A common legend known across the continent states that each river shares a subterranean connection with it. The points on the river best suited for human pilgrimage and ritualism are tributary confluences called **tirthas**. The literal translation of the word (ford, or river crossing) also indicates metaphorically that it is easier to cross the great river of samsara to reach heaven or moksha at a tirtha.

tirtha: a holy space defined by a river confluence

The Kumbha Mela

The largest single religious gathering on earth in the early twenty-first century is not Muslims assembling in Mecca for the hajj but Hindus congregating at a holy tirtha for the Kumbha Mela. In 2013, at least 110 million Hindus gathered to bathe at Prayag ("place of sacrifice"), on the riverside near modern Allahabad, where the Ganges, Yamuna, and invisible Saraswati rivers meet. The pilgrims enter the water at the exact auspicious moment connected with a story in the puranas in which the gods battled the demons over possession of a pitcher (*kumbha*) containing an immortality-giving elixir. After a long struggle, the gods won and became immortal; during the course of the battle, however, four drops of the elixir fell to earth at four places, and the site of the Kumbha Mela is one of them. This gathering draws hundreds of thousands of

Ritual bathers in Varanasi, also known as Kashi or Benares. Located on the western bank of the Ganges and with its riverside ghats dominating the urban settlement, Kashi is the sacred city where pilgrims congregate.

sadhus who are first to immerse themselves in the hyperdivinized river waters; soon they are then joined by millions of householders on pilgrimage, who bathe, offer puja, and sip the ambrosial river water, seeking an infusion of grace.

Pilgrimage in Hinduism is not a requirement of the faith as in Islam, but the benefits are elaborately outlined in the later Hindu texts: healing, good karma, and personal transformation. Pilgrims can go alone on foot or, with increasing popularity, in highly organized groups traveling on airplanes and buses. The goal may be to perform a ritual, such as a mortuary rite for a kin member. The more typical goal, however, is to seek general benefit through darshan and puja.

Sikh Festivals

The commonalities and divergences between Hindus and Sikhs are visible in the Sikh Festivals. These are known as *guru purb,* "guru remembrance" days for remembering the teachers. The birthdays of all ten gurus beginning with Nanak are observed, as are commemorations of the martyrdoms of great leaders. All of these holy days involve chanting of the Adi Granth; during most of them the entire text is read in relay over the forty-eight hours prior to the festival day.

There are three main festivals that coincide with the great Hindu celebrations but also mark key dates in early Sikh history. First in importance is the spring Baisakhi. It is during this festival, which celebrates the creation of the Khalsa in 1699, that new members of this group are initiated. On this day, the Sikh flag flown at homes and at gurudwaras is replaced. The fall festival of lights, Diwali, for Sikhs is the festival celebrating the release of the sixth Guru, Hargobind, and fifty-two followers from imprisonment by the Mughals; the lamps that Sikhs light celebrate their heroic return home. Hola Mohalla, a festival of mischief and play for Hindus, is instead the yearly occasion when Sikhs compete in martial arts and remember the Tenth Guru, Gobind Singh, and the Sikh teaching of protecting the weak and standing up for justice.

The Religious Institutions of Contemporary Hinduism

Although there is no single formal institution that unifies all Hindus, there are standard relationships that support the regular practice of ritual and the transmission of religious ideas. Most families have a relationship with a brahmin family priest whom they call on when there is the need for a life-cycle rite or when someone wishes to perform a special puja.

The predominant religious institution of Hinduism, however, is the temple, and it is thought highly meritorious to build one that houses an icon. Temples built by the great kings demonstrate the most complete expressions of Hindu religious culture. The major temples are more than shrines; they include lands given to the deity and are supported by endowment funds that are continually augmented by the cash offered with puja. Some temples have become fabulously rich over the years: in the summer of 2011, the hidden treasury of the Padmanabhaswamy Temple in southern India was found to hold $22 billion in gold, jewels, and statues.

A Typical Smarta Shaiva Temple

One place of worship that can be found widely in upper-caste communities across the subcontinent is a Smarta temple, attended by a brahmin priest. In it, the major gods of the pantheon we have mentioned are enshrined, with the addition of the sun god, who presides over the astrological deities. Shiva usually is the central god, most often worshipped in his linga icon. The typical Smarta temple has the following standard layout:

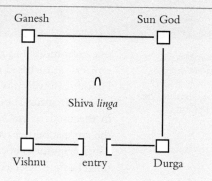

Temple in Madras. Large temples are complex institutions with landholdings, charities, and resident priests.

Temple lands are usually rented out to tenant farmers, with part of the harvest going to the temple; other properties adjacent to the temple are often rented to merchants or artisans. Both rentals provide income for the upkeep of the temple buildings and payment for the priests. Through these relationships, Hindu temples have been integral to the local economies of South Asia, sometimes as the major landowners. Modern land reform has cut back on many of these holdings, forcing temples to find other means of support.

The more organized sects and sadhu orders rely on the *matha*, or monastery, to serve as a venue for schooling and training for ritual service under an abbot. Some modern groups, such as the Ramakrishna Mission, have built their reform movement through a network of mathas. Another familiar institution is the *ashram*, a retreat dedicated to supporting gurus and their disciples, thereby maintaining the relationship that is one of the central lifelines of Hindu culture.

Changes and Continuities: Examples of Postcolonial Hinduism

Hinduism has assumed more forms today than ever in its history, and the linkage of religion to politics is growing. Since there is no one version or center of Hinduism that can stand alone, we will draw on a series of representative case studies to suggest the broad sweep of Hinduism in the postcolonial era: modernizers, guru-based movements *not* influenced by science, and finally proponents of Hindu nationalism who object to India's postindependence character as a secular state.

Modernizers abound in reformist Hinduism. Some teachers and movements begun in the modern era (such as the Ramakrishna Mission) make strong assertions about the compatibility between scientific thought and venerable Hindu doctrines. The "big bang" hypothesis of creation, relativity theory, and the cosmological theories of multiple universes are referred to by these modernizers as compatible with—even anticipated in—the ancient scriptures. Hindu exponents have also proposed scientific explanations for rebirth and karma doctrines. Even the Vedas have been interpreted to credit the ancient seers with awareness of contemporary technological possibilities (e.g., airplanes, genetics, brain waves). Hindu confidence that the traditional teachings will stand up to whatever science discovers is striking among modernists. Just as many scientists around the world (including many in India) refrain from suggesting that their discoveries are ever likely to disprove the existence of God or the reality of spirit, many highly educated Hindus have found no reason to abandon the essentials of their faith. Recent events and developments indicate how Hinduism has endured so strongly among such modernists.

Ganesh's Milk Miracle

A deity who attracts the devotion of nearly all Hindus is elephant-headed Ganesh, divine son of Shiva and Parvati. Ganesh temples are found in nearly every locale where Hindus live. On September 21, 1995, at temples across North India, priests and devotees reported that icons of Ganesh had begun to drink the cows' milk that was being offered to them as part of the daily puja. As the stories spread across the subcontinent, thousands of Hindus from all walks of life rushed to their local temples to offer milk, hoping to witness the phenomenon. As news spread globally via the Internet, Hindus in London, Jersey City, Los Angeles, and Toronto began to report similar experiences.

For believers, this was merely the latest demonstration that the divine is alive, connected to humanity and capable of conferring grace on those who serve the gods. Whatever else this incident reveals about the role of the media and the Hindu diaspora, it also demonstrates that modern believers hold the conviction that the divine is immanent, a traditional view that has shifted little amid all the changes of the modern era.

The reaction was interesting, too: The "miracle" gave rise to widespread public debate and rallies organized by Hindu societies (such as New Delhi's "Guru Busters") whose purpose is to expose charlatans and promote rational faith. Predecessors for these modern skeptics and atheists can be traced as far back as the time of the Buddha (fifth century BCE).

Comic Books and Televised Epics

An important mass media format appearing well after the end of colonialism is the religious comic book. Adopting reformist doctrines and linking far-flung Hindu communities is the Amar Citra Katha series of over 270 titles, in which newly standardized versions of the great stories of Hindu scripture are offered in colorful illustrated formats; the text is written in English and other Indian languages. In recent years they have been adapted into cartoons and animated programs. This series has emphasized for middle-class readers that "true Hinduism" is rational, opposed to violence and superstition, upheld by heroic devotees, and based on the respectful accommodation of other spiritualties (Hindu and non-Hindu) in the interest of national integration.

Television broadcasts of religious epics have also been pivotal cultural events. In 1987 India's national broadcasting system, Doordarshan, began showing in weekly installments its Hindi version of the *Ramayana*, one of the two great religious epics

In India, there are countless comic books devoted to describing the stories of the Hindu gods and human saints. Most are printed in the vernacular languages of the subcontinent, as well as in English. Here, a pivotal scene from the great epic, the *Ramayana*.

that date back to the early classical era. An estimated audience of 80 million watched the program. The media's *Ramayana* gave the nation its first "national version" of the epic, one that celebrates the glories of the legendary Hindu king Rama and his struggle to establish a just and prosperous Hindu nation. Doordarshan has subsequently produced and broadcast an even longer series on Hinduism's second great epic, the *Mahabharata*, as well as dramatizations of other devotional stories centered on the great deities, such as Krishna and Shiva.

The accessibility of lavishly produced TV productions of religious epics, complete with special effects, has in places undercut the relation between priest, teacher, and laity. Many argue, however, that Hindu nationalism has been strengthened by the common experience of viewing these sacred scenes.

The Dilemmas of Religious Suicide: A Bride Commits Sati and a Jain Monk Starves Himself to Death

Following the norms of her caste and the Hindu law books, Roop Kanwar, an eighteen-year-old bride, went to live with her husband's family in the western Indian state of Rajasthan. But seven months later, on September 4, 1987, her husband, Mal Singh, died suddenly. Following ancient custom, the young man's kin prepared to cremate him on a pyre. What happened next shocked India: Roop Kanwar was also burnt alive atop her husband's funeral pyre before five hundred witnesses, becoming a *sati* ("virtuous [one]"), one of forty-two known cases since 1947. What remains unclear were the widow's motivations and how freely she went to her death.

What is not unclear were the motivations of the "fast unto death" or *santhara* undertaken by Jain nun Prekshabai Mahasatiji in 2015, at the age of fifty-two. Jain doctrine defines the soul's bondage in samsara through the karma of physical pollution that binds the soul through both gross and subtle defilements; after a life devoted to vegetarian diet, absolute non-violence, and meditation, final salvation still requires ending one's life by a purifying final fast. According to Jain doctrine, santhara burns up the film of karma that clogs the soul, allowing it to break free from the cycle of rebirth and death. The ordeal must also be approved by one's guru and family members. A nun since the age of 18, Prekshabai had asked her guru for permission to undertake the death fast repeatedly, but, citing her age, he had refused, saying that at fifty-two she was too young. But he changed his mind in June, when her doctors had concluded that chemotherapy could no longer treat her cancer. She took her vow to cut down on food and water, and spent forty-seven days on a hospital bed inside her monastery, with over twenty caring for her as she lost control of her bodily functions. According to press reports, crowds amassed around her, spreading stories about a divine glow. As her guru Muni Shri Prakashsundarji Swami reported, "She had a joy on her face that is indescribable . . . I would look at her and ask, 'Would you like to eat?' and she would smile and say, 'No.'"[7]

Rajasthan state officials were called to act on the Jain religious suicide as well as the reports of sati, both on the basis of India's National Penal Code that holds suicide in any form, including widow immolation, to be illegal and that those who assist are also subject to prosecution. Reformers argued that those connected with Roop Kanwar's death should be prosecuted as murderers; regarding santhara, they contended that it was a form of "elder abuse" in which elderly people were being encouraged to take the vow when they could no longer properly give consent and to free families of the economic burden of caring for the elderly. Under pressure from national politicians and women's groups, members of Mal Singh's immediate family were arrested but no charges were ever filed, as witnesses could not be found who were willing to testify. In Prekshabai's case, although Jain religious leaders defended the practice on the grounds of religious freedom, the Rajasthan State Court formally branded the act, and supporters of any individual doing santhara, as a crime.

Sati is one Hindu practice that the British actively sought to end through explicit legal prohibition. The immolation of widows was held up for ridicule by many Hindu modernizers as evidence of how Indian society needed to break with blindly followed traditions and to reform its ways. Yet in 1987, over 50,000 devotees gathered for a commemorative ceremony for Roop Kanwar held thirteen days after her death; the site of the burning pyre has been transformed into a shrine, outside of which artisans still sell ritual photos and other mementos of Kanwar as a divine figure who was blessed by

GENDER FOCUS: The Divine Feminine and Hindu Women

Considering the role of women in Hinduism is a very confusing task, and the multivocalic nature of great religious traditions is especially clear here.

One impression can be found in viewing a performance of classical Indian dance, *Bharatanatyam*, a tradition that has spread from southern India and is now found across India and is common in global performance. With subtle gestures and bold rhythmically timed steps, the woman dancer portrays the great stories of the Hindu classics.

Another reality about Hindu women is that prescribed in the ancient texts. The *Laws of Manu* instruct men to control their women and for women to accept it as their sacred duty to obey first their fathers, then their husbands, and finally their sons. Lesser good karma is said to be the reason for birth as a female, and the troubles of menstruation and childbirth are accordingly their burden. In public life, the submission of women to men is clear, a norm underwritten by religious sanction. Some temples forbid women from entering the innermost temple sanctuaries, a form of discrimination activists are now contesting. Among the many global Hindu gurus, there are a few women among a large male majority. Only in the esoteric tradition of tantra are women reckoned as equals.

Yet another powerful source of understanding the divine feminine in this tradition is the prominence of goddesses in the Hindu pantheon. There is the peaceful Lakshmi, nurturing goddess of wealth; Saraswati, the sustainer of arts and learning; Durga, slayer of demons; and Kali, the scary embodiment of death's inevitability. No religious tradition in the world has a richer diversity of goddesses who are worshipped, meditated on, and taken as embodiments of the ultimate reality.

and merged with the mother goddess, Devi. The debate about this issue was renewed in 2008 when a seventy-one-year-old wife committed sati in eastern India. With studies suggesting that an average of 450 santharas a year have occurred over the last six years, controversy surrounds the question of whether a religious death was truly voluntary and whether the secular state should regulate this religious practice. Is the secular legal code that prohibits sati and santhara binding? Or, as Hindu traditionalists insist, should the state respect freedom of religion and allow Hindu women to follow this path to seek liberation? In the case of Jain practice, the Indian Supreme Court in October 2015 vacated the state court's ruling that every santhara should be regarded as an illegal suicide.

The Spiritual Marketplace for Neotraditionalism: Popular Guru-Based Movements

Most conspicuous over the last decades has been the rise of cults and sects catering to the urban middle class. Focused on sadhus and drawing inspiration from the reformists and revivalists of the nineteenth century, most of the new sects that have attracted the support of this new middle-class elite have proclaimed their own view of "essential Hinduism" as more belief oriented and less ritualistic. Just as modern technology has undercut to some extent the roles of priest and guru, the new sects have diminished the relevance of caste and regional social identity to spiritual seeking. A number of the new sects have quickly built an international membership. Most also emphasize women's participation. All engage their society and include community development, medical service, and educational initiatives, combining various traditional Hindu doctrines and practices with others adopted from Protestant missionaries.

No modern Hindu saint has drawn devotees from as far and wide across India's urban middle classes as Sathya Sai Baba (1926–2011), a teacher known as much for the miraculous feats credited to him as for his instruction. A vigorous opponent of Western cultural influences on Hindu civilization and individual Hindus, Sai Baba advocated an active life informed by scriptural study and charitable giving. The ashram he established in 1943 marked the beginning of a large global movement toward neotraditionalism.

Sai Baba's fame and stature were based on accounts of his supernormal feats of multiple presence, miracle cures, and materializing items out of the air, including sacred ash, food, books, and even Swiss watches. Through Sai Baba, disciples see one of the perennial themes nurtured in the myriad South Asian traditions: that the divine is alive and appears in human form and that this world is still enchanted with grace. His death in 2011 was reported widely in the global media.

In India today, the most ardent sectarian proselytizers (especially across the northern states) are from the group called Brahma Kumari. The visions and spiritual experiences of the founding guru, Lekhraj (1876–1969), a jeweler from Hyderabad, inspired an early following. In 1936 Lekhraj established the Brahma Kumari sect and turned his entire wealth over to the first community. Their Raja Yoga centers, also called "spiritual museums," draw interested individuals, primarily among urban dwellers. By 2016, these institutions were being maintained by 21,200 full-time religious teachers.

Lekhraj had visions portending the end of the world cycle. He attributed these visions to Shiva, the deity who commands the group's ritual attention. Lekhraj insisted that individuals engage in radical purifications to survive and to inherit paradise. Such cleansing could come only through celibacy, vegetarianism, abstinence from tobacco and alcohol, and specific yoga practices. These traditional disciplines became the core practices of the Brahma Kumaris. The vow of celibacy, long an ideal for Hindu ascetics, is here extended to all householders. As a result, married couples who become disciples have to transform their marital relations to be expressions of "pure, noncarnal spiritual love." This teaching created serious domestic strife in the early community, forcing Lekhraj and his initially small circle of devotees to move to Karachi and later, after partition (1947), to Mount Abu in western India. Once there, the movement was transformed from a reclusive sect to an aggressively outgoing one.

Although its bhakti doctrines and cosmology could be characterized as drawn from premodern Hinduism and its silent meditation practices are drawn from traditional yoga, Brahma Kumari social practices are reformist and focused on women. Brahma Kumaris challenge Hindu society's patriarchal doctrines and ethical norms; the sect invites women to awaken to their divinity through connecting devotionally with the powers of traditional Hindu goddesses.

Indian schoolchildren in Bhopal performing yoga exercises sponsored by the state government of Madhya Pradesh.

In recent years, the Brahma Kumaris have won recognition from India's leading politicians for supporting the establishment of a "value-based society," as members work with UN agencies on educational projects across South Asia. In the last decade, the Brahma Kumaris have claimed status as an independent religion, rejecting the label of "Hindu." In 2016 the group counted membership at 1 million. Over 8,500 Brahma Kumaris centers exist, most in India, but also now in over 100 other countries.

The Connection of Religion with Philanthropy and Social Reform

The impact of Christianity on Hinduism, as we noted earlier, was to suggest the role of modern religious institutions and the scope of religious service in society. Just as Christian missionaries had shown that churches could be linked with schools and hospitals, Hindu reformers (e.g., the Ramakrishna Mission and Sai Baba) have included social welfare initiatives to address the nation's needs. Initially, perhaps, this was done in competition with the Western missionaries; but the idea also found support from many Hindu teachers promoting the spiritual power of selfless, compassionate service and extolling individuals to engage in humanitarian merit-making. As a result, many Hindu mathas have started educational institutions, clinics, orphanages, and hospitals.

New Hindu organizations address the poverty and suffering endemic in South Asia. A prominent example of this engagement with contemporary problems is the pollution in the Ganges River. As governments and corporations elsewhere in the industrial world have done to their rivers, in India 118 urban municipal governments have used this sacred river as a sewer, and 764 private companies have dumped their untreated factory wastes in it. Hence, in many places, the Ganges has dangerous water toxicity and pollutant levels. So pernicious has this problem become that at the end of the great Kumbha Mela pilgrimage in 2013, thousands of Hindu holy men staged two days of protest and filed a lawsuit, threatening to lead others to boycott the next festival unless the government immediately began corrective actions to clean up the river. It remains to be seen, however, whether the convictions of religious leaders can really counterbalance the power of industrialists.

Religious Nationalism: Secular India and Its Discontents

As noted earlier, many of India's anticolonial nationalist leaders were educated in England, and more than a few were unalterably committed to creating modern India as a secular democracy. They knew that religious strife in Europe had led to the formation of most modern Western nations, and they wanted to avoid the problems among the complex and competing religious communities in India that would inevitably result if any sectarian favoritism were shown. In the end, they succeeded, with British help, in marginalizing nationalist groups such as the Rashtriya Svayamsevak Sangh (RSS) that wanted to establish India as a Hindu nation.

In practice, however, the democratic and secular Indian state has proved to be an ally of the high castes, particularly brahmins, in comparison with its British predecessor. This has led to the suggestion that, in its actual workings, India's "secular state" really amounts to a form of "neo-Brahminism": in 2000, brahmins held about 70 percent of civil service jobs but comprised only 3 percent of the population. Yet in a paradoxical development, and despite the state's administration's being biased toward their interests, high-caste politicians have convinced growing numbers of citizens that Hindus have been discriminated against by the laws and policies of secular India. Thus, throughout the 1990s, the Bharatiya Janata Party (BJP), the party controlled by members of the upper castes, campaigned on the basis of promises to establish a strong Hindu nation. Victories in state and national elections came in 1998.

The BJP and its high-caste supporters have sought to reverse the secular state's efforts to uplift Muslims and others equally impoverished among the lowest castes. During the first months of BJP rule, massacres in lower-caste settlements were reported across North India; in most cases investigated, the killings were found to represent efforts to intimidate groups that had voted against high-caste candidates or had sought state intervention to enforce lower-caste rights.

Then, in 2002, anti-Muslim riots in the state of Gujarat, allegedly abetted by its BJP government, resulted in over 2,000 Muslim dead, with 35,000 left homeless. A group of outside, independent judges collected testimony and summarized these horrific events:

> Hindutva hooligans came out into the streets . . . and in all flaming fury, targeted innocent and helpless Muslims. They were brutalized by miscreants uninhibited by police; their women were unblushingly molested; and Muslim men, women, and children, in a travesty of justice, were burnt alive.[8]

International human rights investigators joined in blaming this pogrom on the Vishva Hindu Parishad (see next section) and its youth wing, the Bajrang Dal, for planning these events. Yet few arrests were ever made in Gujarat. Not surprisingly, Muslim resentments, calls for revenge, and terrorist reprisals directed against the Hindu majority have increased across India. Although the BJP lost power in the national Parliament, it once again won in 2014 in the person of Gujarat's chief minister during these riots, Narendra Modi. Modi won by emphasizing his record of economic development and plans to enhance public health, including a cleanup of the Ganges River, but anti-Muslim activities across India and aggressive attempts to revise school curriculums to conform to Hindu fundamentalist ideology have increased as well.

The VHP: Hindu Leaders in Search of a Religious Nation

Vishva Hindu Parishad (VHP): organization of religious leaders that promotes the creation of a Hindu India

Linked to the RSS and the Bharatiya Janata Party, the **Vishva Hindu Parishad (VHP**; Council of All Hindus) was founded in 1964 as an organization of religious leaders who, while retaining their own disciples and spiritual agendas, wished to promote the interests of Hindus and a kind of spiritual Hinduism. In agreement with earlier reformers as well as some European colonialists, the VHP views Hinduism as in decline, seeks the roots of the faith in the earliest texts, and considers the *Bhagavad Gita* to be Hinduism's preeminent scripture.

Violence between communities in India, especially along Hindu–Muslim and Hindu–Christian lines, has increased in recent decades. This photo depicts a Hindu mob advancing in Ahmedebad during the 2002 riots.

The VHP argues that the era before Muslim rule (1200 CE) was a golden age for Hinduism, a time of social egalitarianism, prosperity, just rulers, and a wealth of enlightened seers. But with the Muslim conquest and such actions as the razing of temples to build mosques, Hindu culture declined; subsequent British domination of India made matters worse, causing further stagnation and division among all groups. The VHP views the secular state of India created in 1947 as a further means of dividing Hindus and thwarting the establishment of a great civilization centered on "Vedic spirituality." It further argues that if this secularism can be overthrown, and with it a mind-set of inferiority induced during the colonial period, another golden age can begin. Accordingly, the VHP has voiced support for dismantling any mosques that were (in the party's historical determination) built over Hindu temples in centuries past. The destruction of the mosque in Ayodhya in 1992 attracted attention to the group and support from ultranationalists, as did the VHP's marketing scheme to raise funds by selling bricks for the construction of the new Hindu temple planned for the site. The VHP leaders still express their wish to see other Muslim shrines removed from Benares and Mathura, and many defend the 2002 massacres against Muslims in Gujarat as being brought on by Muslims themselves. Confrontations with the secular constitution of India continue, such as in 2007, when the BJP leaders in the state of Madhya Pradesh passed laws requiring the public school curriculum to include an elementary yoga practice accompanied by devotional chanting. A state court struck down the legislation soon after, enraging the Hindu majority across the country.

Sikh Separatism and Globalization

Because the British invested heavily in irrigation and infrastructure in the Punjab, by the postcolonial era the Sikh home territory had become one of the most productive

SIKHPARK   CREATED BY DALBIR

HINDUS DON'T EAT BEEF, JEWS AND MUSLIMS PORK. WHAT DON'T YOU SIKHS EAT?

BIG MAC WITH MAYONNAISE. IT MESSES UP MY MOUSTACHE.

With greater recognition of the religious pluralism of diverse global communities, differences in ritual beliefs and practices are becoming more widely known. In a parody of the cartoon South Park, Sikh cartoonist Dalbir points out difficulties of following religious law. Although many Sikhs are vegetarian, Sikh dietary rules allow the consumption of all meats if the animal was slaughtered compassionately. Some cartoons have also created inter- and intracommunity conflicts.

agricultural regions of India. But partition was a terrible blow to the Sikhs, as it divided their Punjab homeland and put Sikhs between fleeing Muslim and Hindu refugees, and the shocking massacres each inflicted on the other. Sikhs had to flee to India and abandon holy sites in the Pakistan Punjab; subsequently, Indian politicians divided up the Indian Punjab in ways that were regarded as discriminatory against the Sikh majority. Although Sikhs became one of the wealthiest ethnic groups in postcolonial India, there were many who were left out and felt aggrieved by these events.

Despite Sikh prosperity, these grievances attracted more Sikhs to radical leaders, who in the 1980s revived a demand for a Sikh homeland in Punjab, following the logic that had led to the creation of Pakistan as the homeland for South Asian Muslims. Sikh guerrillas tried to transform this region into a separate state they called Khalistan, extorting contributions they identified as "taxes" from Sikh farmers and merchants while randomly murdering Hindus living there. The movement was funded as well by contributions from Sikhs abroad.

In 1984, after armed secessionist leaders occupied the Golden Temple in Amritsar, the Indian government sent troops to invade this shrine to arrest a separatist militant named Jarnail Singh Bhindranwale. In this operation, Bhindranwale was killed, along with casualties on both sides. The Golden Temple complex also suffered a great deal of damage due to the fighting. Many Sikhs regarded the attack as a desecration of their holiest shrine.

Later in the year, prime minister Indira Gandhi was assassinated by two Sikh bodyguards, who had been outraged by the sacrilege. The murder triggered waves of violence. By the turn of the millennium, the separatist agitation had largely dissipated as moderate Sikhs came back into power in national politics and international support for an independent state declined.

Through the last decades of the twentieth century, the Sikh global migration continued, and now almost 15 percent of Sikhs live outside India. With over 23 million followers worldwide, including a growing number of Western converts, Sikhism is slowly being recognized for its distinctive spiritual development.

A Growing Global Tradition

Hinduism appears in Western awareness through yoga and meditation and the increasing use of "karma" in personal conversations, with much less focus on ritual or law. For many, of course, this interest is confined to the athletic or health benefits, with the religious beliefs underlying the practices often downplayed or tailored to fit the practitioner's existing belief system.

TALES OF SPIRITUAL TRANSFORMATION: Swami Satchidananda's Moksha

"My highest experience . . . of Advaita Oneness was in 1949, a few months after my *sannyas* initiation [as a celibate ascetic]. It was in mid-winter, when I visited Vasishta Cave, where the sage Vasishta performed austerities. I went into the cave, . . . where I reached a large room with a seat. As I sat there and meditated, I had the experience of transcending my body and mind, realizing myself as the Omnipresent. I forgot my individuality. It is impossible to explain exactly what this is. I must have spent several hours in that state. Then I heard a humming sound, OM chanting, coming from a long distance away. Slowly, slowly, it became louder. As it neared I became aware of my mind and body. . . . For some time, I couldn't see anything in the normal way. All over I saw light, light, light. The whole world appeared as a mass of light. There was only peace and peace was everywhere. The state persisted the whole day. I have had this experience very often, mostly when I visit a holy place."

Swami Satchidananda (1914–2002) went on to become a guru whose teaching was centered in North America, founding an ecumenical movement called *Integral Yoga* in 1966. Since 1986, Integral Yoga has been centered in Yogaville, a thousand-acre ashram in rural Virginia, and has spread to twenty-eight countries and nearly 400 centers across North America.

Source: From Sita Wiener, *Swami Satchidananda* (New York: Bantam, 1970), p. 88.

The bow asana, as demonstrated by the yoga master and guru Swami Satchidananda (1914–2002).

The Indian diaspora is increasingly important in the process of Hindu globalization. First and second generations of Indians settled in the United States are the nation's richest ethnic group in terms of per capita income, and the majority, who are Hindu, has supported the internationalization of the faith.

Temples are the natural centers for cultural awareness and revitalization movements among immigrant Hindus. Hindu nationalists have also spread their activism in America through temple institutions and summer camps for youth. The VHP has raised funds for causes back in India, and its members have sought to have public school textbooks in California rewritten to conform to their ideological interpretations of Indian history and Hinduism.

All immigrant Hindus today must submerge many of their regional traditions in joining with coreligionists from all over India to provide a homogenized working definition of "Hinduism." Indicative of this trend is the work of the Pancajanya Project founded by devout Hindus in the Asian-American Hotel Owner's Association: since 2008, they have placed over 150,000 copies of the *Bhagavad Gita* in hotel rooms in thirty states. Converts and immigrant groups also have supported the global extensions of religious centers founded by modern gurus. In the West there are now hundreds of Hindu teachers who travel to the West to give teachings. Several have shifted to ashrams and yoga centers outside India to dedicate their lives to their Western converts and South Asian immigrants. Perhaps the most successful of all the global Hindu gurus was the sadhu Maharishi Mahesh Yogi, who in the 1960s came to prominence by giving spiritual instruction to the Beatles. His movement, **Transcendental Meditation (TM)**, has taken Hindu tradition across the globe and inspired a long agenda for utopian initiatives.

Transcendental Meditation (TM): movement founded by Maharishi Mahesh Yogi that brought yoga meditation teachings to the West

Across Europe and North America, increasingly affluent immigrant communities are building magnificent, traditional Hindu temples. This temple in Omaha, Nebraska, opened in 2004.

As India has become an important player in the global computer and software business, older Hindu institutions and new movements have adopted Internet technology. For example, a famous Ganesh temple in Bombay has set up a website in which viewers can have live darshan of the main icons, hear hymns being sung, and make contributions to sponsor pujas. The website of a Vishnu shrine in the northern state of Jammu offers similar scenes and services, adding maps, regularly updated weather reports, and hostel bookings to aid the estimated 4 million pilgrims who visit the temple annually in person.

Recent observers have discerned the rise of "karma capitalism." Here we can recognize Hindu teachings exerting a new and powerful influence in the global marketplace of ideas. Indian philosophies have been integrated in elite business schools in a variety of ways: "self-mastery" courses that now help to train managers "to boost their leadership skills and find inner peace in lives dominated by work"; Hindu "business gurus" teach that executives should conceive of companies in more holistic ways, to redefine success as larger than monetary profit, including the well-being of employees, customers, and the environment. Human resources initiatives at companies such as General Mills, Google, Aetna Insurance, and Target now regularly include yoga and meditation to benefit their employees and improve corporate productivity. Classical Hindu beliefs and practices have now become a creative influence on the culture of modern multinational business, with many now explicitly managing their enterprises to generate "good karma."[9]

Like immigrant communities across the world today, Hindu parents create programs that instill traditional religious beliefs and practices.

Conclusion

In the twenty-first century Hinduism assumes more forms than it ever has before, and the linkage of religion to politics is growing. Since it is impossible to take any religious tradition as standing for all of "Hinduism," we can only generalize about the broad patterns of change affecting the religion in South Asia. The rapid development of the economic system of the country continues to draw migrants from rural settlements to burgeoning urban areas and transforming the life experiences of millions. In these settings, the Hindu traditions of the premodern world are in decline as new institutions and teachers arise to meet the needs of those living under these new circumstances.

But even with so much change, the belief in the spiritual presence of the gods, in yoga, and in the guru-centered spiritual life remains strong. In the cities, among the rapidly expanding middle class as well as among slum dwellers, there are numerous new incarnations of "organized Hinduisms." Hitherto-independent groups such as sadhus from different regions are forming new organizations to work for common interests. Likewise, laity and priests associated with major temples have pressed for the establishment of management committees to orchestrate rituals and festivals as well as to supervise temple accounts. Thus, what in rural India was a largely preordained relationship with a family priest and local guru, in urban settings has become a matter of individual choice. Hindus in ever-increasing numbers, then, are faced with the "heretical imperative" (as discussed in Chapter 1) of making their own choices about their own religious paths.

In addition, as middle-class South Asians have raised their educational level, experienced rising prosperity, and encountered religions and societies elsewhere, they have been inevitably forced to consider "Hinduism" in comparison to these other belief systems and cultures. Critics have pointed out that Hindu leaders have failed to curb blatant caste and gender discrimination or work for the common good to lessen the rate of India's extreme poverty, with 39 percent of its children malnourished.

Among the many voices of Hinduism today, nationalists seeking a religious state contend with secularists for political power. The voices, aspirations, and wealth of Hindus now living outside of South Asia are also part of global Hinduism when new possibilities and reforms are being envisioned. The daunting task is for Hindus to mobilize their beliefs, values, and conscience to serve the needs of all its adherents, who now number over 1.3 billion.

CONTRASTING RELIGIOUS VISIONS

As the following contrasting visions indicate, every religious tradition is capable of generating both visions that encourage peace and understanding and visions that encourage conflict and violence.

Peacemaker: Pandurang Shastri Athavale and the Swadhyaya ("Truth Seekers")

Pandurang Athavale (1920–2003) grew up in a family that was active in movements sponsored by M. K. Gandhi, the Mahatma. In 1956 he began organizing social uplift programs for the poorest low-caste groups, also drawing on a modernist reading of Hinduism's great spiritual classic, the *Bhagavad Gita*. Living modestly as a householder, Athavale preferred to be called Dadaji ("Elder Brother"), resisting the usual trappings of the title "guru." His social programs have reached an estimated 20 million people living in 100,000 villages. The scope of this movement is due to the practice of *bhaktipheri*, or devotional visits, in which he or his followers spread the message of human service to new communities. His message is simple:

> It is my experience that awareness of the nearness of God and reverence for that power creates reverence for self, reverence for the other, reverence for nature, and reverence for the entire creation. And devotion as an expression of gratitude for God can turn into a social force to bring about transformative changes at all levels in the society.[a]

Acting on this conviction, members of Athavale's organization, called Swadhyaya, help build new temples that are ecumenical and open to all, and community centers for cooperative activities. Swadhyaya has become a worldwide movement, with 350 centers in the United States alone. The magnitude of the work and the authentic spirituality of the movement were the reason Athavale was awarded the 1997 Templeton Prize, the "Nobel for excellence in religious pursuits."

Confrontationalist: Voices from the Vishva Hindu Parishad

Arguing that Hindus have suffered from disunity, mindless pacifism, and Muslim predations over the last millennium, leaders associated with the "Council of All Hindus" have argued for revival by means of changing these old and decadent religious habits. An official inquiry on the Hindu–Muslim rioting in Bombay in 1993 reported that the responsibility lay in gangs of Hindus led by the Shiva Sena ("Shiva's Army"), a VHP ally. Members of this group went on a rampage, setting gasoline fires that burned Muslim businesses and homes. In the end, at least 1,200 Muslims died. A Shiva Sena leader commented several years afterward, "Who are these Muslims? If the Shiva Sena comes to power, everybody will take an initiation of the Hindu religion [to become Hindu]."[b] Similar uncompromising sentiments were expressed by the woman ascetic Uma Bharati, who proclaimed in 1991:

> Declare without hesitation that this is a Hindu country, a nation of Hindus. We have come to strengthen the immense Hindu shakti [force] into a fist. Do not display any love for your enemies. . . . The Qur'an teaches them to lie in wait for idol worshipers. . . . But we cannot teach them with words, now let us teach them with kicks. . . . Tie up your religiosity and kindness in a bundle and throw it in the Jamuna. . . . Any non-Hindu who lives here does so at our mercy.[c]

[a] *Hinduism Today*, June 1997, p. 35.

[b] *India Today*, January 15, 1996, p. 25.

[c] Thomas Hansen, *The Saffron Wave: Democracy and Hindu Nationalism in Modern India* (Princeton, NJ: Princeton University Press, 1999), p. 180.

Discussion Questions

1. Why is a brahmin essential to Vedic ritual?

2. What reasons might be suggested for the transformation of the polytheism of the early Vedic peoples into the monism and theism of later Hinduism?

3. Compare and contrast the spiritual practice of the shaman (Chapter 2) with that of the yoga practitioner. Is it possible to know exactly how different their experiences are?

4. Why would the lowest castes regard the doctrines of karma, caste, and duty as a system designed to subjugate them?

5. What reasons would a woman have for abiding by her dharma?

6. To what extent can karma theory be considered to be a doctrine of fatalism? Do humans still have freedom of action?

7. If you were an Islamic judge in Mughal India, how would you advise the local sultan who asks if his subjects who follow Krishna (as depicted in the *Bhagavad Gita*) are in fact monotheists?

8. How does ritualism express the ideals of bhakti Hinduism?

9. Why was the influence of colonialism on the religions of India powerfully conveyed by the term *Protestant Hinduism*?

10. What reasons are Hindu nationalists giving to support their view that the creation of India as a secular country is a perpetuation of colonialism and a betrayal of Hindu ideals?

11. Explain why M. K. Gandhi's biography reveals many of the factors shaping modern Hindu reform.

12. Critique the following statement, from an ecumenical Hindu organization: "We can follow Jesus without contradiction, for he is none other than another *avatara* of Lord Vishnu."

13. What does it say about the power of ideas regarding the sacred versus the power of profane modern economic interests that the Ganges is now in danger of becoming a toxic waterway?

14. How do Sikh traditions differ from and find agreement with the teachings of the Hindu philosophy and also those of Islam?

15. If you visited a Sikh *gurudwara*, how would the activities there reflect Sikh beliefs?

16. What is lost, and what is gained, by the addition of virtual temple visits to the Hinduism of today?

17. Why have Jains found the career of jewelry and gem trade especially apt given their religious ethics?

Key Terms

Adi Granth
ahimsa
Arya Samaj
ashram
atman
avatara
Bhagavad Gita
bhakti
Bharatiya Janata
    Party (BJP)
Brahman
brahmin
darshan
dharma
Gandhi, Mohandas K.
guru
gurudwara
Hindutva
Janam Sakhis

Kali Yuga
karma
Khalsa
matha
moksha
nirguna Brahman
Om-kara
prasad
puja
puranas
Ramakrishna Mission
Ramanuja
Rammohan Roy
Rashtriya Svayamsevak
    Sangh (RSS)
saguna Brahman
samsara
Sat Guru
satyagraha

Shaivite
shakta
shakti
Shankara
siddha
tantra
Tattvabodhini Sabha
tirtha
Transcendental
    Meditation (TM)
Upanishads
Vaishnavite
Vedas
Vishva Hindu
    Parishad (VHP)
yoga
Yoga Sutras

Suggested Readings

Babb, Lawrence. *The Divine Hierarchy* (New York: Columbia University Press, 1975).
———. *Redemptive Encounters: Three Modern Styles in the Hindu Tradition* (Berkeley: University of California Press, 1986).
Dalrymple, William. *Nine Lives: In Search of the Sacred in Modern India* (New York: Knopf, 2010).
Dimmitt, Cornelia, and J. A. B. van Buitenen. *Classical Hindu Anthology: A Reader in the Sanskrit Puranas* (Philadelphia: Temple University Press, 1978).
Doniger, Wendy. *The Hindus: An Alternative History* (New York: Penguin, 2009).
Dundas, Paul. *The Jains* (New York: Routledge, 2002).
Eck, Diana. *Darsan: Seeing the Divine Image in India*, 3rd ed. (New York: Columbia University Press, 1998).
Embree, Ainslee, ed. *Sources of Indian Tradition*, 2nd ed., 2 vols. (New York: Columbia University Press, 1988).
Hawley, John, and Mark Juergensmeyer. *Songs of the Saints of India* (New York: Oxford University Press, 1988).
Hopkins, Thomas. *The Hindu Religious Tradition* (Belmont, CA: Wadsworth, 1982).

Jaffrelot, Christophe. *The Hindu Nationalist Movement in India* (New York: Columbia University Press, 1996).

Jaina, Padmanabh. *The Jain Path to Purification* (Berkeley: University of California, 1988).

Jones, Kenneth W. *Socio-Religious Reform Movements in British India* (Cambridge: Cambridge University Press, 1994).

Larson, Gerald James. *India's Agony over Religion* (Albany: State University of New York Press, 1995).

Mann, Gurinder Singh. *Sikhism* (New York: Prentice Hall, 2004).

Mittal, Sushil, ed. *The Hindu World* (New York: Routledge, 2004).

Narayan, Kirin. *Storytellers, Saints, and Scoundrels: Folk Narrative in Hindu Religious Teaching* (Philadelphia: University of Pennsylvania Press, 1989).

Smith, David. *Hinduism and Modernity* (London: Wiley-Blackwell, 2003).

Notes

1. Most Sikhs regard their faith as constituting a separate faith that rejects the authority of the Veda, the legitimacy of brahmin priesthood, and the associated ideology of caste. While we will point out how these and other contrasts came to define a very successful and distinctive tradition, we cover this tradition within this chapter for thematic consistency with other chapters treating similar patterns of diversity (Christianity and Islam).

2. Daniel Gold, "Organized Hinduisms: From Vedic Truth to Hindu Nation," in M. E. Marty and R. Scott Appleby, eds., *Fundamentalisms Observed* (Chicago: University of Chicago Press, 1991), p. 581.

3. For the sake of simplicity, in this text we use *brahmin* to indicate the priestly caste and Brahman to indicate the "world spirit," although in fact they are similar Sanskrit words: *brahman* and *brahmana*, respectively.

4. W. Owen Cole, "Sikhism," in John R. Hinnells, ed., *A Handbook of Living Religions* (New York: Penguin, 1984), p. 240.

5. Patwant Singh, *The Sikhs* (New York: Doubleday, 1999), p. 27.

6. Ibid., p. 23.

7. "An End-of-Life Fast Clashes With Indian Law," *New York Times*, August 25, 2015, p. A4.

8. Quoted in the *Financial Times* (London), March 31, 2007, Section FT, p. 1.

9. "Business Filter," *Boston Globe*, October 30, 2006, p. E-2.

Additional Resources

The Hindu Universe (www.hindunet.org). A gateway to many websites for case studies in belief and practice.

Hinduism Today (www.hinduismtoday.com). Online site of a leading magazine covering contemporary events and traditions.

BBC Religions: Hinduism (www.bbc.co.uk/religion/religions/hinduism). Excellent information and useful links, regularly updated.

Jain Dharma Online (www.jaindharmonline.com). Website on Jain texts, traditions, and teachings in a modern perspective.

Sikhs.org (www.sikhs.org). A source for texts in translation and many other topics.

Hindu Ritualism Online (www.onlinedarshan.com) is a clearinghouse for access to temples across the Indian subcontinent; http://shubhpuja.com is a commercial site that offers over 150 pujas and astrological consultancy for clients, who can participate as patrons as the priests perform the rite.

India Pilgrim Tours (http://pilgrimagetourinindia.com/spiritual-pilgrimage.htm). An example of the breadth of spiritual tourist tours now available to affluent Hindus.

BUDDHISM

Paths Toward Nirvana

7

Overview

Popular culture is full of images, stereotypes, and impressions of Buddhism. A long list of celebrities from rock, sports, and show business have identified themselves as followers of the Buddha; the Dalai Lama is by now one of the most recognized religious leaders in the world. The adjective "Zen" is a cliché in advertising, while stress reduction techniques (like "mindfulness") based on Buddhist meditation are increasingly popular. The globalization of Buddhist tradition may be accelerating, but many commonly held Western assertions about Buddhism are incorrect. The goal of this chapter is to convey what has made Buddhism a vibrant living tradition while shedding light on why these superficial impressions have proven so attractive in the West.

When Asian Buddhists meet Western Buddhist converts, they often find their beliefs hard to comprehend. Take, for example, the simple recitation of "going for refuge." This practice is rarely done outside Asia and is largely ignored in America. But for over 2,500 years now, this taking refuge has been a daily practice for Asian Buddhist householders. "Going for refuge" reaffirms one's devotion at the start of any ritual: *Buddham Saranam Gacchami* (I go for refuge in the Buddha), *Dharmam Saranam Gacchami* (I go for refuge in the teachings), *Sangham Saranam Gacchami* (I go for refuge in the community).

◀ Buddhist spiritual practices have proven attractive to many in the fast-paced, often stressful centers of global civilization.

Buddhism Timeline

563 BCE	Birth of Siddhartha [some scholars determine as 463 BCE]
528	Enlightenment of Shakyamuni, the Buddha; creation of the *sangha*, the monastic order
ca. 510	Establishment of nuns' order
483	Death of the Buddha [some scholars, 383 BCE]
482	First Council collects and organizes oral accounts
383	Council of Vaishali leads to the first split in the sangha
273–232	Reign of Ashoka, convert to Buddhism, who spread Buddhism throughout India and beyond (Afghanistan, Burma, Sri Lanka)
250	Council of Pataliputra leads to division into "18 schools"
240	Sanchi stupa and other stupas built across India; relic cult at stupas central to community
ca. 100	Origins of the Mahayana school, beginning with *Prajnaparamita* literature
80	First collections of written canon begun, beginning with the Vinaya, the monastic code; Pali Canon collection begun in Sri Lanka
50 CE–180 CE	Spread of Buddhism into central Asia via the Silk Road
ca. 85 CE	Composition of the *Lotus Sutra*
124	Buddhist monks in western China
ca. 200	Writings of Nagarjuna, the most influential Mahayana philosopher; Madhyamaka school formed
220–589	Buddhist missions reach Southeast Asia, Java, Sumatra, Korea, Japan, Vietnam; Buddhist monasteries established throughout China in era of weak central state
ca. 300	Rituals dedicated to bodhisattvas developed by Mahayana monks
ca. 300	Origins of Pure Land school in India
320ff.	Development of Yogacara school, led by monastic brothers Asanga and Vasubandhu
ca. 425	Writings of a monk who shaped the Theravada school, Buddhaghosa, in Sri Lanka
ca. 500	Rise of the Vajrayana Thunderbolt school in India, which eventually dominates Buddhist communities in northeastern India, Nepal, and Tibet
ca. 600	Formation of the Ch'an school in China inspired by teachings of the legendary Indian monk Bodhidharma
700–1270	Buddhism dominates Sri Vijaya kingdom on Sumatra-Java; rulers build Borobodur stupa
749	First Buddhist monastery in Tibet
760–1142	Pala Dynasty rules North India, patronizes Buddhist monasteries, and promotes Mahayana traditions; tradition in decline elsewhere in India
841–845	Extensive destruction of monasteries in China and defrocking of Buddhist monks and nuns
850ff.	Restoration of Chinese Buddhism, principally the Pure Land and Ch'an schools
ca. 1000	Second introduction of monastic Mahayana Buddhism into Tibet from India

1000–1400	Era of Pagan Kingdom in Burma, establishing one of the great centers of Buddhism
1192	Muslim rule established across northern India; final destruction of Indian monasteries and decline of Bodh Gaya as center of Buddhist pilgrimage
1193–1227	In Japan, formation of new schools: Zen brought from China by Eisei (1141–1215) and Dogen (1200–1253); Pure Land by Honen (1133–1212) and Shinran (1173–1262), and school founded by Nichiren (1222–1282)
1642–1959	Tibet dominated by Gelugpa monastic school under the Dalai and Panchen lamas
1815–1948	Era of British colonial rule; conflicts in Sri Lanka lead to reformist movement styled "Protestant Buddhism" that influences Buddhists across Asia
1864–1933	Anagarika Dharmapala, Sri Lankan reformist, founder of the Mahabodhi Society, who spread reformism across Asia
1871–1876	Meiji state in Japan persecutes Buddhism; 70 percent of monasteries lost as 75 percent of monks marry
1877–1945	Buddhist establishment in Japan supports nationalism, militarism, and territory seizures of Korea, Taiwan, and northern China
1944	Buddhist Churches of America, a Pure Land organization, founded in California
1945	Soka Gakkai established in Japan, a branch of Nichiren school until 1991
1949–1976	Chinese Communist government persecutes Buddhists and seizes 250,000 monasteries and temples, with the Cultural Revolution (1966–1976) a period of intense destruction
1954–1956	Sixth Buddhist Council in Rangoon, Burma, culminating in the marking of the 2,500-year anniversary of Shakyamuni's death
1956	Founding of the Mahasangha Sahayaka Gana in central India, a Buddhist organization
1959–present	Exile of the fourteenth Dalai Lama from Tibet and the era of the globalization of Tibetan Buddhism
1976–present	Slow, partial restoration of Buddhist institutions in China
1982–2009	Civil war against Tamil minority in Sri Lanka polarizes Buddhist community
1987	Founding of Shakyaditya, a worldwide organization of Buddhist women
1989	Founding of the International Network of Engaged Buddhists by Thai activist Sulak Sivaraksa
1990	Revival of Buddhism in Mongolia after 88 years of suppression
1991	Founding of *Tricycle*, a Buddhist mass-market magazine in America
1998–present	Full ordination taken by Theravada nuns in Chinese monasteries, reviving a lost tradition
2007	Monks lead democracy protests in Burma, resulting in fierce government repression of sangha
2008	Uprisings across Tibet lead to Chinese government crackdown
2009	Civil War in Sri Lanka ends
2012–2015	Monks in Burma lead violent mobs that drive Muslims to refugee camps

There is considerable diversity among those who "go for refuge." In the Himalayas, a Tibetan monk seals himself into a cave retreat for three years and three months of meditative solitude. In the heart of urban Seoul, Korea, a media executive declares the opening of a Buddhist cable TV channel at a press conference in the ultramodern headquarters of a major Buddhist reform organization. In Singapore, as householders gather to view 2,500-year-old bone relics of the Buddha, monks chant and extol the blessings of worshipping these mortal remains. All take refuge, all are following their country's Buddhist tradition, yet the diversity is astounding.

Buddhists in all these places revere an image of the Buddha, who is seated in meditation, serene and exemplary, but one cannot help but wonder what the historical Buddha might say today if he heard how differently these disciples now construe his teachings. The oldest of the world's missionary religions and perhaps the most accommodating to adaptation in its global diaspora, Buddhism is in modest revival in most areas of the world today after having suffered setbacks throughout the modern era. To understand Buddhism, we will explore the peoples and cultures of Eurasia: from the homeland on the plains of the Ganges River in South Asia into the high Himalayas, across the tropical states of Southeast Asia and over the central Asian deserts, and throughout the imperial domains of China, Korea, and Japan.

This chapter will examine how Buddhism in its creative diversity has sought to direct devotees to follow the three refuges. We will sketch the life of the Buddha, explore his basic teachings, and chart the various interpretations as the tradition spread by monks, nuns, and merchants reached from northern India to East Asia, Southeast Asia, and in the last two centuries to Europe and the West.

Rough estimates place the number of Buddhists at 395 million, making it the fourth-largest among world religions. Over 98 percent live in Asia. Buddhists today are divided into two factions, those following the **Mahayana**, or "Great Vehicle," and those following the **Theravada**, or "Teachings of the Elders." Roughly 62 percent of people today are adherents of the Mahayana and 38 percent are Theravada followers. With most Mahayanists located in the countries north of the tropics, the label "Northern Buddhism" is sometimes used for this grouping, as opposed to the "Southern Buddhism" of the Theravadins. In a half-dozen Asian states (Sri Lanka, Myanmar, Thailand, Laos, Cambodia, and Japan), Buddhists comprise the overwhelming majority of the population. They are significant minorities in Nepal, China, South Korea, and Singapore, while their presence in Malaysia (10 percent), Indonesia (3 percent), and India is less marked. (It should be noted that specific percentages, figures taken from Western almanac sources, are at best rough estimates, with wide margins for error.)

Although modern Buddhist activists and intellectuals may debate exactly "what the Buddha taught," Buddhism's basic teachings about life, mortality, and spiritual development continue to inspire adherents amid the often-traumatic changes of recent centuries. In every land, venerable institutions and reformist groups alike are seeking to adapt the faith to the changing world and to revive the essential practices that lead to Buddhism's perennial threefold goals: establishing moral community, securing worldly blessings, and realizing nirvana.

Mahayana: "Great Vehicle," the dominant school of Buddhism in Nepal, Tibet, and East Asia

Theravada: traditionalists; school of Buddhism dominant in South and Southeast Asia

A monk rescues texts from a temple ruined by the 2004 tsunami.

Encounter with Modernity: Socially "Engaged Buddhism"

In the aftermath of the devastating tsunami that struck the Indian Ocean on December 26, 2004, killing over 250,000 people, images of lived Buddhism filled the media. Accounts of the first humanitarian responses reported that Buddhist householders immediately gathered medicines, bandages, clothes, and food and headed to coastal areas to help others. Those interviewed in Sri Lanka and Thailand explained that they were strengthened and motivated by their Buddhist tradition's teachings—that suffering is sad but inevitable in life and that acting compassionately is a central duty. This unprecedented tragedy showed how strong the adherence to basic Buddhist doctrines still is today.

Other images of Asian Buddhists are of monks confronting war. In 1991, the monk

Protesting the Vietnam War, a Vietnamese monk commits suicide.

Zen Buddhist leader Thich Nhat Hanh in 2007, at the opening of a three-day requiem for those killed on both sides of the Vietnam War.

engaged Buddhism: reformist movement among global Buddhists seeking to relate the teachings to contemporary suffering

Ghosananda of Cambodia led monks and householders into the countryside to intervene and end hostilities between Khmer Rouge fighters and the new government. Another image, from 1963, is that of a Vietnamese monk sitting cross-legged, engulfed in flames, his suicide a protest of the South Vietnamese government's failure to respect Buddhism and to adopt a policy of national reconciliation. Among the many Buddhist monks who challenged the corrupt South Vietnamese state was Thich Nhat Hanh, who argued that when faced with immense suffering, Buddhists must take action and engage their society.

Inspired by the monks of Vietnam, contemporary Buddhist activists in Asia (and now in the West) are responding to crises posed by environmental despoliation, political corruption, and global hunger. In Asia, these profound changes have disrupted the regions' rural societies, including many of the communities that have long sustained Buddhist monastic institutions. **Engaged Buddhists** refuse to turn away from suffering, counseling instead "mundane awakening." In this way, engaged Buddhists hope to elicit compassion on the part of individuals, villages, countries, and eventually all people, arguing that engagement is as fundamental to Buddhism as the ascetic and solitary practices of the spiritual elite. Especially in urban centers, engaged Buddhists promote new understandings of Buddhism and organize Buddhist action, often confronting politicians and corporations. Can this movement revitalize the tradition from the capitals to the rural hinterlands and mitigate suffering without reducing or compromising its principal values?

Premodern Buddhism: The Formative Era (600 BCE–100 CE)

To understand this concept of "engagement," it is essential to go back to the beginning of the Buddhist tradition. Since it is the life of the Buddha that guides all followers and inspires all the later schools, we first learn about the life of the founder and examine his fundamental teachings. And because the historical destiny of Buddhism, the world's first missionary religion, is centered on the 2,500-year journey of the monastic community (sangha), understanding this institution's origins and development is essential to understanding the faith's expansion across Asia and the West.

The Buddha: Context and Biography

We saw in Chapter 6 that North India during the Buddha's lifetime (563–483 BCE) was a place of spiritual questioning and ascetic searching. The dominant Aryan society was evolving from small pastoral settlements to city-states and a more diverse economy. In the context of this transformation, the old sacrifice-centered Vedic religion controlled by members of the brahmin caste was becoming for some less plausible as an explanation of humanity's connection to the universe. In remote retreats and near to the emerging urban centers, seekers called **shramanas** pursued ascetic practices (yoga) to realize the true essence of human consciousness, life, and reality. The society in which the Buddha was born was ordered by caste and brahmin ritualism. In addition, however, there were nonconformist shramana seekers who questioned almost everything the old Vedic tradition asserted about spirit, morality, and social hierarchy. Some explored various trance states, living as simply and with as little food as possible, while other ascetics advocated materialism, nihilism, agnosticism, or fatalism.

> **shramana:** wandering ascetic, a term applied to Buddhists, Jains, and others

Like the Upanishadic seers, most shramanas believed that life consists of a countless series of rebirths, that these are determined by an individual's karma (a natural and moral causal force that accrues from one's deeds), and that rebirths continue until one "burns off" one's karma to reach a state of liberation. In Buddhism, this state of liberation is termed **nirvana.** The most famous man ever to become an ascetic sought out these shramanas and learned from them, adopting many of their spiritual practices and doctrines. This man, who would later call himself a Buddha, started out life in very different circumstances.

> **nirvana:** blissful state of liberation from rebirth, defined by the extinction of karma

Early accounts of the Buddha's life were passed down orally. What survives today are a variety of ancient accounts. While key events are largely the same across these accounts, specific incidents and thematic emphases greatly differ. What follows here draws on the commonalities of ancient accounts, as well as more recent vernacular biographies.

Siddhartha's Early Life

Siddhartha, the man who was to become the Buddha, was born a prince, the son of warrior-caste parents who ruled a small state in the Himalayan foothills. According to legendary accounts, this boy's birth was accompanied by auspicious celestial signs and a wise man's prediction that the child would be successful as either a universal monarch or a great ascetic. The name Siddhartha means "the one who attains the goal." The boy, whose mother died a week after giving birth, grew up in a palace where his father did everything in his power to ensure his son's destiny to become a ruler. The son trained in the martial arts and was indulged with all the pleasures of rule, including marriage, a harem of concubines, and every form of pleasant artistic distraction.

Siddhartha's life changed when he followed his faithful chariot driver to see the world beyond the palace walls. All the textual legends describe the profound impact of seeing a sick man, an old man, a dead man, and a shramana. These "four passing sights" overturned Siddhartha's carefree assumptions about life. They also offered a vision of the ascetic path he could take to escape the spiritual emptiness he now felt in his sheltered existence. Within days, Siddhartha abandoned his palace and family, including a newborn son. He began at that moment his search for a teacher among the forest-dwelling ascetics. The legends state that he was twenty-nine years old.

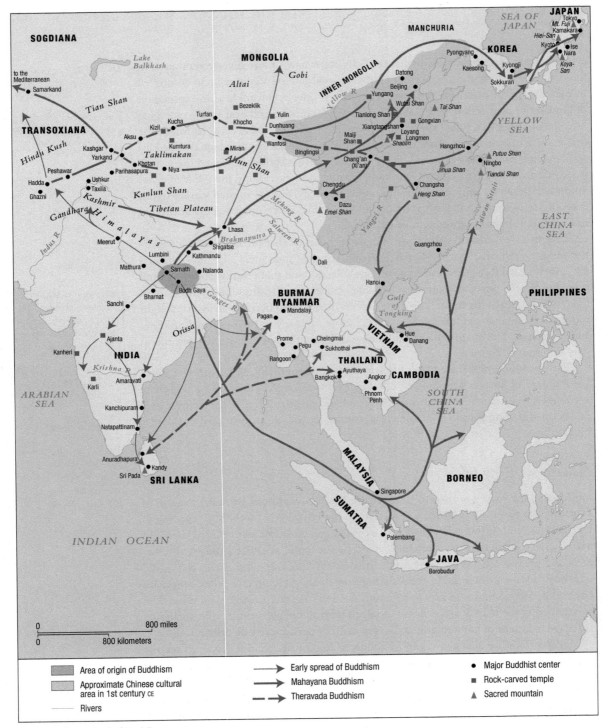

Map 7.1 The spread of Buddhism.

Siddhartha Begins His Quest

Siddhartha found a shramana guru whose way of meditation allowed one to achieve a "state of nothingness." Siddhartha soon mastered this technique, but he also recognized that the accomplishment was limited in value. His quest led to a second teacher, who taught a method of attaining trances that brought an experience of "neither perception nor nonperception." But again Siddhartha found that his mastery of this technique still left him short of the highest goal.

He soon joined five other men, who vowed to explore together a rigorous ascetic practice involving fasting (down to a few rice grains daily), breath control, and long periods seated in unmoving meditation. He adopted this lifestyle for about five years but finally rejected it, also, as too extreme. His fellow seekers, dismayed, ridiculed and abandoned him. Through this experiment, Siddhartha came to understand that the spiritual life is best undertaken as a middle path between the extremes of sensory indulgence (the life in the palace) and asceticism so zealous that it weakens the body. One name for Buddhism, "the Middle Way," stems from this insight.

Despite these setbacks, Siddhartha did not quit. Buoyed by a gift of rice and barley gruel from a village woman, he came to sit beneath a great ficus tree by a river outside the town of Gaya. He vowed to find either success or death in his quest. The legends relate that his revitalized meditations were disturbed by Mara, a supernatural being regarded by Buddhists as the personification of death, delusion, and temptation. Mara summoned his demons, who appeared as armed soldiers to elicit fear and as alluring females to provoke lust. Siddhartha touched his right hand to the earth, asking it to bear witness to his merit and eventual success. This earth-touching gesture, seen often in depictions of the Buddha, brought forth earthquakes and a cooling stream that washed away Mara and his hordes.

The Buddha's bath after his birth, depicted in a Chinese sculpture.

The Bodhi Tree and the Deer Park

Later that night, after resuming his meditations, Siddhartha reached increasingly subtle and blissful perceptions. He even attained such powers as memory of former lives and psychic vision, which allowed him to survey the destinies of all beings according to their karma, as well as the powers of levitation, telepathy, and greatly enhanced vision and hearing. Finally he completely extinguished all desire and ignorance by fully realizing his capacity for insight (**prajna**). This "awakening" to the nature of reality under the *bo* (for *bodhi*, "enlightenment") tree, poetically recounted as occurring at daybreak,

prajna: "insight"; quality of mind discerning reality clearly and calmly, its completeness necessary for enlightenment

The Buddha encountering the "four passing sights" that inspired his religious quest and eventual awakening.

enlightenment: state of "nirvana" or liberation

Dharma: teachings of the Buddha

sangha: Buddhist monastic community

arhat: enlightened being; term applied to the Buddha and his disciples

provides the root meaning of the term *Buddha* that from this moment onward we can properly apply to Siddhartha. He is also referred to as *Gautama Buddha*, using his family surname, and *Shakyamuni*, "the sage," or *muni*, from Gautama's clan, the Shakyas.

For seven weeks the Buddha remained near the bodhi tree, enjoying the bliss of nirvana. The texts recount a story that his very first disciples were householders, merchants who made offerings and received his benediction for their continued worldly success. He also received the veneration of *nagas*, the snake deities, whose submission symbolized Buddhism's claim of "spiritual conquest" over all deities everywhere. Then troublesome Mara returned to tempt the Buddha to remain isolated, enjoying his solitary nirvana. In his attempt to prevent the Buddha from continuing to teach, Mara cited humanity's hopeless stupidity. But the high gods also intervened to request that the Buddha live on to share his doctrine because, they assured him, there were people everywhere capable of realizing **enlightenment** by means of his teachings, or **Dharma**. This request inspired the Buddha's compassion, and he vowed to stay in the world, thus providing the ultimate model of the engaged Buddhist.

He then walked for days to a deer park outside the city of Varanasi, where he found his former ascetic colleagues. Their disdain turned to awe, however, after the Buddha taught for the first time the Four Noble Truths, which culminate in the Eightfold Path. The five ascetics became the first members of the **sangha**, and they were instructed to travel for the purpose of sharing the Dharma with all people of the world.

The Buddha's Life Work

For the next forty or so years, the Buddha empowered his enlightened disciples, called **arhats**, to act on his behalf, admit qualified seekers into the sangha, guide those who wished to meditate, and teach the Dharma to any who would hear it. Shakyamuni converted other ascetics, sometimes whole assemblies of them, as well as solitary shramanas, householders, and rulers. The Buddha's faculty of psychic knowledge allowed him to preach according to the exact capacity of his audience.

As the Buddhist movement grew, new situations arose that required adaptation. In addition to his skill at teaching, the Buddha created a new religious institution in

This Nepalese sculpture shows the Buddha in an earth-touching gesture, a frequently encountered icon that alludes to his calling upon the earth to bear witness to his fitness for enlightenment.

ancient India: the sangha of monks (***bhikkhu***). It was established on the basis of formal ordination and vows to follow the extensive set of rules that the Buddha adapted to the many environments where Buddhist monks came to live.

After much urging (at least according to some legends), Shakyamuni also gave permission, around 510 BCE, for the creation of a sangha for female renunciants. He also bequeathed a mixed message by emphasizing that while women are capable of realizing enlightenment, the nuns (***bhikkhuni***) must subordinate themselves to the monks in personal power and in matters of social etiquette. When admitting nuns, the Buddha

● *bhikkhu/bhikkuni:*
Buddhist monk/nun

also predicted that the tradition would decline. In subsequently allowing the sangha to receive lands, buildings, and other donated communal resources, the Buddha established a framework in which the sangha shifted its focus over time, from wandering to settled cooperative communal existence. This development, which also gave householder disciples a fixed focus for their patronage, in turn strengthened the sangha.

Late in life the Buddha began to suffer from various ailments, and he died in Kushinagar at the age of eighty. His body was cremated and the remains, divided into eight portions, were enshrined in relic mound shrines (**stupas**) that became the focus of Buddhist ritual and the architectural representation of the Buddha's presence across the world.

Shakyamuni's life story became for Buddhists a paradigmatic example of an individual's quest for enlightenment, and his exemplary role for subsequent generations was elaborated in hundreds of stories that describe incidents from this life as well as from his previous incarnations, in which he was reborn as a human, animal, or spirit. These narratives, along with stories of his path to Buddhahood, inspired art and literature across Asia. The Buddha embodies the Dharma, which, as in Hindu practice, is understood as comprising both the ultimate truth and the teachings that lead to that truth.

stupa: Buddhist shrine containing the relics of a Buddha or enlightened saint

Buddhism as the Path to Nirvana

The spiritual tradition we refer to as *Buddhism* arose from the Buddha's wish to help others realize nirvana. The Buddha emphasized the practical, goal-directed orientation of his way and urged his disciples not to engage in idle speculation or mere intellectualism. He taught that humanity comprises persons of different kinds who each have different forms of karma. According to whether they are "ordinary persons," "learners," or "adepts," each is to be instructed differently. Regardless of an individual's level, to be born as a human at all, instead of as an animal or divinity, is a rare opportunity. A human life is not to be wasted; rather, people should live with purpose, with an awareness of the reality of karma, and make efforts to get closer to the highest goal, nirvana.

Unlike the other world religions, Buddhism has but a few universally accepted doctrines. Beyond the three refuges cited at the beginning of this chapter, Buddhists have adopted varying subsets of the Buddha's teachings and rituals, always keeping the monastic community (the sangha) as its central institution. How could a world religion accommodate such pluralism in the course of establishing its essential doctrines?

First, Buddhists (like Hindus) assume that since humanity contains persons of many sorts, many different spiritual avenues are needed to reach everyone. Teachers, therefore, formulated myriad practices, and philosophers offered multiple interpretations of the truth the Buddha had revealed.

The second reason for Buddhism's pluralism lies in an instruction from the Buddha himself: After his death, no one person or institution was to be allowed to fix a single canon or set a single norm of orthodoxy in doctrinal interpretations. As a result, by 600 years after the death of Shakyamuni Buddha, several different canons of collected teachings were made and the sangha aligned under two main divisions: the

The earliest Sanchi stupa with gateway and pathway for ritual circumambulation. This hilltop center in Madhya Pradesh state, central India, was a major Buddhist pilgrimage site in ancient India.

"elder traditionalists" and the Great Vehicle. The elders, or **Sthaviravadins**, in South Asia were more numerous, and their sole surviving school is called Theravada. About 100 CE, the Theravadins collected their scriptures in the **Pali Canon**, and have taught that humanity should aspire to become enlightened arhats. *Mahayana* is the name given to the Great Vehicle division, and many schools survive today, including Pure Land and Zen, each with a great diversity of subgroups. Thus, in many respects it is quite artificial to posit a single "Buddhism" based on a common code or single text. Buddhism in popular practice among the laity, however, does show many continuities, as we will see. The first topic we will discuss is the highest ideal—nirvana.

> **Sthaviravadins:** traditionalists among early Buddhist monastic schools
>
> **Pali Canon:** The Theravada Canon written in the Pali language (derived from Sanskrit)

Nirvana

The word nirvana is based on the Sanskrit verb meaning "to cool by blowing." It refers to the blissful state entered by those who have "cooled" the fevers of greed, hatred, and delusion. These three things inflame desire, create karma, and bind the individual into **samsara**, the world of rebirth and suffering. Buddhists often present the concept

> **samsara:** the world of rebirth subject to the law of karma and the inevitability of death

of nirvana realization by likening it to the extinction of a fire, for as this phenomenon was understood in ancient India, the flames of an extinguished fire had been released to return to a diffuse, unagitated, and eternal state. The state of nirvana thus carries similar associations: freedom and existence in an eternal state beyond all material description. Both men and women, by moral living and mastering meditation, can realize nirvana through the cultivation of prajna, the direct "insight" into the nature of existence.

The Four Noble Truths

Buddha's earliest teaching, the **Four Noble Truths**, provides an analysis of the human condition as well as a diagnosis: the path toward nirvana. The biographies recount that through the realization of these truths in his own experience, Shakyamuni reached final enlightenment.

The first Noble Truth, "All life entails suffering," instructs the Buddhist not to deny disease, loss of loved ones, old age, and death. The intention of this first truth is to encourage clear, realistic observation. Even good times are inadequate, because they are only temporary. The appropriate response to this truth is to make the most of the spiritual opportunities of human birth and to show compassion (**karuna**) and loving-kindness (**maitri**) to alleviate the suffering affecting all other beings.

The second Noble Truth states, "The cause of suffering is desire." This "desire" includes possessions, power, sex, and all that human beings "thirst after." (At the advanced stages of Buddhist practice, desire for doctrinal learning and even the wish for one's own enlightenment must also be rejected to reach the final goal.) The emphasis on desire in the second truth makes plain the need for renunciation, detachment, and asceticism.

The third Noble Truth, "Removing desire removes suffering," is rooted in the central Buddhist idea that the same pattern of cyclical cause and effect, by which desire leads to further suffering, can be reversed and eventually extinguished in nirvana. The emphasis on removing desire also highlights the importance of the sangha as a refuge for individuals who wish to remove themselves from the world of desire.

The fourth Noble Truth, "The way for removing desire is to follow the Eightfold Path," specifies the Buddha's treatment that will "cure" the human condition, with its continuous cycle of rebirth, suffering, and death. As a Buddhist progresses toward enlightenment, moving through moral practice, meditation, and the cultivation of the prajna, an understanding of the Four Noble Truths deepens. There are eight specific elements in the progressive path to nirvana.

The Eightfold Path

The **Eightfold Path** outlines the necessary means for achieving the realization of nirvana:

1. *Right Views*, especially of the Noble Truths, thoughts shaped by detachment from hatred and cruelty
2. *Right Intentions*, staying committed to final realization
3. *Right Speech*, which refrains from falsehood, gossip, and frivolity

---

"The Buddha declares the Law with a single voice,
While sentient beings, each in their own way, construe the meaning."

—Vimalakirti Nirdesha Sutra

Four Noble Truths: primary doctrinal formula describing human life as marked by suffering, distorted by desire, and a path to its extinction

karuna: "compassion," the principal Buddhist social virtue

maitri: "loving-kindness," a Buddhist ethical virtue

"Compared with the man who conquers thousands in battle, the greatest warrior is the man who conquers himself. . . . If a man is strenuous, thoughtful, self-controlled, and morally disciplined, he grows immensely."

—Dhammapada

Eightfold Path: the eight qualities needed to realize nirvana

Basic Buddhist Formula: Buddhist Spiritual Progress and the Eightfold Path

MORALITY	→	MEDITATION	→	PRAJNA	→	NIRVANA
Right speech	→	Right mindfulness	→	Right views		
Right action	→	Right concentration	→	Right intentions		
Right livelihood	→	Right effort				
Social context:						
95% of community		5%		1%		exceedingly rare
						Being a "good Buddhist" for 95% of the community means living a moral life

4. *Right Action*, defined as action free of killing, stealing, and harming
5. *Right Livelihood*, the refusal to earn a living through inflicting harm or killing
6. *Right Effort*, to clear and calm the mind
7. *Right Mindfulness*, the distinctive form of Buddhist meditation that observes clearly the mind and body and that cultivates detachment
8. *Right Concentration*, another form of advanced meditation that attains the mastery of trance states

Another important arrangement of the Eightfold Path was organized according to three central categories of Buddhist practice:

Morality (Shila) entails Speech, Action, and Livelihood
Meditation (Dhyana) entails Effort, Mindfulness, and Concentration
Insight or Wisdom (Prajna) entails Views and Thought

The Eightfold Path emphasizes that moral progress is the essential foundation to successful meditation and that the measure of successful meditation is the awakening and deepening of prajna. The different elements of the path underscore Buddhism's emphasis on effectiveness in improving moral standards, practicing good conduct, promoting the material welfare of society, ridding oneself of desire, restructuring perceptions of the world, and ultimately achieving enlightenment.

The First Community and Its Development

Life in the Buddhist sangha was a true refuge for those who wished to live for spiritual purpose. Material needs of the sangha were met by householders, thus allowing the monks and nuns to meditate and study.

Texts regulating the early monks and nuns, called *Vinayas*, record how the rules of institutional life developed. For example, because the Buddha was sensitive to the state laws under which he lived, he declared criminals, runaway slaves, and army deserters ineligible to join the sangha. He also specified principles to govern the community and insisted that the sangha meet every two weeks so that each monk or nun certified his or her personal compliance. This fortnightly ritual became a central feature of life in the sangha. The Buddha's organizational genius can be seen as well in his cultivation of a householder community that provided for the needs of the sangha. It was Buddhist householders who joined the sangha, and it was the patronage of other good Buddhist householders that established the faith's monasteries and shrines across India and, over time, throughout Asia.

After the Buddha's death, in accordance with his instruction that authority over his community was not to reside in a single person or institution, the monks and nuns settled in separate colonies, which became the monastic centers that perpetuated the faith. They repeated and memorized the sets of sermons they had heard and worked out a distinctive form of communal life. Within the first three centuries there were several councils of monks that met to focus on the exact rules of monastic practice.

Although the early sanghas also found considerable common ground, none of the recorded councils ever achieved exact consensus on matters of discipline or doctrinal formulation. While dissenters practiced as they felt proper in their own monasteries, the monastic codes in the *Vinayas* are remarkably similar. Yet it was disagreements over surprisingly minor points that led to schisms. This early pattern of disciplinary autonomy and doctrinal divergence shaped the regional pluralism found across the Buddhist world right up to the present.

How Buddhism Became a World Religion

Ashoka: ruler whose patronage spread Buddhist institutions and teachings across his empire, and likely beyond

In the first two centuries after Shakyamuni's death, Buddhist monks and converts spread slowly across India. At first, they were simply one of the many shramana groups that emphasized asceticism and rejected the brahmin caste's privileged status, its ritual system, and especially its claim to hold a monopoly on advanced spiritual practice. It was **Ashoka** (273–232 BCE), an emperor of the powerful Maurya dynasty, whose support encouraged Buddhism as a broad-based religious tradition that reached beyond the ascetics. Now it was in a position to unify the social classes of Indic civilization and link the householder population with its monastic elite.

Ashoka, through his personal prestige and imperial edicts as well as the patronage of notable monks, helped spread Buddhism across most of the subcontinent. As a result, the first definite traces of Buddhist monasteries and stupa shrines can be dated to this era, as can the first systematic oral collections of the teachings. Within a century after the end of the Mauryan period, Buddhist institutions dotted the major trade routes leading from the Buddhist holy land, with major shrines, monasteries, and pilgrimage traditions developing at sites associated with the founder's life.

Buddha from Gandhara, in the upper Indus River region, where icons were made by artisans skilled in the Hellenistic style.

The expansion northwest into the upper Indus River region called **Gandhara** and into the Kashmir Valley and beyond into central Asia made these areas Buddhist strongholds for the next millennium. It was here that the Indic world had already met the Hellenic (Greek–influenced), for hundreds of settlements across the upper Indus were populated by descendants of the troops of Alexander the Great (356–323 BCE) who established small states and, in some cases, became prominent regional traders. Many converted to Buddhism. To understand Buddhism's successful rise to popularity among kings and commoners, however, we must comprehend how the sangha became the center of Buddhism across Asia.

● **Gandhara:** area of Indo-Greek interaction, influential in the creation of Buddhist art

Sangha and Monastery: The Institutional Vehicles of Buddhism's Expansion

As Buddhist monasticism spread across Asia, it introduced independent, corporate institutions that transformed local societies and regional polities. It was monasteries and shrines that rooted the faith in every locality. In ancient India, the early sangha admitted new members without regard to caste. In Buddhism's subsequent missionary migrations, acceptance into the sangha offered ordinary citizens an opportunity for spiritual seeking and educational advancement that was otherwise unavailable.

Buddhism could not have existed in society at large without the support of the householders, for it was the laity that ensured the viability of the monastic institution. Throughout the Buddhist world, laypeople made donations to the sangha to "earn merit" as a means of improving their karma and garnering worldly blessings for themselves, their families, and their communities. It was this central exchange, maintained between sangha and society, that kept Buddhism vibrant.

Varieties of Buddhist Monasticism

The typical Buddhist community had its center in a monastery (*vihara*), where monks or nuns would take their communal vows, meditate, and study. Monks also practiced medicine, performed rituals essential to the Buddhist lifestyle of the locality, and served as vihara builders and groundskeepers. Over time, distinctions developed within Buddhist monasticism. At the forest monasteries, meditation and optional ascetic practices could be undertaken (often under the leadership of a charismatic monk teacher). Monasteries in village and urban settlements offered the opportunity to blend compassionate service to the community with individual cultivation and study. A Buddhist monk or nun could move between forest villages and urban monasteries.

In many areas, the focus and inspiration for followers was a monk whose spiritual charisma and exemplary teaching ability drew monastic disciples and donations from the laity. The common biography of such monks mirrors that of Shakyamuni (the Buddha): disillusionments, renunciation, retreat to the wilderness, nirvana realization, and then a return to society to teach.

Practical Mechanisms of Expansion

Many successful monasteries expanded. The pattern was to send out monks to establish satellite institutions following the teachings of the charismatic founder, thereby perpetuating the monastic lineage. This template of Buddhist expansion extended Buddhism into unconverted zones. The resulting network of "mother-daughter" monasteries shaped alliances of all sorts, religious and otherwise, providing the pattern of new Buddhist institution building worldwide down to the present day. This institutional system also resulted in the tendency for aristocratic/dominant caste families to control local monastic lineages. Certain ethnic groups came to dominate Buddhism and, in some regions, their sanghas of "married monks" have been established for generations in specific regions of Buddhist Tibet, the Kathmandu Valley, Japan, and Sri Lanka. In other contexts, Buddhist viharas were instrumental in breaking down ethnic and class boundaries, blurring divisions between peoples, and creating transregional spiritual communities.

Rulers across Asia supported Buddhism because of its emphasis on individual morality, its rituals designed to secure prosperity for the state as well as for its leaders, and the powerful legitimization that monastics could bestow on a regime. History has also shown that states favoring Buddhism often placed controls on the sangha's development. Buddhist exponents, in turn, held up Ashoka as a model for the ideal Buddhist ruler, who today would be called a benevolent dictator. Thus leading monks in the sangha could offer those wielding political power the highest form of legitimation in the eyes of the faithful. In this manner, Buddhist doctrines, officials, and patrons permeated the secular and political lives of the societies Buddhism entered.

In places where Buddhism thrived, some monasteries in cities and villages evolved into complex institutions that were much more than refuges for ascetics. The monastery often promoted literacy by housing the only local school. Many urban monasteries also became lending institutions, appointing treasurers to see that when monies donated at shrines exceeded the sangha's requirements, the surplus was reinvested in the local community. On the trade routes especially, this practice, combined with profits from renting monastery-owned buildings to warehousing or retailing enterprises, garnered considerable income for the monastery treasuries. Such developments explain how Buddhism so often traveled across the Asian landscape on the basis of trade.

Another component in the spread of Buddhist institutions across Asia was the accumulation of lands donated by individuals and the state. Since monks were forbidden to farm, the sangha would rent out the cultivated lands it was acquiring. Whether its laborers grew rice and wheat or cultivated orchards, the monastery derived the food or cash needed for the sangha's upkeep. Until the twentieth century, in fact, many of the large Buddhist institutions were given indentured workers or slaves (usually entire families). Finally, shrines located within the monasteries would also earn income for the sangha in the form of offerings and from levies imposed on artisans who sold icons and votive amulets. All these elements made running a major monastery a demanding job and ensured that both donors and managers wielded considerable influence in the community.

These practices of "monastic landlordism," banking, and shrine management were also central to Buddhism's successful missions across Asia, creating the means to endow the faith with reliable income and a strong material culture. Buddhists attracted a following not only with their spiritual teachings but also with well-constructed, often-remarkable buildings, shrines, libraries, and image halls that complemented the Dharma. Many viharas also organized endowed charities that fed the poor and dispensed free medical care.

But there was one problem. As a practical matter, monastery autonomy and the lack of an overarching authority to regulate the monks' and nuns' obedience to the Vinaya code made political leaders the arbiters of the integrity of Buddhist institutions. These officials had to "purify the sangha" periodically—that is, remove those who were acting contrary to the Vinaya or perhaps had not entered the vihara through the proper ordination. Thus, Buddhism's strength through concentrating wealth and human resources was also its historical weakness: Viharas were vulnerable to the variability of state patronage and royal protection as well as to the devastating effects of internal corruption and civil disorder.

Buddhist monastery estate in ancient China. By the end of the first Buddhist millennium, major monasteries had become complex institutions whose wealth helped popularize the tradition.

Premodern Buddhism: The Classical Era (100–800 CE)

The Pan-Asian Expansion of Buddhism

From the beginning, Buddhism has been a missionary religion, its founder and monastic converts teaching a message directed to and thought suitable for all peoples. By the year 100 CE, Buddhism had entered China through central Asia on the silk routes. As it grew more popular and spread across East Asia over the next six centuries, monks and pilgrims traveled over land and then later on oceanic routes between the two great ancient civilizations of Asia, India, and China. The establishment of Buddhism across Asia constitutes one of the greatest instances of cross-cultural transmission and conversion in world history. Buddhism's original conceptions of space, time, psychology, and human destiny challenged indigenous notions. It also introduced a new social institution that fostered its missionary success: the land-grant monastery, whose members could be drawn from diverse social classes and live free from taxation, forced labor, or military service.

The Core Doctrines

"Enlightened beings are like lotus flowers, With roots of kindness, stems of peace, Petals of wisdom, Fragrance of moral conduct."

SOURCE: *The Flower Ornament Scripture,* translated by Thomas Cleary, from *Everyday Mind,* a Tricycle book edited by Jean Smith

Scholars emphasize the division between traditionalists (Theravada) and adherents of the Great Vehicle (Mahayana), which grew among intellectuals in Buddhism's first millennium. But for most householders, whose practice of Buddhism focused on moral living, merit making, and securing worldly blessings, there was little interest in such doctrinal complexities or philosophical differences. These householders were mainly concerned with the sangha's conformity to the Vinaya code because upright monks and nuns could be relied on for proper performance of rituals that benefited individuals and the community. In addition, householders would earn merit by making donations to the sangha itself.

From the earliest days, monks (or nuns) following very different interpretations of the Dharma coexisted under the same monastery roof. In the following section, we first consider doctrines and ethical norms that all Buddhists shared and then move on to discuss teachings that differed from school to school.

Prajna and Realizing Nirvana

Three Marks of Existence: Buddhist terms for analyzing human reality as marked by impermanence, suffering, and no soul

Necessary for the attainment of nirvana, *prajna* refers to the capacity for deep spiritual discernment. In Buddhism it means "seeing into" reality as it truly is, characterized by suffering, impermanence, and supporting the existence of those traits known as the **Three Marks of Existence.** Buddhist salvation is often referred to as "enlightenment" because prajna eliminates ignorance and completely clears the mind to see reality.

The state a Buddha or an arhat, a fully enlightened follower, achieves at death is referred to as "final nirvana." Nirvana has been described in both negative and positive terms: a deathless realm where there is neither sun nor moon, neither coming nor going, but also a state that is tranquil and pure. Most of the early scholastic treatises recognized nirvana as the only permanent reality in the cosmos. It is not to be seen as "annihilation," which is an extreme position rejected by the Buddha.

"Nonself" Doctrine

The concept of **anatman** ("no-*atman*" or "nonself") is used to reject any notion of an essential, unchanging interior entity at the center of a person. The "atman" the Buddha rejected is the indestructible soul posited in the Upanishads and subsequent Hinduism, as described in Chapter 6. Buddhist philosophers argued that the universal characteristic of impermanence, one of the Three Marks of Existence, applies to human beings. As a result they regarded the human "being" in terms of the continuously changing, interdependent relationship between the five aggregates called **skandhas**.

> **anatman**: "no-atman," the doctrine denying the reality of a permanent, immortal soul or ego at the center of a person

Buddhists see the person as a collection of the skandhas: the physical body, which is made of combinations of the four elements (earth, water, fire, air); feelings that arise from sensory contact; perceptions that attach the categories good, evil, and neutral to these sensory inputs; mental habits (*samskaras*) that connect karma-producing will to mental action; and the consciousness that arises when mind and body come in contact with the external world.

> **skandha**: "aggregate"; term used to identify each of the five main components that define a human being

The spiritual purpose of breaking down this apparently unchanging individuality is to demonstrate that there is nothing (or "no thing") to be attached to or to direct one's desire toward. The no-self concept, however, presented Buddhist doctrine with the problem of moral causality: How can the doctrine of karma, with its emphasis on compensation for one's good and bad moral decisions, operate without the mechanism of the soul? The standard explanation given is that karma endures in samskaras that are impressed in the fifth skandha, consciousness. Although always evolving and so impermanent, one's consciousness escapes the body at death and is reincarnated in the next life form.

While the no-self or no-soul doctrine was at the center of Buddhist thought for the philosophical elite, householders across Asia still typically conceived of themselves in terms of a body and a soul. This contradiction may indicate how unimportant some philosophical doctrines were to the mainstream of popular Buddhist understanding.

Impermanence and Interdependence

Another universally accepted doctrinal formula in Buddhism is one that specifies the patterns of psychic and bodily states conditioning (that is, causing) a person's bondage to suffering and rebirth. Known as **dependent**, or *conditioned*, **origination**, this doctrine views reality as ongoing, impermanent, and interdependent, visualized as a circle

> **dependent origination**: twelve-part formula explaining how individuals are bound to future rebirth until they extirpate desire and ignorance

RITUALS AND RITES: Buddhist Meditation

Then: Tradition of Monastery Meditation

Until about 150 years ago, Buddhist meditation was undertaken only by monastics and was a regular practice only by a minority of this small elite. In ancient India, monks and nuns had varying approaches to this spiritual practice: some were more inclined to textual memorization, rituals, or teaching, while others served as managers and builders of the institution's properties. Those interested in meditation worked with a spiritual mentor, from whom instructions in a specific practice was obtained, and with whom reports of progress and obstacles would be shared. The meditating monk or nun might practice in a monastery training hall, in his own cell, or in an isolated retreat. Some teachers even instructed their disciples that all

activities in daily life could be times of meditation. The traditional Buddhist meditation master would try to discern the state of a disciple's spiritual aptitude (prajna), mainly by interpreting the individual's body, speech, and mind; this caring, personal interaction provided the basis for determining how best for the individual to move forward. Meditation, in short, relied on the communal support of the monastery. Despite this variety of approaches, all are directed to the universal goals: calming the mind and discerning the real.

Now: Online Meditation Guided by Cybermonks

The Buddhist tradition's openness to cultural adaptation continues into the present. Monks, who have always had the role of teachers and scholars,

divided into twelve parts. (See diagram on page 360.) Whatever point of entry you take on this circle, the next clockwise element is the experience conditioned, and the adjacent element in the counterclockwise position is that condition directly affecting the present. Without spiritual exertion, we spin around, life after life, under these conditioning patterns. Used in this way, the twelve-fold formula reiterates the basic doctrines already cited: Craving and ignorance are the two chief causes of suffering (Noble Truths Two and Three); and the human being has no soul, only changing components of bodily life units (skandhas). This complicated formula can also be reduced to two key elements of Buddhism: the interaction of desire and ignorance that keeps humans being reborn in samsara.

Buddhist Moral Precepts

The early Buddhists specified that moral practice is the first foundation for moving toward nirvana. Buddhist ethics involves an "ideology of merit," in which making good karma and avoiding bad karma is the only sensible approach to life. Popular Buddhist stories focus on the reality of rebirth, covering thousands of lifetimes, which leads to the realization that all contemporary beings have been one's parents and children throughout a vast number of rebirths. Thus, it is both natural and logical to act

are becoming increasingly computer literate. So it is the cybermonk who is experimenting today in freeing meditation from the monastery halls. Another profound innovation in Buddhist modernism across Asia has been the democratization of meditation, and its spread to householders. To meet the needs of householders in the West who may be too far from a monastery to practice meditation in a community, contemporary monasteries and institutions now utilize the Internet to foster practice. One example is the Zen Mountain Monastery, in Woodstock, New York. Since 2003, this monastery has posted meditation instructions and a link where distant meditators can contact Cybermonk, "a senior monastic available through e-mail to answer your Dharma questions." While it is uncertain how well these initiatives can actually succeed without the face-to-face guidance of a living teacher, there is no doubt that Buddhist leaders today are embracing social media to pursue missionary outreach. As one cybermonk from Australia, Phra Pannyavaro, has written, "The new 'cyber temple' will become the meeting place for an online Buddhist community of *practitioners*. . . . There is a belief in some Buddhist traditions of a future Buddha, called Maitreya—who it is said will come to revitalise the Dhamma. I cannot honestly see how any future Buddha, or future followers of the historical Buddha, would not naturally use the available technology and be quite at ease surfing the Internet."[a]

[a]Web posting by Venerable Pannyavaro, January 17, 2017, at http://www.buddhanet.net/mag_surf.htm.

morally toward all beings. Buddhist doctrine also emphasizes the wisdom of cultivating detachment, discernment, and compassion (karuna).

The earliest moral rules the Buddha established consisted of five precepts. In South and Southeast Asia, they are chanted regularly in modern Theravada rituals by both monks and laity. In these communities, the precepts are regarded as general ideals applicable to everyone. Mahayana schools tended to regard the precepts more

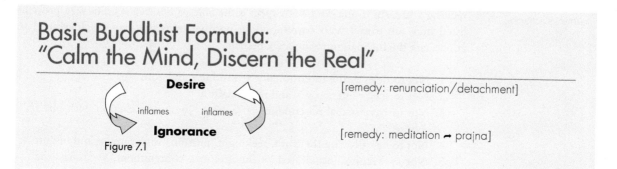

Basic Buddhist Formula: "Calm the Mind, Discern the Real"

Desire

inflames   inflames

Ignorance

Figure 7.1

[remedy: renunciation/detachment]

[remedy: meditation → prajna]

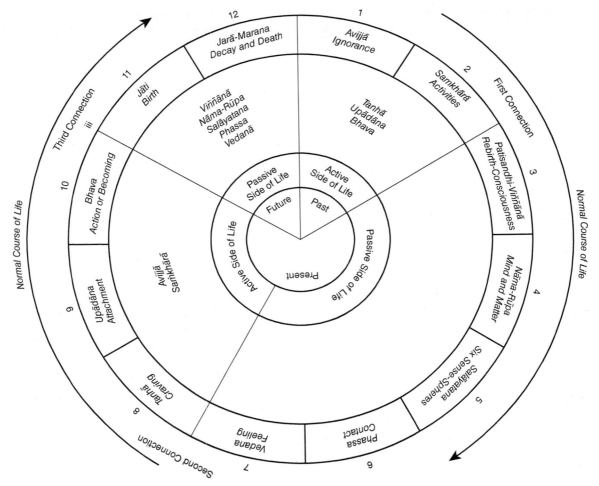

Figure 7.2 Diagram representing the formula of dependent origination, including several interpretive schemes.

as vows, to be chanted only if one intends to follow them completely. (One can omit reciting a precept if one does not expect to be able to observe it.) The five precepts listed here are paired with corresponding positive traits that can be developed to counteract the inclination to violate a precept.

1. Not to destroy life intentionally → kindness and compassion
2. Not to steal → generosity and renunciation
3. Not to have sexual misconduct → seeking "joyous satisfaction with one's spouse"
4. Not to lie → loving the truth, seeking it, pursuing discernment and insight
5. Not to become intoxicated → mindfulness, contentment, awareness via meditation

Later in the history of Buddhism, householders began to observe eight precepts on holy days, involving a stricter observance of the original five along with three additional renunciations:

6. Not to eat (solid) food after noon
7. Not to view shows, dancing, or singing or to wear garlands, perfumes, or jewelry
8. Not to sleep on high or wide beds.

In addition to the eight precepts, there is a set of ten precepts, observed by novice monks and undertaken as a long-term commitment. They comprise the eight but split one of these into two parts and add a final prohibition against handling money. This final rule was made to ensure that begging for food would be the norm for monks and nuns, an exchange between laity and sangha that bound together the Buddhist community.

Karma and Causality

Karma doctrine should not be seen as only weakly fatalistic, as it does determine the form of rebirth. But since one is continually making new **punya** ("merit") or **pap** ("demerit"), this changes the ongoing outcome of karmic destiny. Buddhist karma analysis holds that some good actions (e.g., building a monastery) and bad actions (e.g., harming one's parents) lead to powerful repercussions in the future, in either this life or the next. Nevertheless, the larger reality is that a person's karma, like all phenomena, changes every instant.

> **punya:** "merit"; good karma earned by moral practices, learning, and meditation
>
> **pap:** "demerit"; bad karma earned by breaking the precepts

Further, the Buddhist understanding of causality is that not all occurrences in life are karma dependent. In fact, events are more likely than not to have had causes other than karma. Since only Buddhas can ascertain whether karma or something else is at work in ongoing life, individuals are faced with uncertainty in evaluating events. Buddhists make a "general reading" of karma from the traits discerned at birth (e.g., family status, on the body). To be prepared for the future, however, the logic of the karma doctrine has motivated Buddhists everywhere to cultivate a lifelong practice of making punya and seeking guidance throughout life from astrology. Indeed, texts for householders emphasize that accumulation of wealth is the fruition of good past karma and that giving away wealth to earn merit is the best human expenditure. This giving, of benefit to all, is in a sense the social application of the Buddha's teaching about interdependence. These principles have been incorporated into Four Conditions and **Four Good Deeds**, doctrinal statements that have been as influential for the laity as the Four Noble Truths were for monks and philosophers:

> **Four Good Deeds:** doctrinal formula guiding the laity on the uses of wealth

Four Conditions (to seek)

Wealth gotten by lawful means
Good renown in society
Long life
Birth in heaven

Four Good Deeds (to use wealth for)

Make family and friends happy

Ensure security against worldly dangers

Make offerings to family, friends, gods, and ghosts

Support worthy religious people

The core doctrines we have discussed—prajna and nirvana, anatman (nonself), impermanence and interdependence, and karma causality—comprise the most common foundation for Buddhist belief. For householders, these ideas translate into fostering family ties, striving for economic success, making offerings to hungry ghosts and local gods, pursuing worldly happiness and security, nurturing faith, and seeking heaven.

Now we consider how in specific places and times individual Buddhists and Buddhist communities have focused on these teachings that affect individual life.

The Classical Ideal: Buddhist Civilization

Buddhist civilization was sustained by ritual exchanges between householders and renunciants, the monks and nuns who had abandoned worldly comforts. Many formulations of proper Buddhist practice were made in the course of early Buddhist history to guide the faithful among the spiritual alternatives specified by the Buddha. The triad of moral practice (*shila*), meditation (*dhyana*), and insight cultivation (*prajna*) was an early organizing schema, as we noted in our discussion of the Eightfold Path.

Buddhist monasticism arose to provide refuge and support for renunciants seeking enlightenment, but the tradition survived through relationships with lay followers who provided for the monks' and nuns' subsistence. Drawing on the loyalty of a cross section of all classes, Buddhists laid the foundations for a society with spiritual and moral dimensions. Buddhism adapted to myriad local traditions, yet its community remained focused on the **Three Refuges**: the Buddha, the Dharma (the teachings), and the Sangha (the monastic community).

Three Refuges: the Buddha, the Dharma, and the Sangha

The general ideals of Buddhist civilization were in place very early. Monks and nuns served the world through their example of renunciation and meditation, by performing rituals, and by providing medical services. As preservers, transmitters, and exemplars of the Dharma, the sangha's duty was to attract the lay community's merit-making donations by being spiritually worthy; complementing this, sangha members were to follow the *Vinaya* rules and seek out sympathizers and donors. Based on these guidelines, Buddhist societies came to exhibit common traits: relic shrines as centers of community ritual and economy; monasteries as refuges for meditation, study, and access to material resources; and sangha members who assumed leadership of the community's spiritual instruction and ritual life.

Thus, Buddhism successfully developed a broad vision of the spiritual community and of proper practice. The devout layperson's duty is to help others grow in faith, morality, knowledge, and charity, to live a life worthy of his or her family heritage, and

TEACHINGS OF RELIGIOUS WISDOM: Teachings on Compassionate Living

Given that the First Noble Truth holds that "all life is suffering," then it follows that all Buddhists should do whatever possible to alleviate it and should open their hearts to others. This underlies the universal Buddhist moral emphasis on compassion.

Thus as a mother with her life will guard her son, her only child, let him extend unboundedly his heart to every living being. And so with loving-kindness for all the world, let him extend unboundedly his heart, above, below, around, unchecked, with no ill will or hate.

—The Buddha[a]

In everything you do, simply work at developing love and compassion until they become a fundamental part of you. That will serve the purpose, even if you do not practice the more outward and conspicuous forms of Dharma, such as chanting, virtuous activities, and altruistic works. As a Sutra states, "Let those who desire Buddhahood not train in many Teachings but only one. Which one? Great Compassion. Those with great compassion possess all the Buddha's teaching as if it were in the palm of the hand."

—Tibetan monk and teacher Patrul Rimpoche (1808–87)[b]

[a]*Samyutta Nikāya* (1, 8).
[b]*Words of My Perfect Teacher*, trans. Padmakara Translation Group (1998), pp. 209–10.

to make offerings to the spirits of the dead. The Buddha also revealed short texts (called *mantra*) that, when chanted, help householders achieve material blessings and protections. Given the variety of possible practices, the only sound definition of a "good Buddhist" is simple: one who takes the Three Refuges and practices accordingly.

The Mahayana: Philosophies and East Asian Monastic Schools

Mahayana philosophers and followers were a minority in ancient South Asia, for monks of this persuasion lived in monasteries alongside Sthaviravadins, the predecessors of today's Theravadins. Mahayana only became the "Great Vehicle," the dominant form of Buddhism and the center of a vibrant subculture, in the last era of Buddhism in India (700 CE until its extinction) as well as in Burma, and the Khmer, Indonesian, and Funan regions of medieval Southeast Asia until around 1300 CE.

The contrast between traditionalists (Theravadins) and Mahayanists seems to reflect a universal human tendency to divide religious communities between those inclined to a literal, conservative approach and those inclined to a more open-ended and experimental approach to spiritual matters. The Mahayana in this light might be compared to the Sufis in Islam, opposed to the strict scholars of the law (ulama); the Christian analogy would be the mystics in opposition to the official medieval church.

We shall discuss the Madhyamaka and Consciousness Only schools of Mahayana thought (as well as some minority schools that happen to be well known today) and a tradition called the Thunderbolt Vehicle.

The Madhyamaka

Among the earliest texts expressing Mahayana ideas are those called the *Perfection of Wisdom* (*Prajnaparamita*). In these texts, comments attributed to the Buddha or notable monks poke fun at the Theravadin arhats and seek to undermine their scholasticism. More importantly, however, the *Prajnaparamita* texts represent a search for the ultimate truth behind the words of the oldest Buddhist scriptures. Since Mahayana thought emphasizes interdependence, its exponents saw the Theravadins' focus on an individual's pursuit of nirvana as "selfish" and therefore ignorant of the Buddha's highest teaching. Most Mahayana exponents held that the laity as well as monks could potentially attain enlightenment.

Nagarjuna: influential analytical philosopher of the Mahayana school

Madhyamaka: Mahayana philosophical school whose goal is to clear away all attachments, making realization possible

shunyata: "zero-ness"; the term used to designate the emptiness of all constructs

Opposition to the Theravadins coalesced in the writings of the monk **Nagarjuna** (born ca. 150 CE), one of India's greatest philosophers and founder of the **Madhyamaka** school. Nagarjuna developed a method that reduces all assertions to arbitrary propositions. He argued that all language is conventional and that all classifications set up by language are mere constructions. In other words, language is "samsaric"; using it uncritically to understand reality inevitably warps the mind with samsara's desires and ignorance. In one of the most courageous explorations in the history of religions, even Buddhist terms like *nirvana* and *samsara*, Nagarjuna argued, are mere words. It is through understanding how humans construct reality arbitrarily, positing a "self" and then a "world of things" separate from it, that one reaches a core realization that reality is empty or **shunya** of any "thing" the mind can construe. Through this insight, one can "see into" all illusions and desires, become free from attachments, and find release from the cycle of rebirths. Nagarjuna's aim was to clear away all false assumptions and even the subtle attachment to language and scholastic categories, thus opening the way to Buddhist meditation practices that transcend words in order to reach true refuge and final enlightenment.

"Consciousness Only" School

Cittamatra: Mahayana philosophical school that focuses on consciousness as the center of spiritual realization

The other major school of Mahayana thought continued to develop the Great Vehicle from Nagarjuna's standpoint. The "Consciousness Only" (**Cittamatra**) school largely agreed with the Madhyamaka view of experience as empty but asserted that spiritual transformation can therefore be achieved within human consciousness. This school's great thinkers were the brothers Asanga and Vasubandhu (active ca. 380 CE), who developed theories of consciousness and causality. They described how karma works within the stream of consciousness, where past actions may block pure, passionless seeing. Further, the spiritual life must be devoted to purifying mind or consciousness, since this is all that truly exists. Again, the practical effect of such theories was to promote the traditional Buddhist practice of meditation, as indicated by another name often applied to this faction: *Yogacara*, or "yoga practice," school.

Buddha-Nature School

Buddha-nature school: Mahayana belief that all beings possess the potential for enlightenment

Another Mahayana philosophy emerged in East Asia: the **Buddha-nature** (*tathagatagarbha*) **school**. Its proponents held that if it is true that nirvana and samsara

Manjushri, the bodhisattva of scholars, who holds a lotus containing a Prajnaparamita text in one hand, and in the other a sword symbolizing the prajna that cuts through ignorance and delusion.

cannot be separated in any meaningful way, then nirvana must inter-penetrate all reality. And if this is so, one might say that all beings have a portion of nirvana and so possess the potential for its realization. Even the tiniest thing, they believed, contains the mystery of the universe. Although support for a school centered on this doctrine eventually declined in China, its ideas and meta-phors influenced a Mahayana tradition in East Asia called *Ch'an* in China, *Sŏn* in Korea, and *Zen* in Japan.

The Lotus Sutra and Celestial Bodhisattvas

One of the most popular Buddhist scriptures in East Asia was the **Lotus Sutra**. Originally written in Sanskrit by 100 CE, the *Lotus* develops the Mahayana doctrine of cosmic Buddhahood through parables, accounts of astounding magical display, and hammering polemics. The *Lotus* describes how the Buddha's preaching skill-fully adapted the Dharma to suit the level of the audiences. Even his dying was a show, performed to encourage the active practice of devotees so that they would take seriously the shortness of mortal life. The *Lotus* asserts that the nirvana of arhats is incomplete, merely a preliminary stage in enlightenment seeking. Rather, all beings are destined for Buddhahood through eons of rebirth in samsara.

The religious ideal in the *Lotus Sutra* and in other Mahayana texts shifts from the arhat to the **bodhisattva**, or "future Buddha." Disciples following the Great Vehi-cle are encouraged not to be satisfied with the arhats' limited nirvana, when Buddhahood is the proper, final religious goal for all. Why? Mahayana teachers point out that given the reality of interdependence, no individual can be an enlightened "being" some-how independent of others. Bodhisattvas should therefore not imagine ending their careers until all beings are enlightened, a mind-boggling and very long-term commitment.

The *Lotus Sutra* is only one of many texts that focus on bodhisattvas who have earned the merit necessary to earn rebirth as divinities. These "celestial bodhisattvas" continue to serve humanity by offering compassionate intervention to secure worldly blessings and even the means to salvation. In the popular imagination,

Lotus Sutra: early Mahayana text that reveals the universal cosmic character of Buddhas and the Dharma

bodhisattva: a "future Buddha," either in the present life or in a future life

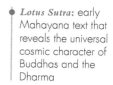

Tara, the popular female bodhisattva who is believed to have arisen from the tears of compassion from Avalokiteshvara.

Avalokiteshvara/
Guanyin: celestial
Mahayana bodhisattva,
popular across Asia

by the end of the faith's first millennium they had become the Buddhist parallels to Hindu or Chinese deities. The most popular and universal celestial bodhisattva was **Avalokiteshvara**, who came to be known as **Guanyin** in China, *Kannon* in Japan, *Chenrizi* in Tibet, and *Karunamaya* in Nepal. Wherever Mahayana Buddhism spread, texts recounting the compassionate deeds of this always kind divine being were spread by storytellers, art, and popular texts. For the great majority of Buddhists in East Asia, being a Mahayana devotee meant performing rituals and asking for blessings from these and other compassionate bodhisattva divinities.

Pure Land Schools

Pure Land: a paradise
for rebirth created by
a bodhisattva, where
humans can achieve
enlightenment

Pure Land Buddhism arose in India, around 300 CE. This school's texts describe how certain bodhisattvas vowed to create celestial paradises on reaching Buddhahood. In these "Pure Lands," there existed all the conditions needed for the individual to be reborn and reach enlightenment. The popularity of this Buddhist orientation, which deferred enlightenment seeking from the human state until rebirth in a heaven, probably had its origins in Shakyamuni's predictions of Buddhism's decline after a thousand years. This expectation allowed for a new spirituality to match the changed times.

Amitabha/Amida:
celestial Buddha whose
Pure Land became
the most popular in
East Asia

The most important of the Pure Land schools was that associated with the western paradise called *Sukhavati*, skillfully created by a Buddha named **Amitabha** in Sanskrit (*Amitofo* in Chinese, **Amida** in Japanese). A system of Pure Land doctrine and practice developed in China and featured the chanting of Amitabha's name as a meditative act and communal ritual. Exponents assured Pure Land followers that by drawing on this Buddha's distinctive cosmic power through chanting and other devotional practices, even those with bad karma could be reborn in Sukhavati.

The Bodhisattva Vow:
"May I be a protector
for the unprotected

A guide for wanderers

A boat, a bridge, a
causeway for those
who desire the other
shore

A lamp for those who
need light."

—Shantideva's
Bodhicaryavatara

Avalokiteshvara, the most popular celestial bodhisattva in the Mahayana tradition. In this sculpture from Tibet, the 1,008 arms convey the divinity's tireless quest to aid those who suffer in samsara.

In Japan, Pure Land Buddhism continued to evolve as devotees were taught that their own "self power" was insufficient to reach nirvana and only the "other power" of celestial Buddhas and bodhisattvas could be relied on. Rituals at death were dedicated to having an individual's lifetime accumulation of merit (punya) be directed to attaining rebirth in the Pure Land. Over the years these schools expanded, and hopes for Pure Land rebirth became extremely popular among the laity. Pure Land schools were also the first to deemphasize the requirement of monastic celibacy by its ordained sangha.

The Meditation School: Ch'an/Zen

By about 600 CE, a Mahayana school called **Ch'an** had formed in China. In contrast to the Pure Land emphasis on "other power," the Ch'an insisted that individual effort to reach nirvana was the Buddha's true teaching. Ch'an masters stressed meditation, this-life realization, and "self power." This school still bases its authority on an unbroken line of enlightened teachers from Shakyamuni onward, with each subsequent enlightened master, in turn, transmitting a "mind of enlightenment" to his key disciple wordlessly, beyond all scriptures.

Less concerned with a single text and formed in close association with Daoist concepts and aesthetics (see Chapter 8), Ch'an lineages respected the Mahayana scriptures but also compiled their own texts recounting the teachings of their own patriarchs and masters, including their approaches to unlocking the gates of nirvana realization. This school also developed the use of paradoxical word problems called **koans** ("cases") that masters forced their disciples to ponder and answer. Answering the koans could lead to small awakenings of prajna or even to complete nirvana realization. Ch'an masters also insisted on the necessity of mindfulness meditation.

The most important figure of this school is Bodhidharma, the patriarch who is said to have brought the mind-to-mind transmission tradition from India to China, early in the seventh century CE. He is depicted as a fierce meditating monk dispensing terse spiritual admonitions. Later known as **Zen** in Japan, the Ch'an school also developed in monasteries upholding strict monastic rules. Its lineages eventually split along the line of those believing in gradual versus sudden enlightenment.

The Thunderbolt Vehicle: Vajrayana

One additional branch to emerge among Mahayana Buddhists was the **Vajrayana**, the **Thunderbolt Vehicle**, a tradition that some scholars would consider to be distinct from the Mahayana school. Also called *tantra* and similar to the Hindu tradition of that name, it developed after the faith's first millennium in South Asia. Perhaps in reaction to the complacency stemming from the mainstream view that final enlightenment would not be achieved until after many future lifetimes, the tantric traditions emphasized the rapid realization of salvation in this lifetime. It was also an esoteric tradition, meaning that it was not public or openly shared but was passed on directly only to those the tantric teacher thought to be capable of understanding and practicing.

Ch'an/Zen: Mahayana school emphasizing meditation, discipline, and individual effort to reach nirvana

koan: spiritual riddle used by Zen teachers to foster spiritual growth

"Unless you enter the great ocean of passions, you cannot get the treasure of full knowledge."
—*Vimalakirti Nirdesha Sutra*

Vajrayana/ Thunderbolt Vehicle: esoteric "vehicle" emphasizing practices that speed progress toward enlightenment

Milarepa, the great tantric saint of Tibet, whose songs are beloved for conveying the struggles of solitary meditation and the joy of enlightenment.

"That by which the world is bound, by that same energy its bonds are released; But the world is deluded and knows not this truth, and he who is deprived of this truth will not gain Enlightenment."

—*Hevajra Tantra*

Tantric Buddhism used Indian yoga techniques and unconventional means under the guidance of an accomplished teacher, and it drew on the Mahayana philosophy that equated samsara with nirvana. It agreed that all beings partake of the Buddha nature (*tathagatagarbha*), and identified the essence of the Buddha's teaching as the pursuit of unshakable, diamond-like insight by whatever means brought immediate success.

The central experience of tantric Buddhism is communion with a celestial Buddha or bodhisattva through the experience of identification with his or her body, speech, and mind. The sage who discovered each path is thought to have experienced this deity as the embodiment of enlightenment. Thus an initiate is taught to place the deity in his or her mind's eye, repeat mantras that resonate with that form, and perform rituals that help to solidify the identification. When complete, one's identification ultimately leads to the attainment of enlightenment equal to that of the divine form.

Some tantric traditions consciously break the norms of orthodox caste society. Men and women assume identities as divine, enlightened consorts, and their sexual union is developed as a unifying experience of the dual energies of the feminine (as insight) and the masculine (as means of practice). Sexual consort yoga was doubtless once an element in some tantric traditions. But as these traditions were systematized in textual form by Buddhist monks after 900 CE in North India, the requirement of literal sexual yoga practice was reinterpreted to allow its replacement by symbolic visualization.

Tantric icon showing visualization of salvific insight and skillful practice as the union of female and male siddhas.

Premodern Buddhism: Buddhist Expansion (400–1500 CE)

As Buddhism expanded across Asia up to the early modern era, in each cultural region monks, nuns, and disciples adapted the traditions to local cultural conditions. Across Asia, all the sanghas developed Buddhist rituals to help individuals through their lives, from birth to death. In applying the faith's resources to fulfilling the religious needs of the householders, monks and nuns from all Buddhist doctrinal schools served their lay communities in a similar manner. We will now survey the wide-ranging, trans-Asian pilgrimage of Buddhism, noting the history of the faith's evolution and the distinctive beliefs and practices that characterize its regional adaptations.

South Asia

With the decline of the great Gupta dynasty in North India by 650 CE, small regional governments controlled the Hindu-Buddhist societies of South Asia. Buddhism survived mainly in the northeast under royal patronage, its presence confined largely to monasteries that had also come to function as institutions of learning.

After Buddhism's successful transplantation in China, Sri Lanka, and Southeast Asia, monks and householders traveled to study in South Asia and to acquire texts. They also completed pilgrimage visits, venerating the "sacred traces" (cremation relics, begging bowls, etc.) of the Buddha and arhats whose remains were entombed in the stupas. The Buddha's enlightenment tree in Gaya and the temple erected nearby were at the center of such visits. As Indic Buddhism declined, pious rulers from Sri Lanka and Burma sent funds and artisans to renovate the Gaya site. By 1296, when the last such donations were recorded, almost every Buddhist monastery in the Gangetic plain had been abandoned and many shrines had been left to decay. The decline of the faith in South Asia was due partly to the successful development of popular devotional Hinduism and by the Hindu monasticism organized by the saint-scholar Shankara, whose Advaita Vedanta school we discussed in Chapter 6.

Another factor in Buddhism's decline was the arrival in South Asia of Islam, another missionary faith that slowly spread throughout the region. By 750 CE, Muslim conquests and conversions to Islam in central Asia and in northwestern India were undermining the predominance of Buddhism. As we have seen, Buddhist monasticism was strongly tied to trade and mercantile patronage; and as the trade moving along the silk routes shifted to Muslim merchants, the monasteries lost a major source of support. In addition, an era of raids into North India culminated in 1192 in the first period of Muslim rule from Delhi. Across the northern plains, most remaining Buddhist institutions were plundered, and the destruction dispersed Indian monks into the Himalayas, to coastal urban centers, and across the seas. In the southern peninsula of the Indian subcontinent, Buddhism also declined slowly, but scattered monasteries existed there as late as the seventeenth century.

Buddhism's dominant region now shifted to East Asia. Because many early versions of the first Buddhist textual collections had been lost, each school settled on surviving texts and scholastic traditions to establish its own doctrinal authority. In East Asia, China became the center of Mahayana Buddhism. The cross-fertilization of Buddhism across Asia was further complicated after 1250, when Tibetan Buddhists exerted strong influences within China, south into the Himalayas, and north into Mongolia.

The island of Sri Lanka embraced Buddhism, and its early kings after 100 BCE supported the sangha and built monuments to express their devotion. Although both Mahayanists and Sthaviravadins practiced there throughout the first millennium, the Theravada school eventually prevailed. The "reforms" instituted by various Southeast Asian kings in the 1300s drew on respected Sri Lankan monks who came to reintroduce Theravada ordination and philosophical traditions. From this time onward, Theravada has remained the dominant tradition in Burma, Siam (now Thailand), and both Laos and Cambodia.

China

In East Asia, Mahayana Buddhism alone flourished, translated in terms compatible with Daoist mysticism, the indigenous gods, and aspects of Confucian morality and state governance (see Chapter 8).

Under the weak regional states of the pre-T'ang era (up until 645 CE), Buddhism found widespread support. Indian and Central Asian monks had begun a determined project of translating the hundreds of Buddhist texts into Chinese. In addition, monks, merchants, and rulers had obtained many precious relics and had them enshrined in monasteries across China. Finally, Chinese Buddhists came to recognize **Wu Tai Shan**, one of China's sacred mountains, as the home of Manjushri, one of Mahayana Buddhism's chief celestial bodhisattvas. This belief grew as devotees who made pilgrimages to this site had powerful meditative visions of this future Buddha. (So strong was belief in Wu Tai Shan's holiness that its fame spread back to India; Chinese annals note that hundreds of Indian pilgrims traveled to China to seek Manjushri's spiritual blessings there!) Through textual transmission, the location of relics in monastic shrines across the country, and the pilgrimages at this (and other) sacred mountains, Asia was unified by Buddhism.

With the consolidation of the T'ang state in Chang-an (modern Xian) and its revival of the traditional Confucian literati class, the destiny of Buddhism rose and fell according to the degree of support from the reigning emperor and his court. Despite the generosity of imperial patrons and wealthy donors who profited from trade along the Silk Road, many Confucian officials in permanent state bureaucracy criticized Buddhism. They argued that monks and nuns were disloyal to parents, country, and

Wu Tai Shan: sacred mountain in China revered as home of the bodhisattva Manjushri

Images of the corpulent and happy Maitreya, the next Buddha, called Mi-lo Fo in China, are popular in East Asia.

ancestors, asserting as well that the rising wealth of the monasteries weakened the overall economy.

Anti-Buddhist sentiment culminated in the great persecution of 841–45. Nearly every Buddhist monastery was dismantled, metal images were melted down for the state treasury, and renunciants were ordered to return to lay life. Buddhism eventually rebuilt and rebounded, but the faith never permeated Chinese society so thoroughly again. From the Sung era onward, it was the Ch'an and Pure Land schools that survived, being less dependent on official recognition or aristocratic patronage. Leading monks repositioned the faith in Chinese society by stressing the compatibility of Buddhism with Daoism and Confucianism.

During the short-lived Mongol conquest of China marking the Yuan dynasty (1271–1368), Tibetan Buddhism became the state religion and its distinctive Mahayana-Vajrayana traditions were granted strong support across the empire, primarily in imperial strongholds. The Mongols' conversion to Buddhism, soon after their thirteenth-century campaigns of violent conquest across Eurasia, marks another point at which Buddhism changed world history, in this case by undercutting Mongol martial values and expansionism.

With the return of native Chinese rule under the Ming (1392–1644), Mahayana traditions were embraced by a large sector of the population: worship of the celestial bodhisattva Guanyin; veneration of the sixteen saints designated as protectors of Buddhism until the coming of the next Buddha; and the practice of releasing animals (typically fish or birds) to earn merit. The corpulent form of the next Buddha **Maitreya** (Chi: **Mi-lo Fo**) appeared as a distinctively Chinese image. From the early Ming, too, the practice of householders keeping detailed merit account books gained in popularity. In China as elsewhere, merit-making and ritual observances dominated the religious life of most Buddhists.

Maitreya/Mi-lo Fo: the next historical Buddha, uniquely depicted in China as corpulent and happy

Southeast Asia

Southeast Asia after 1200 was ruled by regional states that supported the Theravada Buddhist monastic system introduced from Sri Lanka. Buddha relics were imported as well, and stupas in the Sri Lankan style were built across the region. The "reforms" already mentioned effectively reduced the presence of the Mahayana to a few isolated communities, and all of these eventually disappeared. However, the Khmer state for several periods was ruled by kings who favored Hinduism and Mahayana Buddhism, and they constructed magnificent temples and monasteries.

From the early eighth century, the large and prosperous Srivijaya Empire in Sumatra and Java also supported both Hinduism and Mahayana Buddhism. These rulers created the colossal stupa at Borobodur, the crowning monument of this era. But with the empire's decline in the thirteenth century, the smaller states ruled by regional kings favored local religions or (later) the schools of Islam originating in India.

Yet in the majority of the Southeast Asian polities, it was Theravada Buddhism that thrived under rulers who claimed legitimacy under the cosmic law of karma (that is, their past merit entitled them to rule in the present). Their states supported the sangha and sponsored rituals designed to have the powers of the Buddhist universe continually regenerated. In turn, they expected the people to emulate their example by following the Dharma, supporting a just Buddhist order in the territory, and accepting their place in the karma-determined social hierarchy. The many hundreds of grand stupas, image halls, and monasteries built in these prosperous states show the success of premodern Theravada Buddhism. Across Theravadin Southeast Asia, this form of "state Buddhism" survived even after the kingdoms of the premodern era gave way to smaller regional states. However, this form of traditional, hierarchical Buddhism was to be challenged in the modern era as new ideas and political systems emerged.

Japan

Dogen: Japanese monk; founder of Soto Zen school

Eisai: Japanese monk; founder of Rinzai Zen school

Nembutsu: chant of Pure Land Buddhists, reflecting aspiration for rebirth in a paradise

Mahayana Buddhism was adopted across East Asia, originally reaching Japan in the seventh century. By 1230, Japanese monks again had traveled to China to undertake the last transplantations of Chinese schools: two forms of the Ch'an became the Soto Zen school (instituted by the monk **Dogen** [1200–1253]) and the Rinzai Zen school (under the monk **Eisai** [1141–1215]). Both vied for popularity among the aristocrats and warriors who controlled Japanese society in the post-Kamakura era (after 1350).

The Pure Land school also found widespread acceptance through the public preaching campaigns undertaken by monks. Since their simplification of Buddhist practice entailed only the **Nembutsu**, the chant "*Namo A-mi-t'o Fo*," the honorific repetition of Amitabha Buddha's name, householders could hope for nirvana in Pure Land rebirth. A thirteenth-century Japanese monk named Shinran continued the basic rituals and textual interpretations from Chinese Pure Land teachers and added emphasis on *mappo*, the so-called decadent-age doctrine. Shinran argued that human beings were now completely dependent on the Buddha's grace to reach nirvana and had

Archaeological remains of Pagan (Myanmar), one of the greatest Buddhist cities in the world between 1000 and 1400 CE.

simply to acknowledge their grateful acceptance of it to elicit Amida's grace and enter the Pure Land. Shinran's Jodo Shinshu school became a vital separate lineage, and its sangha was the first in Japan to drop the requirement of celibacy.

A third track in this era of new Japanese schools is represented by **Nichiren** (1222–82), a prophetic and charismatic monk who taught that the *Lotus Sutra* is the only true Buddhist text. Practice in the Nichiren school was simplified to three devotional acts: a short honorific repetition of the *Lotus Sutra*'s title (*Nam-Myoho Reng-e Kyo*), meditation on an image of the cosmic Buddha designed by Nichiren, and pilgrimage to the school's national shrine. Later, the monk's followers taught that Nichiren himself was a bodhisattva. Their interpretation of Buddhism emphasized Japan's special significance in leading Buddhism through the declining stage of history, a visionary view that endured to inspire several splinter movements in the modern and postwar eras.

Nichiren: Japanese monk who taught that the *Lotus Sutra* is the only true Buddhist text

The Himalayan Region

In Tibet, Mongolia, and Nepal, Mahayana schools also dominated. Vajrayana traditions came to be regarded as the Buddha's highest teaching. Monks who introduced Buddhism in this region taught that Buddhist belief and practice have both outer and inner levels of understanding, the highest of which was accessible only through tantric initiation and practice. Tibetan scholars translated, commented on, and interpreted

"In short, at all times and all occasions be not separated from these three, namely devotion to your teachers, an open heart to the world and all it contains, and compassion to sentient beings."

—Dolpo Lama's advice

"Nichiren confuses his enemies," a woodcut print by Utagawa Kinuyoshi (1798–1861). Nichiren's disciples followed the teacher's example of practicing aggressive missionary exposition, a trend that has marked the school up to the present.

scores of Sanskrit texts. Ritual masters also applied the texts and teachings to many aspects of life, designing rituals to promote health, prosperity, and the best possible rebirth. Even flags, watermills, and hand-turned wheels were adapted to broadcast the Buddha's teaching, continuously earning merit for individuals and communities.

In Tibet, too, the celestial bodhisattva doctrine was made more accessible to the laity: Extraordinary monks and nuns came to be identified as incarnations of these divinities, and after 1250 these "incarnate lineages" became institutions endowed with lands and households, even assuming power as both religious and political leaders of their regions. Allied with the military might of the Mongols, leaders of the major Tibetan monasteries ascended to rule over central Tibet, a situation unprecedented in any other Buddhist society. The **Gelugpa** school, under the Dalai and Panchen Lamas, came to rule Tibet in 1642, concentrating secular and religious power in its large, land-owning monasteries. Roughly 20 percent of the male population were monks.

Gelugpa: monastic school that came to politically dominate all others by 1640; its head, the Dalai Lama, ruled Tibet until 1959

Buddhism and Modernity

The current condition of Buddhism across Asia is the result of its institutional development and how the tradition evolved in very different social, political, and cultural contexts. The monastic institution that always has been at the center of Buddhist communities faced daunting challenges in the colonial era, while the different crises, influences, and possibilities in each region led to different historical tracks. The general pattern of Buddhism's adaptation in all societies, the diversity that resulted, and the exchanges between monastics and householders that sustained it, are central to this story.

The Potala in Lhasa, Tibet, was the palace of the Dalai Lamas from 1649 until 1959, when the fourteenth Dalai Lama went into exile.

Early Modern Buddhist Polities: Monastics, Householders, Kings

One decisive factor in Buddhist history has been the relation between the institutional religion and political power, a recurring source of controversy from the colonial period until the present. Buddhists have always looked to the legend of Ashoka to define their relationship with rulers as protectors and patrons. Only with such support can the sangha's integrity be ensured, the Buddha's monuments maintained, and the teachings passed down.

For most of its history, the Buddhist sangha has existed in polities ruled by kings or emperors. As a result, a mutually beneficial tradition developed: The sangha adopted rules in harmony with those of states and would applaud exemplary moral leadership on the part of the monarch. In premodern times, monastic Buddhism usually served to promote social stability, accommodating itself to local traditions. The monks also chanted mantras and performed merit-making rituals on behalf of rulers, a custom that continues in modern Japan, Thailand, and Nepal.

Buddhist Monasticism

A monastery (vihara) can be of humble construction or built to imperial, aristocratic standards. Each, however, must have a place for the monks to sleep and a building in which they hold gatherings. Monasteries may also have shrines with Buddha images, one or more stupas, a "bodhi tree," and a meditation hall.

The subsistence of the monks and nuns has remained dependent on the donations of food and shelter by the lay community. Originally, all sangha members gathered their food in morning begging rounds, and the day's solid food had to be eaten by noon. By the modern period, however, Buddhists had developed various routines: In some places members of the laity would come to the monastery on a rotating schedule with food donations; in other places, monks cooked their own foods. Many Mahayana monasteries of East Asia interpreted the moral rules to require vegetarianism of the monks and nuns, but in recent centuries the restriction against alcohol was taken by most to mean "no intoxication," not complete abstinence.

Meditation Practices

Meditation remained essential only for those aspirants, lay and renunciant, actively seeking to move on the final path to nirvana. This practice by monks and nuns, even if only a few, certifies Buddhism's continuing spiritual vitality, inspiring layfolk to respect and take refuge in the sangha. Until the modern era, however, it was almost entirely the elite among monks and nuns who practiced meditation.

Although Buddhism inherited the ancient Indian practice of trance (*samadhi*), as this state does not lead to nirvana realization, it is not given highest priority. The key practice is called *mindfulness meditation* (***vipassana* meditation**): a careful attending to, or being mindful of, the three characteristics of existential reality—suffering (*dukkha*), impermanence (*anitya*), and nonself (*anatman*).

The practice as taught today is simple: While focusing awareness on the breath, the practitioner lets go of all intervening thoughts. This opens up an awareness of the "inner life" we normally ignore. With such heightened awareness, mindfulness meditation shows how suffering and change are inevitable, nourishes personal detachment that diminishes desire, and cultivates the spiritual insight (prajna) that dispels ignorance. The development of prajna and the removal of ignorance eliminate bad karma and create good karma. Perfection eventually leads to the fullness of prajna in a breakthrough, transformative experience of an enlightened mind (*bodhi*).

Mahayana meditations elaborated on these precedents. Ch'an or Zen mindfulness meditation focuses first on the breath. Given the Mahayana teaching that all beings possess the Buddha nature, meditation can comprise any activity practiced with mindfulness, from walking to martial arts to arranging flowers.

vipassana **meditation:** Buddhist meditation practice focusing on breath and body

Japanese and Brazilian monks meditate and chant to bless the Copan Building in downtown São Paulo, Brazil, in 2010. Increasingly, converts and Asian monastics are members of the same sangha.

In Pure Land meditation, the fervent wish to attain nirvana in an otherworldly western paradise (*Sukhavati*) encourages devotees to visualize that paradise as described in the texts. These practices are especially important as death nears, for individuals who can visualize this realm are promised painless passage into heavenly rebirth through the boundless grace of the Buddha Amitabha.

Schools devoted to esoteric Vajrayana innovations developed yet other forms of meditation under the heading of *sadhana*. These tantric practices are based on mind's-eye visualizations of enlightened bodhisattvas and mantra recitations to jump-start spiritual development. By controlling the appearance of mental images, one sees all experience as mind-constructed and thus empty (*shunya*) of any ultimate reality.

Again, however, it is necessary to emphasize that most Buddhists—yesterday and today—concentrated their devotional activities on rituals and on accumulating merit rather than on meditation, and so we turn to gift giving as the foundation of Buddhist practice.

Punya and Dana: The Fundamental Buddhist Exchange

The Buddha set out a "framework of spiritual teachings for disciples." Still used as a guide for modern Buddhist teachers, the sequence counsels progression through the following stages of religious striving:

dana: "self-less giving" to diminish desire: the chief merit-making activity in Buddhist societies

1. ***Dana*** ("self-less giving" to diminish desire)
2. ***Shila*** ("morality")

3. *Svarga* ("heaven")
4. *Dharma-deshana* ("instruction on doctrine") on the Four Noble Truths

Just as merit, or punya, has provided the chief orientation point and goal in the Buddhist layperson's worldview and ethos, dana has always been the starting practice for accumulating it. Merit making for most Buddhists, including most monks and nuns, is the central measure of spiritual advancement. Merit making remains the universal, integrating transaction in Buddhist settings through the modern era, regardless of the respective intellectual elite's orientation toward competing Theravada, Mahayana, or Vajrayana doctrinal formulations or spiritual disciplines.

The wish for merit leading to rebirth in heaven has remained the most popular Buddhist aspiration. Householders can "plant" donations, and the "harvest" in good karma they earn will be great. Punya is needed for a good rebirth, and although Buddhist doctrine holds that heaven is a temporary state, the reward of heavenly rebirth has motivated many to be "good Buddhists."

Merit making can lead one closer to nirvana, but it also has practical, worldly consequences, impacting destiny both now and across future lifetimes. Therefore, Buddhists seek punya to change the karma "account" that affects them in this life as well as to modify future rebirth destiny.

A woman from a Buddhist merit-making society in Hong Kong releases shellfish into Victoria Harbor in 2010.

Selections from a Chinese Buddhist Merit Account Sheet

In East Asia, followers interpreted Buddhist teachings in original ways, in some cases applying the basic ideas into new formulations. By the Ming era, Buddhist monks and householders thought it useful to assign mathematical values to articulate the hierarchy of moral actions, as in this example:

100 Merits: Save one life; save a woman's chastity; prevent a child from drowning; continue a family lineage

50 Merits: Prevent an abortion; provide for a homeless person; prevent someone from committing a serious crime; give a speech that benefits many

30 Merits: Convert another to Buddhism; facilitate a marriage; take in an orphan; help another do something virtuous

10 Merits: Recommend a virtuous person; cure a major illness; speak virtuously; save the life of a good animal; publish the Buddha's teachings; treat servants properly

5 Merits: Prevent a lawsuit; cure a minor illness; stop someone from slandering; make an offering to a saintly person; save any animal; pray for others

3 Merits: Endure ill treatment without complaint; bury an animal; urge those making a living by killing to stop

1 Merit: Give an article to help others; chant a Buddhist scripture; provide for one monk; return a lost article; help repair a public road or bridge

100 Demerits: Cause a death; rape; end a family lineage

50 Demerits: Induce an abortion; break up a marriage; teach someone to do great evil; make a speech that harms many

30 Demerits: Create slander that dishonors another; disobey an elder; cause a family to separate; during famine, fail to share food grains

10 Demerits: Mistreat an orphan or widow; prepare a poison; kill an animal that serves humans; speak harshly to parent or teacher

5 Demerits: Slander spiritual teachings; turn away a sick person; speak harshly; kill any animal; write or speak lewdly; not clear an injustice when possible

3 Demerits: Get angry over words spoken; cheat an ignorant person; destroy another's success; be greedy

1 Demerit: Urge another to fight; help another do evil; waste food; kill insects; turn away a begging monk; take a bribe; keep a lost article

Source: Guide formulated by Liao-Fan Yuan (1550–1624), a Zen master of Jiang-su Province. Translated in *The Key to Creating One's Destiny* (Singapore: Lapis Lazuli Press, 1988), pp. 43–46. Passages edited and in places paraphrased.

Rituals and Festivals

Buddhist monasteries developed ritual procedures and a yearly festival calendar. The monk's vocation came to include priestly duties, performing rituals that linked the Buddha's spoken words with simple gestures. In one universal Buddhist ritual, monks pour water into a vessel as they chant words revealed by the Buddha. Now imbued with healing powers, the liquid can be drunk or sprinkled over the bodies of those needing assistance. All Buddhist schools encourage meritorious offerings of lamps, incense, and flowers to Buddha images, bodhi trees, and stupas.

Theravada monk
sprinkling a householder
with water over which
the sacred words of
the Buddha have been
chanted.

In the Mahayana schools, an important part of a bodhisattva's service to others
is ritual; some monks specialized in chanting sound chains called *mantras*, known for
their spiritual powers. Ritual chanting of the Buddha's own sayings is thought to
further the foundations of spiritual practice and infuse communities with blessings,
including good karma. Ritual service thus came to dominate Mahayana Buddhism in
its missionary program; mantra recitations were thought to activate the unseen cosmic
Buddha powers promised in the Mahayana texts.

The bimonthly Buddhist holiday called *uposatha* occurs each fortnight on the
new-moon and full-moon days. On uposatha, sangha members privately recite the
details confirming that they are monastics in good standing according to the Vinaya
rules. This recitation follows a private confession, to the renunciant's superior, of any
transgressions of the rules during the period. Uposatha continues in the modern era to
uphold the proper standards of monastery discipline in Theravada societies.

Emphasizing the fundamental interdependence between sangha and lay community, householders visit the local vihara on these days to make dana offerings. The regular succession of uposathas and the two half-moon days are when Buddhists typically
undertake meritorious actions, perform rituals, and engage in meditation practices.

In effect, each week has a special day for Buddhist observances. Like other great world religions, Buddhism also formed the basis of distinctive cultures that organized the year with regular monthly and yearly festivals.

The Universal Buddhist Shrine

caitya: Buddhist shrine

For all Buddhist schools, the stupa (or **caitya**, a term that can also signify any Buddha shrine) became a landmark denoting the tradition's spiritual presence. Buddhism eventually recognized "eight great relic caityas" for pilgrimage and veneration in South Asia. Stupa worship thus became the chief focus of Buddhist ritual activity, and this has continued through the modern era to the present. The Buddhist relic cult began early, inspiring monks, nuns, and householders to circumambulate the shrines (in the clockwise direction) and to have their own cremated remains deposited in the same great stupa or in smaller votive stupas located nearby.

Throughout Buddhist history, the stupa has served as a place to go to recall the Buddha's great acts, a "power place" tapping the Buddha's (or saint's) relic's healing potency, a site to earn merit through veneration, and a monument marking the conversion and control of local spirits. In the Mahayana schools, the stupa was also thought of as a symbol of Buddhahood's omnipresence, a center of Mahayana text revelation, and a perfect form showing the unity of the natural elements (earth, fire, air, ether) with the Buddha nature.

Buddhist stupa being whitewashed by a monk in Ladakh, in northern India near the Tibetan border. Monks, nuns, and laity have built these shrines since the Buddha's death.

Later, Buddhists identified stupas as the physical representations of the eternal teachings. They also expanded the possible sacred objects deposited in them to include Buddha's words in textual form. Stupas thus remain the natural sites for Buddhist festivals of remembrance and veneration.

Death Ritualism

In all Buddhist countries today, despite many regional differences, death rituals are the exclusive purview of the sangha and a key time for monks to expound core teachings and receive dana. Buddhist mourners carefully dispose of the corpse, relying on rituals performed by monks to ensure that the dead person does not become a hungry ghost or a demon. They also seek to avert bad destiny for the deceased by making punya and then transferring it to the dead person. In adopting such practices, Buddhists straddle both alternatives to the ancient Indic question of whether destiny is based strictly on an individual's own karma over a lifetime or whether the proper performance of rituals during and immediately after death can override unfavorable karma and manipulate rebirth destiny. Both Theravada monks and—more expansively—Mahayana ritualists apply ritual expertise to this time. The tradition's dependence on after-death ritual service for sangha donations is evident in all modern Asian traditions.

Buddhism Under Colonialism (1500–1960)

The modern era was one of widespread decline for Buddhism across Asia. Medieval states either lost their autonomy or were destabilized by colonialism, first by European powers (the British in Burma, India, Sri Lanka, Tibet, and China; the French in Indochina; the Portuguese and Dutch in Sri Lanka; the Dutch in Indonesia) and later, in the early twentieth century, by Japanese conquest and occupation. In East Asia, the imperial Chinese state was weakened by the colonial powers (primarily Britain), whose aggressive trade

Typical gathering of devotees at the southern shrine of the Swedagon stupa, a Burmese temple in present-day Myanmar.

practices backed by military intervention disrupted the Chinese economy. The civil disorders that followed also undermined Buddhist institutions. (These events are discussed in Chapter 8.)

The impact of European colonialism on Buddhism can be summarized under two broad domains, institutional and doctrinal. Dutch, British, and French colonial governments all eventually declined to fulfill the traditional native king's role of patron and protector of the local religions, including Buddhism. As a result, the accommodations that had evolved over the centuries to perpetuate Buddhism ceased to exist. Colonial administrations also typically ceased enforcement of indigenous land tenure relations and taxation, withdrew from supervision of monastic ordination, and halted ceremonies according respect to venerable monastic leaders, sacred symbols, and temples. The roots of modern crisis and Buddhism's decline across the region are easily traced to this abrupt deprivation of resources and political support.

Challenges from Colonialism, Communism, and Modern Critics (1800–Present)

In the realm of ideas, the colonial powers introduced two often-contradictory systems of thought: on the one hand, the scientific notions derived from the Enlightenment, and on the other, theories of racial, cultural, and religious superiority that were used to legitimate the triumphant expansion of Euro-Christian peoples.

Enlightenment ideals (democracy, modern science, and technology) were imported into Asia through schools built by the colonial governments. The reach of the colonial governments was broader, however, for in fact they were the official and secular extensions of the European home states. In addition, the colonial administrators generally supported the expansion of the Christian missionary presence. It was with such backing that the first modern global Christian missions were created. Across Asia, lay and ordained Christians built churches and established schools, hospitals, and charities. Some proselytized aggressively through public preaching and pamphlets attacking Buddhist beliefs and practices.

After the fall of the Ching dynasty in 1912, socioeconomic conditions remained unstable under the Republic of China. Throughout the twentieth century, the traditional Buddhist schools and Buddhist thought were subject to criticism by leaders of a modernizing faction called the May 4th Movement. To respond to those who claimed that Buddhism was parasitic and corrupt due to its landholdings, China's greatest modern reformer, Taixu (1889–1947), suggested that Chinese Buddhists should follow the ancient Ch'an school's policy of combining field labor with spiritual life, developing a "Buddhist work ethic" within the monasteries. Later, however, the sustained Communist Party policy of destruction, denigration, and disestablishment that began in 1949 had no precedent in Buddhist history.

Although at first disturbed and demoralized, Buddhists recovered from and responded to colonial-era challenges in various ways. Although few converted to Christianity,

Buddhist intellectuals and preachers emerged to engage in the dialogue with science and Christianity. In Sri Lanka, for example, early Protestant missionaries, having assessed Buddhist monks as uniformly indolent and ignorant, felt themselves on the verge of mass conversion. Yet a series of public debates ended badly for those missionaries, a reversal that restored public faith in the ongoing relevance of Buddhist doctrine.

Buddhist reformers involved the lay society of Sri Lanka more fully in Buddhist institutions and spiritual practices, motivating some among the laity to take the place of former royal patrons. The lay reformers, in turn, insisted that monks respect the sangha rules and discipline, and they supported the revival of monastic meditation practice, usually in newly created reformist monastic schools. To publicize these reforms, Buddhists adopted one aspect of Christian missionary methodology: They began by investing in printing technology and undertaking publications that defined reformist doctrines and practices. They also rediscovered the practice of public sermonizing.

Reformers in Thailand, as in Sri Lanka, also articulated new interpretations of "true Buddhism." They taught that Buddhism in its pure form was not concerned with communal rituals or harnessing the cosmic powers of Buddhism to support the secular kingdom. Most reform leaders were critical of—even hostile to—"superstitions," rituals, and other local accommodations. Meditation was now the heart of "true Buddhism," and it was no longer restricted to monks and nuns—all Buddhists could and should feel capable of seeking nirvana.

The Twentieth-Century Buddhist Revival Gains Strength

By the early twentieth century, the revival process in Asia was supported by the first generation of Europeans sympathetic to Buddhism, who saw in the faith a nontheistic spirituality that was a compelling alternative to dogmatic monotheism. Many Western

TALES OF SPIRITUAL TRANSFORMATION: The Enlightenment of Zen Master Sokeian Sasaki

Although the canonical texts counsel monastics not to discuss their own spiritual attainments, the following account of his enlightenment is from a respected modern Zen master.

One day I wiped out all notions from my mind. I gave up all desire. I discarded all the words with which I thought and stayed in quietude. I felt a little queer—as if I were being carried into something, or as if I were touching some power unknown to me . . . and Ztt! I lost the boundary of my physical body. I had my skin, of course, but I felt I was standing in the center of the cosmos. I spoke, but my words had lost their meaning. I saw people coming toward me, but all were the same man. All were myself! I had never known this world. I had believed that I was created, but now I must change my opinion: I was never created. I was the cosmos; no Mr. Sasaki existed.

Source: *Zen Notes* 1, no. 5 (1954), pp. 17–18.

seekers interpreted Buddhism as encouraging spiritual experimentation through meditation rather than requiring blind faith.

Easier travel for Westerners allowed sympathetic Europeans and North Americans to assist native Asian Buddhist modernists as they argued back against Christian ministers. Members of the Theosophical Society, a European group formed to pursue the secret, mystical teachings thought to underlie all the world religions, created new institutions, including English-language Buddhist schools and lay organizations such as Buddhist teaching programs modeled after Christian Sunday schools. In Asia, Buddhist nationalists also became involved in politics, seeking more favorable relations with—and eventually independence from—the European colonial governments.

Early Western scholarship and archaeological expeditions under the auspices of the British colonial government also added to the awareness of modern Asian Buddhists. European scholars used modern critical methods to translate and interpret the earliest canonical texts and then disseminated them globally. In fact, it was common for the newly educated indigenous intelligentsia in Buddhist countries to read their first passages from a canonical Buddhist text in English translation.

As Buddhist literature in English became available and as general literacy increased, voices from outside the sangha joined the contested discussion of "what the Buddha really taught." Thus, throughout the Buddhist world, the leaders of the old Buddhist establishments were often challenged to conform to the standards of discipline set forth in the monastic texts. In most Buddhist countries, colonial and postcolonial governments sought to eliminate sources of political dissent by imposing on the sangha regulations supposedly designed to "keep pure" the local Buddhist institutions.

The global diaspora of Buddhism followed the networks of empire, disseminating through Western converts who became aware of Asian religions as a result of expanding communications and travel. By 1920, Buddhist centers in the West had been established by Euro-American converts and immigrants. As depicted in early popular and sympathetic accounts, the Buddha was a rationalist who rejected ritual as well as a heroic social reformer. Buddhism was seen not as a religion but as an atheistic philosophy, compatible with science. Buddhist meditation, however, was regarded as an authentic, ancient spiritual practice, an aspect that attracted Westerners interested in the new field of psychology.

Euro-American contact with Mahayana Buddhism came earliest with Japanese Zen. Westerners were drawn to Zen's emphasis on meditation as well as its connection with the fine arts. It was in the years leading up to World War II, however, that Japan embarked on an imperialistic course, one that showed the continuing strength of the tradition of Zen leaders supporting aristocratic warriors and rationalizing nationalistic violence.

Once Japan opened itself to the modern world with the restoration of the emperor in 1868, Japan's leaders sought to create a modern industrial state based on nationalism. Shinto was promoted as the shared national faith, and the emperor was revered as a living god. The nationalist movement also involved the deliberate diminishment of Buddhism, which (despite its 1,400 years in Japan) was criticized as "a foreign religion" inferior to Shinto. Many Buddhist monasteries and temples had their lands confiscated and state patronage withdrawn. In response to these changes, some Buddhist organizations instituted reforms that involved undertaking social work, educational initiatives, and the renewal of global missions. Some schools, such as Zen, even issued strong public pronouncements in favor of the government's nationalism and militarism, with prominent monasteries raising money for armaments.

In the years immediately following World War II, Zen Buddhism particularly attracted segments of bohemian and intellectual Western society, furthering an interest that still grows today.

Buddhism and Postmodern Trends in a Postcolonial World

With the end of World War II and, soon after, the demise of colonialism, most Asian nations faced the need to reinvent their societies politically and culturally. Those who sought the rebuilding and renewal of Buddhism in postwar China, Mongolia, Vietnam, and North Korea faced dangerous hostility from communist rulers who regarded Buddhist doctrine as superstition and Buddhist institutions as parasitic on society. These nations disbanded the communities of monks, nuns, and householders, destroyed their buildings and images, and discredited all forms of Buddhist belief and practice. There were other pressures as well, many of which have ultimately exerted more benign effects.

As Asia's rapid industrialization created new wealth, urbanization led to new forms of social dislocation, especially dramatic increases in the numbers of wage-dependent workers and an unprecedented series of ecological crises. At the same time, Asia saw an expansion of higher education and the rise of educated classes alongside new commercial elites. As a result of these changes, Buddhism was transplanted into entirely new social contexts and drawn into political struggles and global dialogues.

Buddhist movements today make use of the same approaches seen across the globe in other faiths. Some leaders reject modernity, seeking to return to traditional practices. Others strive to adapt Buddhism to the global realities of the postcolonial world. Still others blend traditionalism and reform, "rescuing" from the past what in their view is the essence of Buddhism while employing modern technologies to propagate the Dharma. New institutions have been created to champion strict adherence to monastic norms, scholastic learning, and meditation. Most commonly, organizations led by householders have been the most active and effective in adapting Buddhist teachings and practices to the world today.

South Asia

South Asia is the "holy land" where the Buddha was born, was enlightened, and died and where Buddhism has endured over 2,500 years. Among the contemporary

GENDER FOCUS: Buddhist Women

Yesterday and Today

A central issue facing Buddhism today is the sangha's ability to adapt and lead in the postcolonial world. In particular, how the tradition resolves its policies on the status of Buddhist women, especially renunciants, is pivotal.

We have seen how the Buddha reluctantly admitted women into the sangha, albeit with stricter rules and under the authority of monks. With this move the Buddha stated that although women were the spiritual equals of men, capable of reaching enlightenment, they still had to submit to the men in the sangha. The Buddhist sangha from its beginnings offered women a refuge from marriage, house-bound widowhood, and poverty, and the work of women as nuns, devout householders, and patrons was an important factor contributing to its success throughout its history. In the distant past, as today, a visitor to a local Buddhist temple or a remote pilgrimage center would almost certainly find women in the majority of those present doing the rituals, walking the pilgrimage routes, and maintaining the shrines.

In modern times, when monasteries declined and patronage suffered disruption under colonialism, the nun's order in many places disappeared, disrupting the traditional pattern. In the postcolonial era, women in many Buddhist societies have sought ways to restore their role and status in the Buddhist community. In 1987, at an international conference held in Bodh Gaya, 150 devout women formed a worldwide organization called Shakyaditya. The "Shakya Daughters" are dedicated to the restoration of the full ordination of *bhikkhunis* (nuns) among the Theravadins, a lineage most Buddhist monks of this school view as having died out almost a millennium ago. Throughout the Buddhist world today, many highly committed women have adopted an unofficial and unheralded ascetic lifestyle involving meditation, service, or study. In every country today, there is also a male-dominated sangha that controls the Buddhist institutions, and the great majority of monks strongly resist changes in the gender status quo and so oppose taking any action to restore the bhikkhuni order.

Yet some women who have adopted the lifestyle of the nun do not, in fact, even wish to take the full bhikkhuni ordination. Why? According to the Vinaya rules, fully ordained women admitted into the sangha must accept the formal supervision of the senior monks. Presently, in their unofficial status, these renunciants enjoy near-complete autonomy to manage their living arrangements and spiritual training. They argue that since their real loyalty is to the Dharma and their true concern is nirvana-seeking discipline, it is pointless to seek formal recognition. Yet remaining "unofficial" places severe limitations on the women's ability to build their institutions, since they are not recognized for state patronage, and householder donations to them do not yield the same prestige or merit-return that comes from donations to the fully ordained monks. As a result, most of the unofficial "nuns" today remain impoverished, without special honor in their societies at large, and marginal to the dominant Buddhist community.

Since 2000, over 400 women practicing in all the Theravada countries have gone to Chinese Mahayana monasteries (in mainland China or Taiwan) to receive full nun's official ordination, much to the consternation of the traditionalist monks. Can Buddhist traditions facing so many future challenges afford to relegate to the margins of their societies the energy, compassion, and merit of such women?

countries of the region—India, Pakistan, Bangladesh, Sri Lanka, Bhutan, and Nepal—only in the Himalayan regions of the north and on the island of Sri Lanka to the south has Buddhism remained strong.

Remnants of Buddhism in India: Reconstruction in the Places of Origin

Today, Buddhism is found in the modern nation of India only in very small, and recently established, communities. Most important for the faith's revival in the land of its origins are the sacred sites archaeologists discovered during the nineteenth and early twentieth centuries. Among the sites that had sunk into oblivion after the Muslim conquest of South Asia (since 1200 CE), the site where the Buddha was enlightened under the bodhi tree became the most significant and controversial. Identified by British officials in the mid-1800s in the modern city of Gaya, the "Great Enlightenment" temple, called the Mahabodhi, has again become a focal point for Buddhists. Its reformers in the colonial era focused on reestablishing the sanctity of this temple as their first step in reviving Buddhism. In recent decades, over twenty Buddhist monasteries have been erected there, as well as libraries, study centers, and pilgrim hostels. Reformist Buddhists are also attempting to reestablish the site as Buddhism's holiest center and pilgrimage destination, a shrine that unifies all Buddhists. Despite hard work by generations of reformers, this remains an unmet goal.

Even after decades of negotiations, control over the Mahabodhi temple has eluded the Buddhist organizations, for Hindu priests and politicians have failed to turn over ownership of the shrine. By 1992, frustrations at unfulfilled promises peaked: Several resident monks threatened to immolate themselves, and several others began hunger strikes. The provocation for this confrontation was severe: Hindu priests had enthroned a lingam, the phallic icon of Shiva, on a temple altar and performed pujas to treat the five Buddha images in the temple as if they were Hindu deities. As the stalemate continued in 2013, several bombs were detonated near the shrine, injuring five, allegedly in retaliation for Buddhist actions against Muslims in Burma.

"Protestant Buddhism" in Sri Lanka: An Enduring Colonial-Era Reformation of the Faith

The modern reformation of Buddhist tradition begun in colonial Sri Lanka has been described as "**Protestant Buddhism**." The term conveys two distinct but connected historic trends. The first is obvious: the adoption of aspects of missionary Protestant Christianity into the Buddhist framework to revitalize its institutions, practices, and doctrines. The second is an ironic reference to a past marked by the arrogance of missionaries and British colonial discrimination against Buddhism.

The mediator of such "Protestantism" in Sri Lanka was the American convert Henry Steele Olcott (1832–1907), who came to the country and helped activist Buddhist leaders organize their efforts. Olcott emphasized the importance of the laity in revitalization and the founding of Buddhist publications and schools. He also composed a *Buddhist Catechism* (1881) and invented a five-color Buddhist flag, both of which are widely used

> **Protestant Buddhism:** pattern of reform in which Buddhists adopted perspectives of Protestant Christianity

across the world today. Modern Protestant tendencies were evident in the reformist insistence that spiritual and scientific truth be compatible. Furthermore, the reformers believed—in agreement with the Protestant missionaries—that the practice of Buddhism in Sri Lanka had been debased by idolatry, Hindu polytheism, and a corrupt monastic "priesthood." The laity, however, could reestablish "true Buddhism" through adhering to the pure philosophy and meditation practices taught by the human Buddha.

A Sri Lankan protégé, who adopted the name Anagarika Dharmapala (1864–1933), built on Olcott's initiatives, preaching and publishing tracts to spread his vision of revitalized Buddhism. In 1893, Dharmapala addressed an ecumenical conference, the Parliament of World Religions, held in Chicago. He impressed conference-goers with his definition of modernist Buddhism as compatible with science, free from dogma and superstition, tolerant of other faiths, and committed to social reform. After Dharmapala founded the Mahabodhi Society in Calcutta, this organization extended "Protestant Buddhist" reform to other countries in Asia.

Dharmapala also found an enthusiastic reception among the Sri Lankan laity, especially among the newly educated professional elite and the merchant middle class, who owed their rising positions in the world to the changes wrought by the colonial modernization of the country. At the same time, Dharmapala energized the Buddhist reformers in Sri Lanka; his speeches and writings also contributed to the linkage between the faith and the nationalist struggles. He celebrated Sri Lanka as a uniquely pure Buddhist country, elevated the Sinhalese ethnic group as a "chosen Buddhist people," and harshly demonized those opposing the country's Buddhist restoration. Scholars today see these influences as having set in motion the cultural forces that have made the postindependence state, Sri Lanka, a zone of bloody conflict and uncompromising reform.

Buddhism in the Himalayas: No Shangri-La

While it is true that Tibetan Buddhist communities have survived in the remote and picturesque settlements nestled among the world's highest mountains, this region has hardly been a utopian zone for Buddhism in the post–World War II era. Along the southern Himalayan region, the isolation of the states on the Tibetan frontier (Ladakh, Sikkim, and Bhutan) enabled them to retain their independence until the end of World War II. Since religious conservatism also kept the monks and leaders of these states isolated from the modern world, there was little impetus for reform or adaptation to the postwar international political order.

In 1949 most of the territories on the Tibetan plateau ruled by the Gelugpa school's Dalai Lama were declared part of the People's Republic of China, which sent its army to enforce this claim. The far peripheries of India and Nepal once oriented to Lhasa were isolated from the greater Buddhist centers, while central and western Tibet have been ruled by China as "the Tibetan Autonomous Region" until today. Up to the bitter end of China's Cultural Revolution (1976), all religious practices in the region were repressed and most Buddhist temples, monasteries, and shrines were destroyed. Thousands of Tibetans have died since 1949 in conflicts that set Chinese against Tibetan and

Tibetan against Tibetan. The fourteenth Dalai Lama, Tenzin Gyatso, went into exile in 1959, and 15 percent of the population has left the country as well.

After 1980, official toleration of limited worship and monastic ordination returned, as did state-sponsored rebuilding of select monasteries. But increasing Tibetan protests since 1987 met with further restrictions and arrests, while increasing Chinese migration into the region has reduced Tibetans to a minority in their homeland. Buddhist traditions are slowly being restored, but the Chinese government exerts close supervision of monastic training and ritual practices to ensure they are not perceived as promoting Tibetan independence.

Three nations have remained free refuges of Tibetan Buddhism. Nepal has several million Buddhists among the highland-dwelling Tibeto-Burman peoples, in its settlements of Tibetan refugees, and among the Newars of the Kathmandu Valley. Kathmandu is the modern capital of Nepal, and this valley is also Asia's largest center for international institutions connected with the major schools of Tibetan Buddhism.

Tibetan Buddhism also has survived in mountainous areas of northern India (in Ladakh, Himachal Pradesh, and Arunachal Pradesh). India has likewise accepted Tibetan refugees, for since 1959 the Dalai Lama's government in exile has been located in picturesque Dharamsala. Finally, there is Bhutan in the eastern Himalayas, a nation formed in 1907 as the royal kingdom ruled by the Wangchuck family. It is the world's only nation that has Tibetan Buddhism as its state religion.

Most regions where Tibetan Buddhism still flourishes have lost political autonomy. The central, northern, and eastern portions of Tibet were absorbed by China, while Ladakh and Sikkim were absorbed into modern India. Bhutan alone remained independent from India, but only in its internal affairs. In exile and in the isolated enclaves, Tibetan Buddhist institutions have sustained the faith, but these Buddhists struggle as refugees in poverty and as resident aliens within the larger states.

Yet amid the destruction, discrimination, and displacement that came to independent Tibet, there has also been the extensive migration of Tibetan Buddhist teachers into almost every country of the world. While their predecessors were completely out of touch with the modern world and its spiritual challenges, contemporary monk-scholars and meditation teachers are now leaders in "bringing the Dharma to the West." The fourteenth Dalai Lama, Nobel Peace Prize winner in 1989, is well known as a world leader and is certainly the most recognized Buddhist in the world.

Theravada Buddhism Today in Southeast Asia

The first regions missionized in antiquity by Buddhist monks have remained the stronghold of Theravada Buddhism. In Sri Lanka and Burma, a new era began with the withdrawal of the British in 1947. Buddhism became a pillar of the new nations' identity, and the Buddha was elevated to the status of cultural hero and ancestor.

While supportive of the respective struggles for independence, Buddhism in these states had also been enriched and enlarged by revival movements throughout the colonial

Tobi Fudo: Protector of Airline Passengers

The sword-bearing Fudo has long been a protector of Buddhist teachings associated with the tantric school of Japanese Buddhism, Shingon. His dark body and fierce face symbolize his unshakeable devotion to the teachings of the Buddha; yet his nature is compassionate, as he has vowed to be of service to all beings who call upon him. A legend associated with a Fudo in Shoboin, a temple in old Tokyo, recounts the image flying back to the home temple after a monk had taken it on a pilgrimage. This temple's icon in the Edo period (1600–1868) thus came to be called Tobi (Flying) Fudo. Over the last thirty years, the sangha of this temple has sold *ema* boards like the one pictured here—Fudo with a Boeing 747—to Japanese air travelers, who write their flight numbers on the back and leave it at the temple, requesting protection. Carry-on talismans, called "Hiko-Omamori," 飛行守り, are also sold at the temple. The adaptation of Fudo to be a protector of air travelers illustrates the social engagement, creativity, and adaptability of Buddhism in Japan today.

period. Most of these involved the laity in the administration of its institutions and saw the establishment of new monastic schools emphasizing revival through strict discipline, meditation, and social service.

Buddhist leaders in the first decades after World War II were also at the forefront of addressing the relationship between socialism and communism, the political ideologies that had risen as alternatives to capitalism in guiding the newly independent states. Some monks were highly suspicious of communism and allied themselves with aggressive anticommunist campaigns, with one going so far as to say that "killing communists entails no demerit"! However, other, more leftist political activists and high civil servants used Buddhist rhetoric quite creatively to justify participation in communist regimes.

Tooth Relics and Anti-Muslim Riots in Myanmar

The Buddha's cremation relics have always been the most sacred and precious objects for devotees. Not only are they a "sacred trace" of the Buddha's earthly existence; they are also thought to be infused with immense power, and mere proximity to them is believed to confer spiritual and worldly blessings.

In 2011, the Buddha's sacred tooth relic was brought from China to Myanmar for the fourth time. Here, security officials and Chinese Buddhist monks accompany the relic as it is transported to the Kabaaye pagoda in Yangon, Myanmar.

In 1994 (and again in 2011) the Chinese government loaned a tooth relic to Myanmar. Placed in a jewel-embellished palanquin and conveyed from the Boeing 757 to a silk-draped float pulled by an elephant, the relic was taken to its shrine in the Maha Pasana cave in Rangoon, where over the next six weeks a half-million devotees came to venerate it and make offerings. The country's ruling junta, who had sponsored the visit, used the state-controlled media to emphasize that its members were exemplary Buddhists. In 1995 the junta underwrote the construction of a new temple in the capital where the relic has been displayed in 1996 and 2011. Displaying and respecting Buddha relics have been recognized as signs of just rulers in Buddhist states since antiquity, and the junta's generals no doubt intend their sponsorship of tooth relic veneration to win popular approval and counter dislike of their authoritarian rule.

In recent years, political changes in Myanmar have revealed long-suppressed resentments felt by the Burmese Buddhist majority on two fronts: against the Christian tribal groups on their northern borders, and toward Muslim citizens called Rohingyas whose ancestors had immigrated from Bangladesh into Myanmar's southwest border region. Claiming that "Myanmar is a Buddhist country" and challenging the Muslim Rohingyas' right to remain within the country's borders, Buddhist mobs have beaten and killed hundreds and driven 220,000 persons into refugee camps inside and out of Myanmar. Since then, the world press has shown unprecedented photos of Buddhist monks organizing rallies and even leading groups intent on expelling Rohingyas. Inspired by newly awakened Buddhist nationalism, some in Myanmar have even threatened those calling for restraint and attempting to apply Buddhist ethics to all sentient beings.

Monastics and householders of the modernist Dhammakaya school reside in individual tents of mosquito netting on a mass meditative retreat in Thailand.

Three Contemporary Faces of Thai Buddhism

A constitutional monarchy since 1932 and a country never ruled by a European nation, Thailand is another predominantly Theravada country. Thai society supports traditional and reformist Buddhist scholarship, the ancient spiritual practices of forest monks, and pioneering reformist initiatives. Thai reformers have actively participated in modernization through government development programs in infrastructure building, agricultural innovation, education, and health care. Notable independent monks have opposed the state's toleration of corruption, pollution, and environmental destruction. However, mainstream Thai Buddhist monastic institutions have benefited from royal patronage and the rising wealth that accompanied the economic boom of the late twentieth century. Certain charismatic monks and a host of new lay-oriented independent Buddhist institutions are also active in offering leadership to revitalize the faith. The burgeoning urban areas, where neither old community ties nor traditional monasteries effectively meet the needs of the new city dwellers, have been fertile ground for such reformists. Three examples illustrate the sorts of Buddhist innovators active in contemporary Thailand: the Dhammakaya, Santi Asoke, and the work of two monks, Phra Boonsong and Luang Pi Daeng.

The Dhammakaya. The Dhammakaya is the fastest-growing Buddhist reform group in Thailand, attracting the well-educated and newly affluent classes as well as the royal family. Founded by the charismatic monk Phra Monghon Thepmuni in 1978, Dhammakaya spreads its teachings and meditation practices through the use of mass media. The movement has established a presence in every major city and town across Thailand, where its very highly educated monks administer a program of rigorous training for the laity. Another binding force of Dhammakaya is Phra Thepmuni's meditation technique, one that has more in common with Mahayana practices of the Himalayas than with traditional Theravada methods. For its followers, the Dhammakaya has reduced the ritual complexity of the traditional monastery to a few simple practices. It has also emphasized that making money is compatible with Buddhism and has translated utopianism and interdependence teachings through the slogan "World Peace Through Inner Peace." As of 2017, the group numbered its supporters at over 1 million, with branches in twenty-four countries.

Santi Asoke. Santi Asoke differs in many respects from Dhammakaya: It has won a much smaller following (perhaps 85,000, as estimated in 2014) and has garnered much less wealth. Since its founding in 1976, however, movement activists have critiqued what they regard as the complacent establishment monastic schools' compromises with state and business power. Santi Asoke ("Peaceful Ashoka") are named after the first lay ruler in Buddhist history, the Indian emperor who (in Buddhist accounts) spread the faith across India and ruled according to the Buddha's ethical norms. Accordingly, this group seeks to reform Thai Buddhism through a return to austere ethical practices such as abstaining from meat, alcohol, and tobacco as well as avoiding gambling and hedonistic entertainment. Santi Asoke grew out of the work of forest monk reformers who in the 1920s and 1930s sought to revitalize the sangha by a return to an ascetic lifestyle for monks, complemented by rigorous meditation schedules. With its base both conservative and rural, its leaders preach the avoidance of "superstitions" so that its monasteries have few Buddha images and no rituals are focused on them. In recent years, Santi Ashoke has sought to promote ecological activism and sustainable environmental practices, but has lost membership due to involvement in the national political tumults that resulted in a military takeover in 2014.

Phra Boonsong and Luang Pi Daeng. Not all reformers in Thailand have been new institution builders. Phra Boonsong (1941–), the abbot of Phranon Wat in central Thailand since 1972, is a dedicated environmentalist. When he arrived in the area, runoff from the Chin River, which flows by the monastery, was polluting rice fields, and declining agriculture and fishing yields were causing men and women to seek employment in the cities. Phra Boonsong worked to improve the region's ecological balance by appealing to the traditional Thai prohibition against killing inside a monastery. He began by declaring the river adjacent to it a "pardon zone" for all water creatures. Next, from profits made by selling fish food to local Buddhists (who in turn gave it to the fish, earning merit), he was able to add fish stock to the river. The fish multiplied in that nearby stretch of the river, increasing the harvest for local fishermen. He has also begun planting organic orchards and has managed to reduce the use of expensive, watershed-polluting chemicals. The expertise of the Phranon Wat monks in species use, grafting, fertilizers, and marketing is now being shared across Thailand.

TALES OF SPIRITUAL TRANSFORMATION: Maha Ghosananda, Witness to Buddhist Peacemaking in Cambodia

Ordained as a young boy in Cambodia, Somdet Phra Ghosananda (1928–2007) pursued a monastic life through middle age, spending years outside of his native land meditating in Thai forest monasteries and completing a doctoral degree in Pali textual studies. In 1976, when Maha Ghosananda heard of Cambodia's political upheaval and the atrocities of Khmer Rouge rule, he resolved to return to worldly action. He left his forest monastery to work in refugee camps along Thailand's Cambodian border, where he built modest monasteries and trained new monks who helped meet the needs of the suffering population.

After the fall of the Khmer Rouge, Maha Ghosananda returned to Cambodia, where he was named Supreme Monk Patriarch of Cambodia. He was invited to preach Dharma and teach meditation among Cambodian immigrants in the United States, and during his visits there he sought international support for Cambodia's people and to promote anti-landmine activism. While he went on to found over fifty international monasteries, his first priority was to promote peace in Cambodia and foster national reconciliation through Buddhist morality. Even though the Khmer Rouge had murdered his entire family and destroyed his native village, Maha Ghosananda never wavered from his conviction: "It is the law of the universe that retaliation, hatred, and revenge only continue the cycle."

Recognized by the Japanese Niwano Peace Foundation and several times nominated for the Nobel Peace Prize, this beloved, self-effacing monk, called "Cambodia's Gandhi," gave up the satisfactions of scholarship and the bliss of meditation to take decisive action to heal a genocidal national conflict.

Abbot Luang Pi Daeng likewise could not ignore the world outside his monastery, Wat Hua Rin in Northern Thailand. His monastery buildings now include medical examination rooms, handicraft production facilities, and a meeting hall where people with HIV/AIDS come for health monitoring and support group meetings. Taking alms from households with an HIV-infected member to illustrate that the disease cannot be transmitted through casual contact, this monk has worked to end the abandonment of those who have contracted this disease. In addition to providing spiritual counseling, Luang Pi Daeng has applied the Buddhist teaching of suffering and interdependence to this crisis that has deeply affected Thai life: Luang Pi Daeng's work was instrumental in the establishment of the UNICEF-funded Sangha Metta Project, which has trained over 4,000 monks in seven countries about AIDS prevention and treatment.

Buddhist Revival in Postwar Indochina

By 1985, all the countries of the Indochinese peninsula had begun to liberalize their economies and relax restrictions on religious observances. As communist governments retreated from dogmatism to pragmatism and tolerated the enduring popular attachment to Buddhism and indigenous religions, civil authorities in Vietnam, Laos, and Cambodia began accepting the place of Buddhism in national culture and politics.

A French colony until 1953, Cambodia suffered through the Vietnam wars with the French and the United States and, in the aftermath (1975–79), the genocidal conflicts under the rule of the Khmer Rouge, led by Pol Pot. Under Pol Pot's communist regime, Buddhist monks and institutions were targeted for murder and destruction. While several Cambodian Buddhist centers were relocated among refugees over the border in Thailand, only after the withdrawal of the Vietnamese in 1989 did the restoration of Buddhism begin. Several prominent figures seeking national reconciliation have been Theravada monks.

Vietnam has increasingly tolerated the restoration of Buddhist monasteries and temples since 1975. Nevertheless, the government has imprisoned monks it regards as too involved in politics, and the officially sanctioned (and so-named) Vietnam Buddhist Church has won only minimum popular acceptance. Vietnam's population of 75 million resembles China in its religious orientation, with Buddhism the most widespread tradition existing alongside Chinese Daoism and Confucianism, indigenous cults, and Roman Catholic and Protestant Christianity. Vietnamese Buddhism today is predominantly Mahayana in the north, with Theravada monasteries found in the south.

The modern state of Indonesia contains the largest Muslim population in the world, though its western islands of Sumatra and Java were once at the center of an empire that supported both Hinduism and Buddhism. Under a constitution that officially protects all faiths, Indonesian Buddhists are a small minority (1 percent of 205 million), but the faith has undergone a vigorous revival since 1950. Small communities dedicated to predominantly Mahayana Buddhism likewise exist among minority ethnic Chinese communities in Malaysia and in Singapore, the city-state that separated from Malaysia in 1965.

East Asia

Devastated by the destruction of World War II, East Asia embarked on the long road to social, political, and economic recovery after 1945. Communist nations imposed new obstacles for Buddhist adherents and institutions for several decades afterward, but by 2013, only North Korea remained opposed to the tradition's reestablishment across East Asia. The examples that follow illustrate the remarkable rebound of Buddhist tradition, with followers once again drawing on the great ability of the Dharma to be adapted to changing circumstances and times.

Guanyin Rises Again in China

Mahayana Buddhists have long shared a common faith in Avalokiteshvara, whose shrines are found in almost every settlement and home from central Asia to Japan. The celestial bodhisattva has come to be called Guanyin in China and Kannon in Japan. With Buddhism's missionary transplantation across East Asia, this divinity became the refuge for all who desired rebirth in the western Buddhist paradise, for those who met dangerous life circumstances, and especially for women who wanted safe childbirth and sons. As Daoism organized and was systematized in response to Buddhism in China by the T'ang era (618–907), Guanyin was so popular (and Daoism so eclectic) that icons of Guanyin were accepted sights in Daoist temples or in clan temples otherwise dedicated to the veneration of ancestors.

The violently iconoclastic phase of Mao Zedong's Cultural Revolution (1966–69) nearly eliminated Guanyin images from China. Since the mid-1980s, however, Guanyin has returned to favor. Even so, the government's acceptance of the revival of Buddhist devotionalism contrasts to its harsh repression of other faiths that have taken root in China, from Christian sects to the syncretistic Falun Gong (see Chapter 8).

Since the death of Mao Zedong and the end of the Cultural Revolution in 1976, the Communist government of China has slowly allowed many Buddhist institutions to be reopened, including monasteries that train monks and nuns in traditional ritual and meditation practices. Augmented by meritorious gifts from Chinese living outside China, Buddhist institutions have been rehabilitated across the nation as the government has ended restrictions on lay devotees' setting up home shrines and undertaking pilgrimages.

Buddhist Revival in South Korea

The formerly unified Korean culture area, artificially split into North Korea and South Korea after World War II, was strongly influenced by Chinese cultural borrowings, including Buddhism, throughout its history. As South Korea experienced rising economic prosperity from the 1970s onward, it attracted patrons and activists who sought to build the spiritual programs of the monasteries, present the Buddha's teachings in modern media, and reverse the slide of Buddhism in the face of Christian proselytizing and government discrimination.

Despite many setbacks over the last century, the surviving Korean Buddhist institutions remain well endowed with landed income and have created an important niche in Korean society by establishing schools, universities, and lay meditation centers. As in other Buddhist countries undergoing successful economic modernization, Korean Buddhism is experiencing a renewal. Its modern institutions are upgrading monastic education, creating mass media publications and cable networks, and developing an

Boke Fuji ("Senility") Kannon: A New Incarnation of a Buddhist Deity

The late 1980s saw the appearance of icons that depicted the goddess Kannon holding a flower in one hand and opening the other in a gesture of mercy to two elderly people, one male and one female, who clutch at her robes in supplication. Consistent with her renown developed over one and a half millennia for compassionately "mothering" her devotees and bestowing this-worldly boons to those who call on her, this new form of the bodhisattva has arisen as senility or Alzheimer's disease has caused great emotional distress to many in Japan (as elsewhere). Both for the elderly and their families, who share a Confucian responsibility for parental care at this stage of life, old-age suffering has surfaced as a weighty problem, suggesting a creative Buddhist response. Thus temples have established social and spiritual programs, developing amulets, shrines, and pilgrimage routes for devotees to visit in search of preventive blessings. Buddhist priests, aware of physicians' counsel that the best way to keep senility at bay is for the aged to keep active, are encouraging this approach. By organizing pilgrimages, for example, they make available to the elderly enjoyable, stimulating, and hopeful activity, in which the pilgrims can both articulate their worries and acquire peace of mind.

A contemporary Boke Fuji ("Senility") Kannon amulet from Japan.

urban, middle-class Buddhist identity based on householder rituals, meditation, and youth organizations.

Buddhism in Japan Recovers After World War II

Japan, like the United States, is a country of ever-broadening religious expression. Buddhism has contributed to this through its classical monastic institutions and by its doctrines providing starting points for many of Japan's "new religions." In the mid-nineteenth century, the Meiji state's ultranationalist governments deliberately weakened Buddhism. By the 1930s, many abbots of co-opted "establishment schools" were in fact actively fanning the flames of war. World War II left monasteries in ruins and prominent clergy in disgrace. But after the war, the sanghas of the oldest schools retained their nationwide presence under a system of head and branch monasteries developed in the late Tokugawa era (1603–1867), and some communities worked to restore their spiritual integrity. Today, most Japanese families are still registered with a monastery branch of one or the other Buddhist schools for, at the very least, the performance of family death rituals.

The great number of individuals undertaking pilgrimage circuits across the heartland of historical Japan to honor the Mahayana bodhisattva Avalokiteshvara, here called Kannon, attests to Buddhism's importance today. This "pilgrimage boom," as journalists have labeled the popular religious revival, was aided by the proliferation of modern pilgrim facilities. Scholars debate about how much this rapidly increasing pilgrimage is due to religious dedication to Kannon and how much is due to a less pious "cultural tourism."

A final example of a new form of Kannon devotionalism in Japan is the cult organized to seek the forgiveness of the spirits of stillborn, miscarried, and aborted fetuses (*mizuko*, "water children"). Buddhist temples throughout Japan have seen a revival in rituals on their memorial grounds as women have set up icons to which they offer food and other ritual gifts to spirits to whom they denied birth in human form. Kannon and another compassionate bodhisattva, named Jizo, are popular in this form of worship at many temples. Japanese women typically request that the compassionate deities guard and bless these wandering spirits until they fulfill their destiny and continue on to another human rebirth, as in classical Buddhist teachings. The **mizuko cult** has spread widely, promulgated by many temples that not coincidentally benefit from the income derived from the special ritual services they provide.

> **mizuko cult:** in Japan, form of Kannon devotionalism that seeks forgiveness from spirits of stillborn, miscarried, and aborted fetuses

Buddhism Today in Diaspora and in Asia

Buddhism in the West

The economic boom beginning in the 1990s and the global migration of Asians are the most recent developments affecting Buddhism today. To a large extent, newly affluent Buddhists have done what Buddhist householders have always done with a portion of their surplus wealth: make merit through pious donations. This infusion of new wealth has been used to rebuild venerable monasteries and temples, support new reform sects, and modernize Buddhist institutions by establishing schools, starting periodicals, and creating mass media outlets. One exception to the trend of new Asian affluence pushing the international expansion of Buddhism is the Tibetan diaspora, which has depended largely on donations by affluent Euro-American supporters, including Hollywood actors and rock stars.

The global migration of Buddhist monastic institutions and ideas has been so great that a representative of every major Asian school can now be found on every continent, and numerous non-Asians have by now been accepted for ordination as monks and nuns in every nation's sangha. In addition, awareness of the basic Buddhist doctrines of karma, nirvana, and Buddhahood, formerly confined to the educated classes of the world, is now accessible to all via the global mass media.

In the Zen and Tibetan schools in North America, especially, converts now speak of the emergence of new American schools of Tibetan (or Zen) Buddhism.

Facts Regarding Buddhism in America

Self-identified Buddhists: 1.6 million (0.7%)
Those who report meeting a Buddhist teacher "at least a few times a year": 5 million
Those who practice Buddhist meditation: 6 million

"Nightstand Buddhists" who say they read Buddhist literature: 7 million
Those who report "Buddhism has had an important influence on their thinking about religion or spirituality": 28.3 million

Source: Pew Surveys, 2011–2015.

Interestingly, these Euro-American Buddhist schools are selective in their adoption of Asian Buddhist traditions: They have eschewed celibate monasticism, featured meditation, and minimized ritualism, much like the "Protestant Buddhists" of Asia. This expectation of Westerners is especially noteworthy in the Pure Land schools established in America: These centers have found the need to offer programs in meditation for the laity, even though back in Asia their monastic life is more focused on chanting.

In the 1950s the perceived iconoclasm of Zen—its nonconformist appeal—attracted Americans who participated in the Beat Generation culture of jazz, poetry, and experimental literature. The lure of Zen meditation practices has drawn Western practitioners from the 1960s onward. Zen's connection with Japanese fine arts and martial arts also helped Zen-oriented teachers and their institutions across the globe to reach a wider artistic and athletic audience.

The Japanese Soka Gakkai, a modern offshoot of the Nichiren school, has an international following eager to reinterpret Buddhism and take political action to foster the development of a more enlightened world civilization. Pure Land Buddhism has been transplanted among East Asians who have migrated to urban areas worldwide, particularly the West Coast of North America and Hawaii. Indeed, migrants from every Buddhist country in the world have contributed to the globalization of their faith by establishing temples and monasteries in their adopted homelands. The latest groups of Asian Buddhists in America have emigrated from Southeast Asia.

Outside Asia, Buddhists still remain a small minority in the census figures and usually are found in urban areas. Among today's immigrants and Western converts, as in Asia, "being a Buddhist" does not necessarily imply an exclusive identity. Thus, the census figures, which show, for example, roughly a million Buddhists in North America as a whole, do not accurately reflect the penetration of Buddhist concepts and practices in contemporary national culture.

With intellectuals worldwide, however, awareness of Buddhist thought and practice is widespread, although not always to beneficial effect. Advertisers now deploy Buddhist ideas and practices to promote materialistic attachments: Popular advertising since 1999 found the Dalai Lama's image being used to sell Apple computers, a Nike sneaker called "Nirvana," and a designer sandal called "Buddha." The word *Zen* has been reduced to a vapid cliché because it has by now been appended to hundreds of objects, certain to elicit consumer curiosity.

The Reshaping of Buddhism in Asia

In the postcolonial period, Buddhists have had to determine how to situate their tradition in the new secular polities. The effort has included reconstructing sangha–state relations after colonial neglect of the religious institutions, responding to scientific thought and modern medicine, reckoning with the religious pluralism introduced by Christianity and other faiths, and revising law codes in relation to national minorities. The results have been mixed. In Bhutan and Sri Lanka, the dominant ethnic groups have promoted Buddhist nationalism at the expense of non-Buddhist minorities, while in Myanmar, members of the military that once used Buddhist symbols to prop up the legitimacy of their authoritarian regimes, have more recently used Buddhist identity to promote repressive policies and violence.

As ethnic identity has held the loyalty of local communities, often against the demands of modern secular states, "being Buddhist" has drawn individuals to value,

Buddhism as Commodity and Buddhist Imagery as Sales Pitch

Although Zen is not mentioned in it, the ad on the left, for a truck, completely misunderstands the basic message of Buddhism—that possessions and attachment undermine spiritual life. The image on the right makes the equally absurd suggestion that electronic distractions are somehow a kind of spiritual practice.

rediscover, and embrace Buddhism across Asia. In many cases, the postcolonial web of global interaction has shaped the process: The "Buddhism" that reformers discover has been filtered through and influenced by the thinking of Euro-American scholars and Westernized indigenous teachers.

An interesting and early example of this phenomenon occurred in Maharashtra, the modern state in central India. Since 1956, Mahar caste groups relegated to the bottom of the caste system have held mass ceremonies to convert to Buddhism, declaring their rejection of Hinduism and its institutionalization of social inequality. The Mahars' knowledge of Buddhism was informed in part by colonial scholarship; the presence in Maharashtra of ancient Buddhist sites revealed by British archaeology has obvious importance as well. The founder of this movement, Dr. Bhimrao Ambedkar (1891–1956), learned about Buddhism from his studies in the West, particularly at Columbia University, where Euro-American scholarship on Buddhism then held up the image of the Buddha as a social reformer. Statues of Ambedkar abound in Maharashtra villages today, monuments to the reinstatement of Buddhism tradition in the service of a twentieth-century social reform movement.

Buddhism's Affinity for Modernization

At the beginning of the twentieth century, Western scholars questioned whether Buddhism could prove compatible with economic modernization. Since the end of World War II, such skepticism has been laid to rest by the exceptional success of nations strongly influenced by Buddhism. Modern reformers have had many canonical texts to draw on to promote the compatibility between economic development and Buddhism. As an influential reformist monk of Thailand asserted several generations ago, "Education breeds knowledge, knowledge breeds work, work breeds wealth, and wealth promotes happiness."[1]

The economic boom in Asia since World War II has clearly benefited Buddhism as newly wealthy patrons have sponsored various renewal initiatives. Moreover, many do not involve the traditional sangha's leadership. For example, translation of the sacred texts into the global medium of English is emphasized across the world. The Buddhist Publication Society, founded in Sri Lanka in 1956, has offered hundreds of vernacular (and English) translations and interpretive tracts; its work overlaps with that of the Pali Text Society, a group founded in the nineteenth century that publishes scholarly translations of canonical works, including extra-canonical commentaries. Today each of the four Tibetan monastic schools also has a modern publishing house in the West that yearly prints dozens of texts promulgating translations and thematic explanations of Buddhist doctrine by its own monk-scholars. An even larger-scale project was initiated in 1991 by the Japanese industrialist Yenan Numata. His foundation, the Bukkyo Denko Kyokai, is underwriting the scholarly translation into English of the entire Chinese canon. To do all 3,360 scriptures, the project is estimated to span the next 100 years!

Socially Engaged Buddhism: Some Examples

Thai activist Sulak Sivaraksa puts the ancient Buddhist concept of suffering into the framework of today's world:

> In Buddhist terminology, the world is full of *dukkha* ["suffering"], i.e., the dangers of impending world destruction through nuclear weapons, atomic fallout, air, land, and sea pollution, population explosion, exploitation of fellow human beings, denial of basic human rights, and devastating famine. . . . World dukkha is too immense for any country, people, or religion to solve. We can only save ourselves when all humanity recognizes that every problem on earth is our own personal problem and our own personal responsibility. . . . The language of Buddhism must offer answers which fit our situation. Only then will Buddhism survive, today and tomorrow, as it has in the past, influencing humankind positively and generating love, peace, and nonviolence.[a]

An even more forceful exhortation is provided by the Vietnamese monk Thich Nhat Hanh:

> The word *Buddha* comes from the root *budh*, which means "awake." A Buddha is one who is awake. Are we really awake in our daily lives? That is a question. . . . Society makes it difficult to be awake. We know that 40,000 children in the Third World die every day of hunger, but we keep forgetting. The kind of society we live in makes us forgetful. That is why we need exercises in mindfulness. . . . Our earth is like a small boat. Compared with the rest of the cosmos, it is a very small boat, and it is in danger of sinking. We need a person to inspire us with calm confidence, to tell us what to do. Who is that person? The Mahayana texts tell us that you are that person.[b]

[a]Sulak Sivaraksa, "Buddhism in a World of Change," in Fred Eppsteiner, ed., *The Path of Compassion: Writings on Socially Engaged Buddhism* (Berkeley, CA: Parallax Press, 1988), pp. 16–17.
[b]Thich Nhat Hanh, "Call Me by My True Name," in Eppsteiner, *The Path of Compassion*, pp. 34–37.

The Sangha: Adaptive Reformism?

Given the role of the sangha in maintaining the traditional goals in every society, the future of Buddhism is in the hands of the monks and nuns who will become the spiritual exemplars, scholars, teachers, and meditators.

Arguing that the sangha cannot keep Buddhism alive unless the monks keep pace with the educational level of the nation's population, countries such as Thailand have invested in making higher education available to them. This opportunity still attracts many young men from poor rural backgrounds to take ordination. Becoming a monk gives many the chance to live in better material circumstances than their parents could achieve and to gain skills that can be, and often are, taken back into lay life.

But at the same time, many Asian states have created national sangha bureaucracies, placing monastics under political supervision. These governments now scrutinize the preaching and personal lives of monks and crack down on any political activities that might arise in the monasteries. Seeing clearly the threat that the Buddhist Dharma represents to unjust or uncompassionate regimes, politicians have sought to weaken Buddhist institutions even while outwardly honoring them. In recent years, monks in Tibet and Vietnam have felt incidents of stern repression. It is hard to imagine Buddhist monks regaining the power they once enjoyed in the premodern era.

Since World War II, many developments have undermined the classical patterns and exchanges within Buddhist societies. Whereas formerly, monastic schools were an important part of the sanghas' service to local communities and a source of their recruitment, today public education has been removed from the monastery almost everywhere. If connection with and awareness of modern changes are essential to an institution meeting the needs of the lay majority, many question whether the Buddhist sangha today is capable of keeping Buddhist ideas and identity vibrant in the whirl of changes sweeping modern Asian societies. In Japan, Buddhist schools struggle with the loss of support due to the depopulation of the rural areas, and many leaders in the sangha across the country are experimenting with new ways of reaching citizens and utilizing monasteries to serve the common good.

Many progressive Buddhists think not. Noting that the modern sangha has a hierarchy of authority unknown in earlier times, they see little opportunity for young monks to fashion innovative applications of the Dharma in thought or action. Noting how powerful elder monks typically lack vision, purpose, or inspiration beyond the guardianship of ceremonies and tradition, many Asian householders now look to lay institutions for more promising avenues to keep Buddhism vital.

A Thai monk at an ATM in Bangkok. Monks across Asia face the challenge of adapting their lifestyle, defined by monastic laws over 2,000 years old, to the rapidly changing realities of the globalizing world.

The number of men taking monastic vows across Asia has fallen far short of what population increases would predict. As a result, many village monasteries are understaffed, a trend reflecting the breakdown of rural communities that has contributed to the urbanization of Asia. While some Buddhists in Nepal, Korea, and Japan have tolerated sanghas of the "married ordained" to solve the problem of recruitment, these schools on the whole have actually shown even less inclination to revitalize or innovate. Again, it is easy to see why Buddhist reformers have almost always gone outside the boundary of the modern sangha to move ahead with their revitalization programs, at times even having to face opposition from the established monastic community. An important exception is now found in Japan, where in recent years married sangha leaders of a new movement called "Experimental Buddhism" have successfully sought new missions for monasteries (theaters, community meeting centers, fitness centers) and monastic resources (setting up counseling centers and even bars, where Buddhist doctrine can be discussed).

CONTRASTING RELIGIOUS VISIONS

As the following contrasting visions indicate, every religious tradition is capable of generating both visions that encourage peace and understanding and visions that encourage conflict and violence.

Peacemaker: Thich Nhat Hanh

Since his early involvement in the peace movement in his native Vietnam, the Zen monk Thich Nhat Hanh (1926–) has projected a strong and ecumenical Buddhist voice. From exile in the West, he has been a firm advocate of toleration and the centrality of peacemaking when facing both personal challenges and international policy. A leading advocate of "engaged Buddhism" and author of several dozen books, Nhat Hahn has for decades argued that Buddhists must participate in social and cultural activities, with activism informed by the clarity arising from meditation. As he once affirmed, "In times like this, when people suffer so much, the bodhisattvas don't stay in the temple; they are out there."[a] His "12 Precepts of the Order of Inter-being" attempts to express universal principles of life beyond Buddhist sectarianism, rejecting absolutely

Buddhist monks at a mass merit and blessings ceremony for Sri Lankan soldiers.

killing, coercion, dogmatism, and untruthfulness while advocating a meditation-centered life.

Confrontationalist: Political Monks of Sri Lanka's Maha Sangha

Drawing on some of the nationalist pronouncements of reformists such as Anagarika Dharmapala, some monks have formed an entity called the Maha Sangha to engage in political action. These activist monks have urged their government to reply with relentless military action, not negotiated compromise, to resolve the Tamil revolt that has fueled Sri Lanka's tragic civil war since 1983. Citing the Maha Sangha argument that "politics is the monks' heritage," another Buddhist nationalist group, the Bodu Bala Sena ("Army of Buddhist Power") began targeting the substantial Muslim minority scattered across Sri Lanka for criticism as anti-national and anti-Buddhist. In 2013, this group launched a campaign of violent repression calling for the boycott of halal-certified meat; scores of Muslim shops, businesses, and places of worship were vandalized by mobs led by Buddhist monks. As one Buddhist nationalist poet wrote to galvanize support for anti-minority aggression:

My brave, brilliant soldier son
Leaving [home] to defend the motherland
That act of merit is enough
To reach Nirvana in a future birth. . . .
Country, religion, race are my triple gems. . . .
The sangha is ever ready
At the front
If the race is threatened.[b]

[a]Sallie B. King, "Thich Nhat Hanh and the Unified Buddhist Church," in Christopher S. Queen and Sallie B. King, eds., *Engaged Buddhism: Buddhist Liberation Movements in Asia* (Albany: State University Press of New York, 1996), p. 351.
[b]H. L. Seneviratne, *The Work of Kings: The New Buddhism in Sri Lanka* (Chicago: University of Chicago Press, 1999), pp. 272–73.

Tibetan monks engaging in debate training, testing their ability to consistently expound the Buddha's teachings.

State Buddhism and the Poison of Ethnic Passion

With colonialism now gone, shifts in the political, socioeconomic, and intellectual spheres have changed individuals and caused Buddhists to adapt their beliefs and practices to a transformed world. Countries with Buddhist majorities now must decide how to shape society—in economic and political spheres—to best realize the Buddha's ideal of a compassionate civilization. Exponents still debate whether Buddhism should endorse military authoritarianism (on the model of the benevolent dictator Ashoka) or representative democracy (on the model of the sangha's democratic norms). Is it more compassionate to establish a "pure Buddhist state" that privileges Buddhism and Buddhists or to opt for a secular state that guarantees evenhanded tolerance of

A monk from the Ravana Balaya, a Buddhist nationalist group that claims a sacred duty to safeguard Sri Lanka from "minority or outside influences," as he addresses the media during a 2013 protest in Colombo, Sri Lanka.

a multireligious and multi-ethnic society? Can Buddhist ideals be more effectively implemented in a socialist or a free-market system?

As we have seen, in countries such as Myanmar and Sri Lanka, when "political monks" have gathered attention and public support, they have stoked an uncompromising Buddhist nationalism that targets minority ethnic groups of other faiths. In modern China and Vietnam, Buddhist monks are still called on to withdraw, study, and meditate. In India, Sri Lanka, and Thailand, on the other hand, monks have become leaders in political reform movements and in the implementation of economic development projects.

In Sri Lanka, once the nationalistic Buddhist movements had ushered in independence, they turned their efforts inward. By seeking to legislate a "purer Buddhist state" and a restoration of past glories, they created an environment in which activist monks inflamed unprecedented ethnic conflict with non-Buddhist minorities long resident on the island. Paradoxically, Buddhist universalism and the ideology of compassion have not prevented modern attempts at "ethnic cleansing" there or in Burma and Bhutan. Some social historians see the further weakening of Buddhist ethics in the future: As populations rise and resources grow scarcer, politicians of Buddhist Asia, as elsewhere, will be increasingly tempted to use Buddhism to unify majorities to win votes and take power, inviting possible discrimination against non-Buddhists. From 2007 until today, for example, Thai Buddhist monks have called for declaring Buddhism the official religion of the nation, in response to Muslim terrorist acts in its southern region that murdered monks and destroyed Buddhist sanctuaries.

Conclusion

As a refuge of intellectual freedom and spiritual imagination, Buddhist teachers nurtured and enriched the civilizations of Asia. Surveying the belief patterns of the world's Buddhist communities, one is challenged both by the sheer diversity of doctrinal expression and by the complexity of Buddhism's systematic thought. In becoming a world religion, Buddhism in practice has promoted compassionate, medically advanced, disciplined, mercantile, and literate societies. Like other great religions today, Buddhism has shown that its definition of the human condition and its prescribed ways of addressing suffering and mortality have enduring value, even in new societies and in the midst of changes that have shaken the modern and postcolonial world.

The global migration of Asian Buddhists in the postcolonial era is an important source of global revival in the twenty-first century. As these groups grow and prosper in their new countries, they naturally channel a portion of their savings back to the home region. But these immigrants have also paid to sponsor monks and build storefront monasteries in the West and, in the process, internationalized the home country's institutions through a slow grassroots process of development. As Buddhist priests, monks, and expatriates move between their new and old countries, and from rural to urban living circumstances, innovations and resources are being shifted as well. This immigrant-induced exchange also includes the cross-fertilization of ideas moving between Buddhist schools from distant areas of Asia and their Western exponents. It may well be that the future success—or perhaps even survival—of the modern national lineages and schools of Buddhism back in Asia will depend on an international membership, providing worldwide sources of funding and interpretive awareness.

An especially promising development may be the growing presence of Buddhism in the emerging global culture. In the area of human rights, Asian Buddhist exponents

Members of the Thai sangha gather for chanting before a large Buddha in Bangkok.

have made impressive contributions. Buddhist doctrine offers many traditional ideals that have inspired reformers and activists who style themselves as "engaged Buddhists." There is no shortage of examples today of the existential "poisons" that Buddhists have always located at the center of their wheel of life—human greed, anger, and delusion. And new poisons have been churned up in Buddhist countries themselves. Yet the very compassion and selflessness that Buddhists have always embraced as central to their tradition offer the means to lessen suffering of individuals, communities, and the earth itself.

Engaged Buddhism is uniting Asian Buddhists with Western converts, bringing together the energies of householders, monks, and nuns, and finding issues that connect Buddhist activists with similarly committed reformers from other faiths. It remains to be seen whether Buddhist revivalists can offer a compelling interpretation of the Dharma as Buddhists find themselves drawn into the marketplace of globalized capitalism, with its doctrines of individualism and competition and its vigorous encouragement of consumerism.

The late Gene Smith (at right), preserver of thousands of texts brought out of Tibet by refugees, presenting a gift of a hard drive containing thousands of sacred texts to a Tibetan Buddhist abbot. He made similar donations across the Tibetan world in 2008–9.

Discussion Questions

1. Pick three major episodes in the Buddha's life and discuss what lessons they impart to a typical Buddhist householder.

2. In what senses can the Buddha be called the Great Physician?

3. Many modern Buddhists regard the Buddha as a reformer. What teachings can be used to support this interpretation? What historical arguments can be made against this position?

4. Which of the Buddha's teachings are shared with post-Vedic Hinduism?

5. Explain how Buddhist doctrine can argue for reincarnation but against the existence of an "immortal soul."

6. Why is compassion a human ideal that is a logical extension of core Buddhist doctrines?

7. Why is Buddhism known as the *Middle Way*? Give at least three reasons.

8. Support or critique the statement "Vajrayana Buddhism is a school of Mahayana Buddhism."

9. Discuss the state of Buddhism across Asia in the year 750.

10. Why is the *Lotus Sutra* so important in China and Japan?

11. How does popular Mahayana Buddhism resemble and differ from devotional Hinduism?

12. How is the Mahar revival of Buddhism in India indicative of the effects of "Protestant Buddhism" and the backlash from the colonial era within the Buddhist world?

13. Name five aspects of Protestant Christianity that were adopted by Buddhist reformers, shaping the nineteenth- and twentieth-century revitalization movements called "Protestant Buddhism."

14. In your opinion, how would a modern Buddhist revivalist present the Dharma and argue that it remains a religion relevant to life in the twenty-first century?

15. Why might there be so many similarities in the biography of the Jain religion founder Mahavira (see Chapter 6) and the Buddha?

Key Terms

Amitabha/Amida	Avalokiteshvara/	Buddha-nature school
anatman	Guanyin	caitya
arhat	*bhikku/bhikkhuni*	Ch'an/Zen
Ashoka	bodhisattva	Cittamatra

(continued)

Key Terms (continued)

dana	Madhyamaka	samsara
dependent origination	Mahayana	sangha
Dharma	Maitreya/Mi-lo Fo	shramana
Dogen	maitri	*shunyata*
Eightfold Path	mizuko cult	skandha
Eisai	Nagarjuna	Sthaviravadins
engaged Buddhism	Nembutsu	stupa
enlightenment	Nichiren	Theravada
Four Good Deeds	nirvana	Three Marks of
Four Noble Truths	Pali Canon	Existence
Gandhara	pap	Three Refuges
Gelugpa	prajna	Vajrayana/Thunderbolt
karuna	Protestant Buddhism	Vehicle
koan	punya	*vipassana* meditation
Lotus Sutra	Pure Land	Wu Tai Shan

Suggested Readings

Gombrich, Richard. *Theravada Buddhism: A Social History from Ancient Benares to Modern Colombo* (New York: Routledge, 1988).

Heine, Steven, and Charles S. Prebish, eds. *Buddhism in the Modern World* (New York: Oxford University Press, 2003).

Lewis, Todd. *Buddhists: Understanding Buddhism Through the Lives of Practitioners.* (London: Wiley-Blackwell, 2014).

Lopez, Donald, ed. *Buddhism and Science: A Guide for the Perplexed* (Chicago: University of Chicago Press, 2008).

———. *Buddhism in Practice*, abridged ed. (Princeton, NJ: Princeton University Press, 2007).

Nelson, John K. *Experimental Buddhism: Innovation and Activism in Contemporary Japan.* (Honolulu: University of Hawaii Press, 2013).

Queen, Christopher, and S. King, eds. *Engaged Buddhism* (Albany: State of New York University Press, 1996).

Rahula, Walpola. *What the Buddha Taught* (New York: Publishers Resource, 1978).

Robinson, Richard, and Willard Johnson. *The Buddhist Religions: A Historical Introduction*, 5th ed. (Belmont, CA: Wadsworth, 2008).

Seager, Richard. *Buddhism in America* (New York: Columbia University Press, 1999).

Shaw, Sarah. *The Jatakas: Birth Stories of the Bodhisatta* (New York: Penguin, 2006).

Snellgrove, David. *Indo-Tibetan Buddhism* (Boulder, CO: Shambhala, 1987).

Trainor, Kevin, ed. *Buddhism: An Illustrated Guide* (London: Duncan-Baird, 2001).

Wijayaratna, Mohan. *Buddhist Monastic Life* (Cambridge: Cambridge University Press, 1987).

Williams, Paul. *Mahayana Buddhism: The Doctrinal Foundations*, 2nd ed. (New York: Routledge, 2009).

Williams, Paul, and Anthony Tribe. *Buddhist Thought: A Complete Introduction to the Indian Tradition* (New York: Routledge, 2000).

Note

1. Phra Kummsaen, quoted in Kenneth Landon, *Thailand in Transition* (Chicago: University of Chicago Press, 1939), pp. 67–68.

Additional Resources

BBC Religion: Buddhism (www.bbc.co.uk/religion/religions/buddhism). Reliable information and updated links to sites with basic information.

BuddhaNet (www.buddhanet.net). Gateway to sources of scholarly information and current events in the Buddhist world.

Buddhist Studies, The World Wide Web Virtual Library (www.ciolek.com/WWWVL-Buddhism.html). A directory of websites across the Buddhist world.

EAST ASIAN RELIGIONS

Confucianism, Daoism, Shinto, Buddhism

8

Overview

O n days considered favorable for approaching the gods, temples in China, Japan, and Korea are packed with morning visitors. In Beijing, newly married couples flock to the White Clouds Daoist temple to light candles, requesting divine aid to ensure the birth of a son; at family shrines in Seoul, students approach ancestral altars to report their applications to study at universities abroad; in rural Japan, farmers gather to give thanks at the village Shinto shrine for the annual harvest festival. Buddhist monasteries have also attracted new patronage as economic prosperity has enriched the region.

Today in China, public shrines for the sage Confucius are thriving. The Confucian emphasis on education, strong families, individual discipline, and harmonious group relations is seen as holding the center of East Asia's stable societies and orchestrating this region's ascendancy in the global economy. One of the central goals of this chapter is to have the reader understand the Confucian world, in East Asia and beyond. Another is to understand how the Chinese emphasis on harmony was extended to "the unity of the three faiths" (*san-jiao heyi*, still a widely used phrase), meaning Confucianism, Daoism, and Buddhism.

◄ A Japanese woman makes offerings to her recently departed father at a gravesite located in a Buddhist monastery in Tokyo.

East Asian Religions Timeline

1766–1122 BCE	Shang dynasty in China; cult of departed ancestors and oracle bone divination
1122–221	Zhou dynasty in China; yin-yang theory develops; era of intermittent civil disorder
ca. 551–479	Life of Master K'ung (Confucius)
ca. 520–286	Era of first Daoist sages, philosophers Lao Zi (d. 500 BCE?) and Zhuang Zi (365–290 BCE)
450–223	Era of Confucian sage scholars, Master Meng (Mencius, 371–289 BCE), Master Xun (298–238 BCE); origins of Confucian *Analects* and compilation of the *Five Classics*
221–206	Qin dynasty, the first to unify China; Great Wall completed
200 BCE – 220 CE	Han dynasty in China; civil service positions based on mastery of Confucian teachings
220–588 CE	Period of weak regional states and the growth of Daoism and Buddhism
618–907	T'ang dynasty in China; period of Confucian revival; translations of Indian Buddhist texts
668–918	Silla dynasty in Korea, centered on Buddhism as state religion
710–784	Nara period in Japan; Shinto tradition organized; Buddhism made state religion
794–1185	Heian period in Japan, ends with emperor removed from rulership
918–1392	Koryo dynasty in Korea, with ecumenical development of Mahayana Buddhism
960–1279	Song dynasty in China; period of neo-Confucianism (the "Second Epoch")
1130–1200	Life of Zhu Xi, leading neo-Confucian exponent, who reestablished the tradition as preeminent among the Chinese literati
ca. 1150	Goddess Mazu becomes popular in China, recognized by the state
1185–1333	Kamakura era in Japan, era of civil disorder and the rise of new Buddhist schools
1279–1368	Yuan dynasty in China, era of Mongol rule
1336–1600	Era of rule by Shoguns: Shinto-Buddhist syncretism, popularity of Pure Land Buddhism; adoption of Zen among the literati and samurai
1368–1644	Ming dynasty in China, the last era of Han Chinese rule; popularity of doctrines harmonizing the "three faiths"
1380ff.	In China, *The Canonization of the Gods* fixes folk pantheon in hierarchy mirroring state bureaucracy
1392–1910	Yi dynasty in Korea, an era marked by state-favored Confucianism
1472–1529	Life of Wang Yangming, a neo-Confucian who promoted mind cultivation and character development
1501–1570	Life of Yi T'oegye, important Korean neo-Confucian
1534–1582	Life of Nobunaga, Japanese shogun who persecuted Buddhism and gave support to Christianity
1592	Publication of *Journey to the West*, written by Wu Chengen

1600–1867	Tokugawa era in Japan, with new capital in Tokyo; Buddhism under strong state support
1644–1911	Qing (Manchu) dynasty in China; era promoting Confucianism
1815–1888	Oldest new religions in Japan: Kurozumikyo (1814), Tenrikyo (1838)
1850–1864	Taiping Rebellion in China, led by Hong Xiuquan (1814–1864)
1860	Ch'ondogyo movement founded in Korea by Ch'oe Suun (1824–1864)
1868–1945	Return of emperor's rule in Japan and the rise of state Shinto; Japan adopts Western calendar, technology, imperialist political views
1871–1945	Japanese Buddhist establishment joins Shinto nationalists and Christians supporting militarism
1880–present	Best and brightest individuals across the East Asia region studying Western learning, technology to seek rapid modernization
1889–1890	New constitution and Japanese government initiatives draw heavily on Confucian doctrines
1900–1945	Founding of "new religions" in prewar Japan: P. L. Kyodan in 1924, Reiyukai Kyodan in 1925, Soka Gakkai in 1930, Rissho Koseikai in 1938
1912	Fall of Qing dynasty in China, ending state patronage of Confucianism
1946–present	Founding of "new 'new religions'" in postwar Japan: Sukyo Mahikari in 1963, Agonshu in 1971, Aum Shinrikyo in 1989
1949–1976	People's Republic of China established; Communist Party diminishes monks, priests, religious institutions
1966–1976	Cultural Revolution attacks the "Four Old Things": thought, culture, customs, habits
1984–present	Buddhist monasteries and Daoist temples reopen in China
1994	Study of Confucianism in schools officially approved by Chinese state
1995	Aum Shinrikyo sect in Japan launches poison gas attack in Tokyo
1996–present	Images of Mao Zedong and other deceased Communist Party leaders found on popular religious amulets
1999	Falun Gong, a syncretistic Buddhist-Daoist group founded by Li Hongzhi; Chinese government bans the group and begins persecution of practitioners
2007	Chinese government begins funding of the first of 500 "Confucius Institutes" across the world to promote the study of Chinese language and culture
2008	Chinese government declares Qing Ming, "Grave Sweeping Day," an official holiday
2010	Communist Party officially celebrates Confucius' birthday. It places image of Confucius in Tian'anmen Square, Beijing, then removes it a few months later.
2013	Responding to many reports of neglected elders, Communist Party in China passes law requiring children to show filial piety to their parents through visits and calls
2017	Half a billion Chinese officially counted participating in Confucian grave visits and ritualism on Qing Ming

Interreligious pluralism defines East Asia. Throughout the region's history, the great majority of East Asians regarded Confucianism, Daoism, deity cults, and Buddhism as complementary. This applies to Japan as well, between Buddhism and its indigenous religion, Shinto. Most felt that these interrelated beliefs and practices enriched their spirituality. It was rare for individuals—elite or common folk—to feel that "being religious" meant choosing one religious tradition to the exclusion of the others. This openness stands in contrast to the common Western belief that religious conviction means adopting one creed and forsaking all others.

The religions of East Asia today find their common roots in the veneration of ancestors dating back to earliest antiquity. Over time these practices became blended with basic elements of Daoism, Buddhism, and Confucianism, comprising East Asia's **diffuse religion**. Given that roughly 30 percent of humanity is East Asian, no full reckoning of human religious life can be made without taking into account China, Korea, and Japan.

A brief review of the region's geography will help us understand this pattern of cultural diffusion. What is today referred to as "China" is the People's Republic of China (PRC). With more than 1.4 billion citizens, it is the country with the largest population in the world. Although spoken Chinese contains over twenty major dialects, the literate culture of China has used the same written language for more than 2,000 years. This has made the classical literary tradition (including all religious texts) accessible to the learned throughout the entire East Asian region.

China has been the center of the East Asian region from earliest antiquity. The emergence of a central state there predates the unification of Korea and Japan by at least twelve and fifteen centuries, respectively. Most modern national boundaries that

diffuse religion: spiritual tradition centered on family and locality, informed by common ideas from Confucianism, Daoism, and Buddhism

At a shrine atop the sacred mountain Tai Shan in southern China, devotees light incense and candles to honor the local gods. People hang heart-linking locks, hoping to secure the safety and happiness of their family members.

demarcate the region date back to the premodern era. The two Koreas, the region of Tibet, and the republic of Taiwan are exceptions.

In very broad terms, all regions beyond China's early core can be seen as the periphery of Chinese civilization, where states and individuals adapted the essential Chinese cultural forms. These forms include the fundamental material technologies needed for subsistence (intensive rice production, the making of iron, and porcelain pottery); the written Chinese characters used to record the spoken languages; and the beliefs and practices of its great religious traditions. It is true that in every East Asian country today, most people maintain traditions of remembering and venerating their ancestors at graves, temples, and family altars.

Yet despite the overwhelming influence of Chinese culture and the power of the Chinese states, Korean, Japanese, and, at times, Vietnamese peoples preserved their own separate identities. While importing and synthesizing much from China, each nonetheless developed a distinct spoken language, mythology, and spiritual connection to its territory. In all these periphery states, too, the national cultures inspired people to identify with being culturally and politically separate from China, however much their elites admired Chinese culture.

The formerly unified Korean culture area, artificially split into the separate countries of North Korea and South Korea since the end of the Second World War (1945), was most strongly influenced by Chinese cultural borrowings, including Buddhism. In the early modern period until the end of the Yi dynasty (1392–1910), Confucianism was the state religion, and ancestor worship was central. Among South Korea's 48 million people, shamanic traditions are today stronger there than elsewhere in East Asia, and they are practiced by most individuals regardless of any other religious affiliation. Little traditional religious activity is sanctioned or reported among the 24 million people of the modern isolationist and communist state of North Korea.

China also influenced religion in Japan, but beginning later than in Korea. Although Japan never established Daoist institutions, temples devoted to Confucius, or a state bureaucracy administered by men versed in Confucian tradition, most doctrines from these Chinese traditions were transmitted into Japan. These included yin-yang theory, medical principles, and geomancy from the former; with ethical norms, political theory, and ancestor rituals adopted by the Japanese from the latter. Now a constitutional monarchy with all power vested in a parliament and prime minister, Japan had for fifteen centuries been ruled by an emperor and a single imperial line claiming mythological origins. Since the end of World War II, however, Japan's 125 million people have produced the world's third-largest national economy. As elsewhere, this rapid transition has worked in contradictory directions, enriching devotees of every persuasion who have rebuilt institutions and created new ones while changing the society profoundly. This explains why here and across East Asia, thousands of "new religions" have sprung up, offering creative spiritual responses to life in today's fast-moving societies.

Because of the destruction and profound changes that have swept modern China, many religious beliefs and practices originally from China are now best preserved in Korea or Japan. Despite long-standing cultural ties connecting East Asian peoples, the modern era was marked by conflicts between nations that ranged from colonization and warfare to genocide.

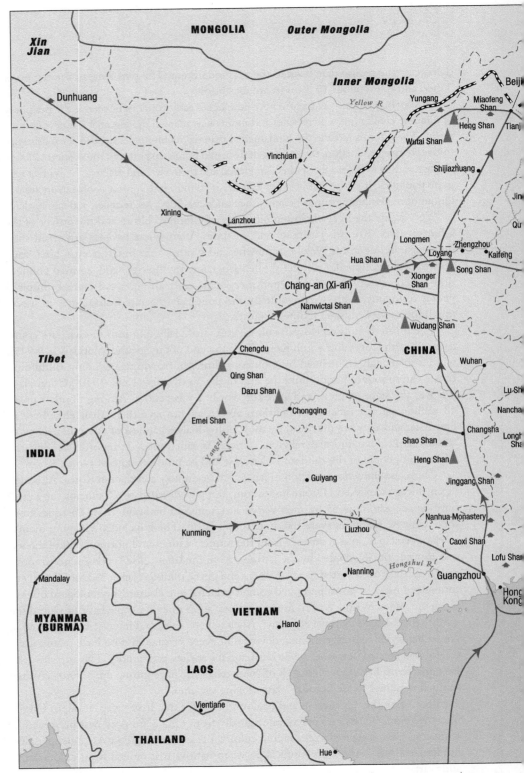

Map 8.1 Modern political map of China, Japan, and North and South Korea showing important religious sites.

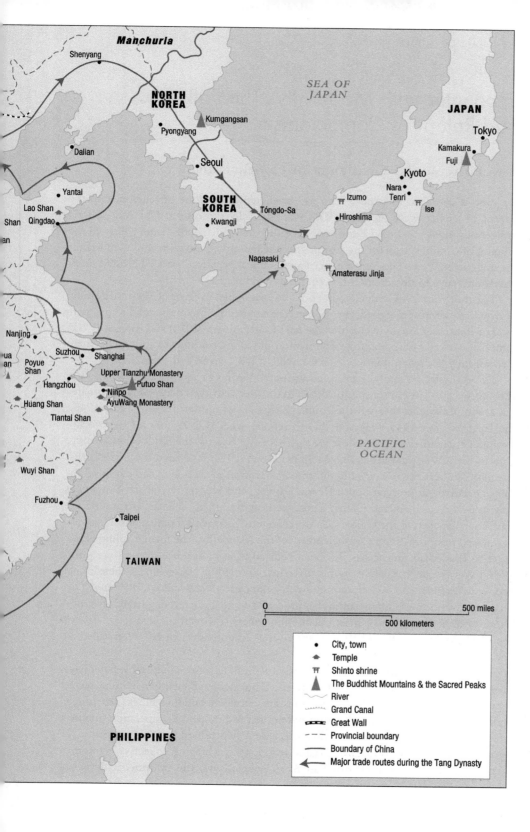

Encounter with Modernity: The Fall and Return of Confucianism

The Postcolonial Challenge of Confucianism

By 1980 it was clear that those who had predicted the decline of religion with the advent of science were incorrect. This was especially the case in East Asia. There, indigenous intellectuals and reformers since the mid-nineteenth century blamed the religion of Confucianism for the region's decadence and failure to defend itself against the imperialist West. The region's social and political problems were all blamed on its blind adherence to decadent Confucian ideals and practices.

The more quickly Confucianism could be abandoned in favor of Western cultural borrowings, reformers argued, the sooner East Asia would be on the road to prosperity. For this reason, many welcomed the fall of the Chinese (1910) and Korean (1912) imperial states and with them the domination of Confucian officials and intellectuals. Yet not only has religion in east Asia survived, it has revived and expanded.

For example, some observers once attributed Japan's prosperity after World War II to its successful Westernization. Although the war destroyed many of Japan's material accomplishments through the country's first era of modernization (1868–1945), the Japanese after 1945 were still able to rebuild what is today one of the world's strongest economies. Scholars now see the success of Japan as the result of much more than its early Westernization: The Meiji era (1868–1912) facilitated the region's first union of Western technology and reformed Confucian social policy. Similar developments occurred in postwar South Korea, Taiwan, and Singapore and are now under way in post-Mao mainland China. Thus, we now find many scholars attributing the East Asians' success to the region's family-centered "bourgeois Confucianism" (as distinguished from the "high Confucianism" of the Mandarins, the former ruling elite).

The East Asian revival has also been realized in each instance by a strong post–World War II state that defines its duty in terms of providing leadership for the national economic agendas and takes responsibility for the nation's collective well-being. This recent reinvention of Confucianism has produced societies that today have low crime rates, social harmony, and efficient economic behavior. Given the disastrous state of the region right after World War II, the overall accomplishment has been called an "economic miracle."

Now what earlier reformers had identified as Confucianism's intractable flaws have been reanalyzed in positive terms: Family-based businesses efficiently maximize scarce capital; tightly woven kin/family relations are excellent building blocks for supply and product distribution; an education system that fosters group cooperation, memorization, and imitation produces individuals able to work hard and master math, science, and technology. With strong states dedicated to achieving collective economic success, it was clear by 1990 that East Asian peoples with this reformed Confucian orientation had created successful twenty-first-century societies. Thus, after East Asians had acquired Western know-how, they effectively drew on Confucian elements in their cultures to mobilize indigenous social resources and create political systems that ensured the social cohesiveness needed to promote national prosperity.

East Asia's success calls into question another former tenet of modernity theory: Must all nations follow the Western model to succeed in the twenty-first century? Or is the Confucian route through strong authoritarian states an alternative for Asia, heralding what might be termed a "Third Confucian Epoch"? To understand better the ideas underlying this encounter with modernity today, we must trace the historical development of religion in East Asia.

East Asian Religions in the Formative Era (1500 BCE–617 CE)

In East Asia, many beliefs and practices documented from earliest antiquity survive up to the present. An example of this conservatism is the deities worshipped by China's imperial court: A list of the gods receiving sacrifices from the last Qing emperor in 1907 matches *exactly* the gods mentioned in a very early record (ca. 1100 BCE), with the sole exception of Confucius (who lived almost 600 years after the Shang court). A survey of the early development of Chinese religions demonstrates the pivotal importance of religion in Chinese civilization and how Chinese religious beliefs and practices spread to other East Asian societies.

Earliest History: Shang (1766–1122 BCE)

In the fertile valleys of the Yellow River, urban societies formed by 2000 BCE. They developed metal technologies, a pictographic writing system, and religious practices. All three of these aspects of civilization are connected in the practice of oracle bone divination, which was discovered among the northern peoples who lived within walled cities and called their rulers the *Shang*. Questions were inscribed on dried large bones of animals. A ritualist then applied a hot metal bar to the bones and discerned answers from the cracking patterns produced. Among the over 150,000 Shang oracle bones found and deciphered to date, most questions had to do with things of this world. There are questions regarding whether to undertake military action, journeys, or ceremonies as well as the interpretation of omens believed to predict weather, illness, or the gender of unborn children.

Shang metal casters made finely decorated bronze vessels that were used in ceremonies to worship deities and ancestors. Inscriptions on the vessels indicate that the Shang rulers boasted of the unrivaled supernatural power of their own ancestors to act on their and the society's behalf. Offerings of drink and food, including animals sacrificed on altars, were made at early Chinese burial sites. This Shang notion of reciprocity between dead ancestors and living kin remains a central aspect of East Asian religions up to the present day.

For the ruling elite, the cult of the dead created large tombs where they were buried with all the essentials for life in the "next world." The early Shang buried sacrificed human servants alongside the nobles; for later emperors, terra-cotta replicas of servants and animals replaced living beings.

Human access to the gods is another important religious belief known from earliest antiquity. The Shang saw gods as immanent in rain, mountains, and rivers. The early Chinese attributed significance to patterns and events in nature and made offerings to particular gods associated with them. Spirits were thought to affect all areas of life, from military battles and foreign relations to business fortunes, marriage, and illness. The presence of gods and ancestor spirits was most dramatically attested to by people who served as spirit mediums and were called *wu/xi* (women/men). Some Chinese turned to the *wu/xi* shamans for divine aid, while others hired them to exorcise the demons blamed for causing personal sicknesses or troubles.

Shang-di: heavenly Lord, thought to preside over early Chinese pantheon

There is also an interesting Shang concept of a high deity called **Shang-di**, "the Lord Above," regarded as so powerful that only the Shang rulers could petition him. The name signifies the elevation of one Shang ancestor to supreme status, though *Shang-di* endured subsequently in popular imagination as the superior deity who monitors human behavior. (Modern Chinese Protestants have used this term as a translation of *God*.)

Thus, the diffuse religion found later in East Asia stems from beliefs prevalent in early China: the view of an interconnected universe peopled by spirits including dead ancestors, and the belief that unseen forces in heaven and on earth could be influenced by the petitions of shamans, oracle readers, and divine kings.

Zhou, Chin, and Han Dynasties (1122 BCE –220 CE)

The millennium from the Zhou dynasty (1122–221 BCE) until the fall of the Han (206 BCE–220 CE) was "formative," in the sense that during this period most of the ideas and practices inherited from the past were developed in more systematic forms and recorded for the first time. It is also in this era that the great sages arose whose teachings would so strongly influence not only the Chinese elite but the entire region.

ancestor veneration: worship, feeding, and petitioning of the souls of dead ancestors

yin-yang theory: twin complementary forces by which the Dao is known

Tu-di Gong: "earth ruler" believed to control fertility worshipped by farmers in early China

Ancestor veneration, deity worship, and the role of spirit mediums all spread as the population of China increased and dispersed southward. This era saw the development of **yin-yang theory** and the five substances theory (*wu-xing*: water, fire, wood, metal, earth) to make observations of nature and natural signs. The cult of **Tu-di Gong**, the "earth ruler" who controls fertility, became widespread among the largely agricultural populations. By Han times, Tu-di was addressed in legalistic petitions, reflecting the growing presence of law in Chinese society.

At court and among commoners, Chinese polytheistic theology regarded the deities as neither good nor evil but as potentially both: They can be agents of illness and disaster or the bearers of blessings. Most of the notable deities by the late Zhou were viewed with both hope and fear, as with the Lord of the Yellow River, whose waters could bring either good harvests or destructive floods. The worldview of most Chinese was that beneficial gods were pitted against malevolent demons. This contrasted with the worldview of the elite, which emphasized abstract reasoning or mysticism.

Ancestor veneration developed further in the formative era. The family tomb became the key place connecting the living and the dead. Texts found in excavated tombs mention belief in a soul that survives into an afterlife, calling it a *chao-hun* ("cloud soul"). The dead were buried with objects that would be useful to a soul revived in the afterlife.

By the Han era, texts deposited in the tombs mention a new supreme overlord, called **Tian di**, who keeps records on each individual soul. Tomb scrolls detail personal acts that seem intended to verify the records kept by Tian di. There are written petitions asking that the deceased be released from blame for any evil deeds performed in life. The belief that proper tombs can facilitate beneficial exchanges between living and dead grew stronger. Rulers had texts compiled to describe the correct rites, and these practices were then widely adopted across Chinese society.

The Zhou era was marked by political instability and militarism. Regional states vied for control of territory and revenues, their rulers and officials showing little regard

☯	
Yin	**Yang**
Dark	Bright
Earth	Heaven
Female	Male
Autumn	Spring
Valley	Mountain
West	East
Po Soul (grave)	*Hun* Soul (heaven)

The symbolism of the *Yi-Jing* was the main system for East Asians conceptualizing the incessantly changing universe, much as math equations are used to express the essential truths underlying the discoveries of modern science. The most common *yin-yang* symbol should be viewed as ever in motion, with the circles in each sector expanding until black becomes white and white black.

Tian di: supreme overlord in Heaven believed in Han-era China to keep records on each individual soul

Terra-cotta warriors, unearthed from an imperial tomb outside Xi'an, China, had been placed with the emperor to serve him in the afterlife.

Daoist: East Asian visionaries who advocated individualistic retreat, learning from nature, and noninterference by the state

Confucianism: culture of literate elite (*rujia*) informed by Confucius and his disciples

Master K'ung: given name of sage later known as Confucius

ren: Confucian ideal of "being fully human"

li: Confucian ethic of correct behavior, which leads to ren

for moral order or respect for human life. Yet individuals arose who formulated the principles on which a just society could be established and by which humane leaders should be guided. These ideas would become the central pillars of East Asian life. Those who advocated individualistic retreat, learning from the natural world, and noninterference by the state as the best ways to ensure humanity's flourishing were called **Daoists**. Those who wished to cultivate their own humanity through disciplined learning, ritual practice, humility, and active social service were called **Confucians**.

Confucius and the Literati Tradition

Although one of the most influential figures in world history, **Master K'ung** (Confucius; 551–479 BCE), failed to realize his own goal of securing an influential position as a state minister. A gifted teacher, his students collected and passed down his oral teachings to their own students. Confucius developed the concepts of righteousness and of **ren**, a term that has many shades of meaning but captures the sense of "being fully human." The chief means to ren was **li**, which consisted of ethical propriety, good manners, and the cultivation of traditional ritual performances. The early Confucians imagined a world led by men, and their ideal was the *jun-zi*, a cultivated gentleman who learns from his teacher in youth and then continues to study, both to develop his virtue and to serve others.

In this textbook, we use the Western term "Confucianism" instead of the corresponding Chinese term, *ruija*, which means "literary tradition." The tradition of the literati, or intellectuals, is rooted in the system of moral observance and ritual performance praised by Master K'ung.

xiao: Confucian ideal of filial conduct; respect for one's parents, elders, and ruler

The most important aspect of the li is the individual's conduct within the family. Here the central principle is filial conduct (**xiao**), or the bond between child and parent. This relationship implies mutual obligations within a hierarchical framework. Protection and nurturing by a superior were rendered in return for selfless service and obedience. Classical Confucianism conceived of this bond as the fundamental human connection and identified four other bonds as extensions of it. The entire set comprised the Five Hierarchical Relationships, which were to lead society toward harmony and "human flourishing." If xiao began with serving one's parents, it was to continue with serving one's ruler, thus bringing to maturity one's own character. Mencius, a disciple of Confucius, described the Five Hierarchal Relationships as follows:

Relationship	Principles of the Relationship
son and father	filial piety ↔ paternal example
minister and ruler	obedience ↔ righteousness
wife and husband	obedience ↔ faithful dominance
young and old	respect ↔ precedence and example
friend and friend	mutuality and trust (*hsin*)

Confucius' theory was that if those who ruled and ministered both followed and encouraged the society's adherence to maintaining these ideals, all would benefit and the state's harmony would be ensured. As set forth in the ***Analects***, the compilation of the master's teachings, anecdotes, and sayings, Confucius became a model for subsequent generations. The cultured human should be at ease while always showing careful respect; he is firm but kindhearted, an advocate for the practice of moderation who finds a natural balance in all endeavors.

Although he is described as being uninterested in the reality of the ghost or other spirits, Confucius was emphatic on the need for individuals to develop a deep respect for others as well as to establish harmony in the personalities of their immediate kin by their careful performance of funeral rituals and the rites of ancestor veneration.

The success of Confucius' teachings was largely due to their advocacy by several great disciples, notably Master Meng (or **Mencius**, 371–289 BCE) and **Master Xun** (298–238 BCE). Mencius argued that human nature is essentially good, that humans are naturally compassionate, dutiful, courteous, and inclined toward learning. Mencius also developed the Confucian view that the well-being of society depends on the virtue of the rulers and that it is the state's responsibility to ensure the flourishing of its citizens. Another especially influential theory of Mencius applied Confucian thought to the destiny of a state: If a dynasty rules by virtue, then it receives the **Mandate of Heaven**, an authorization that can be revoked if rulers cease to be virtuous.

Master Xun, the third of the classical Confucian sages, proposed a more pessimistic, mechanistic, and authoritarian application of Master K'ung's ideas. In his view, humans are inherently antisocial and the universe turns on impersonal forces. But since people can be trained, once shown the good, they will inherently adopt practices that lead in that direction. Hence, Xun turned Confucians toward the careful study of the past, its ancient sages, and the texts that record the human history.

By the late Han (100 CE), the two interrelated elements of the Confucian tradition were established: inner sagehood and outer nobility. Dynasties recorded their histories, officials argued about the Mandate of Heaven, and scholars looked to the earliest sages to model their own lives. We must also note that the notion of Confucius as merely a human sage of this world had already given way to a popular portrayal of him as a demigod.

Early Daoist Philosophy

During the formative era in China, the most important critique of Confucian doctrine came from those who argued that social relations would be harmonious only after

Image of Master K'ung, whose Western name, Confucius, was coined by early Jesuit missionaries.

At 15 I set my heart on learning; at 30, I firmly took my stand; at 40 I came to be free from doubts; at 50 I understood the decree of Heaven; at 60 my ear was attuned; at 70 I follow my heart's desire without overstepping the line.

—Confucius

SOURCE: D. C. Lau, *Confucius: The Analects* (New York: Penguin, 1979), p. 63.

- *Analects:* collection of sayings attributed to Confucius

- **Mencius:** first major disciple of Confucius; systemized Master's thought

- **Master Xun:** influential early Confucian exponent with emphasis on authoritarian rule

- **Mandate of Heaven:** theory that the forces of the universe favor a ruler

"Behave when away from home as though you were in the presence of an important guest. Deal with commoners as though you were officiating at an important ceremony."

—Confucius

Dao: mysterious power that moves the universe and is the source of life for all beings

Lao Zi: "Old Baby"; author of *Daodejing* and founder of Daoism

de: mysterious, spontaneous energy of the universe

wu-wei: Daoist ideal of "noninterference"

Zhuang Zi: the second Daoist classic text, named after a sage of this name

"Standing by the deep valley makes you think deep; Scaling the heights makes you aim high."
—*Book of Yi Xun*

humanity had synchronized itself with nature and with the **Dao**, the mystical reality underlying it.

The first great expression of Daoism is the poetic *Daodejing* (*Tao Te Ching*). This work, traditionally attributed to an anonymous "Old Baby," or **Lao Zi** (Lao Tzu), aims to express the nature of the Dao while paradoxically beginning with the proviso that "the true Dao" cannot be spoken or adequately defined. (The sage's odd name implies the goal of attaining a pristine spiritual state, forever young.)

In this philosophical system, Dao is the prime source of creation, from which the yin and yang forces emerge in ever-shifting harmonies. Dao determines all things and flows as the spontaneous energy (**de**) of the universe, functioning without the will or purpose of a divine creator. To experience the Dao, one must pursue the path of noninterference (**wu-wei**) as in Lao Zi's dictum "Do nothing and nothing will be left undone." The best teacher is (to use the example of the *Daodejing*) water that flows freely yet can overcome all obstacles.

The Daoists felt that the Confucians harmed society through imposing rules that interfered with humanity's natural inclinations. Their political message was to return to primal simplicity, with the state interfering as little as possible with the lives of the people. The highest calling for humans, argued the Daoists, is not state service but retreat into the mountains, where the Dao can be felt most clearly.

The second Daoist classic, the ***Zhuang Zi***, is attributed to and named after the sage Zhuang Zi (365–290 BCE). Through lively parables and mind-boggling paradoxes, his sayings explore the mysterious reality of the Dao in everyday human experiences. The most famous example perhaps is his meditation on waking from a dream of being a butterfly. He asks: Which is "real"? Was Zhuang Zi dreaming of being a butterfly, or is the human Zhuang Zi instead merely that butterfly's dream? This text also explores the acceptance of death. Such acceptance is the necessary step toward experiencing transcendent freedom.

Daoist mysticism provided an alternative to the rules and regulations of strict Confucianism, offering spiritual guidance to those who retreated from government service or active social life. Daoist refuge is found in nature, and the natural world inspired subsequent Chinese artists, including poets and painters.

Lao Zi on an ox. The sage of Daoism depicted in a Ming-era painting.

Defining Terms

Our treatment of multiple East Asian religions in the same chapter calls for a brief explanation of the central terms.

For convenience, we use Confucianism, a Western term originating in eighteenth-century Europe, instead of the corresponding Chinese term, *rujia*, meaning "literati tradition." The tradition of the literati (or intellectuals) is rooted in the system of moral observance and ritual performance praised in the sixth century BCE by Master K'ung (or, in English rendering, Confucius), whose teachings were commented on and extended by subsequent sages. The Confucian tradition was made China's state ideology over two millennia ago, and it became noted for its wisdom books, political institutions, social teachings, and attention to self-cultivation. Scholars during the Sung era and subsequent centuries, known by Westerners as neo-Confucians, edited the foundational texts and reinterpreted their tradition influenced by both Buddhist and Daoist thought. In this cumulative reform the *rujia* neo-Confucian tradition became the most common shared spiritual and ethical culture of China that spread to Korea and Japan. Mastering the tradition's classical texts and central doctrines was at the center of the educational system and government bureaucracy until well into the modern era (1905 in China, 1867 in Japan, 1910 in Korea). Reflecting this diversity, we use *Confucianism* without imputing to the tradition a singular creed, ritual, or institution.

Daoism can refer to loosely connected philosophical and religious traditions and so always needs further specification. All traditions of Daoism build on the earliest texts attributed to Laozi and Xuangzi, that articulate the path to cultivate an immediate sense of personal connection with the primal force or reality of the universe, one that its sages labeled "the Dao," using a character that means "way" or "path." The sages of religious Daoism themselves are revered as humans who had realized supernatural physical powers or spiritual immortality. Through meditation or alchemy, this strand of Daoism advocated the sages' path to immortality and divinity; eventually monastic traditions (on the model of Buddhism) were developed to sustain communities of seekers and maintain cults to enshrined immortals. Many aspects of "applied" Daoism were developed as "secular" traditions to manage worldly life in East Asia: acupuncture to adjust the flow of the life force flowing in the human body, *feng shui* to help humans live their lives in harmony with the natural energy flowing in the natural and built environment, *Yi-Jing* and other forms of prognostication to determine the proper moment to perform important tasks (marriage, travel, etc.), *wu-shu*, or the martial arts, to focus human powers in order to overcome enemies.

Deity cults in traditional East Asia were universal. Springs, rivers, remarkable geographic features—particularly mountain peaks—are still thought to have extraordinary divine inhabitants whose spiritual force, or *ling*, is immanent. Each sector of the earth, in fact, is thought to have a resident deity who serves as the counterpart of the government official in charge of the village, the town, the province, and the state itself, with a hierarchy of gods mirroring the human civil service. Across East Asia, the common popular perception is that the deities exist and that they can be contacted at temples, especially mountain shrines. A person will question a god and then, through ancient divination rituals, attempt to discern an answer. In the popular conception, deities, like local officials, can be paid to provide favors; the big gods may be induced to discipline lesser gods (or demons) who cause troubles. Humans out of mutual respect are obliged to show the gods thanksgiving regularly for life, health, and prosperity. Gods in China who failed to provide assistance were reviled and abandoned.

Defining Terms *continued*

Diffuse religion is the useful term that indicates what for most East Asians consists of a spiritual life that is centered within the family unit and immediate locality. It has its roots in the ancestor veneration and spirit worship of earliest antiquity but incorporates general and basic elements of Confucianism, Daoism, and Buddhism. The unity of a region's diffuse religion derives from the long-established state bureaucracy practice of promulgating full expressions of the common traditions; at times, scholars were assigned to codify the myriad texts and practices to give them coherence. From medieval times until now, traditional printed almanacs have been important texts that record such teachings and orchestrate yearly practices based on the lunar calendar for families and localities. Among the major elements of the diffuse religion is belief in deities and in rituals relating to them. There is also a sense that the universe has fundamental forces and powers, requiring humans to seek harmony with them to achieve health and long life. Further, the world is believed to have certain natural hierarchies that must be acknowledged and respected, in forms prescribed by the ancient traditions. This requirement of hierarchical respect extends to one's departed kin.

The sectarian religions in East Asia were institutional Buddhism and Daoism and the sects that arose periodically, often with the goal of overthrowing the state. Such separate religions were meaningful primarily for the very small elites who joined an order, adopted a singular discipline within one tradition, or sought individualistic sectarian goals. But over time, many sects ceased to advocate the singularity of their approach alone.

Thus it is hard to find firm boundaries separating the spiritual traditions of East Asia. The Dao is a concept shared by all schools, for example; indeed, the Buddhists used the term to define the Buddha's teaching (Dharma) in early translations. The goal of harmony is also common in each spiritual path. We are able to treat East Asia's religions under a single heading precisely because of the commonality of this "diffuse borrowing," the nexus of the diffuse religion in the home and among kin rather than in large institutions, and the pertinent attempts by elites and commoners alike to harmonize these rich traditions. In each nation, the inclusive harmonizing trait has been expressed with only slight variation: in Japan, "Shintoist in youth, Confucian as an adult, Buddhist in old age"; in Korea, "Confucian by obligation, shamanist at heart"; in China, "Confucian in the office, Daoist outside."

"Religious Daoism" (Dao Jiao)

qi: vital life force in individuals and in nature

religious Daoism: tradition devoted to attaining individual immortality through alchemical infusions or meditative practices

The basic philosophical ideas of ancient Daoism were developed into various religious traditions, which differed according to the spiritual disciplines required for individuals to achieve immortality. There were two main avenues to reach this goal. The first required meditation aimed at strengthening and multiplying the life force (**qi**), typically through breathing exercises, fasting, and sexual practices. These practices create a spiritual essence that can survive the physical body's death.

A second path involved the study of alchemy, the art of transforming such substances as mercury and gold into an elixir that, when ingested, gives birth to an "inner child" whose body and soul are invincible to decay or death. Through these two paths, Daoist mystics and alchemists contributed to the development of Chinese science and medicine as well as to the martial arts traditions. **Religious Daoism** also focused on temples dedicated to the divine immortals, who were called upon to help in practical as well as spiritual matters.

Daoism Traditions: Basic Beliefs

Philosophical Daoism evolved from the *Daodejing*. Three key ideas from this elite tradition remain important across East Asia. First is the Daoist notion that humanity is interconnected in a web of natural forces, all shifting and reversing direction when they reach their apex. Reality is best perceived through this interconnection, for in this movement the power of the Dao can be discerned from moment to moment. The classic text describing "the state of the moment" is the *Yi-Jing*, and it has helped East Asians determine the various combinations of yin and yang forces at work in a given setting.

The second important Daoist notion is that some individuals can attain a state of ultimate transformation, transcending mortality via alchemical, dietary, or meditative practices that impart the power to know and control unseen forces. The human body is potentially perfectible, even though those who attain immortality are few. Here, Daoists join with Confucians in seeing the world as redeemable through human agency, with nature occupying a dual role as humanity's true home as well as teacher.

The third important Daoist notion is that the pursuit of simplicity is essential for spiritual development as well as for the betterment of society. Only the "natural person" who "goes

Deity from a Daoist temple, where immortals are worshipped to secure blessings.

● **philosophical Daoism:** tradition articulating path to harmony for individuals and society based on understanding and flowing with natural forces

A recluse in the mountains. Hermits like the one in this fourteenth-century Chinese painting looked to nature for inspiration and as a source of primal energy (qi).

Stages of Creation in Daoism

ONE		TWO		THREE		MYRIAD THINGS
a state of eternal union with the Dao	∝	yin and yang in perfect harmony (*through taming the thought processes via meditation*)	⇒	essence (*jing*), life energy (*qi*) (*each "fixed" through alchemical practices*)	⇛	self amidst ∞ combinations of yin and yang

The Daoist sage seeks to reverse the process of creation, by engaging in meditative practices to preserve jing and move it toward the head, multiplying qi, finding harmony within the self and the universe, then merging with the Dao.

---

with the flow" (wu-wei), avoiding unnatural action, can find the truth, and only a society whose citizens live in a simple manner can find true peace and justice. Daoism thus, with Buddhism, provided a counterculture to the Confucian establishment, by serving those who wished to withdraw from society or to critique the excesses of those in power, and even, at times, bolstering a rebel group's intention to overthrow the regime.

State Religion: The First Confucian Epoch (220 BCE–200 CE)

The first full unification of China was brought about by the first Qin emperor of the Qin dynasty (221 BCE–206 BCE). He instituted a central bureaucracy and state religion, both designed to promote social unity by harmonizing the forces of nature with imperial rule. Although he made good on many of his lofty ambitions, this emperor obsessively sought personal immortality through Daoist alchemy and ruthlessly suppressed viewpoints he considered deviant. His Mandate of Heaven lasted only fifteen years (221–206 BCE). Many later Chinese emperors would act as though, and even assert, they were divine.

The next unification of China occurred under the Han (200 BCE–220 CE), who established an imperial university and examination system that was based exclusively on Confucian teachings. By the later Han (ca. 175 CE) the content of the **Five Classics** had been officially established. These five classics are the *Yi-Jing* (*Book of Changes*), *Shu Jing* (*Book of Documents*), *Shi Jing* (*Book of Poetry*), and *Li Jing* (*Book of Rites*) and a historical work that records events in early Chinese states for the purpose of assessing blame and praise. The classics promoted a tradition of learning from the past to guide future governance, and they supported the view that for full development, a human must integrate historical, social, political, and metaphysical awareness.

"The mysteries of Heaven and earth are embodied in the inhalation and exhalation. . . . Your internal energy must be gathered in its three forms: generative, vital, and spiritual energy. Once the soul is merged into this unified spirit, it must be nourished. Vital, it will leave the body, ascend to the heavens, and become immortal."

—Daoist Sage Wang Ch'ung

Five Classics: Confucian canon of five works attributed to Master K'ung

TEACHINGS OF RELIGIOUS WISDOM: Daoist

The need for individuals who seek to understand the universe to travel to mountains and rivers to discuss ultimate principles is conveyed in this parable by the great Daoist sage Zhuang Zi.

A frog in a well, restricted in his environment, is unable to talk about the ocean. A summer insect, confined to its season, cannot talk about ice. A poor village scholar, restricted by his learning, cannot discuss the Dao. A person can find spiritual truth only by leaving his home cliffs and riverbanks and gazing upon the mighty ocean. Only then can the seeker perceive his own place and begin to understand the Great Dao.

—Zhuang Zi

Source: Adapted from D. Howard Smith, ed., *The Wisdom of the Taoists* (New York: New Directions, 1980), pp. 82–83.

The state religion developed in the Han placed the emperor as chief priest, advised by Confucian experts on ritual performance. Daoist thought was integrated in imperial religion by specialists who used Daoist techniques to interpret omens in the natural world. On behalf of the kingdom, the emperor alone could sacrifice to the spirits of the departed imperial ancestors; as the Son of Heaven, he revered heaven and earth as his symbolic parents and worshipped the primary cosmic spirits. The emperor held the Confucian Mandate of Heaven as long as he acted for the well-being of the empire; earthquakes, eclipses, and unusual weather were interpreted as signs that heaven might be withdrawing its mandate.

Being Human: The Individual, the Family, and the Ancestors

In the Confucian worldview, each person is at the center of multiple relationships, determined by gender, generational location in the family, and status in the empire. According to the norms of filial piety, the young owe obedience to parents, women to men, citizens to rulers. This worldview is very different from the individualism that dominates the West and has spread across the globe through modernization.

The Confucian ideal was for the family to benefit in old age from the reciprocities that required their deference earlier in life and to have their political obedience rewarded by heaven's blessings. To support this understanding, Daoism contributed the belief that since human beings are a combination of heaven (*yang*) and earth (*yin*), which in their exact balance determine gender, personality, and health, they must pursue harmony in their social relations and so respect these primary relations.

All persons are also seen as benefiting after death from the Confucian ordering of life, since the living descendants are expected to perform the necessary rites to ensure their best possible destiny in the afterlife. Indigenous beliefs going back to the Shang era later merged with Buddhist notions to create a composite understanding of the individual's fate after death. What emerged in classical China (and was accepted in Korea and Japan, too) was a belief in the Buddhist concept of *karma* and an understanding that after death all souls undergo processing in a netherworld. Here divine

Modern Chinese family gravesite in Singapore, sited and designed in accordance with the principles of feng shui. Here family members gather twice yearly to feast and make offerings to their ancestors.

magistrates carefully calculate karma and then send the soul on to its proper destiny. In this way indigenous Chinese and Buddhist ideas coexisted in harmony.

In conception and in practice, then, ancestors live on in the East Asian family's presence and receive ongoing ritual attention: in the grave, in an ancestral tablet (located in the home altar or clan temple), and potentially in the underworld, especially in the first years after death. The Korean and Chinese practice of burning paper replicas of items considered useful in the underworld is thought to send relief to loved ones who are waiting out an intermediate state before reincarnation.

By the end of the Han, after centuries of state support, Confucian ethics centered on hierarchy and mutual obligation had thoroughly permeated Chinese society. The key elements of the "diffuse religion" were widely shared and had come to include the notions of yin-yang theory, geomancy (*feng shui*), the major deities of the pantheon, and the understanding of souls going to an afterlife. The Confucian literati were also convinced that they could unite the society around a common ritual discipline, with ancestor rites the universal and civilizing norm.

Among gentlemen, rites for the dead are taken as the way of man; Among the common people, they are taken as matters involving demons.

—Master Xun

SOURCE: D. C. Lau, *Mencius* (New York: Penguin, 1970), p. 191.

Development of the Multiple Traditions in Post-Han China

We now move into the fractured China of the post-Han centuries (220–617), a time when the Confucian tradition fell out of power as well as when Buddhist missionaries arrived and secured a permanent place in China for their faith.

Arrival of Buddhism

The transplantation of Buddhism from India into East Asia is one of the greatest cultural conquests in world history, matched in importance only by the conversion to Christianity of the peoples of Europe and the Americas and the conversion to Islam by many peoples of Eurasia. Buddhist monks reached China on the Silk Road through central Asia by 120 CE and later over the sea routes.

Mahayana Buddhism entered Asia through merchants and missionary monks but became firmly established everywhere owing to the patronage of emperors and aristocracy. Most East Asians came to believe in karma and added the Buddha and celestial bodhisattvas as additional divinities for their devotions.

Chinese literati criticized Buddhism for its rejection of family life and service to one's kin and the worship of deities who originated from "barbarian" peoples outside China. The Buddhist ideal of monastic retreat for personal enlightenment was construed as an antisocial behavior. But in splintered China after the fall of the Han, the Confucian literati lost their power.

These Confucian anti-Buddhist arguments would be recycled at various times, but for almost all of its first 500 years in East Asia, Buddhism was widely and deeply incorporated into the region's religious life, finding support in the imperial courts and eventually among all segments of society, from philosophers to farmers. As time went on, Chinese, Korean, and Japanese monks would formulate their own interpretations of the many Buddhist teachings, creating distinctive East Asian schools of textual interpretation and ritual practices.

With a sacred mushroom in his pocket, a Daoist immortal plays his flute in paradise.

The Institutional Development of Daoism

Another effect of Buddhism's rise was to motivate adherents of Daoism to systematize their texts and teachings and to create institutions modeled after Buddhist monasteries. The meditative regimes and elaborate rituals that eventually developed in the Daoist monasteries gave individuals many avenues for practicing Daoism.

By 300, several branches of religious Daoism had formalized early practices. Guo Hong (283–363) was the most prominent figure, known for his seeking to harmonize the tradition with Confucianism. Beginning with the notion that heaven's greatest creation is life itself, he argued that pursuing longevity and immortality must be the greatest human goal. Guo prescribed a path to that goal based on moral goodness, social service, and alchemy utilizing two metals: gold (which neither corrodes nor diminishes if buried or melted) and cinnabar (a red mercury ore that keeps changing as long as it is heated). This "inner alchemy" culminated in the practitioner's ingesting wild herbs and these refined, cooked substances along with breath meditation to achieve profound transformation and oneness with the cosmos.

Daoism competed with Buddhism for favor at the imperial courts, and devotees among the emperors spread the reformed and newly organized tradition across China. The new monastic orders strengthened Daoist traditions. Daoist scriptures were catalogued and organized, and later commentaries expanded the tradition's literature by thousands of additional works. However, organized Daoism never penetrated Korea or Japan.

Shinto: indigenous religion of Japan that reveres native deities, including the Emperor

The eight immortals of Daoism, depicted in a Qing dynasty hanging scroll, with the Three Stars and the Queen Mother of the West. These were the chief divinities enshrined in Daoist temples from the Ming period onward.

Religion Under the Early Japanese Imperial State: Buddhism and Shinto

In Japan, as elsewhere, Buddhism began among the elite, who saw in it a means to unite a fragmented land. Indeed, it was under the royal sponsorship of Prince Shotoku (d. 622) that Buddhism became the state religion. By 741, an edict called for officials to establish a Buddhist monastery and temple in many Japanese provinces, enroll at least twenty monks and ten nuns, and recite texts and perform rituals for the benefit of emperor and state.

But Buddhism was not the only foreign belief system to shape the development of Japan: Confucian texts and teachers from China and Korea were also influential in the early courts. A seventh-century reform established a Confucian bureaucracy modeled after that of China. Daoist ideas of natural harmony and energy flow, both in the environment and within the person, along with yin-yang analysis, were part of this broad cultural influence. However, neither Daoist monasteries nor Daoist monks ever existed. Moreover, the Japanese never ceased to worship their own distinct divinities, the *kami*, believing the islands themselves to have been established by these native deities. This religious tradition is called **Shinto**.

The Shinto Pantheon of Japan

In many respects, the Shinto tradition in Japan shares basic assumptions and practices regarding deities found throughout East Asia. Shamanism also developed in Japan, because its mediums gave the community access to the gods as well as to their departed ancestors. Pilgrimages to mountains thought to be divine abodes were common.

However, as Shinto mythology developed, it was adapted, systematized, and disseminated by the early state. These accounts portrayed Japan as a unique spiritual territory filled with the distinctive deities called **kami**. Legends focused on the kami enabled Shinto priests to enshrine a unique pantheon. This helps explain why the Japanese, despite the importation of many other aspects of the country's religious life from China and Korea, were less ready to adopt Chinese deities and folk traditions.

The Shinto pantheon is headed by the goddess **Amaterasu**, the kami of the sun, credited in Japanese myth with having aided in the creation of the country and with being a progenitor of the royal family. Other kami are associated with wind and weather, geological features, plants and animals, and ancestral spirits. Shinto shrines often display mirrors as symbols of Amaterasu and for their symbolic meaning of an ideal purity and brilliance.

Until the modern era, Shinto priests of major shrines inherited their positions and learned the rituals from their fathers; thus they were always males from aristocratic families. Over the last 150 years, priests have had to pass a state-prescribed course of training at an institution such as Kokugakuin University, founded for this purpose. The role of the *shinshoku*, as the priests are usually called, involves mastery of the daily gestures of respect offered to the kami, the annual rituals of the shrine, calligraphy, and complex forms of ritual purification. Shinto has never developed any "inner" spiritual practices. As we shall see, in the modern period, the state regulated and reformed Shinto as a vehicle for modernization. For its contemporary exponents, however, the artful rituals oriented to the deities throughout the seasons offer a means of achieving refined sensitivity and moral transformation.

kami: Japanese deity associated with places, certain animals, and the emperor

Amaterasu: kami of the sun; progenitor of Japanese imperial line

"The belief is that the new year is given to us by . . . the kami of years. What comes from the realm of the kami is inherently good. . . . So we look out upon the possibilities of the new year, and we want to purify our blunders and cast off whatever evil influences we may have accumulated in the old year."

—Shinto priest Uesugi Guji (1987)

SOURCE: John K. Nelson, *A Year in the Life of a Shinto Shrine* (Seattle: University of Washington Press, 1996), p. 207.

Wood-block print of the sun goddess Amaterasu, legendary progenitor of the Japanese people.

East Asian Religions in the Classical Era (645–1800 CE)

Classical Imperial China (645–1271 CE)

During the T'ang Dynasty (618–907), China ended four centuries of fragmentation and Buddhism enjoyed extraordinary development. At first, Buddhism in northern China appealed to the non-Han conquerors, and it succeeded in the south through popular and charismatic monastic preachers. But in the T'ang era, more unified monastic networks developed into seven doctrinal schools. Each school took as its highest authoritative source a different text that was thought to contain the Buddha's highest teachings.

T'ang China, with its capital in Chang'an (modern Xi'an), was the world's most advanced civilization. Living within the high city walls were merchants from across the Eurasian world; distributed in neighborhoods were Nestorian Christians, Hindus, Manicheans, Zoroastrians, and Muslims. These resident aliens mixed with Buddhists and Daoists, who had their own numerous monasteries and temples. The wealth from trade, efficient taxation, and imperial patronage underwrote a golden age that found expression in all the fine arts while spreading Buddhist influences and religious practices across the empire and into both Korea and Japan. Adventurous Chinese monks, such as the renowned Xuan Zang (d. 664), even traveled to India for fourteen years in search of additional texts and teachers.

This pluralistic, tolerant world was disrupted in 845, when edicts by Emperor Wu-zong forced 250,000 Buddhist monastics to return to lay life and confiscated all but forty-nine monasteries throughout the empire. The emperor was partly motivated by considerations of personnel and finances: With the success of Buddhism, more lands were being donated to the monastic community, thereby losing their taxable status; and men and women were joining Buddhist orders, exempting themselves both from taxation and, in the case of the men, from military service. Wu-zong's second motivation was religious. He was an ardent Daoist eager to advance the tradition's popularity. Buddhism was never again to dominate China's religious landscape.

The later T'ang was a time of resurgent Confucianism. This tradition had continued to guide the familial life of commoners, and Confucius himself was used as a symbol of national unity. The groundwork was being laid for a brilliant assimilation of Buddhism and Daoism.

Song Dynasty: The Second Epoch of Confucianism (960–1279)

The so-called Second Epoch of Confucianism reinvigorated the older ideology of human relatedness based on hierarchy, age, and gender. Neo-Confucianism moved to the center of Chinese religious life, later influencing Korea and Japan, as well.

Song dynasty administrators restored Confucian learning as the basis for winning a position in its burgeoning civil service. This measure encouraged a return to the Confucian classics as a subject for study, further scholarship, and teaching. As the best minds of the day once again were drawn into reinterpreting the indigenous tradition, private academies that instilled virtue and erudition flowered.

The Confucian tradition's great "Second Master" was **Zhu Xi** (1130–1200). The works compiled and commented on by him, entitled *Jinsi Lu* ("Reflections of Things at Hand"), were immensely influential. Zhu Xi gave students the order in which to study the classics and crafted strong arguments against Buddhism and Daoism. Zhu Xi also codified the system of thought known as **neo-Confucianism**.

Despite its apparent criticism of Daoism and Buddhism, the neo-Confucians in fact were strongly influenced by both. Of equal importance in securing the success of neo-Confucianism was Zhu Xi's compilation of a ritual manual that imparted Confucian procedures for all life-cycle rites, including the non-Buddhist and non-practices around which the majority of Chinese ordered their lives. This ritual text, like the *Jinsi Lu*, was influential across East Asia.

Neo-Confucianism's strength was that it provided both the individual and the state with a convincing philosophy for understanding the world. The neo-Confucian philosophers emphasized that education was needed to perfect human awareness of li and that inner meditative cultivation (a borrowing from Buddhism), which Zhu Xi called "investigating the nature of things," was needed to perfect the qi. Almost all the neo-Confucians assumed the reality of karma as one of life's causal agents.

Only under the guidelines set forth by the neo-Confucian masters did the literati tradition acquire its own systematic regime of spiritual training. The first stage of training was "disciplining the body" by means of the six arts of Confucian education: ritual, music, archery, calligraphy, horsemanship, and mathematics. All were defined very broadly. For example, *ritual* means conducting religious rites as well as mastering the proper ways of eating, walking, and asking questions. The *Analects* provide many instances of seemingly trivial events associated with Confucius, but those events had their use in just this context of providing the sage's life as a model for disciplined training.

Beyond foundational training, all the neo-Confucian subschools called for the "rectification of the heart-mind" and prescribed new practices: discipline manifested by outward zeal in investigating the external world as well as the personal goal of knowing oneself. The aim was to become a perfected person, a *sheng-ren*, who has achieved fully his or her complete human nature.

The popular convergence of the classical traditions in late traditional China was inspired by neo-Confucian figures like Zhu Xi who sought harmony by learning from all orientations. The "diffuse religion" still extant in contemporary East Asia stems from their brilliant syntheses of ancient sources.

Zhu Xi: great Neo-Confucian master who integrated elements of Buddhism and Daoism into Confucianism

neo-Confucianism: tradition seeking to harmonize early Confucian humanism with elements of Daoism and Buddhism

"The ideal sage is one who is first in worrying about the world's troubles and last in enjoying its pleasures."

—Fan-Chung-Yen (989–1052)

SOURCE: Arthur Wright, *Buddhism in Chinese History* (Stanford, CA: Stanford University Press, 1959), p. 43.

Neo-Theories of Order, Hierarchy, and Relatedness

The Confucian notion of the self that became reinforced in family norms and in state law is decidedly not that of the isolated individual but of the person as "a center of relatedness." This concept can be understood as a series of concentric circles, with the assumption that to reach their highest potential, persons must act harmoniously within their families, local communities, and states and with heaven beyond. This scheme clearly implies that engagement in culture and community is necessary for both the person and humanity overall to flourish. As the Confucian classic, the *Great Learning*, states:

> The ancients who wished to bring order to their states would first regulate their families. Those who wished to regulate their families would first cultivate their personal lives. Those who wished to cultivate their personal lives would first rectify their minds. Those who wished to rectify their minds would first make their intentions sincere.
>
> Those who wished to make their intentions sincere would first extend their knowledge. The extension of knowledge consists of the investigation of things. . . . Only when the personal life is cultivated, the family will be regulated; when the family is regulated, the state will be in order; and when the state is in order, there will be peace throughout the world.[1]

The elaboration of meditative practices and multidisciplinary studies by the neo-Confucian masters established a rich tradition designed to develop the individual's integral relations with each circle. Such later figures as Zhang Zai (1020–77) went on to combine this concentric conception with the Daoist ideal of finding "full humanity" by merging with the cosmos:

> Heaven is my father and Earth is my mother, and even such a small creature as I finds an intimate place in their midst. Therefore that which fills the universe I regard as my body and that which directs the universe I consider as my nature. All people are my brothers and sisters, and all things are my companions.[2]

The Development of Buddhism, Daoism, and Confucianism in Korea and Japan

In Korea, Buddhism flourished under imperial support once the country had been united under the Silla dynasty (668–918). Ties to Chinese Buddhism were strong, and almost all of the Chinese schools had Korean counterparts. Korean monks were notable in China, and their commentaries on major texts were studied in both Japan and Tibet. Yet over time, Korean monks were most successful at finding harmony rather than division in their development of the tradition from the various schools and teachings.

Religion in the Koryo dynasty (918–1392) continued in this mode. Uniquely Korean was the centrality of Son (Ch'an/Zen) Buddhism, which was to become the most influential school in subsequent Korean Buddhist history. It assimilated the scholastic schools introduced from China and closely adapted Buddhism to Korean culture.

In Japan, the assimilation of Buddhism had ecumenical aspects as well. It had continued strongly when the capital was moved to Kyoto in 800 CE, as various elements of Mahayana Buddhism and Daoist theories of yin-yang imported from China were effectively integrated with Shinto practices.

The later Kamakura era (1185–1333) was marked by military leaders who usurped the power of the emperor and established a social system closely akin to that of European feudalism. The next 700 years was an age of widespread contact with China, as trade grew and Buddhist monks were instrumental in bringing the two schools that had survived the persecutions in post-T'ang China: Pure Land and Ch'an/Zen. Notable monks of this era also brought neo-Confucian learning, literature, and the arts to Japan.

The disorder and suffering in the Kamakura also led to dramatic changes in Japanese religions, especially Buddhism. Kamakura religious leaders in Japan established the framework for subsequent schools that remained relatively stable until the early modern era.

The most popular Buddhist school was Pure Land, and its advocates taught that an individual's salvation was completely in the hands of the Buddha of the Pure Land, whom they called Amida, from the Sanskrit name Amitabha. They emphasized the practice of repeating Amida's name as faith alone in the degenerate **mappo** age could enable rebirth in a realm where nirvana realization was certain. Pure Land teacher Shinran ended the requirement of monastic celibacy, and Pure Land remains the largest Buddhist school in Japan today.

mappo: Buddhist doctrine of world in decline

The second new school established during the Kamakura era was Zen, and it, too, was brought from China, by two Japanese monks, Eisai (1141–1215) and Dogen (1200–1253). In adopting sitting meditation, mind puzzles (koans), and unusual teaching methods, Zen masters created an innovative uniquely East Asian lineage of Buddhism. It also was very traditionalist, however, in rejecting the concept of mappo and resisting the other schools' radical simplification of Buddhism into mere ritual repetition and reliance on faith. Zen teachers insisted that each individual had to win his or her own salvation on the meditation mat through persistence and self-power alone.

Another remarkable Buddhist leader of this era was **Nichiren** (1222–82), a monk who attributed the decline in Japanese life to the neglect of the *Lotus Sutra*, which he viewed as containing the Buddha's supreme teaching. The Nichiren-shu advocated chanting the name of this text as the means for personal transformation as well as national renewal. (It is a practice continued to the present day in the **Soka Gakkai**, a modern Nichiren-derived school that now spans the globe.)

Nichiren: monk who founded new Buddhist school based on primacy of the *Lotus Sutra*

Soka Gakkai: twentieth-century offshoot from Nichiren school, now a global Buddhist organization seeking world peace

In the Kamakura era, ideas regarding Shinto–Buddhist accommodation were heard from both sides: Shinto exponents argued that the Buddhas and bodhisattvas were really indigenous gods, and the Buddhists built Shinto shrines in their monastic

Use Buddhism to rule the mind, Daoism to rule the body, Confucianism to rule the world.

—*Emperor Xiao Zong (1163–1189)*

SOURCE: Wing-sit Chan, *A Sourcebook of Chinese Philosophy* (Princeton, NJ: Princeton University Press, 1973), pp. 497–98.

Although the Three Teachings are different, in the arguments they put forward, they are One.

—*Liu Mi (active 1324)*

SOURCE: Timothy Brook, "Rethinking Syncretism: The Unity of the Three Teachings and Their Joint Worship in Late-Imperial China," *Journal of Chinese Religions* 21 (1993), 17.

If someone is a Confucian, give him Confucius; if he is a Daoist, give him Lao Zi; if he is a Buddhist, give him Shakyamuni; if he isn't any of them, give him their unity.

—*Lin Zhao'en (1517–98)*

SOURCE: Ibid., 18.

courtyards, consistent with the view that the kami were in fact protectors or bodhisattvas. This urge to harmonize the various spiritual traditions was one that Japan shared with China and Korea.

East Asian Religions in the Late Classical Era (1400–1800)

The four centuries preceding the modern era show few religious innovations across East Asia. For Buddhism, this era is characterized by elaborations of traditional practices and the modest growth of monastic networks.

Across East Asia, the diffuse religion remained central, as ancestor ritualism, local cults to important deities, and the role of the spirit mediums defined the religious field in cities and villages alike. For Ming-era China (1368–1644), the popular text *Feng Shen Yan-yi* ("*The Canonization of the Gods*") was especially influential in promulgating the idea of an orderly pantheon of Chinese divinities in a hierarchy that included Buddhas, immortals, gods, and local spirits. Throughout China, a standard organization for the state's official religion was fixed in each province. There would be a Confucian temple with major disciples, a military temple featuring the war god Guan Yu and other notable heroes, and a **city god**, who supervises all the village earth gods.

"The Unity of the Three Traditions": Late Ming to Early Qing Eras in China

The Chinese emphasis on harmony was also extended to "the unity of the **three faiths**," meaning Confucianism, Daoism, and Buddhism. Many philosophers who were exclusively committed to one of these faiths still argued that their tradition was superior in answering the fundamental spiritual questions. But more popular were teachers such as Jiao Hong (1540–1620), who regarded all three teachings as in fact "a single teaching," stating that each merely uses separate language to articulate its truth and that all three could and should be believed.

Among Confucians who most powerfully conveyed this ecumenical ethos was Wang Yangming (1472–1529), whose view of the "true gentleman" was based on the assumption that everyone can know the good and that "self-perfection" means knowing this goodness to the maximum. Wang argued, in language mirroring the "all beings have the Buddha nature" doctrine of Mahayana Buddhism, that all humans have the potential to achieve self-perfection, since all share a primordial awareness.

Buddhism by the end of the Ming dynasty (1368–1644) had worked out its permanent place in Chinese civilization. We thus find influential teachers such as Chuhong (1535–1615) preaching that the essence of Buddhism was social activism as expressed through charity and moral action. He also emphasized that to be a filial child and a loyal subject was to be a "good Buddhist." This view was expressed by many subsequent Chinese Buddhists.

Buddhism and Neo-Confucianism in an Enduring Ming Tale

The *Journey to the West* (or "monkey story"), written by the Confucian scholar Wu Cheng-en (1500–82), is an example of the Ming-era harmonization of the "three faiths." It recounts the journey of the great Buddhist monk Xuan Zang (d. 664) to search for texts in India. In this dangerous quest, he is assisted by the Monkey King, Sun Wukong, a figure from the Chinese folk pantheon. While ostensibly the account of the great Buddhist monk's journey, recurring incidents in the long tale (spanning four hefty volumes in English translation) are employed

to teach self-discipline—a personal trait valued by both traditions—to the Monkey King and Confucian wisdom to the monk. In many episodes, the success of Xuan Zang's mission depends on the Monkey King's aid and on the monk's timely learning how common people think about the ways of the world. Translated into opera and folk ballads, the monkey story became one of China's most popular narratives, its major characters defining important personality stereotypes while conveying the pattern of Confucianism dominating the literati culture of the Ming dynasty.

The Monkey King leads the Buddhist monk Xuan Zang and other companions, illustrating a scene from the Ming dynasty tale, *The Journey to the West.*

The Ming dynasty also saw the beginning of regular contact with Europe, first with the Portuguese in 1514. With these traders and then with growing numbers of missionaries, the Chinese found little to admire and much resented the "barbaric manners" of most of their guests. In this early era of contact, failure to institute good relations with the Europeans or to attempt to understand the world beyond China set up the problematic and confrontational geopolitical environment of the colonial era.

The Qing dynasty (1644–1912) brought outsiders again in control of China, this time in the form of the Manchurians, who continued most traditional state administration. Confucian imperial ritual remained central to the state, and mastery of the classics was the basis for the selection of the literati who ran it.

Confucian ideas and practices throughout China were strengthened by the *Sheng-tu* (*Pictures of the Sage's Traces*), captioned accounts of Confucius' life and exemplary tales of ethical practices. The stories appeared on stone tablets installed in temples (Daoist as well as Buddhist), on silk paintings, and in widely disseminated books. Many versions of the great teacher appeared, some with Confucius as a human being

Forming one body with Heaven, Earth, and the myriad things is not only true of the great man. Even the heart-mind of the small man is no different. . . . Therefore when he sees a child about to fall into the well, he cannot help feeling alarm and commiseration.

SOURCE: Timothy Brook, "Rethinking Syncretism: The Unity of the Three Teachings and Their Joint Worship in Late-Imperial China," *Journal of Chinese Religions* 21 (1993), 22.

One scene from the Sheng tu, carved in marble in a Beijing temple, here depicting how a son should show filial piety (xiao) to his ailing mother.

living an exemplary ethical life, others describing miracles and magic, while still others emphasized the sage's commending great ritual exertions. Many of these publications were also exported to Japan, where they influenced the efflorescence of Confucian studies and related arts in the Tokugawa era (1600–1868).

Zen and the Shoguns (Twelfth to Nineteenth Centuries)

In Japan during medieval and early modern times, there were no Daoist temples competing with institutional Buddhism or Shinto shrines, nor did the deities of "diffuse Chinese popular religion" find their way across the water. Instead, Shinto theologians presented the nation's deities in a uniquely Japanese pantheon, although the relationships between them varied by region and were not systematized nationwide until the modern era.

Zen Buddhism, however, also exerted an ecumenical influence in this period. The Zen school's strong relationship with China fostered studies in both Daoism and Confucianism. It also promoted the idea that Daoist concepts and Confucian morality could be harmoniously combined. Zen, the vehicle for Japan's cultural elite, adopted art forms from China, but Japanese masters soon took them to new levels of originality in such fields as ink painting, poetry, and tea ceremony.

Zen and the other Buddhist schools were closely tied to the ruling elites, who were a source of protection and patronage for their favorite monasteries and teachers. This relationship also led Buddhists in Japan to vie for support among the top ranks in society, which most of them tended to view uncritically. The habit of overlooking discrepancies between Buddhist teachings and rulers' practices continued right into the modern period, when most monks were more concerned about accommodation with the elite than with reforming Japanese society or preventing war.

The Shoguns Persecute Christians and Promote Buddhism

Although Buddhism enjoyed official support during most of the shogunate, Nobunaga (1534–82) waged an anti-Buddhist campaign, going so far as to burn the great monastery center on Mount Hiei, outside Kyoto, where Japanese Buddhism was first established. It was dislike of Buddhism that probably led Nobunaga to be receptive to the first Jesuit missionaries, giving Christianity more early support than it received anywhere else in East Asia. Much to the chagrin of the European missionaries, however, most Japanese had trouble seeing in Christianity anything but an obscure form of Buddhism: Catholic rituals appeared to be similar to certain monastic rites; and the concept of a heavenly Lord whose son became incarnate to serve humanity was not unlike Mahayana Buddhism's doctrine of the cosmic Buddha whose sons, the compassionate bodhisattvas, also served humanity.

But squabbles that developed among European Christians, as well as some missionary attempts to manipulate Japanese politics in the name of their home countries, convinced Iyesu, the first Tokugawa shogun, to outlaw Christianity in 1606. When in 1616 he expelled all remaining missionaries, there were already an estimated 300,000 Japanese converts. The next decades saw attempts by the Japanese state to root out Christianity. Some of these efforts at removing Christianity were gruesome, and many converts who would not recant their faith were tortured. A Christian–government conflict in 1637–38 that resulted in over 37,000 deaths confirmed for its Japanese opponents the disruptive potential of the foreign faith.

From this time onward, every Japanese family was required by law to be registered with a Buddhist temple, in an effort to regularize ties with Buddhism and to emphasize that in Tokugawa times being Buddhist was inherently part of being Japanese. (This position was to change dramatically in the nineteenth century.)

The Regional Spread of Neo-Confucianism

Neo-Confucian thought spread under the Tokugawa shoguns. Confucianism finally found its own strong supporters in a succession of prominent Japanese philosophers, many of whom were not part of the samurai elite. For some, Confucian teachings gave those of lower birth ideals to uphold against the hierarchical system instituted by Japan's hereditary nobility. Unlike in China, the ideals of Confucianism spread among both the merchant class and the samurai as Japanese intellectuals throughout the Tokugawa era studied and defended the positions of all the major neo-Confucian sages. Efforts were also made to rationalize Shinto beliefs with Confucian doctrines.

TALES OF SPIRITUAL TRANSFORMATION: Confucian

The Sage ideal of the Confucian tradition is indicated in a text that prescribes total commitment to truthfulness that, if fully put in practice, can be a path to cosmic harmony.

Only one who is perfectly truthful can give full realization to his human nature; able to give full realization to his human nature, he is then able to give full realization to the human nature of others; able to give full realization to the human nature of others, he is then able to give full realization to the nature of other creatures; able to give this, he can then assist in the transformative and nourishing processes of heaven and earth. If he can assist in the transformative and nourishing powers of heaven and earth, he can then form a triad with heaven and earth.

Source: *Maintaining Perfect Balance*, a neo-Confucian classic, in Daniel Gardiner, *The Four Books* (Indianapolis: Hackett, 2007), p. 124.

East Asian Religions in the Early Modern Era

Disruptive European Intrusions

A Shinto priest bestowing a blessing to a group of restaurant employees by waving a sacred "sakaki" branch over them.

Post-Enlightenment colonialism, or imperialism, represents the first modern attempt to establish a global world order. Europeans forced Asian societies to change on European terms, abruptly imposing new ideas, technologies, and institutions that had evolved naturally over many years in Europe. European imperialism undermined most institutions in premodern East Asia, with organized religions especially subject to disruption and decline.

Colonialism was a brutal enterprise at times. It forcibly changed every regional economy, promoted trafficking in narcotics when the opium trade was profitable, challenged East Asians' fundamental understandings regarding humanity and cosmos through science and Christian missions, and undermined the long-held view of Asia's ruling classes that their civilizations were the world's greatest.

The crisis of colonialism forced East Asian elites to contend with the Western world and its technologies. From about 1850, across the region, the best minds in East Asia chose to learn about the West first and about their own traditions hardly at all, with the result that the Enlightenment mentality infiltrated the cultural heritage of modern East Asia. Among a large portion of this Western-influenced elite, agnosticism or atheism replaced belief in their own indigenous spiritual traditions.

It would be wrong, however, to see the history of modern East Asia as dictated solely by European actors and external forces. There were important internal dynamics at work in Korea, China, and Japan, and the different processes already under way in each shaped their different destinies under colonialism. Finally, although the effects of colonialism were overwhelmingly destructive, the fusion of older traditions with modern changes led to a number of religious innovations that were compelling and original.

Traumatic Transitions of the Modern Era

The era of colonialism was perceived across Asia as a time of repeated crises. The common terms used to express the peoples' sense of inundation and powerlessness across East Asia convey this: *humiliation (chi)* in Chinese, *bitterness (hahn)* in Korean, and *patient endurance (nin)* in Japanese. Although each nation had differing reactions to the experience of modernization, it is essential to appreciate the magnitude of colonial-era disruptions to understand the changes in religious life across East Asia.

The Decline of Confucian Ideology and Exponents

The rapid changes brought by imperialism ended the influence of the Confucian elite in China, Korea, and Japan. The Confucian worldview and social ideology were subjected to critiques by the native-born reformers of each nation, who attempted to save state sovereignty and match the wealth, knowledge, and power displayed by the Western colonizers. In addition, many young people abandoned the traditional curriculum to pursue "Western learning" and critiquing the Confucian tradition. Finally, the fall of the Korean and Chinese states, whose political and economic resources supported Confucianism, ensured that this tradition would lose its central place in the region's early modernization.

Confucianism was now blamed for every problem. The failure to develop modern trade was blamed on the classical ranking of social classes by occupation, which in the Confucian view of the good society placed scholar-officials at the top and merchants at the bottom. Confucius himself had no respect for merchants, whom he called "parasites."

The traditional Confucian educational system was also blamed for stifling the nation's technical development, inasmuch as it rewarded rote memorization and imitation, not independent thinking. Moreover, for the critics, the Confucian view of history as cyclical had made the elite disinclined to pursue innovation or progress.

The strongest terms of rejection were directed toward Confucian social norms and, at their center, family relations. Reformers found these rigid relationships to be an obstacle to modernization in many respects. Individuals who placed loyalty to family first, for example, were unable to extend trust to others as needed in a modern economy. Similarly, filial deference to elders made individuals dependent on the collective family, thwarting creativity and giving too much power to those who were merely of senior rank. Both East Asian reformers and Western social scientists until the 1970s agreed that Confucianism was the key obstacle to the region's modernization.

A reconsideration of the characteristics fostered by Confucianism, however, suggests that these Confucian elements also played a role in the region's ultimately successful response to the challenges of the postcolonial era. These include, for example, the emphasis on education, the practice of carefully studying problems before taking action, the expectation that state officials will act for the good of the whole, and the intellectual elite's acceptance of responsibility for the nation's well-being. But what is certain is that the imperial system that supported the Confucian literati tradition was overthrown completely in China and Korea. By contrast, in neighboring Japan, the emperor-led state after 1868 melded nationalism and Confucianism with its own form of colonialism. Whatever Confucianism means exactly in the present day, a break with the past had irrevocably occurred. We must first turn to the important exception of Japan and its distinctive fusion of belief systems: melding modernization with Confucianism in the form of nationalist **neo-Shintoism**.

neo-Shintoism/state Shinto: reformation of Japan's indigenous religion after 1869, with the divine emperor at its center

State and Civil Religion in Japan: Neo-Shintoism

By 1882, fifteen years after the restoration of the Japanese monarchy in the person of the Meiji emperor, the Shinto tradition was officially adopted as the state religion. To bring this about, most shrines and temples were integrated into a single system under government supervision. The emperor was revered as a divinity on earth, whose presence was a blessing to the nation. This idea was expressed at the national shrines in the capital and then in rituals regularly conducted in every local shrine as well; Japanese were directed to worship daily facing the emperor in Tokyo, just as Muslims worshipping Allah face Mecca. The reformed educational system also centered its curriculum on the sanctity of the emperor, and all citizens were expected to honor him by working for the good of the nation. This was one of the Confucian elements in Japan's modernization.

A constitution adopted in 1889 limited Japanese citizens' freedom to express any opinions critical of Shinto doctrines and practices, especially the imperial ties to the indigenous deities, but it guaranteed religious freedom to followers of other religions as long as they did not undermine Shinto and were loyal to the nation. Those affected included Buddhists and Christians, as well as the "new religion" sects that multiplied throughout the modern era.

The Meiji state religion, or state-Shinto, can be labeled neo-Shintoist, for it was associated with the ancient religious tradition that reveres the indigenous deities of the Japanese islands. However, the "civil religion" constructed around Shintoism by the Meiji elite was thoroughly Confucian in character. It emphasized loyalty to the state, filial piety, self-sacrifice, and dedication. Moreover, it heralded the contributions of individuals that would be needed to make the modernization of Japan a success. Finally, a Confucian vocabulary was used to define the emperor's and the nation's mission, with special emphasis on the emperor's Mandate of Heaven. Thus, Meiji Japan was the first political entity in East Asia that harnessed reformed Confucian values to meet the challenges of modernizing and adopting the technologies pioneered in the West.

Institutional Buddhism

As we noted in Chapter 7, institutional Buddhism took root in Asia by way of a monastic system in which monasteries became landlords who relied on lay farmers to tend the crops and on charitable donations from the faithful. At times of economic hardship or when the state could not extend customary protections, Buddhism declined. In general, the crises of the modern era across East Asia deprived Buddhism of economic support and deprived Buddhist monasteries of new monks and nuns. Instead, the most gifted people now wanted to learn about the West and to lead their countries in modernizing national industries, governments, and military establishments.

Procession bearing the local god (kami) through Kamakura, Japan, during the Spring Festival.

In nineteenth-century China, there were few signs of innovation and few Buddhists who rose to contribute to the national struggles. In Japan's long Tokugawa era (1600–1867), on the other hand, the military leaders supported Buddhism strongly, including the promotion of Buddhist pilgrimage as a means of having the Japanese acquire a sense of national integration. But the Meiji reformers felt it essential to reverse course, both to weaken pro-Buddhist foes and because they believed that Buddhist influences were contrary to Japan's Shinto-centered revitalization. Shinto-based nationalism and the state-encouraged challenges to institutional Buddhism forced followers to shift their emphases and rethink their doctrines in light of the changes under way in their society. The Buddhist establishment after 1876 tried to prove its patriotism and relevance. Major Buddhist schools competed to implement Meiji social and national programs, and they, too, fanned the rising flame of anti-Western feelings.

Compared with elsewhere in Asia, early movements led by Japanese householders to reinterpret Buddhism in terms of modern philosophy were few. Instead, religious reformers were more likely to begin their own sects, drawing on doctrines as they liked, without trying to work through the Buddhist establishment.

In Korea, Confucianism was strongly supported in the nineteenth century and Buddhism was increasingly marginalized, as the government also tried to limit the economic power of monastic estates by consolidating schools and seizing lands. State decrees prohibited Buddhist monks from major cities.

The same observations about Chinese monastic Buddhism in the modern era apply to Daoist monasticism as well. The institutions carried on, but they brought little to the discussion about creating the new China in the radical intellectual climate of the early twentieth century. Daoism, too, was attacked from the standpoints of science and democracy.

Later Christian Missions in China, Japan, Korea

The Jesuits, the first Christians to proselytize in Ming China, focused on the elite, not the masses, for conversion. Unlike their counterparts in Japan, who were expelled after

Scenes from missionary life in China: an American family resident in China ca. 1898 shown in formal Chinese dress; a classroom in a Methodist boarding school for girls; a group of Chinese converts and missionaries with shipments of Bibles and evangelical publications.

an era of toleration, they did succeed at winning imperial approval for their presence. The Chinese were far more interested in the Jesuits' knowledge of European sciences (particularly astronomy, mathematics, and ballistics) than they were in Christianity. Missionary efforts were also hampered by the bitter controversies that broke out between Jesuit and Dominican Catholics, particularly on the issue of whether to tolerate Confucian morality or ancestor veneration. An imperial edict banned Christianity in 1724, but the censure was not as thoroughly enforced as in Japan.

The Protestant presence was significant only after 1800. Their missionary efforts were directed to the masses, and a Chinese translation of the complete Bible appeared in 1815. As elsewhere, the missionaries were less successful at mass proselytizing than at transmitting Western medicine, schooling, and new technologies. By 1877, there were 347 missionary schools and an estimated 400,000 Chinese converts.

Outlawed in Japan in 1606, its missionaries expelled in 1616, and its followers violently persecuted, Christianity survived there underground among remarkably faithful converts. Once granted religious freedom in 1863, Japanese Christians built churches and publicly asserted their faith. Soon, however, like the Buddhists, the Christians began to feel the need to prove their religion's nationalistic credentials. They supported the war efforts launched by the state and proclaimed that Christianity strengthened Japan by supporting ethics in national life, resisting radicalism, and combating communism.

Korea remained closed to Christian missionaries until the late nineteenth century, when representatives primarily from American Methodist and Presbyterian denominations settled and attracted converts while building schools and hospitals. Korean Christians, like those in Japan, also had to prove their patriotism by emphasizing their independence from Western churches. Scholars are still uncertain as to why Korea embraced Christianity so much more readily than other Asian countries. (Latest surveys have found that 32 percent of South Koreans are converts.)

The Appearance of New Religious Movements and Religions

From the imperial era until the present, "**new religions**" have emerged across Asia, underscoring this period as one of social dislocation, dissatisfaction, and cross-traditional synthesis. It also signals the extent to which the "established religions" of the region (Confucianism, Daoism, Buddhism) had lost their allure for some who were increasingly drawn to ideas from the West.

For the majority of peasants and artisans, the crises that resulted from foreign domination were a disaster for local subsistence economies. Non-elites continued to have faith in their own deities, shamans, and ancestors and indeed turned to them in times of trouble. Yet given the turmoil of the modern era, it is not hard to imagine that countless rituals failed and a great many prayers went unanswered. For all these reasons, the modern era in East Asia is marked by the unprecedented flowering of "new religious movements" that did not rely on old deities, institutions, or rituals. Most often, they arose from the lower classes through sects entirely independent of the traditional institutions of Daoism, Buddhism, and (premodern) Shinto.

Taiping Rebellion in China (1850–1864)

In China, a rebellion led by a Chinese convert to Christianity nearly ended Manchu rule. The nineteenth-century **Taiping Rebellion** began with a humble and failed village scholar, **Hong Xiuquan** (1814–64).

After an illness during which he was delirious for several weeks, Hong, with the help of an American Southern Baptist missionary, interpreted his fevered visions as Christian revelations. Despite limited knowledge of the Bible, Hong established his own form of Christianity, convinced that he had seen God, who had charged him with saving humanity and destroying demons, and that he had met Jesus, who was revealed to be Hong's "older brother." A charismatic preacher whose apocalyptic predictions captured the imagination of many, Hong organized his followers into a militant sect called the Taipings. Although the Western missionaries rejected his teachings, to some Chinese they offered a prophetic, utopian vision of a future "Heavenly Kingdom of Great Peace" based on egalitarianism, shared property, and gender equality. One of his Old Testament–inspired proclamations was that all idols be destroyed, be they Buddhist, Daoist, or even Confucian ancestor tablets. He also insisted that those joining his group adopt a puritanical moral code, abstaining from alcohol, tobacco, and opium.

"new religions": new sects formed since the nineteenth century combining elements of Buddhism, Daoism, and Confucianism with ideas imported from the West

Taiping Rebellion: violent revolt led by Chinese converts to Christianity, who established a separate state with its capital in Nanjing

Hong Xiuquan: charismatic instigator of the Taiping Rebellion; claimed to be younger brother of Jesus

Hong vilified the Manchu elite as demons standing in the way of the sect's radical transformation of China. The Qing state, in turn, persecuted the group, stepping up its efforts after 1850, by which time the Taipings had over 10,000 members. Thus provoked, Hong gathered an army whose bloody campaigns likely comprised the most destructive civil war in world history. Most of China was affected, and an estimated 20 million people perished. The Taiping army captured Nanjing in 1853 and occupied it for ten years, establishing a separate regional state ruled by Hong and his neo-Christian ministers.

Ultimately, however, the movement fell apart, owing to internal divisions, refusal to cooperate with potential allies, the leadership's ruthless brutality and paranoia in governing the Taiping community, and their hostility to the Confucian elements deeply embedded in China's population. Nanjing was retaken in 1864, all Taiping leaders not killed in battle were executed, and the first Asian-Christian "new religion" was utterly eradicated.

"Religion of the Heavenly Way": Ch'ondogyo in Korea

The **Ch'ondogyo**, which merges elements of Confucianism, Daoism, shamanism, and Roman Catholicism, was founded by Ch'oe Suun (1824–64) in 1860. Its original name, *Tonghak* ("Eastern learning"), signals its origins as an indigenous response to the challenge of newly imported Christianity (called "Western learning" in Korean). According to the sect's scriptures, Suun received a direct revelation of a new "Heavenly Way" (*Ch'ondo*) designed to awaken each person to the totality of life in the universe and the divinity immanent in each person and all creation. Sunn was inspired to reverence the Ultimate Reality, called *Hanullim*, an impersonal force with whom each person can have a direct connection.

The essential path to individual realization is through repetitive private and communal chanting. To invoke Hanullim to enter into personal awareness, the "21-syllable Incantation" is intoned.

Drawing on Confucianism for ethical principles and on Korea's folk religion for the communal rituals, Suun organized his movement on the notion that those who shared belief in that one God constituted a separate and distinct community within Korean society. Suun attracted a large following but was martyred by the government. The Ch'ondogyo continued to grow under Suun's successors, becoming one of the major religions of the Korean peninsula. Ch'ondogyo appealed especially to the lower classes, who were told that they, along with scholars and high officials, could achieve salvation through disciplined effort. Like Korean Christians, Ch'ondogyo members were active in resisting Japanese rule. Although banned in North Korea since 1949, recent reports mention its survival there; the group remains very popular in the south. There is an institutional center in Seoul, and in 2005 its membership, governed by an elected body, was reported to number over 3 million.

The collected writings of the first three leaders became the sect's chief scriptures. Ch'ondogyo's theology is expressed in one simple phrase: "Humans bear

Ch'ondogyo: Korean movement reaffirming the truth of human dignity and the vitality of Daoism and Confucianism

Ultimate Energy being all around me, I pray that I feel that Energy within me here and now. Recognizing that Hanullim is within me, I will be transformed. Constantly aware of that divine presence within, I will become attuned to all that is going on around me.

—Ch'ondogyo incantation

SOURCE: Robert Buswell Jr., ed., *Religions of Korea in Practice* (Princeton, NJ: Princeton University Press, 2007), p. 450.

divinity." The ethics of the sect emphasize respecting this universal divinity in others. The injunction "Treat others as divine" seems tame today but was revolutionarily democratic in the status-conscious Korea of the late nineteenth century. A heavenlike earthly existence marked by widespread social cooperation is their utopian goal.

Older "New Religions" in Pre-Meiji Japan

By the end of the Tokugawa era, the medieval social order in Japan had begun to break down, and for some the vitality of Buddhism and traditional Confucianism had waned. Of the several dozen spiritual movements that arose in this period, three grew to become denominations among the postmodern "new religions" of the early twenty-first century.

Each of these movements began with a charismatic individual who experienced extraordinary revelations after a serious illness. Having shared their discoveries with others, these leaders began building communities of followers who felt the teachings helped them reorder their lives on new spiritual principles. Almost every "new religion" thus offered a path to salvation out of the maze of choices that had developed along the way of Japanese religious history: Buddhism, neo-Confucianism, elements of Daoism, Shinto. All later were harmonized with the Meiji state's neo-Shintoism, eventually becoming regarded as "Shinto sects." Two of the more prominent Shinto sects are Kurozumikyo and Tenrikyo.

Kurozumikyo ("Kurozumi's religion") was founded by Kurozumi Munetada (1780–1850), a charismatic teacher who in 1815 was possessed by the Shinto sun goddess Amaterasu, whom he asserted to be the single Lord of the Universe. Soon after his initial experience he began preaching and attracting disciples, who spread his revelations across Japan.

Followers of Kurozumikyo believe that all humans are emanations of the kami and that individual believers may become kami, or become one with them, securing eternal life, by adopting the moral and spiritual practices of these Japanese deities. The potential for all to realize the divine state explains the Kurozumikyo emphasis on the equality of all people, a radical idea in pre-Meiji Japan, where class completely determined individual destiny. Kurozumikyo grew dramatically after winning Meiji recognition. Its leaders had a central shrine established in Okayama City, and the group numbered perhaps 700,000 by 1880. In 2010, 361 centers were counted in Japan, and its membership had dropped to just more than 200,000.

Tenrikyo ("Religion of Heavenly Wisdom") began with messages its founder, Nakayama Miki (1798–1887), received while in a trance. The source of these communications, he reported, was a spirit Nakayama called "God the Parent" (Oyagami). Regarded by followers as the one true god of the universe, Oyagami commanded Nakayama to be his medium and to further his mission through healing and preaching. Tenrikyo claimed that its newly released universal doctrine of harmonious living would usher in a new world order, a divine kingdom in which humanity would enjoy

"True Sincerity is the one thing we must be most thankful for; with sincerity alone the Earth can be a family. In this world of ours we have come together to form a circle; let us pray to be joined by the Heart of all our hearts."

—Munetada, founder of Kurozumikyo

Tenrikyo: Tenrikyo ("Religion of Heavenly Wisdom") was founded by Nakayama Miki (1798–1887) and became a recognized Shinto sect in 1838; essential for salvation are a dance ritual, an initiation ("receiving the holy grant"), and performance of daily social service for others

blissful union with God the Parent. In the sect's view, the "one, true kami" in the universe had created humanity to see it find harmonious life and then entered into creation in the form of ten other kami. Tenrikyo adherents believe that Oyagami made his new revelation to Nakayama to rectify growing human selfishness, a shortcoming that has undermined the original divine intent.

Tenrikyo became a recognized Shinto sect in 1838 and rapidly spread throughout Japan. Like the other Shinto-related sects, after the Second World War the group made efforts to "purify" Tenrikyo of its Shinto and nationalist associations. By 2013, there were over 3.75 million members, who had established over 16,000 centers in Japan, with an additional 20,000 mission centers worldwide.

Nichiren-Related Sects of the Meiji Era

As the Meiji reforms opened and transformed Japanese society after 1867 and government calls to modernize Japan multiplied, the spirit of renewal found religious expression as well. Numerous laity-led groups arose because the Buddhist "establishment" offered few opportunities for those wishing to reinterpret the doctrines or apply them in the context of modern scientific discoveries from the West. Many modern groups formed in association with the Nichiren school, with its focus on the *Lotus Sutra*'s teachings of compassion and interconnectivity an inspiration to engage with modern problems. Directly stemming from this school is the largest new religion of modern Japan, the lay organization called *Soka Gakkai* ("Value Creation Society"). Established formally near the end of World War II by the Nichiren disciple and educator Makiguchi Tsunesaburo (1877–1944), the Soka Gakkai aims to foster a "Third Civilization" based on Nichiren's teachings, one in which the true Buddhism would spread throughout the world. Its members believe that repeatedly chanting the *Nam-Myoho-renge-kyo* (the name of the great Buddhist text, the *Lotus Sutra*) is a means for changing the world. The Soka Gakkai also considers its mission to work for world peace and human welfare, and after 1960 it established a political party in Japan (the Komeito) to achieve this goal there. It has also sent missionaries to every major country of the world. By 2013, the Soka Gakkai had registered 12 million Japanese members and claimed 1.4 million international adherents.

Also originated by and for Nichiren laity, *Reiyukai Kyodan* ("Spiritual Friends Association") was founded in 1925 by Kubo Kakutaro (1892–1944) and Kotani Kimi (1901–71). The group emphasized ancestor worship by the laity and attributed the upheavals of the era to ancestral distress over the ineffectiveness of the contemporary Buddhist leaders. The Reiyukai also emphasizes conservative social values and expects its members to work hard to strengthen the Confucian "three bonds" (between ruler and minister, father and son, and husband and wife). In addition, the Reiyukai are strong supporters of imperial veneration and other conservative causes in Japanese society. One of the most active proselytizing new religions, the Reiyukai by 2013 had 5 million members and centers abroad in twenty-six countries.

East Asian Religions and Postmodern Trends in a Postcolonial World

The coming of the Marxist state to mainland China in 1949 and the imposition of totalitarian rule by the officially atheistic Communist Party began an era of sustained religious repression. Chinese religions suffered the destruction of properties and religious institutions through unprecedented governmental attempts to exterminate any vestige of traditional religious teaching or spiritual training. In China, this repression lasted for almost two generations, until 1976.

But as we discussed in Chapter 1, such persecution has not led to the end of religion in China. Far from it. State-sponsored substitution of modernist Marxist ideologies, utopian mythology, and the orchestration of a personality cult centered on Mao Zedong represented attempts to substitute a communist Chinese civil religion for Confucianism, Daoism, and Buddhism. The effort failed, though it did weaken the bond between most mainland Chinese and their traditional organized religions.

Since the reform era that began soon after the death of Mao in 1976, the gradual restoration of religion in China has proceeded under the supervision of the state. A popular upsurge of practice at Daoist temples, family graves, Buddhist monasteries, Christian churches, and mosques is evident, however. Countless Chinese have seized the opportunity to make pilgrimages, reopen shrines, and resume the ritual practices of their ancestors. We discuss here both the surviving traditions and new religions that have multiplied the pluralism characteristic of the postcolonial era.

Continuities and Transformations in the East Asian Religions

A knowledgeable visitor to Osaka, Seoul, or Shanghai today would be intrigued to see how traditions endure amid signs of extraordinary changes: Shinto shrines tucked

TALES OF SPIRITUAL TRANSFORMATION: Daoist

This Daoist tale describes how Zhuang Zi learned from his wife's death and explained his spiritual realization to a friend who discovered him drumming and singing instead of maintaining the expected Confucian decorum of solemnity.

I pondered over her beginning before she was born; not merely before she was born but when there was as yet no body; not merely when there was no body but not even a vital spirit. Within an inchoate confusion there took forth a transformation and there was

vital spirit. The vital spirit was transformed and there came forth form, and with the transformation there was life. Now once again there is a transformation and she died. What happened may be compared to the four seasons. . . . Now she is lying in peace in a small room. For me to follow after her weeping and wailing would be an indication that I have no thorough understanding of human destiny.

Source: Smith, *The Wisdom of the Taoists*, p. 88.

into spaces between skyscrapers, new Confucius Institutes being built by the Chinese government, Buddhist television stations broadcasting from corporate headquarters in Korea. New religions are being formed, even as old ritual practices are being applied to new human problems. As global awareness is further influencing East Asian religions, they are also expanding to Asian communities across the globe. These trends now merit our attention.

The Reality of Gods and Spirits in China

Ancient Chinese myths mention deities of mountains, rivers, rain, and the earth that have remained part of the diffuse Chinese religion. Interestingly, most deities appearing later in East Asia have human origins, as heroic ancestral spirits have become gods. This is true of **Guan Yu**, the god of war (in real life, a Han general), various deified statesmen, Confucius, and even, in recent years, Mao Zedong. Most other important deities have been Buddhist in origin.

In regional and local contexts, the East Asian pantheon has always been in flux as new heroes arise and the deities are obliged continuously to show their power (**ling**), to prove themselves worthy of the investment of further offerings. Those manifesting strong healing powers or success in responding to popular appeals win devotees, patrons, and new temples. Alternatively, other deities have faded from popularity. Thus, the East Asian understanding of and experience with divinities has not been based so much on faith as on experiential encounters.

The most common deities found on altars in Chinese homes and temples are icons of the "triple gods": Longevity, in the form of a vigorous old man; Wealth, embodied by a Confucian official; and Blessings, symbolized by a male god holding a baby boy.

Another prominent deity, Tian Shang Sheng-mu ("Holy Mother in Heaven"), is popularly known as *Mazu* ("Grandmother"). Her origins can be traced to a girl born in the ninth century who saved her father and brothers at sea by exercising magical powers acquired via Daoist practice. She died young, and soon apparitions and miracles attributed to her were reported. By the mid-twelfth century, the state had recognized Tian Shang Sheng-mu and Mazu cult and temples that spread along the eastern coast of China, where the goddess remains popular today.

In the kitchen of every traditional Chinese and Korean home (but not in Japan) is a figure of the deity Zao Wangye, the "**kitchen god**." He records the household goings on and composes a yearly report right before New Year's Day. Individual kitchen gods and earth gods of each community were believed to present these records to the nearby city gods, who in turn informed the celestial Jade Emperor on New Year's Day. This notion of a divine, hierarchical officialdom reflects popular understanding in China of what happens when a person dies: The earth god of the locality reports to the city god, who

Guan Yu: Chinese god of war, worshipped for protection today

ling: spiritual force possessed by geographic places, deities, and sages

kitchen god: in China and Korea, deity residing in every household

Image of Mazu, the protective deity worshipped along the Chinese seacoast.

Representations of the "triple gods"—Blessings, Wealth, and Longevity—found on many altars in Chinese homes, restaurants, and temples.

then escorts the soul to the underworld to appear before ten judges who determine punishments and karmic destiny.

Ritual Practices

In many respects, East Asia derives its unity as a religious and cultural area from the shared ritual practices in its temples and at family graves. These rituals are an extension of the human custom of feasting an honored guest, in these cases an ancestral spirit or a deity. Along with food and drink, other items presented in East Asian rituals include candles, flowers, oil lamps, and incense. In keeping with the idea that the deities are senior but essentially human is the practice of full prostration (*ketou*, or "kowtow") before icons or tablets, a gesture of respect that junior kin also make before their living elders at festival times.

For most occasions in daily life, priests (be they Daoist, Buddhist, or shamans) are not needed. This is because senior householders and state officials, even at the highest level, have ritual tasks to perform according to their status. In particular, Confucian filial piety is shown at a parent's death through careful carrying out of the appropriate rituals. The reward is the soul-spirit's blessings and the promise of a reunion with kin after the children's own demise.

Participation in a funeral is one of the key events binding families and transmitting family values. The funeral itself involves the largest and most ostentatious procession that can be afforded, with musicians and mourners carrying large paper replicas of items the deceased is expected to need in the afterlife. The traditional death rituals

Items for burning to be sent to the dead by the affluent Chinese of Shanghai and Singapore.

end with the priests ritually transferring the soul to two places for future worship, inviting it to reunite with the previously deceased ancestors. The cremation remains are brought in a procession to the family grave or clan temple. Here they are left in an urn, and a grave tablet with the deceased's name is written. The yin (earthly) soul stays with these remains. The yang (heavenly) soul is carried to the family's home and ritually installed on the family altar as a permanent tablet inscribed with the person's name is set in place. On the altar near tablets for other senior kin and images of various deities, this spirit receives all the offerings made to the gods. Moreover, any important event in the family is announced to the tablets as if the ancestors resided there.

Although not all families can afford family gravesites, all wish to have them, since with such a burial the family can most directly ensure the happiness of the earthbound souls. Some Buddhist temples in Japan cultivated family patronage by creating cemeteries on their grounds. Families possessing graves go to them on two occasions each year to tidy them, make sacrifices, and then eat and drink among the family's ancestral graves. Thus, cemeteries in East Asia are not dreaded locales but places one can go to feel close to one's deceased kin as well as to conform to the basic Confucian requirement of caring for them after death.

The Religious Institutions: Monasteries, Temples, Shrines

The religious institutions that sustain the three traditions in East Asia vary widely. For their surrounding householder communities, Buddhist monasteries have temples with images of compassionate bodhisattvas and include monks who specialize in healing and death rituals. The temple in all these religions is considered as simply a house

GENDER FOCUS: Women and East Asian Religions

In the Asian traditions, the great sages are all male, as are the preponderance of major gods. The great monastic traditions that were formed by Buddhists and Daoists all rendered nuns as secondary figures who exerted little institutional control. This pattern of religious traditions providing legitimation for gender inequality is also clearly seen in Confucian thought, which held that the control of women by men is necessary for the establishment of a harmonious society. The fact that men are instructed to act in ways to deserve this power by ensuring the flourishing of women and girls does not alter the reality of male control. Nor did the doctrines of the Daoists, seeing harmony in the universe based on a balancing of yin and yang, including male and female, exert any counterforce to the gender hierarchy found across East Asia.

In China, the subjugation of women found extraordinary expression in the practice of women binding their feet. Widespread in Chinese society from 1000 CE until the mid-twentieth century, this custom involved the excruciatingly painful process of young girls (ages five through seven) having the bones of their toes and arches broken, then bound in place inward, creating an incapacitating

deformity. Scholars have interpreted foot binding as an expression of gender relations in conformity with the dominant neo-Confucian tradition. Although this contradicts a central ethical principle of this tradition that prohibits individuals from mutilating their bodies, that ideal seems to have been applied to men alone. Instead, foot binding was part of the male-regulated family, in which bound feet rendered women dependent on their families, particularly their men, and became a symbol of chastity and male ownership.

Attention to gender and the male control of Confucianism, Daoism, and Buddhism makes it especially understandable that women were drawn to the hundreds of "new religions" established across East Asia. Many were founded by, supported by, and, to a greater extent than in the older faiths, run by women. Under conditions of modernity, women seeking power, prestige, and careers outside the traditional boundaries of family life found many new options in these new religions that cultivated their membership. The changing familial, educational, and economic conditions for women seen across Asia today are also forcing the long-established religions to reform their institutions to attract females as devotees.

for humanlike divinities. They can be modest roadside boxes where humble images are kept, or they can be massive palaces housing gilded images flanked by hosts of attending demigods.

The larger temples in China share certain characteristics. The aesthetic in them is highly baroque: with curving roof lines and eaves, every beam and column painted with bright colors, decorations bright with gold surfaces, the statues wearing silk vestments.

The greatest temples contain all the major deities of the pantheon. The entrance always opens to the south, an auspicious direction, and is guarded by statues of protectors. In larger establishments these guardians are lodged in a gatehouse through which all visitors must pass. In larger compounds, the main deity will be in the last hall on the same axis as the entrance, with halls containing lesser deities arrayed on the same line and separated by courtyards. Before each icon is an altar for receiving offerings,

(left) Chinese temple, the home of the gods, featuring the ornate pillars and roof tiles of the palace style. (right) Main gate, or torii, of the Fushimi Inari Shinto Shrine in Kyoto, Japan.

most commonly candles or incense sticks. Kneeling cushions are supplied as well as a means of divination for posing questions to a deity: Two half-moon wooden blocks are thrown to derive a "yes" or "no" answer, based on their resting alignment.

The larger Daoist temples are usually served by a resident priesthood and by mediums. The mediums specialize in exorcisms and help private clients make offerings. Resident priests may assist in rituals such as exorcisms but have also mastered complex Daoist death liturgies and wear more formal attire.

Japanese Shinto shrines (*jinja*) are notable for their natural wood, plain roof tiles, and restrained aesthetic. Every jinja is also marked by a gateway called a *torii*. Given the emphasis on purification in Shintoism, water sources for rinsing the face and mouth are always present where devotees approach the main shrine. These distinctive features of Japan's Shinto architecture delineate a transition from the ordinary world into sacred space.

After purification, devotees proceed to the main and subsidiary shrines. Facing the main icon, they present their petitions. Before making a request, a visitor can ring a shrine bell. Ending the ritual by clapping shows respect.

The Diffuse Religion in Practice: The Major Religious Festivals

In our discussion of the religious practices of China, Korea, and Japan, we have pointed to the "diffuse religion" that gives the region a characteristic unity, drawing on elements of the three traditions. Festivals express this diffuse religion most clearly, since Confucian, Daoist, and Buddhist elements have been woven into the yearly cycle of life. The globally familiar Chinese system of twelve-year cycles, lunar days,

A small Shinto shrine (jinja) dedicated to the protector of cows, the cow kami.

and solar seasons is still used in many areas and has been intermixed with the Western calendar. Indicative of its rapid Westernization in the nineteenth century, Japan shifted many of its holidays to fixed "Western" days.

National holidays have grown out of a variety of origins: mythic events or deities indigenous to the particular nation, days accentuating Confucian values, or relatively recent events that the nation's leaders wish to mark in the country's "civil religion." For example, Japan celebrates the Cherry Blossom Festival (April 1–8) to thank the kami of the forests for the renewal of life seen in the blossoming of the trees.

Every major deity in every locality is thought to have a "birthday" each year, either a day celebrated nationally or the day a more local deity's temple was first established. On these annual occasions, the priests and temple supporters arrange for ritual performances, local devotees make offerings (and petitions), merchants and artisans sell their wares, and theatrical performances are staged to entertain deity and devotees alike.

Most common festivals of East Asia have Chinese or Buddhist origins. New Year's Day is a time for gathering family and friends, settling debts, and seeking blessings and divine protection for the year ahead. The day in China and Korea is called *Spring Festival*, although it falls usually just after the middle of winter. In traditional preholiday rites, householders send the Kitchen God (Zao Wangye) off to heaven by burning

Daoist New Year
celebrations in Beijing.

his paper icon and installing a new paper icon; they also post ancient characters on doorways to invite prosperity for the year ahead. The essentials of Confucian family life are marked in sacrifices offered to ancestors at their tablets. It is customary for junior family members to kowtow to seniors, who then in turn receive gifts of money in special red envelopes.

Qing-Ming: annual spring festival when Chinese tend to family graves and make offerings to the ancestors

Ancestor's Day, or **Qing-Ming** ("Pure Brightness Festival"), is the first of two dates over the year when families must visit the ancestral graves to maintain them, make sacrifices, and feast together there with the departed spirits, usually in early April. In Japan, this festival has been fixed as the vernal equinox (March 21) and is called *Higan* ("Further Shore"), with a second Higan on the autumnal equinox. Buddhist priests are also expected to come to the home on a short visit, during which they recite sacred scriptures. The merit earned for this good deed is dedicated to the dead.

Japanese Buddhists mark the Buddha's birthday on April 8, when people anoint images of baby Buddha with flowers and scented water, just as the texts describe the local deities doing at the actual birth of Siddhartha. Chinese and Korean Buddhists do the same on the eighth day of the fourth lunar month. Confucius' birthday is celebrated today only in Korea and always on September 28. In Taiwan, on Teacher's Day, Confucius is honored with colorful rituals and elaborate sacrifices laid out before the sage's temple tablets.

All Souls Festival: summer event when families perform rituals to connect the living with their ancestors and ensure ancestors' comfort in the afterlife

All Souls Festival is a summer event when the gates of purgatory are thought to be momentarily held open. On this occasion, families integrate practices from all three traditions to connect the living members with their departed kin. Buddhist and Daoist priests perform rituals to aid families in their effort to ensure their ancestors' comfort in the afterlife.

Scene in Chengudu, China from the Qing-Ming festival, the yearly family ritual for feasting and honoring the ancestors.

The early fall **Full Moon Festival** is a time to worship the harvest moon, also known as the "full rabbit moon." In the popular Buddhist scriptures, the Buddha was once born as a rabbit who rendered such extraordinary service to his fellow animals that the gods placed his image on the moon's surface; in the Daoist perception, a rabbit can be seen on the moon, using a pestle to pound the herbs of immortality in a mortar. Across East Asia, people view the rising moon on this night to ask for blessings that in rural communities include a good rice harvest in the month ahead.

Full Moon Festival: fall festival to feast with kin and celebrate the harvest moon

The Return of Religion to China: Case Studies

Between 1949 and 1976, the Communist Party–led government of China dispersed the religious specialists (monks, nuns, and priests) and destroyed much of the formal infrastructure of the organized religions of China, demolishing Buddhist and Daoist monasteries and image shrines as well as the deity temples that before 1949 could be found in every community. The party also pushed religion underground, since in the most active phase of the **Cultural Revolution** (1966–69), any attempt to pray, meditate, or read religious literature was potentially a capital crime. We now examine a few examples in pursuit of understanding the extraordinary phenomenon of religion's return to the People's Republic of China.

Cultural Revolution: period in Communist China under Mao Zedong when religious traditions and practitioners were persecuted

Mao in the Rearview Mirror

The Forbidden City in Beijing is the immense, walled complex from which the Yuan, Ming, and Qing emperors ruled all of China. It was at the top of the

Contemporary Mao amulet, inscribed with prayers for good fortune and safe travel, of the kind found widely in China today adorning rearview mirrors in cars.

palace's southern gateway, called the Gate of Heavenly Peace (Tian'anmen), that Mao Zedong proclaimed the establishment of the People's Republic of China in 1949. Despite all the changes that have swept China since Mao's death in 1976, his immense painted portrait still hangs over that gateway. The image serves as a constant reminder of Mao's heroic and determined role in leading the Communist Party's triumphant success.

The style of the Tian'anmen Square portrait suggests that Mao is the ascetic servant of the people, a true communist leader whose deeds are legendary. He bravely fought the Japanese, and in the Long March of 1934 he led the troops in strategic retreat halfway across China. For Mao and so for the early Chinese Communist Party leaders, religion and religious institutions were "enemies of the people." Mao was a rationalist who critiqued "superstitious" religious ideas that allegedly blocked the people's attempts to understand the world; he never ceased to highlight the classic modernist goal of setting the world free from the wrong thinking stemming from belief in supernatural "magic."

People who grew up during the decades of Mao's dictatorship later painfully realized how full of "superstition" they had been in uncritically following the Communist Party and especially in showing reverence for Chairman Mao. Yet today, more than forty years after his death, Mao retains his standing among many Chinese as a sincere and uncorrupted champion of China's renewal who tried to seek justice and the common good. But regard for Mao endures in ways that even he did not anticipate. For example, many Chinese now regard Mao as a deity. In their homes, or even on their persons, you may find an amulet of Mao that is believed to confer protection and even business success to the bearer. The transformations under way in China today and the restoration of religion among the Chinese people are embedded in this striking turn of fate: The most powerful man in East Asia, while alive an atheist who suppressed religion, is in death a powerful spirit.

While his transformation to a revered protective spirit and god of wealth would doubtless have dismayed Chairman Mao, it does demonstrate the global pattern of religious traditions responding to the needs of local life. As the state and party have moved since the early 1990s away from collectivist policies to emphasize individual and private enterprise, leaders have exhorted the Chinese people that "to get rich is glorious." At the same time, the government has retreated from promises of guaranteed state employment, pensions, and universal medical care. So is it really surprising that an unassailable icon would be adopted as the god of personal protection and wealth?

The Force of Feng Shui

Ideas about what constitutes "religion" in China not only fascinate modern scholars but have been repeatedly debated by officials of the Communist Party. In the reform era, as pressure has been exerted to reintroduce almost every sort of former spiritual practice, the East Asian organized religions, with their potential for reestablishing nationwide institutional networks, have had to deal with deliberate governmental attempts aimed at controlling and regulating them. A few ancient practices, however, were left almost entirely unmolested. One of these is *feng shui*, the school of applied religious Daoism that seeks to maximize human flourishing in natural and constructed environments. (The name, which means literally "wind-water," refers to the principal bearers of environmental energy used in geomancy.)

Feng shui consultants are today found everywhere across mainland China, where they advise builders of the new hotels, residences, and factories rising so quickly across the country. The goal of feng shui is to determine the most auspicious building sites, architectural designs, and living arrangements. Both private concerns and state ventures with party approval now take the "science" of mapping the qi, the inherent energy of a place, quite seriously.

The state's support of feng shui has given credence to the classical religious worldview regarding humanity and the environment. It is based on Daoist principles of balancing yin and yang, channeling the subterranean and atmospheric flow of their qi, and pursuing health and prosperity through expert arrangement of harmonious design features. The government's policy reflects the perennial Chinese emphasis on religion's practical, this-worldly benefits.

Nor is mainland China the only area to see the effect of this revival of the ancient worldview: As significant numbers of Chinese people have migrated overseas, real estate brokers from London to San Francisco are having to take account of feng shui analysis in marketing their properties.

A feng shui master holds a compass, or lopan, used to determine auspicious environments.

Nationalism and Confucianism Revived

Perhaps even more striking is the return of Confucius to an honored position in modern China. In the retreat from communism, China has been beset by corruption accompanying its hastily instituted market reforms. Many Chinese writers have pointed out the crisis in faith and values as the profit-seeking motive has been unleashed over the last four decades. Since 2011, a rising theme in the China press has been the decline of moral values and the lack of civic virtues, highlighted by noted cases where strangers refused to help injured children or elders.

The Communist Party, in apparent recognition of this potential source of chaos, embarked on another great reversal by turning back to Confucius. The restoration of Confucius to respectability is part of its promotion of a more primordial Chinese tradition on which to anchor its permanent power base: nationalism.

Regardless of whether they support the communist government, Chinese people widely share great pride in their civilization and its culture. Party strategists see the world economy as developing in a direction leading to eventual domination by China. Thus, in the interest of guiding the country to reach this pinnacle, they have all but ended any demands that the people accept ideologies contrary to Chinese traditions.

The People's Republic of China has permitted Confucianism in order to evoke nationalistic pride, another complete reversal by the Communist Party leadership. During the Cultural Revolution, Mao required Red Guards (a fanatical pro-Mao student movement) to denounce Confucius, tarring the master as an apologist for feudalism and exploitation, a symbol for all the traditions that the Communist Party was out to replace. The Party also attacked the core Confucian virtue of filial piety, seeking the individual's highest loyalty for itself.

Yet the excesses of the Cultural Revolution may have sparked renewed interest in Confucian thought in China. In 1994, to mark the 2,545th birthday of the great sage, the party launched an initiative to revive Confucian thought. A series of international conferences were convened, the Confucian temple in Beijing was restored and reopened to the public, and Confucius' home temple in

With the allowance for religious freedom after the Cultural Revolution, traditional Daoist priests have enjoyed their restoration to temple service across China.

RITUALS AND RITES: Ancestor Veneration

Then: Traditional Funerals

In its zeal to end wasteful expenditures on the rituals of death and ancestor veneration, which for some traditional families meant going into nearly inescapable debt for extravagant funerals, the Chinese Communist Party in 1956 issued strict regulations limiting funeral observances and—a radical break from the past—required secular cremation while also prohibiting rituals at ancestral graves. This attempt to break with the Confucian tradition went even further during Cultural Revolution, when the Red Guards ransacked and destroyed gravesites throughout China, including parts of the great imperial tombs. Mao was trying to destroy the familial tradition, which he saw as dividing "the people" and so undermining the party's quest to promote the collective good.

Beginning in the early 1990s, the practices of traditional funeral processions and burial of the dead in family graves slowly began to return, largely in villages and smaller towns, but hardly at all around major cities such as Beijing, where until 1996 the government posted signs threatening punishment for those burning paper money at gravesides. Since 2008, when the Chinese government reinstated Ching Ming as a national holiday, ancient cemeteries have been restored and new ones established to accommodate families' wishes to reestablish the old family traditions. (According to government statistics, more than 520 million people—almost half of China's population—visited cemeteries during this festival in 2017.) Ideal sites near Beijing and Shanghai now command very high prices and one sees burial places of elaborate design, including permanent brick structures with nameplates affixed. Even government-owned shops can be found selling the items used in this popular observance, as the traditional belief again affirms that the state of one's ancestors' graves determines one's own destiny.

Now: Online Memorial Rituals

Across Asia, during the Ching Ming Festival, virtual possibilities exist if individual mourners can't take time off, are allergic to incense smoke, or the family grave is too far away. Instead, one can simply go online. A growing number of websites in China and Taiwan are dedicated to ancestor worship, as well as thousands of online memorial halls. These prayer websites offer convenience, with many featuring a special form users can fill in to send good wishes, messages, and even presents.

While some find this a meaningful innovation, others express the opposite view, that such virtual ancestor worship just cultivates laziness and insincerity.

Qufu was celebrated as a place to visit. In 2010, China for the first time under Party rule celebrated Confucius's birthday; in 2014, the Party passed a national law requiring children to visit and support their elderly parents, not mentioning its efforts to undermine such filial piety during the Cultural Revolution. By the year 2016, China's presidents and high officials readily quoted from Confucius in public speeches, popular books and television series in China explored Confucius and Confucian thought, and the Communist Party funded the creation of Confucius Institutes across the world.

Qi Gong

qi gong: discipline of cultivating the vital individual life force

Another area in which religion has returned to mainland China in the guise of applied therapy is in the practice of **qi gong**. This healing art, like feng shui, draws on Daoist theories of vital energy in the body.

In some governmental circles, there is ambivalence about such applied spirituality. Although the modern official press features an occasional article, often by a prominent scientist, that denounces "phony qi gong" as "harmful" and criticizes individual practitioners for "feudal and superstitious activities which use the flag of qi gong as a cover for swindling others," it continues to allow the practice to flourish, even in state-controlled temple precincts. Thus, while this medically oriented practice is mixed with other therapies (Chinese and Western), qi gong, like feng shui, now affirms the credibility of the most elemental ideas of classical Daoism.

Falun Gong and Eastern Lightning: The Limits of Religious Freedom

In general, there were fewer "new religions" in the People's Republic of China under communist rule than in Korea or Japan; but barely a quarter century after Mao's death, the party leadership discovered that its relaxation of earlier repressive policies had allowed the formation of powerful new Chinese religions called Buddhist Law Power (*Falun Gong* or *Falun Dafa*) and Eastern Lightning (Dongfang Shǎndiàn).

Founded in 1990, Eastern Lightning emerged into public awareness near the end of 2012, when it widely publicized that the end of the world was about to begin.

Sales clerk at an ancestor worship shop, Shanghai. Government shops across China now sell the paper money, candles, and incense needed for this ancient practice, once prohibited by official regulations. Recent additions available in upscale memorial supply shops include paper replicas of iPads, Android phones, and computers.

Women performing a *qi gong* ritual in Shanghai, with gestures designed to cultivate and concentrate the qi energy in the body.

The group would be led by a woman from central China, "Lightning Deng," who has been identified as "Jesus Christ incarnated"; her mission is to "slay the great red dragon," the Communist Party. Her most widely distributed book, *Lightning from the Orient*, proclaims itself "the Word of God." It claims the first coming of Christ was to redeem humanity, while hers as the second is "to conquer men's hearts and defeat Satan." Recruiting with aggressive means, Eastern Lightning leaders have attracted over a million followers. Anticipating these last days, many withdrew all their money from banks and sold their property. The Chinese government launched a campaign of arrests against members, declaring it a dangerous cult and "a social cancer and a plague on humankind."

Founded in 1992 by Li Hongzhi, Falun Gong quickly attracted millions across China. Falun Gong's principal practice of qi gong exercises promises to promote individual health and spiritual transformation through the generation of extraordinary energy, in line with Daoist traditions at least two millennia old. Falung Gong leaders began to attract government criticism, and its members were persecuted. In late April 1999, the group staged a protest against these actions, with 10,000 members surrounding the Communist Party leadership compound in central Beijing. Arriving undetected, Falun Gong followers sat in silent, nonviolent protest throughout the day and then dispersed without incident. The massive sit-in provoked an all-out propaganda offensive, capped by the arrest of Falun Gong leaders, who were charged with antigovernment subversion. Within months, the group had been outlawed as a "pernicious superstition."

Falun Gong and Eastern Lightning resemble the new religions we have described in Korea and Japan: Their doctrines comprise an original recombination of Buddhist,

Daoist, and Christian millennial doctrines, and their founders both claim supernormal status "on a level the same as Buddha and Jesus." Falun Gong's principal practice of qi gong exercises promises to promote individual health and spiritual transformation through the generation of extraordinary energy. Falun Gong, in particular, is an apt example of a new East Asian religion in the age of media technology, when so many regional faiths are becoming global.

Shrines in Chinese Village Squares, Shops, and Front Doors

Across mainland China since 1976, devotees have worked to reestablish shrines, temples, and the ritual practices destroyed or prohibited under government orders dating back to 1949. Exactly where the Communist Party's line of toleration lies has varied according to the region and its succession of officials. Tensions still exist over what is "superstition," which is strongly discouraged by the government, versus what is considered "religion." Individuals have a constitutional right to practice a religion, but the state reserves the right to grant or withhold this designation for a given belief system.

Accounts of village life cite the near-universal attempt of rural peasants to use part of their new earnings to build (or rebuild) the public temples that house the local and regional gods. None is more telling than the practice of making offerings to the local earth gods (**Tu-di**). In pre-Maoist China, earth god shrines were found in homes, neighborhoods, villages, government offices (where they received offerings from state officials), and even Buddhist monasteries. People believe that, if petitioned properly

Tu-di: "Earth Ruler," local god who is worshipped across modern China to control the earth's fertility

Rituals performed at a Daoist temple in Xi'an.

and sincerely, the earth gods protect against locusts, mildew, disease, and other obstacles to a rich harvest as well as solve any other difficulties in their domain. These shrines and this cult have returned everywhere.

Clearly, the Chinese government has accepted the return of China's diffuse religion, as long as the new organizations do not threaten the Communist Party's ruling power. By being sensitive to the importance and meaning of religion, we can comprehend how China's spiritual traditions are changing to meet the needs of the common people. As the party expands economic opportunity but ends the social safety-net protection programs (guaranteed employment, medical insurance, housing) people increasingly feel that to prosper, they need all the luck, and divine assistance, they can attract. Accordingly, the quest to satisfy the perceived need for good fortune is so intense that the official proponents of communist doctrine are reluctant to suppress practices many old Communist Party members consider "an opiate of the masses."

Japan's Creative Diversity: Old Traditions and New

Whereas in China the Cultural Revolution postponed the expression of religious awakening until after Mao's death in 1976, in Japan this era of innovation commenced in 1945, with the necessity of rebuilding the war-ravaged country both physically and spiritually. After the devastation of World War II, Japan had to reinvent a form of government, redesign its economic system, and rebuild its major cities without reference to the emperor as their divine leader. Japan's surrender in 1945 was spoken by Emperor Hirohito in his own voice, and during the occupation he was compelled to renounce his divinity (as a Shinto kami) explicitly and to underscore his purely ceremonial presence in Japan's political future.

The state system of neo-Shintoism was discredited and discarded. Shinto then survived largely in its myriad shrines dedicated to divinities in neighborhoods, villages, and regions and attended to by hereditary priests. Establishment Buddhism, like the rest of Japan's cultural institutions, also had to overcome the stigma of having uncritically supported the fascist state. As the economic system flourished, Japan's wealth eventually was used to rebuild these institutions, accelerating the traditional religion's material recovery and, in some cases, expansion.

The Claim of "Having No Religion" and the Reality of New Year's Rituals

Educated Japanese and oftentimes their friends in intellectual Western circles are fond of proclaiming that the Japanese are "lacking in religion," an Enlightenment attitude common among educated East Asians. While few Japanese today care to learn much in depth about Shinto mythology or Buddhist doctrine, widespread indifference does not prove that Japan "lacks religion."

Beyond the unprecedented growth of the new religions, one has only to know where and when to seek a wealth of examples that dispel this widespread stereotype about a Japanese people somehow being different from everyone else. Contemporary New Year's Day observances provide an example of the strength of "diffuse popular religion" in modern Japan.

During the Meiji era, Japan had legislated a shift away from the Chinese lunar calendar's determining the date of the "new year" festival and adopted the Western (or Gregorian) system that has the year begin on January 1. On this day and days around it, Japan shuts down its industrial economy. Families begin the process of renewal through a special cleaning of the house. On New Year's Eve or early New Year's morning, long lines of family members arrive at their local Shinto shrine to pay their respects to their neighborhood's kami. People then consign to bonfires all the family amulets accumulated over the past year. That evening or the next day, a family member will purchase new amulets to arrange on the newly purified family altar.

In a recent survey of those who visited Shinto shrines, 65 percent of men and 75 percent of women reported experiencing *aratamatta kimochi*, "a feeling of inner peace," afterward.[3] Many ritual activities at these shrines seem to indicate religious conviction—clapping the hands together, bowing before an image, making an offering, buying an amulet. Thus, contemporary New Year's Day traditions in Japan as well as everyday activities at Shinto shrines fit perfectly into the "religion" framework we introduced in Chapter 1.

A powerful and poignant indication of enduring religiosity of the Japanese was seen in the aftermath of the 2011 earthquake and the tsunami and nuclear disaster it caused, a catastrophe that claimed several thousand lives. Prominent monks in the months following pointed out that the community's response is indicative of the Buddhist tradition's enduring place there: showing patience, resilience, and self-sacrifice in the face of tragedy. The absence of looting, the many acts of self-sacrifice, and workers facing dangerous radiation for the common good epitomized the Buddhist bodhisattva ideal. To memorialize the dead, priests read scripture and chanted sutras before bodies were cremated. And for bodies washed out to sea, there were prominent and nationally televised mass memorials for the dead.

Then, as people began rebuilding their homes and lives until the present, Shinto moved to center stage. People turned to Shinto rituals performed by priests to restore the balance between the human and the divine, bless the construction sites, and pacify the local kami. At the Otsuchi shrine that stood undamaged in a small town devastated by the waves, throngs of survivors stopped by daily in the first months to bow and ring the bell at the main shrine. As one CNN report noted, "Their prayers to this local kami in the first months were heartbreaking, as residents asked for help in finding missing relatives before continuing the grim task of searching for their bodies. Others asked for strength in the face of the horrific post-tsunami reality."

Daruma-san:
Japanese name of legendary Indian sage who brought Zen tradition to East Asia; a folk icon in Japan

The Zen of Daruma-san

If any single religious icon could be said to embody the paradoxes of religion in Japan today, it might be **Daruma-san**. The name and identity of this figure derive

Buddhist temple damaged by the 2011 earthquake and tsunami in Yamamoto, Japan.

from Bodhidharma, the sage renowned as the transmitter of the Buddhist medita-tion tradition from India (around 600 CE) that became Ch'an in China and Zen in Japan. Daruma-san became a Zen saint, and legends about him are part of the scriptural lore of this school. They celebrate his unbending commitment to med-itation retreats and his terse replies to students and patrons. Images of Daruma-san came to be popular in Japan. His visage adorns kites, toys, knockdown dolls, and sake cups. Several dozen major Buddhist temples feature his icon and offer a full range of amulets.

Today, the most widely used images of Daruma-san are limbless round papier-mâché icons that are employed for making vows or proclaiming formal wishes. The standard ritual consists of making a wish and coloring in one eye of the statue, which is then placed on the family altar. When there is success in the matter wished for, the other eye is colored in and the doll (like all other amulets) is eventually discarded, fuel-ing the next New Year's temple bonfire. The Daruma-san icon is used in the same manner by businesspeople undertaking new ventures and politicians beginning elec-tion campaigns.

Thus with Daruma-san we witness the domestication into popular Japanese ritual life of the founding saint of Zen Buddhism, a fiercely ascetic meditation master who has become transmuted into an ostensibly comic figure, who nonetheless commands a following of millions. The subtle meanings of Daruma-san stand in stark contrast to the extreme teachings of a recent Japanese cult, one that attempted to use the Buddha's Four Noble Truths to rationalize a premeditated attack with nerve gas on innocent citizens.

Daruma images, round Japanese dolls modeled after Bodhidharma.

The Rise and Fall of the Aum Cult

In March 1995, as government investigators were about to arrest its leaders, at least ten members of the Aum Shinrikyo sect executed a terrorist poison gas attack in the Tokyo subway. Twelve people were killed and 5,500 were injured. The terrorist disciples were acting on the orders of the sect's guru, Shoko Asahara, a semi-blind forty-year-old who claimed to be an incarnation of Jesus and a spiritual master who had distilled the final truths of tantric Buddhism, Hindu yoga, the LSD psychedelic experience, New Age astrology, and the self-proclaimed sixteenth-century seer Nostradamus. In 1989, Asahara applied for and received registration as a tax-exempt religious organization for Aum Shinrikyo ("the True Teaching of Aum"). Then he set about building his sect around a core of commune-living disciples, many of whom were highly educated, successful people who commanded considerable wealth. Devotion to Asahara himself reached fanatical cultic proportions, with Aum members buying bottles of his bathwater.

In the aftermath of the attack, the Japanese cultural elite and the media questioned what this group's success said about the moral and cultural state of the nation. How large was the young population that was so alienated from tradition that they could accept such an unlikely collection of ideas from a dropout who claimed to be both Buddha and Jesus? Most disturbingly, what led followers to murder innocent fellow citizens? And why have followers kept the organization going until today, under its new name, Aleph?

The Aum tragedy also brought to popular attention the thousands of post–World War II "new religions" that claim the loyalty of an estimated 20 percent of modern Japanese; our survey of religion in Japan today concludes with a sampling of them.

The Newer "New Religions" in Japan

Although a new generation of Japanese spiritual leaders has formed independent groups to meet spiritual needs, the attraction of "new religions" must be kept in perspective; most Japanese today have not joined them. The majority find the older traditions or being nonreligious more to their liking.

Shinto shrines remain reference points for many modern Japanese today. These rocks conjoined by sacred hemp rope are located near Ise, symbolizing the union of the first kami.

Some of the new "new religions" were synthesized by charismatic founders from Japan's long-extant traditions along with aspects of modern nationalism, elements of Christianity, or scientific principles. Many of the "new religions" began in some measure as responses to the dislocations that shook Japanese society during its sudden opening to the outside world in the late nineteenth century and the headlong modernization and Westernization of the Meiji era. Almost every older "new religion" splintered with the passing of its founder and the struggles of interpretation and succession that followed, adding to the number of groups. But most of the popular "new religions" today are more recent in origin, attracting followers who find themselves disconnected from the old pattern of melding Shintoism and Buddhism that satisfied their ancestors.

In 2016 there were over 18,600 "new religion" organizations officially registered with the Japanese government. The great majority are small in size and rarely active. Many are hard to distinguish from poetry circles, philosophy clubs, or groups formed around health practitioners. The major new religions, however, are an important part of today's spiritual landscape; roughly 20 percent of Japanese people surveyed in recent years reported that their predominant religious affiliation is with one of the "new religions."[4]

While Aum's mass murder plot is completely atypical of the new religions, other aspects of that cult are not. Most form around a charismatic leader whose personal struggle to find the truth becomes paradigmatic for disciples drawn to the movement. Some sort of shamanic experience or performance is the most common ritual.

Zen painting depicting Bodhidharma, founder of the Ch'an/Zen Buddhist school.

Although members of most are taught to reject the diffuse eclecticism of Shintoism or Buddhism, many of the "new religion" worldviews draw on ancient traditions such as Buddhist karma and reincarnation doctrines, Confucian moral teachings and ancestor rites, or Shinto styles of worship. Some also import practices from the West or from India. Each new religion also tends to be this-worldly in its goals and imbued with the mission of ushering in a new divine era.

The most successful sects are built around a new "sacred center," a shrine that expresses the sect's mission and a priestly-bureaucratic administration that manages the organization. Membership in most new religions is open, but there is typically an initiation that requires individuals to make a personal commitment to the group.

The most successful new religions have built schools, colleges, and hospitals; some offer residential communities and athletic facilities to sustain their members from cradle to grave. These resources are also useful for proselytizing purposes and for demonstrating the power of the new path itself. The Tenrikyo, for example, one of the most successful new religions, has centers in every urban area of Japan; its headquarters, called Tenri City (near Nara), is a center for pilgrimage comparable to Salt Lake City for Mormons.

Sociological surveys have shown that devotees of the new religions are most commonly those excluded from dominant avenues to prestige in modern Japan. That is, with certain exceptions, members do not typically have prestigious jobs in the large corporations but run small family businesses. Within the group there are hierarchies and internal ranks to which individuals can aspire. Women typically outnumber men in membership and serve as leaders; their proselytizing is notable for its distinctly maternal style.

The new religions present themselves as experts at solving human problems. Whatever their supernatural beliefs, all hold that sickness, economic failure, and all interpersonal relations can be fully under individual control. Life will improve, they assert, if devotees will only discipline themselves in realizing the core values of Japanese culture: harmony, loyalty, filial piety, selflessness, diligence, ritual service. Problems can be solved by making a concerted effort to practice these virtues, to perfect the self, and to harmonize it with all levels of life. The sects differ in the prescriptions for accomplishing these goals, and we can give here only a representative sampling of the "new, new religions," groups formed in the postmodern era.

Rissho Koseikai. Rissho Koseikai was founded by Reiyukai member Niwano Nikkyo (1906–99), who retained the Nichiren Buddhist school's focus on the *Lotus*

Sutra. After 1969, the group's focus shifted to the individual's personality development through special counseling sessions led by trained lay "teachers" and the goal of world peace. Members sit together in a circle, creating an intimate atmosphere for open discussion. Rissho Koseikai teachers are trained to bring the Mahayana teachings, particularly those highlighting the universal Buddha-nature within all beings, to bear on all problems. The member's vow, repeated daily, shows its Buddhist center and its commitment to bring the teachings to life in the modern world.

As of 2016, the Koseikai was Japan's second-largest new religion, organized uniquely according to government unit lines and claiming over 2 million member households. It has 245 centers in twenty countries, the great majority in Japan. Missionary movements have brought Rissho Koseikai to Korea, Brazil, and the United States.

Perfect Liberty Kyodan. Another among the most popular groups is the Perfect Liberty Kyodan (P. L. Kyodan, or PL), whose primary slogan, "Religion is art," indicates its emphasis on the spiritual value of practicing the fine arts in everyday life. Its focal practice is liturgical: prayers choreographed with stylized prostrations, gestures, and offerings. The theology is monotheistic, but there is a strong emphasis on the human mind's central role in discerning divine warnings and receiving divine instruction through the sect's training. PL claims 500 churches in ten different countries, with more than 1.25 million members; its official aim is, according to its website, "to make true world peace a reality by inspiring people to understand and appreciate their power to create and plan, judge and decide, and make the world a true utopia."

Agonshu. A new religion founded in 1971, Agonshu also has a Buddhist identity. The group was founded by Kiriyama Seiyu (b. 1921), a charismatic spiritualist who claimed that the true teachings of Shakyamuni Buddha were revealed to him. Kiriyama's distilled "essence of Buddhism" is that the ancestors must be properly "turned into realized Buddhas" through performing special rituals for them in the afterlife, a belief that would be disputed by traditional Buddhist monks and scholars. Agonshu teachings attribute the world's troubles to the influence of the dead, who afflict the living to protest neglect. In the group's view, Kiriyama has rescued for the good of the entire world esoteric practices to pacify and enlighten the dead, particularly through fire rituals kept secret for centuries by the tantric Buddhist school in Japan called *Shingon*. The greatest yearly practice of this Agonshu rite, called *hoshi matsuri*, or "star festival," has become one of the most spectacular events in modern Japanese religion. Attracting a half-million pilgrims to the site, Agonshu priests set massive twin fires, one to benefit the ancestors, the other to promote the personal welfare of all participants, who contribute millions of small boards to fuel the flaming blazes.

Sukyo Mahikari. Sukyo Mahikari, founded in 1963, is an ethnocentric new religion that presents a narrow, sectarian view of salvation. It teaches that the postwar occupation unnaturally imposed democracy and materialism on the Japanese people, causing them to be possessed by evil spirits angry over the corruption of the country.

We, members of Rissho Koseikai,
Take refuge in the Eternal Buddha Shakyamuni,
And recognize in Buddhism the true way of salvation,
Under the guidance of our revered founder, Nikkyo Niwano.
In the spirit of lay Buddhists,
We vow to perfect ourselves
Through personal discipline and leading others
And by improving our knowledge and practice of the faith,
And we pledge ourselves to follow the bodhisattva way
To bring peace to our families, communities, and countries and to the world.

—Rissho Koseikai vow

SOURCE: http://www.rk-world.org/ (November 10, 2007).

Let's do it!
I will certainly succeed!
I am blessed with very good luck!
I will certainly do well!
I will definitely win!

—Agonshu chant

SOURCE: Ian Reader, *Religion in Contemporary Japan* (Honolulu: University of Hawaii Press, 1991), p. 100.

Then communism was sent by the gods to warn humanity of a coming ordeal, or "baptism by fire," that will claim all but the elect, who must restore patriotic ties to the emperor and demonstrate their loyalty to other Confucian relationships (between parents and children, husbands and wives). Those who follow this vision will be the "seed people" to restart the world in its proper order. Since the founder's death and the succession of his daughter to leader, the group has emphasized an ordination ritual that conveys "the transmission of light energy that purifies the spiritual aspect of people" and environmental activism, including community cleanup campaigns. Sukyo Mahikari claims close to a million adherents and has established branches in 75 countries.

Korea's Strong Confucian Tradition Accommodates Diversity

With the tradition of Confucianism entrenched in family rituals, marriage arrangements, and the moral education programs in the public school curriculum, South Korea today is the "most Confucian" nation in East Asia. Institutions dedicated to Confucian studies thrive in Korea, and exponents use the mass media to preach Confucian values.

Some among the Korean political elite (like many others in East Asia) believed Confucianism to be harmful to the nation, hindering its progress in the modern world. From this viewpoint, Westernization, agnosticism, and/or Christianity served as an antidote. However, Confucianism as the cultural center of Korea has endured even among Christian converts, most of whom openly observe their family's older rituals in honor of ancestors. South Korea adopted national economic goals in a Confucian framework: The central government takes responsibility for the citizenry's education and economic well-being, supports the family as the basis for social stability, accepts the intelligentsia as the conscience of the nation, and invests in education as the essential foundation for both material and cultural progress. The government has likewise supported major institutions dedicated to Confucian studies.

In the nation of North Korea, an emphasis on Confucian civil religion with communist characteristics remains. Much as in the Maoist era, citizens are expected to sacrifice themselves for the common good, and participate in the "cult of personality" centered on the modern nation's ruling patriarch, Kim Jong Un. In recent years, both modest Christian and Buddhist groups have been permitted.

As with Japan, we highlight groups that are shaping the diverse religious environment in modern South Korea.

Confucian Revival: The T'oegyehak Movement

Since learning the lessons of history is a strong Confucian value, it is not surprising that an important South Korean group emphasizes a prominent figure in its own historical tradition, the philosopher Yi T'oegye (1501–70). Master T'oegye developed the ideas of the most famous neo-Confucian Chinese thinker, Zhu Xi, whose Second Epoch leadership we have discussed, and T'oegye was responsible for making his system of thought prominent in Korea.

The Korean industrial leader Lee Dong-choon (1919–89) started the traditionalist **T'oegyehak** movement group by publishing the prolific writings of Master T'oegye. The T'oegyehak, which is a presence not only across East Asia but among East Asians living in the West, promotes detailed studies of the Confucian values as interpreted by Chinese and Korean masters. The organization has sponsored numerous conferences and made copies of the Confucian classics available across the globe.

T'oegyehak: modern Korean Confucian group based on teachings of master Yi T'oegye

Buddhist Revival

Despite many setbacks over the last century, the surviving Korean Buddhist institutions have established an important niche in Korean society through the monastery schools and lay institutions they founded. The Son Buddhist school, the Korean version of Zen, has sent several prominent teachers to the West, winning international support and renown.

A new school calling itself Won-bul-gyo, styled **Won Buddhism** in English, arose in 1924. Its founder, Soe-Tae San (1891–1943), claimed to have been enlightened through his own independent ascetic practices. He and his disciples sought to revive Buddhism by simplifying its doctrines and combining Pure Land and Zen teachings. The only Won ritual involves the worship of a picture of a black circle in a white background, symbolizing the *dharmakaya*, the cosmic body of the Buddha.

Won Buddhism: Korean school of Buddhism that combines Zen and Pure Land teachings

Only after the death of San and the end of Japanese occupation did the group find popular acceptance across Korea. Typical of reformist "Protestant Buddhist" groups elsewhere in Asia (see Chapter 7), Won Buddhism has been especially popular in major urban areas and emphasizes that Buddhist doctrines are compatible with modern thought. It also makes Buddhism attractive to the laity by translating classical texts into vernacular Korean and through weekly congregational worship involving chanting, simple rituals, and sermons. The group encourages women to be leaders and active participants. Won Buddhist monks or nuns, who lead the ritual services, can marry.

Another aspect of Won Buddhism that resembles reform Buddhism as practiced outside Korea is the encouragement of lay meditation and social service. For the former, members try to cultivate the "Buddha nature in all things" and bring this awareness to all work done in everyday life. For Won social engagement, the Buddhist ideal of nonself (*anatman*) is sought through service offered to the public, and these activities are also seen in classical terms as a means to address the universality of suffering. This is summarized by the founder's often cited exhortation:

> The Truth is one.
> The World is one.
> Human beings are one family.
> The World is one work place.
> Let us cultivate One World Community.

The primary form of social service undertaken by Won Buddhists has been in building schools, from kindergartens to universities.

By 2016, this school's temples are now found on every continent and the group claims 960,000 followers. Won Buddhists have pursued ecumenical relations with other faiths, both in Korea and with Japanese Buddhist groups.

Christianity in Korea

What makes Korea a unique stronghold of Christianity in Asia? Similarities between emotional Protestant rituals and the shaman tradition have been suggested along with several elements unique to the recent Korean historical experience, such as the Buddhist cooperation with Japan's imperial rulers, churches' prominent involvement in the struggle against Japanese occupation (1910–45), and Korean Christians' subsequent leadership in human rights activism. With the exception of some churches tolerating shamanism and reinterpreting ancestor ritualism within a Christian framework, there has been little doctrinal innovation outside the traditional denominational frameworks. As of 2016, approximately 32 percent of the South Korean population was Christian, with Protestants outnumbering Catholics by 4 to 1. There are now dozens of "megachurches" in Korea, with the Yoido Full Gospel Church in central Seoul the largest Christian congregation in the world, with over 830,000 members!

Persistence of the Shaman's Drum

mudang: Korean shaman

Amid a rising number of Christian converts and modest revivals under way among the various Buddhist schools, one finds a steady reliance on shamans, or **mudang**, in South Korea. As discussed in Chapter 2, shamans in Korea enjoy uniquely high status and popularity. Once demonized by Christian missionaries and denounced as charlatans by the early post–World War II South Korean governments, in 2016 shamans are lauded as bearers of "intangible cultural assets" and now have a following.

TALES OF SPIRITUAL TRANSFORMATION: Buddhist Satori

The greatest experience in Buddhism is the realization of ultimate truth of a reality "beyond words." Zen masters preserved stories of the conditions existing at the pivotal moments when disciples broke through to deeper, transformative realization. Like this one, for example.

Late one night a female Zen adept was carrying water in an old wooden bucket when she happened to glance across the surface of the water and saw the reflection of the moon. As she walked the bucket began to come apart and the bottom of the pail broke through, with the water suddenly disappearing into the soil beneath her feet and the moon's reflection disappearing along with it. In that instant the young woman realized that the moon she had been looking at was just a reflection of the real thing . . . just as her whole life had been. She turned to look at the moon in all its silent glory, her mind was ripe, and that was it . . . satori ("Enlightenment").

Source: Zen Master Chiyono, *No Moon, No Water.*

Shamans have thrived in modern Korea through dramatic rituals such as this one, in which the mudang subdues a troublesome local spirit.

Roughly 200,000 active registered shamans exist in South Korea, and many now have connections to establishments such as "*saju* cafes" where clients can consult as they sip coffee. Commercial websites also give new lines of access to specific healers. Scholars speculate that it is shamanic traditions that have helped foster Korea's harmonious and richly pluralistic religious culture.

Korean "New Religions"

As in Japan, the collapse of the traditional order in the nineteenth century precipitated a host of religious responses. The "new religions" formed to meet a three-part challenge: rebuilding the nation, restoring its spiritual center, and supporting individuals who were coping with rapid and often-traumatic changes.

Also conforming to the pattern seen in Japan's new religions, most Korean groups have been founded around men who claim a new supernatural revelation, usually based on traditional doctrines from Buddhism, Daoism, Confucianism, or Christianity. Korean new religions focus on this-worldly problems rather than the afterlife; some also imagine playing a leading role in establishing Korea as humanity's global leader and/or creating a utopia on earth. Most have developed their doctrinal teachings into a comprehensive worldview and have created supportive social institutions. The total number of new religion adherents was last determined in 2016 by the government to number about 1 million, or 2 percent of the South Korean population. (We discuss the most prominent Korean new religion, the Unification Church, in the next chapter.)

Conclusion: Have We Entered a Third Confucian Age?

The vibrant religious and philosophical ferment felt by many Chinese is clearly visible in the new art being produced by artists such as Zhang Huan. This installation, called *Peace Bell II* (2001), is intended to suggest, in the artist's comments, "The act of ringing the bell—slamming the figure of the artist into the record of his ancestry to produce a beautiful and powerful sound—suggests that artistic struggle with the circumstances of and inheritance from family is both necessarily violent and richly generative."

Our study of the religions of East Asia shows that contrary to assertions of many among the modern elites of China and Japan as well as numerous Western scholars, religious beliefs and practices are central to the life and culture of the region. Moreover, only by understanding the religious dimensions of Shintoism and Confucianism can one comprehend the nationalism and cultural foundations of Japan's and China's post-WWII rise to create two of the world's leading economies. Likewise, only by recognizing the religious dimensions of Maoist communism is it possible to fathom how in China the Communist Party has sustained its place of power since 1949, a topic we'll return to in Chapter 9.

Nevertheless, Confucianism and Daoism present a challenge to the Western monotheistic model of "being religious," with some scholars claiming that these belief systems are not "religions" at all. Rather, their diverse aspects, as we illustrated, suggest another way for humans to be religious: not centering the sacred on a single God above but seeing as sacred this world "below," in which humans live together and within nature. Respect and reverence are the central religious emotions. Confucianism and the diffuse religions of East Asia have both cultural and supernatural dimensions. They create in each society circles of reciprocal relatedness, making social relations sacred, harmonizing human existence with vital energies of nature, and respecting the creative power of the universe. In the supernatural dimension, they envision a world affected by deities, and reverence the survival of ancestors as spirits with whom relations can endure forever.

The general ethos promoted by all East Asian religions can be characterized as optimistic toward human life and human potential, seeing the improvement of the individual and improvement of society as sacred goals. Respect for the past serves to uphold acceptance of pluralism and the tolerance of religious diversity. The "diffuse religion" supports family cohesion as the center of a moral society, and the Confucian core of East Asia supports education for its role in cultivating character and in the acquisition of practical knowledge. This sort of "pragmatic idealism" calls for improving the world for the sake of this-worldly concerns, not as the dictate of a transcendent deity. The success in the modern global marketplace of this complex of religion and culture rebuts those Western scholars who had argued that East Asian religions were obstacles to modern economic development. New syncretistic religious understandings, informed by growing global connections, seem destined to develop further in China.

If the Confucian system of family/ancestral devotion is regarded as the central pillar of Chinese tradition, then it is clear that it, too, has survived the criticisms and persecutions and that it has done so strongly. However, in recent years there have been signs that the "Confucian family revival" in China was not as vibrant as originally thought. The market economy made extended family living difficult, so the elderly were left behind as jobs required moves; the Party's "one-child policy" placed the burden for elder care on one individual adult child; and the Party's suppression of children's literature promoting filial piety deprived today's adults of that teaching during their childhood. These effects of earlier government policies became clear as press reports in 2012–13 exposed adults who had been scandalously unfilial: parents forced to live in unheated rooms, eat only gruel, and survive on their own in rural poverty. Shocked and dismayed, the Communist Party passed a law in 2013 requiring children to call parents regularly and act on their filial piety. Can a law change the pressures of the market economy to restore Confucian virtue?

It is possible that the future revival of religion in China will threaten regional stability. A large state trying to hold together diverse groups and disparate regions faces certain inherent problems, and difficulties loom large in the present relationship between communist China and its principal minorities. In particular, it is across religious issues that major fault lines affecting modern China are to be found, in particular with Muslims in Xinjiang Province and with Buddhists in the Tibetan cultural region.

Ascribing East Asia's economic revival mainly to its Confucian roots remains, for some, a contested position. According to "Third Epoch" proponents, the traumas of the modern era succeeded in liberating the Confucian worldview from the trappings of power that had developed in the imperial systems of China, Korea, and Japan. Under them, the application of the highest Confucian ideals had been corrupted by government officials and the organized religious academies, which turned "mastery" of the classics into a mere exercise in memorization needed to pass imperial examinations.

Now the Confucian revival movement seeks to return to the basic teachings of the early sages (Confucius and Mencius, of the First Epoch) and do what Master Zhu Xi and other reformers accomplished in their time (the Second Epoch of neo-Confucianism). Believers in "Third Epoch" Confucianism, working on the periphery of China and increasingly finding supporters in

Confucian schools promoting the classical Confucian humanities are being reinvented in China in the twenty-first century.

In 2010, the Chinese government placed an image of Confucius in Tian'anmen Square, Beijing, forty-one years after the sage was reviled by Communist Party Red Guards during the Cultural Revolution. Early in 2011, it was removed without comment, an indication of the persistence of ambivalence in the Chinese Communist Party leadership.

mainland China as well, are now addressing the challenges of economic and cultural globalization.

Such efforts to revive this spiritual tradition have made "Third Epoch" Confucians critical of the global modernizing process, especially insofar as it has caused the fragmentation of society, promoted the vulgarization of social life, disregarded the public good, or overglorified wealth. The vast majority of modernist Confucians adopt this critical stance while also being committed to empirical science, democratic politics, gender equality, and the economic development in their own countries. In early twenty-first-century China, interest in promoting Confucianism as a means of forming the character of citizens is winning widespread support among intellectuals and parents and even within the Communist Party itself. A host of newly approved schools include in their curriculum the study of traditional Confucianism; "Harmonious Society," the 2002 slogan for the nation's future that has been adopted by Xi Jinping, the new Communist Party president, has Confucian overtones. The theme of the 2008 Beijing Olympics, "One world, one dream," also projected the early Confucian ideal of a world led by ethical ideals.

The global vision of "Third Epoch" exponents is to bring the Confucian tradition into the debate about how the twenty-first century's global order should be conceived. They aim to foster dialogue between the Confucian worldview and the ideologies of sociopolitical modernization and consumerism prominent in the Euro-American world. Informed by very different notions of religious truth and by ethnocentric visions of their own central places in the cosmos, will the world's people outside East Asia be interested in such a dialogue?

Discussion Questions

1. In terms of the discussion in Chapter 1, is ancestor veneration really a "religious tradition"? Why?

2. What beliefs from each of the three religious traditions of the region might explain the East Asian peoples' unique capacity for sustaining the three without choosing just one?

3. Why do purity and brightness sum up the ethos of Shintoism?

4. Why, from the Daoist perspective, were disasters in the natural world taken so seriously by Chinese emperors?

5. How is the cult of ancestor veneration related to the norms of Confucian character formation and family morality?

6. A Chinese novelist in the colonial period described the Chinese family as "a prison ward" that denies basic rights to the individual, exploits women, and wastes the energy of the young. How would you defend Confucian ideals against these criticisms?

7. What features of East Asia's "diffuse religion" would a Christian missionary find most important to resist? What features would be compatible?

8. How might neo-Confucianism be seen as an attempt to harmonize Buddhism, Daoism, and early Confucianism?

9. In Korea, does shamanism reinforce ancestor veneration or undermine its practice?

10. Critique the following proposition: China's religious revival was postponed by the Chinese communists, who imposed a "forced conversion" of the nation to Marxism-Leninism, the "new religion" it had imported from Europe.

11. For all the nations of East Asia, the colonial era was very destructive. But certain individuals fused ideas from global culture with older beliefs, creating new and original religious understandings. Cite an example of this process in China, in Korea, and in Japan.

12. What influences from the West might have influenced elites in East Asia to claim that the Chinese (or the Japanese) are "not religious"?

Key Terms

All Souls Festival	city god	Daruma-san
Amaterasu	Confucianism	de
Analects	Cultural Revolution	diffuse religion
ancestor veneration	Dao	Five Classics
Ch'ondogyo	Daoist	Full Moon Festival

(continued)

Key Terms (continued)

Guan Yu	neo-Shintoism/state	Tenrikyo
Hong Xiuquan	Shinto	three faiths
kami	"new religions"	Tian di
"kitchen god"	Nichiren	T'oegyehak
Lao Zi	philosophical Daoism	Tu-di
li	qi	Tu-di Gong
ling	qi gong	Won Buddhism
Mandate of Heaven	Qing-Ming	wu-wei
mappo	religious Daoism	xiao
Master K'ung	ren	yin-yang theory
Master Xun	*Shang-di*	Zhu Xi
Mencius	Shinto	*Zhuang Zi*
mudang	Soka Gakkai	
neo-Confucianism	Taiping Rebellion	

Suggested Readings

Ashiwa, Yoshiko, and David L. Want, eds. *Making Religion, Making the State: The Politics of Religion in Modern China* (Stanford, CA: Stanford University Press, 2009).

Buswell, Robert E. *Religions of Korea in Practice* (Princeton, NJ: Princeton University Press, 2007).

Chau, Adam Yuet. *Miraculous Response: Doing Popular Religion in Contemporary China* (Stanford, CA: Stanford University Press, 2006).

Earhart, H. Byron. *Japanese Religion: Unity and Diversity*, 4th ed. (Belmont, CA: Wadsworth, 2003).

Gardner, Daniel. *The Four Books* (Indianapolis: Hackett, 2007).

Hardacre, Helen. *Shinto: A History*. (New York: Oxford University Press, 2016).

Kendall, Laurel. *Shamans, Housewives, and Other Restless Spirits: Women in Korean Ritual Life* (Honolulu: University of Hawaii Press, 1985).

Lee, Peter H., ed. *Sources of Korean Tradition: From Early Times to the 16th Century* (New York: Columbia University Press, 1996).

Lopez, Donald S., Jr., ed. *Religions of China in Practice* (Princeton, NJ: Princeton University Press, 1996).

Nelson, John K. *A Year in the Life of a Shinto Shrine* (Seattle: University of Washington Press, 1996).

Park, Jin Y. *Makers of Modern Korean Buddhism* (Albany: State University of New York Press, 2010).

Picken, S. D. B. *Shinto: Japan's Spiritual Roots* (Tokyo: Kodansha, 1980).

Reader, Ian, and George J. Tanabe Jr. *Practically Religious: Worldly Benefits and the Common Religion of Japan* (Honolulu: University of Hawaii Press, 1998).

Reid, T. R. *Confucius Lives Next Door: What Living in the East Teaches Us About Living in the West* (New York: Vintage Books, 1999).

Robson, James. *The Norton Anthology of World Religions: Daoism.* (New York: W.W. Norton, 2015).

Sommer, Deborah. *Chinese Religion: An Anthology of Sources* (New York: Oxford University Press, 1995).

Sun, Anna. *Confucianism as a World Religion.* (Princeton: Princeton University Press, 2015).

Swanson, Paul, and Clark Chilson, eds. *The Nanzan Guide to Japanese Religions.* (Honolulu: University of Hawaii Press, 2006).

Thompson, Laurence G. *Chinese Religion: An Introduction,* 5th ed. (Belmont, CA: Wadsworth, 1996).

Notes

1. Quoted in Stephen Teiser, "Popular Religion," *Journal of Asian Studies* 54, no. 2 (1995), p. 378.
2. In Wing-sit Chan, *A Sourcebook of Chinese Philosophy* (Princeton, NJ: Princeton University Press, 1973), pp. 86–87.
3. In Donald E. MacInnis, *Religion in China Today* (New York: Orbis, 1989), p. 206.
4. S. D. B. Picken, *Shinto: Japan's Spiritual Roots* (Tokyo: Kodansha International, 1980), p. 56.

Additional Resources

Marukoto: The Teaching of Roundness (http://www.kurozumikyo.com/marukoto_e.html). An introduction to the Japanese "New Religion," Kurozumikyo.

Reiyukai (http://www.reiyukai.org/). Website for this Nichiren-related sect.

Rissho Kosei-kai (http://www.rk-world.org). Worldwide Buddhist organization founded in Japan that combines the wisdom of both the *Lotus Sutra* and the foundational teachings of Shakyamuni Buddha.

Agon Shu (http://www.agon.org/en/). Website for this new Buddhist group that emphasizes relic veneration and rituals for ancestors.

Jodo Shu (http://www.jodo.org/about_js/history.html). Website for the oldest Pure Land Buddhist lineage in Japan.

International Association of Shinto Shrines (www.jinjahoncho.or.jp/en/). Information on shrines, rituals, and festivals. Site with links to many major shrines, with additional information about festivals and shrine practices.

Korean Shamanism Web Site: (http://www.neomudang.com). The site offers an interactive map where one can click on a region of Korea and find a list of shamans who practice there along with their specialties.

GLOBALIZATION

From New to New Age Religions

9

Overview

Debbie belongs to a Baptist church in Atlanta and regularly attends services on Sunday mornings and Wednesday evenings. However, she has other religious interests as well. Indeed, she regularly checks her astrological chart in the newspaper to see what kind of day she can expect to have. And on Tuesday nights she practices Zen Buddhist meditation with a small Zen group that meets at the house of her friend Sherry. In fact, Sherry, who is Jewish, is the organizer and leader of the group, or "sangha," as Buddhists call it. Moreover, next week, she and her friend are going for a three-day Zen meditation retreat that she hopes will help deepen her spirituality both as a Christian and as a practitioner of Zen. Last week, Debbie's friend Michael talked her into going to a program led by a psychic medium who offers to put people in touch with their dead relatives. She is not sure what she thinks about this but is open to giving it a try. Likewise, Debbie has been reading *Dianetics*, by Scientology founder L. Ron Hubbard, just to see what it is all about.

All these activities mark Debbie as one of countless individuals who are on a personal quest that is typical of new age religion: They are eager to explore the mystery of the "self" and its perfection. Debbie has another friend, Marcus, who thinks she is too self-absorbed and needs to pay more attention to issues of social justice in a global culture dominated by mass media and multinational corporations, and marred

◀ The Baha'i Temple in Chicago.

487

by racial and economic exploitation. Marcus is trying to get her involved in a small interracial activist group inspired by the life and teachings of Martin Luther King Jr. These activities of Debbie and her friends, as we shall see, could all be grouped together under the heading of *new age religion*.

In this chapter we will first explore what we mean by "new" religions and then focus primarily on "new age religions"—the distinctive forms that new religions and new ways of being religious have taken in response to globalization. New religions represent the integration of influences from multiple religions and cultures, resulting in the creation of new variations and expressions of known religious practices. In one familiar pattern, a new prophet or sage reveals new understandings of an existing tradition, given to him or her in religious experiences or revelations.

In the past the messages of prophets and sages reflected primarily local situations—typically the incursion of elements imported from nearby religions and cultures. Today, however, many new religious movements reflect not just a response to local diversity—to this or that movement that has entered the environment of a relatively stable culture. Rather, they indicate an awareness of global religious diversity as a whole, past and present. This awareness is fostered by mass communications, especially the Internet and cable television, and widespread access to international transportation, made possible by modern science and technology.

"The New Age is partially an offshoot of the Age of Science. . . . Children of the Age of Science, myself included, prefer to arrive firsthand, experimentally, at their own conclusions as to the nature and limits of reality. Shamanism provides a way to conduct these personal experiments, for it is a methodology, not a religion."

—Michael Harner, *The Way of the Shaman*

Encounter with Modernity: The Challenge of Global Diversity to the "Purity" of Tradition

In the twenty-first century, Christianity, like all other religious traditions, seeks to communicate its understanding of truth on a variety of websites. Many of these websites address the concerns of those who hold fundamentalist beliefs and seek to educate their believers against the dangers of "new age religion." Such websites often contain warnings such as "'New Age' Religions and Why Christians Can't Participate." Such websites warn a Christian like Debbie (described in the Overview) that she is in danger of worshipping false gods. She is warned that she is failing to be faithful to the Gospel of Jesus Christ, who offers the one and only path to God and salvation. In postmodern societies, Christianity is not alone in facing the problem of keeping its followers "true to the tradition." Other traditions, especially the monotheistic traditions of Judaism and Islam, also warn their "faithful" to "be faithful" and keep to the way of Torah or the way of the Quran, as the case may be.

Globalization presents challenges to believers of all traditions. Persons involved in postmodern spirituality, however, do not see themselves in an "either/or" situation. They do not see themselves as having to choose one spiritual practice or path to the exclusion of others. In fact, they see themselves in a "both/and" situation. For the new age believer, one can be a Jew and still engage in Buddhist rituals and meditation; one can be a Catholic and still practice Hindu meditation and ritual; and so on.

The problem of keeping the tradition "pure" may be more challenging for monotheistic religions than it is for the religious traditions of India and China, where different religious paths have often interpenetrated. Nevertheless, people of all religions and cultures often have reservations when they see their children departing from strict adherence to the "sacred traditions" as they have known and practiced them. In every tradition this can seem quite threatening. The issue presented by globalization is whether it shall lead to greater understanding and cooperation among religions and cultures, or greater defensiveness, prejudice, and even violence. The answer, as we shall see, is that globalization can lead to both.

New Religions

Old Religions and New Religions in the History of Religions

From a historical perspective, as this book has amply indicated, no religion has ever managed to remain unchanged. Indeed, while every chapter in this book began with an "overview" description of the religious beliefs and practices of the tradition, in every case we went on to say that such a snapshot was no more than a broad generalization that did not accurately reflect the tremendous diversity found among practitioners, yesterday or today. There is not one Judaism but many, not one Buddhism but many—likewise there are many Christianities, many Islams and Hinduisms, many Daoisms and Confucianisms.

New religions test and transform boundaries. Every tradition tolerates a tremendous amount of diversity. An emerging movement that at first is treated as a form of error may finally be accepted into the fold or at least tolerated as a distant cousin. It may, for example, be seen as a reform within the tradition to bring it back to its original purity. But then there are other movements, perhaps brought about by new religious experiences and extraordinary revelations, whose "errors" seem too great. Changes that had started out as reforms may present such a dramatic break with past beliefs and practices that they come to be perceived not as a continuation of the old tradition but as a fatal error—a deviation from the true path. The new tradition, of course, sees the error lying not in itself but in the old tradition, which had somehow lost its way.

Although before the common era there was more than one form of Judaism, Christianity, which began as a Jewish sect called the *Nazarenes,* came to be seen, and to see itself, as crossing a boundary that made it no longer a Jewish alternative but a "new religion." And while Christianity also encompasses tremendous diversity, when Islam emerged in Arabia in the seventh century it was seen by Christians as a new and heretical religion, even though Muslims recounted many of the same biblical stories and saw their faith as the continuation and culmination of God's revelations handed down through Moses and Jesus. Moreover, Islam developed two major branches, Sunni and Shiah, as well as many schools of theology and law. However, in nineteenth-century Persia, when the Baha'i movement claimed to bring a final revelation that included all the religions, East and West, it came to be viewed as "not true Islam," but a new belief system.

When we look at Asian religions we find the same pattern. Hinduism encompasses great diversity, yet as Buddhism grew and developed it was seen, and came to see itself, as a "new religion." Buddhism, too, splintered into many Buddhisms, some claiming to be more advanced than others.

In every tradition, some movements emerged and then disappeared. Even so, in century after century, many of "today's" new religions become tomorrow's old and established religions. We can illustrate the character of new religions with a few examples before turning to our primary concern, examples of "new age" religions that have appeared in our emerging global civilization. The relatively recent history of Christianity in North American culture presents an interesting illustration of how a new religion comes to be.

In the 1800s, Christian denominationalism began to emerge as a way of moving beyond the hostile sectarianism that had divided Christians, and by the late twentieth century there was a broad spectrum of "acceptable" religious diversity in America. Nevertheless, a number of very distinctive religious movements that originated in the nineteenth century tested the limits of denominationalism. As a rule, contemporary mainline Christian denominations (i.e., those representing widely established, long-accepted church traditions in America, such as the Methodists, Presbyterians, and Episcopalians) tend to regard these unique movements as having strayed beyond the boundaries of Christianity. Mormonism provides us with a good example; Jehovah's Witness provides another.

The Church of Jesus Christ of Latter-day Saints: A New American Christianity

The Church of Jesus Christ of Latter-day Saints, or Mormonism, was established on April 6, 1830, by Joseph Smith Jr. It appears to have arisen in response to the confusion and conflict created by the incredible sectarian diversity of nineteenth-century Christianity. Joseph Smith believed he had been led by angels to discover a revelation that would overcome this confusion. The new revelation, contained in the Book of Mormon, was understood by Smith and his followers as a continuation of the revelation given in the Bible. It was a revelation that had been given first to Native Americans, as descendants of the lost tribes of ancient Israel. Mormons believe that these tribes had migrated to the North American continent, where the risen Christ visited them and gave them new revelations. Eventually the book containing these pronouncements was buried by a Native American named Mormon, who was killed by tribesmen who rejected the new message and wanted to suppress it. It was these "pagan" natives who met Columbus in 1492. But the revelation could not be suppressed forever, and so Joseph Smith was guided by angels to find the Book of Mormon so that it could flourish once more.

Earlier, in Chapter 4, we noted the incorporation into Christianity of traditions specific to Africa and Asia. Similarly, Mormonism links biblical religion to the history of an indigenous population—in this case producing a distinctively American Christianity, one that includes visits of the risen Christ and several of the risen apostles to a new land, to guarantee the purity of Mormon revelation and so set it apart from existing "human interpretations" of Christianity. The capstone of the message was the promise that at the end of time, in the "latter days," Christ would return to establish a "New Jerusalem" in America. The growing stature of Mormonism in America is illustrated by Mitt Romney as the first Mormon candidate for president of the United States in 2012. Mormonism, with its emphasis on family, community, and healthy, wholesome living, flourishes today, with well over 15 million members worldwide.

Jehovah's Witnesses—Another American Vision of the End Time

The nineteenth century saw the emergence of other apocalyptic movements looking for the coming of a New Jerusalem in America. William Miller (1782–1849), a farmer in upstate New York and considered the founder of the Seventh-Day Adventists, predicted the second coming of Christ would occur on March 21, 1843. When that did not happen, he recalculated and predicted March 21 a year later. Another end-time thinker, Charles Taze Russell (1852–1916) was swept up in the apocalyptic fervor of movements similar to the Millerites. Russell, founder of the Jehovah's Witnesses, may have learned from the failure of those predictions, for he embraced an interesting twist on the apocalyptic belief that Christ was coming soon. He suggested that Christ had already spiritually returned as an invisible presence in 1874, initiating a 40-year period for the ingathering of true believers that culminated in 1914, the beginning of World War I, as the beginning of the time of apocalyptic sufferings that would announce the second coming.

After Russell's death, the movement was led by Joseph Franklin Rutherford (1869–1942). In the twentieth century, Jehovah's Witnesses grew into a significant international movement with a presence in Europe, Asia, Latin America, and the Middle East. In the year 2000, the Watch Tower Society separated out from the

Joseph Smith Jr. receiving the sacred plates of the Book of Mormon from the Angel Moroni.

Watch Tower Bible and Tract Society, and the new Watch Tower Society's governing board assumed leadership authority in the global movement.

The Jehovah's Witnesses take their name from the Hebrew name for God, the four letters of the tetragrammaton—YHWH. There are no vowels in biblical Hebrew, so they adopted the practice of pronouncing this as "Yehovah." They refer to themselves as Yehovah's Witnesses, those who are called to champion the oneness of God. Although they consider themselves Christians, they do not adhere to the teachings of the ancient church councils that affirmed the trinitarian theology accepted by both the Catholic Church and the Protestant Reformation traditions of Luther and Calvin, all of which consider God to be one, yet three—Father, Son, and Holy Spirit, all equal in status. For Jehovah's Witnesses, "trinity" is not found in the Bible. For similar reasons they do not celebrate traditional Christian holidays like Christmas and Easter, which they see as later pagan nonbiblical additions to Christianity.

Like the Millerites or Seventh-Day Adventists, Jehovah's Witnesses are distant inheritors of the traditions of the Anabaptist wing of the sixteenth-century Protestant Reformation, who were known for their distrust of government as the work of the devil. Indeed, the Jehovah's Witnesses have a reputation as "conscientious objectors" who refuse to cooperate with any government's conscription into military service. Like the Adventists, Jehovah's Witnesses strongly identify with the Jewishness of early Christianity, before its explicit doctrinal move into Trinitarianism. Russell saw 1914, the beginning of World War I, as a spiritually pivotal time that marked the end of the gentile domination over Israel and the beginning of the difficult end times predicted in the Bible. Indeed, Adventists present in Nazi Germany during World War II were courageous in their resistance to the Nazis and Nazi anti-Semitism. Like Jews, they became targets for imprisonment in the death camps.

Charles Taze Russell, founder of the original Watch Tower Bible and Tract Society.

Civil Religion in China—A Blend of Confucianism and Marx's Secular Apocalyptic Vision

Civil religions represent yet another form in which new religious traditions can play very traditional roles in a society. In most times and most places throughout the history of civilization, religion and politics permeated all of culture and were like two sides of the same coin. It was, as we have seen, modernity that introduced secular nation-states and the idea that government should not impose on citizens the obligation to join or practice any particular religion. But having removed religion as a legitimizer of their own authority, these modern states faced a new problem—winning loyalty from their citizens without the traditional appeal to religion. The result has been the creation of a distinct entity we shall call *civil religion*. Civil religion reintroduces religion under

Mao Zedong, founder
of the People's Republic
of China.

the disguise of "indigenous cultural history and tradition" to reinforce the authority
of new and more secular modern nations.

When the Red Army gained control of mainland China in 1949, Communist
Party leader Mao Zedong ascended the southern gateway to the emperor's old palace
(the "Forbidden City") to proclaim the creation of the People's Republic of China.
This moment was later pictured on currency and in popular prints, and soon thereafter an immense portrait of Chairman Mao was mounted over the ancient gateway.
Over the next twenty-five years, the Communist Party drew on a variety of religious
conceptions to legitimate its position in China and to wield power. Essential to this
was the communist millennial doctrine of a final age of harmony imported from
Russian revolutionaries. Early on, the government integrated this with ancient Confucian imperial doctrine to promote the cult of Mao himself as the sage-philosopher
leader of the nation. His words and teachings were pivotal for national salvation, and
his character radiated the morality of communist truth. Statues of Mao were put up
in public spaces around the nation, his portrait replaced images of family ancestors in
home shrines, and during the Cultural Revolution (1966–76) his "Little Red Book"
became a sacred text to be memorized, followed, and always possessed. Officially, the
Communist Party disavowed religion as superstition and railed at long-dead Chinese
emperors as feudal exploiters of the masses. Nevertheless, it is not hard to see how
party strategists adapted powerful religious ideas from both European and Chinese
traditions to create a civil religion to confirm the legitimacy of its dictatorship.

The New Age and New Age Religions

Postmodernism and the New Age

The collapse of colonialism, especially after World War II, was followed by the emergence of globalization. This globalization was fostered by the development of international corporations, global mass transportation, and global mass media, carrying modern science and technology around the world. Logically enough, then, since the 1960s and 1970s new patterns of religion have appeared that reflect a global consciousness. Although incredibly diverse, these religions, shaped by science and technology as well as by the traditional considerations, are often grouped together under the title *new age religions*. Not all new age religions are postmodern as we have defined that term. Indeed, many are content to continue the modernist pattern of privatization rather than seek a new public role for religion. But global consciousness has been a significant factor in the emergence of all new age religions. In this section and the next, we will look at examples of modernist and postmodernist new age religions.

In the first chapter we cited Jean-François Lyotard's definition of *postmodernism* as the collapse of metanarratives, the grand stories or myths that gave each civilization a sense of meaning, purpose, and identity. The great metanarratives created a relationship of identity between religion and culture, giving us Hindu civilization, Christian civilization, Islamic civilization, and so on. Each civilization was centered in its own grand stories and the social practices that came from the vision of life the stories promoted. Modernism, with its myth of scientific progress, was a relatively recent addition.

The resurgence of religions around the globe since the 1970s may well represent the need to fill the vacuum created by the tendency of secularization to purge events of meaning. The problem with a secular understanding of time, history, and society is that the significance and drama provided by the grand narratives of religions are missing. Pluralism may have collapsed the grand metanarratives into smaller stories, but there is still a great hunger for such stories, and new age religions help people discover the meaning and significance of time and their place in it. New age religions provide a rich feast for the religious imagination as seekers attempt to penetrate the mysteries of their time and to explore the wonders they offer.

Postmodern culture represents the loss of a normative center in every culture that has been touched by global mass media, international corporations, and global mass transportation. Postmodern culture is pluralistic, relativistic, and eclectic—seemingly without any public norms or standards. The choice between "truths" is said to be intellectually "undecidable" and so is decided pragmatically, in terms of "what works for me." Truth, goodness, and beauty are in the eye of the beholder. People mix and match beliefs, practices, and aesthetic choices to their own taste in all areas of life—whether music, clothing, architecture, intellectual beliefs, or religion.

A young Buddhist monk at a school in Burma looks at his photo on a laptop.

Globalization provides the social context of postmodernism. Globalization "marbleizes" all cultures so that the world's religions are accessible in everyone's hometown. Today, much more than in the past, in the same community you will find Jews, Christians, Muslims, Hindus, Buddhists, and many others. Such pluralism is a powerful social force inducing the collapse of metanarrative, whereby a story that was once embraced by almost all people in a given culture is now simply one of many stories. In this situation religions are challenged first to relinquish their position of being identical with the culture and then to accommodate an existing cultural pluralism. Almost all religious communities have had to embrace denominational type identities in this context, accepting the existence of other beliefs and practices, although fundamentalist communities strive mightily to resist such an accommodation. This denominational accommodation, we have said, was what sociologist Peter Berger meant by saying that all religions have become "Protestant." But for most new age groups their religious practices have gone a step further, moving from organizational pluralism (denominationalism) to eclecticism.

Many of the "new age" religions, like older "new religions," represent the integration of the diverse influences from different traditions. The new age religions are not based solely on the great world religions; often they incorporate elements of primal religions, exhibiting a special interest in shamanism. Moreover, today these eclectic belief systems typically reflect not only global religious diversity but the global influence of science and technology as well.

A group in the Netherlands performs a ritual based on the Thirteen Moon calendar of the Maya.

The New Age—Modern and Postmodern?

New age religious movements can be divided into modernist forms, which continue to privatize religion, and postmodernist public forms of religious practice, which seek an active role, socially and politically, in transforming society. Most modernist new age religions are highly diverse in their practices and beliefs, with minimal organizational structure. Nevertheless, there are some very important instances of highly structured new age movements; as we shall see, Scientology is one and Baha'i is another. What unites new age seekers, despite their diversity, however, is the quest for the perfection of the self. Their goal is to realize a "higher self" through intense personal experiences of transformation.

Many new age seekers are not interested in joining religious organizations. They typically integrate a variety of interests into their personal style of spiritual practice. Many read "spiritual" books and go to workshops and seminars intended to guide them to self-realization. Modernist "new agers" are interested in such shamanistic practices as channeling information from otherworldly spiritual beings, contacting the dead through mediums, spiritual healing, and the cultivation of ecstatic out-of-body experiences (sometimes referred to as *astral projection*). They are also interested in the mystical traditions and meditation practices of all religions as well as the ancient divination practice of astrology. Some combine these interests with the teachings and practices of transpersonal psychologists such as Abraham Maslow (1908–70) and Fritz Perls (1893–1970); others embrace speculative visions that combine the "new physics" with religion, believing that science itself is finally coming to discover and affirm ancient religious and metaphysical insights. The final test of each seeker's synthesis is personal experience and pragmatically evaluated usefulness.

The growth of new age religiousness is deeply rooted in this Romantic reaction to the rationalism of the Enlightenment. The Enlightenment emphasized universal rationality (i.e., the sameness of human nature everywhere), science, and progress. Its philosophers rejected the ancient, the archaic, the traditional, the idiosyncratic, and the nonrational. The Romantic reaction, a stage we are still in, did just the opposite, embracing in all their diversity the emotional, the experientially transformational, the historically unique and particular, as well as the "primitive" and traditional aspects of human history.

Like fundamentalist forms of evangelical Christianity, modernist forms of new age religions are expressions of the human need for transformative experience, a need as old as shamanism and as recent as the Romantic reaction to Enlightenment rationalism and its expression in evangelical pietism. Both deemphasize rationality and focus on the experiential transformation and perfection of the self through deeply emotional experiences of the kind we have called religious. And both share the conviction that all social change begins by changing the self (i.e., by being born again).

The Age of Apocalypse or the Age of Aquarius?

Two new age models of religious meaning are playing a role in our emerging global civilization—the apocalyptic and the astrological. These models share a vision of the conflict and discord of the past and present giving way to a future era of global peace and harmony. Among Christian evangelicals the popularity of the belief that the end of time is near is evidenced by sales of tens of millions of books such as Hal Lindsey's *The Late Great Planet Earth* and the *Left Behind* series of novels. As indicated by the popularity of biblical prophecies of the end times among evangelical Christians, there are still many heirs to the apocalyptic religious vision of the medieval monk Joachim of Fiore, who anticipated a "third age" (the age of the Spirit) as a time of global peace and harmony. However, the third age will be preceded by the biblical apocalypse, which in turn will bring the cataclysmic end of time. The belief that there will be a cataclysmic end to time followed by a new age of peace and harmony is also illustrated in late-twentieth-century movements such as Aum Shinrikyo (Chapter 8). But first we will turn to the alternative vision—the astrological vision of the age of Aquarius.

A gentler vision of the new age, the age of Aquarius, has been offered by some astrologers in recent decades:

> We are passing out of 2,000 years of Piscean astrological influence into the influence of Aquarius, which will affect all aspects of our culture as we move from Piscean structures of hierarchical devotion to more fluid and spontaneous relationships that dance to an Aquarian rhythm.[1]

Predictions of the coming of a new age by others not of the apocalyptic tradition include the writings of José Argüelles. In his book *The Mayan Factor*, this new age author used ancient Mayan and Aztec astrology to calculate that the age of Aquarius would begin in 1987, on August 16 or 17.[2] When that did not happen, new interpretations or perhaps misinterpretations of Mayan texts emerged predicting a more traditional apocalyptic view of the end of the world which would occur when the Mayan calendar ends (according to some) on December 21, 2012. As of 2018, that has not happened either. In these Aquarian times, many forms of new age religion tap into a very ancient type of religious experience found in primal animistic and early urban polytheistic religious practices—that of the shaman. As we saw in Chapter 2, in his or her ecstatic or out-of-body experiences, the shaman explores the spirit world, the realm of contact with spiritual beings and dead ancestors.

Everywhere in the world, shamanism was the earliest form of religious experience. And everywhere, the great world religions emerge with the discovery that the realm that a shaman visits when he or she leaves her physical body to travel to the domains of the spirits and of dead ancestors is really an intermediate spiritual realm between the earthly physical world and a higher unitary reality. For example, in the Vedas of Hinduism the highest realities (devas) are the many gods and goddesses of nature, but in the Upanishads the discovery is made that the gods are part of the order of this world of samsara and that there is a higher power beyond their realm, the reality of Brahman.

The emergence of monotheism out of polytheism in the Mediterranean world (in Judaism, Christianity, and Islam) provides another example. The polytheistic realm of the gods was not denied. It could not be denied because many people continued to have shamanistic-type experiences of another realm inhabited by spiritual beings. So this realm of the deities was reassigned to a different kind of spiritual being and renamed the realm of angels and demons. Like the devas or gods of Hinduism, angels were recognized as spiritual beings, yet they were part of the cosmic order created by a higher reality, God. In China this concept of a higher unitary reality was given the impersonal name of Dao.

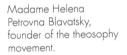

Madame Helena Petrovna Blavatsky, founder of the theosophy movement.

For all the differences between ancient urban religious cultures and religions in postmodern society, there is at least one profound similarity between them: Both premodern urban society, as typified, for instance, by the polytheistic culture of ancient Rome, and postmodern society, with its myriad eclectic religious practices, lack an integrating center. In both, being religious is not so much about belonging to "a religion" as it is about selecting from the chaotic variety of available beliefs and practices, a mix that will serve the pragmatic purposes of finding health, happiness, and meaning—that is, of having the unseen powers that govern your destiny on your side.

Theosophy, Christian Science, and the Unity School of Christianity

The precedents for many forms of new age religion go back to the interest in esoteric religious beliefs and practices that flourished in the nineteenth century, when historical and ethnographic researchers were just beginning to catalog the diverse practices of primal (tribal) and archaic (early urban) religions. From Europe, the teachings of Emanuel Swedenborg (1688–1772) and Franz Anton Mesmer (1734–1815) spread belief in the validity of the shamanistic experience of other worlds and in the animistic unity of all things, which made spiritual healing possible. In America, Ralph Waldo Emerson (1803–82) and others popularized a school of thought called *transcendentalism*, which integrated certain Asian religious beliefs (especially from Hinduism) with American philosophy, affirming the existence of a "world soul" that all beings shared. In this context the practice of spiritualism also flourished, with psychic mediums performing in private séances the ancient shamanistic rituals for contacting spirit beings and dead relatives.

One of the most important movements to emerge at this time was Theosophy, founded in New York by Helena Petrovna Blavatsky (1831–91) in 1875. Like the transcendentalists, theosophists found great spiritual wisdom in esoteric teachings, especially in the ancient teachings of Hinduism, with their focus on the interconnectedness of all beings through the universal Brahman. In the theosophical view, all world religions have a hidden unity of message and metaphysical reality, which could be sought through the truths of esoteric texts as well as through the help of leaders who claimed to receive guidance from "living masters," residing in the Himalayas. The Theosophists had considerable influence among Asian reformers who were trying to modernize Buddhism. This growing interest in global religious wisdom is illustrated by the first Parliament of World Religions in Chicago in 1893, at which representatives of all the world's religions convened to share their views.

This historical milieu gave birth to two important nineteenth-century precursors of new age religion, both with roots in the New Thought movement: the Church of Christ, Scientist (Christian Science) and the Unity School of Christianity. Women were leaders in both movements. Mary Baker Eddy (1821–1910) was the founder of the Christian Science movement, and Emma Curtis Hopkins (1849–1925), a former disciple, broke with Eddy to form the Unity School. The two movements drew on popular forms of philosophical idealism, and the Unity School emphasized Hindu teachings, as well. These influences were integrated with an aura of "science" to affirm the higher reality of mind over matter and therefore the possibility of spiritual healing and spiritual control over the events of one's life.

Emma Curtis Hopkins, founder of the Unity School of Christianity.

"The lofty reasonings of Science are the sunshine of the Spirit. They are the works of Truth. Truth is in us. Let it shine. Truth performs great tasks. Let it shine on miracles of health, cheering, enlightening the nations."

—Emma Curtis Hopkins

Scientology

As the new age religions began to appear in the twentieth century, the religious fascination with the authority of "science" broke free of its earlier linkage to Christianity in movements of the "Christian Science" type. One result was the emergence of *Scientology*, founded by L. Ron Hubbard (1911–86). In 1950 Hubbard published

Mary Baker Eddy, founder of the Church of Christ, Scientist (Christian Science).

Dianetics: The Modern Science of Mental Healing, in which he claimed to have discovered a cure for all human psychological and psychosomatic ills through the realization of a state of mind he called "Clear." Hubbard went on to establish the Hubbard Dianetic Research Foundation in Elizabeth, New Jersey. Later he moved the organization to Phoenix, Arizona, where the Hubbard Association of Scientologists was founded in 1952.

Although born in Tilden, Nebraska, Hubbard was exposed to Asian religion and culture as a child because he traveled with his father, who was in the navy. As a young man with an adventurous spirit, Hubbard was involved in three Central American ethnological expeditions. He received a commission in the navy during World War II, during which service he was pronounced dead twice. In one instance he apparently had something like a shamanistic out-of-body experience in which he acquired spiritual knowledge that gave him his life's mission.

In *Dianetics: The Modern Science of Mental Healing*, which became the foundation for Scientology, we learn that the mind is made up of two parts, the analytic and the reactive. Traumatic experiences in early life or even in the womb are said to imprint themselves on the reactive mind as *engrams*, which cause psychological and psychosomatic problems if they are not dissolved. The way to dissolve these traumatic impressions is to work with a counselor called an *auditor*, who leads the individual into reenacting the events that caused the trauma, thus releasing or liberating the individual from the engrams' negative effects. Hubbard called this state of release "Clear," and devotees of Scientology work hard to attain it.

Scientology, however, went beyond the psychological orientation of Dianetics to develop an elaborate mythology according to which all humans were once advanced beings Hubbard called *Thetans*, all-powerful, eternal, and omniscient. The first Thetans relieved their boredom by playing mind games in which they used imagination to create different physical worlds. However, they soon forgot their true identity as creators and found themselves trapped in these worlds, living as mortals who died, only to be reincarnated again and again. At each reincarnation, people accumulated more psychological baggage, or engrams. To be liberated from this pattern and realize one's true identity, it is necessary to gain insight into one's engrams. Upon finally achieving the "Clear" state of mind, a person gains control over both mind and life. The auditing process that leads to this liberation came to involve the use of a machine that works somewhat like a lie detector. This device, the E-meter, it is believed, measures reactions of resistance to words and other symbols that reveal undissolved engrams. After achieving "Clear," one can go on to higher states that involve out-of-body experiences.

TALES OF SPIRITUAL TRANSFORMATION: A Scientologist's Account of Achieving "Clear"

As with other religious movements throughout history, Scientologists seek to undergo spiritual death and rebirth, or being "born again." In such rebirth experiences the old way of experiencing the world is replaced by a dramatically new one. The following example is taken from a publication of the Church of Scientology of California dated 1970.

There is no name to describe the way I feel. At last I am at cause. I am Clear—I can do anything I want to do. I feel like a child with a new life—everything is so wonderful and beautiful. Clear is Clear! It's unlike anything I could have imagined. The colors, the clarity, the brightness of everything is beyond belief. Everything is so new, I feel newborn. I am filled with the wonder of everything.

Source: Quoted in Robert S. Ellwood and Harry Partin, eds., *Religious and Spiritual Groups in America*, 2nd ed. (Upper Saddle River, NJ: Prentice Hall, 1988), p. 140.

In 1954 Hubbard established the first Church of Scientology in Washington, DC, and in 1959 he started the Hubbard College of Scientology in England. Whereas many new age religious movements stress individualism and are quite loosely organized, Scientology has an elaborate bureaucratic global organization, similar to the modern international business corporation, with its penchant for technical language, efficient organization, and the dissemination of polished communications to interface with the world. And yet all this organization and efficiency is focused on bringing about a powerful experience of enlightenment or rebirth that perfects the self and opens it to the spiritual world that shamans have traversed throughout the ages. Scientologists have also shown a keen interest in Buddhist teachings; there may be Taoist influences as well, and of course the parallels of the auditing practices to depth psychology are obvious. The achievement of "Clear" shows the movement's affinity with both Western experiences of being "born again" and Eastern experiences of enlightenment.

L. Ron Hubbard, founder of Scientology

Scientology is, in many ways, the perfect illustration of the global eclectic integration of the elements that make up new age religions: science (especially psychology), technology (corporate and technical structure), Asian religions (reincarnation and the quest for liberation), and shamanism (out-of-body spiritual explorations). A Thetan, according to Hubbard, goes "through walls, barriers, vanishes space, appears anywhere at will and does other remarkable things."[3]

The Baha'i Global Religious Vision

As we transition from the nineteenth into the twenty-first century, the Baha'i tradition presents us with a powerful example of the embrace of globalization in a new religious movement that links the biblical religions of Judaism, Christianity, and Islam in a sweeping vision that comes to embrace the religions of Asia as well.

"Philosophic knowledge is only valuable if it is true or if it works. . . . A philosophy can only be a *route* to knowledge. It cannot be crammed down one's throat. If one has a route, he can then find what is true for him. And that is Scientology."

—L. Ron Hubbard

The Baha'i tradition emerged in nineteenth-century Persia (Iran today) in a world dominated by Islam. There is a kind of logical development that goes on among the biblical religions. Arising out of the religious traditions of an ancient Israel, Judaism began to emerge after the Babylonian Exile as the first biblical witness to the oneness of God through its Torah and eventually Talmud. In the first century, Christianity, starting as a Jewish sect, broke off from Judaism to become a new religion. Christians claimed that Jews had failed to recognize Jesus as Messiah and Son of God, who fulfills the ancient Jewish prophecies that Christians believe are contained in the Torah. For Christians, Jesus is the final fulfillment of the Bible; nothing and no one else is needed after him. So Christians added the New Testament to the Torah to make a new Bible in two parts: Old Testament (an adaptation of the Torah) and New Testament.

Then in the seventh century, in Arabia, Muhammad emerged as a new prophet, who teaches that both Jews and Christians have strayed from the straight path God had laid out in his revelations in history. Just as Christianity did not deny that God revealed himself to Jews first, but asserted Jesus completed God's revelation in Christianity, so Muslims argue that revelation is only completed by God's working through the "seal of the prophets," Muhammad, the last and final prophet who received the truth of God's will. The Quran, like the New Testament, embraced the great figures of biblical revelation, such as Adam, Abraham, Isaac, Jacob, Moses, David, and Jesus and even recognizes Jesus as the Messiah who will return at the end of time, but it does not call him, as Christians do, Son of God.

In the nineteenth century in Persia, a new religious movement, Baha'i, emerged and claimed to be founded on a new revelation to Shirazi Sayid Ali Muhammad, who came to be known as the Bab, in 1844. The Baha'i emerge out of Shiite Islam, which emphasizes the primacy of political leadership by divinely inspired Imams rather than the Sunni Ulama or scholars sharing authority with political leaders or caliphs. One Shiite branch, The Twelvers, held that there would be twelve such Imams. The twelfth disappeared and is said to have gone into occultation, a state of being not unlike Jesus' ascension into heaven, to come again at the end of time. In fact, some teach that Jesus and the twelfth Imam—the Madhi—will appear together at the end of time. Around this time this messianic expectation for the reappearance of the twelfth Imam—Mohammad al Madhi—was heating up, leading to the expectation that since it was one thousand years since the disappearance of the "hidden Imam," his promised return was eminent.

The Bab was the first Shiite Muslim messianic leader to break away from Islam to forge a new religious movement. Mirza Husayn ali Nuri was imprisoned in Tehran during a persecution of the Babis in 1852. While in prison he came to believe he was indeed called to be a divine messenger. He became known as Bahaaullah—"the splendor or glory of God." He authored the *Kitab al-aqdas* or the "Most Holy Book" of the Baha'i faith. In 1863, while in exile in Baghdad, he publicly embraced his role as God's promised messenger. He was imprisoned in Acre (in Israel) for nine years and later settled in Haifa in what is now Israel. He died in 1892. Haifa is now the site of the Baha'i World Center.

Baha'i teaching claims that God's revelation did not end with Jesus, nor with Muhammad, nor even with Bahaaullah, but God provides a new messenger or

"Manifestation" for each new age of humanity. Naturally, Muslims take exception to the idea that Muhammad is not the seal of the prophets, just as Christians reject the Muslim view that Islam corrects and supersedes Christian teachings, and just as Jews take exception to Christian and Muslim claims to have superseded Judaism. The teachings of the Baha'i complicate this picture further by arguing that God has provided other revelations in Asian religions, like Hinduism and Buddhism through Krishna and Buddha, that are a part of God's "Great Covenant" of continuing revelations to all humanity; Baha'i is just the most recent example. According to Baha'i teaching, all these prophets or "mirrors" of God are part of God's continuing manifestations leading the whole human race into a new global unity. The global vision of the Baha'i teaches the oneness of God, the oneness of all God's prophets around the world, and the oneness of humanity. Baha'i calls on all to establish this oneness as a fact in a global harmony beyond all divisions of nationality, religion, race, or gender.

The Baha'i Gardens and the Shrine of the Bab in Haifa, Israel.

Baha'i teaching offers a parallel to the vision of history of progress through the three ages of the human race. This view was adopted in Western Enlightenment philosophical thought. Kant brought together the Stoic dream of cosmopolitan citizenship with the Christian millennial hope that at the end of time all the tribes of the earth would live together in perpetual peace. Kant's ideals came to be embodied in the experiment with the League of Nations from 1920 to 1946 and the birth of the United Nations in 1945.

Parallel commitments are expressed in Baha'i teachings that have established a global "House of Justice" and Spiritual Assemblies to provide a model for—and encouragement of—the global unification of the human race in peace and universal harmony. Baha'i teachings do not see the teachings of Bahaaullah as competing with these other trends toward globalization but rather see in them the multiple instances in which God is working to unify the human race in confirmation of the Baha'i vision. Under Shoghi Effendi, the laws and institutions needed to promote the unity of the human race became organized into "the Administrative Order" of the Baha'i community. This institution exists at the local, national, and finally the international level through which Baha'i's work promotes the establishment of world harmony and God's kingdom on earth. This emerging kingdom, they believe, will pass from a stage of crisis through a lesser peace gradually established by agreements among the nations, to the "Most Great Peace," which results from finally realizing the truth of Bahaaullah's teaching by the masses as a "coming of age" of the whole human race. Baha'i teaching and practice provide global leadership through The World Centre of Baha'i Faith and its "International Teaching Center" in Haifa, Israel. The estimated population of Baha'is in the world today is over 5 million.

Conclusion: The Postmodern Challenge—Can There Be a Global Ethic in a World of Religious Diversity?

In 2014, a Pew poll noted that the second largest religious population group in the developed world had become "Nones"—those who do not report a religious affiliation. Nearly 25 percent in the United States fit this description. Many of these are "new agers" who have given up all institutional affiliations but are still quite into personal spirituality and believe in reincarnation, for instance. Those who claim to be either agnostic or atheist seem to be overwhelmingly white and male. That latter presents an interesting case: Can atheists be religious?

In 2010 various atheist groups in the United States and Britain began an advertising campaign, affirming on billboards and other media that you can be "Good Without God." This, of course, was shocking to many pious people in both countries.

However, from the perspective of the comparative study of religions, atheism appears to be a culturally relative phenomenon. It seems to depend on the versions of monotheistic belief generated by the biblical religions of Judaism, Christianity, and Islam. Many Buddhists, it is often noted, have no belief in God yet are deeply religious and morally courageous. One of the attractions of Buddhism in a world shaped by modern science is to offer educated persons a way to be religious without believing in God. The real question for the global future of religions is this: Can there be a shared global ethic in a world of diverse worldviews, whether theistic or nontheistic?

Beyond Atheism: The Challenge of Postmodern Secular Relativism

As we noted in the first chapter, religion is about what people hold sacred, and what they hold sacred is their way of life. God, gods, or spirits are often introduced in sacred stories to explain why a group's way of life is sacred, but that way of life may be considered sacred even if such beings are not appealed to. A good example of this is revolutionary Russia, which declared itself an atheist state yet whose mass extermination of its own citizens under Stalin rivaled the devastation of the Holocaust. The Soviet Union was an atheist state that considered its way of life sacred and so executed countless numbers who threatened the new communist way of life.

The interesting question is not whether one can be good without God but whether one can be good without being religious—and here the answer seems to be no. For even those who champion a secular humanist morality hold some things sacred, especially human dignity and human rights. In the United States, atheists have sometimes embraced a kind of fundamentalism. Some have challenged whether a city council, a state government, or even the U.S. Senate violates the First Amendment to the U.S. Constitution by beginning proceedings with a prayer. Many championing atheism have argued that no prayer should ever be said as part of a government proceeding. The First Amendment, however, forbids two opposing things in one sentence—(1) "the establishment of religion" (where the government gives official preference to one religion over all others) and (2) any government attempt to restrict the "free exercise of religion." According to the Constitution, the state should show no preference but should support religious diversity. If we understand that even atheists hold their values and way of life sacred, then they are religious and should be neither forbidden nor favored by government. Globalization relativizes all worldviews, including atheistic ones. The true challenge to religion in a global civilization is not atheism but relativism. If all views, whether theistic or atheistic, are relative, then who can say how human beings ought to live? If good is in the eye of the beholder, then even Hitler and Stalin can be made to seem good. To affirm human dignity against the brutality of such figures is to reject relativism and affirm the unique sacredness of human dignity.

Among religious modernists a different solution was sought to the challenge of scientific rationality and theistic belief. As explained in Chapter 4, on Christianity, the difference between fundamentalists and modernists stems from an argument about the impact of science on traditional religious beliefs. Theistic fundamentalists often seem to believe they must oppose science to reaffirm traditional religious beliefs, while atheistic fundamentalists seem to believe that they must oppose religion in order to affirm scientific beliefs. Modernists attempt to embrace science, preferring to find a rational balance between science and religious beliefs.

Traditional theistic fundamentalists generally had no objection to the use of science to invent things like the automobile or to create better medications. When science impinged on religious beliefs concerning the origins of humanity and the right way to order society, however, many drew a line. If the human self and society do not have sacred origins but are only the result of biological evolution and human decisions, then the human self and society seem to be set adrift in a relativistic world without meaning, purpose, or ethical norms.

As modern science and technology—and the worldview they foster—were carried around the world by colonialism, the impact of modernity was felt in different ways in different societies and cultures. Not every religious tradition emphasizes orthodoxy ("right beliefs") the way Christianity does. For example, Hinduism, Judaism, and Islam place far more emphasis on orthopraxy ("right actions"), the maintenance of a sacred way of life. Thus the most common feature of the fundamentalist reaction to modernity across religions and cultures is the desire to preserve the premodern sacred "way of life" against the threat of secularization and the normless relativism it seems to engender.

The social sciences of the nineteenth century promoted a technological understanding of society. According to this understanding, society itself can be redesigned through public policy decisions, just as engineers periodically redesign cars. While the use of scientific and technological inventions per se was relatively uncontroversial, many rejected the way social science treated the social order in a secular and technological fashion, as if society could or should be shaped and reshaped by human choices, without regard to the sacred ways of one's ancestors. In our chapter on Christianity (Chapter 4), we pointed to the emergence of existentialism as a watershed moment in the history of modernization, opening the door to postmodern relativism by calling into question the idea of *human nature*. For many, this seeming disappearance of human nature is terrifying, suggesting that we as human beings know neither who we are nor what we ought to do. This is the mindset Nietzsche was addressing when he said that "modern man" had murdered God and so now wandered the universe without a sense of direction. In fact, as we noted in Chapter 4, the one thing Christian fundamentalists and Nietzschean atheists have in common (unlike Christian modernists) is that both see science and the Bible as incompatible. Depending on which camp you are in, either God or science has to be rejected. For many theistic fundamentalists today, it seems that the secular "technologized" understandings of self and society can only lead to moral decadence—a decadence in which the family and the fabric of society will be destroyed. Those who believe that secularization is robbing humanity of an understanding of its sacred origins and destiny reject scientific-technologized understandings of self and society. As an antidote, they favor a return to the sacred fundamental truths about human nature that governed life in premodern times.

Modernization is often presented in terms of a story about the secularization of society, that is, the liberation of the various dimensions of cultural life from the authority of religion. Since religion in premodern societies preserves the sacred by governing every aspect of life, modernization and secularization are threats to traditional societies everywhere. Nevertheless, sacralizing society to protect a divinely ordered way of life is not the only role religion has played in history. Moreover, as we have noted, secular ways of life that appeal to the rationality of science have also become sacred. Paradoxically, the most successful critiques of the sacralization of society have come from religions. The great sociologist Max Weber pointed out that religion not only sacralizes and reinforces the unchanging "routine" order of society (as the French sociologist Émile Durkheim held); sometimes it also "charismatically" desacralizes and transforms society. Religion, like reason, sometimes criticizes and transforms sacred order rather than functioning as its defender. Brahmanic Hinduism sacralized caste society in ancient India, but Buddhism began as a movement to desacralize the priestly elite and see all persons in the caste system as equal and capable of achieving spiritual deliverance. Sacralization readily accommodates hierarchies (e.g., a caste system, or hierarchical social order), whereas desacralizing breaks with caste, inviting pluralism and equality.

Because religions (even in the same traditions) often manifest dramatically opposing values and orientations, the sociologist Jacques Ellul has argued that it is helpful in understanding the role of religion in society to distinguish between two terms that are typically used interchangeably: sacred and holy. In his view, the experience of the sacred leads to a view of society as an order that is itself sacred and must be protected from all profane attempts to change it. The experience of the holy, on the other hand, calls into question the very idea of a sacred order. It desacralizes (or secularizes) society and seeks to introduce change in the name of a higher truth and/or justice. Thus, the call for human dignity and rights is really a manifestation of the holy rather than the sacred. According to this view, the same religious tradition can express itself in opposite ways in different times and places. In India, early Buddhism called into question the sacred order of Hindu caste society, but later Buddhist societies developed their own sacred orders. Early Daoists in China called into question the sacred hierarchical order of Confucianism but later also integrated themselves into the sacred order of Confucian society by means of a neo-Confucian synthesis.

In the West, early Christianity, sharing a common ethos with Judaism, called the sacred order of Roman civilization into question, but medieval Christianity resacralized Europe. Then later, Protestantism desacralized the medieval European social order and unleashed the dynamics of modernism, which is also in danger of sacralization. From this perspective, the struggle between fundamentalism and modernism in the contemporary world that we have surveyed in this textbook is an example of the conflict between the sacred and the holy, the sacralizing and desacralizing (secularizing) roles of religion.

Traditional religious fundamentalists express the desire to preserve the sacredness of human identity in a rightly ordered society against what they perceive as the chaos of today's decadent, normless secular relativism. Secular fundamentalists express a desire to preserve the sacredness of the scientific and rational way of life against the chaos introduced into society by diverse forms of religious absolutism. To restore the sacred normative order, religious fundamentalists tend to affirm the desirability of achieving the premodern ideal of one society, one religion. In the case of secular fundamentalism, what is to be preserved is the sacredness of the way of life made possible by scientific rationality in an age of progress. Both religious and secular or atheistic fundamentalists remain uncomfortable with the religious diversity that thrives in a secular society.

Religious modernism as it emerged in the West rejected the fundamentalist ideal, adopted from premodern societies, of identity between religion and society. Instead of dangerous absolutism, modernists looked for an accommodation between religion and modern secular society. They argued that it is possible to desacralize one's way of life and identity in a way that creates a new identity that preserves the essential values or norms of the past tradition, but in harmony with a new modern way of life. Modernists secularize society and privatize their religious practices, hoping by their encouragement of denominational forms of religion to ensure an environment that supports religious diversity.

What we are calling religious postmodernism, like religious modernism, accepts secularization and religious pluralism. But religious postmodernism, like fundamentalism, rejects the modernist solution of privatizing religious belief and practice and seeks a public role for religion. It differs from fundamentalism, however, in that it rejects the domination of society by a single religion. Religious postmodernists insist that there is a way for religious communities in all their diversity to shape the public order and so rescue society from secular relativism. The chief example of this option is the model established by Mohandas K. Gandhi. Because his disciples rejected the privatization of religion while affirming religious diversity, Gandhi's movement must be defined as a postmodern new age religious movement rather than a modernist one.

"Passing Over": A Postmodern Spiritual Adventure That Responds to the Challenge of Globalization

All the great world religions date back a millennium or more, and each provided a grand metanarrative for the premodern civilization in which it emerged—in the Middle East, in India, and in China. In the past these world religions were relatively isolated from one another. There were many histories in the world, each shaped by a great metanarrative, but no global history.

The perspective of religious postmodernism arises from a dramatically different situation. We are at the beginning of a new millennium, which is marked by the development of a global civilization. The diverse spiritual heritages of the human race have become the common inheritance of all. Modern changes have ended the isolation of the past, and people following one great tradition are now very likely to live in proximity to adherents of other faiths. New age religion has tapped this condition of globalization but in two different ways. In its modernist forms it has privatized the religious quest as a quest for the perfection of the self. In its postmodern forms, without rejecting self-transformation, it has turned that goal outward in forms of social organization committed to bettering society, bringing personal and social transformation into balance.

The time when a new world religion could be founded has passed, argues John Dunne in his book *The Way of All the Earth*. What is required today is not the conquest of the world by any one religion or culture but a meeting and sharing of religious and cultural insight. "The holy man of our time, it seems, is not a figure like Gautama [Buddha] or Jesus or Mohammed, a man who could found a world religion, but a figure like Gandhi, a man who passes over by sympathetic understanding from his own religion to other religions and comes back again with new insight to his own. Passing over and coming back, it seems, is the spiritual adventure of our time."[4]

This postmodern spiritual adventure occurs when we pass over into another's religion and culture and come to see the world through another's eyes. When we do this, we "come back" to our own religion and culture enriched with new insight not only into the other's religion and culture but also into our own—insight that builds bridges of understanding, a unity in diversity between people of diverse religions and cultures. The model for this spiritual adventure is found in the lives of Leo Tolstoy (1828–1910), Mohandas K. Gandhi (1869–1948), and Martin Luther King Jr. (1929–68).

Two of the most inspiring religious figures of the twentieth century were Mahatma Gandhi and Dr. King. They are the great champions of the fight for the dignity and rights of all human beings, from all religions and cultures. Moreover, they are models for a different kind of new age religious practice, one that absorbs the global wisdom of diverse religions, but does so without indiscriminately mixing elements to create a new religion, as is typical of the eclectic syncretism of most new age religions. Yet clearly these religious leaders initiated a new way of being religious that could occur only in an age of globalization.

Martin Luther King Jr. often noted that his commitment to nonviolent resistance, or civil disobedience, as a strategy for protecting human dignity had its roots in two sources: Jesus' Sermon on the Mount and Gandhi's teachings of nonviolence derived from his interpretation of the Hindu sacred story called the *Bhagavad Gita*. Gandhi died when King was a teenager, but Dr. King did travel to India to study the effects of Gandhi's teachings of nonviolence on Indian society. In this he showed a remarkable openness to the insights of another religion and culture. In Gandhi and his spiritual heirs, King found kindred spirits, and he came back to his own religion and culture enriched by the new insights that came to him in the process of passing over and coming back. Martin Luther King Jr. never became a Hindu, but his Christianity was profoundly transformed by his encounter with Gandhi's Hinduism.

"I simply want to tell the story of my numerous experiments with truth, and my life consists of nothing but these experiments. . . . They are spiritual, or rather moral; for the essence of religion is morality."

—M. K. Gandhi

Just as important, however, is the spiritual passing over of Gandhi himself. As a young man, Gandhi went to England to study law. His journey led him not away from Hinduism but more deeply into it, for it was in England that Gandhi discovered the *Bhagavad Gita* and began to fully appreciate the spiritual and ethical power of Hinduism.

Having promised his mother that he would remain a vegetarian, Gandhi took to eating his meals with British citizens who had developed similar commitments to vegetarianism through their fascination with India and its religions. It is in this context that Gandhi was brought into direct contact with the nineteenth-century theosophical roots of new age globalization. In these circles he met Madame Blavatsky and her disciple Annie Besant, both of whom had a profound influence on him. His associates also included Christian followers of the Russian novelist Leo Tolstoy, who, after his midlife conversion, had embraced an ethic of nonviolence based on Jesus' Sermon on the Mount (Matthew 5–7).

At the invitation of his theosophist friends, Gandhi read the *Bhagavad Gita* for the first time, in an English translation by Sir Edwin Arnold, entitled *The Song Celestial*. It was only much later that he took to a serious study of the Hindu text in Sanskrit. He was also deeply impressed by Arnold's *The Light of Asia*, recounting the life of the Buddha. Thus, through the eyes of Western friends, he was first moved to discover the spiritual riches of his own Hindu heritage. The seeds were planted in England, nourished by more serious study during his years in South Africa, and brought to fruition on his return to India in 1915.

From his theosophist friends, Gandhi not only learned to appreciate his own religious tradition but came to see Christianity in a new way. For unlike the evangelical missionaries he had met in his childhood, the theosophists had a deeply allegorical way of reading the Christian scriptures. This approach to Bible study allowed people to find in the teachings of Jesus a universal path toward spiritual truth that was in harmony with the wisdom of Asia. The power of allegory lay in opening the literal stories of the scripture to reveal a deeper symbolic meaning based on what the theosophists believed was profound universal religious experience and wisdom. From the theosophists, Gandhi took an interpretive principle that has its roots in the New Testament writings of St. Paul: "The letter killeth, but the spirit giveth life" (2 Corinthians 3:6). This insight would enable him to read the *Bhagavad Gita* in the light of his own deep religious experience and find in it the justification for nonviolent civil disobedience.

Mohandas K. Gandhi, whose techniques of nonviolent civil disobedience led to the liberation of India from British colonial rule in 1947.

Gandhi was likewise profoundly influenced by Tolstoy's understanding of the Sermon on the Mount. The message of nonviolence—love your enemy, turn the other cheek—took hold of Gandhi. And yet Gandhi did not become a Christian. Rather, he returned to his parents' religion and culture, finding parallels to Jesus' teachings in the Hindu tradition. And so he read Hindu scriptures with new insight, interpreting the *Bhagavad Gita* allegorically, as a call to resist evil by nonviolent means. And just as King would later use the ideas of Gandhi in the nonviolent struggle for the dignity of black citizens in North America, so Gandhi was inspired by Tolstoy as he led the fight for the dignity of the lower castes and outcasts within Hindu society and for the liberation of India from British colonial rule.

Gandhi never became a Christian and King never became a Hindu. Nevertheless, Gandhi's Hindu faith was profoundly transformed by his encounter with the Christianity of Tolstoy, just as King's Christian faith was profoundly transformed by his encounter with Gandhi's Hinduism. In the lives of these twentieth-century religious activists we have examples of "passing over" as a transformative postmodern spiritual adventure. Whereas in the secular forms of postmodernism all knowledge is relative, and therefore the choice between interpretations of any claim to truth is "undecidable," Gandhi and King opened up an alternate path. While agreeing that in matters of religion, truth is undecidable, they showed that acceptance of diversity does not have to lead to the kind of ethical relativism that so deeply troubles fundamentalists. For in the cases of Gandhi and King, passing over led to a sharing of wisdom among traditions that gave birth to an ethical coalition in defense of human dignity across religions and cultures—a global ethic for a new age.

By their lives, Gandhi and King demonstrated that, contrary to the fears raised by fundamentalism, the sharing of a common ethic and of spiritual wisdom across traditions does not require any practitioners to abandon their religious identity. Instead, Gandhi and King offered a model of unity in diversity. Finally, both Gandhi and King rejected the privatization of religion, insisting that religion in all its diversity plays a decisive role in shaping the public order of society. And both were convinced that only a firm commitment to nonviolence on the part of religious communities would allow society to avoid a return to the kind of religious wars that accompanied the Protestant Reformation and the emergence of modernity.

The spiritual adventure initiated by Gandhi and King involves passing over (through imagination, through travel and cultural exchange, through a common commitment to social action to promote social justice, etc.) into the life and stories and traditions of others, sharing in them and, in the process, coming to see one's own tradition through them. Such encounters enlarge our sense of human identity to include the other. The religious metanarratives of the world's civilizations may have become "smaller narratives" in an age of global diversity, but they have not lost their power. Indeed, in this Gandhian model, it is the sharing of the wisdom from another tradition's metanarratives that gives the stories of a person's own tradition their power. Each person remains on familiar religious and cultural ground, yet each is profoundly influenced by the other.

Tolstoy, Jesus, and "Saint Buddha": An Ancient Tale with a Thousand Faces

Although at first glance the religious worlds of humankind seem to have grown up largely independent of one another, a closer look will reveal that hidden threads from different religions and cultures have for centuries been woven together to form a new tapestry, one that contributes to the sharing of religious insight in an age of globalization. In *Toward a World Theology*, Wilfred Cantwell Smith traces the threads of this new tapestry, and the story he tells is quite surprising.[5] Smith notes, for example, that to fully appreciate the influence on Gandhi of Tolstoy's understanding of the Sermon on the Mount, it is important to know that Tolstoy's own conversion to Christianity, which occurred in a period of midlife crisis, was deeply influenced not only by the Sermon on the Mount but also by the life of the Buddha.

Tolstoy was a member of the Russian nobility, rich and famous because of his novels, which included *War and Peace* and *Anna Karenina*. Yet in his fifties, Tolstoy went through a period of great despair that resolved itself in a powerful religious conversion experience. Although nominally a member of the (Russian) Orthodox Church, Tolstoy had not taken his faith seriously until he came to the point of making the Sermon on the Mount a blueprint for his life. After his conversion, Tolstoy freed his serfs, gave away all his wealth, and spent the rest of his life serving the poor.

A key factor in Tolstoy's conversion was his reading of a story from the lives of the saints. The story was that of Barlaam and Josaphat. It is the story of a wealthy young Indian prince by the name of Josaphat who gave up all his wealth and power and abandoned his family to embark on an urgent quest for an answer to the problems of old age, sickness, and death. During his search, the prince comes across a Christian monk by the name of Barlaam, who tells him a story. It seems that once there was a man who fell into a very deep well and was hanging onto two vines for dear life. As he was trapped in this precarious situation, two mice, one white and one black, came along and began to chew on the vines. The man knew that in short order the vines would be severed and he would plunge to his death.

The story was an allegorical parable of the prince's spiritual situation. Barlaam points out that the two mice represent the cycle of day and night, the passing of time that brings us ever closer to death. The paradox is that like the man in the well, Josaphat cannot save his life by clinging to it. He must let go of the vines, so to speak. He can save his life only by losing it. That is, if he lets go of his life now, no longer clinging to it but surrendering himself completely to the divine will, his spiritual death will lead to a new life that transcends death. This story and its parable touched the deeply depressed writer and led him to a spiritual surrender that brought about his rebirth. Out of this rebirth then came a new Tolstoy, the author of *The Kingdom of God Is Within You*, which advocates a life of nonviolent resistance to evil based on the Sermon on the Mount.

The story of the Indian prince who abandons a life of wealth and power is of course a thinly disguised version of the life story of the Buddha. Versions of the story and the parable can be found in almost all the world's great religions, recorded in a variety of languages (Greek, Latin, Czech, Polish, Italian, Spanish, French, German, Swedish, Norwegian, Arabic, Hebrew, Yiddish, Persian, Sanskrit, Chinese, Japanese, etc.). The Greek version came into Christianity from an Islamic Arabic version, which was passed on to Judaism as well. The Muslims apparently got it from members of a Gnostic cult in Persia, who got it from Buddhists in India. The Latinate name *Josaphat* is a translation of the Greek *Loasaf*, which is translated from the Arabic *Yudasaf*, which comes from the Persian *Bodisaf*, which is a translation of *Bodhisattva*, a Sanskrit title for the Buddha.

The parable of the man clinging to the vine may be even older than the story of the prince (Buddha) who renounces his wealth. It may well go back to early Indic sources at the beginnings of civilization. It is one of the oldest and most universal stories in the history of religions and civilizations. Tolstoy's conversion was brought about in large part by the story of a Christian saint, Josaphat, who was, so to speak, really the Buddha in disguise.

The history of the story of a great sage's first steps toward enlightenment suggests that the process leading to globalization goes back to the very beginnings of civilization. Therefore the line between new religions and new age (globalized) religions may not be as sharp as previously assumed. We can see that the practice of passing over and coming back, of being open to the stories of others, and of coming to understand one's own tradition through these stories is in fact very ancient. Thus when Martin Luther King Jr. embraced the teachings of Gandhi, he embraced not only Gandhi but also Tolstoy and, through Tolstoy, two of the greatest religious teachers of nonviolence:

Leo Tolstoy, the famous Russian novelist, whose writings on Jesus' Sermon on the Mount inspired Gandhi.

Jesus of Nazareth, whose committed follower King already was, and Siddhartha the Buddha. So, from the teachings of Gandhi, King actually assimilated important teachings from at least four religious traditions—Hinduism, Buddhism, Judaism, and Christianity. This rich spiritual debt to other religions and cultures never in any way diminished King's faith. On the contrary, the Baptist pastor's Christian beliefs were deeply enriched, in turn enriching the world in which we live. The same could be said about Gandhi and Hinduism.

Gandhi's transformation of the *Bhagavad Gita*—a Hindu story that literally advocates the duty of going to war and killing one's enemies—into a story of nonviolence is instructive of the transforming power of the allegorical method that he learned from his theosophist friends. The *Bhagavad Gita* is a story about a warrior named Arjuna, who argues with his chariot driver, Krishna, over whether it is right to go to war if it means having to kill one's own relatives. Krishna's answer is yes—Arjuna must do his duty as a warrior in the cause of justice, but he is morally obliged to do it selflessly, with no thought of personal loss or gain. Gandhi, however, transformed the story of Arjuna and Krishna from a story of war as physical violence into a story of war as active but nonviolent resistance to injustice through civil disobedience.

If the message of spiritual realization in the *Gita* is that all beings share the same self (as Brahman or Purusha), how could the *Gita* be literally advocating violence, for to do violence against another would be to do violence against oneself? The self-contradiction of a literal interpretation, in Gandhi's way of thinking, forces the mind into an allegorical mode, where it can grasp the *Gita's* true spiritual meaning. Reading the *Gita* allegorically, Gandhi insisted that the impending battle described in the Hindu classic is really about the battle between good and evil going on within every self.

Krishna's command to Arjuna to stand up and fight is thus a "spiritual" command. But for Gandhi this does not mean, as it usually does in "modern" terms, that the struggle is purely inner (private) and personal. On the contrary, the spiritual person will see the need to practice nonviolent civil disobedience: that is, to replace "body force" (i.e., violence) with "soul force." As the *Gita* suggests, there really is injustice in the world, and therefore there really is an obligation to fight, even to go to war, to reestablish justice. One must be prepared to exert Gandhian soul force by putting one's body on the line, but in a nonviolent way, through civil disobedience. In so doing, one leaves open the opportunity to gain the respect, understanding, and perhaps transformation of one's enemy.

The lesson Gandhi derived from the *Gita* is that the encounter with the other need not lead to conquest. It can lead, instead, to mutual understanding and mutual respect. King's relationship to Gandhi and Gandhi's relationship to Tolstoy are models of a postmodern spirituality and ethics that transform postmodern relativism and eclecticism into the opportunity to follow a new spiritual and ethical path—"the way of all the earth"—the sharing of spiritual insight and ethical wisdom across religions and cultures in an age of globalization.

On this path, people of diverse religions and cultures find themselves sharing an ethical commitment to protect human dignity beyond the postmodern interest in personal transformation fostered by the modernist ideal of privatization. Gandhi and King were not engaged in a private quest to perfect the self (although neither neglected the need for personal transformation). Rather, each man embarked on a public quest to transform human communities, socially and politically, by invoking a global ethical commitment to protect the dignity of all persons. The religious movements associated with both men fit the pattern of the holy that affirms the secularization of society in order to embrace religious pluralism. Gandhi and King recovered the premodern ideal of religion shaping the public order but now in a postmodern mode, committed to religious pluralism.

Martin Luther King Jr., who led the civil rights movement for racial equality in the United States, using the techniques of nonviolent civil disobedience inspired by Gandhi.

The Children of Gandhi: An Experiment in Postmodern Global Ethics

In April 1968, Martin Luther King Jr., sometimes referred to as "the American Gandhi," went to Memphis to support black municipal workers in the midst of a strike. The Baptist minister was looking forward to spending the approaching Passover with Rabbi Abraham Joshua Heschel. Heschel, who had marched with King during the voter registration drive in Selma, Alabama, three years earlier, had become a close friend and supporter. Unfortunately, King was not able to keep that engagement. On April 4, 1968, like Gandhi before him, Martin Luther King Jr., a man of nonviolence, was shot to death by an assassin.

The Buddhist monk and anti–Vietnam War activist Thich Nhat Hanh, whom King had nominated for a Nobel Peace

Prize, received the news of his friend's death while at an interreligious conference in New York City. Only the previous spring, King had expressed his opposition to the Vietnam War, largely at the urging of Thich Nhat Hanh and Rabbi Heschel. King spoke out at an event sponsored by Clergy and Laymen Concerned about Vietnam, a group founded by Heschel, Protestant cleric John Bennett, and Richard Neuhaus, then a Lutheran minister. Now another champion in the struggle against hatred, violence, and war was dead. But the spiritual and ethical vision he shared with his friends, across religions and cultures, has continued to inspire followers throughout the world.

These religious activists—a Baptist minister who won the Nobel Peace Prize for his leadership in the American civil rights movement, a Hasidic rabbi and scholar who narrowly escaped the death camps of the Holocaust, and a Buddhist monk who had been targeted for assassination in Vietnam but survived to lead the Buddhist peace delegation to the Paris peace negotiations in 1973—are the spiritual children of Gandhi. By working together to protest racial injustice and the violence of war, they demonstrated that religious and cultural pluralism do not have to end in ethical relativism and, given a commitment to nonviolence, can play a role in shaping public life in an age of globalization. The goal, Martin Luther King Jr. insisted, is not to humiliate and defeat your enemy but to win him or her over, bringing about not only justice but also reconciliation. The goal, he said, was to attack the evil in systems, not to attack persons. The goal was to love one's enemy, not in the sense of sentimental affection or in the reciprocal sense of friendship, but in the constructive sense of seeking the opponent's well-being.

Nonviolence, King argued, is more than just a remedy for this or that social injustice. It is, he was convinced, essential to the survival of humanity in an age of nuclear

A Buddhist monk meditates during a moment of silence near the finish line of the Boston Marathon bombings on the one-week anniversary of the April 22, 2013, attack.

TEACHINGS OF RELIGIOUS WISDOM: Thich Nhat Hanh on the Shared Wisdom of Buddhism and Christianity

Thich Nhat Hanh was nominated by Martin Luther King Jr. for the Nobel Peace Prize for his nonviolent struggle to establish peace between North and South Vietnam during the Vietnam War in the 1960s. In his writings, especially *Living Buddha, Living Christ,* he insists that religious language is about direct religious experience, not about abstract metaphysical beliefs. On this, he says, both Buddhist and Christian contemplative monks agree.

Once the ultimate is touched, all notions are transcended: birth, death, being, non-being, before, after, one, many and so forth. Questions like "Does God exist?" or "Does nirvana exist?" are no longer valid. God and nirvana as concepts have been

transcended. . . . For the one who has had an experience of God or nirvana, the question "does God exist?" is an indication of the lack of insight. (p. 189) . . . The practices of prayer and meditation help us touch the most valuable seeds that are within us and they put us in contact with the ground of our being. . . . When the energy of mindfulness is present, transformation takes place. When the energy of the Holy Spirit is within you, understanding, love, peace, and stability are possible. God is within. You are, yet you are not, but God is in you. This is interbeing. This is non-self. (p. 167–68)

Source: Thich Nhat Hanh, *Living Buddha, Living Christ* (New York: G. P. Putnam and Sons, Riverhead Books), 1995.

weapons. The choice, he said, was "no longer between violence and nonviolence. It is either nonviolence or nonexistence."

Truth is to be found in all religions, King said many times, and "injustice anywhere is a threat to justice everywhere. We are caught in an inescapable network of mutuality, tied in a single garment of destiny. Whatever affects one directly affects all indirectly."[6] The scandal of our age, said Abraham Joshua Heschel, is that in a world of diplomacy "only religions are not on speaking terms." But, he also said, no religion is an island, and all must realize that "holiness is not the monopoly of any particular religion or tradition."[7]

"Buddhism today," writes Thich Nhat Hanh, "is made up of non-Buddhist elements, including Jewish and Christian ones." And likewise with every tradition. "We have to allow what is good, beautiful, and meaningful in the other's tradition to transform us," the Vietnamese monk continues. The purpose of such passing over into the other's tradition is to allow each to return to his or her own tradition transformed. What is astonishing, says Thich Nhat Hanh, is that we will find kindred spirits in other traditions with whom we share more than we do with many in our own tradition.[8]

The Future of Religion in an Age of Globalization

Will the global future of religion and civilization be shaped by this Gandhian model of new age spiritual practice? It clearly offers an alternative to both traditional denominational modernist religions and the more privatistic modernist forms of new age religion. The Gandhian model also offers an alternative to the fundamentalist rejection of modernization and secularization by showing that religious pluralism does not have to lead to relativism. On the contrary, it can lead to the sanctification of life and the promotion of an ethic of human dignity across religions and cultures. The challenge is that the sharing of spiritual wisdom does require seeing the religions and cultures of others as having wisdom to share, and not all will accept this presupposition. Nevertheless, the emergence of religious postmodernism means that in the future, the struggle among religions will most likely be not so much between fundamentalism and modernism, nor between theists and atheists, but between religious fundamentalist exclusivism and postmodern religious pluralism—both as forms of religion that shape not only private but also public life.

Discussion Questions

1. What is the difference between a "new religion" and a "new age religion"?

2. How do modernist new age religious belief and practice differ from postmodernist new age religious belief and practice? Give an example of each.

3. How does new age religion relate to the split between faith and reason (the *via moderna* and the *devotio moderna*) that shaped the emergence of the modern world through the Enlightenment and the Romantic reaction it provoked?

4. In what sense is "civil religion" a new way of being religious, and in what sense is it a very old way of being religious?

5. What do the authors mean by suggesting that in a postmodern society, atheism can itself become a form of fundamentalism?

6. In what way is the postmodern path of religious ethics opened up by M. K. Gandhi and Martin Luther King Jr. similar to fundamentalist ideals for society, and in what way is it different?

Suggested Readings

Bruce, Steve. *Religion in the Modern World* (New York: Oxford University Press, 1996).

Dunne, John S. *The Way of All the Earth* (1972; rpt., Notre Dame, IN: University of Notre Dame Press, 1978).

Ellwood, Robert S., and Harry B. Partin, eds. *Religious and Spiritual Groups in Modern America*, 2nd ed. (Upper Saddle River, NJ: Prentice Hall, 1973, 1988).

Fasching, Darrell J. *The Coming of the Millennium* (San Jose, CA: Authors Choice Press, 1996, 2000).

———. "Stories of War and Peace: Sacred, Secular and Holy," in Sarah Deets and Merry Kerry, eds., *War and Words* (Lanham, MD: Rowman and Littlefield, 2004).

Fasching, Darrell J., Dell deChant, and David Lantigua. *Comparative Religious Ethics: A Narrative Approach to Global Ethics*, 2nd ed. (Oxford: Blackwell, 2011).

Jones, Lindsay, ed. *Encyclopedia of Religion*, 2nd ed., 15 vols. (Detroit: Macmillan Reference USA, 2005).

Juergensmeyer, Mark. *Terror in the Mind of God* (Berkeley: University of California Press, 2000).

Laderman, Gary, and Luis Leon, eds. *Religion and American Cultures*, vol. 1 (Santa Barbara, CA: ABC Clio, 2003).

Lewis, James R., ed. *The Oxford Handbook of New Religious Movements* (New York: Oxford University Press, 2004).

Melton, J. Gordon. *Finding Enlightenment* (Hillsboro, OR: Beyond Words Publishing, 1998).

Rothstein, Mikael, ed. *New Age Religion and Globalization* (Aarhus, Denmark: Aarhus University Press, 2001).

Notes

1. William Bloom, *The New Age: An Anthology of Essential Writings* (London: Rider/Channel 4, 1991), p. xviii. Quoted in Steve Bruce, *Religion in the Modern World* (Oxford: Oxford University Press, 1996).

2. Sarah Pike, "New Age," quoted in Robert S. Ellwood and Harry B. Partin, eds., *Religious and Spiritual Groups in Modern America*, 2nd ed. (Upper Saddle River, NJ: Prentice Hall, 1988), p. 140.

3. L. Ron Hubbard, *Scientology: The Fundamentals of Thought* (Edinburgh: Publications Organization Worldwide, 1968); originally published 1950. Quoted in Ellwood and Partin, *Religions and Spiritual Groups in Modern America*, p. 147.

4. John Dunne, *The Way of All the Earth* (Notre Dame, IN: University of Notre Dame Press, 1978), p. ix.

5. Wilfred Cantwell Smith, *Toward a World Theology* (Philadelphia: Westminster Press, 1981), chap. 1.

6. Martin Luther King Jr., "Letter from Birmingham Jail," in King, *I Have a Dream: Writings and Speeches That Changed the World*, ed. James M. Washington (San Francisco: HarperSanFrancisco, 1992), p. 85.

7. Abraham Joshua Heschel, *Moral Grandeur and Spiritual Audacity: Essays [of] Abraham Joshua Heschel*, ed. Susannah Heschel (New York: Farrar, Straus & Giroux, 1996), pp. 241, 247.

8. Thich Nhat Hanh, *Living Buddha, Living Christ* (New York: G. P. Putnam and Sons, Riverhead Books, 1995), pp. 9, 11.

Additional Resources

Cults a.k.a. New Religious Movements, Ontario Consultants on Religious Tolerance (http://www.religioustolerance.org/cultmenu.htm)

This site devoted to religious tolerance offers comprehensive, balanced information on new religions, "cults," and the anti-cult and counter-cult movements. Principal new religions are profiled, including their history, beliefs, practices, publications, and conflicts with government or other groups. Offers an overview of the conflicts, including references supporting the various sides of the conflicts.

GLOSSARY

Adi Granth: the scripture worshipped by Sikhs

Aggadah: the stories of the Tanak and the Talmud that communicate spiritual truths

ahimsa: nonviolence, the ideal of doing no killing, especially for its karmic effects

al-haram al-sharif: the noble sanctuary

All Souls Festival: a summer event when the gates of purgatory are thought to be held open; families perform rituals to connect the living members with their departed kin and ensure their ancestors' comfort in the afterlife

Allah: God

al-Quds: the holy city (i.e., Jerusalem)

Amaterasu: the kami of the sun and progenitor of the Japanese imperial line

Amitabha/Amida: the most important and highly developed of the Pure Land schools created by a Chinese Buddha named Amitabha in Sanskrit (Amitofo in Chinese, Amida in Japanese), featured chanting Amitabha's name (*Namo A-mi-t'o Fo*) as a meditative act and communal ritual

amoraim: the generation of sages that created the Gemara

Analects: collection of sayings attributed to Confucius

anatman: "nonself," the doctrine denying the reality of a permanent, immortal soul as the spiritual center of the human being

ancestor veneration: worship, feeding, and petitioning of the souls of dead ancestors at family graves, temples, or home altars

animism: religious tradition whose basic perception entails belief in an inner soul that gives life and ultimate identity to humans, animals, and plants and that places primary emphasis on experiential rituals in which humans interact with other souls

arhat: an enlightened disciple, according to the Theravada school; an advanced disciple, according to the Mahayana

Arya Samaj: religious organization that redefined and defended reformed Hindu traditions

Ashkenazi: Jews whose traditions originated in central and eastern Europe

Ashoka: (273–232 BCE), ruler whose patronage spread Buddhist institutions and teachings across his empire, and likely beyond

ashram: center of religious practice following a guru

atman: in Hindu thought, the soul that resides in the heart, is the source of both life energy and spiritual awareness, and transmigrates after death

Augustinian: refers to views of St. Augustine, for example, his view of the separation of church and state, in which the state is answerable to the church in religious matters while the church is answerable to the state in secular matters—yet both exist to promote the spread of the Gospel

Avalokiteshvara: *see* Guanyin

avatara: "incarnation" of a god that descends to earth; avataras assume life forms that aid creation, usually to defeat demons and overcome evil

ayatollah: literally, "sign of God"; title used by certain Shiah religious leaders who are widely reputed for their learning and piety

bar/bat mitzvah: the rite of passage for boys (bar mitzvah) whereby they become full members of the religion of Judaism who are able to read and interpret Torah; in modern times a parallel rite for girls (bat mitzvah) has been established in some forms of Judaism

Bhagavad Gita: Hindu scripture inserted into the great epic, the *Mahabharata*, extolling the divinity of Krishna as the ultimately real deity

bhakti: devotionalism to a divinity, a means to reach salvation from the world of rebirth

Bharatiya Janata Party (BJP): Hindu nationalism party that rose meteorically in popularity in the 1990s and assumed national rule in 1998

bhikkhu/bhikkhuni: Buddhist monks or nuns

Bodh Gaya: the site of Shakyamuni Buddha's enlightenment, under a tree

bodhisattva: a Buddha to be, either in the present life or in a future life. In the Mahayana tradition, all individuals should aspire to be Buddhas; hence, the bodhisattva is the highest human role. Some future Buddhas can be reborn as deities; hence, in Mahayana Buddhism there are also bodhisattvas who can assist humans.

Brahman: world spirit that arises at creation, which Hindus hold is either in impersonal form, nirguna Brahman, or human form, saguna Brahman

brahmin: member of the highest caste, innately possessing the highest natural purity; the men traditionally specialize in ritual performance, textual memorization and study, and theology

Buddha: literally, one who has "awakened," ended karmic bondage, and will no longer be reborn; one who will enter nirvana

Buddhaghosa: (fifth century CE), great Theravadin monk-scholar

Buddha-nature school: a Mahayana Buddhist belief that all beings have a portion of nirvana and so possess the latent potential for its realization; a reversion to belief in the soul that also reinforced the need for traditional meditation practices

Bwiti: a West Central African religion that incorporates animism, ancestor worship, and Christianity into its belief system, along with a specially cultivated hallucinogen

caitya: a term that can also signify any Buddha shrine; *see also* stupa

caliph (khalifah): successor of Muhammad as the political and military head of the Muslim community

Catholic: those churches that define their Christian authenticity through apostolic succession

Ch'an: a Mahayana Buddha-nature tradition in East Asia called *Ch'an* in China, *Sön* in Korea, and *Zen* in Japan

Ch'ondogyo: Korean movement reaffirming the truth of human dignity and the vitality of Daoism and Confucianism

Christ: from Greek translation of the Hebrew word meaning "messiah" or "anointed one," the title Christians apply to Jesus of Nazareth

circular time: the awareness, more prevalent in hunter-gatherer than industrial societies, that life is governed by the rising and the setting of the sun, the phases of the moon, and the seasons of the year

circumcision: the cutting of the foreskin of the penis as a sign of the covenant of Abraham

Cittamatra: Mahayana philosophical school that focuses on consciousness as the center of spiritual realization

city god: Chinese deity with influence on spirits living within city precincts, to whom every family's kitchen god reports at year's end

civil religions: the beliefs and rituals of modern "secular" societies that treat their social order as sacred due to the "cultural" influence of the religions that shaped their origin and development

colonialism: the political, social, cultural, and economic domination of one society by another

Confucianism: culture of the literate elite (rujia) informed by Confucius and his disciples, who mastered the classics and rituals; the moral tradition upholding the "three bonds" and the "three principles" as the basis of social life; the spiritual tradition of revering ancestors as part of the family bond

Confucius: *see* Master K'ung

Constantinian/Constantinianism: view of the unity of church and state attributed to the first Christian Roman Emperor, Constantine, in which the state exists to rule over and protect the church as the official religion of the empire

cosmogony: mythological account of the creation

covenant: the agreement between God and the people of Israel whereby they are chosen to be God's people; God agrees to guide and protect them; the people agree to follow God's commandments (*halakhah*)

Cultural Revolution: period from 1966 to 1976 when China's Communist Party, under the leadership of Mao Zedong, attacked religious traditions and practitioners

dana: one of the four merit-making activities in Buddhist culture, "self-less giving" to diminish desire

Dao: mysterious power that moves the universe and all beings

Daoist: East Asian visionaries who advocated individualistic retreat, learning from the natural world, and noninterference by the state as the best way to ensure humanity's flourishing

dar al-Islam: the house or abode of Islam, as opposed to the house of war; territory controlled and ruled by Muslims

darshan: seeing the divine; making eye contact with a god, holy site, or guru

Daruma-san: Japanese name for the monk Bodhidharma, who brought a meditation-centered Buddhist tradition to China, which would be called Zen in Japan

dawah: call, missionary work, proselytization

de: mysterious and spontaneous energy of the universe

deism: Enlightenment view that God created the world the way a watchmaker creates a clock and leaves it to run on its own without interference

dependent origination: a twelve-part formula explaining how individuals are bound to future rebirth until they extirpate desire and ignorance

dharma: "duty" determined by one's caste and gender

Dharma: the Buddha's teaching, one of the three refuges; more broadly, the truth at the center of Buddhism, the basis for realizing enlightenment

dhimmi: literally, protected non-Muslim peoples; refers to Jews and Christians (later extended to others) who were granted "protected" status and religious freedom under Muslim rule in exchange for payment of a special tax

Diaspora: the dispersion of a religious people outside their geographic homeland, where they must live as a minority among others

diffuse religion: spiritual tradition centered on family and locality, informed by common ideas from Confucianism, Daoism, and Buddhism

divine: highest spiritual reality; representative of the gods

Dogen: (1200–1253), Japanese monk; founder of Soto Zen school

Dreamtime: in Aboriginal legend, the time when the world was being created

dual Torah: the scriptures of Rabbinic Judaism, composed of the written Torah (Tanak) and the oral Torah (Talmud)

Eightfold Path: the eight qualities needed to reach nirvana, concerning morality, meditation, and salvific wisdom

Eisai: (1141–1215), Japanese monk; founder of Rinzai Zen school

engaged Buddhism: a reformist movement among global Buddhists seeking to relate the teachings to contemporary suffering

enlightenment: *see* nirvana

evangelical: refers to pietistic Christian movements that arose in response to the Enlightenment and also dogmatic divisions within Protestantism; emphasizes the unifying power of conversion as an emotional transformation rather than a rational/dogmatic one

fana: in Sufi usage, annihilation of the ego-centered self

faqih (pl. fuqaha): jurist, legal scholar; one who elaborates *fiqh*

faqir: ascetic mendicant mystic ideal; Sufi *shaykh*

fatwa: legal opinion or interpretation issued on request by legal expert (*mufti*) to either judges or private individuals

fiqh: understanding; science of Islamic law; jurisprudence; human interpretation and application of divine law

Five Classics: Confucian canon attributed to Master K'ung: *Book of Changes (Yi-Jing)*, *Book of Documents (Shu Jing)*, *Book of Poetry (Shi Jing)*, and *Book of Rites (Li Jing)*, and a historical work that uses events in the early Chinese state to show how to assess praise and blame

Four Good Deeds: a doctrinal formula guiding the laity on the uses of wealth, advising the pursuit of happiness, security, philanthropy, and ritual

Four Noble Truths: a doctrinal formula focusing on diagnosing the human condition as marked by suffering and distorted by desire and then prescribing the Eightfold Path as a solution

Full Moon Festival: an early fall festival to worship the harvest moon with special sweet "moon cakes"; across East Asia, people view the rising moon on this night to ask for blessings; rural communities request a good rice harvest in the month ahead

fundamentalist: term first emerged to refer to evangelical Protestants who believed that certain fundamental truths of the Gospel were threatened by modern interpreters; in general, fundamentalist movements in all religions see modernity as corrupting the fundamental truths and practices of a society as they were expressed in the premodern stage of their respective traditions

Gandhara: area of Indo-Greek interaction, influential in the creation of Buddhist art

Gandhi, Mohandas K.: (1869–1948), iconic leader who inspired mass support and led India to independence combining religious and political reforms

Gelugpa: monastic school that came to dominate all others, whose head, the Dalai Lama, ruled Tibet until 1959

Gemara: *see* Talmud

gentile: anyone not Jewish

Ghost Dance: a shaman-led nationwide movement aimed at reviving the indigenous nations of North America; ended in 1890 when the U.S. Cavalry massacred up to 300 of the men, women, and children gathered for the Ghost Dance at Wounded Knee, South Dakota

globalization: for the purposes of world religions, the idea that all the world's religions have members in every country or society; anyone using the Internet can view the major temples, shrines, churches, mosques, or monasteries from around the world and offer ritual prayers or make monetary offerings to them

Gospel: literally, "good news"; usually refers to the four Gospels of the New Testament, which retell the words and deeds of Jesus of Nazareth; can also refer to other, similar ancient writings not included in the Christian scriptures

grace: expresses the idea of unmerited divine love and assistance given to humans

Guan Yu: Chinese god of war, regarded as protector of merchants

Guanyin: the most popular and universal celestial bodhisattva was Avalokiteshvara, known as Guanyin in China, Kannon in Japan, Chenrizi in Tibet, and Karuna-maya in Nepal

guru: a teacher in matters spiritual and cultural, whom disciples regard as semidivine

gurudwara: Sikh temple

hadith: narrative report of Muhammad's sayings and actions

hajj: annual pilgrimage to Mecca; all Muslims should make the *hajj* at least once in their lifetime, but it is recognized that individual circumstances may make compliance impossible

halakhah: the commandments of God revealed in the Tanak and commented on in the Talmud; the word means "to walk in the way of God" by obeying his commands or laws

haredim: Jewish ultra-Orthodox movements that reject all modernist forms of Judaism

Hasidism: a form of Judaism emerging in the eighteenth century, focused on piety and joy, with strong roots in Jewish mysticism

heresy: comes from the Greek term that means "choice"; came to be used as a negative term for choosing to believe doctrines viewed as erroneous by those who considered themselves to be "more orthodox"

heretic: from the ancient Greek, meaning "to choose"; in our postmodern world every religious person becomes a heretic, that is, one who is not simply born into a given religion or identity but must choose it, even if it is only to choose to retain the identity offered by the circumstances of his or her birth

hijab: Arabic word for veil or external covering; can consist of headscarf alone or full body covering; also known as *chador* (in Iran) or *burqa* (in Afghanistan)

hijra: migration; Muhammad's *hijra* from Mecca to Medina in 622 marks the first year of the Muslim lunar calendar

Hindutva: Hindu-ness

Holocaust: meaning "burnt sacrifice," one name given to the attempt by Nazi Germany to eliminate the Jewish people

Homo religiosus: religious humanity; a term coined by comparative religions scholar Mircea Eliade to indicate that religious practice was universal to all humans

homoousios/homoiousios: first term was used to assert that the Word of God through which all things were created is "the same as" God; second term was used to assert that this Word was "like God"; Council of Nicaea (325 CE) affirmed the first and rejected the second

Hong Xiuquan: (1814–64), charismatic instigator of the Taiping Rebellion, whose trance experiences led him to believe that he was the "younger brother" of Jesus, charged with establishing a new state in China

Huang-di: "Yellow Emperor," first immortal in religious Daoism

hudud: Quranically prescribed crimes and punishments for consumption of alcohol, theft, fornication, adultery, and false witnessing; some countries have adopted these punishments as evidence of the "Islamic" nature of their political rule and law

ibadat: worship, ritual obligations

ijma: consensus; in Islamic law, refers to agreement of scholars on interpretation of legal questions; some have reinterpreted this principle to justify the right of a parliament to enact legislation

ijtihad: human interpretation or independent reasoning in Islamic law

imam: in Sunni Islam, the prayer leader and the one who delivers the Friday sermon; in Shiah Islam, refers to Muhammad's descendants as legitimate successors, not prophets, but divinely inspired, sinless, infallible, and the final authoritative interpreter of God's will as formulated in Islamic law

incarnation: the eternal Word of God is embodied in the flesh of Jesus during his earthly life. There were two basic formulations of this: "the Word became flesh" and "the Word bodily dwells in the flesh" of Jesus.

Islam: submission or surrender to God

Israel: either Jews as a religious people or the land and state of Israel, depending on the context

jahiliyya: the period of ignorance in which justice is guaranteed and administered not by God but by threat of retaliation by family or tribe

Janam Sakhis: traditional stories about life and teachings of Guru Nanak

jihad: to strive or struggle; exerting oneself to realize God's will, lead a virtuous life, fulfill the universal mission of Islam, and spread Islam through preaching and/or writing; defense of Islam and Muslim community; currently often used to refer to the struggle for educational and social reform and social justice as well as armed struggle, holy war

jun-zi: a Confucian gentleman who has cultivated character and learning

justification by faith: Protestant Reformation doctrine formulated by Martin Luther, asserting that humans are saved by faith as a gift rather than through works of obedience to the law

Kabbalah: Jewish mysticism; the most important Kabbalistic work is the *Zohar*; for Kabbalists, God is the *En Sof*, the limitless or infinite, who manifests himself in the world through his *Shekinah*, or "divine presence" in all things; the reunion of all with the infinite through mystical contemplation will bring about nothing less than the messianic kingdom

Kali Yuga: the dark age the world has now entered, when human spiritual capacity is thought to be diminished; a view shared by some Hindus and Buddhists

kami: deity of Japan associated with places, certain animals, and the emperor

karma: literally "action" but also meaning the effects of actions that, through a hidden natural causality, condition a being's future; Hindus fix karma as acting on the inborn soul, and Buddhists define its effects on the consciousness and habits

karuna: compassion, the quality that motivated the Buddha to preach and the principal Buddhist social virtue

Khalsa: Sikh organization for the defense of the faith, marked by their uncut hair (covered with a turban), short trousers, steel wristlet, comb, and sword

khatam: seal or last of the prophets; Muhammad

khutba: sermon delivered at Friday prayer session in the mosque

Kingdom of God: the kingdom occurs whenever humans live in accord with the will of God and especially at the end of time, when God will be all in all

"kitchen god" (Zao Wangye): deity residing in every household, thought to observe and report on family events to his celestial superiors yearly

koan: a Buddhist spiritual riddle designed to foster spiritual growth, posed by monastic teacher to junior monks, such as "What is the sound of one hand clapping?" or "Does a dog have Buddha nature?"

kosher: what is *halal,* suitable or fit, used especially in reference to foods permitted by Jewish dietary laws

Lao Zi (Lao Tzu): "Old Sage," reputed author of *Daodejing* and founder of Daoism

li: in Confucian thought, individual performances needed for personal development, including manners, service to others, and rituals

liberation theology: emerging in twentieth-century Latin America, its goal was to show that the Gospel was more radical than Marxism in its promotion of justice for the poor

ling: spiritual force possessed by geographic places, such as rivers, mountains, and caves, as well as by deities and charismatic sages

literati tradition: *see* Confucianism

Lotus Sutra: one of the earliest and most influential Mahayana Buddhist texts, which reveals the cosmological nature of a Buddha and the universal character of Buddhist truth

Madhyamaka: a Mahayana philosophical school that posits the provisional and incomplete nature of all assertions; its goal is to clear away attachment even to words, making realization possible

Maharishi Mahesh Yogi: (1917–2008), founder of the Transcendental Meditation movement

Mahayana: the "Great Vehicle" that was the dominant school of Buddhism in Tibet and East Asia; the Mahayana philosophical schools developed cosmological theories of Buddhahood and envisioned the universe as permeated by bodhisattvas, some of whom were like deities and the focus of ritual veneration

Mahdi: expected or awaited one; divinely guided one who is expected to appear at the end of time to vindicate and restore the faithful Muslim community and usher in the perfect Islamic society of truth and justice

Maitreya: the next historical Buddha, uniquely depicted in China as corpulent and happy

maitri: loving-kindness, a Buddhist ethical virtue and topic of meditation

Mandate of Heaven: theory that the forces of the universe favor the ruler

mappo: Buddhist doctrine of the world in decline, especially that humans cannot practice meditation as well as in the time of the Buddha

Marranos: the Jews of Spain who were forced to convert to Christianity during the Inquisition but secretly continued to practice their Jewish faith

Master K'ung: given name of the sage (551–479 BCE) to whom Catholic missionaries later gave the Latinate name Confucius

Master Xun: (298–238 BCE), influential early Confucian exponent with emphasis on authoritarian rule

matha: monastery

Mencius: first major disciple of Master K'ung; a systematizer of Confucian ideals who lived 371–289 BCE

merit: *see* punya

metanarrative: a grand cosmic and/or historical story accepted by the majority of a society as expressing its beliefs about origin, destiny, and identity

millennialism: beliefs about an age of peace (1,000 years) at the end of time that have their origin in the New Testament Book of Revelation

Mi-lo Fo: *see* Maitreya

minbar: pulpit in the mosque from which the Friday sermon (*khutba*) is preached

Mishnah: *see* Talmud

mitzvot: the commandments of God requiring deeds of loving-kindness

mizuko cult: a new form of Kannon devotionalism in Japan organized to seek the forgiveness of the spirits of stillborn, miscarried, and aborted fetuses and transfer merit to them until they fulfill their destiny and continue on to another human rebirth

modern: a civilization that separates its citizens' lives into public and private spheres, assigning politics to public life while restricting religion to personal and family life; a dominant scientific metanarrative provides the most certain public truths people believe they know; society and politics are governed by secular, rational, and scientific norms rather than religion

modernist: the liberal wing of the Evangelical movement of the early twentieth century that embraced modern science and progress as promoting the goals of the kingdom of God on earth

moksha: "release" from samsara, freedom from future rebirth and redeath (i.e., salvation)

morality: the rightness of any human action

mosque (*masjid*): Islamic temple, from *masjid*, "place of prostration"

muamalat: social interactions

mudang: Korean shamans, predominantly women, drawn into the role through either troubling personal experiences or inheritance

muezzin: one who issues the call to prayer from the top of the *minaret*

mufti: legal expert, adviser, or consultant; one who issues *fatwas* to judges and litigants

mujaddid: renewer; one who comes to restore and revitalize the Islamic community; one who purifies and restores true Islamic practice; one *mujaddid* is to be sent at the beginning of each century

mujtahid: expert in Islamic law; one who exercises *ijtihad*, or independent reasoning, in legal matters; one capable of interpreting Islamic law

Muslim: one who submits or surrenders himself or herself to God and his will; one who follows Islam

myth: from the Greek *mythos*, meaning "story"; a symbolic story about the origins and destiny of human beings and their world; myth relates human beings to whatever powers they believe ultimately govern their destiny and explains to them what the powers expect of them

n/um kausi: shamans of the Kung people

Nagarjuna: (born ca. 150 CE), influential analytical philosopher of the early Mahayana school

nationalism: belief in the nation as a sacred entity

Native American Church: a "Pan-American" movement among American Native peoples that has factions related in varying ways to Christianity but that are united in their ceremonial use of the cactus peyote as the group's own communal sacrament

Nembutsu: repetition of the name of the Buddha Amitabha, for the purpose of making merit and gaining rebirth in the Pure Land

neo-Confucianism: tradition originating in the Song dynasty and developed subsequently by masters such as Zhu Xi who sought to harmonize early Confucian humanism with more cosmological theories of Daoism and karma doctrine of Buddhism, adopting meditation techniques from both

neo-Shintoism (or state Shinto): Meiji state's adoption of Shinto as state religion, with emperor as focal divinity, which lasted from 1868 to 1945

new age religions: religions that emerge by breaking with traditional beliefs and practices, typically through the influence of other religious practices around the globe due to the influence of modern science, global media, and global travel

new religions: religions that arise as new revelations within a tradition that change it in ways that traditional adherents do not accept, often through the influence of new religious prophets and the influence of other religions in their local environment

"new religions": sects arising in Japan from the early nineteenth century combining elements of Buddhism, Daoism, and Confucianism with ideas imported from abroad; term may also be applied outside Japan

Nichiren: (1222–1282), Japanese monk who taught that the *Lotus Sutra* is the only true Buddhist text and that chanting its title was an essential salvation practice; founded new school based on these ideas

nirguna Brahman: *see* Brahman

nirvana: a blissful state achieved by individuals who have cut off their karma by ending desire, attachment, and ignorance; after death, they enter the final trans-personal state for eternity, free from future rebirth

nonviolence: a strategy for dealing with the violence of others through nonviolent acts of civil disobedience

numinous: the human perception of the sacred

OM: also written in full phonetic rendition as AUM, one of the most prominent symbols of Hinduism; repeated as part of almost every mantra for offerings and meditation as well as written calligraphically on icons and other symbols

Om-kara ("Divine One") and Sat Guru ("True Teacher"): Sikh terms for the impersonal ultimate reality

original sin: the sin of Adam and Eve, who disobeyed the command of God not to eat the fruit of the tree of knowledge of good and evil; said to have affected all human beings by corrupting their will so that they are often unable to do the good they intend

orthodoxy: acceptance of "right beliefs" or "doctrines" based on sacred texts as formulated by religious authorities

orthopraxy: the practice of "right actions" or rituals as prescribed by sacred traditions

Pali Canon: the only complete canon among the early collection of Buddha's teachings, in this case in the Pali language derived from Sanskrit; it is split into three divisions: *Vinaya* (monastic code), *Sutras* (sermons), and *Abhidhamma* (advanced teaching formula)

pap: "demerit"; bad karma earned by breaking the precepts

passing over: the act of imagination whereby one sees the world through the eyes of another's religion and thereby gains new insight into one's own religion

Pentecostal: refers to churches that emphasize possession by the Holy Spirit and speaking in tongues

People of the Book (*ahl al-kitab*): those possessing a revelation or scripture from God; typically refers to Jews and Christians, Muslims, and sometimes includes Zoroastrians

philosophical Daoism: tradition articulating path to harmony for individuals and society based on understanding and flowing with natural forces

postmodern: a society typified by diversity in both beliefs and social practices that has no single dominant metanarrative (other than the narrative of diversity) and is skeptical of finding either certain knowledge or norms in any public form of truth, whether religious, ethical, or scientific

prajna: the "insight" or "wisdom" necessary for enlightenment in Buddhism, comprising the ability to "see clearly" into the nature of existence as marked by suffering, impermanence, and absence of a soul

prasad: the remains of any substance (food, flowers, incense, etc.) used in a ritual offering, thought to be medicinal because it has been in contact with the divinity

premodern: a civilization in which there is no separation between religion and society; a dominant religious metanarrative provides the most certain truths people believe they know; by being a member of that culture, one automatically participates in its religious vision and lives by its religious norms

Protestant: the churches, beginning at the time of Martin Luther, that teach salvation by faith rather than works and also reject the mediation of the church through apostolic succession as necessary for salvation in favor of a direct personal relationship with God in Christ

Protestant Buddhism: a term signifying a pattern of reform in which Buddhists protested colonial rule yet adopted perspectives and missionary techniques of Protestant Christianity

Protestant ethic: term coined by sociologist Max Weber, who noted that the Calvinist branch of the Reformation fostered a belief in working hard and living simply for the glory of God and as proof that one was among those destined to be saved; such an attitude, Weber said, contributed to the accumulation of wealth needed for investment and fueled the Industrial Revolution and the flourishing of capitalist societies

puja: a ritual offering to a Hindu or bodhisattva deity, Buddha, or bodhisattva

punya: merit, or the good karma that enters into the content of an individual's life, earned in Buddhist doctrine by moral practices, learning, and meditation

puranas: texts extolling the histories, theologies, and necessary rituals for expressing the Bhakti faith for the different Hindu deities

purdah: seclusion of women from men who are not relatives; segregation of the sexes

Pure Land: in Mahayana Buddhism, the belief that Buddhas and advanced bodhisatt-vas can through their inexhaustible merit create rebirth realms where humans can easily engage in Buddhist practices conducive to enlightenment

qi: vital force of life within individuals and in nature

qi gong: discipline of cultivating the vital individual life force that can be used for worldly goals such as healing or to reach immortality

Qing-Ming: yearly spring festival when Chinese visit and clean family graves and then feast after making offerings to the ancestors

qiyas: legal term for analogical reasoning

Quran: revelation, recitation, message; Muslim scripture

Rabbinic: a rabbi is a teacher; the name came to designate the Judaism of the *dual Torah* introduced by the Pharisees, which came to be normative in the premodern period

Ramadan: month of fasting; ninth month of the Muslim calendar

Ramakrishna Mission: founded by Swami Vivekananda to further the teachings of his guru, Ramakrishna; an influential Hindu missionary and reform organization that today runs hospitals, schools, and temples and has centers in over a dozen countries

Ramanuja: an influential theologian (1025–1137) who argued that the ultimate reality humans could relate to was saguna Brahman

Rammohan Roy: pioneering religious figure who called for the reform of Hindu beliefs and practices

Rashtriya Svayamsevak Sangh (RSS): "National Union of [Hindu] Volunteers"; group advocating "Hinduism" as devotion to "Mother India"

redemption: root meaning is "to be rescued or freed," especially from slavery; used in both a literal and a metaphorical sense: God redeemed Israel from slavery in Egypt and exile in Babylonia; God redeems sinners from punishment and death due to sin

religion: from the Latin *religare*, meaning "to tie or bind," and the root *religere*, which has the connotation of "acting with care"; expresses a sense of being "tied and bound" by obligations to whatever powers are believed to govern one's destiny—whether those powers be natural or supernatural, personal or impersonal, one or many; ancient peoples everywhere believed that the powers governing their destiny were the forces of nature

religious Daoisim: tradition devoted to attaining individual immortality through alchemical infusions or meditative practices

ren: Confucian ideal of being "fully human" in ethics, manners, and cultivation

ritual: actions that connect the individual and the community to each other, through the sacred

sacraments: ritual actions, such as baptism and holy communion, said to impart the grace of God to Christians, usually through the mediation of ordained clergy

saguna Brahman: *see* Brahman

salat: official prayer or worship performed five times each day

samsara: "the world" of rebirth subject to the law of karma and the inevitable reality of death, a religious understanding shared by Hinduism, Buddhism, Jainism, and Sikhism

sangha: the Buddhist monastic community of monks and nuns

Sat Guru: "true teacher"; Sikh term indicating the active mode of Om-kara

satyagraha: Gandhi's central principle of "grasping the truth"; with roots in the Hindu and Jain doctrine of nonviolence (ahimsa) and in Christianity's injunctions to love one's enemy and turn the other cheek (as a reaction to being struck in the face), Gandhi required those opposing the government to confine their protests to nonviolent acts, to accept suffering for the cause, to love the opponent, and to be disciplined in personal life

Second Coming: belief that Jesus, who died on the cross, arose from the dead, ascended into heaven, and will return at the end of time to raise the dead and establish a new heaven and a new earth

secular: sociologically used to mean "nonreligious"

Sephardic: Jews whose traditions originated in Spain and Portugal

shahadah: declaration of faith, witness, testimony; refers to the declaration of Muslim faith: "There is no god but God and Muhammad is His Messenger"

Shaivite: devotee of Shiva

shaktas: devotees of Devi

shakti: innate, creative force of this universe, understood as feminine

shaman: *see* spirit medium

shamanism: the traditions focused on individuals who can leave their bodies to enter the realm of the afterlife and spirits where they can learn higher spiritual truths and the arts of healing to bring back to one's people; has its roots in ancient animistic and polytheistic cultures

Shang-di: Heavenly Lord, thought to preside over early Chinese pantheon; term Christians used as translation for *God*

Shankara: Hindu philosopher (788–820) and monastic organizer, whose monistic interpretation of the *Upanishads* became the most influential expression of nirguna Brahman doctrine

sharia: Islamic law; straight path

Shema: the essential declaration of monotheistic faith as found in Judaism: "Hear O Israel, the Lord our God, the Lord is One"

shen: usual term in Chinese for a kindly god or goddess

Shiah or Shii: follower(s), partisan(s); refers to those who followed the leadership of Ali, the nephew and son-in-law of Muhammad, as Muhammad's successor; those who believe that leadership of the Muslim community should belong to Muhammad's descendants

Shinto: indigenous religion of Japan that reveres the deities of the islands, including the emperor

shirk: polytheism, idolatry, association of anyone or anything with God; the most serious sin in Islam

shramana: wandering ascetic known at the time of the Buddha

shunyata: "zero-ness"; the term used to designate the emptiness of all constructs

siddha: tantric saint

skandha: an aggregate, used in Buddhist thought to identify each of the five components that define a human being: the physical body (*rupa*), feelings (*vedana*), perceptions (*samjna*), habitual mental dispositions (*samskaras*), and consciousness (*vijnana*)

Soka Gakkai: Nichiren Buddhist offshoot, now global religion seeking world peace through Mahayana Buddhist teachings

Son of God: title applied to Jesus of Nazareth

sorcerers: mediums who manipulate the spirit world and coerce the supernaturals without their consent, often for their own benefit and against community values

spirit flight: "soul journey"; a shaman's attempt to locate another person's soul, perhaps because it has wandered off in this world or needs assistance to reach the afterlife of the clan's ancestors

spirit medium: person who communicates with deities and spirits through ritually induced trance

state Shinto: *see* neo-Shintoism

Sthaviravadins: the traditionalists among the early Buddhist monastic schools, the only surviving school today being the Theravadins

stupa: the distinctive Buddhist shrine, a raised mound surmounted by a ceremonial pole and umbrella; contains the relics of a Buddha or enlightened saint, either the literal bodily relics or other items left behind, such as words in textual form or clothing items worn

Sufi: literally "one who wears wool"; Muslim mystic or ascetic

Sufism: Islamic mysticism or asceticism

Sunnah: example; typically refers to Muhammad's example, which is believed by Muslims to be the living out of the principles of the Quran; *Sunni* is derived from this word

Sunni: those who accept the *sunna* and the historic succession of the caliphs; the majority of the Muslim community

surah: chapter, particularly of the Quran

Swami Vivekananda: Ramakrishna's foremost disciple

sympathetic imagination: empathy; necessary to understand the religious languages and messages of different times and places

synagogue: a community centered on the study of Torah and prayer to God; the buildings used to house these activities also came to be known as synagogues

syncretism: the weaving together of alien and indigenous religious beliefs and practices; or the combining of elements from different practices to create a new religion

syncretistic: the identification of the gods of one religion with the gods of another so that one's own gods are seen as the same as those of the other's religion but under different names

t'i: affection for siblings, in Confucianism a marker of character

T'oegyehak: modern Korean Confucian group based on teachings of master Yi T'oegye (1501–70)

taboo: forbidden

Taiping Rebellion: nineteenth-century revolt in China led by converts to Christianity, who established a separate state in the city of Nanjing; resulting civil war was bloodiest in world history

Talmud: the oral Torah, recorded in the *Mishnah*, and the commentary on the *Mishnah* called the *Gemara*; there are two Talmuds: the Bavli (Talmud of Babylonia) and the Yerushalmi (the Jerusalem Talmud); the former is considered the more comprehensive and authoritative

Tanak: the written Torah, or Hebrew Bible, made up of Torah (the first five books, from Genesis to Deuteronomy), Neviim (the prophets and historical writings such as Jeremiah and 1 and 2 Kings), and Ketuvim (the wisdom writings, such as Proverbs, Job, etc.)

Tannaim: the generation of sages, beginning with Hillel and Shammai, that created the *Mishnah*

tantra: the esoteric tradition common to both Hinduism and Buddhism that employs unorthodox practices including sexual yoga to transform the body and lead individuals quickly to experience moksha/nirvana

Tattvabodhini Sabha: a colonial Hindu sect, powerful around Calcutta, that promoted the "modern Hindu's" adaptation to India's new economic and political realities; merged the values of working hard, living honestly, saving rationally, and promoting altruism with the individual controlling personal desires; along with Rammohan Roy (1772–1833), they saw reformed Hinduism now being led by the "godly householder," not the premodern elite of world-renouncing ascetics

tawhid: oneness, unity, and uniqueness of God; absolute monotheism

temple: a place to worship God or the gods in diverse religions; in Judaism only one temple was allowed for the worship of God in Jerusalem, whereas each Jewish community would have a synagogue for study and prayers

Tenrikyo: Tenrikyo ("Religion of Heavenly Wisdom") was founded by Nakayama Miki (1798–1887) and became a recognized Shinto sect in 1838; essential for salvation are a dance ritual, an initiation ("receiving the holy grant"), and performance of daily social service for others

Theravada: traditionalists, the last surviving Buddhist school of elders (Sthaviravadins) that is now dominant in South and Southeast Asia

three faiths: Chinese grouping of the three great traditions: Confucianism, Daoism, and Buddhism

Three Marks of Existence: the Buddhist terms for analyzing human reality as marked by impermanence, suffering, and no soul

Three Refuges: *see* Triratna

Thunderbolt Vehicle: *see* Vajrayana

Tian: "heaven," understood as impersonal yet responsive to human actions

Tian di: a supreme overlord believed to keep records on each individual soul, according to texts found in Han-era tombs in China

tirtha: a holy space defined by a river confluence

Tisha B'Av: a day of mourning to commemorate tragedies affecting the Jewish people, particularly the fall of the First and Second Temples in Jerusalem

totem: symbol taken from the natural world that stands for a social group possessing a common origin and essence

transcendent: beyond all finite things

Transcendental Meditation (TM): a movement founded by Maharishi Mahesh Yogi that brought mystical Hindu teachings to the West through mantra-centered meditation

Trinity: God as Father, Son, and Holy Spirit; meant to suggest that the transcendent God can be immanent in the world without losing his transcendence—when God acts in the world (as Son or Spirit), God does not cease to be father and Creator of the universe; therefore, God is not many gods but one God in three persons

Triratna: the "Three Jewels" that every Buddhist takes refuge in for all rituals: the Buddha, the Dharma, and the Sangha

Tu-di: "Earth Ruler," local god who is worshipped across modern China to control the earth's fertility

Tu-di (or Tu Chu) Gong: the cult of the "earth ruler" who controls fertility, widespread among farmers in China during the millennium from the Zhou dynasty (1122–221 BCE) until the fall of the Han (206 BCE–220 CE)

tutelary spirit: a supernatural agent, often an ancestral spirit, whose help is required by a shaman to perform the difficult soul journeys, negotiate with evil spirits, compel a soul to return, or increase the shaman's healing powers

two natures, one person: doctrine affirmed by Council of Chalcedon (451 CE); in the one person of Jesus are two natures (divine and human) said to coexist in unity but without confusion or mixture, so Jesus is fully human in everything except sin, and yet the fullness of God is also present in him and united to him

Tzaddik: in the Hasidic tradition, a "righteous man," as powerful as the rabbi in a traditional Talmudic community but revered for mystical piety and devotion, not Talmudic scholarship; for the Hasidim, the Tzaddik was especially chosen by God as a direct link between heaven and earth, whose holiness was so powerful that, like Moses (Exodus 32:11–14), he could intervene on behalf of the faithful and change the mind of God

ulama (sing. *alim*): religious scholars

ultimate reality: that which is the highest in value and meaning for the group

***ummah*:** Muslim community of believers

Upanishads: appendices to the Vedas that record early Hindu speculations on Brahman, atman, the means to realize their identity, and moksha

Vaishnavite: devotee of Vishnu or his incarnations

Vajrayana: the Mahayana-derived Buddhist tantric "vehicle" of belief and practice that uses unorthodox means, including sexual experience, to propel individuals quickly toward enlightenment

Vedas: the collection of the earliest Hindu hymns directed to the pantheon of deities, including ritual directions and chanting notations for their use

"Venus" figurines: small prehistoric Eurasian stone sculptures of females with large breasts and hips, often with their genitalia emphasized, thought to indicate a worship of fertility in small communities

***via analogia*:** a way of knowing spiritual reality through the use of analogy, for example, "God is my shepherd"

***via negativa*:** the mystical way of knowing the highest spiritual reality (God, Brahman, etc.) by negating all finite qualities and characteristics; Hindus, for instance, say Brahman is "neti . . . neti"—not this and not that (i.e., Brahman is not a thing, Brahman is no-thing and therefore is pure nothingness, Brahman is beyond imagination and cannot be imaged, Brahman can only be known by a mystical experience of unknowing)

vihara: a Buddhist monastery

***vipassana* meditation:** the widespread Buddhist meditation practice focusing on calming the mind and discerning the truly real

Vishva Hindu Parishad (VHP): an organization of religious leaders founded in 1964 to promote the interests of Hindus and advocate for India to be recognized as a "Hindu state"

wali: friend or protégé of God; Sufi term referring to saint; one reputed to have the power to bilocate, cure the sick, multiply food, and read minds

white shamans: Westerners who create global organizations propagating a purported "universal" shamanic tradition, charging high fees for tours, courses, initiations, and healing services, some pledging to use some of the proceeds to assist indigenous shamans

Won Buddhism: a new Korean school of Buddhism founded in 1924 by Soe-Tae San (1891–1943); it ritualizes worship of a picture of a black circle in a white background, symbolizing the *dharmakaya*, the cosmic body of the Buddha; the group is named *Won* from the Korean reading of the Chinese character "round"

Wu Tai Shan: sacred mountain in China referred to as home of the bodhisattva Manjushri

wu-wei: "noninterference" or "non-[forced] action," an ideal in Daoism

xiao: Confucian ideal of children honoring their parents, attitude that extends to the ruler

yin-yang theory: twin forces by which the Dao is known, each complementing the other (female/male, valley/mountain, etc.)

yoga: a term meaning "union" that refers to the various means of realizing union with the divine; earliest use of yoga refers to ascetic practices but expands to include the path of philosophical inquiry, bhakti, and tantra

Yoga Sutras: codification of yoga practices, attributed to Patanjali

zakat: almsgiving, one of the Five Pillars of Islam: 2.5 percent tithe of one's net worth to help the poor is required of all Muslims

Zen: the Japanese Mahayana Buddhist school focused on meditation practice, as transmitted from and organized in China as the Ch'an

Zhu Xi: (1130–1200), great Chinese master of neo-Confucian thought who integrated into Confucianism elements of Buddhism and Daoism and established core rituals of subsequent tradition

Zhuang Zi: second great Daoist classic, named after a mystical sage of the same name

Zionism: the desire to return to the land of Israel as a homeland; in modern times, the secular movement started by Theodor Herzl that led to the formation of the state of Israel

Zohar: major book of Jewish Kabbalism: *The Book of Splendor*

CREDITS

INDEX